THE
COLLECTED
WORKS OF
MAX HAINES

THE COLLECTED WORKS OF MAX HAINES

by Max Haines

The Toronto Sun Publishing Corporation Limited

Other works by Max Haines:

Bothersome Bodies (1977)

Calendar of Criminal Capers (1977)
  (with Andy Donato)

Crime Flashback #1 (1980)

Crime Flashback #2 (1981)

Crime Flashback #3 (1982)

The Murderous Kind (1983)

Murder and Mayhem (1984)

The Collected Works of Max Haines, Vol. 1 (1985)

That's Life! (1986)

True Crime Stories (1987)

True Crime Stories, Book II (1988)

True Crime Stories, Book III (1989)

True Crime Stories, Book IV (1990)

THE COLLECTED WORKS OF MAX HAINES - Volume 2

Published by the Toronto SUN Publishing Corporation Limited
333 King Street East, Toronto, Ontario Canada M5A 3X5

Editor: **Glenn Garnett**

Copy Editor: **Maureen Hudes**, B.A., B.Ed

Cover and Book Design: **Vince Desai**

General Manager: **Joseph P. Marino**

First printing: September 1991

Canadian Cataloguing in Publication Data:

Haines, Max

The Collected Works of Max Haines

ISBN 0-919233-37-6 (v.2, bound)

ISBN 0-919233-38-4 (v.2, pbk.)

1. Murder. I. Title.

HV6515.H355 1985 364.1'523 C86-008656-9

To the memory of
Samuel Mosher

Acknowledgments

In the world of true crime, many individuals contribute to the final product.

Employees of the Texas Archives went beyond the call of duty to dig up little-known facts about famous Texan gunslinger Ben Thompson. The good folks of Lancaster, Penn. shared their folklore and information about Wilburt Hess, enabling me to write about Pennsylvania's Hex Murder.

Numerous citizens of Glasgow, Scotland contributed to the story about multiple murderer Peter Manuel. The late Gordon Sinclair helped with the saga of Kid McCoy. Jane Stafford shared details of being personally abused by her husband. Thurston Fields, the chief of police of Jewell City, Conn. walked me through the woods, just as he did while pursuing a serial killer. Det. Insp. Bill McGregor shared his frustration of not being able to identify a murder victim. David Star trudged through snow and slush until we located the final resting place of swindler Cassie Chadwick.

Special thanks to Toronto *Sun* head librarian Julie Kirsh and her staff - Joyce Wagler, Glenna Tapscott, Katherine Webb Nelson, Sue Dugas, Chris Eyton, Barb White and Robert Smith.

This work would not have been possible without the efforts of editors Glenn Garnett and Maureen Hudes.

- M.H.

Contents

Part 1
CONS AND SCAMS

Part 2
THE POISONERS

Part 3
CANADIANA

Part 4
THE DOCTORS

Part 5
NASTY LADIES

Part 6
ALL IN THE FAMILY

Part 7
FAMOUS NAMES

Part 8
MONSTERS

Part 9
AMERICANA

Part 10
AROUND THE WORLD

Part 11
QUESTIONABLE CASES

1

CONS AND SCAMS

SASSY CASSIE

Some children play doctor or nurse. Others prefer being railway engineers. From childhood Cassie Chadwick played fraud.

Cassie was a rather pudgy, tightlipped lass with no obvious ability or talent. Yet this plain Jane from rural Ontario was able to fleece hard-nosed American bankers out of an estimated $3 million.

Born Elizabeth Bigley in Eastwood, Ont., near Woodstock, in 1857, she displayed a keen but not exceptional mind in school. At the ripe old age of 21, Liz gave the very first inkling of what was to follow. She had pale blue personal cards printed, exclaiming for all the world to see, 'Miss Lizzie Bigley, Heiress to $18,000.'

If anyone questioned Lizzie's claim, she took great glee in displaying a lawyer's letter from England, which explained that she had been left $18,000 by a recently departed uncle. Lizzie was able to purchase several gowns and an organ based on this bogus letter.

When our heroine was unable to pay for any of her purchases, she was arrested and brought to trial. For the very first time, Lizzie displayed her not inconsiderable acting ability. She mimicked the judge, laughed uncontrollably at nothing at all, and sometimes broke into religious hymns. It worked. The judge found the poor girl not guilty, remarking that it was obvious she was insane and should receive some sort of treatment.

After her acquittal, Lizzie took the show on the road. She visited a married sister in Cleveland. Coincidentally, her sister picked that very time to visit the folks back home in Eastwood. While sis was away, Lizzie mortgaged all her furniture. When Lizzie was unable to pay, the furniture was repossessed. History does not reveal how Sis felt upon returning to an empty home.

Undaunted by this minor setback, Lizzie continued to live by her wits. One of her favorite scams was to pierce her gums with a pin until they bled. In obvious distress she would inform some friend that she required a sum of money for an operation. Lizzie, a keen student of psychology, knew just how much cash she could realistically extract from each mark. Lizzie's gums came to resemble a pincushion.

In 1883 Lizzie, using the name Alice Bastado, entered the blessed state of matrimony. Well, just barely. The marriage lasted only 12 days, which is a quickie even by today's standards. Then again, Lizzie was about 100 years ahead of her time in most things.

She met Dr. Wallace S. Springsteen at a party in Cleveland and quickly let the good doctor know that she was an Irish heiress. At that very moment Dr. Springsteen had need of a cash transfusion to set up his medical practice. He proposed. Lizzie accepted.

Within a week our girl had purchased expensive gowns, rugs, and fine furniture, which was just great with Springsteen, except for one thing. Lizzie neglected to pay for anything. When bill collectors came calling, Lizzie, cool as a cucumber, informed her new husband that the clothing and furniture were little tokens of affection from him to her. The doctor said no way. The bill collectors repossessed everything, including the nuptial bed. Springsteen took to the hills, obtaining a divorce along the way.

Lizzie busied herself for the next two years by marrying an Ohio farmer and taking him for enough cash to set up shop as a clairvoyant in Toledo. She used the name Mme. de Vere. Honest, Lizzie had a crystal ball and everything. She proceeded to successfully shear the sheep who called at her establishment.

One of her sheep, or I should say lamb, because this meek father of five children did have the rather unfortunate name of Joseph Lamb, was shorn of $1500, his entire life's savings. Lamb bellowed. Lizzie assured him that all was not lost. Together they would swindle Richard Brown, a well-known broker, out of a whopping $40,000. The scheme didn't work.

Lizzie and Lamb were both arrested and stood trial. Lamb swore that Lizzie had hypnotized him. Evidently the jury believed him. Lamb was acquitted, but Lizzie drew nine and a half years in the Ohio State Prison. Four years later, Gov. William McKinley granted our Lizzie a pardon.

On the day of her release from prison she headed for Cleveland, changed her name to Mrs. Cassie Hoover, and opened a massage parlor. In walked Dr. Leroy Shippen Chadwick, a prominent Cleveland physician. Dr. Chadwick had lost his wife four years previously and dearly longed for sympathetic female companionship. He also suffered from an extremely painful back condition.

He didn't know it, but he was meeting the only woman in all of Cleveland who could cure both maladies. Cassie proved to be a whiz in the massage parlor, as well as a real charmer in the companionship department. Dr. Chadwick fell in love.

Now Dr. Chadwick was not Cassie's average choice of husband. No siree, he was a bona fide member of Cleveland society and well-off financially. In short, a fine catch. In 1897, he and Cassie became husband and wife.

It took Cassie about four years of constant spending to decimate the doctor's fortune. Remember, those were the days when a dollar was a hundred cents. It is estimated that Cassie went through a quarter of a million dollars. The Chadwick home was converted into a showcase. Expensive paintings hung on the walls. Fine Persian rugs covered the floors. One Christmas Eve Cassie remodeled the entire house as a surprise for her husband.

In 1902, Dr. Chadwick could take the indiscriminate spending no longer. He closed out his bank account and headed for Europe. Cassie departed for New York, where she pulled off her greatest scam, for which she is remembered to this day.

In order to obtain credit in Cleveland, Cassie told financiers a fantastic tale, which she then proceeded to prove. She told them she was a niece of Frederick Mason, a lifelong associate of multi-millionaire steel magnate Andrew Carnegie. She added that she was heiress to $7 million of Carnegie's securities by virtue of the fact that she was Carnegie's illegitimate daughter. Cassie felt that as Carnegie was getting up there in age, it was time the old boy let her have a few million to come and go on.

Cautious Cleveland bankers decided to check out her story. They suggested that their own lawyer accompany Cassie to the Carnegie estate and have Carnegie sign a few million dollars worth of notes. Cassie thought it a great idea.

A fancy carriage pulled up outside 2 East 91st St. in Manhattan. Cassie suggested that her eccentric millionaire father might not like a lawyer barging in on him unannounced. She would go in, break the ice, and then call for the lawyer. Cassie walked up to the front entrance bold as brass and rang the bell. As the lawyer watched, Cassie chatted with a servant and was then ushered into the mansion.

Fifteen minutes later she reappeared, dejected. Her daddy didn't want to meet any lawyers, but all was not lost. Cassie extracted two $500,000 notes signed by Andrew Carnegie, as well as a wrapped package, which Cassie explained 'held a bunch of bonds.'

Cassie returned to Cleveland, where word of her genuine claim as Carnegie's illegitimate daughter had preceded her. She walked into Cleveland's Wade Park

Banking Co., then controlled by Rockefeller interests. Secretary treasurer of the bank, Ira Reynolds, greeted her with open arms. Cassie had two little items with her. She passed Reynolds a promissory note signed by Andrew Carnegie for $500,000 and requested storage space for a package, which she offhandedly remarked contained $5 million in securities. The list of securities was neatly itemized on the outside of the parcel.

Reynolds was delighted to receive the goodies. He suggested that Cassie open an account with his bank in the amount of $50,000, giving her access to pin money. Cassie agreed. As she rose to leave, Cassie stopped short. A smile crossed her face. She wasn't a very astute business person. Shouldn't she get a receipt for the $5 million in stocks and bonds?

"Of course," replied the banker, and hastily signed a receipt listing the securities without ever having opened the package. Cassie had pulled it off. She now had in her possession a legitimate receipt for $5 million in nonexistent securities.

Cassie shifted into high gear. She next appeared in Oberlin, Ohio, where she presented herself to Charles T. Beckwith, president of the Citizens National Bank. Beckwith was stunned at his good fortune. Cassie passed over two half million dollar promissory notes bearing Carnegie's signature. She also showed Beckwith the list of securities being held in trust for her at Mr. Reynold's financial institution.

Small town banker Beckwith had to catch his breath. But wait, there was more. Cassie explained that estate planning was not her long suit. She really needed two intelligent men to handle her affairs. Would Beckwith be interested at $10,000 a year? Beckwith choked on his cigar and jumped at the chance. He offered his head cashier as the second man. It was settled. Cassie walked out of the bank, firmly entrenched as the bank's most prominent customer.

Three weeks later she borrowed $5000. In the succeeding months she borrowed larger amounts. Beckwith was delighted. It wasn't every banker who had Andrew Carnegie's signed notes in his safe.

Within a year Cassie was into the bank for $240,000. Beckwith had forced $102,000 of his own money upon her, in an attempt to pick up the high interest rates, which didn't seem to concern Cassie at all.

Employing much the same scheme, Cassie proceeded to fleece other financial institutions. She ran up the tab at the Wade Park Banking Co. to $400,000. Elyria Savings Bank coughed up $100,000 and the American Exchange Bank in New York City went to the well for $380,000. The Euclid Avenue Savings Bank was taken for $420,000.

Cassie didn't confine her skullduggery to banks. Dear friend Herbert Newton was swindled out of a whopping $500,000.

What did Cassie do with the veritable Niagara of funds flowing into her coffers? She spent it, that's what she did. It was the turn of the century. A family could live on $9 a week. Cassie gave porters $20 tips. Her home was a showplace, housing *objets d'art* from around the world. She maintained a stable of servants who jumped to fulfil her every whim and travelled with an entourage to the capitals of Europe. Once, when the mood struck her, she purchased 12 grand pianos and gave them away as gifts. Befitting a woman of her stature, she adorned herself with diamonds worth a king's ransom. Never one to forget those less fortunate, Cassie donated large sums to charity.

The first tiny crack in Cassie's pyramid of subterfuge appeared in 1904 when her good friend, millionaire Herbert Newton, became tired of waiting for Cassie to pay up. He sued her for $190,000. It didn't take long for the house of cards to tumble.

As soon as it became known that Cassie didn't have the ability to pay Newton the relatively small sum of $190,000, the good people of Oberlin, Ohio started a run on the Citizens National Bank. Poor Beckwith had to close the bank's doors. He admitted that the $240,000 owed by Cassie was four times the entire capitalization of the bank.

Reporters reached Andrew Carnegie, who informed the world he not only never had an illegitimate daughter, he had never even heard of Cassie Chadwick.

It was all over. Cassie was arrested in New York. On March 6, 1905, she was brought to trial, charged with forgery and abetting bank officials with misappropriation of funds. Cassie's trial was the most publicized court event in a decade. Carnegie attended the trial and enjoyed it immensely. Charles Beckwith didn't attend. He died of a heart attack, which many believe was brought on by his personal bankruptcy.

Cassie was found guilty and sentenced to ten years in the Ohio State Penitentiary. Back in prison Cassie's health deteriorated rapidly. In the summer of 1907 she was transferred to the prison hospital, where she died that same year.

In her home town of Eastwood, they still love to relate how Cassie drove up to Carnegie's mansion and was ushered inside by a servant, thereby laying the groundwork for her master swindle. It was easy. Cassie impressed upon the servant her urgent need to use the bathroom. The servant sympathetically obliged.

DISHONEST ABE

Abraham Sykowski's father was an industrious Polish immigrant who worked long and hard in his tailor shop located in New York's teeming Lower East Side. Abe's father lectured his bright son on the virtues of honesty, truthfulness and diligence. Abe didn't listen. He preferred to lie, cheat and steal.

From the age of 14, 5 ft. 5 in. Abe was in and out of trouble. He was caught stealing vegetables from tenement buildings, but was let off with a warning when his father swore his Abe would never as much as jaywalk the rest of his life.

Abe had two genuine talents. He had the natural ability to learn and speak foreign languages. He mastered six, which were to stand him in good stead in later years. Abe also learned to contort his supple body into strange shapes. That's how he found himself in vaudeville. In 1915, 20-year-old Abe was good enough to be hired by Barnum and Bailey's circus. P.T. billed him as the Human Frog.

Abe loved being the Human Frog, but longed for the big money that the frog business simply couldn't provide. He gave common theft a try, was caught and sent to prison for nine years.

While in prison Abe dreamed up a con game that was to provide him with a minimum of $125,000 per year for the next 25 years. In good years he made $375,000. That isn't half bad when you consider that in 1930 you could purchase a hotdog and a coke for a dime. Of course, Abe did have the inconvenience of spending a couple of years in prison during that span, but then every occupation has its drawbacks.

Let's look in on Abe's scam during his salad days in the summer of 1946.

Abe, posing as Count Alexander Navarro of Madrid, Spain, checked into a luxurious suite in Montreal's Windsor Hotel. Abe was invited to Montreal's better social functions.

At one of these rather formal affairs, he let it slip that he was in dire need of a good lawyer. Someone suggested he contact 60-year-old Washington attorney Otto

Dunning. Count Navarro called the lawyer, informing him that he had been given his name by a friend at a party. He required top-drawer reputable legal advice since he was about to dispose of a third of a billion dollars.

Dunning cleared his throat. He could get away immediately. There was one other little matter the Count mentioned as an afterthought. Did Dunning know anyone who would be interested in investing a piddling $125,000? The loan would be fully guaranteed, would pay a high interest rate and be payable in 90 days. Dunning thought he could dig up someone.

Count Navarro, decked out in his very best custom tailored lightweight threads, welcomed his guests into his suite of rooms. Dunning had brought along Sigmund Janas, the president of Colonial Airlines, as his investor. After offering the men two of the finest Havana stogies to accompany their Remy Martins, Count Navarro got to the point.

Faking embarrassment, the nifty little con artist explained that he was worth many millions of dollars. His face grew crimson when he admitted he had made every cent illegally as Al Capone's partner and financial advisor during that gentleman's bootlegging career.

Otto Dunning was well aware that Big Al had been stashed away because of income tax evasion. He ventured to inquire if the Count had paid income tax on his many millions. Count Navarro responded to this query by leading the two men to a hotel safe, where he displayed a stack of letters purportedly from famed lawyer Clarence Darrow to Henry W. Morgenthau, Secretary of the Treasury of the U.S.

The letters were eight years old, having been written before Darrow died. Among the papers were cancelled cheques totalling $84 million to cover all taxes owed by the Count to the U.S. government. It was obvious that Darrow had acted as legal counsel for the Count. The last letter in the stack was from Morgenthau to Darrow, advising him that Count Navarro's tax bill was paid in full. The boys from Washington were duly impressed.

Count Navarro continued talking in that low confidential voice. He explained that he had only a year to live and planned to give his money away to charity, where it would do the most good. He also required assurances that his good works would be carried on after his demise. To start the ball rolling he wanted to donate $50 million immediately to a list of charities in case he was called away to his great reward without prior notice. In this way, Count Navarro pointed out, he could meet St. Peter with a clear conscience.

Dunning looked at Janas. Janas looked at Dunning. They were obviously in the presence of a highly moral human being. Still, business is business. Dunning gingerly inquired as to his fee for such big time giving. The Count stated that ten percent seemed fair to him, making the rather serious point that Dunning's credentials had to check out before the deal could be consummated.

Dunning was quick with figures. He didn't need a pencil. Ten percent of $50 million dollars worked out to a cool five million. Dunning agreed that the fee seemed fair enough.

Count Navarro had a minor problem. He produced clippings from the Montreal Star describing the robbery of his hotel suite some two weeks previously. The Count's passport was one of the items stolen. He had to wait for a new passport from Spain, which might take months. In the meantime the third of a billion dollars was stashed away in 33 safety deposit boxes in New York City and he simply couldn't leave Canada without a passport. One of Dunning's duties back in Washington would be to pull whatever strings necessary to speed up delivery of the passport.

Navarro explained that he didn't just leave the addresses and numbers of the safety deposit boxes lying around anywhere. Naturally, the boxes had been rented under fictitious names. The Count produced a Bible. He told the two Americans that the bogus names, box numbers and locations of the banks were written in the Bible in invisible ink. A hot iron applied to the pages would reveal all.

The hook was in. The little con artist could see the greed mounting in his guests' eyes. Still sipping those Remy Martins, Janas got up enough courage to ask about the $125,000 investment. His question met with an unusual response. Navarro doubled up with laughter. Wiping tears from his eyes, he had to admit the plain truth. He was temporarily stone dead broke. He began laughing again. His two guests laughed. It was humorous, a man with a third of a billion dollars broke. When the tears cleared, Navarro explained that he required the $125,000 for incidental living expenses until he retrieved his millions from the safety deposit boxes in New York.

Janas agreed to send a cheque as soon as he returned to Washington. The Count wouldn't hear of it. There was the matter of references. He would have his people check out Dunning. After all, it was only proper. If all was in order, he would call the lawyer in Washington.

On July 2, 1946, six days after their first meeting, Dunning received the all-important phone call. He was informed that his references were impeccable. Dunning and Janas caught a plane to Montreal. They passed over a cheque for $125,000 to Count Navarro and received a promissory note due in 90 days at a whopping rate of interest. The two men returned to Washington, where Dunning was to attempt to procure a new passport for the Count.

Ten days passed. Dunning called to give his client a progress report. The Windsor Hotel informed him that Count Navarro had moved out ten days earlier. Little beads of sweat formed on Dunning's forehead. He called Janas' bank. Yes, the cheque for $125,000 had been cashed and cleared some days earlier.

The lawyer and the airline executive had been taken. Abraham Sykowski had struck again. This time Abe's luck ran out. The FBI located him four months later in Willemstead, Curacao, living in a luxurious suite with a set of blonde twins.

Brought back to New York, Abe pleaded guilty to swindling Janas and was sentenced to five years imprisonment. While in prison, he had plenty of time to think about the con business. Abe made up his mind that when he was released, he would swindle King Farouk of Egypt. But that's another story.

In August, 1951, Abraham Sykowski, con artist extraordinaire, was released from prison. He headed for France with the express intention of conning King Farouk. Where he obtained the financial assistance to carry out his plans, no one knows. In preparation for his scam, Abe rented several safety deposit boxes in New York City banks and stuffed them with newspapers.

Abe arrived in Cannes in style, driving up to the Carlton Hotel in a white chauffeur-driven limousine. King Farouk was staying at the Carlton. His heavy Majesty dined at the same table each night. An extravagant tip to the maitre d' assured Abe of an adjoining table.

That first night, Abe walked into the dining room with three well-endowed blondes. The three ladies had been coached and well-paid to dote over Abe all through the meal. Farouk, whose appetite for bad girls was only surpassed by his penchant for good food, couldn't help but notice the action at the next table. Each evening, 59-year-old Abe repeated the performance.

Eventually His Majesty's curiosity was tweaked. He inquired as to how Abe, at his age, managed to keep three ladies so very happy, satisfied, or whatever. Abe, a master at small talk, soon became a friend of the King of Egypt.

Little by little he let the king know he had a third of a billion dollars in safety deposit boxes in New York. The money had been earned illegally. No taxes had been paid on the cash. As a result, Abe couldn't travel to New York to pick up his ill-gotten gains.

King Farouk checked out Abe's story. His investigator confirmed that Abe had indeed rented several safety deposit boxes in various New York City banks.

Farouk had a plan. If Abe signed access to the boxes over to him, he would see that Abe obtained his money under certain conditions. Farouk's fee for his services would be ten percent, or $33 million. In addition, Abe would guarantee to invest $100 million in Egyptian enterprises.

Gee, Abe told the king, His Majesty drives a hard bargain. He would have to think it over. Abe even confided to the king that he was short of cash. This was no problem to Farouk. He insisted that Abe move into the Royal Suite with him. Abe accepted. But still, a man required a certain amount of independence, say $100,000 worth of independence. Farouk had no intention of letting his pigeon off the hook because of such a paltry sum. He turned over $100,000 to Abraham Sykowski.

At that precise time in history an event took place back in Egypt over which Abe had no control. Gamal Abdel Nasser, a spoilsport army officer, was causing all sorts of unrest. The powers that be suggested that King Farouk leave the ladies alone for a while and come home. Farouk agreed, and invited Abe to accompany him. That's how the tailor's son from the Lower East Side of New York became a more or less permanent guest at Abdin Palace in Cairo. Abe had everything his heart desired. He literally lived like a king.

The good times lasted five months. In July, under Nasser's leadership, the country revolted. Large King Farouk was unceremoniously sent back to the Riviera, this time in exile.

Abe skipped. He has never been officially heard of again. However, acquaintances spotted him in a plush Paris restaurant in the mid-fifties. Abraham Sykowski was decked out in a tuxedo and was accompanied by two shapely Parisienne beauties.

THE CARDIFF GIANT

"There were giants on the earth in those days." -Genesis 6:4

George Hull looked about his cigar factory in Binghamton, N.Y. and thought to himself that there had to be something more to life than tobacco. Surely, in his allotted span of three score and ten, he could perform some act of renown or achieve some measure of fame so that the recorders of the unusual would remember him after he departed his mortal coil.

While thus pensively disposed, George travelled to Ackley, Iowa in 1871 to visit his sister. George's sister was a woman who feared the Lord, her husband, and the fires of hell, pretty well in that order. She made it a point to attend revival meetings and insisted that George accompany her to hear the good words as expounded by Evangelist John Turk.

George nodded at the right places. He even mouthed the expected responses, but his heart wasn't in the revival business. His head snapped forward. What was the Reverend Turk saying? There were giants on the earth in those days? Of course there were. George would see to it. He would make his own giant. But first there was some research to attend to.

"Tell me, Rev. Turk, what size were the giants which roamed the earth in those times?" inquired George. Without a pause in praising the Almighty, the Rev. Turk replied, "I would imagine they were at least 12 feet tall."

That's all George wanted to hear. That night he tossed and turned. He could think of nothing else. Bright-eyed and bushy-tailed, George rose the next morning and visited stone quarries located near Fort Dodge. He found just what the doctor ordered - a hunk of gypsum measuring over 12 feet long and 4 feet wide. George bought the five ton mammoth piece of gypsum on the spot.

There were problems. How does one transport a five ton piece of gypsum without having to answer a lot of questions? George developed a cover story. He was collecting unusual mineral specimens from each state for an exhibit taking place in Washington. The locals swallowed that one.

Now all he had to do was transport that rock 30 miles to the railway station. This proved to be no mean task. George broke several wagons, but finally had the gypsum and himself on a train heading for Chicago. Once there, he stored his unusual cargo in the barn of an acquaintance.

George had the time, the money and the patience. Besides, he knew exactly what he was doing. He hired an artist and a stonecutter. He assured them they would be well paid for their efforts and gave them strict instructions. George wanted the end product to be a huge naked giant. The facial expression would have a distinct look of pain and horror, depicting the way he died. The two men were sworn to secrecy. For five months they labored. Gradually, a face, complete with eyes, nose and mouth took form.

All this hacking and chiselling had reduced the size and weight of the giant to a mere 10 feet 4 inches and 3000 pounds. Needle point hammers produced pore-like tiny holes in the gypsum. Aging was accomplished with the aid of sulphuric acid.

George had the giant crated and shipped to Binghamton, N.Y. Then he looked up his cousin, Bill Newell, who lived on a farm near the small town of Cardiff, about 13 miles south of Syracuse. Bill was game to turn a dishonest dollar. Equipped with four horses and assorted trusted relatives, the giant was lugged to Bill's farm, where it was buried face up five feet underground. The area was then seeded with clover.

George had planned to wait up to a year before "finding" the phenomenon of the ages. As luck would have it, the process was speeded up. A farmer plowing his field in Onondaga Valley unearthed some bones, which were sent to Cornell University and authenticated as genuine fossils. George instinctively knew that the time was ripe. He told cousin Bill to let his neighbors know that his well was running dry and he would soon need to dig for a new one. Bill agreed to co-operate in return for 10% of the take.

Cousin Bill had no difficulty leading the unsuspecting dowsers to where he wanted them to dig. He left the well-diggers to do their work. Bill went to Syracuse.

When he returned there was some excitement taking place on the farm.

Who would believe it, a giant! A petrified giant found right on Bill Newell's farm. Word spread like wildfire. Everyone talked about the giant. Reporters from all over the nation converged on the Newell farm. Soon European correspondents arrived on the scene.

Bill erected a tent around the giant. To limit the unscientific, he charged 50 cents a peek. It was quite a sight. The mammoth naked man had been lying underground for centuries, uncovered only by the sheerest of accidents by well-diggers. Surely, this was living proof that the Bible was literally true. There were giants on the earth in those days. Someone labelled the huge fossil "The Cardiff Giant" and the name stuck.

Picking up on the religious angle, preachers from across North America came to view the biblical giant. All agreed. The giant was authentic. Under George's instructions, Bill raised the admission price to $1. Business boomed. On one Sunday alone, 2,800 gullible folks viewed what was now being hailed as the eighth wonder of the world.

As summer gave way to winter, George realized that it would become increasingly difficult for customers to make their way to the Newell farm. Reluctantly, he accepted $30,000 from a group of Syracuse businessmen for a 75% interest in the giant. They moved the giant to a Syracuse exhibition hall, where it was displayed before thousands.

Eminent scientists and archeologists declared the Cardiff Giant to be a genuine fossil. Dr. James H. Drator, head of the prestigious New York State Museum, proclaimed, "The statue is remarkable and is authentic. It is a link between the past and today." The curious lined up in droves.

Not everyone was fooled. Dr. Andrew D. White of Cornell University examined a sliver from the giant and declared, "It's pure gypsum." Sculptor E.D. Palmer took one look and said, "The Cardiff Giant is a hoax." But the public refused to accept the word of these experts. They were deemed to be anti-religious.

P.T. Barnum, of "there's a sucker born every minute" fame, wanted a piece of the action. George wouldn't hear of moving the giant out of the area. P.T. was not to be denied. He had a duplicate giant manufactured and displayed it in New York as the one and only Cardiff Giant. George took him all the way to the New York State Supreme Court. That august body ruled that P.T. had just as much right to display his giant as George had.

Surprisingly, both giants continued to draw well for some time. George went on tour with his Cardiff Giant, billing it as the one and only. Eventually business dropped off in Barnum's New York museum. He stored his giant near Buffalo, where it was destroyed by an explosion in 1904.

Reporters gnawed away at the history of the giant until they uncovered the true story of George's trip to Iowa, the manufacturing of the giant and its burial. Despite proof positive that the Cardiff Giant was a hoax, a curious public continued to pay to see it long after it was exposed. Before being placed in storage, the giant was displayed at the Pan Am games in Buffalo in 1901.

In 1939, the Cardiff Giant was acquired by the New York State Historical Society and placed on display outdoors at the Farmers Museum in Cooperstown, New York, where I viewed the eighth wonder of the world.

Ms Rabbit Goody, Supervisor of Domestic Arts at the Museum, has informed me that since my visit the Cardiff Giant has moved indoors. It is now on a platform, with appropriate bunting above and below the display, duplicating the manner in which it was exhibited over 90 years ago.

Some visitors say the Cardiff Giant's craggy visage has developed a slight smile.

ARTIE'S LUCK
RAN OUT

Artie Pais was a pleasant, round little man with a bald head. He made his living as a mechanic in a New Rochelle, N.Y. garage, where he was the most popular man on the staff. Artie had a girlfriend, Ida, who lived and worked in the same neighborhood. In the years after World War II, he saved his money and opened his own garage in nearby Larchmont. No question about it, Artie was the salt of the earth.

It was while running his own establishment that Artie met Angie John. Angie, a horse trainer by profession and a schemer by inclination, introduced Artie to the exacting science of betting on the nags at the nearby track in Yonkers. In the course of following the ponies, the two men made the acquaintance of Frankie Mateo. Frankie came highly recommended. He was a navy deserter and small-time thief.

The three men became fast friends and might have remained that way for years had Artie's garage remained solvent. Never mind that he was raiding the cash register in order to place friendly wagers on slow horses. It makes no difference. The garage went under.

Artie and Angie put their heads together. Artie was a mechanic without a garage. Angie was a horse trainer without a horse. There seemed little else they could do but rob a bank. They picked a small branch of the County Trust Co. in Mount Vernon. Things went smoothly. The boys took their time, tied up four employees and left with a cool $97,000.

The employees told police that the two robbers were friendly, relaxed and appeared to be in no hurry to leave the premises. They had spent 35 minutes in the company's offices and left no clues to their identity.

Artie and Angie bought a horse for $7,000. Angie, the expert on horseflesh, went for breeding. Their new acquisition, Battleover, claimed Man o' War as his grand-daddy. The boys shipped themselves and Battleover to Florida and waited for the money to roll in. Battleover was a fine looking animal, but displayed a decided dislike for jockeys. In his first two starts, he threw his jockey. Then he went lame.

Back in Manhattan, Ida was getting impatient. Artie had promised marriage as soon as Battleover started winning. In due course, Battleover recovered sufficiently to take part in the balance of the winter racing season. Now completely cured of tossing jockeys off his back and with all four legs in working trim, the temperamental animal was entered in several races. Battleover was consistent. He didn't win a race.

Dejected, and with their trust company loot growing dangerously low, Artie and Angie headed north with the first signs of spring. Before leaving for northern climes, inconsiderate Battleover, in a temper tantrum, kicked Artie in the derriere. In the ensuing weeks, Battleover's hoofprint developed into an ugly sore on Artie's bottom.

Once back in New York, Ida insisted that Artie see a doctor. Reluctantly, Artie had his rump examined. The hoofprint had developed into a non-malignant cyst. It hurt like hell. An operation was scheduled for the immediate future.

In the meantime, the two men renewed their acquaintance with Frankie Mateo. Money was running low and ungrateful Battleover was eating like a horse. The partners decided to rob a bank. Frankie, good friend that he was, would assist.

The boys picked the County Bank Co. in Port Chester as the location for their next unscheduled withdrawal. They noted that a middle-aged woman, Mary Kostolos, was the first to arrive at the bank each morning. The conspirators stole a car, equipped it with stolen licence plates, and proceeded to trail Mary from a grocery store to her home. It was 10:15 p.m. Artie and Frankie jumped into Mary's car and almost scared her to death. Artie explained, "Everything is going to be all right, lady. All we want is the bank's money."

Mary informed them that the vault could only be opened at 8 o'clock the next morning by another bank employee. Frankie was devastated. He insisted that they stop and inform Angie of this revolting development. Angie, trailing in the stolen car, lost his nerve. He told his partners that he wanted to go home. Artie and Frankie were welcome to rob the bank should they still feel up to the task.

Artie needed time to think. He drove Mary's car around the streets of Port Chester for a couple of hours. Frankie was nervous, Mary petrified.

Surprise number two was in store for the inept bank robbers. With a degree of urgency, Mary announced, "I have to go to the bathroom." That was the final straw for Frankie. He declared, "I want to go home." Artie found a ladies' room in a gas station, which nicely attended to Mary's immediate needs. Then, reluctantly, he drove Frankie to his White Plains home.

The whole well-planned evening was turning into a fiasco, but still Artie wouldn't throw in the towel. He proceeded to the bank, parked Mary's car in the parking lot and had Mary open the bank's front door with her key.

It was 4 a.m. Artie had four hours to wait until the vault could be opened. He passed by some time by leading Mary to the washroom and tying her to the toilet. Considerate Artie left the door ajar so he and Mary would not get lonesome.

While Artie and Mary were enjoying each other's company, Angie and Frankie met. What the heck, they decided, let's see if Artie went through with the robbery. It was around 7 a.m. when they cruised by the bank in the stolen car. Artie happened to peer out the bank's window as his partners drove by. Some friends, he thought, they never even dropped in.

Around 7:30 a.m., bank employees showed up. One by one, Artie tied them and deposited them in the lavatory. Finally, Purdy Ungemack, the man who could open the vault, walked in. He, like all the other employees, figured there were several armed men robbing the bank. Only Artie knew he was all alone. Patiently, Artie waited until 8 a.m.

Customers gathered outside the door waiting for the bank to open. At last, 8 a.m. arrived. Ungemack opened the vault. Artie rushed in. There was money everywhere but, darn it all, he had forgotten to bring something in which to carry away the loot. Scampering about the bank, Artie found a cardboard box. He crammed it full of bills, but it didn't hold all the money. In desperation, he filled a wastebasket with bills.

Artie ordered Ungemack to help him carry the money out to the car. He instructed Ungemack to tell those nosy customers that he would be back in a moment. Ungemack never dreamed that this relaxed, bald-headed little guy was robbing his bank single-handed. Customers grumbled at the delay, but said good morning. A police officer, parked nearby in his cruiser, waved. Artie waved back.

In moments, Artie was steering Mary's car through rush hour traffic. He drove to a supermarket parking lot, where he had left his own car. He leisurely transferred his two containers of money to his car and drove home. When he dumped the money on his bed, counting it proved to be quite a task. The take was a whopping $188,784.51.

Well, now, who should show up at Artie's home but those fair-weather friends,

Frankie and Angie. They insisted on some small compensation for services rendered. Artie dickered before giving each man $30,000.

Police swarmed over the bank. Employees were questioned about the gang. What did they look like? How many were there? The press dubbed the robbery a "perfectly executed operation with army-like precision."

Artie's unbelievable luck ran out. That very night, a citizen reported that he had seen a man transfer two packages to a vehicle from the auto that was identified as belonging to Mary Kostolos. The nosy parker even jotted down the licence number.

Artie was traced, his home searched, and his portion of the loot recovered. He readily confessed, implicating his two friends. Angie and Frankie were picked up without incident. All but $2,000 of the bank's loot was recovered.

The three men were tried and found guilty. Angie received a sentence of 25 years in prison. Frankie got 22 years. Artie, who co-operated throughout with authorities, was sent away for 18 years.

When asked if he had anything to say before sentence was passed, Artie said that he would appreciate if the wheels of justice would speed up a bit. His cyst was killing him and he was scheduled for surgery that very day.

2

THE

POISONERS

SARAH DISPENSED ARSENIC

Poisoners as a group are the most insidious of all murderers. I am not referring to those poisoners who add a dash of arsenic here and there to rid themselves of a frigid spouse. Heavens, no. I am alluding to those ladies and gentlemen who, for one reason or another, see fit to administer their deadly potions to several of their fellow human beings over a period of years. Sometimes the poisoners are in a position to solicitously nurse their victims into the grave.

Sarah Jane Robinson did, but we will get to all that soon enough.

When Sarah was only fifteen, she and her sister Annie, nine, arrived in the United States to join a brother who had preceded them from Ireland. Like many natives of the Emerald Isle, they settled in New England.

Both girls were rather pretty and as they grew up had no trouble attracting suitors. Sarah eventually married Moses Robinson and raised a family in Cambridge, Massachusetts. Annie married an insignificant gentleman with the regal-sounding name of Prince Arthur Freeman.

There you have it. Two children, making their way in the New World, marrying and raising families. Some called them the salt of the earth. We will never know what initially possessed Sarah to switch from salt to arsenic. We do know that she became well-known among her family and friends as a sort of prophet. Sarah would close her eyes on an overcast summer evening, go into what appeared to be a trance, and declare that the sun would shine bright and clear the next day. She was right more often than she was wrong.

The family was somewhat startled one night in 1881 when Sarah closed her eyes and declared that their landlord, one Oliver Sleeper, who lived in the same house as the Robinsons, would become gravely ill. The family was perversely delighted when almost immediately Sleeper commenced to suffer from nausea.

That Sarah could really call the shots. When she declared that the landlord would not recover, the family awaited developments with baited breath. They didn't have long to wait. In a few days Oliver became a permanent "sleeper." The poor man had succumbed to stomach trouble, or consumption, or whatever.

For the next several months Sarah batted only .500 on the weather-prediction scale but proved to be flawless when it came to death. A tear rolled down her cheek as she sadly told her children that their father was not long for this world. As if set upon by supernatural powers, Moses took ill. It was only a year after Mr. Sleeper took his permanent leave when Moses was laid to rest. Sarah collected $1,000 insurance. Sarah and her three children, Lizzie, William, and Charlie, continued to live in the same house without incident for the next three years. We can only assume that she contented herself with weather predictions during this dry spell. Then all hell broke loose.

Sarah's sister Annie came down with a case of pneumonia but was recovering nicely when Sarah insisted that Annie move right into her house to be nursed back to health. Strangely enough, instead of improving, Annie went rapidly downhill under her sister's loving care. After lengthy bouts of nausea and vomiting, she expired.

Prince Arthur and his son Tommy moved in with the Robinson clan. This move was not a wise one.

Quite suddenly, Tommy became sick. "The Lord works in strange and wonderful ways," declared Sarah. "The boy will be leaving soon to join his Uncle Moses." Those members of the family who remembered Sarah's accurate and deadly prediction of three years before sat up and took notice. Within a few days Tommy joined his mother and his Uncle Moses.

Next to the interred in the rich New England soil was Prince Arthur, who had the decency to leave in his wake the princely sum of $2,000, a fortune in those days. Sarah, of course, was the next of kin.

Prince Arthur Freeman and his family were no more. Did Sarah rest? No, she did not.

This cold, heartless woman turned to her own children. Lizzie began to suffer from spells of nausea. Her mother told neighbors it was no use. Moses would soon be coming to take her away. Sarah was right on the money again. Lizzie was buried, and Sarah collected the insurance loot. A few months later, William joined his sister. He was the fifth member of the family to expire in eighteen months. Little Charlie Robinson, the last remaining member of the family, must have been expecting one of his mother's dreaded predictions, but merely by chance he was to be spared.

Sarah Jane Robinson's name had shown up so often at the offices of the United Order of Pilgrim Fathers, a benevolent organization which had carried insurance on the lives of Sarah's victims, that they began to think she was a member of the staff. The Pilgrim Fathers decided all was not kosher with Sarah and called in the police.

A cursory investigation was all that was necessary to figure out that a woman who correctly predicts five illnesses and five deaths in eighteen months can't be all good. An indignant Sarah was taken into custody. The five most recent victims were exhumed, and all were found to be liberally laced with arsenic. Police delved further into Sarah's history and exhumed husband Moses and landlord Sleeper. Both bodies contained arsenic.

How in the world did Sarah evade detection for so long? It must be remembered that we are relating Sarah's murderous ways in hindsight. At the time, the doctors who attended her victims were faced with a pleasant, concerned woman, who apparently loved her family. She had tirelessly nursed all of her patients before they died. The symptoms of arsenic poisoning can readily be mistaken for those of several stomach ailments. Before the turn of the century refrigeration as we know it did not exist. Tainted food was often consumed, resulting in stomach trouble and occasionally death. Epidemics did wipe out entire families.

In 1886 Sarah was tried for the murder of her son William. Her guilt was not easy to prove. It was never revealed how she acquired arsenic. No one had actually seen her administer the poison. At her trial no reference could be made to her other victims. Sarah swore that vengeful, wicked people were at work to destroy her because of her God-given talents as a seer. The jury was unable to reach a verdict.

The state then tried Sarah for the murder of her brother-in-law, Prince Arthur. This time they received permission to delve into the murder of Annie Freeman as well. It was argued that Annie was murdered in order to remove an heir to Prince Arthur's $2,000. At this second trial Sarah's motive was clearly proven to be murder for insurance money.

Sarah was found guilty and sentenced to hang. At the time of her sentencing she gave an elaborate, emotional speech professing her innocence. Her sentence was later commuted to life imprisonment.

Once in prison Sarah continually decorated photographs of her victims with fresh cut flowers. She served almost twenty years in prison before dying there in 1906.

CHAMPION HOCH

Henri Landru, known as "Bluebeard," seduced scores of women for fun and profit. "Brides in the Bath" Smith married several ladies before fatally dunking them in their baths. Both gentlemen were unquestionably unique, but for sheer quantity of wives, none surpasses the champ of champs, the groom of grooms, the one and only Johann Hoch.

Johann left his native Germany around 1881, and for the next ten years roamed the United States performing menial tasks to keep the wolf from the door. In 1882 he settled in Chicago, gaining employment in the meat-packing business. Somewhere along the way, Johann got the bright idea that it was extremely profitable to marry lonesome ladies and either abscond with their money or kill them. Once he got the hang of it he became the all-time world's champion marrying man.

Mrs. C. A. Mayer has the distinction of being the very first lady to fall for the chunky, magnetic little man with the big black moustache and thick German accent. Three weeks after the holy union the former Mrs. Mayer died of convulsions. Of course we know that nasty Johann had slipped a substantial quantity of arsenic into his loved one's porridge.

Two months later Johann tied the knot with Mrs. Harriet Irick. Harriet was laid to rest fifteen days later. The year 1893 was an off year for Johann. His lone marriage that year was to a Mrs. S. Hauck of Peoria, Illinois, whom he quickly deserted after she turned over her life savings of $400. The following year Johann married again. This wife's fate is unknown to this day. She simply disappeared from the face of the earth.

Mrs. Martha Steinbrecher married Johann and lived happily for four months. Unfortunately she died of convulsions, screaming that she had been poisoned. Her attentive husband swore to the heavens that if he ever found out that his wife had been poisoned he would pound the culprit to a pulp. No one paid any attention to either him or Martha. Johann reluctantly sold the property Martha left him for $4,000.

At about this time in his murderous marrying career, Johann decided to speed up his operation. He believed in advertising. His ads brought scads of inquiries from lonely ladies, who immediately fell under the hypnotic spell of the little German.

Mary Rankin never even made it to the bedroom. Our boy took the money and ran before the marriage had been consummated. Then there was Janet Spencer. Poor Janet was left high and dry a few weeks after her marriage.

Charlotte Andrews is deserving of mention. She set a record of sorts. Charlotte was deserted exactly two hours after the ceremony.

Ironically Johann met Mrs. Mary Hoch of Wheeling, West Virginia. As soon as he heard the familiar last name Johann knew he would have no trouble. He wooed, wed and poisoned Mary, all within a few weeks. Mrs. James Huss lasted three months and coughed up over $2,500. Barbara Brosset married Johann on September 22, 1896, after a courtship of exactly three days.

The list goes on and on. From city to city, always marrying, sometimes deserting, sometimes poisoning, Johann kept up the frantic pace. Early in December 1904, he placed an ad in a German-language newspaper. The advertisement read: "Matrimonial - German, own home, wish acquaintance of widow without children, object matrimony."

Nothing catchy. Direct and to the point - that was our Johann. Yet the advertisement brought an immediate response from divorced Julia Marie Walcker. Her reply read: "Dear Sir, In answer to your honorable advertisement, I hereby inform you that I am a lady standing alone. I am 46 years of age and have a small business, also a few hundred dollars. If you are in earnest I tell you I shall be. I may be seen at 12 Willow St."

Julia had nothing to fear. Johann was earnest, all right. Within twelve days Julia became Mrs. Johann Hoch. She sold her tiny shop for $75, which she dutifully turned over to her new husband, together with her life savings of $300. She and Johann moved into a rented cottage, which Julia believed belonged to her attentive husband.

Soon after occupying their new home, Julia became quite ill. Johann called in Dr. John Reese who diagnosed Julia's illness as being inflammation of the bladder. He left her some medicine. In the days that followed, Julia's condition worsened. Johann called Julia's sister, Mrs. Amelia Fischer, and asked her to visit. Mrs. Fischer responded to the call immediately. She stayed awhile, made her sister comfortable, cleaned up the cottage, cooked a hot meal, and in general acted as a good sister should.

Johann walked Mrs. Fischer to the streetcar one evening. He was charming, attentive, even flattering. No question about it, our boy knew how to turn them on. Next day Mrs. Fischer was back for more of the same. It got so bad that the once staid Mrs. Fischer acted overly friendly with Johann right in front of her very ill sister. Julia berated Mrs. Fischer in a voice loud and clear. Mrs. Fischer turned up her nose, threw on her coat, and marched right out of the Hoch cottage.

Julia Hoch's condition deteriorated rapidly. Wracked with excruciating pain, she mercifully died one month to the day after her marriage. Johann's grief was so great he had to be restrained at graveside.

Speedy Johann proposed to his sister-in-law on the ride back from the cemetery. Mrs. Fischer accepted. Four days later she became Mrs. Hoch. On her wedding day she turned over $750 to her new husband. That night Johann flew the coop.

Two days later the talkative Mrs. Hoch informed police that she had been married, swindled, and deserted, all within twelve hours. Chicago police put out the word and were immediately deluged with inquiries from all over the country. Could this be the Mr. Hoch I was married to? All the ladies fortunate enough to be alive were correct. Johann had married them all.

As the tale unfolded the name "Hoch" became a household word. Every suspicious woman in America was on the lookout for the marrying man. Mrs. Katherine Kuemmerle of New York City recognized Hoch's description as fitting one of her roomers. Mrs. Kuemmerle called the police, and the elusive Johann Hoch was taken into custody.

Women came out of the woodwork to pull the plug on Johann. Still, there were many who were too ashamed or embarrassed to admit that they had been taken in by the not very attractive little man with the black moustache and the piercing eyes.

Authorities were able to document twenty-four marriages. At least twelve of the new brides died suddenly soon after walking down the aisle. Johann denied murdering anyone, although when taken into custody he was carrying a large quantity of arsenic. It is estimated that he married at least fifty times. He readily admitted to the twenty-four proven marriages and conceded that there must have been many more, but for the life of him he couldn't remember the names or the details.

Once resigned to his fate, Johann proved to be a remarkable character in many ways. Even while in custody he still held a strange fascination for women. Detectives and guards had to admit that he was an excellent conversationalist and an amusing companion. He loved to explain that his unusual hold over women could be attributed to his use of flattery.

On May 19, 1905, Hoch was found guilty of murder and sentenced to death. While awaiting execution, his last wife, Amelia Fischer, stood by her husband even though she knew very well that he had murdered her sister.

Does a leopard change his spots? No sir. Johann proposed to a cute little police matron while awaiting his date with death. Unfortunately his date with the executioner was one rendezvous Johann Hoch was forced to keep.

He was hanged on February 23, 1906.

HOME SWEET HOME

J im Archer and his wife, Amy, struggled for years to save enough money to open the Archer Home for Elderly People in Windsor, Connecticut. Amy, a deeply religious graduate nurse, had a dream. She saw herself easing the discomfort of those feeble elderly people who didn't have that much time left on this good earth.

Right from the beginning the Archer Home flourished. In 1910, after only three years in operation, the home was the well-established domicile of twenty elderly guests. Amy usually charged a lump sum upon accepting a guest into her home. Amounts ranging from $1,000 to $2,000 were turned over to her in exchange for the necessities of life for whatever years remained.

Amy was a fine nurse and an excellent administrator, scurrying from dawn to dusk, caring for the myriad needs of her elderly guests. Her reputation was enhanced when she donated the handsome sum of $1,000 towards the purchase of a new organ for the local church. No question about it, 50-year-old Amy had arrived as a well-liked, respected pillar of the community.

All were saddened when James Archer died, leaving all his worldly goods to his wife. Three years later Amy married one of her elderly guests, Michael W. Gilligan. Unfortunately, after only four months of marital bliss, he chose to depart these mortal climes in favor of whatever lies beyond. Considerate Michael managed to make out his will only hours before the end. Amy inherited the tidy sum of $5,000.

It is only proper to note that death is not a stranger in homes for the aged. The Archer Home was no exception. In fact, it seemed that hardly a month went by without a visit from the local undertaker. No one was overly concerned.

On May 30, 1914, guest Frank Andrews rose bright and early, had a hearty breakfast, and prepared to paint a fence. By mid-afternoon Frank had completed his work. He sat down to the dinner table, displaying his usual good disposition. Shortly after dinner Frank complained of not feeling well.

At about 11 o'clock that same night, Amy called Frank's sister, Mrs. Nellie A. Pierce, who lived a few miles away. She told Nellie that Frank was not feeling well, but it didn't seem to be anything serious. She would call Nellie again in the morning when Frank felt better. Ten minutes after Amy made this call, Frank Andrews was dead. Dr. H. F. King, the county medical examiner, attributed death to gastric ulcers and so signed the death certificate.

Neighbors talked. It just didn't seem right. Frank Andrews was painting the fence in the afternoon, ate a hearty meal that evening, was vaguely ill at 11:00 p.m., and was stone dead ten minutes later. When these rumors reached Dr. King, he was furious at the malicious neighbors besmirching the good name and good works of Amy Archer-Gilligan. The doctor reminded the gossips that many of Amy's guests could only afford small lump-sum payments and were in fact subsidized by Amy herself.

Not satisfied with this explanation, several neighbors contacted a Hartford newspaper, which in turn informed police of the suspicious deaths taking place at the Archer Home. Detectives investigating the matter felt they were dealing with a mass murderer, but with so little concrete evidence to go on they proceeded slowly. It wasn't until May 8, 1916, two years after Frank Andrews' death that authorities felt they had enough evidence to proceed against Amy. She was taken into custody and placed in the Hartford jail.

Soon accounts of Amy's foul deeds appeared in the Hartford newspapers. The heat was on. The number of deaths which had taken place at the Archer Home was now being studied by police. A total of 48 deaths had occurred in five years, an average of one death every six weeks. The Old People's Home in Hartford had buried exactly the same number, but as everyone was quick to grasp, the Hartford home had six and a half times as many guests. Other comparisons were made, and in each case the incidence of death was between six and ten times greater at the Archer Home.

One fact puzzled everyone for a while. Amy had not gained in any material way from the deaths of her guests. Only her late husband had had anything to leave. What could be her motive?

Police delved painstakingly into Amy's operation. They came to realize that her motive for murdering her guests lay just below the surface, but it was there nevertheless - evil, cunning greed. By shortening the lives of her guests she increased the frequency of lump-sum payments by new guests. Even if a new guest didn't immediately arrive to take the place of a dead one, Amy still gained by cutting down on the overhead.

Could Amy have murdered all 48? Everyone took part in the guessing game. The one person who knew for sure swore from the jail that the whole thing was insane. She was a nurse, not a murderer.

The state of Connecticut exhumed bodies all that autumn of 1916. As a result of their investigation Amy was charged with the murder of her second husband, Michael W. Gilligan, as well as the murders of guests Charles A. Smith, Frank Andrews, Alice Gowdy, and Maude Lynch.

Five murders is a nice round figure. While the state hinted that arsenic was found in several other victims, they proceeded only with those cases which appeared easiest to prove.

Amy's trial took place in June 1917. Although the prosecution wanted to proceed with five charges, it was ruled that only one charge could be presented at one time. The State chose the case of Frank Andrews. Andrews' body had been exhumed and his vital organs were found to contain large quantities of arsenic. The prosecution followed up by proving that Amy had purchased arsenic a short time before Andrews' death, ostensibly to kill rats in her home. It was proven that the Archer Home was singularly free of rodents of any kind.

Amy was found guilty of murder in the first degree and sentenced to be hanged on the morning of November 6, 1917. While there was no doubt as to Amy's guilt, the idea of hanging a woman was reprehensible to many influential people. It had been more than a hundred years since a woman had been hanged in the state of Connecticut.

Amy was granted a reprieve. The governor of the state then granted a stay of execution, and finally the Supreme Court of Appeals ordered a new trial. Basically, the court ruled that evidence pertaining to the poisoning of other victims had been erroneously admitted as evidence.

In June 1919, at Middleton, Connecticut, Amy once more stood trial with her life in the balance. At the last moment she pleaded guilty and was sentenced to life imprisonment. It had taken three years for the Amy Archer-Gilligan case to reach its conclusion.

In the end no one really knew how many victims had succumbed to Amy's poisonous ways. Surely some of the 48 deaths at the Archer Home were due to natural causes. Still, there are those who believe that Amy gave every one of the 48 victims a gentle push towards the grave. If so, Amy was one of the most prolific mass murderers of all time.

ENTER GESINA, EXIT LOVERS

Before scientific tests were developed to detect the presence of arsenic in recently deceased relatives and friends, unsavory characters had the vile habit of dispensing the deadly poison with reckless abandon. Ladies found the nasty white powder particularly convenient in hastening the departure of unwanted lovers and oh, so tired husbands.

The subject of this story, Gesina Gottfried, was a comely fraulein who operated in various German towns and cities in the 1820s. Old records revealed that she had a delicate figure and finely chiselled features. No question about it, the boys looked up from their Pilsener and pretzels whenever Gesina strolled by.

Herr Mittenberg appeared to be a wealthy businessman, and as such became a target for our Gesina, even though she was only seventeen. Gesina played out the line; Mittenberg nibbled, then took the bait and proposed. Gesina said *ya*, and soon became the youthful and lovely Frau Mittenberg. No sooner was the honeymoon over when Mittenberg revealed the true state of affairs to his young bride. Instead of being loaded, he was heavily in debt. Gesina didn't take her husband's deception well. In fact, she grew to hate Mittenberg with a passion.

The pair quarrelled constantly. Despite this lack of true love, Gesina found it in her heart to forgive and forget at least twice. The squabbling couple had two children.

Mittenberg was soon drowning his sorrows by downing copious quantities of schnapps. One dull day, when he was in his cups, he hauled off and put the slug on

Gesina. It was a mistake. Then and there she decided that one day she would kill her husband. Come to think of it, the children were annoying as well. Gesina made a mental note to dispose of them when the time was ripe.

Around this time in her troubled, but so far not criminal, career, Gesina met a young man named Gottfried. For the first time in her life she fell in love. It was fun rolling in the hay with Gottfried, but the intrigue was tiring. If only Mittenberg, the spoilsport, would die, she would be free to marry her true love. While such fanciful thoughts danced through her head, Gesina observed her mother liberally lacing some cheese with a white powder. Inquisitive Gesina found out that the powder was deadly arsenic. Mittenberg's fate was sealed.

A more than sufficient quantity, dissolved in Mittenberg's beer at suppertime, was all that it took. He clawed at his stomach, grew clammy, brought up, and writhed in agony. Gesina washed the dishes. A broad smile crossed her lips when she leaned over her husband and found that he was breathing no more. Herr Mittenberg was hastily buried without incident.

Gesina was free to marry her lover, but wouldn't you know it, there was a catch. Her parents didn't cotton to Gottfried, and that upstanding gentleman insisted that her parents had to accept him before he would promise to love, cherish, and protect forever. Try as she might, Gesina couldn't talk her parents into accepting Gottfried.

Ever thoughtful, Gesina had a solution. One night, while a guest in her parents' home, she insisted on preparing the evening meal. Presto, Gesina's parents toppled over dead. Once again Gesina showed up at graveside, dabbing at her bloodshot eyes as her parents were laid to rest.

Surely Gottfried would marry her now. Gesina was wrong. Stubborn Gottfried felt that he could not in good conscience marry her because of her two children by Mittenberg. Gesina did what had to be done. She fed arsenic to her two children who were promptly removed from the scene.

Now, if you are keeping score, that's five deaths in the same family. Yet no real suspicion fell on Gesina. The bad luck which seemed to have befallen Gesina's family was not particularly unique.

All obstacles had been overcome. Gottfried would be hers at last. When the subject of matrimony was broached, instead of being eager, Gottfried hesitated. Gestina listened to his lame excuses. The thought entered her head that she had fooled everyone except Gottfried. He had somehow guessed the truth and was scared silly of his everloving Gesina.

Gesina was fit to be tied. Imagine, knocking off her husband, her parents, and her children, only to be rebuffed by the object of her affection. She would show him. This time she had to be careful.

Slowly Gottfried was fed arsenic. He became ill. Each day the pain was a little more severe. Gesina moved into his home to nurse him back to health. Often the subject of their much-delayed wedding was brought up. When Gottfried's suffering was most intense he consented to the marriage. Quick as lightning, Gesina set up a bedside wedding, which was followed by Gottfried making out a will, naturally leaving all his worldly possessions to his dear wife. Gesina waited a few months before feeding her husband a massive dose of arsenic. He died in agony within twenty-four hours. That was that.

For several years after her killing spree, Gesina was the mistress of many wealthy men. She lived in relative comfort. Once again she tried her hand at marriage, and once again she murdered her husband after having him make out a will in her favor. Our heroine was now converted from a murderer who kills for love and revenge to one who kills for gain. She lived well, but slowly went through her victims' wealth.

Gesina's home in Bremen was heavily mortgaged. The holder of the mortgage, Herr Rumf, agreed to purchase the house. One of the terms of the agreement had the Rumf family, including wife and children, move into the home, with Gesina acting as housekeeper. Little did they know they were moving into a veritable lion's den.

With her usual cunning, Gesina came to the simple conclusion that she would have everything the Rumf family owned. Frau Rumf was fed an unpleasant mixture of arsenic and porridge for breakfast one morning. So much for Frau Rumf.

The man of the house turned his children over to the kind care of his housekeeper. The children soon were placed to rest beside their mother. Doctors had no hesitation in signing the death certificates.

Gesina went to work on Herr Rumf. With no one else in the once active home, Gesina and Rumf were together constantly. A touch, a whispered word, and gradually Herr Rumf was smitten. After she was firmly established as his mistress, Gesina broached the subject of a will. She was quite willing to forsake marriage, but she thought it only fair that Rumf provide for her should anything unforeseen happen to him. Rumf did as he was told. Gesina decided to poison him slowly, no doubt concerned that suspicion would fall on her as the only survivor of the entire household.

All good things come to an end. One day Rumf was home alone feeling ill. He thought that he may have eaten tainted pork and decided to investigate. Upon examining the side of pork from which the meal had been carved, he was amazed to find that it was completely covered with a fine white powder.

A light snapped on in Rumf's mind. He cut off a slab of pork and rushed to the police. They quickly summoned a chemist and, in no time at all, it was established that the white powder was arsenic.

Gesina was arrested on March 5, 1828, and charged with the murder of Frau Rumf and her children. Once in custody Gesina proved to be an open book, confessing to many crimes not even thought of by the authorities. She claimed that she was responsible for fifteen deaths during her murderous career. At no time did she show remorse or concern about the fate which awaited her.

She was quickly tried, sentenced to death, and executed.

SWEET AUNT CARRIE

What does a 14-year-old schoolboy from London, England, have in common with a matronly 63-year-old darling from Sydney, Australia? Quite a bit. Both were compulsive poisoners who had stumbled upon colorless, tasteless, and odorless thallium as the instrument they employed to send friends and relatives to that great world which lies beyond.

In 1962, before his sixteenth birthday, Graham Young was convicted of poisoning his mother, father, sister, and a school chum. Confined to Broadmoor, an institution for the criminally insane, Graham was released after nine years. Within sixty days he was dispensing his deadly concoction of thallium and tea to fellow employees in the tiny village of Bovingdon. After killing two colleagues and poisoning scores more, Graham was taken into custody. When questioned as to his motives, Graham replied, "I liked the power it gave me." He is presently confined to prison, where he presumably will remain for the rest of his life.

Down in Sydney, Australia, Carrie Grills had been married for close to forty years to her husband, Richard. Her whole life changed when the Grills moved in 1947 to a rat-infested apartment and Carrie discovered a commercial product called ThalRat. She was amazed at the product's efficient deadly qualities.

When she administered ThalRat to her stepmother, Christina Mickelson, our Carrie discovered that her new-found friend worked just as efficiently on humans as it did on rodents. After all, Christina was 87 and an absolute bore.

Next in line to bite the dust was a family friend, Mrs. Angelina Thomas, an 84-

year-old who had known Richard Grills since he was a boy. It appears that at this point in her fledgling career as a poisoner, Carrie felt that anyone over eighty was fair game. Whether by design or not, it is a fact that deaths of the elderly are not investigated with the same degree of concern as those of younger people.

John Lundberg was a mere youngster of 60 when he made the fatal error of joining the Grills on their vacation. John, who was married to Richard Grills' sister, began to feel a marked numbness in his legs. Soon his hair started to fall out. They buried John in October 1948.

Several years before this epidemic of death, Carrie's brother had passed away from natural causes. Honest. Now it was his widow Mary Mickelson's turn to bear the brunt of Carrie's wrath. She began to lose large tufts of her hair. When they buried Mary, poor Carrie, crying profusely, had to be led away from graveside.

If you are keeping score, we are now up to four, and not even an iota of suspicion had been cast in Carrie's direction. The chubby, round-faced obliging Carrie was everyone's friend. Serving tea, bringing cakes and cookies to family functions, Carrie was a rock among grieving relatives.

When John Lundberg went to his great reward after his not so delightful vacation with the Grills, he left behind a mourning wife, Eveline, and an adult daughter, Chrissie, who was married to a streetcar driver, John Downing. John and Chrissie lived on the same street as Eveline. Since the untimely death of her husband, it was quite natural for Eveline to spend a lot of time with her daughter and son-in-law. She would often pass the time of day sitting on their veranda.

Eveline was somewhat concerned. In recent days she had felt a certain numbness in her legs and arms. She also noticed that when she brushed her hair an inordinate quantity of it was left clinging to her hairbrush. Come to think of it, Chrissie and John didn't seem that well either. Not to worry; Aunt Carrie would drop in that day, as she did most every day. Carrie always cheered them up with her infectious good nature.

And so it happened. On April 13, 1953, John Downing was sitting in his kitchen while good-natured Aunt Carrie brewed up some tea to share with Eveline on the veranda. Was it John's imagination or had he really seen Aunt Carrie pause on her way to the veranda? Did her hand go to her dress pocket and then hesitate over one of the teacups as if she was surreptitiously slipping something into it? Next day Eveline seemed to be in great discomfort. A week later, when Aunt Carrie visited, John watched her carefully. The same thing happened. There could be no doubt - Aunt Carrie was putting something in the tea.

John knew he would cause a scene, but he didn't care. he waited until the spiked cup was placed before his mother-in-law. Then, despite Aunt Carrie's incredulous protests, he commandeered the cup of tea and took it to the police. An analysis of the contents revealed the presence of thallium.

Sweet, motherly Carrie Grills was taken into custody. Bodies were exhumed, and soon her murderous trail of thallium was uncovered. Initially Carrie was charged with four murders and three charges of attempted murder. Eventually, to expedite matters, the Crown proceeded with the attempted murder of Eveline Lundberg. Mrs. Lundberg had been left permanently blind as a result of the thallium administered to her by Carrie. She was assisted into the courtroom by her daughter and son-in-law, who had escaped without ill effects from the crazed obsession of dear Aunt Carrie.

While irrefutable evidence piled up against her, Aunt Carrie remained her cheerful, unflappable self. She retained her composure while bodies were exhumed and tests were conducted, all proving that she was some kind of a monster. Carrie's personality can best be illustrated by her response when she was told that the body of her stepmother, Mr. Mickelson, contained thallium. "Fancy that," Aunt Carrie replied, and would hear no more of such a distasteful subject.

Carrie was found guilty of attempted murder and sentenced to life in prison. Why did she snuff out four lives and leave another human being permanently blind? She never gained materially by any of the deaths, nor did she ever reveal any other motive for her poisonous spree. In fact, her lack of motive was the main thrust of her defence during her trial.

Of course, we know better. We have the benefit of Graham Young's words uttered almost twenty years later when he said, "I liked the power it gave me."

POISONING
IN JAPAN

Sadimacha Hirasawa is an embarrassment to an entire nation. He is living far too long and his country, Japan, is reluctant to execute him.

There is little doubt that the murders which took place at precisely 3:20 p.m. on Jan. 26, 1948, were the strangest and most infamous in Japan's criminal history. On that day, Manager Takejiro Yoshida beckoned to an employee to secure the doors of Tokyo's Teikoku Imperial Bank. The last customer left the bank, but just before the doors were locked one individual gained entrance. He wore a white cotton smock. An armband indicated that he was a welfare department health officer.

In those long ago days of 1948, Japan was governed by U.S. Occupational Forces under the command of General Douglas MacArthur. The Japanese were forced to follow scores of rules and regulations, many of which pertained to preventive medicine in an attempt to avoid epidemics.

The welfare department official approached manager Yoshida. He introduced himself as Dr. Jiro Yamaguchi. He explained that the U.S. authorities were concerned about an outbreak of dysentery in the area. They also feared a typhoid epidemic. He went on to state that his mission was to have all 15 bank employees take medicine to prevent a typhoid outbreak. He assured the manager that he was making the rounds of all business establishments in the area. Yoshida listened. The doctor made a certain degree of sense. He summoned his 14 employees and explained the reason for the doctor's visit.

Dr. Yamaguchi then took over. He reviewed his assignment, advising that each employee would be required to take two doses of medicine. He suggested they procure their personal teacups. Everyone did. Then the doctor demonstrated the method of taking the rather disagreeable medicine in one gulp. He extracted a large bottle from his official looking case and poured the liquid into each of the 15 cups. At the command, "Dozo," everyone gulped down the liquid.

Many gasped. Some complained of a burning sensation. The doctor quickly explained as he filled the cups for the second time that this cup would neutralize any bad effects. Once again, the employees drank from their personal cups. Several dashed to a water fountain in an outer office, but it was no use. Like rag dolls, they crumpled and fell in agony. All the while, the man known as Dr. Yamaguchi calmly stood by watching his victims die. He then scooped up 164,400 yen in cash and a cheque for 17,400 yen, at the time the equivalent of about $800 American. Dr. Yamaguchi strolled out of the bank and disappeared.

Inside the bank, lying in grotesque heaps, were the bodies of the madman's victims. Of the 15 employees in the bank that day, 12 were dead. Only the bank manager, Takejiro Yoshida, Mrs. Masako Takauchi, and one other employee, survived. Mrs. Takauchi crawled over her dead comrades toward the door and raised the alarm.

Within hours, the liquid left in the teacups was analysed. It contained potassium cyanide. The following day, news of the weird robbery and murders was given wide publicity. Soon the case became the most widely publicized and discussed crime ever committed in Japan. Despite the publicity, on the day following the murders, a careless teller cashed the 17,400 yen cheque stolen from the bank.

Investigating officers were amazed to discover that two previous attempts had been made to rob banks using the same method as at the Taikoku Bank. Three months before, a bogus doctor, introducing himself as Dr. Shigeru Matsui, entered the Yasuda Bank. He presented his personal card to the manager and convinced the 18 member staff to take medicine. The employees became ill, but there were no fatalities. The phony doctor left the bank without being apprehended. Later, the liquid was found to contain potassium cyanide, but the mixture was too weak to cause death.

Just nine days before the murders, a second attempt to rob a bank failed. This time a man posing as Dr. Jiro Yamaguchi presented his card to the manager of the bank. When the manager became suspicious, the man fled.

Detectives knew they were after one man. Eyewitnesses identified him as middle-aged, with a mole on the left cheek and a scar under his chin. The killer had left his personal card at each bank.

The card bearing the name of Dr. Matsui was traced to the real Dr. Matsui, a respected physician, who had absolutely nothing to do with any crime. Dr. Matsui informed police that he had ordered 100 personal cards, and had only four left in his possession. Each time the doctor gave out his card, he received one in return, as is the custom in Japan. Someone had used one of his 96 cards in the robbery attempt.

Police undertook the arduous task of tracing the 96 cards in Dr. Matsui's possession. The job took weeks. Finally, 95 suspects were cleared, leaving only one name to be checked. The card belonged to a well-known artist, Sadimacha Hirasawa. Hirasawa belonged to several prestigious art societies and was indeed an unlikely mass murder suspect. Dr. Matsui remembered exchanging cards with the renowned artist while travelling on a ferry to Hokkaido.

When questioned, Hirasawa readily admitted meeting Dr. Matsui on the ferry and exchanging personal cards. In fact, Hirasawa recalled that the doctor had written an address on his card with a fountain pen before giving it to him. When asked to produce the card, Hirasawa claimed that it had been stolen by a pickpocket. Dr. Matsui told police that the artist must have been mistaken. He never carried a fountain pen.

There was other strong evidence against Hirasawa. Samples of his handwriting matched the signature on the cheque cashed the day after the murders. Shortly after the robbery, he displayed large amounts of money, but could give no explanation as to how it came into his possession. Hirasawa also had a mole on his left cheek and a scar under his chin. A search of his home uncovered a brown suit and white smock identical to those worn by the killer.

Pleading innocence, Hirasawa was arrested and taken into custody. His arrest caused a sensation throughout Japan. Could this mild mannered artist, who had a clean record all his life, be the diabolical killer who calmly watched his victims die? Many believed that there had to be some kind of mistake.

Two survivors of the mass murder positively identified Hirasawa, but the third victim wasn't sure. The employees of the first two banks could not identify him positively.

Police claimed that Hirasawa, faced with the seemingly insurmountable evidence against him, admitted, "I am the man." Five months later he recanted his confession, stating that it had been forced out of him by the police.

Hirasawa was tried in 1950, found guilty of murder, and sentenced to death. His case has never ceased to fascinate the Japanese. Many feel that Hirasawa did not confess, or that if he did, his confession was obtained by force. They believe that he was made a scapegoat because police were under intense pressure to apprehend the killer. His supporters continue to press for a new trial for the condemned man. There is even a Save Hirasawa club in Japan today.

In all, Hirasawa has appealed his conviction five times. Each appeal has been turned down. Under Japanese law, only the minister of justice can trigger an execution by sealing the death warrant. Not one of Japan's ministers of justice has been willing to take this unpopular step since Hirasawa's original conviction.

Today, 93-year-old Sadimacha Hirasawa languishes in a Sandai prison, located about 200 miles north of Tokyo. He has been under sentence of death for 35 years.

VELMA'S
POISONOUS WAYS

Kind, generous, caring. These are the words used by acquaintances to describe Velma Barfield. Members of her own family describe her as "a wonderful mother" and "a loving grandmother." Well, folks, Velma may have been all these things. Unfortunately, she was also a cold-blooded murderer.

Margie Velma Bullard first saw the light of day in Sampson County, North Carolina on Oct. 23, 1932. Velma's daddy worked in a cotton mill, which only afforded the Bullards and their eight children the necessities of life.

When Velma was 17, she dropped out of the eleventh grade, ran away with Pepsi Cola truck driver Thomas Burke and became Mrs. Burke. Thomas was 16. The Burkes settled in the small town of Parkton (pop. 500), where Velma gave birth to her children, Kim and Ron.

For 15 years the Burke family led a normal, happy existence. Then disaster struck and marital harmony flew out the window. Thomas lost his position with the Pepsi organization. This revolting turn of events was followed by a car accident in which Thomas received head injuries. At loose ends, without employment, Thomas took to the devil rum. Just for fun he sometimes passed the time of day by beating Velma.

Not one to let grass grow under her feet, Velma had Thomas admitted to the Dorothea Dix Hospital in Raleigh, N.C. In an attempt to hold her family together, she obtained employment in a department store in Fayetteville. When Thomas was discharged from hospital, he continued his abusive ways right up until 1969. He stopped then and with good reason.

One night he went to bed smashed to the gills. He was smoking at the time and apparently succeeded in setting the bed on fire. By the time help arrived, Thomas had swigged his last slug and puffed on his last cigarette. Many believe our Velma assisted her husband to his great reward, but we have no proof of the validity of this accusation, so we mention it only in passing. Velma always denied giving Thomas the great push.

Velma's second husband, Jennings Barfield, whom she married two years after Thomas' demise, didn't fare nearly as well as Thomas. He lasted only six months. Doctors declared that Jennings died of natural causes. His heart stopped beating. Velma always maintained that she had absolutely nothing to do with Jennings' big step to the other side.

Now, then, these untimely deaths did nothing for Velma's nerves. She began taking tranquillizers to calm herself down. What's a girl to do when the darn things fail to have their desired effect? She upped the dosage. I mean right up there until she became a bona fide pill addict.

Her two teenage children did everything to discourage Velma's self-destruction. They poured pills down sink drains, into toilets, anything to get their mother off the capsules. Velma was furious. She berated her children and found new hiding places for her stash.

Despite her consuming passion for pills, Velma had one other driving force in her life. She attended church three times a week and taught Sunday school at the First Pentecostal Holiness Church.

A steady supply of drugs doesn't come cheap. Velma was having an increasingly difficult time financing her habit. In 1974 she obtained a $1000 loan from the Commercial Credit Corp., posing as her mother, Lillie Bullard. The fat was in the fire. Velma knew very well her 64-year-old mother would raise Cain when she learned of the deception. How to avoid a scene and very possibly a jail sentence? Simple. Velma sashayed down to the local hardware store and bought a supply of a handy little product called Ant Terro.

That very evening Velma placed a liberal quantity of the arsenic-based ant exterminator into mother's soup. For good measure, she shook a dash into mother's Coke as well. That was it. Mother didn't survive the night. Her death was attributed to natural causes.

Two years later, Velma found herself employed as a live-in maid for 85-year-old Dollie Edwards. While in Dollie's employ, Velma's star shone brightly. God fearing, churchgoing Velma took exceptional care of the elderly lady and her home. She became more a member of the Edwards family than an employee. Her kindness impressed Stuart Taylor, Dollie Edwards' nephew.

Now Stuart was something of a drinker, but under Velma's influence he swore off Johnny Barleycorn and commenced to accompany Dollie and Velma to church, not once but thrice a week. Stuart was in the process of divorcing his wife and told everloving Velma he would soon be free to marry her if she would have him. Velma said yes.

In February 1977, Dollie Edwards felt poorly. No wonder. Velma had been up to her old tricks. This time it was a concoction called Singletary Rat Killer. Dollie took three days to die. Velma cried and cried and cried. At the cemetery she cried some more. It was touching.

Every cloud has a silver lining. The pastor of Velma's church heard that Velma was at loose ends. He highly recommended her to Mrs. Margie Lee Pittman, who was at that very moment looking for a live-in housekeeper for her parents, 80-year-old John Henry Lee and Record Lee, 75. What luck! Mrs. Pittman hired Velma.

With all this action taking place, we mustn't forget that Velma still required her pills on a daily basis. Her $75 a week salary simply didn't cover her pill purchases. One day she found a blank cheque in the Lees' home. Velma couldn't resist the temptation. She forged Mrs. Lee's name on a $50 cheque. Folks, Velma was sorry the day after she forged that cheque. Surely old man Lee would run to the police as soon as the forgery was discovered.

Back to the cure-all - arsenic-based Ant Terro. Within a month John Henry was gone. An astute medic signed the death certificate "acute gastroenteritis." Velma was a rock. She accompanied Mrs. Lee to the cemetery.

With John Henry gone, it just wasn't the same. Velma changed jobs, accepting employment at the Lumberton United Care Rest Home, who were delighted to obtain her services.

These were exciting times for Velma. Gainfully employed, she looked forward to her upcoming marriage to Stuart Taylor. Life was coming up roses, but darn it all, a girl has to have her drugs. Velma took a chance. She forged and cashed two small cheques in Stuart's name. The first time he was mad. The second time he was furious and told Velma in no uncertain terms that if she ever forged another cheque he would turn her over to the police and that would be the end of the marriage plans. Velma couldn't live without her pills. She cashed a third cheque. Once again, someone had to die. It was Stuart Taylor's turn.

On the way home from a Rex Humbard revival meeting with Stuart, Velma dropped into a drugstore and picked up a supply of old reliable Ant Terro. That evening she spiked Stuart's beer with the poison. For three days Stuart convulsed in agony while Velma continued to feed him arsenic. On day four Stuart died. Cause of death - acute gastroenteritis.

Velma's luck didn't hold. Stuart had a family who couldn't understand how a healthy, robust man could expire in four days. They demanded an autopsy, which indicated arsenic poisoning as the cause of death.

Velma, the only person with Stuart during the last days of his life, was immediately suspected. She confided to her son that she had indeed killed Stuart. Ronnie Burke accompanied his mother to the police station. Under questioning, Velma shocked her interrogators by admitting to the murders of her mother Lillie Bullard, Dollie Edwards, John Henry Lee, and Stuart Taylor. She never did admit to poisoning husbands Thomas Burke or Jennings Barfield.

Velma stood trial for the murder of fiancé Stuart Taylor, was found guilty and sentenced to death. On Nov. 2, 1984, after spending six years on Death Row, Velma Barfield was wheeled into a specially constructed chamber at Central State Prison in Raleigh, N.C., where massive quantities of procuranium bromide were pumped into her veins. She was the first woman to be executed in the U.S. in over 22 years.

DR. JIMMY AND
PRUSSIC ACID

A few eyebrows were raised when Dr. James Cockburn Belany up and married beautiful Rachel Skelly of Sunderland, England. You see, Dr. Jimmy was 43; Rachel an unsoiled virgin of 20. The pair wed on Feb. 1, 1843.

Rachel's widowed mother owned several properties, as well as a portfolio chock full of stocks and bonds. Mum was so flush that Dr. Jimmy gave up his practice to devote full time to the administration of her fortune. In fact, the newlyweds moved into Mother's home, presumably to live happily ever after.

The doctor and Rachel were married only five months when Mother suddenly took ill. Her son-in-law took care of her medical needs. Dr. Jimmy didn't do that good a job. Mrs. Skelly died a short time after being stricken. Dr. Jimmy stated that the dear soul was carried away by "bilious fever," whatever that is.

Ah, but even the Grim Reaper has his brighter side. All of Mrs. Skelly's worldly goods were left to Rachel. Not one to let grass grow under his feet, Jimmy saw to it that Rachel drew up a will with him as beneficiary.

With the coming of spring Jimmy planned a trip to Germany to take part in his favorite sport, falconry. He had a bit of a problem. Rachel was somewhat pregnant, but this inconvenience was overcome when it was decided that she would spend some time in London while Jimmy continued on to Germany.

Excitedly, plans were drawn up. On June 3 Jimmy and Rachel rented rooms at a Mrs. Heppingstall's home in London, England. A Captain Clark and his daughter, who were friends of the doctor, lived close by. It was Jimmy's plan to spend a few days in London with Rachel while she became acquainted with the Captain's daughter, who would act as her companion during his absence.

On the day of her arrival, a Tuesday, Rachel was in fine spirits. She attended the theatre that evening with her husband, Captain Clark and his daughter. Next day Rachel didn't feel well and stayed in bed. On Thursday, she felt so well she went shopping at 10 in the morning. She didn't return home until 5 o'clock.

Later that evening Dr. Jimmy called on an old friend, a surgeon named Donoghue. Dr. Jimmy explained that he had been taking tiny quantities of prussic acid for medicinal purposes for years and required a small quantity. Next morning Dr. Donoghue sent a one ounce bottle of the deadly poison to Jimmy's rooms.

Early on Saturday morning the landlady, Mrs. Heppingstall, heard the happy couple moving about in their rooms. Shortly after 7 a.m. Dr. Jimmy requested a tumbler of hot water and a spoon. Mrs. Heppingstall brought them to his room. At about 7:30 Dr. Jimmy walked out of his bedroom into an adjoining sitting room and proceeded to write letters.

Thirty minutes later Dr. Jimmy screamed for help. Mrs. Heppingstall came on the fly. She found Rachel lying unconscious in bed, frothing at the mouth. Dr. Jimmy was excited, but did not seem to react to the seriousness of the moment. Mrs. Heppingstall hurriedly instructed her maid, Sarah Williams, to fetch Captain Clark. Meanwhile, Rachel went into convulsions. When Mrs. Heppingstall implored Dr. Jimmy to do something, he replied, "It is no fit. It is a disease of the heart from which her mother died some months ago."

Finally Clark arrived, took one look and dashed out, returning moments later with his own physician, Dr. Garrett. They were too late. Rachel died with her head on Mrs. Heppingstall's shoulder. Dr. Garrett informed the bereaved husband that an inquest and autopsy would be necessary.

The results of the autopsy indicated that Rachel had died from prussic acid, which was found in her stomach. An inquest revealed enough incriminating information to charge Dr. Belany with his wife's murder.

Dr. Jimmy's trial, which began on Aug. 21, 1844, became a celebrated one, chiefly because the jury was asked to weigh a preponderance of circumstantial evidence against one basic possibility.

An array of witnesses were called to the stand and swore that Dr. Jimmy and Rachel had been an ideal couple who had apparently been very much in love. Preliminaries dispensed with, everyone got down to the business at hand.

Sarah Williams, Mrs. Heppingstall's maid, told the court that she had found the prussic acid bottle and a used tumbler on a small table near Rachel's bed. The neck of the bottle was broken. After Rachel's death Sarah had also found broken glass on the steps of the front door, but not in the room where Rachel died. Later the prussic acid bottle was nowhere to be found. Dr. Jimmy stated that he had thrown it away in a vacant field, but it was never recovered.

Dr. Garrett testified that Jimmy had called on him several times after his wife's death inquiring about the cause of death. On one occasion he told Garrett that he had been taking three drops of prussic acid daily for years and had purchased some from Dr. Donoghue before Rachel died.

He went on to explain that on the day of the tragedy he was attempting to take his daily dose when he broke the neck of the prussic acid bottle while taking out the stopper. Some of the acid spilled on the bedroom floor. Trying to be careful with the remainder, he poured it into a tumbler and left the room to write letters. Dr. Jimmy told Garrett, "I heard a scream. I immediately went in and found my wife in convulsions. She said, ' Oh, dear me! I have taken some of the strong drink out of the tumbler. Give me some cold water.'"

It must be pointed out that this statement was given to Garrett before the autopsy revealed that prussic acid had been the cause of death. It is well known that prussic acid gives off a strong smell of bitter almonds. Dr. Garrett stated that he did not smell bitter almonds when he entered Rachel's bedroom. If some had been spilled on the floor, the odor would have been obvious.

There you have it. It was definitely proven that Dr. Jimmy purchased prussic acid, that Rachel drank the prussic acid, and that Jimmy stood to inherit his wife's fortune upon her death.

A guilty verdict appeared certain until the solicitor general instructed the jury - "The question you have to decide is whether the prussic acid had been taken by the wife by mistake or whether the accused had been guilty of the capital offence of administering it to her or purposely placing it in her way in order that she might take it herself."

The jury took only one hour to find the defendant not guilty. However, matter's didn't end with the verdict. Dr. Jimmy, who most probably was guilty of murder, was so hated by the public that he was forced to leave London for Sunderland the day of his release. He arrived home in time to witness his effigy being set on fire in front of his house. Three days later his home was burned to the ground by an angry mob. Dr. James Belany was fortunate to escape with his life. It is reported that he made his way to Newcastle and was never heard of again.

AN UNUSUAL POISON

*"**D**o you solemnly swear, that you will be loyal to the profession of medicine; that into whatever house you shall enter, it shall be for the good of the sick to the utmost of your power; that you will exercise your art solely for the cure of your patients and will give no drug, perform no operation for a criminal purpose."*

Hippocratic Oath (abridged)

I am certain that Dr. Carlo Nigrisoli of Bologna, Italy, started out in the practise of medicine convinced that he would uphold every single one of old Hippocrates' tenets. After all, the good doctor came from a long line of distinguished physicians who had practised medicine in Bologna for generations. He had no reason to stray from the straight and narrow.

What went wrong? Iris Azzali, that's what.

Iris strolled into Carlo's clinic one day with a minor ailment. The doctor cured what ailed her, and other things as well. Iris was a willowy, long-legged beauty, with big brown eyes, full seductive lips, and a body that would make the Leaning Tower of Pisa stand up straight and take notice.

From that very first meeting, the older man with a wife and three children at home thought of little else but beautiful, youthful Iris. She, in turn, thought the debonair society doctor so much more intelligent and mature than her regular companions.

How can one put it delicately yet retain a degree of candor? Carlo and Iris met clandestinely at her apartment where their signs of affection soon graduated to physical fulfilment. Oh, what the heck, they hit the sack at every opportunity.

Sure, there were a few anxious moments. Take the time Iris became a tad pregnant. She cried and in general carried on something fierce, but Carlo rose to the occasion. He escorted her to another city, where she obtained an abortion. Presto, her troubles were over.

Now, folks, all this intrigue did not have a good effect on Carlo's wife Ombretta. She realized that Carlo was no longer the loving husband and attentive father he had once been. When Ombretta attempted to discuss her husband's changing attitude toward her, he flew into a rage. Ombretta became nervous and distraught. Something definitely was rotten in the state of Bologna.

The unhappy couple's best friends, Anna and Carlo Frascaroli, soon became aware of the tension between Carlo and Ombretta. Frascaroli, who was also a doctor, had been approached by Carlo, who told him that Ombretta was suffering from nervous exhaustion. Dr. Frascaroli prescribed a series of injections. He began giving the injections himself, but for convenience sake both doctors agreed that Carlo Nigrisoli would continue to give them to Ombretta at their home. Of course, the Frascarolis were totally unaware of Carlo's extracurricular activities with Iris.

Meanwhile the affair grew warmer. Carlo and Iris couldn't stay away from each other. They took little trips together into the country. Ombretta was miserable. She was losing her husband. The father of her children was no longer interested. On the other hand, Carlo now regarded his wife as an obstacle standing in the way of his happiness with firecracker Iris.

The potentially dangerous triangle exploded on March 14, 1964. It was around midnight when Carlo raced from his bedroom shouting to the servants, "I must get Signora Nigrisoli to the clinic. She has had a heart attack."

Poor Ombretta was rushed to her husband's clinic, but died without regaining consciousness. Carlo explained, "I had given her a heart stimulant by injection, but it doesn't seem to have succeeded." Carlo was completely distraught, but did muster up enough presence of mind to suggest to the doctors in attendance, "Put on the death certificate that she died from coronary thrombosis." The doctors disagreed with Carlo, feeling that they did not have enough information to be certain of the cause of death.

Suddenly Carlo extracted a neat little pistol from his inside coat pocket. Raving like a lunatic, he shouted that he would kill himself unless the doctors signed the death certificate. Instead, they calmed him down and called police. In minutes the blubbering Carlo was in a police station answering embarrassing questions. When

Italian detectives found out that he had been giving his wife a series of injections, they decided to hold him until the results of the post mortem were revealed.

These results caused a sensation throughout the country. The autopsy showed that Ombretta had died from an injection of curare. Curare is not your average poison, not by a long shot. It's a rare vegetable poison derived from certain South American plants. Some South American Indian tribes treat the tips of their arrows with it for use in warfare. The poison causes paralysis of the muscles, which is quickly followed by an inability to breathe. It has been used medically as a relaxant prior to operations. Dr. Frascaroli stated definitely that he had never used nor prescribed curare for Ombretta's condition.

Dr. Carlo Nigrisoli was charged with his wife's murder. His trial began on Oct. 1, 1964. It was the first trial held in Italy where curare was used as the instrument of death. It was also Italy's first televised murder trial. Adding to the uniqueness of the proceedings, Carlo obtained permission to testify from his cell via a sound system especially set up for that purpose. At no time was he actually in the courtroom, although his voice could be heard and he could hear everything which transpired.

Iris testified, admitting to her affair with the accused man. Dr. Frascaroli related that he had prescribed a nerve tonic for Ombretta to be taken intravenously. Dr. Frascaroli dramatically added that he had instructed Carlo to discontinue the injections a few days before Ombretta died.

It was proven that Carlo continued to give the injections. The prosecution painted the cruel picture of Carlo injecting his wife with curare, which rendered her helpless. He then cleaned up the evidence of his deed and watched as his wife took 20 minutes to die. It was only then that he ran for help.

A well-known neurologist, Prof. Domenico Zanello, surprised the court when he testified that Ombretta had discovered a hidden bottle of curare in her bathroom on the day before her death. Realizing that her husband might very well be about to murder her, she visited the professor for advice. He told her to go directly to the police, but she wouldn't listen. She insisted on trying every possible method of winning back the affection of her husband. The professor did convince her to take a trip the next day in order to be out of Carlo's reach. The advice came too late. On the day following Ombretta's visit to the professor, she was dead.

On Feb. 14, 1965, the 117-day trial came to an end. Dr. Carlo Nigrisoli was found guilty of murder and sentenced to life imprisonment.

A PASSION FOR POISON

Despite the late Velma Barfield's recent venture into the poisoning business, that vile art has not flourished for some time. This is attributable to two rather depressing factors. Forensic science has succeeded in garnering the ability to trace poisons in the human body during autopsy and indeed long after death. It has also become progressively more difficult to purchase perfectly reliable, old fashioned poisons without giving nosy pharmacists your life history.

Because of these encumbrances, we have to go back to the good old days when poison was used with reckless abandon to speed victims to their great rewards.

Louise Jane Taylor obviously had a penchant for older men. In March 1882, her husband, a navy man of questionable mental prowess, passed away at the age of 70. It was presumed his death was due to natural causes. Louise was a mature but sprightly 36 at the time. Her beloved husband left her a tiny pension, which served nicely to augment her income as a clerk in a millinery shop in Woolwich, England.

Now Louise could have left well enough alone, but she chose instead to sally forth to the home of Mr. William Tregillis and his good wife, Mary Ann. The Tregillises lived in nearby Plumstead. They occupied two rooms on the second floor of a cottage. The ground floor was occupied by the landlords, Mr. and Mrs. Thomas Ellis.

The Tregillises were not spring chickens. Far from it. Willie was 85, Mary Ann merely 82. Willie had recently been released from a mental institution, where he spent several months before returning to his wife's side. Outside of Willie's little mental problem, both he and Mary Ann were in excellent health for their advanced years.

When Louise called on Willie, it was no surprise. You see, Willie, an old navy man himself, had been a great friend of the late Mr. Taylor. Despite their cramped quarters, the Tregillises graciously took Louise in. Generous to a fault, Willie moved out of his wife's bed, offering that time honored space to Louise. Willie slept alone in the other room.

About three weeks after Louise showed up, Mary Ann's health took a turn for the worse. She shivered and complained of being chilly most of the time. In general, she just wasn't the old Mary Ann.

Willie and Louise called in Dr. Smith, who noted the obvious symptoms as well as observing that Mary Ann's teeth were turning black. Dr. Smith called on his patient each day, but could do little for her other than prescribe the usual potions and pills. Gradually his visits became less frequent. The truth is, Dr. Smith probably felt his patient was deteriorating from old age and would soon die.

Willie was understandably distraught at his wife's sudden illness. If anything happened to Mary Ann, he would lose his companion of a lifetime. It also occurred to Willie that he might be sent back to the mental institution if there was no one around to take care of him in his twilight years.

Willie thought something was amiss when Louise presented him one day with her will. She had left everything to him and his wife. Despite rowing with only one oar in the water, Willie thought the matter of the will most unusual. After all, he was about 50 years older than Louise. He also believed she didn't have a penny to leave him if she left a hundred wills.

Before Willie could express his amazement, Louise had another bright idea. Why didn't she and Willie just leave Mary Ann? Willie showed his true mettle. He would have none of it. He couldn't leave his poor suffering wife. Besides, he would never go away with anyone without marrying them first. Obviously Willie had acquired his high moral standards while serving in the navy.

Meanwhile, Mary Ann suffered from nausea on a full-time basis. Louise had other diversions. One Edward Martin, who pursued the delightful occupation of watercress salesman, was a frequent visitor. He claimed to be Louise's nephew, but Ed didn't fool anyone. It was obvious that he and Louise were lovers. Willie found himself in a bind. Morally he didn't approve of Ed and Louise carrying on in his home, but being of a practical bent, he realized that to object would be to jeopardize the free help he had in nursing Mary Ann.

It was then that Dr. Smith made two important observations. He noted that Mary

Ann's gums had developed a distinctive blue line often found in cases of chronic lead poisoning. He also recalled that Louise had ordered sugar of lead from him on several occasions. In those long ago days, lead acetate was not on the poisons list, but its toxic properties were well known. The poisoner using sugar of lead had to have patience. Louise had the patience of Job.

Dr. Smith came to the disagreeable conclusion that he had not only supplied poison to his patient but also was the doctor of record during Mary Ann's illness. He sought a second opinion. A police surgeon confirmed his worst fears. Mary Ann Tregillis was being slowly poisoned.

Louise Taylor was taken into custody. Poor Mary Ann was hurriedly asked to give testimony under oath by a presiding magistrate. There was great fear that she would die before being able to give evidence at Louise's impending trial. The stricken woman testified from her bed.

Old records reveal that Mary Ann was "a little incoherent and wandering", but she managed to state that all medicine given to her was administered by Louise Taylor. She had enjoyed excellent health until Louise came to live with her and her husband. Every time Louise gave her medicine, she became nauseous. When she complained, Louise told her, "You must. What is the good of a doctor if you do not take his medicine?"

On Oct. 23, Mary Ann Tregillis died. Louise Taylor's murder trial took place in London's famed Old Bailey. The highlight of the dramatic trial occurred when Willie testified, "I believe she wanted to get my pension and put me into a lunatic asylum after my wife was gone." No one could put it in more precise language. Old Willie was believed by all.

The jury took only 20 minutes to find Louise guilty of murder. They did not recommend mercy. No one, not even Ed Martin, came to visit her while she awaited her fate.

On Jan. 2, 1883, Louise Taylor was hanged at Maidstone.

DEATH AT THE SCHOOLHOUSE

The good folks of Tuttletown, California, enjoyed their Friday night socials. Why, as long as anyone could remember, almost everyone from miles around danced until the dust rose from the schoolhouse floor.

The beautiful spring night of April 26, 1929, was no exception. Steve and John Rablen fiddled their hearts out, as they did every Friday night. Kind of sad about Steve's son, Carrol. Young Carrol had come home from the First World War stone deaf. Then there was that hasty marriage to Eva. Not that Eva wasn't a good-looking woman, mind you. Quite the contrary. Eva was an attractive blonde. It was just that folks said that right after her first husband was planted back in Texas, she commenced advertising. Can you imagine, advertising for a man?

Anyway, Eva had placed an ad with one of those matrimonial agencies. Carrol Rablen answered the ad, and before you could say caveat emptor, the two young people were husband and wife.

Right off, Eva enjoyed the Friday night socials. It was a strange situation. You see, because Carrol was stone deaf, he sat in his car outside the schoolhouse while Eva danced her little legs off inside. That's the way it was on April 26, 1929, when it happened.

Considerate Eva pushed through the crowded room with a cup of coffee and a plate of sandwiches. She bumped into a lady dancing, excused herself and made her way outside to her husband's car. This was not unusual. Eva always walked out to the car three or four times during the evening to see Carrol. He usually urged her to go back in and enjoy herself. This night would be different.

Eva gave her husband the coffee and sandwiches and turned to go back to the dance floor. Carrol drank some coffee, let out a piercing shriek and slumped to the floor of his dilapidated auto. The fiddling stopped. Everyone ran outside. Carrol was gently lifted from the car and laid on the ground. He was deathly pale.

Steve Rablen was one of the first at his son's side. Frantically, he leaned over Carrol and shouted, "Speak to me boy, what's the matter?" Carrol groaned. Then he wet his lips and whispered, "That coffee was bitter." His voice trailed off. Carrol died where he lay.

Police were summoned and the new widow Rablen questioned. Eva, through sobs of grief, informed the police, her father-in-law and the assembled crowd, "This is terrible. We were so happy together. I can't understand it. Maybe it was a stomach attack, but he seemed so well when we started out for the dance."

Questioned further, Eva told police what everyone knew. Because her husband was stone deaf and couldn't hear the music, he sat out in his car while she took part in the Friday night social. Despite Eva's assurance that Carrol had been content with his lot, there were those around Tuttletown who knew him to be a quiet, morose man because of his affliction. The investigating sheriff brought up the question, "Do you think it was suicide? Could he have put something into his own coffee after you turned away?" Eva thought not. "I doubt it very much," she told the sheriff.

The day after Carrol's untimely demise, the questioning began in earnest. The townsfolk had their own opinions, and these opinions didn't include kind words concerning Eva Rablen. Everyone, even her father-in-law, suspected her of hastening Carrol's departure from this mortal coil, but there was no proof.

No poison or poison container was found in the car or on Carrol's body. Had he poured poison into his coffee, he would have had to do the job in a split second or his wife not to have seen him. Eva said she hadn't seen him put anything in his coffee. Suicide just didn't add up.

The contents of Carrol's stomach were examined by a chemist from a nearby town. No trace of poison was found. An autopsy failed to disclose the cause of death. The death of Carrol Rablen was fast becoming a mystifying puzzle.

Steve Rablen was disconsolate over his son's death. He ridiculed the suicide theory. Steve was sure his son had been murdered. He visited the sheriff and told him in no uncertain terms, "Carrol was murdered and I'll tell you who done it - his wife." The sheriff warned the old man of the gravity of his accusation, but Steve was adamant. He figured Eva poisoned Carrol for his $3,000 life insurance. The meeting ended with the sheriff promising to search the crime scene once more.

Next morning, the sheriff got down on his hands and knees on the very spot where Carrol's car had been parked. With his fingers probing the earth and grass, he crawled around in an ever-increasing circle until he came to the schoolhouse steps. From his unusual vantage point, he noticed a board missing from under the second step. The sheriff stuck his hand in the opening and groped until his hand came in contact with a hard, smooth object. From under those stairs, the sheriff pulled out a tiny bottle. It was labelled "Strychnine" and had been purchased at Bigelow's Drug Store in the small town of Toulumne, located a few miles away.

Druggist Warren Sahey consulted his poison book. He had sold the strychnine to a woman who had signed her name as Mrs. Joe Williams. The sale had been made on April 26, the day of the dance. Warren remembered that the woman had told him she wanted to kill gophers.

The sheriff, who had brains to spare, told the druggist he would be back shortly with a woman for him to identify. The druggist was instructed to act in a normal manner when faced with the suspect. The sheriff called on Eva, and in the friendly way of western sheriffs, questioned his suspect. He then suggested a leisurely drive to ease the tension of the investigation. Eva accepted. Let's give her credit for not giving herself away when she walked into Bigelow's Drug Store with the sheriff. Later, Warren Sahey swore that Mrs. Joe Williams, who had purchased the poison, was none other than Eva Rablen.

Eva was confronted with the damaging identification. She adamantly denied ever purchasing poison at Bigelow's. Mr. Sahey was simply making a terrible mistake.

District Attorney C.H. Grayson was given the facts of the case. Like everyone else, he was sure Eva had poisoned her husband. He was also convinced that he didn't have enough evidence to gain a conviction. In desperation, he asked Edward Oscar Heinrich, then considered to be the greatest scientific criminologist in the U.S., to assist in the investigation.

Heinrich listened to the story of Carrol Rablen's death. He insisted that everyone at the dance that night be questioned until they found the woman who had bumped into Eva as she was taking coffee and sandwiches out to her husband. The woman was located. Mrs. Alice Shea remembered the incident well. Heinrich's analytical mind had guessed correctly. Mrs. Shea recalled the incident because several drops of coffee had spilled on her dress. She had not had the dress cleaned and willingly turned it over to the sheriff's men.

Heinrich took several items to his laboratory in Berkeley. These included the contents of Carrol's stomach, the empty cup which had contained the coffee, as well as Carrol's car.

Using methods and equipment then the state of the art in crime detection, Heinrich identified strychnine in the coffee crust on the bottom of the cup. He also detected the deadly poison in the coffee stain on Mrs. Shea's dress, as well as on the front seat of Carrol's car. Most important of all, he discovered strychnine in Carrol's stomach. The small town chemist, who had subjected the stomach contents to elementary tests, had not been equipped to carry out the more complex experiments conducted by Henrich. There was little doubt in anyone's mind that Eva had placed the poison in her husband's coffee in the schoolhouse. On her way back from Carrol's car, she had tossed the bottle under the school steps.

Eva Rablen was taken into custody and charged with her husband's murder. She was the first woman to be accused of murder in that part of California. Her hearing was such a popular event that no building was big enough to hold the crowd. It was decided to conduct the hearing outdoors so everyone could join in the fun. There, under the blue California sky, was held what was probably the most picturesque court proceeding ever assembled.

On June 4, in a four-minute court appearance, Eva Rablen pleaded guilty. She was sentenced to life imprisonment at San Quentin on condition that she never be paroled and her sentence never commuted.

THE REVEREND WAS A RASCAL

Reverend Clarence Virgil Thomas Richeson was a definite rascal.

The Reverend's early years revealed little to prepare us for what was to follow. Born in Rose Hill, Virginia, to dirt poor mountain folk, Clary worked from dawn to dusk. As a teenager he wandered over to Carrolton, Missouri, where he didn't better himself all that much. He caught on as a farmhand and worked like a dog. Enough farming for our boy.

Clary gravitated to St. Louis, where he worked for a while as a clerk in a hardware store before turning his hand toward operating a streetcar. That's when Clary saw the light.

Try as I might, I have been unable to discover what connection the streetcar conducting business had with the Lord's Prayer. Maybe he would have heeded the calling regardless of his occupation.

In 1900, Clary joined the Third Baptist Church in St. Louis, not as a follower, but as an extremely active member. He taught Sunday school, chaired the men's club meetings and, in general, took to religion with a vengeance. Shortly after receiving the word, he left his job as streetcar conductor for the more remunerative position of bread delivery man.

In 1902, Clary enrolled in the William Jewell College, a small Baptist school located in Liberty, Missouri. The old institution, founded in 1849, is still going strong today. They are not that proud of alumnus Clary.

While a student, Clary met an instructor's daughter, Patsy Fells, who, it must be pointed out, fell hard for the attractive divinity student. Clary and Patsy had an on and off affair for the next few years.

Although not a graduate, by 1904 Clary was doing some pastoral work at Bethany Church in Kansas City when an embarrassing incident took place. Three young female members of the flock unceremoniously interrupted services one day and loudly declared for all to hear that, on various and sundry occasions, our Clary had bedded down with all three. The trustees of the church, feeling that this triple play was not in keeping with the previous immaculate standards of their pastors, suggested that the Reverend Clark seek employment elsewhere, preferably far, far away.

The Reverend caught on at the Budd Park Baptist Church in Kansas City. After Clary had ministered to his flock for only a few months, a young widow of the congregation had the audacity to accuse Clary of horizontal activities completely devoid of ecclesiastical connotations. Even worse, the widow's brother wanted to make hamburger out of the pastor. Clary moved on.

It should be pointed out that Clary did not attend divinity school on a regular basis, and so it took him until 1908 to graduate. However, graduate he did. Young, intelligent Rev. Clarence Richeson accepted a position in Hyannis on lovely Nantucket Sound.

It so happened that a sweet young thing, Avis Linnell, sang in the choir of the Reverend's church. Avis took one look at tall, handsome Clary and her defences crumbled away to dust. The Reverend didn't require all that much encouragement. Folks, those two were at it all the time. Unfortunately, at that very period in the turbulent saga of the Reverend Richeson, he took up with Violet Edmands. Miss Violet was not your average Cape Cod gadabout. No, sir. Violet was the daughter of Moses Grant Edmands of Chestnut Hill, the head honcho of the Baptist Missionary Society of America. Suddenly, Clary could see the light at the end of the tunnel. A marriage to Violet would in one fell swoop, give him a beautiful wife, an influential father-in-law to further his career and cold, hard cash. Who could ask for anything more? Clary and Violet became engaged.

Wouldn't you know it, Avis picked this inopportune moment to inform Clary that she was heavy laden with child. Obviously, Avis tried harder. To say that the Reverend was on the horns of a dilemma would be an understatement. But there was a way out. It was so very simple. Kill Avis and make it appear that she had become so distraught at losing charming Clary that she had ended it all by her own hand.

That's the way it looked on Oct. 14, 1911, when Avis was found nude and dead in her bathtub. The recently departed Avis had moved to Boston to further her singing career. At the time of her death she was living at the YWCA.

An autopsy was performed, revealing that Avis had died as a result of potassium cyanide poisoning and, even more startling, that she was several months pregnant. To the unsuspecting, it appeared that, finding herself in a shameful position, she decided to kill herself. Remember, folks, the date was 1911. However, Avis had a bulldog of a brother who had never liked the preacher man down at the church. He was convinced that Reverend Clary had something to do with his sister's death. Armed with his suspicions, he hustled down to the police station and demanded action.

Reverend Clary was questioned. He admitted that some months before he had been engaged to Avis, but she longed for a singing career and so they had broken up. Despite the suspicions of Avis' brother, things might have quieted down were it not for an annoying pharmacist, William Hahn.

The pharmacist, who hailed from nearby Newton, had heard of Avis' untimely demise and the subsequent questioning of her pastor. He told police that four days before Avis' death, Reverend Clarence Richeson had entered his shop. The man of the cloth had requested a quantity of poison to destroy an unwanted dog. Hahn went on to state that while he was offering the Reverend a small amount of poison, Clary had interrupted, asking for a larger quantity so that the canine's death would be quick and merciful.

Rev. Richeson walked out of the shop with 15 grains of potassium cyanide. As he left the store, Clary reminded Hahn that he had been invited to the wedding and to be sure to show up. As an afterthought, he suggested that Hahn say nothing about the poison purchase. Sensitive parishioners might not take kindly to their preacher killing a dog.

The revelations of William Hahn were acted upon immediately. Clary was located at the mansion of his fiancée. Protesting his innocence, he was arrested and lodged in jail. Naturally enough, his betrothed's family was devastated. Tearfully, the wedding was cancelled. More tears were shed as Violet returned wedding presents.

In the days following the arrest, detectives proceeded to build a case against Rev. Richeson. It didn't take long to discover that Clary had been slipping away to Boston at every opportunity. Avis had told some of her singing student companions of her true love. Police were able to positively place Avis and Clary together in Boston on the afternoon before her death. Not much question about it. That rascal preacher man had deceived Avis into thinking that the substance he had given her would, when taken together with a hot bath, induce an abortion. Unsuspecting Avis had taken the poison and died.

On Dec. 20, 1911, guards rushed to the Reverend's cell in response to moans and groans. They found Clary drenched in blood. He had managed to sharpen the top of a marmalade tin can on the cement floor of his cell. Using the tin, he had successfully emasculated himself. The pastor was rushed to hospital, where doctors managed to save his life.

A couple of weeks later, Reverend Clary wrote out a detailed confession, admitting his diabolical scheme to kill the one person who stood between him and a lifestyle which was almost in his grasp.

The Reverend stood trial for murder. Well, not exactly. Because of his recent injury, Clary was allowed to sit during the proceedings. He pleaded guilty and was sentenced to death.

On May 20, 1912, at precisely 12 minutes after midnight, Rev. Clarence Virgil Thomas Richeson, was electrocuted in the state of Massachusetts' electric chair.

THE CANDY KILLER

If I've told you once, I've told you a thousand times: Don't consume food or drink delivered anonymously by mail. Often the gifts contain unwelcome toxic ingredients guaranteed to give you a nasty tummy ache, or even worse, hasten your departure from this mortal coil.

Too bad Oddvar Eiken and Anders Muren didn't take my advice. The two young Norwegian men were medical students in Lund, Sweden. Both had fled their country before the Nazi invasion and served as fighter pilots during the Second World War. Now in their late twenties, they were attempting to make up for lost time and spent most of their waking hours either in class or studying.

There was another bond between the two men. Oddvar was engaged to marry Anders' beautiful sister, Randi. The lovers had met the summer before, when Oddvar visited his friend's home in Vraadal, Norway. The tall, handsome war hero took one look at 23-year-old blonde, beautiful Randi and said, "That's for me."

Soon they were engaged. Both families were delighted with the match. Randi would continue her studies at the Kristiansand Teachers Training College and marry during the following Easter recess.

On March 12, 1949, Oddvar received a package through the mail. Because it was postmarked Kristiansand, Norway, he assumed the parcel was from Randi, although there was no return address. The outside wrapping was quickly torn away. Inside was a short note from Randi, suggesting he eat all the contents himself, four large pieces of chocolate. Oddvar laughed at the suggestion. He gave one chocolate to eight-year-old Marianne Svenson, his landlady's daughter. Marianne generously shared her candy with a chum, Barbro Jacobsson. Oddvar and Anders shared one piece. Two pieces remained untouched.

Next morning, all four were violently ill. Rushed to a nearby hospital, they were quickly diagnosed as suffering from arsenic poisoning. Doctors managed to save all the victims except little Marianne Svenson. She slipped into a coma and died.

Investigators questioned Oddvar and Anders. Both men steadfastly stated that despite the note, Randi simply could not be responsible. The two uneaten chocolates were tested. Arsenic had been injected into both candies.

Detectives, armed with the note signed by Randi and all the wrappings which had held the fatal candy, travelled to Kristiansand to question Randi. She proved to be a straightforward, if somewhat puzzled, young woman. Randi was amazed at the whole chocolate story, claiming that at no time had she sent any candy to her fiancé. Shown the note, she admitted that the signature looked like hers, but was definitely not genuine.

Handwriting experts compared the signature on the note to a sample of Randi's handwriting. They concluded that the note had been written by someone else, who had obviously attempted to copy the young student's handwriting. Now convinced of Randi's innocence, detectives questioned her regarding anyone who might want harm to come to her fiancé.

Randi remembered a strange series of events. Sometime earlier, she had received notes in the mail informing her that Oddvar was having an affair with another woman. She checked with her boyfriend and found out that he, too, was receiving letters informing him that she had a lover.

When both she and Oddvar disregarded these letters, she received one more letter, signed by a Signe Lundgren. Miss Lundgren stated that she was pregnant with Oddvar's baby. She wanted Randi to break off her engagement, so that Oddvar could marry her. Randi immediately got in touch with Oddvar, who swore he didn't know anyone named Signe Lundgren.

The questioning switched back to the survivors of the poisoning. Oddvar revealed that about two weeks before the chocolates arrived, he had received a bottle of liquor by mail. There was no note or return address, but he had assumed the gift was from Randi. From his hospital bed, Oddvar told police where they could locate the bottle and its wrappings.

Police found the discarded packaging and the bottle in Oddvar's room. Newspapers which had been used to protect the bottle had one word scrawled across the front page. The word was "Flemming." Randi told police that she had once had a Danish suitor named Flemming Rosborg. When she became engaged to Oddvar, she had broken off with Rosborg.

Rosborg, now a prime suspect, was located in Copenhagen. He was questioned for three days and swore he knew nothing about poisoned chocolate. Meanwhile, the bottle of liquor was tested. It contained enough arsenic to annihilate a hockey team. Rosborg gave police a detailed account of his activities, and proved without a doubt that he had absolutely nothing to do with the poisoning.

While they were coming up with negative results, police were stunned when another gift of poisoned chocolates was brought to their attention. Carstein Brekke, a student at the same teachers college which Randi attended, reported receiving poisoned candy. He had eaten a small quantity of the candy and became ill. Testing indicated that the chocolate had been injected with small quantities of arsenic. To add to the mystery, Carstein knew all the principals in the case. He considered himself Randi's dear friend. Randi agreed that they were good friends, but nothing more.

All five young people involved in the case, Randi, Oddvar, Anders, Flemming and Carstein, were exactly as they appeared to be - fine, upstanding students who planned to be either teachers or doctors.

On a hunch, a sharp detective thought of showing Randi the box and wrapping that had been used to send the poisoned liquor to her fiancé. Immediately upon seeing the box, she said, "It's the egg box I returned to Carstein." She went on to explain that Carstein had often given her eggs from his parents' farm. She always gave the box back to him to use again.

Now with a concrete clue, detectives searched Carstein's room. They found scraps of paper with Randi's signature repeated over and over again. He had obviously practised writing her signature. Carstein Brekke was taken into custody. After five hours of questioning, he not only confessed, but insisted on writing the confession in longhand.

Carstein admitted that it was he who had written the poison pen letters in an attempt to break up Randi and Oddvar. He loved Randi dearly, but she viewed him only as a friend. He had invented the name Signe Lundgren and had orchestrated the entire plot. By scrawling Flemming on the old newspaper, he knew police would make the connection with Randi's old boyfriend.

Although the murder of Marianne Svenson had taken place in Sweden, Norwegian officials insisted that Brekke stand trial in Norway because the poison had been sent from that country.

Brekke was examined by psychiatrists and adjudged to be sane and fit to stand trial. He was found guilty of several charges relating to attempted murder, as well as manslaughter in the case of little Marianne Svenson.

In May 1951, Carstein Brekke was sentenced to 15 years imprisonment.

3
CANADIANA

UNDER THE MICROSCOPE

Murder most foul doesn't often visit Edmundston, New Brunswick. The peaceful mill town of 12,000 inhabitants, situated on the St. John River directly across from Madawaska, Maine, is better known for its hunting and fishing than acts of violence. Yet, on May 13, 1958, an unusual murder was to take place in Edmundston, one which would utilize atomic energy for the first time ever in a criminal investigation.

Gaetane Bouchard, 16, arrived home from school and chatted with her mother before going downtown shopping. It was 4:30 p.m. She never returned.

By 7:30 p.m. Gaetane's father, Wilfred, was growing increasingly apprehensive over his daughter's failure to show up for supper. It wasn't like her to be late. Mr. Bouchard phoned several of her friends but could locate no one who had seen her after 4:30 p.m.

He did find out that Gaetane sometimes kept company with John Vollman, an American from across the river in Madawaska. Mr. Bouchard drove to Madawaska and located Vollman, who worked as a reporter with the *St. John Valley Times*. Vollman, a clean-cut, pleasant young man, readily admitted knowing Gaetane but told her distraught father that, although he had been in Edmundston that afternoon, he had not seen Gaetane.

Mr. Bouchard reported his daughter missing to the RCMP. Meanwhile, he couldn't sit still. With his son, Jean Guy, fifteen, and a neighbor, Stanley Gauthier, he cruised the streets of Edmundston in vain.

The three men decided to search the secluded lovers' lane which can be found in every small town. They made their way to an abandoned gravel pit on Boucher Office Road. Using flashlights, they scanned the area. It was Jean Guy who found his sister. She was lying face down on the gravel.

Within minutes RCMP officials were on the scene. Dr. J.B. Gaudreau examined the body. It was an eerie sight. Mounties had positioned their vehicles so that their headlights illuminated the still form.

Gaetane had been stabbed repeatedly in the neck and back. Some skin had been scraped away from her bare legs. A bloodstain on the ground some twenty-five feet from the body indicated the point from which she had been dragged.

Searching on their hands and knees, officers found tire prints. Nearby were two tiny chips of green paint, which could have dropped from a vehicle when particles of gravel were thrown up under the wheels as it drove away.

Next morning little else was discussed in Edmundston. Who could have committed such a horrendous crime? The RCMP went to work, tracing Gaetane's last known movements. On her way home from school she had walked with friends, had a soda at Soucy's Restaurant, and purchased two Caramilk chocolate bars.

After dropping her books off at home, she was again seen in front of the restaurant at about 5:00 p.m. by Marcel Bosse, a farmer who was parked nearby. Bosse noticed Gaetane about to cross the street when a green Pontiac pulled up. He heard the driver say, "Do you want a ride?" Gaetane replied, "No," and the Pontiac drove off. Bosse observed that it had a yellow Maine licence plate.

Several girlfriends had also seen the green Pontiac shortly after 5:00 p.m. They stated that Gaetane was in the front seat with the driver, a dark, good-looking young man. Paul Emile Levesque spotted the same car and occupants turning onto Boucher Office Road. It was apparent to the RCMP that Gaetane had eventually accepted a ride with the driver of the Pontiac and was driven to the gravel pit and her death.

An autopsy revealed that one of the stab wounds had pierced the heart, causing death. A portion of partially digested chocolate in the stomach further indicated that death had taken place not more than three hours after the chocolate was eaten.

Gaetane had consumed some of the chocolate bars at 4:00 p.m., which meant that death had occurred between 4:00 and 7:00 p.m. As she had been seen alive shortly after 5:00 p.m., the time of death was narrowed to a little under a two-hour span. Although the autopsy revealed that Gaetane had died a virgin, police firmly felt that they were dealing with a sex-motivated crime.

Gaetane's girlfriends were questioned in an effort to discover if any particular boy was paying special attention to her. Maine authorities assisted in tracing a 1952 green Pontiac. Both these avenues of investigation bore immediate results.

Sergeant J.R. LaPointe of the RCMP found out from Gaetane's girlfriends that one boy, John Vollman, had tried to pick them up on the afternoon of Gaetane's murder. The girls told LaPointe that Vollman had a reputation for not being content with necking. He wanted to go all the way and, when repulsed, would fly into an uncontrollable rage. They wanted no part of him.

The Mounties were informed by the head of the Criminal Investigation Division of the Main State Police, Otis Labree, that they had located a car dealer who had sold a green Pontiac with Maine plates three weeks before the murder. The purchaser had been John Vollman.

Together with Maine officials, the Mounties called on Vollman at his place of employment. His 1952 green Pontiac was parked outside. Examination of the rocker panel under the right front door revealed a tiny scar in the paint. The larger of the two chips of green paint found at the scene of the crime precisely matched the scar on Vollman's car.

Vollman readily admitted knowing Gaetane Bouchard but vehemently denied having anything to do with her murder. Yes, he had been in Edmundston the day of the murder covering a story but claimed that anyone who thought he had been with Gaetane was mistaken. He also pointed out that green Pontiacs were the most popular automobiles in the area.

Vollman's car was impounded. Microscopic examination revealed that the chip of paint found in the gravel pit was the same type and color as his car, certainly incriminating evidence, but not conclusive. Vollman could have been in the gravel pit prior to the murder. A partially consumed lipstick-smeared Caramilk chocolate bar was found in the glove compartment of Vollman's car. The lipstick was the same shade and brand used by Gaetane, but it was also a popular brand sold by many stores in the area.

The web of circumstantial evidence was rapidly closing in on John Vollman. Still, there was no hard evidence to place him in the gravel pit with the victim at the time of the crime. It was then that the case took an unusual turn.

When the autopsy had been performed, a single strand of hair two and a half inches long was found clutched in the victim's hand. That single strand of hair was forwarded to the RCMP laboratory in Ottawa along with samples of Vollman's hair. It must be pointed out that up to this time microscopic examination of hair was not considered a foolproof method of establishing positive identity.

The Ottawa lab sent the lone strand of hair taken from Gaetane Bouchard's hand to the Atomic Energy of Canada Laboratories in Chalk River, Ontario, where scientist Dr. Robert E. Jervis was experimenting with an entirely new method of hair identification.

It was his theory that trace elements in human hair would be different from person to person due to heredity, nourishment, environment, and other factors. Jervis found that by bombarding the hair samples for various lengths of time in a nuclear reactor, he could, by complicated experimentation, measure the quality of trace elements in the hair sample. The resulting measurements were unique to each person's hair.

In this way, the hair found clutched in Gaetane's hand was identified as being identical to hair samples taken from Vollman's head. It was the first time this method, known as neutron-activation analysis, had been used in a criminal case.

John Vollman was arrested and charged with the murder of Gaetane Bouchard. On November 4, 1958 he stood trial in Edmundston where for the first time anywhere, scientist Francis M. Kerr of the RCMP explained the new method of hair identification from the witness stand.

On the last day of his trial, Vollman took the witness stand and confessed. Gaetane had repulsed his advances. There was a struggle. They fell to the ground outside the car, where he stabbed her repeatedly with a hunting knife.

John Vollman was sentenced to be hanged. Four days before his scheduled execution, his sentence was commuted to life imprisonment. He has since been released.

CALGARY
DESPERADO

At the turn of the century, Calgary was the most exciting city in Canada. Immigrants poured into the territory around the bustling cow town to take up ranching. Many had done well at ranching in the United States and felt they could duplicate their success starting off with cheap, and oftentimes free land. Others moved to Canada to start life anew after breaking the law in the United States.

One such young man was Ernest Cashel, an 18-year-old brown-eyed desperado who had begun his life of misadventure four years earlier by running away from home. He stole as he went from state to state, finally getting tossed into jail for a year while he was still only 15 years of age.

In jail he not only met real criminals but read extensively about outlaw Jesse James, who became something of a hero to him. By the time he hit Alberta he strutted as he walked, wore a wide-brimmed hat, and made his living playing poker. This dubious vocation lasted only as long as his luck.

One day Ernie found himself dead broke. In order to get a stake, he forged a cheque in a Calgary store. The storekeeper remembered his face, and soon the law was looking for bad Ernie Cashel. But Ernie, who could always anticipate heat, had disappeared. Once the Calgary police assured themselves their man had left town, they notified the North West Mounted Police.

At that time the commanding officer of the Mounties in Calgary was a Superintendent Sanders. He learned that the wanted man's family had moved from the United States to Ponoka, Alberta. He contacted Red Deer and instructed Constable Rubbra to pick up Ernie. Rubbra apprehended his man without incident and returned to Red Deer with his prisoner. Ernie was turned over to Rubbra's superior for the train trip to Calgary.

As the train sped through the night Ernie thought of nothing but escape. His plan was simple enough, having been used many times before and since. He asked permission to use the washroom and never returned. The door to the washroom was forced. Ernie had leaped through an open window into the night.

No law-enforcement agency likes being duped. The Mounties were no exception. Word went out across the plains of Alberta: Get Ernie Cashel. It would prove to be a difficult task.

Ernie was traced to a rancher at Lacombe who had sold a horse and saddle to a stranger who called himself Ellsworth. The stranger, who fit Ernie's description, had never returned to pay for the horse.

A month passed before word of Ernie's exploits drifted back to Calgary. He had been spotted near Haynes Creek, about thirty-eight miles from Lacombe, on his stolen horse. It was reported that he had stayed a few days at a small ranch owned by Rufus Belt. Constable Macleod was instructed to travel to the Belt ranch and interview the owner.

When the Mountie arrived at the Belt spread he could sense that something was drastically wrong. There was no sign of Rufus anywhere. The doors and windows of the ranch house were wide open although it was the middle of November. Rufus' distinctive dark cream pony, new saddle, shotgun, brown suit, and about $250 in cash were missing. There seemed little doubt that Rufus Belt had met with foul play.

The harsh cold winter fell over the west. Mounties wondered how Ernie, a relative tenderfoot, could survive the winter without making contact with someone. He was now wanted for forgery, horse theft, and possibly murder. Now and then the wanted man would be sighted, but always he was one step ahead of the frustrated Mounties.

Finally Ernie made the mistake of selling Belt's brown coat near Kananaski. There was a blood-stained hole in the garment which immediately aroused the suspicion of the purchaser. He informed the Mounties who rushed to the scene of the transaction and recaptured Ernie without incident.

With Ernie safe in custody in Calgary, the Mounties made a concerted effort to find the body of Rufus Belt. They hadn't long to wait.

On July 23 a naked body surfaced in a remote creek. A friend of Belt's positively identified the body by a distinctively deformed left big toe. Belt had been killed by a bullet fired directly into his left breast. The hole in the coat and the entry wound on

Belt's body matched perfectly.

Ernie Cashel stood trial for murder. His trial was followed with great interest across the country. Ernie was found guilty. A sentence of death was passed with the execution date set at December 15, 1903. As his date with the hangman drew near, Ernie acted with a certain degree of bravery, never once displaying a semblance of fear. His guards felt he was emulating what he thought would be Jesse James' behavior in a similar situation.

Like Jesse, Ernie had a brother who visited him often. John Cashel was an honest citizen who had never committed a criminal act in his life.

On December 10, Ernie Cashel's twenty-first birthday, his brother John paid a visit to the jail. Later that day Ernie's three guards made their daily search of the condemned man's cell. One guard accompanied Ernie outside the cell while the other two conducted the search. Once the search was completed, the guards beckoned Ernie to return to his cell. Ernie didn't move. Instead he took his hands out of his pockets. He was holding two revolvers. "You speak or move, either of you, and I'll let you both have it." The guards froze. Ernie backed the three men into his cell, "I don't want to shoot you but I'm in a bad position." Knowing the desperate man had only five days to live, the guards didn't doubt him for a minute.

John Cashel was taken into custody within a half-hour of the escape. It was obvious he had provided his brother with the two revolvers.

Once more the word went out. Ernie Cashel must be brought in. But again Ernie proved to be a slippery adversary. In typical Jesse James fashion, he showed up on December 15, the date set for his execution, at a vacant farmhouse near Calgary, where he stole a $1,000 ring. Ernie left a note letting the owners know that he would repay his loan of $1,000 in six months.

Ernie was once again a fugitive in frigid western Canada in the deep of winter. From time to time a farmer would report being held up in his own home. Ernie raided the farmhouses of food and clothing but never neglected to read whatever newspapers he could find detailing his exploits.

Meanwhile, on January 21, John Cashel was convicted of aiding in his brother's escape. The Mounties believed Ernie would make his way back to the Calgary area to learn of his brother's fate. With the aid of many citizens, search parties were formed to conduct house to house searches.

It was in this manner that the Mounties stumbled across Ernie's hiding place, a deserted ranch shack near Nose Creek. Constable Biggs, accompanied by two other Mounties, entered the small structure. Biggs made the mistake of opening a trap door leading down to a cellar. A bullet whizzed by his head. Biggs managed to scamper up the ladder to safety. The three officers obtained reinforcements and immediately surrounded the shack.

Inspector Duffus, the senior Mountie at the scene, decided to smoke Ernie out. He placed hay against the shack and lit it. Soon the tiny structure was filled with smoke.

The Inspector shouted, "Cashel, you had better come out!" A hollow-sounding voice echoed from the cellar. "I'm not coming out. I'm going to kill myself."

The flames leaped higher. Ernie had to act. Finally he shouted, "For God's sake, put out the fire! I don't want to be roasted!"

Surrounded by Mounties, with his hands raised high above his head, Ernie emerged from his cellar hideout. Soon he was joking with his captors and was openly delighted to learn that his brother had received only one year's imprisonment for helping him escape. He admitted that he returned to the Calgary area with the intention of helping his brother had he received a longer sentence.

On February 2, after confessing to the murder of Rufus Belt, Ernie Cashel was hanged.

Jesse would have been proud.

THE MISSING WIFE

When Cyril and Betty Belshaw took their year-long sabbatical from the University of British Columbia they had no way of knowing that before the year was out tragedy would descend upon them both, leaving Betty dead and Cyril accused of her murder.

Professor Belshaw, the respected head of the anthropology department of the university, planned to spend the last half of his sabbatical in Montana-Vermala, Switzerland, with Betty, who was also employed at U.B.C. as an English instructor. All went well until early in 1979 when the urbane, cultured Belshaws decided to take a trip to Paris.

According to Professor Belshaw, he and Betty left Montana on January 13, stopping over that night at the Relais PLM Beaune, arriving at the Novotel Bagnolet in Paris the next day. The Belshaws didn't leave their room for the rest of that day.

On the morning of the fifteenth, Cyril and Betty had a continental breakfast in their room. Betty planned to do research at the Bibliotheque Nationale. Cyril would get in some shopping.

The Canadian couple left the hotel and caught the subway. They separated at Bourse Station when Betty left the subway. Cyril watched her departure. According to his statement later given to police he never laid eyes on his wife of 37 years again.

At 1:00 p.m. Cyril waited for Betty at their prearranged meeting place, the Galleries Lafayette, Paris's largest department store. Betty didn't show up.

All that day Cyril waited for word from his wife. When he hadn't heard from her by the following day, he reported her missing to the police. He also called on the Canadian Embassy and gave the official all the details of the disappearance. Then he phoned his two adult children back in Canada and advised them of their mother's strange absence. On January 18, Belshaw returned by car to Montana, Switzerland.

This, then, was the sequence of events later related by Belshaw. Staid, correct Betty Belshaw, who had never been anything but a well-organized, punctual individual, had mysteriously disappeared from the streets of Paris without explanation.

On March 28 laborers repairing a road near Le Sepey, Switzerland, found the nude body of a middle-aged woman. The body had been wrapped in garbage bags and tied with twine before being thrown down a ravine often used as a garbage-disposal site. Animals had mauled the body, making identification extremely difficult.

Initially there was no connection between Betty Belshaw and the decomposed, partially consumed body found at Le Sepey. One must remember that Mrs. Belshaw disappeared in Paris, while the unidentified body was discovered in Switzerland. Eventually Interpol inquired if the body could be that of the Canadian woman who vanished from the streets of Paris.

As a result of this inquiry, Professor Belshaw was asked for his wife's dental charts, which he volunteered to procure himself. Belshaw then provided the police with Betty's charts, which were compared with the teeth of the corpse found at Le Sepey. The comparison indicated that the corpse was definitely not that of fifty-five-year-old Betty Belshaw. Professor Belshaw returned to Canada.

Despite this seemingly conclusive proof, Swiss authorities contacted the RCMP in Vancouver and requested Mrs. Belshaw's dental charts be sent to them directly from her dentist. The RCMP were compelled to call upon Professor Belshaw to obtain the name of his wife's dentist.

Knowing that precise records would be forwarded to Switzerland, Professor Belshaw wrote out a statement which he delivered to a Vancouver detachment of the RCMP. In the statement he admitted altering the dental charts which he had initially provided to the Swiss police. He gave as his reasons the fact that he could not face "the psychological trauma of possibly identifying my wife without the presence of family and friends, or the delays in returning to my home and family after many months of hope that my wife might be found alive."

Professor Belshaw further stated that he had acted foolishly and on impulse. The unaltered dental charts proved that the corpse found at Le Sepey was indeed the body of Betty Belshaw.

Strong suspicion centred on Professor Belshaw. Swiss detectives arrived in Vancouver to question him. He refused to return to Switzerland, but on November 1, 1979, was arrested in Paris, where he had flown to attend a United Nations conference. The Swiss immediately instituted extradition proceedings in order to transfer Belshaw to Swiss soil and charge him with his wife's murder.

On December 3, 1980, Cyril Belshaw, then editor-in-chief of *Current Ethnological Sciences*, author, former member of the Academic Board of British Columbia, and advisor to the U.N. Bureau of Social Affairs, stood trial for the murder of his wife.

At Belshaw's trial the prosecution claimed that the falsification of the dental records was the action of a guilty man. They further stated that the motive for the murder was Belshaw's involvement with Mrs. Elida Harris of Vancouver, a married graduate student at the university. It was proven that Mrs. Harris had visited with the professor alone in his chalet in Montana for over a week before the Belshaws took occupancy. Upon returning to Canada Belshaw saw Harris about once a month.

The prosecution contended that Betty Belshaw was murdered because she found out about the prolonged affair. They claimed Mrs. Belshaw never reached Paris but was killed either in Montana or on the way to Le Sepey where the body was found. Hotel employees where Belshaw stopped over on his way to Paris, and in Paris itself, could not recall ever having seen Mrs. Belshaw.

In his defence Professor Belshaw admitted falsifying the dental records and admitted to his affair with Mrs. Harris but vehemently denied murdering his wife. He claimed that if his wife had found out about his affair he would have been admonished by her, but their relationship was such that the incident would not have broken up their marriage.

A panel of three judges and a six-member jury acquitted Cyril Belshaw of the murder of his wife. He walked out of court a free man.

The murder of Betty Belshaw remains unsolved to this day.

UNCONTROLLABLE DESIRES

There are monsters among us. Psychiatrists describe them as pathological personalities of the antisocial type. This is the story of one such deranged individual.

On the night of March 1, 1974, Judy Barksey, 19, purchased a pizza and two bottles of pop to take with her. She already had a chocolate bar. Judy was making her way home that night in Strathroy, Ontario, when she was attacked.

Later, her assailant was to describe the incident in his own words: "It was late at night. I was at home watching a hockey game and I decided to go uptown to get some raffle tickets on the game at the News Depot. After getting the tickets I started for home. I noticed a girl walking on the street in front of me. I started fantasizing sex with her and I was trying to build up nerve to approach her. As we walked along I finally built up enough courage, or else my sickness was coming to a head, that I grabbed her after we crossed over the tracks. I told her what I wanted. She struggled and refused. I grabbed her by the throat. She goes down, then I panicked, took my jackknife out and stabbed her in the throat. I got scared and I went into her purse and took some money."

Judy Barksey's monster cleaned off his bloody jackknife in a mud puddle and went home to his wife.

The morning after the attack, Dallas Allan, 66, left his home at 11:45 to mail a letter. As he walked by a fertilizer shed he looked to his left and spotted the body of a young girl lying on the ground. A pizza, two bottles of pop, and a chocolate bar were strewn around her. Moments later police were viewing the body of Judy Barksey.

Despite an extensive investigation, detectives were unsuccessful in tracing the killer.

A year and three months later the man with the uncontrollable desires was absently looking out the window of his home as Rosalie Winters, 18, wandered into Alexandra Park. Strong hands clamped around her neck. Schoolbooks flew into the air. Rosalie lost consciousness. She was raped and left in the park. She was unable to give a good description of her attacker.

On October 20, 1975, exactly four months after the attack on Rosalie Winters, the unknown assailant struck again. Twenty-four-year-old Denys Jenner arrived home from work and entered his Strathroy home by the back door. His wife, Louise, was lying dead on the kitchen floor. Someone had slashed her throat and tightly tied a black bootlace around her neck.

Realizing his wife was dead, and fearing for his baby's life, Deny's walked over his wife's body to his daughter Rachel's room. He found Rachel unharmed in her crib. Mrs. Jenner had been sexually attacked but had been given the opportunity to dress before she was killed.

Ontario Provincial Police detectives theorized at the time that Louise's killer was known to her. Photographs were found on a chesterfield as if an acquaintance had been scanning them. Possibly Mrs. Jenner had excused herself to change her baby's diapers upstairs, giving the killer time and opportunity to undo his bootlace. When Mrs. Jenner came back downstairs, the killer struck.

A 74-year-old neighbor of the Jenners reported seeing a late-model cream or yellow vehicle, possibly an Oldsmobile, enter the Jenner driveway on the day of the murder. She said the occupant of the vehicle, a white male with dark, collar-length hair, had been at the Jenner door three or four minutes before entering the house.

Police conducted thousands of interviews in the Jenner investigation. One man, Chris Magee, loosely fitted the description given by the Jenners' neighbor. He knew Mrs. Jenner, as well as Judy Barksey. His father owned a light-colored Oldsmobile.

Magee remained a suspect, but there was nothing of a definite nature to label him a killer. When interviewed he vehemently denied having any knowledge of the murders.

Sylvia Holly Jennings, 19, was hitch-hiking to London. She accepted a lift. She was driven well past her destination to an abandoned side road near Mount Brydges, where she was raped, beaten with a Coke bottle over the head, and left for dead. Miraculously, she survived the attack.

James Frayne, 16, of Forest, Ontario, drove a farm tractor and hayrake to a farm his family owned about four and a half miles from his home. When he arrived at the abandoned farm site he spotted a leg and knee in the grass.

Initially James thought someone was sunbathing. He blew the tractor horn and went about changing the hayrake for a mowing machine. James commenced to cut hay, but the sight he had seen upon entering the property bothered him. He returned to the spot and took a much closer look. What he thought was a sunbather was in reality the body of 15-year-old Susan Lynne Scholes.

Susan had been raped and stabbed in the throat. The Scholes family resided in London but was spending the summer at their cottage in nearby Hillsboro Beach.

At 1:00 p.m. Susan had left the cottage with her brother Geoffrey to go to Forest to buy batteries for her portable radio. Geoffrey dropped Susan off in town. She purchased the batteries and was seen walking out of town towards County Road 12.

McFarlane's Tile Yard is situated on that road. Mrs. McFarlane heard of the murder on the radio and immediately went to the police. She reported seeing the murdered girl walking in front of the tile yard at 1:30 p.m. Susan was wearing a distinctive green sweater with the word "Hillsboro" printed in white letters across the front.

Mrs. McFarlane's son had been using a fork-lift to transfer tile to the yard when he saw Susan, who he knew through his association with her brother Geoffrey. As he watched, a truck stopped and gave Susan a lift. He recognized the truck as the one used in the area to pick up and dispose of dead animals.

OPP inquiries soon uncovered that the suspect truck, a 1975 Ford, was owned by Mr. John Grinsven, a Strathroy-based dealer in dead stock. On the day of Susan's murder the truck was operated by none other than Chris Magee, the suspect in the Barksey and Jenner murders.

Taken to the OPP detachment in Forest, Magee admitted picking up Susan but claimed that he dropped her off and continued on his way. He told the investigating officers that he was married, had two children, and that he and his wife had recently separated. He and his children were presently living with his father in Strathroy. Magee had no police record but had been dismissed from various jobs because of petty theft.

Investigating officers found out that Magee's truck was usually outfitted with a filleting knife, used in his work with dead animals. When the truck was searched, the knife was missing. It was later found on Grinsven's property, sharpened and cleaned. It was obvious that all traces of blood had been thoroughly cleaned away by Magee.

On October 21, 1977, Chris Magee was arrested and stood trial for the murder of Susan Scholes. At no time did he confess to the crime. He was adjudged to be not guilty by reason of insanity and sent to the Mental Health Centre at Penetanguishene.

Magee, always suspected of committing the other crimes in the area, was reinterviewed on May 11, 1979, by OPP Constables P. De Vlugt and B. Linker. They learned nothing new from their two-hour session with Magee, but a half-hour after they left the institution they received a radio message that Magee wanted to see them again.

When they returned Magee blurted out a confession to the two officers: "I'm guilty of everything you suspect me of." He went on to give detailed statements concerning the murders of Barksey, Jenner, and Scholes, and the rapes of Winters and Jennings.

On January 18, 1980, Chris Magee stood trial for the murders of Barksey and Jenner. Once again he was found not guilty by reason of insanity. He is presently confined to the Mental Health Centre at Penetanguishene.

WAKAW MURDER

The hard-working farmers of Wakaw, Saskatchewan, had no reason to believe that the spring of 1916 would be any different than those of previous years. It was true that hail in the Wakaw area had destroyed 35 per cent of the crops that year, but the Ukrainian immigrants, most of whom couldn't speak a word of English, had overcome such hardships in the past.

Life would go on. Soon the heat of summer would bring tourists from Prince Albert and beyond to partake of the excellent fishing and boating on the crystal clear lakes surrounding the village.

Then it happened. The Royal Northwest Mounted Police Division Headquarters at Prince Albert received a telegram from Constable Dey of the Wakaw detachment: "Six people reported dead near here. Murder suspected. If possible send help."

And so began one of Saskatchewan's most diabolical and cold-blooded murder cases.

Inspector Duffus and Detective-Sergeant Prime, together with two other Mounties, journeyed to Wakaw to assist Dey. They discovered that the home of Prokop Manchur had been burned to the ground. His barn, sheltering horses and oxen, had also been destroyed by fire, cremating many of the animals trapped inside. Some oxen were inexplicably lying dead just outside the barn doors.

As the ruins cooled, the Mounties searched for bodies. Prokop Manchur, 46, was found in the kitchen, burned almost beyond recognition. The charred remains of his two daughters, Antone, 15, and Paulina, 20, were recovered in the same general area. Paulina was married to a farmer, Mike Syroshka, but the marriage didn't last, and Paulina had returned to live in her father's house.

The primitive farmhouse had not yet given up all its dead. Entrance to the cellar was gained by lowering a ladder through the floor of the living room. Here the Mounties found Prokop's wife, Mary, and the youngest member of the family, two-year-old Olga.

Mary's legs were grotesquely caught in the bottom rungs of the ladder, while her head, what was left of it, rested on a large stone on the floor. A portion of the unfortunate woman's brains lay on the floor. Her baby lay beside her.

This was no accidental fire. Constable Dey realized that murder had taken place that April day in the farmhouse of Prokop Manchur. While pondering the magnitude of the tragedy, Dey was informed that yet another body had been found. The soot-covered body of John Mychaluk, Prokop's brother-in-law, was discovered a short distance from the farmhouse. The body had not been burned. There was no doubt as to the cause of death. A bullet had entered Mychaluk's forehead and travelled directly through his head. Another had pierced his chest. It was the opinion of the coroner that either wound would result in instant death.

The bodies of the Manchur family were examined, and revealed the horror of their last moments before someone had set fire to their home. Mary had two bullet wounds in her arms. Baby Olga had also taken two bullets to the body. The three victims who had met their deaths in the kitchen, Prokop and his daughters, had all been shot.

Who had wiped out an entire family? The Mounties went to work.

Initially it was ascertained that John Mychaluk's body had been dragged out of the farmhouse through a window by neighbors who were the first at the scene of the fire. This accounted for the soot and grime on the unburned body. Mychaluk had a room in his brother-in-law's farmhouse and had lived there for some time.

The investigators deduced that Mary Manchur had fled to the cellar with her baby in a futile attempt to escape the carnage taking place in the kitchen. The murderer caught up with her while she was still on the ladder. No doubt the force of the two bullets in her arms sent her plunging onto the stones below, splitting open her head. The killer must have then taken aim and shot the baby in cold blood.

After killing all the occupants of the farmhouse, the killer had set the house and barn on fire. Several oxen made their way out of the blazing inferno only to be shot down by the mad, but obviously cool, assassin.

Paulina's husband, Mike Syroshka, was the first individual to come under suspicion. It was alleged that he had treated Paulina cruelly. After three years of marriage, at the instructions of her father, she had left him and returned to the family farm. Syroshka didn't take the separation well. He had been heard to threaten the entire family if Paulina didn't return to him.

When questioned, Syroshka admitted that bad blood had existed between him and the entire Manchur clan, but he vehemently denied any connection with the crime. He claimed that he had not set foot on the Manchur farm for over a year.

On the night of the fire, at exactly midnight, he, his mother, and other members of his family, had watched the reflection of the fire from his parents' farm. Syroshka willingly showed the Mounties the clothing he had worn on the night of the tragedy. They found no stains nor any other evidence to connect him to the multiple murder. Besides, when Syroshka confided to the Mounties that he had loved Paulina they were inclined to believe him.

The Mounties now turned their attention to the burned out ruins and a .32 Winchester rifle found amidst the debris. When the rifle was recovered there were eight live cartridges in the magazine and one exploded cartridge in the chamber.

A meticulous examination of the burned-out house recovered bullets which had been embedded in a wall. These bullets matched those recovered from the bodies of the victims. Empty cartridge cases were found in the ruins. They were all .32 Winchester centre-fire cartridges. It was apparent that one person, using the Winchester, was responsible for all the murders.

No one could identify the rifle. Friends and acquaintances swore that they had never seen any member of the Manchur family or John Mychaluk in possession of such a weapon.

The first break in the case occurred when Prokop Manchur's father informed the police that he had found a sheepskin coat near his son's farmhouse on the night of the fire. He had thought nothing about it at the time, but now, realizing that it might be connected in some way to the murders, he turned it over to the police.

The coat was quickly identified as belonging to John Mychaluk. He was seen wearing it on the night of the tragedy. Inside a pocket of the coat the Mounties found a box containing three .32 Winchester centre-fire cartridges. Also tucked away in the box was the name of the store in Wakaw where the cartridges had been purchased.

While shown this evidence, the Wakaw shopkeeper's memory was jogged. It was he who had sold the cartridges and rifle to Mychaluk.

The investigating officers now turned their attention to the possibility that Mychaluk may have been in some way involved in the murders. There were powder buns around his wounds, indicating that he had been shot at close range.

It was alleged that Mychaluk had made improper advances to Paulina Manchur. Was it possible that she was about to expose him, thereby providing him with a motive for murder? Some claimed that Mychaluk had argued heatedly with Prokop Manchur over money. Did these arguments precipitate the annihilation of the entire family?

These theories all pointed to Mychaluk as the killer, except for one undisputable fact. According to the coroner, either the bullet to Mychaluk's head or the one to his chest would have caused instant death. Dead men simply can't get off a well-aimed second shot.

To Inspector Duffus goes the credit for solving the mystery. So sure was he that Mychaluk had wiped out the entire Manchur family before turning his own rife upon himself that he was convinced that the coroner had erred. Inspector Duffus knew that if by chance the chest wound had not caused death there would be internal hemorrhaging. Only an autopsy would prove his point.

Duffus was correct. An autopsy revealed that Mychaluk's chest cavity was swimming with blood. There was now no doubt in the coroner's mind that Mychaluk had lived for some time after receiving the chest wound.

John Mychaluk had killed all the Manchurs and then turned his rifle upon himself. Instead of ending his life instantly with a bullet to the heart as he had planned, the bullet missed its mark and he remained alive. Now, certainly dying, but conscious enough to feel the heat of the flames advancing towards him he managed to lean the Winchester to his forehead and pull the trigger.

On April 14, 1916, a coroner's jury found the Manchurs' deaths to be the sole responsibility of John Mychaluk who, immediately following the murders, had committed suicide.

THE FIFTY CENT
MURDERS

Not many men have attempted to get rich by counterfeiting 50 cent Canadian coins. Herbert McAuliffe not only attempted the trick but did a fairly good job. Unfortunately, Herbie's rather comical criminal endeavors ended in tragedy when his bungling efforts turned to murder.

Born in North Bay, Ont., Herbie was an above average student during his formative years. He showed a natural mechanical bent and attended a technical school before leaving North Bay for the tobacco belt around Simcoe.

In 1939, together with thousands of other young Canadians, Herbie joined the army. While in the service, he used his mechanical ability to good advantage and quickly rose to the rank of staff sergeant. However, there must have been a little larceny in his heart even then. In 1944, he was dishonorably discharged for stealing money from his comrades.

Herbie gravitated to Windsor, Ont., taking with him one of the army's .45 calibre Thompson sub-machine guns and eight automatic pistols, but we have no reason to believe that he intended to use the army weapons. No, Herbie had other devious plans. He had decided to counterfeit Canadian 50 cent pieces, something never accomplished in this country before.

To facilitate his operation, Herbie rented a double garage from Germain Noel on London St., using the alias Frank West. Noel listened as Herbie explained that his work was rather noisy and was a top secret government project concerning the invention of a revolutionary new weapon.

Now that his cover was established, Herbie wrote away for books and manuals on coin minting. For weeks he pored over the technical articles. There was one immediate problem - the lack of funds. In order to implement his scheme, he required money to purchase machinery. This minor difficulty was overcome with ease. Herbie became extremely adept at holding up service stations and grocery stores.

Coincidental with his successful robberies, a steady stream of rather sophisticated machinery arrived at the garage on London St. A turret lathe, dies and punch presses worth over $15,000 were delivered to Herbie's factory. A $10,000 hydraulic press for stamping out the coins was installed at the garage. Herbie didn't do things half way.

It was hard work. Herbie carried out his experiments from scratch. He had no assistants and no technical advisors. His painstaking experiments continued for four years, interrupted and financed by his periodic stickups.

At last his technique was perfected. He had invented his own alloy and was actually able to stamp coins out of cheap metal and coat them with silver in an electroplating bath. The end result looked perfect. Just for fun, Herbie produced a bucket full.

That same night, Herbie tested his newly minted 50 cent pieces at a gambling joint in Detroit. He knew betting quantities of 50 cent Canadian coins would be unusual and focus attention on him, but he wanted the coins to be examined. If they would be accepted in a gambling den, they would be accepted everywhere. Herbie and his phony fifties passed with flying colors. His coins were identical to the real thing.

Next day, back at the garage, Herbie decided to figure out just how much he would net from his operation. He added up his expenses and was dumbfounded to find out that it cost him 48 cents for every 50 cent coin he produced. If he threw in his own labor he was losing money.

There was a solution. If he had the capital to modernize his plant with new equipment, he could lower costs. Herbie decided that the quickest way to raise capital would be to rob a bank.

In his usual methodical manner, Herbie drove throughout the countryside looking for a suitable bank. He found it in the Imperial Bank of Canada at Langton, Ont. Now, Langton was not a hustling, bustling metropolis. Located about 20 miles from Simcoe, it was not likely that the 250 souls who called Langton home would interfere with Herbie's nefarious scheme.

In preparation for the heist, Herbie stole a car in Windsor. Into it he threw his

.45 calibre Thompson sub-machine gun, a Luger and a .45 revolver. He tossed in a brown paper shopping bag to hold his anticipated loot.

Herbie walked up to bank accountant Henry Thompson and announced, "This is a stickup. Listen, chum, if you don't open up the combination on that vault I'll be back tonight to drill you dead." Thompson filled Herbie's paper shopping bag with $22,577 in bills and coins. Herbie waved his gun menacingly and herded 11 customers into the bank vault. He then took off for his waiting car, but in his haste our boy neglected to lock the vault door.

Inside the vault Arthur Lierman, a 31-year-old tobacco farm owner, pushed the door open. As he did so he shouted to William Goddyn, 24, "Come on, Bill, I've got a .22 calibre rifle in my Buick. Let's get him."

Herbie knew he was being followed. A few miles down the road near Frogmore he stopped, took out his sub-machine gun and fired a burst at the pursuing car. Lierman and Goddyn died in a hail of 30 bullets.

Herbie abandoned the shopping bag full of money on the front seat of his stolen car and took off into the bush. Word of the dramatic daylight bank robbery and the murders of two popular citizens of the area spread like wildfire.

The hunt was on. Herbie was headline news across the nation. The largest manhunt in Canadian history up to that time was organized. For three days Herbie hid out in barns, stole food from farmers, and swatted mosquitoes until Graham Haggerty, a 20-year-old farmhand out deer hunting, discovered Herbie in an old shack near Straffordville.

Initially, Herbie was identified as Frank West or George Walker, the two aliases he had used during his years developing fake 50 cent pieces. Eventually his true identity and his counterfeiting career were uncovered and revealed to the public.

Herbie was tried in Simcoe, found guilty of murder and sentenced to death. On Dec. 19, 1950, he was given the last rites of the Catholic church and walked briskly to his death on the scaffold at the Simcoe jail.

So ended the career of Herbert McAuliffe, who will go down in Canadian history as the only man to successfully produce counterfeit 50 cent pieces.

MYSTERIOUS DISAPPEARANCE

Whatever happened to Fred Johnsen?

It is eight years since Fred disappeared from his luxurious new home at 93 Old Forest Hill Rd. in Toronto's ultrarespectable Forest Hill area, and still the mystery of his disappearance remains unsolved.

Fred didn't always live in Forest Hill. Born in New Brunswick, he was adopted from a Saint John orphanage by Mr. and Mrs. Edward Johnsen of New Denmark, N.B. Fred was brought up in New Brunswick's potato belt. A high school dropout, he worked hard on the family farm for years.

In 1958 Fred hitch-hiked to Toronto to begin a new life. He was eminently successful. What Fred lacked in formal schooling, he made up for with an uncanny ability to smell out a profitable business deal.

His first venture into the world of business was modest enough. Fred opened a second hand store selling used television sets and electrical appliances. He made contacts in the U.S. and brought in large quantities of television sets which had been purchased from hotels and motels. The business prospered.

In 1962 Fred married Lisa, a native of Denmark. Hard-working Fred and his wife bought a home in King City. Call it luck, call it intuition, Fred recognized the potential profit in nursing homes. He purchased a part interest in King City Lodge. Within two years the government of Ontario extended the Ontario Health Plan to include nursing home care. This decision was a turning point in Fred Johnsen's financial life. Almost overnight nursing homes had become a profitable, viable business.

Within the next eight years Fred bought and sold nursing homes in King City, Toronto, St. Thomas, St. William, Southampton and Wiarton. In the U.S. he had an interest in homes in Texas, Florida and California. Fred branched out into other enterprises. During the few years before his disappearance he acquired interests in British United Automobiles, Downtown Fine Cars, Vintage Grand Touring Automobiles and Coventry Motors Ltd.

His holding company, Komar Investments, controlled three electronics firms. Together with his brother-in-law, Youcef Debabi, he owned Home Juice Corp.

No question about it, Fred was a wheeler-dealer who could recognize a profitable situation and take advantage of it. He was also one of those venturesome breed of businessmen who use their credit and income from one company to finance a new enterprise. Fred's various businesses often suffered from cash flow problems. Still, he had come a long way from the potato fields of New Brunswick.

On Aug. 28, 1979, Fred Johnsen, 44, was plucked from his Old Forest Hill Rd. home. The large stone house had just been purchased by the Johnsens for $446,000. Extensive renovations raised the total cost to the $800,000 range. There was a $387,000 mortgage on the house.

The Johnsens' Porsche and Rolls Royce were parked in the driveway that night. Lisa's sister Evy and her husband Youcef Debabi were visiting. Their Jaguar was parked beside the Johnsen vehicles.

The doorbell rang. Lisa answered. Later, she described the man as "short, very fat and quite ugly." The man produced a parcel and requested that Fred Johnsen sign for it. Lisa called to the kitchen for Fred. When he appeared the fat man leveled a small handgun directly at his chest. Fred ran out of the room with the intruder in pursuit. Evy and Youcef Debabi gasped. Lisa ran next door and had a neighbor call police. They arrived a few minutes later, but it was too late. Fred Johnsen was gone and has not been seen since that fateful night.

Initially the kidnapping was thought to be a case of a man of substance being held for ransom, yet kidnappings of that type are usually executed by an efficient gang, not a lone, rather innocuous intruder.

About a week after the abduction, a ransom demand was received. Explicit instructions outlined the type of packaging and twine to be used to wrap the ransom money. The kidnappers demanded two separate packages of 20,000 twenty dollar bills and another with 20,000 ten dollar bills, a million dollars in all.

Before delivering the money, an ad was to be placed in the classified section of a Toronto newspaper giving the precise dimensions and weight of each parcel. In this way, the kidnappers could verify that the one million dollars was in readiness. For some reason, police interpreted the ransom note to be for $800,000. When they placed the ad, the dimensions and weights were incorrect. Whoever made the ransom demand was never heard from again. Was it a hoax or were the real kidnappers scared off?

Toronto hoodlum Howard "Mugsy" Dean contacted lawyer David Humphrey, who at the time was acting on behalf of concerned business associates of Johnsen. Dean told Humphrey that while he was not personally involved in the kidnapping, he knew where Johnsen was being held and why. He informed Humphrey that Johnsen owed underworld characters some $28,000 plus interest of $25,000. For a fee, Dean would deliver Johnsen.

Dean's claims were not dismissed out of hand. He managed to extract $1000 from Johnsen's business acquaintances before being charged with extortion. Mugsy was later convicted and sentenced to five years imprisonment for his involvement in the Johnsen affair.

Exit Mugsy, enter the Fat Man.

Thirty-eight-year-old Alan Bazkur stood 5 ft. 7 inches tall and weighed in at somewhere over 200 pounds. Big Al had a buddy, Sandra Cohen. Sandra told Al that in order to avoid a traffic violation, she had performed a sex act with a police officer. Al saw the incident as a golden opportunity. He instituted a campaign for compensation for Sandra. The police officer in question resigned, but Al wanted cash.

His campaign made him highly visible. Here was a fat man who bore a striking similarity to the fat man described by Lisa Johnsen. Two things happened. Lisa Johnsen picked Al out of a lineup and Al couldn't account for his exact whereabouts on the night of the abduction.

Alan Bazkur was arrested and stood trial for Johnsen's kidnapping. The Crown's case fell apart when Bazkur remembered spending the evening of the kidnapping at the Hampton Court Hotel on Jarvis St. The barman corroborated Bazkur's story. He had not come forward sooner because Bazkur had used a phony Chargex card in the name of G.W. Watson. Handwriting experts agreed that Bazkur had signed Watson's name to the Chargex cards. To further corroborate his presence at the hotel on the night of the kidnapping, a CBC reporter recalled having a prolonged discussion with Bazkur in the bar. Both men swore that Bazkur was in the bar from 5:30 p.m. till after midnight. Alan Bazkur was acquitted.

Much has been dredged up about Fred Johnsen's private life. He may have lacked funds to close the biggest deal of his life just before he was kidnapped. We know he was accustomed to making several gambling trips each year to Caesar's Palace in Las Vegas, where he often won and lost $30,000 in a single night. Did he orchestrate his own disappearance after skimming off funds from his various interests and flee to a life of luxury on some Caribbean island? Or was he killed in gangland fashion for reneging on a loan?

Lisa Johnsen has been successful in having her husband declared dead in a Surrogate Court, which clears the way to having his will probated. Three insurance companies, Sun Life Assurance Co., Crown Life Insurance Co., and Metropolitan Life Insurance Co. carry policies on Fred's life totalling $3 million. Lisa and other beneficiaries are pressing for payment. The Supreme Court has upheld the Surrogate Court's decision. However, a motion in the Supreme Court asking for payment has been thrown out and the Insurance companies have been granted a stay of proceedings. So far no money has changed hands.

The hunt for Fred Johnsen goes on. Metro Police investigating officers have probed a cement wall in Toronto, checked out a burial site in Kearney, Ont., and looked into sightings of Johnsen in Arizona and California. All these leads and many others have proven fruitless.

The truth is no one knows what happened to Fred Johnsen since that night of Aug. 28, 1979 when an ugly fat man forced him from his home on Old Forest Hill Rd., where such things simply don't happen.

THE DEMETER FILE

O n Dec. 4, 1974, intelligent, wealthy real estate developer Peter Demeter was sentenced to life imprisonment for procuring the murder of his wife, Christine.

Christine's body was found on the garage floor of the Demeter home in Mississauga. She had been bludgeoned to death.

The gates of Millhaven Penitentiary closed behind the tall, debonair builder as they have closed behind hundreds of convicted murderers who preceded him.

Most are never heard of again.

But Peter Demeter was different. He was not an average man, or more precisely, he was not an average prisoner. European born, university educated, he was poles apart from the three-time losers and impulsive killers with whom he came in contact.

After Demeter was classified and commenced serving his sentence, word drifted back to the law enforcement community that he harbored a grudge against the Peel Regional Police, who had gathered the evidence which had convicted him of his wife's murder. In particular, he had a passionate hatred for Deputy Chief William Teggart.

In Millhaven, Demeter made a friend. Some say a friend who received payment for his services, for Demeter had entered Millhaven with a net worth in excess of $1 million.

Mike Hodgson, better known as "The Butcher," was Demeter's bodyguard. To harm Demeter was to cross the Butcher's path. Hodgson, serving time for manslaughter, cast a long shadow. Few dared mess with Peter Demeter at Millhaven.

After Demeter had served four and a half years at Millhaven, Hodgson was transferred to the medium security facility at Warkworth. Three days later, Peter Demeter, now without his bodyguard, was attacked by a fellow inmate in his cell. Demeter let it be known that without protection he was a dead man. As if by magic, within 72 hours, he was transferred to Warkworth.

During the intervening years and, in fact, from the day of Christine Demeter's murder in 1973, the couple's daughter, three-year-old Andrea, lived with Peter's cousin, Dr. Steven Demeter and his family. Peter readily gave Dr. Demeter power of attorney, enabling him to act on Peter's behalf in financial matters.

By 1981, the over $1 million insurance on Christine's life had accumulated to over $3 million, including interest. Peter initiated legal action against the three insurance companies in order to lay his hands on the money. He also instructed Dr. Steven Demeter to initiate an action on Andrea's behalf against the same companies. The Demeters lost the lawsuits. Both appeals were dismissed.

Dr. Demeter approached Peter with $30,000 in legal fees which the insurance fight had cost him. Peter refused to pay, and the two former friends had a falling out. Dr. Steven Demeter was secretly placed on Peter Demeter's hate list, along with the Peel Regional Police and Deputy Chief Teggart.

Dr. Demeter didn't have long to wait to hear from his cousin. In April 1982, he received a threatening letter from Peter. He travelled to the prison and informed Peter that the letter would be turned over to the authorities should anything happen to him. Dr. Demeter also expressed his concern to parole authorities, as well as Dep. Chief Teggart. From that day to this, there has been no communication between the two cousins.

Andrea Demeter had initially been told that her father was on a prolonged business trip in Europe. As the years passed, this pretense was dropped and the little girl was told the truth about her father. In 1979, at the age of nine, Andrea was visiting her father at Warkworth. She had difficulty coping with the visits. At times, her father was rude and abusive. Finally, she stopped visiting.

Meanwhile, Mike Hodgson was paroled from prison, and had become involved in a fraud-related matter in Hamilton. He skipped to England, where he stayed a short time before returning. Once back in Hamilton, he lived with Anthony Preston, 48, a former prison inmate, who had spent eight years behind bars.

By the summer of 1983, Peter Demeter had himself spent over eight years in prison. His status had greatly changed since his Millhaven days. He was domiciled at Edmison House, a halfway house in Peterborough. He was required to spend from 12 a.m. to 7 a.m. each day at the house. He also had to return to Warkworth each weekend.

Demeter, with an I.Q. of 146, considered to be in the genius category, had no difficulty ingratiating himself with prison officials who controlled his destiny. He had the key to the parole officer's home and often attended family barbecues there.

Demeter spent many pleasant evenings at his parole officer's home. Occasionally, he took the official's two children swimming.

Demeter visited his living unit officer's cottage in the Muskokas, and has admitted giving gifts such as liquor, to the families of other correctional facility officials. His classification officer's son received a gift of designer jeans. On one occasion, charming Peter took the boy to Toronto and lined him up with a prostitute.

Correctional authorities maintain a Life Skills office at 331 Rubige St. in Peterborough, where six inmates counsel institutionalized inmates on how to cope with life on the outside. Peter Demeter ran the office.

That summer of 1983, Demeter arranged a meeting with Anthony Preston and Mike Hodgson at the Holiday Inn in Peterborough. Shortly after the meeting, Hodgson returned to Hamilton and turned himself in to the police. Two months later, Demeter set up another meeting with Preston at the House of Chan on Eglinton Ave. in Toronto. For the first time, Peter Demeter told someone in an ambiguous manner that he had a job he needed done. Preston listened and was interested. He returned to Hamilton, but was once more summoned by Demeter, this time to Peterborough. Coincidentally, they met a mutual friend, Mike Lane, an ex-convict on parole from a life sentence for murder. Lane left the meeting. Demeter and Preston sat around a picnic table in the park.

According to Preston's later testimony, Demeter said, "My cousin's been cheating me out of my money." Demeter went on to accuse his cousin of stripping his house in Mississauga of valuable paintings and of turning his daughter against him. At this time, Demeter was well aware that Dr. Demeter had applied to the public trustee to be appointed Andrea's legal guardian.

The meeting continued. Preston claims Peter said, "While in jail I have worked out a three part plan. I spent an awful lot of time working it out."

In essence, Peter wanted his home in Mississauga burned to the ground in order to collect the insurance of $138,000 to finance the rest of his scheme. The second phase involved the kidnapping of his cousin's son, Stuart Demeter, 19, a computer science student. He was to be lured to a parked van on the pretext of obtaining summer employment. Preston would want a van for this purpose.

When the unsuspecting boy opened the door of the van, Peter Demeter would be secreted inside and shoot him dead. Preston later testified, "Demeter said Stuart was going to have to be sacrificed, because Dr. and Mrs. Demeter had to pay for what they had done to him." After the murder, the boy's teeth were to be removed and his fingers amputated to deter identification. The body was to be placed in a body bag and burned.

The third phase of the overall scheme was the kidnapping of a Progressive Conservative fundraiser living in Rosedale. The kidnappers were to appoint Peter Demeter as mediator. The goodwill generated by Demeter in returning the politician to his family, would go a long way with the parole board.

Preston agreed to the razing of Demeter's house, but was leery of Demeter and his talk of murder and mutilation. The sum of $8,000 was agreed upon for the torch job. Demeter passed over a down payment of $500 to Preston. Preston returned to Hamilton, and made up his mind to go through with the arson job, but to have nothing to do with the murder and kidnapping.

In subsequent meetings between the two men at Hy's Restaurant on Richmond Ave., Hemingway's on Cumberland and the Long Bar in the Sheraton Centre, Preston received a further $3500 in cash and a ransom note to be read over the phone to Dr. Demeter after the job was done.

On Aug. 15, 1983, the Mississauga Fire Dept. extinguished a blaze at Demeter's vacant house at 1437 Dundas Cres. in Mississauga. Seven days later, on Aug. 22, the house again mysteriously caught fire, but burned itself out. The very next night, the luxurious home burned to the ground.

Anthony Preston had done his job well, but wanted nothing more to do with Demeter, who made several attempts to contact him. Preston feared for his life. He gave a copy of the ransom note to his girlfriend, instructing her to go to the police with it if anything ever happened to him.

On Sept. 3, 1983, Police Chief D. K. Burrows and Dep. Chief William Teggert of the Peel Regional Police met with Insp. Noel Catney, a veteran of 18 years police work and 46 murder investigations. They advised him that they felt that Peter Demeter was behind the suspected arson of his home. Insp. Catney was given the green light to consider the arson a major project. He hand-picked his team of investigators.

Five days later, Catney was advised that Peter Demeter would be at the site of his burned out home. Catney made a point of being there. The two men met. The master manipulator gazed at the ruins of the home which he hadn't seen for nine years. Catney, the professional cop, asked Demeter if he had any idea how the house had burned down. Demeter replied that he didn't know. Catney promised Demeter he would find out who set the fire. At the time he had no idea that he would live and breathe the Peter Demeter saga for the next two years.

Three weeks later, the arson was to take a back seat when Insp. Catney received a phone call from Insp. Bob Lewis of the Peterborough Police Dept. Lewis had a strange story to tell. The night before, Mike Lane, 32, a parolee who had somewhat of a reputation as a strongman, had flagged down a police cruiser. Lane reported that Peter Demeter had approached him with a proposition to lure a 19-year-old boy to a van in a parking lot, where Demeter would shoot the boy. He went on to relate many of the same details that Preston would later reveal to the police. Mike Lane wanted no part of Demeter's murderous scheme.

Insp. Catney had questioned the Demeter family during the arson investigation and knew that the intended victim was Stuart Demeter. Catney travelled to Peterborough and received Mike Lane's promise of co-operation. Meetings were set up between Demeter and Lane at the Holiday Inn in Peterborough. Unknown to Demeter, video and audio tapes were made of these conversations.

Demeter went through his entire plan to kidnap and murder Stuart Demeter. He had purchased a home at 426 Donegal St. in Peterborough. The old home had a crawl space with a dirt floor. Part of Lane's job, for which he would receive $10,000, was to dig a hole in this crawl space. Demeter wanted the hole to be six feet four inches long. Stuart Demeter's exact height. The hole was to be Stuart Demeter's grave.

On Oct. 19, 1983, Insp. Catney arrested Peter Demeter. He was charged with two counts of counselling to commit murder, three counts of arson, and one count of conspiring to commit arson. At the same time, Anthony Preston was taken into custody and charged with arson. He would later be found guilty, and sentenced to nine months imprisonment. He also told police of Demeter's plan to murder Stuart Demeter. He even turned over a ransom note complete with Peter Demeter's fingerprints.

Noel Catney's two year odyssey was over. Today, Catney says, "Peter Demeter is probably the most dangerous individual I have ever been involved with during my police career. He should never be considered for parole."

On July 8, 1985, Peter Demeter, 54, was found guilty of two counts of counselling to commit murder.

ENOUGH IS ENOUGH

Jane Stafford looked at the 280 lb. hulk of a man snoring in the cab of the family's half-ton Jeep truck, the man who had been the source of her hell on earth for five long years. Then she said to Allan, her 16-year-old son, "Get me a gun." Allan brought out a 12-gauge shotgun, passed it to his mother and returned to the house.

Jane, relating the sequence of events to me, stated, "I put the gun in the window of the cab and just fired."

It was the night of March 11, 1982 when Jane Stafford, 33, blew the head off Billy Stafford, her common-law husband. Jane didn't know that in the months to follow her case would be discussed across the nation. She didn't know that many would claim that she crystalized the plight of battered and abused women everywhere.

No - Jane knew only one thing that March evening. The beatings to herself, her family and her neighbors had to stop before Billy killed her or someone else.

Jane Stafford has not had an easy life. Born in Brooklyn, N.S., not more than 30 miles from Bangs Falls, she has rarely left the beautiful south shore area of Nova Scotia where she was born and raised. She vividly recalls her career Army father abusing her mother, so that later, when she became the victim of her second husband's abuse, she felt that this was the natural order of things.

Jane left school in Grade 9. She had married and given birth to her eldest son Allan by the time she was 15. For ten years she lived with an alcoholic husband. Her second son James was born before she obtained a divorce in 1976.

While still married, she met Big Billy Stafford, a friend of her husband's. Soon after her divorce she moved in with Billy.

For a short while, her common-law husband, a part-time fisherman and lumberman, treated her with some semblance of decency. Jane didn't know that Billy Stafford had already had two disastrous relationships with women. His first wife, Pauline, almost drowned when Billy submerged her head in a bucket of water. He terrorized their five children with lit cigarettes and knives until one day, while Billy was fishing, Pauline took off with her five children for Ontario. She never returned until after Billy's death.

Billy's next relationship with a woman fared no better. His first common-law wife left for Calgary after sampling Billy's lifestyle.

Now it was Jane's turn. Jane gave birth to Billy's son, Darren. When I met Darren, he played hide and seek with me in the Nova Scotia Legal Aid offices.

From all outward appearances he is an attractive, normal youngster, but Darren's short life has been full of the trauma of literally having a monster for a father. When he was only two, his father would pick him up by the hair and hold him in the air before dropping the terrified child to the floor. Sometimes Billy would hold a gun to the boy's head and tell him, "I'm going to blow your head off." On other occasions he would hold a knife to the boy's throat.

Allan Ferrier, the Nova Scotia legal aid lawyer who defended Jane, told me, "Darren has received psychiatric treatment and counselling for almost two years and there is every reason to believe he will be fine. However, he shocked psychiatrists when he told them he wished he was as big as his father Billy and his father was as small as he, so that he could be mean to Billy like Billy was mean to him."

Billy directed his abuse towards Jane after Darren's birth. He had apparently wanted a girl and knew he wouldn't have one after Jane had a hysterectomy. Jane's life became a series of degrading acts and beatings.

When I met with Jane Stafford I thought one of her outstanding features was her flawless even white teeth. I mentioned this and was shocked at her reply, "Oh, they're all false. That happened when Billy kept striking me with the butt of his rifle until I was unconscious. My oldest son Allan found me on the floor and thought I was dead. The few teeth which weren't knocked out later had to be extracted by a dentist. I told the dentist I was in a car accident and struck my head on the steering wheel. I was laid up in bed for two weeks after that beating."

Coverups, such as lying to the dentist, served to isolate the life Jane was leading, but many knew the nature of the man with whom she was living. Most, if not all, were fearful for their lives if they messed around with Big Billy Stafford.

Once he forced the captain of a scallop dragger to bring his vessel to shore. Billy was charged with mutiny on that occasion, but in the end no one would testify against him. The charges were eventually dropped, but Billy found himself blacklisted by the fishing industry.

Sometimes friends would become the object of Billy's anger. For no apparent reason he would beat them up and throw them out of his home. Once he beat up Jane's father. Soon friends stopped dropping in at the Staffords'.

Billy drank daily, used drugs, and terrorized anyone who crossed his path. Police were told to approach the Stafford home armed and with caution. They rarely did.

Just for fun Billy, who sometimes claimed he was placed on earth by the devil, would load the truck with his family and roar down the highway on the wrong side of the road. Eyes popping, mouth frothing, he laughed in the face of death while his passengers cringed in fear.

But it was against Jane that most of Billy's anger was directed.

On two occasions he fired his .22 calibre rifle at Jane, once while she was tending her garden and once while she was working in the house. Billy explained that he was just seeing how close he could come to her.

There were other, far worse, indignities and sexual abuses, some of which are so abhorrent that it is not necessary to repeat them here.

James escaped most of his stepfather's abuse as he stayed much of the time with Jane's parents. Allan was beaten up approximately once a week.

Why didn't Jane leave? Some way, somehow, taking such abuse herself and seeing her children terrorized, why didn't she simply run away?

Jane explained to me, as she earlier explained to the court, that Billy had often bragged to her that he had once murdered a man by throwing him overboard. In actual fact, a man was lost at sea while Billy was aboard, but nothing ever came of Billy's involvement. Billy assured Jane that if she ever left him he would kill her parents. Jane didn't doubt him for one minute.

Life went on. Big Billy called the shots and Jane and her children danced to his tune. There were rules. When you drove in the Jeep you were not allowed to get out before Billy. If you did, you were beaten. Some evenings Jane and Billy played cards. It was a strange game. If Jane played the wrong card she was beaten to the floor and made to struggle back onto her chair and continue playing. No Bible or prayer books were allowed in the Stafford home.

Most people knew that big Billy was in some state of drunkenness every day. They knew he got into minor scrapes with the law. Some, who asked to remain anonymous, thought that he might kill someone some day. But only Jane knew first hand the violence that was Billy Stafford.

During the last few years of her life with Billy, Jane was helped and consoled in her plight by Margaret Joudrey, an older woman who lived in a trailer adjacent to the Stafford property. For years Billy had been arguing over the boundary line between the two properties. When Margaret's common-law husband passed away without a will, it became a legal possibility that Margaret did not hold title to the property. Billy taunted his neighbor with this fact at every opportunity.

The turbulent existence that was Jane Stafford's life polarized on March 11, 1982. That morning, Billy rose early and worked in the woods with his eldest stepson, Allan, and Ronald Wamboldt, 44, an alcoholic who at that time was rooming with the Staffords. Wamboldt had often unintentionally displeased Billy, and he too had been the recipient of periodic beatings.

The men returned from the woods around noon and started drinking. By 4:30 p.m. Billy and Ron were drunk. Billy was becoming progressively wilder. They decided to visit a friend, Leona Anthony, in Charleston, five miles away. Darren and Allan were left at home. Jane drove the truck to Charleston, where the drinking continued.

By 8:30 that evening Ron Wamboldt was dead drunk. He remembers none of the events which took place that night. On the way home, Jane drove the Jeep. Ron sat next to the passenger door, while Billy was propped up in the middle. Billy bragged that once they got home he was going to burn out Margaret Joudrey. Then he would beat Allan to a pulp. No doubt it would be Jane's turn next.

Jane guided the truck onto the dirt road leading to her modest home. She pulled into the yard. Ron staggered out of the vehicle, entered the house and fell into bed. Billy was asleep in the cab. Jane hesitated before leaving the Jeep, knowing she would be breaking one of Billy's rules if she left the truck before he did.

Jane beeped the horn. When her son Allan appeared, she asked him to fetch a gun. She stepped down from the truck. Sixteen-year-old Allan gave his mother the shotgun and returned to the house. That's when Jane, by her own admission, figured, "To hell with it. I'm not going to live like this any more." She "put the gun in the window and just fired."

Billy Stafford would inflict no more indignities on his common-law wife. The shotgun blast had blown off his head. Blood, pieces of bone, and brain fragments spattered the interior of the cab. Some blood splattered on Jane's clothing. Bits and pieces of Billy's skull lay on the cab floor.

Now in a dazed condition, Jane acted in an irrational manner. Jane Stafford, who had never harmed a living creature in her life, now shouted to her son to go to Margaret Joudrey's to phone her parents and tell them to meet her at nearby Charleston. She also told Allan to get rid of the shotgun. Without hesitation he threw it in the Medway River.

Jane jumped into the cab beside the bloody body of what had once been Billy Stafford and drove five miles to Charleston, where she met her parents. Jane merely parked the truck with its grisly cargo beside the road. She accompanied her parents to their home, changed her clothing, and had them drive her back to Bangs Falls. That night she stayed with her sons.

Next morning, a resident of the area, Carl Croft, walked past the truck and spotted the headless corpse. He contacted police. Later that day, when Jane was informed that Billy's body had been found, she fainted.

Three days after the shooting, Jane Stafford was arrested and charged with first degree murder. A friend put her in touch with Allan Ferrier, a Nova Scotia legal aid lawyer.

Ferrier, 33, a graduate of Dalhousie Law School, had never been in private practice. His entire career had been spent with the province's legal aid department. The Stafford case was his second murder trial. His first defence in a murder case had resulted in an acquittal. Ferrier, a laid-back Maritimer, wears blue jeans and a t-shirt to the office. One gets the impression that the legal aid office in Bridgewater won't be able to hold bright, articulate Allan Ferrier much longer. He is a young man on the rise.

As I sat in Ferrier's office, he explained that he realized the Crown would allege that his client's life was not in danger at the time of the killing. After all, the victim was snoozing in the cab of his truck. However, Ferrier quoted Section 37 of the Criminal Code which reads, "Everyone is justified in using force to defend himself or anyone under his protection from assault, if he uses no more force than is necessary to prevent the assault or the repetition of it." Ferrier argued that Jane Stafford was defending her son, who was under her protection. She also had no other recourse, nowhere to turn, no one to help her.

The Nova Scotia jury of ten men and one woman had four verdicts to consider: guilty of first degree murder, guilty of second degree murder, guilty of manslaughter, or not guilty. They took 18 hours to find Jane Stafford not guilty. When the verdict was read, the crowded courtroom burst into applause. Scores of friends and spectators tried to hug Jane, slap her on the back, wish her well. It was as if abused women everywhere had won a moral victory.

Epilogue: Since her trial, Jane Stafford has taken an upgrading course with the Nova Scotia Department of Education and has received the equivalent of a Grade 12 certificate. She is taking a course in Bridgewater leading to a Certified Nurses' Assistant Certificate.

The Attorney General's office of Nova Scotia has served notice that they are appealing the jury's verdict in the Stafford case.

The Stafford case is no longer unique. On Dec. 8, 1982, James Clarkson, 44, of Durham Bridge, N.B. was found shot to death in his home. His wife Lana was charged with second degree murder. At Mrs. Clarkson's trial witnesses stated that the alcoholic Clarkson continually beat his wife and children. After deliberating a little over one hour, the jury found Lana Clarkson not guilty.

WHO IS THE NATION RIVER GIRL?

Detective Inspector Bill MacGregor of the Ontario Provincial Police stared down at a photograph of two partial dentures taken from the unidentified body of a young woman. MacGregor, like the three previous detectives who attempted over nine long years to identify the body, is no nearer today than they were to solving the mystery of the Nation River girl.

Claude Legault was working the south section of his farm at approximately 10 a.m. on May 3, 1975 near Casselman, Ont., when he spotted what he thought was a dead animal floating in the Nation River. Upon closer inspection, he realized it was the almost nude body of a human being. Claude returned to his home and called the Casselman detachment of the OPP.

The partially decomposed body was nude from the neck down. The wrists were tied in front with a man's navy blue necktie decorated with red maple leaf emblems. The victim's ankles were tied with two neckties, one blue and grey, the other a loud red and white patterned affair. The killer had tightened a blue body shirt around her neck. A J-Cloth and an ordinary hand towel were wrapped around the dead girl's head.

A distinctive linen towel, manufactured in Ireland, was found with the body. It bore illustrations of meat, fish and drink, and was entitled Food and Drink. On the towel were printed six tips for drinking at parties. For example, number one suggested: "Eat or nibble as you drink, particularly at a cocktail party. But concentrate on protein foods that digest slowly . . . sardines, salmon, shrimp, caviar, meat and eggs."

Strangely enough, a curtain rod runner with a plastic wheel was found under the girl's left armpit. Among the crude array of materials, police found a 24-inch piece of T.V. coaxial cable. Two large sections of green cloth held the gruesome bundle in place.

Pathologist J. Hillsdon-Smith performed the autopsy. His findings confirmed that the cause of death was "strangulation by a ligature." The victim was between 25 and 35 years old. Her shoulder length dark brown hair had been dyed a reddish blond. She had had restorative dental work on her upper and lower dentures. Sometime in the past her appendix had been removed. She had never given birth. Her fingernails and toenails were painted with common pink nail polish. The Nation River girl was 5 ft. 3 in. tall and had weighed between 100 and 110 pounds.

Attempting to establish the date of death proved to be a problem for Hillsdon-Smith. The body appeared to have been in the river from one to four weeks, establishing a murder date at somewhere between April 5 and April 26. However, as temperature had a direct effect on the rate of decomposition, there was an outside chance that the victim may have been killed just before the river froze the previous fall.

Tiny bloodstains were discovered on the Nation River bridge. The quantity of blood was too small to establish a blood type, making it impossible to ascertain whether it was that of the victim. However, the position of the spots was compatible with someone lifting a body over the bridge railing. If investigating officers were to assume that the blood on the bridge was that of the victim, they could narrow the perimeters of the murder dates. A heavy rain had fallen on April 19, which would have obliterated the bloodstains on the bridge. It was then reasonable to assume that the girl had been tossed in the river between April 19 and April 26.

The multitude of physical clues found with the body gave OPP officials every reason to believe that the body would be readily identified and the killer apprehended. Such was not to be the case.

Initially the victim's fingerprints were checked against all missing person's in Canada with negative results. The FBI had no record of her prints. Interpol couldn't help.

One by one the items found with the body were traced. The neckties had been manufactured in Montreal and sold in large quantities through Ontario and Quebec. The colorful towel had been imported from Ireland by Ralph Hunter Linens Co. of Toronto. They had been sold in 50 dozen lots up to 1972. The towels retailed for $1.69 and proved to be untraceable. The coaxial cable was manufactured by

Amphenol Canada Ltd. and sold by thousands of feet throughout Ontario and Quebec.

So it went with every item found with the body. All were impossible to trace. The dentures, often the means of positive identification, proved the most frustrating to the officers. The materials used in the manufacture of the dentures were of the highest quality, but the workmanship was inferior. Denturists in Toronto believed that such inferior workmanship would not be acceptable in the Toronto market, but might have been manufactured in the province of Quebec.

One by one, denturists in Ontario and Quebec were interviewed. All swore that they had not made the dentures. When it was suggested that the dentures might have been manufactured in Halifax, a member of the OPP flew there, but once again the work was not identified.

The green material wrapped around the victim's head could have been part of a curtain. With this in mind all hotels and motels for miles were canvassed to match the material, but nothing came of this avenue of the investigation.

Waitresses and entertainers who had abruptly left their places of employment were tracked down. Scores of girls, many of whom were go-go dancers in Ontario and Quebec towns, were traced and found to be alive and well.

In 1977, the Ontario Dental Association held a convention in Toronto. Posters with an illustration and description of the dentures were distributed at the convention, but no one identified the dental work.

Det. Insp. MacGregor believes that the dentures are the key to identifying the dead girl. Prior to 1975, many dentures were being bootlegged by unlicensed technicians. Materials may have been imported from Germany and the dentures manufactured in a one man lab. When the licensed denturists were canvassed these individuals would have been missed.

I travelled to the Long Sault detachment of the OPP and watched as Cpl. Earl Bowes unsealed the small cardboard carton containing the items which were found with the victim over nine years ago.

Who once wore these neckties? Who wrapped the victim's head with the various items which must have been close at hand? These questions remain unanswered.

For years, the Nation River girl's body lay frozen in the Toronto morgue waiting to be identified. No one came forward. The unidentified body was buried in 1986.

HE DIDN'T GET AWAY WITH MURDER

O n March 28, 1981, Jeanette Kelly plunged to her death from the seventeenth floor of her luxurious Palace Pier apartment overlooking Lake Ontario.

Two years later, her husband Patrick, a former RCMP undercover officer, was charged with her murder. This is the story of their lives together, culminating with Jeanette's death and with Patrick standing trial for her murder.

When Pat Kelly was still a child, his family moved from Toronto to Victoria, B.C. He attended school in Victoria, graduating from Mountain View High School after completing Grade 12.

Pat Kelly, a clean cut, bright young man, tried his hand at banking. He obtained employment with the Bank of Montreal in Port Alberni, B.C. and was soon transferred to Dawson Creek. It was only a matter of a few months before Pat knew that the regimented life of a banker was not for him. He left the bank and caught on with a logging company, but here too, a restless streak, maybe an adventurous one, made Pat look to greener pastures. What could hold more promise of adventure than the RCMP?

On Nov. 2, 1970, Pat Kelly joined the Mounties and was assigned to Regina for basic training. Six months later he graduated and was sent to Toronto, where he spent four months on duty at Pearson International Airport. Next step in Pat's law enforcement career found him stationed at the RCMP detachment at Owen Sound. Here he obtained his first taste of undercover work, becoming involved in drugs and customs investigations. A year later, he was transferred back to Toronto to enrol in a French course, which lasted 18 months. Pat was then assigned to the drug squad. Soon he was an undercover drug squad operator.

In 1974, Pat's superiors sent him to the University of Javaria in Bogota, Colombia to take part in a total immersion course in Spanish. Later, while vacationing in Acapulco with fellow RCMP officer Wayne Humby, Pat met his future wife, Jeanette Hanlon.

The daughter of an automobile dealer in Glasgow, Scotland, attractive Jeanette hit it off with Pat right from the start. She was an employee of Avianca, Colombia's national airline, and was stopping over in Acapulco on her way back to Scotland after setting up a computer program for an airline in New Zealand. Jeanette and Pat were seldom apart during the week they spent in Mexico.

Jeanette, who had a full airline pass, continued on to Scotland to visit her family. She and Pat kept in constant touch by phone for a few weeks. Then she joined him in Toronto. The lovers discussed marriage. Jeanette was smitten. She returned to Scotland, but three months later emigrated to Canada to live with Pat Kelly. Ten months after her return, on Sept. 20, 1975, Jeanette and Pat were married.

They had become good friends with another couple, Dawn Tabor and John Pinkerton Hastey, better known as Pinky. The pair had been childhood friends in Maine. A short time after they arrived in Toronto, Dawn and Pinky married. They lived at 1900 Bloor St. East in Mississauga. Pat and Jeanette lived at Applewood Towers in Mississauga. Dawn Hastey is a name to remember. Sometime later, in the tangled web of the Kellys' life, Dawn would play a starring role.

By 1976, Pat and Jeanette purchased their first home from Pat's cousin, Jack McKay, at 16 George St. in Cookstown. Jeanette discovered she had a flair for interior decorating. The young couple worked several months renovating their new home.

Once they were nicely settled, Jeanette opened a craft shop specializing in homemade quilts. She named it The Quilt Shop. Farmers' wives around Cookstown brought their homemade quilts to Jeanette, who sold them at a profit. The trendy shop gradually caught on. While it didn't produce a large profit, it did pay its own way. In the summer of 1978, the Kellys sold their shop at a small profit.

That summer of 1978, Pat was deeply involved in an RCMP undercover drug operation. It was a rather stressful time for Pat. He had been attempting to sell his home in Cookstown and purchase a condominium in the Palace Pier apartment building in the west end of Toronto. The house in Cookstown had been up for sale with no takers for over 10 months. This was of some concern, since Pat had put

$3000 down on the new apartment, but required a further $5700 to close the deal toward the total price of $87,000.

Later, Pat would testify that he had several sources from whom he could have borrowed the balance of his down payment. However, all his problems appeared to evaporate when, in August, the Cookstown house burned to the ground. At the time of the fire, Pat claimed that he was at a lodge in Algonquin Park, while Jeanette was visiting her family in Glasgow. Pat phoned Jeanette, who flew back to Toronto.

Arson was strongly suspected. Jeanette was understandably shocked when Pat was charged with setting fire to the house, along with two counts of attempting to defraud the insurance companies. Their marriage deteriorated into a strained relationship. In Pat's own words, ". . . basically a platonic relationship took place. I didn't get in her way and she didn't get in mine. We would often socialize together and go to a movie perhaps or go to dinner." It was quite remarkably a congenial atmosphere considering the circumstances.

For some time after the fire took place, Pat and Jeanette lived at the Holiday Inn in Don Mills under police protection. The drug probe involving Pat had been finalized in July and the fire had taken place in August. There was a grave suspicion that Pat's life was in danger. To this day, Pat claims that criminals burned his house shortly after his cover was blown.

Others obviously had a different theory, but things took a turn for the better for the Kellys. Pat was discharged on the arson charges. He collected $60,000 in insurance for the house and $55,000 for contents, in all $115,000.

Pat and Jeanette took a holiday in Mexico. The Kellys grew much closer now that the terrible possibility of a conviction and prison sentence had been lifted from their shoulders. When they returned to Toronto, there seemed little reason not to move into the Palace Pier.

On Oct. 3, 1978, the Kellys moved into their luxurious new apartment.

Although the Kellys' domestic situation improved, there were other women in Pat Kelly's life. Let's start with Dawn Hastey.

Before Pat and Jeanette married, they made the acquaintance of Dawn Tabor and Pinky Hastey. The two couples became close friends in a short period of time. In the summer of 1975, both couples married. Five years later, when Dawn had marital difficulties, it was only natural that she discuss her problems with her close friends, the Kellys. Both Pat and Jeanette were sympathetic to her plight. They suggested that she would be welcome to stay with them should she leave her husband.

The very night this discussion took place, Dawn had a heart to heart talk with her husband. Next day she moved into the Kellys' one bedroom apartment. Dawn slept on a pullout couch in the den.

A few weeks after Dawn moved in, Jeanette took a trip to Italy. Pat flew to Vancouver on personal business. The arrangement was working our rather well. The Kellys had an old English sheepdog, appropriately named Kelly, a 90-pound animal which took some looking after. Dawn would take care of the dog.

Pat returned from Vancouver unexpectedly at 8 o'clock the next morning. Dawn was sleeping on the pullout couch in the den. One thing led to another. Dawn had intercourse with her best friend's husband. It didn't stop there. Over a period of time, they made love again and again.

In various statements, Dawn has admitted, "It could have been ten times." On other occasions, she testified, "From the first time we made love until the last time, I don't know. I mean, I could say three times or say ten times." Obviously, it would have been too much to ask Mrs. Hastey to keep a score card. She is even on record as saying, "Probably every night when I was there."

Pat, who denies ever being intimate with Dawn, well recalls arriving at his apartment after an early morning flight from the west coast. ". . . She was sleeping in the den, and when I came in, I asked her if she wanted a coffee and I was going to make one for myself, and I made a coffee for her and took it into the den. She mentioned she hadn't slept well and asked for a back rub. I started to give her the back rub, and at one point she turned over and reached up to me and pulled me toward her to kiss her, and I said I would make another cup of coffee and got up."

There were other women in Pat Kelly's busy life. In 1978, during the course of an official investigation, Pat met librarian Jan Bradley. Every few months or so thereafter, he dropped into the library and took Jan out for coffee. For reasons of his own, he told her his name was Pat McLean. This rather casual relationship continued until January 1981, when Pat took Jan out for dinner.

Later that month, he and Jan spent a weekend at the Briars, a resort near Sutton, Ont. They slept together for the first time. Pat informed Jan that his real name was Kelly, not McLean. She didn't take the deception well. The weekend was cut short, but the lovers made up and Jan Bradley, like Dawn Hastey, would play a large part in the future lives of the Kellys.

Pat had other diversions besides his wife, Dawn, and Jan. In the summer of 1980, he met a young lady named Cheryl. Their relationship lasted until the Christmas season of that year. Pat claims it was a casual affair - movies, dinner, drinks, that sort of thing. Another lady, Leslie, was being courted in the same manner.

How did Patrick Kelly manage it all: an expensive car, luxurious apartment, European vacations and his constant squiring of a string of women?

In 1980, Pat left the service of the RCMP. During his career as an undercover agent with the Mounties, he made many important contacts, particularly in Colombia. Pat acted as courier for wealthy Colombians who wanted to get their money into the U.S. or Europe due to the instability of the Colombian government. Pat received healthy commissions for his services and never reported these commissions as income.

Pat, who clearly had a keen eye for turning a fast dollar, also acted in bringing seller and purchaser together for the sale of real estate in Mexico. Sellers desiring only cash for property would be put in touch with buyers who wanted to purchase properties at healthy discounts. Once the deal was consummated, Pat received commissions from both parties. Here again, Pat never declared this income.

Years earlier, Pat had attended junior high school with Victor Simpson in Victoria. The school chums kept in touch. Victor became a lawyer, while Pat became a law enforcement officer.

In 1980, Victor Simpson formed a company known as K & V Enterprises, which acted as a holding company for any type of financial transaction. In September, 1980, Pat became an employee of K & V Enterprises, with the title of executive manager. His main duties, according to Simpson, were "to investigate and locate investment opportunities for the company." Pat received a salary of $1200 a month from K & V and a car allowance of $225 per month. Pat also invested large amounts in K & V from time to time to facilitate deals which K & V consummated in French and Spanish speaking countries. In essence, almost everything funnelled into K & V came back to Kelly in wages, allowances, or loans from the company.

Apparently, Jeanette Kelly was unaware of just how her husband made his living. She did, however, know that they had collected a tidy sum in insurance after Pat had been discharged concerning the Cookstown fire. She also knew that she lived in a luxurious apartment, drove a late model Porsche and could afford to slip away to Europe whenever the fancy struck her.

In fact, in 1980, Jeanette travelled to Italy, accompanied by Dawn, who was then separated from her husband. Pat not only financed his wife's expenses, he also loaned $4000 to Dawn so that she could travel with Jeanette.

Jeanette and Dawn separated after they landed in Rome. Dawn took a room at the Holiday Inn in St. Peter's Square, while Jeanette had a liaison with a friend, Marchello Rodocachi. According to Dawn's later testimony, Marchello and Jeanette were madly in love. They travelled together to Austria.

Dawn claimed Jeanette had confided in her that she had to make a decision on whether to return to Pat in Canada or stay with Marchello as his mistress in Europe.

Dawn returned to Toronto in August, a few days before Jeanette. She stayed at the Kelly apartment, but her affair with Pat had waned during her absence. Nothing happened. When Jeanette returned, Dawn noticed that she and Pat were extremely cool to each other. It was obvious to her that Jeanette was sorry to be back in Toronto. Dawn moved out of the Kelly's apartment and into a friend's home in Burlington.

Within a few weeks, Dawn and Pat discussed Jeanette's attitude. Dawn told Pat that Jeanette had mentioned divorce. Pat replied that if there was a divorce, Jeanette would end up with nothing. Jeanette was not aware of many of his debts. He had told Jeanette his feelings on the matter. According to Dawn, Jeanette told her she was concerned about her lifestyle and had decided to leave things exactly as they were. Dawn Hastey paid back the $4000 she owed Pat Kelly for the European holiday and shortly thereafter moved to the United States. In February 1981, Dawn returned to Toronto.

That winter was a hectic one for all the participants in the Kelly affair. Pat was seeing Jan Bradley on a regular basis. They slipped away to New York for pleasant and rather expensive weekends at the Park Plaza and Algonquin Hotels. Their relationship intensified right up until March 28, when Jeanette Kelly plunged to her death from the seventeenth floor of the Palace Pier.

Two distinct versions exist as to how Jeanette Kelly met her death. This is the version Pat Kelly told witnesses at the time of the tragedy and which he would relate from the witness stand three years after the events took place.

The Kellys awoke around 9 a.m. that fateful day. They had tea and toast on the balcony. It was going to be a busy day for Jeanette. She was flying to Italy that evening at 6 p.m. and was busy packing. Pat helped. Then he and Jeanette slipped out for brunch at the Magic Pan in Sherway Gardens. They returned at 2 p.m.

Pat went downstairs to a storage area and carried up his wife's Samsonite luggage. They continued to clean up the apartment and packed Jeanette's clothing until around 3:15 p.m. At that time Pat suggested a pot of tea. He went into the kitchen to prepare the tea. Jeanette strolled in, mentioning something about a rattle on the balcony. She picked up a stool and walked out to the balcony.

Pat went back to preparing the tea when he heard his wife cry out. He dashed to the balcony and saw Jeanette falling. He clutched at his wife and managed to get both hands around the upper part of her legs, but as she was still in motion, he couldn't maintain his grasp and Jeanette fell away.

Pat phoned the doorman, instructing him to call an ambulance. He then ran to the elevators and was beside his wife's body in minutes. Pat felt Jeanette's pulse. There was none. Pat Kelly closed his wife's eyes. He followed the body in a separate ambulance to St. Joseph's Hospital. Pat was beside himself with grief.

On April 1, the day Jeanette was buried, Pat demonstrated to Sgt. Michael Duchak of the Metro Police just how the accident had occurred. According to Duchak, he and Kelly stood about three feet apart. Kelly lunged at Duchak and put his arms around the police officer's waist. He put his right cheek to the right side of the police officer's chest and held on. Then Duchak states, Kelly let go and said, "She was already over the balcony, we were face to face, I remember looking at her face. I was leaning over the rail. I was too weak to hold onto her and she fell."

Prior to his wife's death, Pat claims he had arrangements to take a trip to Hawaii with Jan Bradley. Now, completely broken up over his wife's tragic death, he decided that the trip might be just what he needed to take his mind off his troubles. On April 6, 1981, eight days after his wife's untimely death, Patrick Kelly flew off to Hawaii for a holiday with Jan Bradley.

When Pat and Jan returned, Pat found it embarrassing to continually have to explain how the accident occurred. Later, witnesses were to state that Pat claimed his wife fell while hanging plants on the balcony. Others stated he told them she was attempting to fix a noisy rattle. Pat moved to Victoria for the summer.

Back in Toronto, Jan was being questioned by police. Pat sent her money and advised her to retain a lawyer. Meanwhile Pat, who apparently was never one to let grass grow under his feet, kept company with several other women. Three years later, Crown counsel would insinuate that, as a former police officer, Kelly was cunning enough to keep company with other women in order to divert suspicion from Jan Bradley. Pat, of course, claimed his involvement with other women was not serious.

Jan couldn't stand the pressure. She left her employment and flew to Victoria to discuss matters with Pat. In June, the couple vacationed in Florida. That fall, Pat decided to sell the Palace Pier condo, which held bitter memories, and move to the south of France. He could well afford the move.

In September, 1981, Pat collected life insurance from London Life Insurance Co. on three policies totalling $221,813.83. In addition to these policies, he collected $43,324.80 from Confederation Life, who covered the group plan at Canadian Pacific

Airline, where Jeanette was employed. In all, the insurance proceeds on Jeanette Kelly's life amounted to $271,138.83.

In December, 1981, Jan Bradley drove with her mother from Toronto to Montreal's Mirabel Airport. Pat arrived on a flight from Victoria. Together, they flew to France. Later, Mrs. Bradley would attend her daughter's wedding in the south of France.

Pat and his new wife adjusted nicely to their lifestyle. They often took pleasant junkets to the Bahamas for the weekend. Pat bought new suits by the dozen.

Meanwhile, Toronto police, who had their suspicions from the day of Jeanette Kelly's death, went about gathering evidence. An autopsy had been performed on Jeanette Kelly's body the day after the fall by Dr. John Deck, staff neuropathologist at the Toronto General Hospital. From his examination, Dr. Deck indicated that Jeanette Kelly contacted the ground in a sitting position, resulting in severe injuries to the base of the spine as well as the back of both legs. There were no major external injuries above the waist.

Dr. Deck pointed out that abrasions to the left breast, in his opinion, had not been incurred as a result of the fall. He felt the abrasions were consistent with a blow of some kind. The doctor further pointed out small scrape marks near the deceased's nose, injuries to the upper and lower lip and an abrasion over the jaw, which were not consistent with those major injuries connected to the fall. Later, in answer to prosecution counsel's question, "Are those injuries you noted to the face, the nose and the mouth consistent or inconsistent with a punch, one or more punches?", Dr. Deck replied, "I think they are quite consistent with more than one punch."

Paul Malbeuf, a member of Toronto's Metro Police Emergency Task Force, took part in an interesting experiment. An exact duplicate of the pertinent areas of Apt. 1705 were constructed. A policewoman was positioned on the stool allegedly used by Jeanette Kelly. The stool was placed beside the balcony rail. Malbeuf, an all-around athlete, was positioned in the kitchen beside the kettle, where Kelly claimed to be when his wife cried out.

When the police woman screamed, Malbeuf, a former 100 yard dash champion, equipped with running shoes, was to race to her aid before she fell over the rail. Malbeuf extended himself, but try as he might, he never once reached the policewoman in time to grasp her before she fell, as Kelly claimed had happened with his wife. In fact, the experiment was tried several times, but Malbeuf never came close to making contact with the policewoman.

To add substance to the results of Officer Malbeuf's experiments, Eric Krueger of Toronto's Centre of Forensic Sciences, an expert in velocity, stated that Jeanette could not have fallen from the balcony as Pat Kelly claims. Krueger takes into account that from balcony to street level in 140 feet, Jeanette Kelly, 5 ft. 3 in. tall and weighing 132 pounds, would have been on the ground in three seconds. The fastest a runner could make it to her side was four seconds. Besides, according to Krueger, if Jeanette accidentally lost her balance, she would not have landed on her spine.

On a visit to Canada in 1982, Patrick Kelly was arrested on three charges of credit card fraud involving $125,000. He was then charged with his wife's murder.

Much of evidence related here came from expert testimony and from witnesses who observed Pat Kelly's guilty actions. But the Crown's star witness was not an expert. Dawn Tabor/Hastey/Bragg, the Kellys' dear friend, claimed to be an eyewitness to Jeanette Kelly's murder. By the time Pat came to trial, Dawn had married for the second time.

Dawn Bragg stated she was in Apt. 1705 on the day of Jeanette Kelly's death. On March 29, 1981, Dawn drove up to the Palace Pier and entered the building via a back door, using keys given to her by Jeanette some months earlier. Both Pat and Jeanette were in. They were arguing. Dawn offered to give Jeanette a lift to the airport.

Meanwhile, she was asked to take a seat in the den. She could hear her friends arguing about a divorce. Jeanette was adamant about refusing to grant Pat a divorce. The Kellys raised their voices. Suddenly, Jeanette screamed. Dawn walked out of the den to find her friend Jeanette on the floor. Pat picked up the limp form of his wife. He carried her over to the balcony and opened the doors. From the witness stand, Dawn Bragg would state, "He took Jeanette out to the balcony and dropped her over the edge."

Dawn went out to the balcony, looked down and collapsed. In an instant Pat was at her side, consoling her, telling her everything would be all right, telling her he loved her. Pat hurried Dawn to the elevators. They went up a few floors. All the while, Pat told Dawn to be quiet, to go out the back way and to go home. She listened and did as she was told. After all, she and Pat had been lovers.

Dawn remembered well one night at the Palace Pier Club when Pat had discussed taking care of Jeanette. He had said he would take Dawn to France. He told her he was in love. He also told her there was no way anyone could tell how a person fell off a balcony.

According to Dawn, Pat had previously confided to her how he set fire to his home in Cookstown. He took Dawn to the lodge where he supposedly was when his house burned. He explained how he went to bed that night, got up and drove to Cookstown. He spread gasoline throughout the house and lit it. Then he drove back to the lodge without being seen.

The day after Jeanette fell to her death, Dawn Bragg was in a dilemma. Three years later, as the Crown's star witness in the murder trial of Pat Kelly, she attempted to explain when she was asked, "What were your feelings on March 30?"

"I was afraid," Dawn answered. "Afraid of what I had seen and I was afraid of Pat. I was afraid I knew too much." A couple of days after Jeanette's funeral, Pat called Dawn. He told her he was going away alone and would call her if he needed her.

Dawn Bragg's story was fascinating. If true, it branded Pat Kelly a cold-blooded killer. Yet, there were doubts concerning her testimony. Why did she wait two years to inform police that she was a witness to Jeanette's death? Quite possibly Dawn Bragg felt she could be charged with conspiracy to commit murder. Given the promise by Metro Police Sgt. Ed Stewart that any statement she might give would not be used against her, she decided to reveal to police that she was in Apt. 1705 when Jeanette was killed. Sgt. Stewart, who had doggedly gathered evidence for close to three years, would later earn a commendation for his relentless work on the Kelly case.

Defence Counsel Earl Levy pleaded that much of the prosecution evidence was theatrical and circumstantial. If Dawn Bragg, an admitted liar, was still lying when she claimed to be an eyewitness to the murder, then the prosecution's case was without merit.

Crown Counsel L. Budzinsky contended that even without Dawn Bragg's testimony, the circumstantial evidence against Kelly was overwhelming. If her evidence was taken at face value, Pat Kelly was guilty of first degree murder.

The jury agreed with the Crown. Pat Kelly was found guilty of murder in the first degree. He was sentenced to life imprisonment with no possibility of parole for 25 years.

Kelly appealed his conviction. The Ontario Court of Appeal upheld the conviction. Mr. Justice Bert MacKinnon stated on behalf of the three man court, "There was no miscarriage of justice."

DEATH JILTED
THE BRIDE

A few miles north of London, Ontario, lies the tiny, peaceful hamlet of Arva. Paved roads have replaced the old dusty thoroughfares, but once you venture off the main road, the area is much the same as it was 91 years ago when intrigue and bloody murder paid a visit to the Ontario countryside.

Joe Sifton had gone through two wives and was 55 years old if he was a day. You had to hand it to Joe, he looked ten years younger.

Joe lived on his son Gerald's farm, but the two men never got along. It didn't matter what the topic - if Joe said black, Gerald said white. In order to keep peace in the family, Joe moved away to his own farm nearby. Truth is, Joe owned several choice acres in the area. The Sifton clan was never considered to be poor.

Mary MacFarlane was a fresh, 20-year-old dairy maid who worked for Gerald on his farm. The decaying trial transcript of the case reveals the facts, but only the imagination can do justice to Mary. One can picture the rosy-cheeked lass at the butter churn or scurrying around the farm doing her chores. Mary was engaged to Martin Morden, a fine broth of a lad who had formerly worked on Gerald's farm. The young people were to marry the following spring.

Who knows how it started. Maybe it was those rosy cheeks. Maybe Joe was one of those men who required a woman's company. Whatever the reason, 55-year-old Joe took a shine to 20-year-old Mary. Actually, he took more than a shine. He took Mary.

Now don't go blaming Joe. It takes two to tango and the evidence indicates that

Mary simply loved to dance. Well, folks, Joe and Mary danced to such an extent that lo and behold, Mary noted the distinct absence of the regular monthly biological occurrences which had never deserted her in the past. Yes, of course, she was pregnant.

Mary approached Joe on Thursday, June 27, 1900 with the disconcerting news. Joe took it well. They would get married. Indeed, there were certain complications. There was the little matter of Mary's engagement to Martin Morden. Mary assured Joe that it was nothing more than a childish infatuation to be ignored. Number two wasn't as easy to dismiss. Gerald would be furious. He stood to inherit his father's substantial estate. The marriage would change all that. Joe assured Mary that Gerald would just have to grin and bear it.

The die was cast. Joe would make arrangements with the Reverend Cooper. The date and time were set. The wedding would take place at 5 p.m. on the following Sunday.

Weddings were never meant to be secret. Mary revealed her marriage plans and delicate condition to Gerald. He reacted as expected and flew into a rage.

That very evening Joe called on Mary. He was discreet enough not to knock on the farmhouse door, but parked his buggy in the yard. Mary ran out and the pair drove away. That night they told Mary's mother of the impending nuptials. Mrs. MacFarlane was none too happy with the match, but in the end reluctantly gave her blessing.

At 11 p.m., Joe parked his buggy in his son's yard. Before Mary could depart, farmer Edgar Morden suddenly appeared on the scene. Edgar had startling news. In a whisper, he told Joe, "You better get away - out of the country, your life is in danger." Edgar, good friend that he was, insisted that Mary and Joe stay over at his house for their own safety.

The couple took Edgar's advice. They were served supper by Edgar's wife, after which they sat around the stove before going to bed.

On Sunday, Mary awoke brimming with joyful anticipation. This was to be her wedding day. Joe told her the plans. They would drive over to his place, where he would change into his best clothing. From there they would make their way to the church. Despite Edgar's warning, Joe couldn't believe he was in any real danger. After all, Gerald was his own flesh and blood.

Joe had just put on his Sunday best suit when Gerald showed up with hired hand Walter Herbert, ostensibly to return some equipment. They would place it in the barn. Joe said he would give them a hand when he finished dressing. Mary implored

Joe not to go, but he insisted.

Shortly after, Walter Herbert ran to the house and excitedly blurted out, "Oh, Mary, Mr. Sifton has fallen out of the barn and killed himself!" He then called across the road to neighbor John Sinker, "Mrs. Sifton fell out of the barn and killed himself!"

Sinker asked, "How did he fall out of the barn?"

"He was knocking boards out of the haymow and fell out of the barn."

Sinker ran to assist his fallen neighbor. He noted an axe and some bricks not far from Joe's head. The badly injured man was carried indoors.

Gerald and Walter rushed the short distance to Dr. David McNeil's home. Gerald told the doctor, "Father is terribly hurt. He fell out of the barn and may not be alive when you get there." Reverend Cooper, a neighbor of Dr. McNeil's, overheard the conversation and he too showed up at Joe's side a few minutes after the doctor. That afternoon, Joe Sifton died.

Initially, Joe's death was considered to be an accident. Then rumors began to spread throughout the area. Rev. Cooper remembered seeing two pools of blood beside Joe's fallen form, rather unusual for a fall. There were also the axe and bricks close to Joe's head. Dr. McNeil, who was also the coroner, became suspicious.

Twenty-five days after the tragedy, Joe's body was exhumed. There were two distinct and terrible wounds to the scalp. Police were called in. They learned that Gerald had offered James and Martin Morden $1,000 each if they would help him kill his father. Gerald had suggested a fake suicide. Both men, who had been approached separately, refused the offer. Later, when the investigation into Joe's death intensified, Gerald offered the brothers $1,000 not to tell the authorities of his proposition.

The police, headed by famed Det. Insp. John Wilson Murray, picked up Gerald Sifton and Walter Herbert. Both men were charged with murder.

A short time after being taken into custody, Walter confessed. He told authorities that the night before the tragedy, Gerald had offered him $1,000 to be a witness "in case anything should occur to make people suspicious about the job." Walter said that he would go with his boss but would have nothing to do with putting old Joe out of the way.

After breakfast on the day of the murder, they left Gerald's house in a horse-drawn cart. When they arrived at Joe's, Gerald fetched an axe and entered the barn. He then took a large hammer and proceeded to knock boards off the top of the barn up in the haymow. Gerald told Walter, "If my father comes up in the mow, hit him in the head with the axe."

Soon, Joe came into the barn and climbed up the ladder into the haymow. Walter crouched low. "When his father came up, I struck him with the axe. Gerald came over and struck him three or four blows on the top of the head with the hammer. His father's legs seemed to cave in and he fell through the trap door. His legs went through the rungs of the ladder and he hung there. Gerald told me to get down and shove him up. I did so and Gerald pulled him out of the hole and hit him two or three more blows.

"Then we picked him up into the mow and placed him on his back. Gerald picked up the axe and hit him again a couple of times. Gerald took hold of his shoulders and I took his feet and we carried him over and threw him out the end of the barn."

Gerald then told Walter to fetch some bricks and put blood on them. Gerald threw the axe out of the barn and instructed Walter to run to the house and tell Mary of the horrible accident.

A year later, Gerald Sifton was brought to trial. Rarely has a more graphic tale of murder been related in a Canadian court. Defence counsel produced doctors who felt that had Joe received the terrible punishment outlined by Walter Herbert, his injuries would have been more severe. After deliberating six hours, the jury reported that they could not reach a verdict.

Another long year went by before the entire process was repeated. Once more the crowded courtroom was transfixed by Walter Herbert's account of the murder. After almost five hours of deliberation, the jury returned a verdict most startlingly at odds with the evidence - not guilty. Gerald Sifton was a free man.

Walter Herbert, who had confessed to murder, which the court had ruled was not murder at all, was allowed to change his plea from guilty to not guilty. He too was set free.

The notoriety of the murders and the two trials forced the two main participants in the drama to leave the area forever.

FUN ON THE FARM

The quaint villages with their large churches and hard-working farm folk that make up rural Quebec are a strange backdrop for murder most foul. Yet, even here, the passions which simmer, boil and erupt into bloody murder have found their way.

Back before the turn of the century, the tiny village of St. Canute was a remote community. The God-fearing French farmers led a hearty, healthy and for the most part happy existence. But not Cordelia Poirier.

You see, Cordelia was unhappily married to Isidore Poirier. Now Isidore wasn't a bad fellow, really. It was just that he was about as exciting as maple sap dripping into a bucket. Isidore worked hard, was a respected member of the community and attended church regularly. But he was oh so very colorless. Isidore made love as though it was a duty rather than a pleasure. Besides, he was well into his forties while Cordelia had not yet celebrated her thirtieth birthday.

Sam Parslow, the Poiriers' young hired hand, had none of Isidore's finer qualities. But what he lacked in stability, he more than made up for in bed. Many a chilly winter night, when Isidore was away for one reason or another, Sam would dim the lantern in Cordelia's room and partake of the forbidden fruit which lay within. Some nights Sam attempted to harvest the entire orchard, so eager was Cordelia for his substantial charms.

In 1895, as luck would have it, Isidore received an opportunity to work in California for several months. He jumped at the chance. Cordelia practically pushed him out the door. Sam and Cordelia's sack time increased dramatically.

Mon Dieu, could this go on in a quaint French village without tongues wagging? Of course not. The lovers sometimes went out together. They held hands and occasionally stole a kiss in public. Mind you, all the while that Cordelia was performing between the sheets with Sam, she was attending mass regularly. In fact, both she and Sam sang in the choir. Cordelia also played the organ during mass.

Can't you just hear the whispers? "A disgrace, and poor Issie in California;" "They should be horsewhipped for carrying on so." It couldn't go on.

Finally, Sam's mother, who felt that her son was being led away from the straight and narrow by the wicked Mrs. Poirier, went to the parish priest, Father Pinault, and asked him to save her boy. The good father, obviously a man of few words, sent a note to Isidore in California. "Come back at once, or else take away your wife."

Isidore didn't take the insinuation. He wrote a scorching letter to Father Pinault, telling him in no uncertain terms that he had the utmost faith in his wife. Isidore, never one to keep a secret, wrote dear Cordelia about the priest's ridiculous accusations. Cordelia replied that he was right - they were ridiculous.

In due course, Isidore returned to his home in St. Canute. We can only assume that Sam moved out of the master bedroom and into the hired hand's quarters. The gossip grew to a crescendo. Cordelia, by far the most dominant personality in our triangle, knew she had to do something. It didn't take her that long to come up with a murder plan which would turn a dishonest dollar at the same time. She would insure her husband's life before she and Sam killed him.

After paying her insurance agent a brief visit, Cordelia wrote him a letter. The letter is so incriminating we reproduce it here: "I told my husband that I had been to see you with regard to our policy. I forgot to ask you for books in French. My husband wants to understand the thing before disbursing too much money. He is well decided to continue, but he wants first to understand whether if he should die by any means - by being killed or by accident, or by poison or by railway accident - your company would pay, because he has spoken to several people and they say you would not. It seems to me you told me I would be paid no matter what death my husband would meet. My husband today is in perfect health. Reply and I will arrange with you."

The agent assured Cordelia that his company would pay off no matter how Issie might meet his death. In due course, Isidore Poirier's life was insured for $2,000.

With financial matters in place, Cordelia proceeded to cajole, urge and otherwise convince Sam that the only proper thing to do was to kill Isidore. They would allow a decent interval to pass before marrying. Sam didn't need much persuading. He thought it was a great idea.

On Nov. 21, 1898, Isidore attended mass as usual. Cordelia and Sam filled the church with ecclesiastical melodies. After mass, Isidore stopped off at the blacksmith shop, where he and Smitty Bouvrette had a few blasts out of a whisky bottle the blacksmith kept handy for just such occasions.

Cordelia knew Isidore would take a nap when he arrived home. The opportunity she and Sam had been waiting for was at hand. Sam hid in the house, fingering the new butcher knife he had purchased in Montreal. Isidore went to bed. In minutes, Sam and Cordelia could hear Isidore snoring. Sam sneaked up to the bed. He was scared stiff. He aimed the knife at the sleeping man's throat, thrust forward, but failed to inflict a fatal wound. Isidore woke up. The two men struggled. Cordelia shouted, "Kill him, kill him!" Thus encouraged, Sam stabbed Isidore in the neck and about the face. Finally, Isidore was dead.

The conspirators lifted the body onto the bed and placed the butcher knife in the dead man's hand. They put a half empty bottle of whisky beside the body. Then Cordelia slipped out of her bloodsoaked dress and burned it in the stove. If you didn't look closely, the gory mess might have passed for a suicide.

Cordelia put on her Sunday best and returned to church, where she played the organ as usual. After services she travelled to her father's home in St. Jerome and spent the night. Next morning she returned to St. Canute to play the organ for a wedding at the church. Cool as cucumber, Cordelia conversed with several villagers, her parents and the parish priest, without giving any signs that her husband lay dead for over 24 hours, his head almost severed from his neck.

On the way home from church, Cordelia told blacksmith Bouvrette to walk through the house with her. We all know what they found in the bedroom. The parish priest was the first one called. Father Pinault reluctantly announced that it looked like suicide to him. Cordelia smiled.

A nosy farmer noted that the ashes in the stove didn't look like residue left from wood. He scooped out the ashes and discovered a number of hooks and eyes. Of course, we know they were all that remained of the bloody dress Cordelia had been wearing.

Someone thought a more experienced individual should be brought in to ascertain the cause of Isidore's death. Detective K.P. McCaskill was dispatched from Montreal. He took one look at the bloody footprints on the floor and knew he was investigating murder. One of the prints matched Cordelia's shoe, another matched Sam's. The jig was up. Cordelia and Sam were taken into custody. Cordelia, by far the stronger personality, immediately confessed, claiming Sam was the instigator of the plot and the actual killer. No one believed her. Both she and Sam were found guilty and were sentenced to hang.

On March 10, 1899, 800 screaming ticket-holders were allowed into the prison yard at St. Scholastique to witness the execution. It was a gala affair. They sang songs and even took a few shots at the scaffold.

Sam Parslow had to be practically carried to the noose. Cordelia walked with head erect. When she saw Sam's condition she shouted in disgust, "Stand up!" Then she and her lover plunged into eternity.

TO NEWFOUNDLAND WITH LOVE

Unlike the British and Americans, we Canadians do not regularly ship sundry bodies across our fair land in assorted trunks and suitcases. But one must not rush to the conclusion that our criminal history has been devoid of the certain elan associated with a body speeding over land and sea. Nothing could be further from the truth.

Why, back in 1960, all of Canada spent the quiet summer months enthralled with fast-breaking developments concerning the case of the C.O.D. corpse.

Turn over, Agatha, wherever you are, here we go.

Down in Argentia, Newfoundland, CNR station agent Thomas Donovan had just polished off a heaping plate of salted cod and boiled potatoes before returning to his job at the station. Tommy was more than a little bit perturbed. You see, there was an unclaimed trunk addressed to a Mrs. Williams hanging around the station. No one had claimed the trunk, no one had paid the C.O.D. charges of $17.68. Above all, there was the distressing matter of the odor. It was getting a tad worse every day.

Tommy decided to take a peek. He was relieved to discover that the beat up old trunk was full of nothing worse than some used clothing and blankets. Tommy removed a blanket. Whoops. There, staring vacantly up at the grey, overcast Newfoundland sky, were the unseeing eyes of a dead woman. Tommy let out a yell that could be heard all the way to Joe Batts Arm.

RCMP Inspector D.O. Bartram took over the investigation. He found 60 individual pieces of clothing in the trunk and, of course, the unidentified dead woman. No discernible marks were found on the body to indicate how the poor lady had met her death.

Within two days Inspector Bartram was heartened in his task by a Newfoundland lady who positively identified the partially decomposed body as that of her long lost daughter, with the very coincidental name of Frances Elaine Haines. Frances had married a sailor and moved away ten years earlier. Was someone playing a sadistic joke by returning Frances from whence she came? No, not really. Frances was found in the U.S., alive and well. Mother had simply been mistaken.

After dispensing with this temporary red herring, the Mounties, in conjunction with Metro detectives, concentrated their efforts in Toronto where the C.O.D. corpse had originated. Detectives found that CNR Express Agent William Squires had handled the death trunk. He vaguely remembered helping someone unload the trunk on May 4, a little over a month before Tommy Donovan took his famous peek in Argentia. Squires could give no description of the man who turned the trunk over to him.

An autopsy on the unidentified woman revealed no signs of violence. A week after the body was discovered, a routine fingerprint check in Ottawa positively identified the victim as Mrs. Marjorie Scott. Marjorie had a police record. She had been a hard-drinking, hard-living woman who, while she had no future, had quite a past.

Marjorie was born Marjorie Sagar in 1923 in Napanee, Ont. Folks there remember her as being a wild teenager. When she was 17 she married ex-con Clement Scott in Kingston. It didn't work out. Clement hanged himself in New Westminster, B.C. in 1958.

At the age of 20, Marjorie had her first rather serious brush with the law. She was convicted of theft from a farmhouse near her home in Napanee and received a suspended sentence. In 1944, she looted a Whitby home, was apprehended and sentenced to three months in the Mercer Reformatory.

Marjorie apparently favored gentlemen who had spent some time behind bars. She met hard-drinking ex-convict Leonard Ede when she was a young but extremely experienced 21. Although legally married to the still living Clement Scott, she bigamously married Ede on Dec. 5, 1946. Their turbulent relationship was to continue off and on for the next 14 years until Marjorie ended up in that battered old trunk.

Lennie drank heavily. No, that's an understatement. Would you believe that some days he killed six bottles of the very cheapest wine money could buy? Marjorie joined him whenever possible, which was pretty well all the time. They fought incessantly. Sometimes the police were called to break up the combatants. On other occasions one or the other would leave for months at a time, but for better or worse, they always returned to live together.

On May 3, 1960, the odd couple was living in a double room with kitchen on Granby St. in Toronto. They commenced drinking in the afternoon. Soon they were arguing. According to Lennie, Marjorie came at him with a kitchen knife. He disarmed her. Incensed, Marjorie picked up a broom and swung at Lennie. He ducked and punched Marjorie hard across the mouth. She went down, but got up fighting mad. Lennie then grabbed her by the throat and shook her. Marjorie quieted down. Later she asked Lennie for a drink of water. Lennie gave her the water. Marjorie lay down and fell fast asleep.

Next morning Lennie woke up. Marjorie didn't. She was dead. What to do? Lennie picked up the phone to call police, but thought better of it. In the past, the police had often been to Granby St. to quell fights. No one would believe that he hadn't killed Marjorie. There had to be another solution.

Lennie solved his immediate problems by picking up six bottles of wines. After serious meditation, he remembered a friend who had an old steamer trunk. Lennie picked up the trunk, explaining to his friend that he had to move. Returning to Granby St., he placed Marjorie's clothing in the trunk and ever so gently deposited Marjorie. He then covered the clothing and the deceased with blankets. It was an unsettling experience. Lennie dropped over to the Avonmore Hotel to have a few beers.

On the way home, he met one armed truck driver Rollie Tremblay, who innocently agreed to help deliver the trunk to Union Station. Lennie and Rollie drove over to Granby St. where, with the help of unsuspecting fellow roomer, Pete Campbell, they loaded Marjorie aboard the truck. The trunk weighed 172 pounds.

When Lennie arrived at the station, he was asked to give the trunk's destination. It was a trick question, but Lennie rose to the occasion. Years before, while in the navy, he had been stationed in Argentia, Nfld. It was the furthest place he could think of, and so by chance Marjorie began her 1,500 mile odyssey across land and sea.

Rollie Tremblay and Lennie became so friendly that Rollie invited Lennie to join him at his home for an impromptu wine and cheese party. Lennie picked up four bottles of wine. There is no record that Lennie purchased any cheese.

Next day, Lennie took a bus to Cleveland, knowing that sooner or later someone would open a trunk in Argentia, Nfld. He obtained part-time work and stayed sloshed. Each day he purchased the Toronto papers looking for the inevitable. One night while drunk he called Pete Campbell in Toronto fishing for news, but there was none.

Once the body was identified and Lennie's relationship to the dead woman established, the police were actively hunting Leonard Ede. They located Rollie Tremblay, who told them of taking the trunk to Union Station. Pete Campbell readily related how he helped place the trunk onto Tremblay's truck. He also told of receiving a phone call from Ede in Cleveland. Circulars, complete with pictures, were widely distributed to Cleveland police.

Sure enough, a Cleveland police officer spotted Lennie on the street and took him into custody. Lennie seemed relieved that the whole thing was coming to an end. He co-operated with police officers, waived the extradition and was returned to Toronto.

Initially, Lennie was charged with murder, but this charge was dropped. While medical evidence indicated that Marjorie had died of asphyxiation, doctors were unable to determine what caused the asphyxiation. There was no evidence of foul play, either internally or externally, on the body.

However, Lennie wasn't completely out of the woods. He was immediately charged with public mischief and causing indignities to a human body. Leonard Ede pleaded guilty and was sentenced to 15 months in Burwash Reformatory.

GREAT CANADIAN CROOK

Geordie Lemay is unique. Strongly suspected of one murder, acquitted of another, he was also the brains behind one of Canada's most dramatic robberies. Toss in recent capers such as assorted burglaries and trafficking in drugs and you begin to get the idea.

George was born to a well-to-do Montreal family. His early years gave no hint of what was to follow. His mother employed George in her successful real estate business.

In 1950, George met beautiful 19-year-old Huguette Daoust, a Montreal bank secretary. Huguette was petite, weighing no more than 105 pounds, with dark hair which accentuated her large, bright eyes. George fell hard. He pursued Huguette with a passion, until the lovely girl from the respected family consented to marry him.

On May 19, 1951, over the objections of her family, Huguette and George were wed. They honeymooned in Florida, familiar territory to George, who had often been on fishing expeditions to the Sunshine State.

When the newlyweds returned to Montreal, it was evident that they were having difficulty adjusting to married life. For one thing, George didn't seem to be very interested in working for a living. For another, he displayed a nasty temper.

Seven months passed, strained months for the good-looking young couple. When George suggested a second honeymoon in Florida, Huguette thought it a great idea. On Dec. 27, the Lemays drove to Miami in George's red Studebaker convertible. They rented a room and fished every day.

On Friday, Jan. 4, 1952, they went fishing along the Florida Keys, stopping at Tom's Harbor Bridge #4. According to George, they were fishing off the bridge at around 8 p.m. Huguette, clad only in a halter and shorts complained of the cold. She told George that she was going to the Studebaker to change into something warmer.

Fifteen minutes passed. When George's fishing line broke, he walked the hundred feet to the car to get a new line. It was only then that he missed his wife. George shouted. He peered into the car. His wife's shorts and halter were on the seat. A sweater and a pair of jeans were missing. No doubt Huguette had wandered off, but as time passed, George became frantic. He raced to a toll gate and, crying hysterically, told attendant Les Baker, "My wife has been kidnapped! Stop all cars! Have them searched!" Baker called the Florida Highway patrol.

Despite an extensive investigation, and despite the suspicion that George may have been involved in his wife's disappearance, no trace of Huguette Lemay has ever been uncovered since that day 39 years ago when she went fishing with her husband.

For the next ten years, George, who maintained a chalet near St. Jerome in the Laurentians, continued to get into minor scrapes with the law. On the Dominion Day weekend of 1961, he graduated to the big time. That's the weekend he directed the novel and daring break-in of the St. Catherine St. branch of the Bank of Nova Scotia in Montreal.

Lemay had rented a building across the street from the bank. Using walkie talkies, he directed his confederates as they worked all weekend digging a tunnel into the bank's safety deposit box vault. Three hundred and seventy-seven safety deposit boxes were looted. The official loss reported was well over $600,000, but it's believed that many victims were reluctant to disclose the amounts removed from their safety deposit boxes. Some feel that George relieved the bank's clients of over $4 million that weekend.

Within two weeks, the gang was rounded up. Andrew Lemieux, 27, his brother Yvon, 19, their sister, Lise, Jacques Lajoie, 37 and Roland Primeau, 35, were taken into custody. The four men were convicted and given lengthy prison sentences. Lise pleaded guilty to being an accessory and was sentenced to time already served. Later, she would become George Lemay's second wife.

But where was our George? The answer to that question was partially revealed two weeks later, when George's 42-foot cruiser was found docked near Miami. George had piloted the cruiser almost 2,500 miles from Montreal to Florida. The police had the cruiser, but its owner was long gone.

Meanwhile, a raid on George's St. Jerome chalet uncovered a small portion of the loot taken from the bank's safety deposit boxes. Police found a few thousand dollars secreted in a false panel in George's bedroom.

Two years later, RCMP, FBI and Scotland Yard co-operated in using an Early Bird satellite for the first time to send pictures of internationally wanted fugitives across the U.S. In this manner, Lemay's picture showed up on TV screens in Florida. Sure enough, a boatyard worker in Fort Lauderdale recognized the wanted Lemay as Rene Roy, the owner of the 43-foot sloop, the *Tirana*. Within the hour, Roy was fingerprinted. He was indeed the internationally-sought bank robber from Canada, George Lemay.

Lodged in Dade County jail while deportation proceedings were being instituted, George seemed to take a great interest in strengthening his somewhat flabby, squat physique. He also found time to marry Lise Lemieux. Active George was successful in turning on the charm and bribing the guard with a whopping $35,000 to aid him in his escape. It was a daring venture in the Lemay style.

George was allowed to slip out of his first floor cell and take the elevator to the seventh floor, where he entered a room with an unbarred window. He fastened a rope to a radiator and made his way seven floors down the rope to freedom. Now everyone knew why George had been devoting so much time to building up his strength. He had, as usual, planned every facet of his escape.

The FBI, RCMP and Interpol searched for George throughout the world. It took them almost a year. On Aug. 19, 1966, the FBI received a phone tip. They picked up Robert Palmer in the Golden Nugget Casino in Las Vegas. Fingerprints proved that Palmer as really our George. To change his appearance, George had shaved off the remaining hair from his almost bald head.

It took four months to get George back to Canada to face the music. On Nov. 16, 1966, he was charged with the old Dominion Day break-in of the Bank of Nova Scotia. His confederates described in detail how he had masterminded the entire operation. They related that, when their hard tunnelling had been completed, George had, like a conquering general, insisted on being the first to enter the vault.

In January 1969, after one of the longest criminal trials in Montreal history, George was found guilty and sentenced to eight years imprisonment.

After serving his sentence, George was out of jail only a short time before being picked up on a drug trafficking charge. While back in jail awaiting trial, George and three confederates are believed to have orchestrated the killing of one Pierre Quintal to prevent him from testifying against them. Despite Quintal's death, they were convicted on the drug charge.

In 1984, George stood trial for Quintal's murder. He was acquitted, but still had to serve the remainder of his drug related sentence. Once again, George completed his term in prison and was released.

Where is George now? Your guess is as good a mine. Quebec prison officials assure me that George is now "on the streets." They nonchalantly add that they expect him back any time. George is like that.

OTTAWA TRAGEDY

When Stuart and Mary Poulin gave birth to their third daughter, their 12-year-old son Robert moved into a basement bedroom. For the next six years Robert lived in a private, secretive world behind closed doors.

Outwardly, everything was normal. Robert's father, in his fifties, was a former armed forces pilot who taught elementary school in Ottawa. His mother, a nurse, was active in community affairs. Their two-and-a-half storey Tudor style home on Warrington Dr. was spacious, their family close-knit. Unknown to his parents or his friends, Robert was spending more and more time in a fantasy world, a world he could enter at will when he closed his bedroom door.

Robert Poulin's parents respected privacy. The bedroom was Robert's place. They knocked on the door for permission to enter.

In his early teenage years, Robert had a newspaper route. For some time he worked in a pizza parlor. He attended church every Sunday. For relaxation he played complicated war games over the phone with friends or by himself. Robert attended St. Pius X Catholic High School. In the 12 months preceding Oct. 27, 1975, Robert's parents never once saw the interior of their son's room.

When Robert was in Grade 10, he became acquainted with Kimberley Rabot. At his parents' request he invited Kim to his home. The two students played Risk, a beginner's war game.

To the outside world, Robert Poulin's actions were normal, but his secret life was taking hold. It would soon erupt into one of the most horrendous crimes ever committed in Canada's capital city.

Sex occupied more and more of Robert's thoughts. By the time he was 17, he had covered his walls with Playboy centrefolds. Normal for a 17-year-old? Maybe. But Robert went further than pictures. He purchased women's underclothing and acquired books on bondage. He bought weapons - a snub-nosed .38 calibre revolver and an ivory handled knife. He kept a scrapbook of nude men and women.

Robert wrote about bondage, rape, murder and suicide in his diary. From his writings we learn that Robert grew to fear his own obsessions. In an attempt to alleviate his urge to rape a girl, he purchased a life-sized vinyl inflatable doll for $29.95 from a mail order house in California. The ad appeared in magazine circulated throughout the U.S. and Canada.

Robert was extremely disappointed in his life-size doll. His fixation with aberrant sexual behavior increased. On Monday, Oct. 27, it would explode into violence.

Robert left his home at 8 a.m. but returned 15 minutes later. He entered his basement room through the garage. His mother heard him but paid little attention. Around 10 o'clock Mrs. Poulin went down to the basement and inquired through a curtained off partition if she could speak to her son. "Yeah, but don't come in," Robert replied.

Mother and son talked through the curtain. Behind that curtain Robert had already raped and killed Kim Rabot. She had been handcuffed to Robert's bed. Robert Poulin was now acting out his fantasies. He was no longer the normal boy outsiders knew.

Shortly after 11 a.m., Robert came up to the kitchen, chatted for a moment with his mother, had a peanut butter sandwich and watched TV. At 11:30, Mrs. Poulin left her home and returned at 1:30. The back door was open. Robert was gone. Black smoke was pouring out of a second storey window. Mrs. Poulin called for help. Firemen found Kim Rabot's body handcuffed to Robert's bed. She had been raped and stabbed to death.

Robert had purchased a Winchester shotgun, model 2200, for $109 four days before, and sawed 15 inches off the barrel. He set his house on fire before heading for St. Pius X High School on his 10-speed bicycle.

Father Robert Bedard was just beginning to conduct his Grade 13 theology class. It was a little after 2 p.m. Late students straggled in. By 2:20 p.m. Father Bedard was well into the lesson. The door to the class opened one more time. Robert Poulin stood in the doorway with a shotgun. He smiled. Then he fired.

Seventy-eight students ran for cover. Some threw chairs through windows and climbed out. Four times the pump action sawed-off shotgun roared. Mark Hough, 18, was critically wounded in the neck and head. He would die from his wounds. Barclay Holbrook, 17, was wounded in the chest. Terry Vanden Handenberg, 18, was hit by pellets in the right shoulder and back of the neck. Mark Potvin, 18, Benggawan

Kurniadi, 18, Renzo Catana, 18, and Mark Holleran, 18, received minor wounds. All but Mark Hough would recover.

Robert stepped back from the doorway. One last shot was fired. Then nothing but moans, cries and blood. Outside classroom 71, Robert Poulin had blown away half of his head.

Back at the Poulin residence, it was discovered that a plastic bag had been placed over Kim Rabot's head. She had been stabbed 14 times. The knife used to take her life was found taped to Robert's chest.

What strange urges were at work in Robert Poulin's mind that day which would cause him to take three lives, including his own? Robert left a diary. He wrote that he planned to have intercourse with a girl, to burn down his family's home and then to kill himself. He was depressed and at the breaking point.

Robert had suffered from acute loneliness and had even advertised for a friend. He placed an ad in the Ottawa *Journal* from Oct. 3 to Oct. 10, 1975. It read: "Male, 18, looking for companionship. P.O. Box 4021, Station E." The box had been rented by Robert to receive his supply of pornographic material. He never responded to the three homosexuals who answered his ad.

Robert's main disappointment in life had been his failure to be accepted for officer's training in the militia. Deeply resentful, he joined the Cameron Highlanders as a private for the summer before his October nightmare. As his fantasy world became more dominant, Robert could no longer control his urge to act out the fantasies contained in his pornographic literature.

In truth, a once normal boy had lost contact with reality.

WHO KILLED THE PROFESSOR?

The day I drove to the portable emergency command post of the McMaster University campus, Sgt. John Reid of the Hamilton-Wentworth Regional Police was a harassed man, shouting directions, answering phones and deploying men.

It was a few days before Christmas of 1983. Dr. Edith Wightman had been murdered in her Chester New Hall office on campus. The crime was unusual in many ways. Dr. Wightman had no known enemies nor was she sexually attacked. Who would murder a university professor in broad daylight in her office?

Later, a much more relaxed Staff Sgt. Reid recalled every detail of his most intriguing murder investigation. "There is no doubt about it, it was my most interesting investigation in 24 years as a police officer. There were many reasons: the status of the victim, the international aspects of the case, and the wide publicity given to the investigation. Besides, initially there was a real possibility that the crime had been committed by a student or a colleague."

The call came in on Dec. 17, 1983. A murder had been committed on the McMaster campus. Sgt. Mike Driscoll and Sgt. John Reid would become partners in heading the investigative team attempting to track down the killer. It would take them 24 days.

A security officer had opened Dr. Wightman's fourth floor office. It was he who had called police. Edith Wightman was found face down on the office floor. Her hands were handcuffed behind her back, her eyes and lips taped shut. One of the professor's boots had been removed and her slacks had been pulled down.

All about the campus, there were signs of the impending holiday season. The city of Hamilton was bedecked in green and red for Christmas. Around McMaster, young people were dashing about, preparing to travel home for their Christmas break. It was the time and place of fellowship and good cheer. Inside Edith Wightman's office it was the time and place of death.

Who was the professor who had her life so ignominiously snuffed out while working in her office? Edith Wightman was born in Edinburgh, Scotland. Early on, she showed extreme promise as an intellectual and as a musician. She became a member of the National Youth Orchestra of Great Britain, playing the cello. Later, she attended St. Andrews University, where she developed an interest in archeology and ancient history. Edith graduated from St. Andrews with the highest of honors and enrolled in post graduate studies at Oxford. She received a diploma in archeology and a PhD in Roman history.

In 1969, at the age of 31, Edith obtained the position of assistant professor in McMaster's history department. She quickly fit into university life. Edith Wightman was no shrinking violet. She had opinions and expressed them at university functions. Those who knew her recognized and respected her brilliance. During her first few years at the university, she wrote a book, *Roman Trier and Treveri*.

It was somewhat of a shock to Edith's acquaintances when she dated admitted homosexual Gregoire Brown. Edith should have known better. Brown, a native of New Zealand, was an unstable, erratic musician, who immigrated to Hamilton to enrol in their music program. His instrument was the cello. Eventually, he played with the McMaster Symphony Orchestra, where he met Edith Wightman. Ninety days after their first meeting, Gregoire moved in with Edith.

Gregoire Brown, in one fell swoop, had a home, a car, enough money to indulge his passion for antiques and, at the same time, an attentive, intelligent companion. Edith appeared to be in love. She was 36, Gregoire 23, when they married.

It didn't take long for cracks of disharmony to appear in the relationship. Gregoire's well-known temper tantrums became more frequent. Perhaps in his eyes, his mediocre career paled compared to the brilliance of his clever wife. Edith's book was now acclaimed internationally. She was a bona fide rising star on the academic horizon, while Gregoire's musical career sputtered and fizzled.

To alleviate the situation, Gregoire suggested he continue his studies in Europe. Surprisingly enough, Edith agreed to finance the venture. Off Gregoire went to London, England, where he soon took a homosexual lover. Two years later, Edith filed for divorce.

Another man, far more in keeping with Edith's intellectual ability and social status, was to enter her life. Archeologist John Hayes, associated with the Royal Ontario Museum, was to become Edith's good friend and co-worker on several projects connected with the Roman empire.

It was John Hayes who had an appointment with Edith on the day she was killed. He had just arrived from Toronto. It was 11 a.m. He tried the door to Edith's office and then knocked without getting a response. It wasn't like Edith not to keep an appointment. A few hours later, he tried phoning. Still no response. Finally, around 3 p.m. he called the university security office. The guard opened the door, and so began the most sensational murder case in Hamilton since pieces of John Dick's body were found scattered over Hamilton Mountain in 1946.

Reid and Driscoll and their team of investigators had little difficulty tracing the last known actions of the victim. After she completed normal Saturday morning activities, Edith went to her office a little after 10:30 a.m. John Hayes pounded on her door around 11 a.m. In that short space of time, someone had entered Edith's office, placed handcuffs on her wrists, taped her eyes and mouth, removed one boot and pulled down her slacks. She later died on her office floor.

While Edith Wightman shopped and made her way to her office in anticipation of John Hayes' visit, another individual was preparing for his activities that Saturday.

Michael Crowley was a quiet, 27-year-old chemical technician employed at Welmet Industries in Welland. Although a bit of a loner, Crowley, a big man standing over six feet and weighing 230 pounds, was well-liked by fellow employees. What his colleagues didn't know was that Michael Crowley was a transvestite. He had a particular penchant for university campuses and had often roamed the grounds of Brock University in nearby St. Catharines. On this Saturday, he would visit McMaster University in Hamilton.

Crowley left his Welland apartment and headed for Hamilton in his brown van. En route he stopped, crawled into the back of the van and began his weird transformation from husky man to grotesque woman, as he had done so many times before.

Crowley disrobed. He tugged on his pantyhose, put on a blouse and skirt. Boots and a winter overcoat completed the clothing, but not the illusion. The dark beard had to be covered. Out came the makeup kit. Blush was carefully applied. A touch of eyeshadow and lipstick and the job was done. In the strange world of Michael Crowley, he was now a woman. To those who observed him, he was a large caricature of something either to be laughed at or pitied.

Michael Crowley was prepared. He carried with him the paraphernalia of robbery, if not murder. His equipment that day included handcuffs, tape and a chloroform-soaked rag in a bottle. Crowley parked his van and walked to Chester New Hall. He walked to the top floor. Two floors below, Edith Wightman, unaware of the terror stalking the halls above, worked at her desk. Crowley found every office door on the top floor locked. Disappointed, he walked downstairs to the fourth floor. He saw only one person, Edith Wightman, sitting at her desk with her back to him.

Silently, he approached the unsuspecting woman. Another step and he could reach out and touch her. Suddenly, Edith turned and recoiled at the sight facing her. According to Crowley, she said, "What do you want?" before he was on her cramming, the chloroform rag into her mouth. In moments, Edith was unconscious. Crowley locked the office door from inside. Edith's wrists were handcuffed behind her. Tape was applied to her eyes and mouth.

Crowley pulled down his victim's slacks, but her boots made the task difficult. He decided to remove the boots. One boot was wrenched free, but then the unexpected happened.

Just like infamous English mass murderer Reginald Christie, Michael Crowley was confronted with the fearful possibility of being discovered in the very act of murder. There was a knock on the door. Crowley, crouching over the still form of Edith Wightman, didn't move a muscle. Another knock, louder. Then nothing. On the other side of the door, John Hayes thought to himself that it wasn't like Edith not to keep an appointment. No use to keep knocking. He walked away.

Whatever thought may have been in Michael Crowley's mind before the knock on the door were now gone. Frantically, he rummaged through Edith's purse. He pulled out a driver's licence and credit cards, opened the office door and left Chester New Hall without being seen.

The strange looking man dressed as a woman went shopping. Using Wightman's stolen credit cards, he made purchases at a Canadian Tire Store and a Towers store. In St. Catharines he stopped at the Penn Centre, where he picked up tools at a Canadian Tire Store and a TV converter at Robinsons. At the latter store, he had an anxious moment. He was asked to give a home phone number. Crowley had to think fast. He blurted out a number. Later, it was discovered that the first three digits corresponded with his phone number in Welland. No one bothered to check if the signatures written by the strange looking woman were similar to that on the credit card. There was no similarity whatsoever.

Michael Crowley made his way to his Welland apartment. That Monday, he reported to work at the Welmet Industries plant as usual. There was one great difference, though. Michael Crowley read in the newspaper that Edith Wightman was dead. Police were searching for her murderer.

Sergeants Reid and Driscoll believed that someone who knew Wightman might be the killer, maybe a disgruntled student or a shunned lover. However, as time passed, they homed in on the theory that the murder was the result of a robbery gone awry. They felt it was unusual for Professor Wightman not to have a driver's licence or credit cards in her purse.

To this day, Reid talks about the feeling of invading a murder victim's privacy when searching their home for clues. The day after the Wightman murder, he found himself, together with Sgt. Rae Greenwood, meticulously sifting through every item in the Wightman home. They found the first solid clues, which were to assist in leading them to the killer - credit card receipts, but no cards.

The robbery theory was fortified. The killer had stolen Wightman's credit cards. A small army of policemen was dispatched to stores in an effort to find out if the killer had used the stolen cards. They struck paydirt. Cashiers who had handled Crowley's transactions remembered the strange looking man disguised as a woman. They gave descriptions to police, enabling them to make a composite drawing of the suspect.

Lending credence to the suspicion that the culprit was a transvestite, police immediately received reports that a transvestite had often been seen roaming the grounds of the McMaster campus.

At this stage in the investigation, Reid felt that an arrest might be imminent. "We had a lot to go on, although it was a huge puzzle that had to be brought together. We believed the killer was a transvestite. We had a sample of his handwriting. We had his description. We knew he had chloroformed Dr. Wightman and that she had choked on the rag stuffed in her mouth. We had a fingerprint believed to be the killer's, which we had lifted off a filing cabinet in Professor Wightman's office. We even thought he might be from Welland, because he gave the Welland exchange when asked for his phone number. What we didn't know was the identity of the man we sought."

Transvestites were questioned throughout the Niagara Peninsula. Samples of their handwriting were sent to Toronto Centre for Forensic Sciences to be compared with that of the suspected killer. All came back negative. Reid and Driscoll worked around the clock. New Year's came and went. The killer remained at large.

Following reports that a transvestite had been seen on the Brock University campus, police set up an investigative office at the university. Sergeants Grant Scobie and David McCulloch of the St. Catharines office felt that publicity might help. It was now 20 days since the murder. They asked the editor of the Welland-Port Colbourne Tribune to review the murder in the newspaper, appealing to the public for information.

Sure enough, a citizen reported knowing a transvestite who resembled the composite drawing. This call in itself was not unusual, but when the caller added that this particular transvestite had been seen carrying handcuffs, the detectives believed they had their man. His name was Michael Crowley.

Crowley was picked up leaving work. His handwriting was matched against that of the man who had used Dr. Wightman's credit cards. Even to the inexperienced eye, the writing was identical. The hunt was over. A search of Crowley's apartment yielded leather harnesses, whips, rope and handcuffs. He also had stacks of pornographic magazines, most featuring bondage.

When taken into custody, Crowley implored the officers to believe him. "It was an accident!" he sobbed, over and over. He handed over a capsule containing potassium cyanide to Sgt. McCulloch. Crowley had planned to commit suicide rather than be taken into custody, but had changed his mind.

Michael Crowley wrote out a full confession in longhand, detailing the attack on Dr. Wightman. He pleaded guilty to first degree murder and was sentenced to 25 years with no possibility of parole for 15 years.

Dr. Edith Wightman had choked to death on a chloroform-soaked rag stuffed into her mouth. What was the killer's motive when he stalked the offices of Chester New Hall? Because Dr. Wightman's boot was removed and her slacks pulled down, many believe the motive was sexual. Others believed the prime motive was robbery. Did Crowley intend to kill his victim, or was it all an accident as he maintained?

It matters little. The Canadian Criminal Code is clear. When death is caused during an act of criminal confinement, the charge is first degree murder.

Michael Crowley is presently serving his sentence at Kingston Penitentiary. Staff Sergeants Reid and Driscoll have long since moved on to other cases. Future generations of McMaster students will walk past Chester New Hall oblivious to the terrible crime which took place there on a Saturday, when a brilliant professor turned in her chair and exclaimed in fear, "What do you want?"

THE DI PALMA
DISAPPEARANCE

In 1972, when Lee Marie Conway graduated as a registered nurse from St. Joseph's Hospital in Toronto, the future looked bright. She was now qualified to pursue a satisfying and honorable profession. Besides, she had met someone she really cared for - Joe Di Palma. Affection turned to love, and on Oct. 20, 1973, Lee and Joe became husband and wife.

Eventually, the couple moved to Angus, Ontario. In April 1979, a son, Anthony, was born. Joe had a good sales position with Rothmans of Pall Mall Ltd. The pieces were falling into place for the Di Palma family.

Sure, there were a few rough spots. Joe had the exasperating habit of putting off fixing things around the house. When Anthony hit the terrible twos, he proved to be a hyper youngster. Lee also felt a bit confined in her rural home and often expressed a desire to live closer to Toronto. But these small differences or complaints were superficial. The Di Palmas had a very successful marriage.

All this was to change on Tuesday, Sept. 21, 1982. On that day, quite by chance, Lee was to cross paths with an amoral monster.

On that fateful morning, Joe got up as usual and left at 7:30 a.m. for his employment in Toronto. Lee's parents, Kevin and Audrey Conway, who had spent the previous night at the Di Palmas, rose and had breakfast with their daughter. They left the house at 10:30 a.m. to visit their son in Levack, Ont.

Lee Marie cleaned up the dishes and tidied the house. She then dressed Anthony for the short ride into Barrie in her black and silver 1972 Buick. At 12 o'clock, Lee pulled into Don and Ron's Sunoco Service Station in Angus to purchase gas. Promptly at 1:15 p.m. she dropped little Anthony off at the Barrie YMCA. The one hour between 12:15 and 1:15 p.m. is unaccounted for. Quite possibly, Lee went window shopping and had lunch. There is also the possibility that she was being stalked by a madman.

Anthony was enrolled at a Stay and Play program at the 'Y.' Each Tuesday and Thursday, Lee would drop him off at 1:15 p.m. and pick him up at 3:15 p.m.

The previous day Lee had made a hairdressing appointment for that Tuesday at 1:30 p.m. at the House of Bellini's located in the Bayfield Mall. She never kept the appointment. Later that afternoon at 3:15 p.m., when she failed to arrive at the 'Y' to pick up Anthony, social program director Heather Fraser grew apprehensive. She called the Di Palma residence and the Royal Victoria Hospital, where Lee worked as a part-time nurse. When she could find no trace of Lee Di Palma, she called police.

At 8:44 that evening, Lee's Buick was found parked in the Bayfield Mall opposite the Pit Stop Gas Bar. The car was unlocked, the window open and an interior garbage container was overturned, all conditions which were foreign to Mrs. Di Palma.

At the request of Barrie police, the Ontario Provincial Police were brought into the case. Inspector Norton Rhiness headed the investigative team. Rhiness had precious little to work with. Mrs. Di Palma had disappeared as if swallowed up by the earth.

Lee Marie Di Palma's past was scrupulously investigated. There were no hidden boyfriends, no affairs, no logical reason why this housewife, nurse and mother would meet with foul play. The disappearance was given wide publicity. A dramatization of the mystery appeared on television. Police were deluged with tips from well-meaning citizens. All had to be checked out. One tip was thought at the time to hold real significance. A citizen came forward stating that she and her daughter had been on a bus on Oct. 22, 1982, a month after Mrs. Di Palma's disappearance. She claimed that she chatted with Lee.

The woman, who was travelling to Sudbury, overheard Lee saying that she was going to Calgary. She said a friend had a large dog. She talked about places she had visited in Calgary and people she had met there two years earlier. She complained that her husband was negligent in fixing things around the house.

The woman said she had often been to Bayfield Mall in Barrie. She talked about her sister Nancy and said she had a small son. The blonde woman with the shoulder bag even stated that her husband once drove a van for Rothmans. Unbelievably, each one of these statements was dead on. They all applied to Mrs. Di Palma. However, the woman on the bus was not Lee Marie Di Palma.

Other sightings occurred in Calgary, Blind River and Vancouver. On Dec. 20, about three months after the disappearance, an alcoholic confided to a friend that he had murdered a woman near Barrie. He then committed suicide. For a while, he too was considered a prime suspect.

On May 15, 1983, eight months after Lee Marie failed to pick up her son, her body was found. Malcolm Urquhart and his wife Pauline were out picking mushrooms on Laurence Henderson's property in nearby Mulmur Township. Urquhart noticed a white object on the ground. At first he thought it was a puffball. It turned out to be the skull of Lee Marie Di Palma. Police were soon at the scene. Nearby, they found evidence that before death, Lee had been tied up with shoelaces and the straps from her shoulder bag.

Five months after Lee Di Palma's disappearance and before her body was found, Lindley Charles McArthur first came to the attention of police. McArthur was accused of kidnapping a 13-year-old girl and driving her to a secluded area, approximately three quarters of a mile from where Mrs. Di Palma's body was eventually found. The youngster was sexually attacked. McArthur was arrested at this time and lodged in the Barrie Jail.

Once in jail, McArthur had an overwhelming urge to talk about the Di Palma murder. Several convicts were told details of the murder. Some thought he was lying, others didn't care one way or the other. Many grew tired of listening to him.

During the spring of 1983, McArthur was transferred to the Mental Health Unit at Penetang for assessment. That May, Mrs. Di Palma's body was found. McArthur told a psychiatrist that he thought fingerprints would connect him to the Di Palma killing. After the assessment was completed, McArthur was sentenced to two years less a day for the assault on the 13-year-old girl. He was returned to the Barrie Jail to serve his time.

Insp. Rhiness, aware of McArthur's loose tongue, decided to place an undercover agent in McArthur's cell. Fabricating a story that he had been picked up on Highway 400 and was being held until he could be returned to Calgary to face a rape charge, the undercover agent ingratiated himself with his cellmate. Soon McArthur was confiding in his new friend. "Yeah, I expect to be charged with murder in the first degree." When the undercover police feigned ignorance, McArthur went on, "So you never heard about Di Palma. The broad was taken from her car and strangled."

Two days later, McArthur was charged with murder. He told the undercover policeman, "I'm charged with murder. As far as I know, they have three things on me.

I hung around there. I was in town that day and I know the area where the body was found. Man, after a year, I thought it was over." Then McArthur, cool as a cucumber, took in a movie on television. He really enjoyed the horror movie, *The Changeling*.

During his stay in jail, McArthur revealed details only the killer would know. He told one inmate that he jumped out of his truck, ran to the driver's side of Mrs. Di Palma's car, stuck his hand through the open window and caught her by the throat. She said, "Please don't hurt me." He dragged her from her car to his truck.

Who was Lindley Charles McArthur?

McArthur was born in Collingwood on Sept. 21, 1962. He successfully completed Grade 12 at Collingwood High School. He was married on Feb. 28, 1982, but at the time of his confinement was already separated. Factors leading the the breakdown of his marriage were his long stretches of unemployment and his desire for non-stop sex. His wife told police that McArthur demanded sex sessions that sometimes lasted for 12 hours. He was also rough and abusive during sex games. On some occasions, he insisted on performing the sex act as many as 15 times a day.

McArthur's wife revealed that the day after the sex attack on the 13-year-old girl, her husband shaved his beard. He did the same thing the day after Lee Di Palma was reported missing. Mrs. McArthur also told police she noticed that her husband had inexplicably lost the laces to his blue Adidas right after the new abduction. She had purchased a new pair.

What had triggered the abduction, rape and murder of a defenceless woman? As McArthur told one of his fellow prisoners, "I done it for kicks." The day he murdered Lee Di Palma was his twentieth birthday.

In June 1984, Lindley Charles McArthur was found guilty of first degree murder. He was sentenced to life imprisonment with no possibility of parole for 25 years.

4
THE
DOCTORS

DARLING MRS. SPARLING

Canada's most infamous medical murderer was Dr. Neill Cream, who took tremendous delight in poisoning unsuspecting ladies before the turn of the century. Less well known but every bit as wicked was London, Ontario's Dr. Robert MacGregor.

By the time he was 30, Dr. MacGregor had left London and set up practice in the village of Ubly in Huron County, Michigan. One January afternoon in 1909, Carrie Sparling, the 45-year-old wife of dairy farmer John Wesley Sparling, walked into the doctor's office with a distressing bit of dust in her left eye.

Although Carrie was the mother of four strapping sons, she had the appearance of a girl of 25. Dr. MacGregor took one look at the bad eye, coughed and said, "Kindly disrobe." The doctor started by staring at Carrie's toes and after several pauses on his way northward finally concentrated on the sore eye. Dr. MacGregor extracted the dust and told his patient that he would drop in on her the next time he was near her farm in Sanilac County, about an hour's buggy drive from Ubly.

Dr. MacGregor was a tall, attractive man. Carrie didn't exactly repulse his advances. The doctor did have a meek, rather ugly wife of his own, who was forgotten from the very day Carrie showed up with that bad eye.

A week after Carrie's visit, Dr. MacGregor travelled to the Sparling farm, where he met big husky, John Wesley and his four sons, Ray, 20, Scyrel, 21, Albert, 23, and Peter, 24.

The doctor thought it best to give Carrie a physical examination. One never knew what damage dust in the eye could inflict. Dr. MacGregor and Carrie were directed to the bedroom by trusting John Wesley. An hour later they emerged and advised Mr. Sparling, "Everything was just fine, even better than we had hoped."

From then on Carrie suffered from a series of minor ailments. The doctor came every second week or so and never failed to cure what ailed her.

After several months had passed, Dr. MacGregor confided to his best friend Xenophon A. Boomhower, who lived in the neighboring village of Bad Axe, that he suspected John Wesley Sparling had Bright's disease. A few months later John Wesley was confined to his bed. Despite Dr. MacGregor's care, the poor man was called to that great dairy farm in the sky.

The doctor, who was now considered a dear family friend by the four boys and something altogether different by Carrie, met with the Sparling family. He advised the boys to take out life insurance. Considering the untimely demise of their father, the four lads thought it good advice. By coincidence, the doctor's father was an insurance agent back in London. He sold them Sun Life of Canada policies.

A year later Dr. MacGregor informed his friend Boomhower that Pete Sparling had acute pancreatitis. Everyone was shocked. Poor Pete. He was laid to rest beside his dad less than a year after the elder Sparling had departed this mortal coil.

Distraught, Carrie decided to sell the farm and purchase a smaller one in Huron County, a stone's throw from Dr. MacGregor's office in Ubly. Coincidental with the Sparlings' move, good friend Xenophon Boomhower was appointed county prosecutor.

The wood was hardly stacked for the winter at the Sparlings' new farm when Albert took ill. The doctor explained to Boomhower that Albert had lifted a heavy piece of farm machinery and had suffered internal injuries. A few months later Albert joined Pete and John Wesley down at the family plot.

It was vacation time. Dr. MacGregor took his wife on a motoring trip throughout Ontario. While the doctor was away, Carrie bought a house in Ubly for investment purposes. It was only a few streets removed from Dr. MacGregor's office. When the MacGregors returned, Carrie suggested that they move out of their present home and rent from her. It seemed like a good idea, and that's how the MacGregors became tenants of Carrie Sparling.

Mrs. MacGregor took ill. Her husband suggested she return to Ontario to visit relatives and rest up. Mrs. MacGregor left the scene. She was no sooner gone than Carrie took to visiting the good doctor. Sometimes she stayed all day. When the fancy struck her she stayed all night. Tongues wagged, but the untimely death of Scyrel Sparling interrupted the gossip.

The death appeared to puzzle Dr. MacGregor. He suggested an autopsy, which he conducted with another doctor in attendance. It was a cursory affair. Dr.

MacGregor took one look and said, "Well, well, cancer of the liver." The other doctor agreed without really taking part in the examination. Scyrel joined the other members of his family down at the eternal place of rest.

Shortly after Scyrel's tragic passing, a village busybody observed Carrie leaving the doctor's residence at dawn. She informed elderly John Sparling, an uncle of the late John Wesley, who waited until he spied Carrie enter Dr. MacGregor's home. He then climbed up a ladder and peered into the bedroom. Land sakes! The rumors were true. There were Carrie and Dr. MacGregor, coupled.

Things got hot. Old John informed Prosecutor Boomhower, who secretly had Scyrel's body exhumed. Vital organs were sent to the University of Michigan. The university report stated that Scyrel's organs were laced with arsenic. Albert's body was also exhumed. It, too, contained arsenic.

When Dr. MacGregor told Boomhower that the one remaining Sparling son, Ray, had taken ill, he knew he had to take immediate action. Unknown to Carrie, he visited the bedridden Ray at the farm and told him the whole sordid story. He advised Ray to pretend to take Dr. MacGregor's medicine but to save it for analysis. The medicine proved to be laced with arsenic.

Dr. MacGregor was taken into custody and charged with Scyrel's murder. Carrie was charged with being an accomplice. During the trial, Prosecutor Boomhower forcefully pointed out that both Albert's and Scyrel's bodies had contained arsenic. Dr. MacGregor was found guilty and sentenced to life in Michigan State Prison. The charges against Carrie were dropped.

As soon as the prison gates closed behind him in 1912, Dr. MacGregor began a campaign of letter writing proclaiming his innocence. One such letter reached Gov. Woodbridge Fuller, who was appalled that testimony concerning Albert's poisoning had been admitted as evidence at a trial which concerned Scyrel's death only. The governor interviewed several members of the jury, who said they would not have found MacGregor guilty if the evidence concerning Albert's death had not been presented.

Gov. Fuller pardoned Dr. MacGregor after he had served four years in prison. Once outside, the doctor was the object of ridicule. Friendless, he applied for the position of physician at Michigan State Prison. The appointment was granted. Dr. MacGregor ministered to the prisoners for 12 years, never leaving the institution until he died within its grey walls in 1928.

DR. LOOMIS AND THE OTHER WOMAN

Everyone who ever met Grace Loomis liked her very much. Yet I know for a fact that there was an exception. That person hit Grace flush in the face three times with a blunt instrument, killing her instantly.

We know the exact time the fatal blows were struck. At precisely 9:06 on the night of Feb. 22, 1927, a Detroit telephone operator, diligent Doris McClure, plugged in a telephone line and heard a woman's blood-curdling, terror filled scream. Abruptly the scream stopped. The operator then heard a terse male voice say, "Never mind." The line went dead. Diligent Doris didn't call police, but made a note of the time - 9:06.

At 9:06 p.m. Tom Blockson and Ethel Bell were walking in the street close to Frank and Grace Loomis' home. They heard a loud shriek coming from the house, followed by a windowpane shattering. They thought Dr. Loomis was treating a patient and didn't call police. Tom and Ethel never did explain what type of pain they thought shattered windows.

The cause of all the commotion at the Loomis residence became clear at 9:45. That's when Dr. Frank Loomis ran from his home and summoned his neighbor, Mrs. Mildred Twark, with the unoriginal but nevertheless informative phrase, "My wife has been murdered."

The doctor and Mildred returned to the Loomis home. Unlike glamorous Hollywood corpses, poor Grace lay in the sun parlor with one leg drawn under her, her neck twisted, and both arms spread out. The upper portion of her body was covered with blood. All in all a horrible sight.

The sun parlor was spattered with blood, reaching to the ceiling. Several pieces of furniture were in odd positions and had obviously been pushed aside during the brief struggle Grace had put up for life.

At Mildred Twark's urging, Dr. Frank checked on his children. Upstairs, Ralph, eight, and Jeanette, five, were fast asleep. The doctor then ran the one block to summon police.

The first officer at the scene asked Dr. Frank, "Did you move anything?", to which the doctor answered, "Yes, and the coroner won't like that. I know this looks bad for me." The officer did a double take.

Senior officials arrived to take Dr. Frank's statement. He told them that he arrived home before 9 o'clock. He talked to his wife briefly, telling her that he was going to take a walk. This was not unusual for the doctor, who was in the habit of taking health walks at every opportunity. Before he left he gave his wife $100 to go shopping for children's clothing the next day.

It was drizzling out. The doctor put on his rubbers and left at exactly 8 o'clock. He outlined his route for detectives and stated that he had arrived back home at 9:45 to find his wife's battered body sprawled in a pool of blood. He had run to her side, put his head to her heart, and at one point attempted to move her to a divan, but gave up. Grace weighed 165 lbs.

It may be noted that the doctor's story accounted for his bloodstained suitcoat, vest and pants. The doctor added his personal theory that maybe a peeping Tom had seen him pass over the $100 to his wife and had killed her six minutes after he left the house. The money was nowhere to be found.

Within 48 hours homicide detectives had pieced together a series of facts which simply didn't jive with Dr. Frank's theory. For starters, isn't it a bit unusual to take a walk in the rain? Walking slowly, a policeman covered the route taken by the doctor in 34 minutes.

An examination of the Loomis furnace uncovered two pearl shirt buttons. Dr. Frank had been asked to turn over the clothing he had been wearing on the night of the crime. Everything was blood splattered, except for his spotless white shirt. Did the doctor take off his blood-saturated shirt and burn it in the furnace, accounting for the two pearl buttons found there? Police thought so. They also found a fence with two by four stakes attached to fence wire rolled into a coil in the Loomis basement. One of the two by four stakes was missing, which led detectives to believe that the doctor may very well have burned the murder weapon.

Dr. Frank was taken into custody. Investigating officers were sure that the doctor, who was known to have a violent temper, had killed his wife during an argument. If he had not gone for a walk at all, he would have had plenty of time to set up all the physical evidence to fit his story and dispose of the murder weapon in the furnace before dashing over to Mildred Twark's house at 9:45.

Counteracting police theories was the fact that Frank and Grace were a happily married couple. The doctor was a devoted family man with an unblemished reputation. Then there was the little matter of motive. There was absolutely none. Despite police suspicions, Dr. Frank was released from custody.

That isn't to say Frank was home free. Not by a long shot. Detectives followed the doctor in the hope that he would lead them to the motive for killing his wife. Once released, Dr. Frank attended to his most pressing problem first. He buried Grace. After disposing of this pedestrian inconvenience, he led police to one of the oldest motives in the distressing history of murder - the other woman.

Her name was never made public, but we do know juicy tidbits about her. She was not the type of lady one would think would appeal to Dr. Frank. The object of his affection hung around shady bars and loved partying. The doctor visited her every day before his wife's untimely demise. The lady in question would say no more than that she was a good friend and patient of the kindly doctor.

Now equipped with a motive, police arrested Dr. Frank and charged him with his wife's murder. As there was no evidence of premeditation, it was felt that there was no hope of convicting the doctor of first degree murder. At his trial the jury never got to hear that the doctor was having an affair while his wife was alive. No one knows to this day why the unsavory lady wasn't called to testify.

Prosecution attorneys felt that Dr. Frank would crack on the witness stand; the state would accept a manslaughter plea and everyone would be happy. It didn't turn out that way. The doctor was found not guilty.

Dr. Frank was never the same man after his acquittal. He sent his children to their grandparents in Brooklyn, Mich., and concentrated full time on his lady friend. The doctor was completely at his love's mercy. When things went well, which wasn't too often, he was ecstatic. When he had a lovers' quarrel he sank into the depths of depression. His practise suffered until it was non-existent. He moved frequently. Nothing mattered to him except his girlfriend.

On May 19, 1929, a year after his acquittal, he opened his office at 1 o'clock in the morning, had a few blasts of whisky, read the Bible, wrote a couple of letters professing his innocence, and hooked himself up to a gas stove. Dr. Frank Loomis was found dead at 8:30 that same morning.

THEORA NEVER RETURNED

Alice and Beatrice Bustin, two Ohio State University students, had reason to be concerned. Their roommate, Theora K. Hix, had left their room at the women's residence on campus at about 7 p.m. on a warm June evening in 1929. She never returned. Next day, with no word from Theora, the two sisters reported her absence to police.

When detectives read the missing persons report, they knew there was no need to search further for Theora Hix. Earlier that day her body had been found in deep grass behind a shooting range about five miles northwest of Columbus, Ohio.

The 24-year-old second year pre-medical student had been stabbed many times. She had also received several blows about the head, possibly inflicted by a ball-peen hammer. Her jugular vein and her carotid artery had been slashed. Strangely enough, three fingers on her right hand were crushed. The victim had not been sexually attacked.

Alice and Beatrice Bustin were questioned extensively, but could shed little light on their roommate's private life. Theora was a quiet girl who kept to herself. As far as they knew she had no boyfriends. However, they told detectives she had the habit of leaving their room each evening at about 5 p.m. and not returning until after 10 p.m. Knowing that Theora was a very private person, the Bustin sisters never inquired about her absences and Theora never volunteered any information.

An examination of the victim's body indicated that she had met her death sometime before a heavy rain had fallen on Thursday, the night before her body was found. The time of death was further narrowed by Constable John Guy, who was at the shooting range that Thursday evening.

Guy stated that up until 8 p.m. the shooting range was being used by two competing shooting teams. From 8 p.m. to 10 p.m. the range was deserted. At 10 p.m. Guy had concealed himself in an adjoining field in order to apprehend thieves who were stealing livestock from a nearby farm. Had the murder taken place after 10 p.m., Guy would have witnessed it.

Around 10:20 p.m., there was a heavy rainshower. Guy discontinued his surveillance. Since the victim had been killed before the rainfall, it was reasonable to assume that the murder had taken place between 8 and 10 p.m. on Thursday night.

Unknown to Theora's friends, she was keeping company with a man. This fact was revealed to authorities when a university instructor, after being promised anonymity, came forward with the information that he had often seen her driving with Dr. James Howard Snook in the doctor's blue Ford.

Dr. Snook was an unlikely suspect. The lean, balding, bespectacled 50-year-old Snook was a professor of veterinary medicine on the medical facility at Ohio State University. He was married and had an exemplary reputation.

Snook had an interesting hobby. He was an excellent pistol shot, having represented the U.S. ten years before in the 1920 Olympics. At one time he was a world champion, and on six occasions was U.S. champion.

When questioned, Snook remained aloof from his interrogators, answering all questions in a curt, brief manner. He immediately admitted having known Theora Hix for three years and volunteered that for some time he had assisted her in paying her university tuition. They often went for drives together in his car and she was an intelligent, interesting conversationalist. Dr. Snook assured detectives that there was nothing further to their relationship.

Columbus police were positive they had their man, but the good doctor was admitting nothing. Then the unexpected happened. Mrs. Smalley, an astute lady who rented furnished rooms on Hubbard Ave., saw photographs of Dr. Snook and Theora Hix in the local newspaper. She had quite a story to tell.

Four months earlier, on Feb. 11, 1929, Dr. Snook had rented a room from Mrs. Smalley, supposedly for himself and his wife. The doctor arranged with Mrs. Smalley that his wife would do the day to day cleaning of the room, while she would give the place a good cleaning once a week. In the four months Dr. Snook and Theora occupied the room, Mrs. Smalley caught a glimpse of Theora only once. She remembered her as she was impressed by the age difference between the doctor and his wife.

Mrs. Smalley went on to state that on the Friday Theora's body was found behind the firing range, Dr. Snook told her he had to leave the city immediately. His wife would be staying until Sunday to wind up their affairs. While Mrs. Smalley wished Dr. Snook good luck, Theora Hix's unidentified body lay in a Columbus funeral home.

Dr. Snook proved to be one cool cucumber. The first hint that his iron-like composure wasn't emotion free occurred when Mrs. Smalley was brought into his presence. Without hesitation she said, "Good evening, Mr. Snook." Snook replied, "Good evening, Mrs. Smalley."

It was story changing time. Dr. Snook admitted that he had set up the little love nest with Theora, but vehemently denied any involvement in her death.

Now hot on the trail, Columbus detectives discovered that Snook had taken a suit to a dry cleaning establishment on the day Theora's body was found. The suit was examined. There were bloodstains on the jacket sleeves and the knees of the trousers. The blood type was the same as Theora's.

While Mrs. Snook looked on helplessly, police raked through ashes taken from her furnace. They recovered bits of fabric, which they were able to prove came from pyjamas owned by the slain girl.

Snook weakened when faced with this overwhelming array of evidence and admitted killing his lover. It was a brief and skimpy confession, hinting that Theora had been a cocaine addict who had badgered him for money on a daily basis. However, an analysis of Theora's internal organs revealed no signs of her having been an addict.

On July 24, 1929, Dr. Snook stood trial for the murder of Theora Hix. Defence attorneys attempted to prove that his confessions had been obtained under duress and that the doctor was insane anyway. No one was buying.

Dr. Snook took the witness stand in his own defence. He told the court that he had attempted to break off his affair with Theora and return to his wife. He said Theora became incensed, cursing and striking him as he drove his car. He stopped, tried to calm her, but then in a rage rained blows to her head with a hammer. Again, no one was buying the doctor's story. The girl had been attacked with knife and hammer. Her jugular had been severed by the deliberate stroke of a knife. Dr. Snook did clear up one minor mystery. Theora had incurred the three crushed fingers when he accidentally slammed the car door on her hand.

Dr. James Howard Snook was found guilty of murder. On Feb. 28, 1930, he was executed in the electric chair, courtesy of the State of Ohio.

PRESCRIPTION MURDER

Down through the checkered history of crime, certain professions have had a disproportionate number of murderers. The practice of medicine has had more than its share of men determined to shorten life rather than prolong it. Robert George Clements was one such doctor.

Dr. Clements was born in Belfast, Ireland. He became an M.D. in 1904, at age 24. The young general practitioner was a bit different than his colleagues right from the beginning. For one thing the good doctor liked the good life. Clements dined in the best restaurants. He attended the theatre regularly, more often than not with a bright-eyed Irish colleen on his arm. The good life necessitated more funds than the doctor earned at his humble practice, so he was often strapped for ready cash. This situation served to gall the man of medicine, but a sure cure was just around the corner. Her name was Edyth Ann Mercier.

Now Edyth was not your average sweet young thing. She was a good ten years Clements' senior. What's more she was plain. But there were compensating factors. Edyth's daddy was an extremely wealthy grain merchant. On the day of his marriage, Dr. Clements came into a tidy sum of cash. Then, as if on cue, Edyth's daddy died of natural causes 18 months after the marriage. He left Edyth £25,000, a princely sum in 1913.

While there is no proof that Dr. Clements had anything whatsoever to do with his father-in-law's death, you should know, in light of future events, that he was Mr. Mercier's doctor during his last illness. Dr. Clements signed the death certificate, stating cancer to be the cause of death.

The Clements' financial status, now substantially improved, allowed the doctor to partake of the good life he so craved. The couple joined several exclusive social clubs, contributed heavily to reputable charities and, in the main, were considered to be an integral part of Belfast's status-conscious society.

Seven years later, the bloom was definitely off the rose. Edyth was aghast to discover that they, or to be more specific, her husband, had gone through their entire fortune. To add insult to injury, nasty rumors were being bandied about, referring to the doctor's unmedical dalliances with younger lady friends.

Coincidental with their financial and domestic difficulties, Edyth fell ill. Her husband told friends that she suffered from sleeping sickness and that the prognosis was not good. Clements was correct. Edyth died in 1920, leaving the doctor so distraught that he personally signed the death certificate, sold his practice and moved to Manchester.

One thing you can say for Robert George Clements - he was a fast worker. No sooner was his shingle swaying in the Manchester breeze than he was the steady escort of a bevy of that city's most eligible and rich ladies. A year after Edyth's death, Clements married for the second time. Mary McCleery, the daughter of a wealthy Manchester industrialist, became wife number two. Once more, the doctor was in the chips. Once more, he spent money with, as they used to say, reckless abandon. Once more, his wife grew ill just as the money was running out. Mary lasted until 1925, when she suddenly expired. Dr. Clements signed the death certificate, listing the cause of death as endocarditis.

Three years later, Dr. Clements went to the well for the third time. Katherine Burke was not of the same mould as numbers one and two. Katherine was not wealthy and was acquainted with Clements' previous wives. There is even a possibility that Clements actually cared for Katherine and there is undeniable evidence that his practice had prospered to the extent that he was able to live in the grand manner without outside help.

This state of affairs lasted until 1939. Poor investments in the hotel business reduced Dr. Clements' funds to a dangerously low level. That's when the doctor let it be known that Katherine was suffering from tuberculosis. She died, even after Dr. Clements brought in a young colleague at the last moment. The grieving husband suggested that tuberculosis had carried Katherine away. The young doctor agreed.

For the first time in his murderous career, Dr. Clements was suspected of foul play. A friend of his most recently departed wife was a lady doctor, Dr. Irene Gayus. She personally disliked Clements and when she learned that he had signed the death certificates of his previous two wives, she grew downright ugly. Dr. Gayus ran to the police, suggesting they delay Katherine's burial. However, they were too late. Katherine had been cremated only a few hours before police arrived at the scene.

There is no evidence that Clements had knowledge of this near miss. He went on is merry way. Wife number four was Amy Victoria Barnett, a lady 20 years the doctor's junior. Papa Barnett was loaded. And what's more, he conveniently died in 1940, leaving his daughter and her husband a cool £22,000 and his opulent residence in Southport.

Wouldn't you just know it, seven years later, Dr. Clements was telling his acquaintances that he wife wasn't well at all. He had a colleague, Dr. John Holmes, look in on her, but the doctor couldn't pinpoint the problem. A few evenings later, Dr. Holmes received an urgent call from Dr. Clements that his wife was gravely ill.

Dr. Holmes had the stricken woman admitted to the Astley Bank Nursing Home, where she was immediately examined by Dr. Andrew Brown. Brown noticed that Mrs. Clements' eyes had pinpoint pupils, her skin had turned bluish and she was having difficulty breathing. He thought she was suffering from an overdose of morphine. Next morning, at 9:30 a.m., Amy Victoria Clements died.

Upon hearing the distressing news, Clements suggested his wife had suffered from a brain tumor. Dr. Brown disagreed and insisted on performing an autopsy immediately. Dr. James Houston, a young pathologist who knew the Clements well, assisted Dr. Brown. The brain was examined, but no evidence of a tumor was found. Dr. Houston, for reasons never explained, destroyed the vital organs he removed from the body. However, he later reported that his testing of blood samples indicated that Mrs. Clements' death was caused by mycloid leukemia.

This conclusion did not sit well with Dr. Brown. He contacted the coroner, who in turn contacted police. The local gendarmes took a long look. When they discovered Dr. Clements had been writing prescriptions for large quantities of morphine for patients who had never been treated with the drug, they decided to act. A second autopsy was ordered, and Dr. Houston was notified of this decision.

When police went to question Dr. Clement, they found him unconscious in his kitchen. He died hours later, leaving behind a short note. The note read: "To Whom it May Concern, I can no longer tolerate the diabolical insults to which I have recently been exposed."

The second post mortem proved to be most revealing. Remember that vital organs had been destroyed, so the pathologist had little to work with. However, he was able to establish that death had been caused by an overdose of morphine. A search of Clements' flat turned up large quantities of morphine tablets hidden in bottles.

A few days later, Dr. Houston was found dead in his laboratory. He had taken 300 times the lethal dose of sodium cyanide. Poor Houston, despondent over wrongly certifying that Mrs. Clements had died of leukemia, had ended it all.

On Tuesday, June 25, 1947, an inquest into the weird events leading successively to the deaths of Mrs. Clements, Dr. Clements and Dr. Houston, was held in Southport. Three days later the jury came to the conclusion that; a) Mrs. Clements was murdered by Dr. Clements; b) Dr. Clements committed suicide; and c) Dr. Houston took his own life in a state of depression. It was learned that Dr. Houston had committed a series of medical errors, which had caused him to become severely depressed. The Clements' case was the last straw.

And so ended the case of the doctor who married and poisoned four wives.

5

NASTY

LADIES

LAURA LAUGHED LAST

Women scorned develop oh-such-nasty traits. They are forever running around shooting and sticking knives into the men who "done them wrong." Made famous in song and prose, they are, nevertheless, an occupational hazard for those men all too anxious to take advantage of what was once called the weaker sex.

Let's clear the dust and cobwebs off the old records and reveal for all to see the loves and follies of one such lady.

Laura was born in Holly Springs, Mississippi, in 1937. By the time she was 16 she had all those attributes associated with girls a few years older. Laura had all the attributes in all the right places too.

One fine day a liquor dealer, William H. Stone, already a dirty old man at 36, fell hard for Laura. Before you could say Jack Daniels, the booze salesman married Laura, but we mustn't dwell too long over Stone. A year later he died from partaking of a steady and overabundant supply of his own products.

Heartbroken at the trick fate had played on her, Laura entered a convent to forget her great loss. She managed to put the tragedy behind her rather quickly. Two months later she left the convent and married Thomas J. Grayson.

Tommy was a barrel of fun. Somewhat of a sharpshooter, he loved to come home drunk at night and shoot at the walls of the bedroom. One night, just for the novelty of it all, he took Laura out behind the house, entered a chicken coop, and proceeded to blast the heads off fifty chickens.

Laura, quite understandably, took a dim view of all this. She gathered up her mother and took off for San Francisco. Then she divorced Tommy.

Are you ready for number three? Colonel William D. Fair was a country lawyer who seemed like a pleasant-enough character if somewhat unstable. Maybe he was more unstable than pleasant. Two years after he and Laura were married, he shot himself as dead as doornail with a bullet well placed between the eyes. The Colonel was different in one respect. When he departed this world he left Laura with a bouncing one-year-old daughter, Lillias Lorraine.

Having thrice gone to the altar, and striking out on each occasion, Laura felt that it was time to make a living on her own. She gathered up her mother, as was her custom, and little Lillias, and headed for Virginia City. The wild, open city, booming in 1863, appealed to Laura. She borrowed money to open a hotel, which she named the Tahoe House. It was an instant success.

At last Laura was self-sufficient. That's when she met Alexander Parker Crittenden. Crittenden wasn't just any old Southern gentleman, no siree. He was a West Point man, having graduated the year Laura was born. Shunning the military life, he took up law. By the time he met Laura, he was an established and respected lawyer, as well as a powerful politician. If you can picture Colonel Saunders in a pinstripe suit, holding on to a mint julep, you pretty well have Crittenden.

Crittenden always stayed at the Tahoe House when he travelled to Virginia City. It wasn't long before he and Laura were spending their afternoons together. Sometimes the afternoon ran right into the evening. Actually three times a week Crittenden would tiptoe across the hall and stay all night with Laura.

Laura, being the marrying kind, began pressing for her fourth trip to the altar. It seems Crittenden always had a big deal coming off in a month or two. He kept Laura on the hook for nine months. Then one day the mint juleps hit the fan. Laura found out that the love of her life, the man who was sharing her bed, already had a wife and son as well. Laura had a *tete-a-tete* with Crittenden. Under pressure, that scalawag told Laura that he had kept his little secret from her in order to spare her feelings. He had planned to reveal all after he obtained a divorce.

It is a tribute either to Laura's gullibility or Crittenden's gift of gab that Laura accepted the story. Just before Christmas of 1864, to illustrate his good faith, Crittenden purchased a house for Laura. Together with Lillias, she moved in, lock, stock, and barrel. Mama stayed at the Tahoe House to take care of business.

Then Crittenden did something that couldn't possibly augur well for the future. He told his wife, Clara, about his dear friend Laura. Of course he didn't reveal his activities between the sheets with his dear friend. Never one to leave well enough alone, he invited the wife to visit with Laura. Down Clara came from San Francisco to

Virginia City. Crittenden managed to convince each woman that he was faithful to her, and her alone.

Crittenden thought it would be best for all concerned if he stayed with his wife while she was in town. Each evening he would have dinner with both women at the Tahoe House. Then he would accompany his wife back to their hotel suite. Once she was fast asleep, he would dash back to Laura and spend a few hours doing what came naturally. Excusing himself, as befits a gentleman, he would still get back to his wife's side before dawn. He convinced Laura that he and Clara were married in name only. Finally, Clara went back to San Francisco, and Crittenden got some sleep.

For years Crittenden promised Laura that he would divorce his wife, but he never did. His mistress often had fits of rage but always returned to her lover. Seven eventful years went by before things came to a head. During those years Laura had made a small fortune in the hotel business and moved to San Francisco to be near Crittenden.

Crittenden arranged to have his wife move out of San Francisco. In October 1870, he promised Laura faithfully that he would get a divorce and marry her. Laura really believed him this time. She bought a new wardrobe. The lovebirds made plans for an extensive honeymoon. No sooner was the great plan hatched than Crittenden informed Laura that his wife was returning to San Francisco.

Laura pleaded with Crittenden not to see his wife, but he said out of decency he had to meet with her one last time. He swore he wouldn't even hold her hand.

For reasons known only to herself, Laura visited a gunsmith and purchased a revolver. On October 29, Crittenden took the ferry to Oakland to meet his wife. Unknown to Crittenden, Laura had followed him on the boat. As the El Capitan docked at Oakland she watched the reunion. Crittenden's wife locked arms with her husband. They both smiled. Crittenden affectionately tousled his fourteen-year-old son's hair. Laura couldn't take the touching family scene any longer. She walked briskly over to her lover, extracted her revolver from her pocket, and shot Crittenden directly through the heart and both lungs. Then she approached the captain of the ferry and said, "Yes, I did it, and I meant to kill him. He ruined me and my child."

Laura's murder trial lasted 26 exciting days. Her defence of "emotional insanity" didn't sit well with the jury. She was found guilty and was sentenced to death, the first woman ever to receive the death sentence in the state of California.

After being granted a stay of execution, Laura's lawyers appealed to the Supreme Court. Surprisingly, the Supreme Court reversed the previous decision on legal technicalities and granted Laura a new trial.

Two years later Laura gain stood trial for murdering her lover. This time the jury returned with a verdict of not guilty. When the verdict was read, Laura fainted.

Laura went on to live a peaceful if somewhat lonely life in San Francisco. She outlived her defence attorney, the prosecuting attorney, the judge, and most of the jury who had convicted her at her first trial.

In October 1919, neighbors thought it strange that cats belonging to an old lady living in a converted store were crying. They decided to take a look. Laura, at the ripe old age of 82, had died peacefully in her sleep, forty-nine years after she killed the man who done her wrong.

MATA HARI

It is now well over sixty years since the unusual name "Mata Hari" was a household word around the world. It is one of those names which everyone has heard. Let's see now, she was an actress who got into trouble. No, she was the general's wife who played around. That's not right either - she was a . . . But let's dispense with speculation.

Margaret Gertrude Zelle was a beautiful Dutch girl of twenty when she answered an ad in an Amsterdam newspaper. In replying, she was to begin a journey through life which was to lead to disaster.

Captain Rodolf Macleod had been an army man all his adult life. Now in his early forties, he was taking his annual leave in Amsterdam, having just returned from a tour of duty in the Andes. One day he remarked to a friend that life had become somewhat of a bore. Macleod's friend knew what was missing from his life. he needed a wife.

The friend took it upon himself to place an ad in the newspaper: "Captain from the Indies, spending vacation in Holland, seeks suitable wife, preferably with a little money. Letters, etc. exchanged."

It was this ad which Margaret Zelle answered. MacLeod received scores of replies, but her letter and photo were far and away the most interesting.

The pair arranged to meet. Six weeks later they were married. The following January, Margaret gave birth to a son, Norman. On May 1, 1897, the MacLeods were posted to Semarang, Java. Soon the Captain was promoted to Major, and the union was blessed with a second child, Jeanne-Louise.

On the surface the MacLeods appeared to be an average army couple, but all was not going well. Margaret hated Java and her restricted life as an officer's wife. The pair had monumental battles. MacLeod continually berated Margaret for flirting with other men. To make matters worse, Norman took ill suddenly and died. The incessant arguing continued.

In 1901 the MacLeods returned to Amsterdam. A short while later the Major was shattered to discover that his wife was plying her not inconsiderable wares three or four times a week at a house of ill repute. After many screams and lectures he told her that she was no longer welcome under his roof. Actually he said, "Get out, you whore!"

Margaret Zelle's story really begins after her divorce from MacLeod. She left Amsterdam and made her way to Gay Paree, arriving there in October 1903. Margaret made her living as best she could as a model for sculptors and artists. She also wasn't above plying those same wares which had served her so well in Amsterdam. But it wasn't until Margaret decided to try dancing that she hit the jackpot. She was an instant sensation for a couple of very good reasons. She got the bright idea to perform in private salons, where her various seductive gyrations could be viewed in the raw. Soon she came up with the stage name, "Mata Hari," which in Malay means "Eye of the Dawn."

Her dancing held men enthralled. Adorned with bangles and other assorted brass ornamentation, her coffee-colored skin glistened; as veils dropped, mouths opened, and elderly gentlemen's hearts palpitated dangerously. She was by far the most sensational performer in Paris. Her Eastern dances, which she had supposedly learned during her youth when she was initiated into the mystic ceremonies of Hindu cults in the Vishnu temples of Beneares, were self-taught. Ambassadors, ministers, generals, and the very rich flocked to see her perform. No one ever suspected that she was the daughter of a hatshop clerk from Leeuwarden.

As a much-sought-after celebrity, Mata Hari cultivated important friends in several countries. The capitals of Europe - Vienna, Berlin, Moscow, and of course, Paris - paid homage to the exotic dancer. As war clouds gathered over Europe, Mata Hari at first displayed no outward sign of loyalty to any particular country. After all, did it really matter? She had from time to time gone to bed with some of the most important military and financial men in all of Europe.

It is believed that she first came to the attention of French intelligence when she rode triumphantly through the streets of Berlin with Herr von Jagow, Chief of Berlin Police, on the day the First World War was declared. A year later she returned to Paris. While filling out registration papers she claimed that she was born in Belgium. The false information was uncovered and gave the French another reason to keep an eye on the famous dancer.

From this point in Mata Hari's career it is a bit difficult to separate fact from fiction. Was she a spy for France or Germany or, as many informed sources state, for both? It is certain that during the course of the war she had close contact with senior German intelligence officers and in fact often dined at German headquarters.

In 1916 she visited Vittel, where the French were building an airdrome in the strictest secrecy. From Vittel she made her way to Madrid. Spanish ports at the time were full of German submarines waiting to pounce on French troop transports moving over the Mediterranean. Mata Hari supposedly cultivated young French officials, extracting information concerning troop movements. The information was passed along to the German legation, which in turn informed the submarine commanders.

If this in fact did happen, our happy hooker may very well have been responsible for about 21,000 French deaths. Now under strong suspicion as a German spy, Mata Hari was arrested when she left Spain, bound for Holland via England. British authorities intercepted the suspected spy at Falmouth and placed her in the Tower of London, where she underwent extensive interrogation by Sir Basil Thompson, Chief of Scotland Yard. Thompson later revealed that it was during this interrogation that Mata Hari confessed to him that she was a spy in the employ of the Germans and, as it was not her intention to land on British soil, he let her continue on her way.

Mata Hari returned to France, where incriminating documents were supposedly found on her person. She was arrested and charged with espionage. Her secret court martial concluded on July 25, 1916. She was found guilty as charged.

As soon as her conviction became public knowledge, a great effort was put forward by high-ranking French officials to save her life. Many of these men were not sure whether or not they had given Mata Hari information useful to the enemy. Men reveal strange secrets while in bed with beautiful women.

At her trial Mata Hari swore that she was paid by many Frenchmen for making love, not war. As her execution day approached, Mata Hari displayed a certain degree of courage. This display of courage has given rise to the theory that she was convinced that the firing squad would be using blank cartridges. She was wrong.

On October 15, 1917, comforted by two nuns, she was escorted to a rifle range at Vincennes. Mata Hari was offered a blindfold, which she refused. She defiantly held herself against the stake without being tied. Some accounts of her death state that just before the fatal shots rang out, Mata Hari threw open her dress, revealing her seductive body for the last time.

After her death, Mata Hari's many influential friends sought to vindicate her memory. Captain Georges Ladoux, who at the time of Mata Hari's execution was the head of French counter-intelligence, came under great suspicion as a spy himself. Mata Hari's former bedmates insisted that he had framed the well-known dancer. As a result Ladoux was arrested and tried as a traitor. The court martial acquitted him without ever bothering to review the evidence. Within two weeks he was promoted to the rank of major.

Mata Hari's strange life has always been a source of fascination. Movies, books and plays have exaggerated her exploits, but she simply refuses to remain buried.

In 1933, Ladoux died, leaving papers indicating that Mata Hari was indeed a double agent. She was receiving $500 a month from the French government, as well as a bonus for particularly useful information. Ladoux was sure she had much the same deal with the Germans.

As recently as 1955, Mata Hari once more made the wire services. Her personal papers were sold at a London auction. They brought $560.

POOR JESSIE

Some cities seem to specialize in interesting murders. So it is with Glasgow, Scotland. For some reason, good old Glasgie Town has provided us with many of the most bizarre and fascinating murders ever perpetrated.

This particular case centres around a house on a street in the west end of Glasgow with the picturesque name of Sandyford Place. In this house, in 1862, dwelt the eminently respectable Fleming family. Three generations of Flemings lived under the one roof. John Fleming was an accountant whose son, John, Jr., worked with him in his office. Mrs. Fleming had passed away some years before. The patriarch, James, was about 80 years old at the time of our little drama. He lived in a basement apartment in the house, and while the rest of the family gained a degree of respectability, James lagged far behind.

Ten years earlier, when the elder Fleming was only 70, he got into a bit of trouble which caused his entire family some embarrassment. James, who was obviously young at heart, was responsible for a servant girl becoming pregnant. Not only did this cause the normal amount of consternation, but it spurred the church in which James the Naughty was the eldest member to unceremoniously kick him out of the congregation. Or, if I may put it in their very words, "For the sin of fornication with Janet Dunsmore." Still, time heals all wounds, and after a few years James was reinstated in his church.

John Fleming and his son always spent their summer weekends at their cottage on the Clyde. They left the elderly James at Sandyford Place with a maid, Jessie M'Pherson, who had worked for the family for years. On Friday, July 4, 1862, the two younger Flemings left the house in the morning for their place of employment, after which they would go directly to their cottage. The weekend passed, and on Monday they went to the office, not returning home until 4:30 Monday afternoon.

When they arrived home they were greeted by the old man and immediately noticed that the maid, Jessie, was nowhere in sight. James said that she must have left the house, because he hadn't seen her since the previous Friday. Not only that, her bedroom door was locked. The two men looked at each other and secretly wondered why James hadn't done anything about a missing servant and a locked door for the entire weekend.

They gained entrance to the bedroom and found Jessie lying practically nude beside her bed. A piece of carpet had been thrown over her head, and there was a great deal of blood in the room. A doctor and the police were summoned. They examined the body, which was horribly cut and bruised about the head. Jessie's arms and hands were badly cut as well. She had obviously tried to fend off her attacker. Strangely her head and neck had been washed. Even the floor appeared to have been recently washed, despite the blood splatters evident around the perimeter of the room. Outside the bedroom there were several blood smears, indicating that Jessie may have been killed elsewhere in the flat and dragged into her bedroom. In the bedroom the police discovered a perfect bare footprint imprinted in a large puddle of blood.

It was ascertained that two of Jessie's dresses were missing as well as several pieces of the family's silverware. On the surface it appeared to be a case of murder during the commission of a robbery. The police did wonder at the elder Mr. Fleming's not noticing any of the blood smears throughout the flat, nor could they comprehend why he did not react sooner to his maid's disappearance. On the other side of the ledger was the respectability of the Fleming family and James's advanced years. The bloody footprint was not that of the deceased or Fleming. Medical men felt that the print had been made by a woman.

A description of the articles taken from the house received a great deal of coverage in the press. A pawnbroker came forward and described a woman who had pawned the silverware at his shop. When provided with the description, James told the police of a friend of the dead servant, one Jessie M'Lachlan, who might shed some light on the mystery. Mrs. M'Lachlan was questioned and said that she was given the silver by old James on July 3, the day before the murder, and had not been in the house over the weekend. Her home was searched and the missing dresses were found. Then her footprint was checked against the bloody footprint found at the scene of the murder. They matched perfectly.

Jessie M'Lachlan was arrested and tried for murder on September 17, 1862. The jury took only fifteen minutes to bring in a verdict of guilty. Then in an extremely dramatic turn of events, before sentence could be passed, the accused, through her lawyer, asked to be heard. The judge granted the request and Jessie's lawyer read a startling statement.

In essence it stated that Mrs. M'Lachlan was innocent. She told of visiting the house on Sandyford Place and being met at the door by James. He asked her to go and get him a bottle of whisky, which she did. When she returned she found her friend Jessie M'Pherson lying moaning on the floor. Her head had been severely cut. Mrs. M'Lachlan ran to her friend while James was muttering something about an accident. She got the old man to fetch water and started to wash the blood from the injured woman's face and neck. The wounded woman regained consciousness, and Mrs. M'Lachlan told her she was going to get a doctor. The trembling victim begged her not to leave. While this was going on James commenced to wash the floor around the fallen woman. Then they both carried her to her bed. As Jessie's condition grew worse, Mrs. M'Lachlan went to the front door, desperately trying to get assistance. She was startled when she heard her friend screaming. She ran back to the bedroom and witnessed the old man raining blows on Jessie's head with a meat cleaver.

Mrs. M'Lachlan begged the old man, "For the love of God, let me go away!" James Fleming assured her that she would come to no harm. He explained that they were both in the same boat. He could blame her as easily as she could blame him. He claimed that if she did as told, they would both get away undetected. Then he gave her the dresses and silver to make it appear that a robbery had taken place. Mrs. M'Lachlan claimed she left the house knowing that her friend had been killed while resisting the old man's advances but kept silent thinking that no one would believe her story.

The statement took forty minutes to read and impressed everyone with its ring of truth. Everyone, that is, except the judge, who remarked, "There is not upon my mind a shadow of suspicion that the old gentleman had anything whatever to do with the murder."

Mrs. M'Lachlan was sentenced to death. Because her statement accounted for all the physical facts of the case, the newspapers came out strongly in her favor. Eventually her sentence was commuted to life in prison. She spent fifteen long years in the H.M. General Prison of Perth before being paroled.

The woman who probably was only guilty of being in the wrong place at the wrong time, emigrated to the United States. She rejoined her husband who had come to America while she was in prison. Jessie M'Lachlan died on New Year's Day, 1899, at the age of 66, in Port Huron, Michigan.

CHOCOLATES, ANYONE?

In the weird and wonderful world of murder, there is something classical, yet cowardly, in injecting arsenic in chocolates. The perpetrator of such an act must have a singular disregard for whoever partakes of the deadly gift. After all, chocolates are a treat, something to be shared.

Many of us aficionados are familiar with Christiana Edmunds who, in 1871, in Brighton, England, first attempted to poison her doctor's wife by injecting arsenic in chocolates. Christiana mailed the arsenic-laced chocolates to her intended victim, but the ruse didn't work. Not content with this unsuccessful attempt, she purchased chocolates from several sweet shops in town, and after injecting her purchases with poison, returned them to the shop to be resold to the general public. Diabolical Christiana caused the death of one innocent youngster before being discovered and sent to the Broadmoor Lunatic Asylum, where she later died.

John P. Dunning was doing nothing more sinister than strolling through Golden Gate Park in San Francisco on a sunny summer day in 1892. It was to be a day John would remember for the rest of his life.

All was right with the world. John, in his mid-twenties, was happily married and had just become the proud father of a bouncing baby boy. He shaded the sun from his eyes as he idly walked along the park pathways. My, what an attractive lady sitting on that bench, John thought. No harm in striking up a conversation with her. The lady on the park bench proved to be Mrs. Cordelia Botkin. At a mature 38, Cordelia was an attractive morsel, who readily responded to John's advances.

Cordelia's husband, who had the rather pleasant first name of Welcome, had been a banker in Kansas City before moving to California and setting up housekeeping in Stockton. Cordelia and Welcome had an adult son by the time she met John Dunning in the park. Obviously the Botkins were not on good terms, for Cordelia spent all of her time in San Francisco, while Welcome remained throughout our narrative in the environs of Stockton.

Let's get back to the park. Cordelia found John attractive in many ways, not the least of which was his youth. At 38, the thought had no doubt occurred to her that the number of years left to turn men's head was diminishing rapidly. John, a war correspondent, had exciting tales to tell, so very different from her stuffy husband, whom she hardly saw anyway. Dunning thought of his wife. Then he thought of his baby. Then he looked at Cordelia. Then he rented a room.

John and Cordelia embarked on a prolonged affair. Cordelia rented a room on Geary Street. For convenience sake, John took a room in the same house.

Poor Mrs. Dunning felt that something was rotten in the state of Denmark. John paid scant attention to her and the baby. Many nights each week he didn't even bother to come home. When questioned about his negligence and absences, he explained, as a war correspondent, he had to work late many nights each week. Mrs. Dunning didn't have to be a mental giant to realize that there were not that many wars being fought at that particular time on the streets of San Francisco. She packed up her baby and went home to Mummie and Daddy in Dover, Delaware.

The set-up suited John just fine. As soon as the wife was safely back east, he and Cordelia came out of the closet. They dined at the best restaurants, were constant theatregoers and regularly visited the racetrack.

You had to call John's relationship with Cordelia more than a casual affair. For six years the pair were inseparable. Then, as so often happens in the affairs of men, John felt that enough was enough. The break came suddenly. On March 8, 1898, John was assigned by the Associated Press to report to Puerto Rico. When he broke the news to everloving Cordelia she thought it a great idea. She would accompany him.

John cleared his throat and explained that he would be going alone, and what's more, that he didn't intend to return to California. In fact, the thought of a reconciliation with Mrs. Dunning back in Delaware had crossed his mind more than once in the past few months. Cordelia was incensed. She let John know loud and clear that thoughts of Mrs. Dunning hadn't seemed to trouble him while they were frolicking between the sheets for the past six years.

It was no use. John explained as best he could that all good things come to an end.

That night John left San Francisco by train. During a tearful farewell, Cordelia lost her cool and made a dreadful scene. John smiled, boarded the train, and figured that was that. He was wrong.

Back in Dover, Delaware, Mrs. Dunning was pleasantly surprised to receive warm, caring letters from her husband, who had lo these many years been anything but an ideal mate. Was there still hope of a reconciliation and a normal life for her and her boy?

On August 9, 1898, Mrs. Dunning, her sister, Mrs. Dean, and two of the Dean children had just finished the evening meal. That afternoon one of the children had picked up the mail at the post office. It was the family's custom to relax on the front porch after dinner to read the newspapers and go through the day's mail. Mrs. Dunning was particularly interested in the mail since the contents of her husband's letters had taken a decided turn for the better in recent months.

On this day the mail contained a small special-delivery package addressed to Mrs. Dunning and postmarked San Francisco. Had some friend remembered her from years before when she lived in the Bay area? Mrs. Dunning opened the parcel with some degree of anticipation. The package contained chocolate creams and a dainty new handkerchief. The accompanying note read, "Love to yourself and baby, Mrs. C." How pleasant, thought Mrs. Dunning, but for the life of her she couldn't remember anyone named Mrs. C.

Never look a gift horse in the mouth. Mrs. Dunning sampled one of the chocolate creams. They were delicious. She passed the box along to Mrs. Dean and the Dean children. As this peaceful family scene was taking place, two young women, Miss Bateman and Miss Millington, passed in front of the house. They lingered to chat with Mrs. Dunning and her sister. They were delighted to sample several of the delicious chocolate creams. Jokingly, they remarked that it was not good to eat too many sweets, not the best thing for the teeth and the figure, you know. The two girls soon were on their way. Mrs. Dunning and her sister had several more chocolates before retiring for the evening.

In the middle of the night Mrs. Dunning experienced severe cramps. She doubled up in pain and just managed to drag herself to the bathroom, where she was surprised to find her sister and the two Dean children also suffering excruciating nausea. A doctor was summoned. He immediately pumped the stomachs of all four patients. He then administered medication and confined all four to their beds. All were considered seriously ill.

The doctor was no sooner back at his own residence when he was called upon to make another house call. Miss Millington was found to have exactly the same symptoms as Mrs. Dunning, Mrs. Dean, and the children. Next morning it was discovered Miss Bateman had also suffered from extreme cramps during the night.

What could all of these people have eaten which could have caused such sudden and severe illness? Of course, we know, don't we? It was those delicious, innocent-looking chocolate creams.

For some days all six lingered between life and death. Gradually Miss Bateman and Miss Millington recovered, as did the Dean children. After lingering in agony for eleven days Mrs. Dean died; Mrs. Dunning followed a day later.

Post mortems performed on the two ladies revealed lethal quantities of arsenic in both bodies. Chocolates which had not been consumed were found to be impregnated with the deadly white powder.

Who hated the family enough to hatch such a callous, diabolical plot? The sender could not even be sure who would consume the deadly chocolates. John Pennington, the father of the two victims, seemed to recall that his daughter, Mrs. Dunning, had received an anonymous letter some months before informing her that her husband was seeing another woman in San Francisco. At the time Mrs. Dunning had shown the letter to her father. He thought the handwriting resembled the handwriting on the note which accompanied the chocolates.

Meanwhile John Dunning was notified in Puerto Rico of his wife's death. He rushed to Dover, took one look at the note, and knew immediately who had written it. Hubby John, who does not come off as a knight in shining armor in this narrative, decided to tell all. He started by relating his first meeting with Cordelia in the San Francisco park and ended with leaving her at the train station when he departed for Puerto Rico. There was no doubt about it - Cordelia had written the fateful note.

A Dover detective was dispatched to San Francisco to work with the California police. It was no contest. Cordelia may have been a great lover, but she was a lousy murderer. Detectives came up with enough evidence to convict her ten times over.

For starters, handwriting experts swore that Cordelia had written the note which was enclosed in the deadly parcel. Detectives were successful in tracing the candy shop where the chocolates had been purchased. A clerk in the store readily identified Cordelia as having bought the chocolates about a week before they arrived in Dover. She remembered Cordelia because it was the first time a customer had requested a plain box which did not have the name of the store on it. After going to all this trouble with the chocolates, bungling Cordelia neglected to remove an identification tag from the handkerchief. It was readily traced to a linen shop where again Cordelia was identified as the purchaser.

On the day Cordelia bought the chocolates and the handkerchief, she had been living in Room 26 at the Hotel Victoria. Wouldn't you know it, a conscientious porter found a partially destroyed seal on the floor. It was a seal used routinely at the candy store to wrap boxes of chocolates. Cordelia had made sure to take it off before sending the chocolates away in the mail.

As if all this wasn't enough, Cordelia even encountered one of those long shots which stretches coincidence to its limit. When she mailed her special-delivery parcel, she made an indelible impression on the postal clerk handling the transaction. The parcel was addressed to Mrs. John Dunning. The postal clerk's name was John Dunnigan. He remarked on the similarity of the addressee's name to his own and chatted with Cordelia for some time. He remembered her well.

It never rains but it pours. Frank Grey, a pharmacist at the Owl Drug Store, identified Cordelia as the lady who purchased two ounces of arsenic from him. Here, too, Cordelia managed to stand out from the crowd. She claimed she wanted the arsenic to clean a hat. The druggist offered her several other products which he claimed would do the job better, but Cordelia insisted on arsenic. Mr. Grey identified his customer easily.

On February 4, 1899, Cordelia was found guilty of murder and sentenced to prison for life. Normally the gates of prison should have closed behind her, leaving only the memories of her sensational poison case, but Cordelia was not your average lady. She had her lawyers appeal her case on a technicality. While awaiting the disposition of this appeal, she was allowed to serve her time in a San Francisco jail rather than in prison.

Several months after the conclusion of her trial, Judge Cook, the very judge who had presided at the trial, was on a downtown streetcar. Gazing idly out a window, he spotted Cordelia Botkin aboard another trolley. The judge couldn't believe his eyes. Here was a convicted murderer he had just sentenced to life imprisonment strolling around the streets of San Francisco.

Judge Cook made some inquiries and discovered that Cordelia had again turned on the charm. She had seduced two of her jailers. In return Cordelia had a suite of rooms, clothing, excellent food brought in from the outside, special bedding, visitors, and the freedom to do a little shopping downtown when the mood struck her. It beat prison.

The judge's discovery hit the papers and a minor scandal followed but soon subsided. Cordelia continued to live in relative luxury while in jail.

It took five years for the court to decide that the judge at Cordelia's trial had instructed the jury that circumstantial evidence was superior to direct evidence and had so weighed the evidence against the accused. Cordelia was granted a new trial but again was convicted of murder. She appealed once more. It wasn't until 1908, ten years after her first trial, that this appeal was turned down.

Cordelia Botkin was transferred to San Quentin Prison where she died four years later of natural causes.

LITTLE EVA COO

For a town located off the superhighways, Cooperstown, New York, has a lot going for it. James Fenimore Cooper's home still stands there in much the same condition as it was when he wrote *The Last of the Mohicans*. Down the street the most imposing structure in the town houses the Baseball Hall of Fame.

Back in 1934 Cooperstown became internationally prominent for quite another reason. It was here that a murder case unfolded which contained all the intangible ingredients which set it aside from other acts of mayhem and caused it to become a celebrated place.

Little Eva Coo wasn't little at all. She tipped the scales at 170 pounds, give or take the odd pound. Eva ran a road house at the edge of town. It was one of those establishments where you could get your booze served up by a hostess, who did more hosting than she did serving. Eva's place was known by the motto "Anything Goes." Some times the leading citizens of the community would discreetly patronize Eva's funhouse. No questions asked - everyone had a good time.

There were two men in Eva's life. By 1934 she had been living for three years with Harry Nabinger. Harry had a wife and kids back in Detroit, but the set-up was so comfortable at Eva's that he was inclined to overlook that little detail. The other gentleman in Eva's life was Harry Wright. This Harry was an alcoholic cripple whose mother had died. He was taken in by Eva on a temporary basis and stayed for four years. To give you an idea of Harry Wright's personal habits, it was rumored that Eva used to take him down to the lake every month or so in order to force him to bathe. Eva fed, clothed, and gave him shelter and saw to it that the poor guy had enough booze to see him through each day.

Whatever else she may have been, little Eva obviously had a big heart. Besides the bevy of hostesses she supported she had taken in another stray, Martha Clift. Martha had been thrown out of her own home by her parents because of her wanton ways.

On June 15, 1934, this little group of happy-go-lucky characters was jarred out of its complacency when Harry Wright's broken body was found in a ditch not more than a hundred yards from Eva's establishment.

At first Harry's death was attributed to a hit-and-run driver. A few days later the sheriff who was investigating the death quite naturally questioned the girls who worked at Eva's. He discovered that Eva had taken out several small insurance policies on Harry's life. Both Eva and her friend Martha Clift were questioned separately about their activities on the evening of June 14. By telling the two women that each had confessed, blaming the other, the police managed to get two confessions made to order. Each, in fact, did place the blame on her friend.

By the time Eva's trial started on August 14, the details of the macabre evidence which was to unfold was public knowledge. The laws governing the reporting of crimes were not as stringent as they are today. Well-known reporters from all over North America swarmed into Cooperstown. They and the public were not to be disappointed.

Without actually admitting to murder, Eva's confession was cold-blooded enough. She claimed that she found Harry dead. In order to get a double pay-off from the insurance policies because of accidental death, she took the body up Crumhorn Mountain with her trusting friend Martha at the wheel of the family chariot. Eva admitted placing Harry on the road and having her friend run over the body two or three times. At one point they were interrupted by an approaching car. This intrusion was overcome by having Martha park directly over Harry. Eva coolly passed the time of day with the occupants of the car until they finally drove away. Then Eva placed Harry's body back in the car, drove down the mountain, and threw Harry into the ditch not far from the roadhouse.

It was a dandy little story which conveniently circumvented murder. Eva's friend Martha told much the same story but with a subtle change. She claimed that Harry was alive and well when they started up the mountain, ostensibly to gather some wild shrubs. Martha stated from the witness stand that Eva killed Harry by clubbing him to death with a mallet. Then, scared stiff, and under Eva's orders, she ran over the dead man.

Martha further stated that Eva had talked incessantly to her about killing Harry in the weeks preceding the murder. They had discussed poison, car accidents, and several other methods to hasten Harry's demise before Eva settled on simulating a hit-and-run accident. With a friend like Martha shooting off at the mouth Eva didn't need any enemies.

The prosecution came up with other goodies. It was discovered that several of the policies on Harry's life contained a cute little clause leaving extra cash to the beneficiary if his death occurred before his fiftieth birthday. A stone cutter, Arthur Stanley, testified that Eva had come to him and had him change the date of Harry's birth on the family stone in the graveyard. He changed the date of birth from 1880 to 1885, making Harry just under 50 when the alleged hit-and-run accident took place.

On September 6, Eva was found guilty of murder and was sentenced to be executed on October 15. Three days before her date with death she received a reprieve so that her appeal could be heard. The appeal failed. On June 28, 1935, Eva Coo was put to death in the electric chair at Sing Sing Prison.

Martha Clift was tried separately for the murder of Harry Wright. She was found guilty and sentenced to twenty years in prison.

BEST FRIENDS

The peaceful little town of Wylie, Texas is a good place to live. Located about 25 miles northeast of Dallas, many of its 3500 residents are employed in the booming computer industry that has blossomed in recent years throughout the area.

Typical of the prosperous young families living in the neat middle class homes were the Montgomerys. Pat, 35, and Candy, 30, had been married for 10 years. They had two children; Jenny, seven, and Ian, five. Pat was an electronics engineer with a Ph.D. degree.

On the evening of June 12, 1980, Jenny Montgomery's best friend, seven-year-old Alisa Gore, slept over at the Montgomery home. Next day, Alisa wanted to stay over an extra night. Everyone agreed it was a good idea. Alisa's father, Allan, who was also employed in the electronics industry, was out of town on business, leaving his wife Betty and their 11-month-old baby daughter, Bethany, alone in their home at 410 Dogwood St. in Wylie.

There was one minor detail which popped up that morning. Alisa had to attend her swimming lessons. Candy decided to drive over to the Gore home to pick up the youngster's bathing suit.

It was hot that summer in Texas, one of the hottest on record. The picture of domestic tranquility presented by the Montgomery and Gore families camouflaged the turbulent emotional lives being led by the four adults. You see, Candy Montgomery and Allan Gore had carried on a torrid love affair for 10 months. The affair had been terminated seven months earlier.

The Gores and Montgomerys attended the same church - the United Methodist Church of nearby Lucas. It was here that bored, restless Candy Montgomery became infatuated with Allan Gore. Her own husband, Pat, deeply involved in a budding career, was preoccupied with his job and children. Candy's sex life with an attentive, but passive, husband left a lot to be desired.

Candy picked Allan Gore. It wasn't just sex. She wanted someone she could talk to, who would understand and sympathize with her predicament. One suspects Candy also sought the adventure and thrills the clandestine affair would afford. Allan was vulnerable to her offer. His wife, Betty, was high strung and prone to minor ailments. The idea of an affair appealed to him. Theirs was no impetuous, damn the world affair, but rather a well thought out plan of action, where both parties would receive mental stimulation as well as sexual gratification. The two lovers met each week in a motel for ten months.

It was Allan who broke off the affair. Their church had instituted a program to assist troubled marriages. The counselling seemed to bring Betty and him closer together. He no longer required Candy's solace. There were no tears, no recriminations. Candy wasn't pleased, but she and Allan had entered the relationship with the understanding that they would harm no one and would break off the relationship whenever either one desired it.

Candy Montgomery drove her own children and Alisa Gore to Bible school that Friday morning in June. Ironically, it was Friday the thirteenth. Candy taught the first class and then took the opportunity to hop over to the Gores' to pick up Alisa's bathing suit. From the moment Candy drove her white station wagon into the Gore driveway, we have only her word as to what transpired. A few hours later, the Montgomery and Gore families would never be the same again. Indeed, most of the U.S. would soon learn of the dreadful deed which took place in the utility room at 410 Dogwood St.

Later, under the glare of a much publicized murder trial, Candy testified that she had chatted briefly with Betty that fateful morning. Bethany was asleep in her crib. After several minutes of small talk, Candy asked for Alisa's bathing suit. Without warning, Betty looked in her friend's eyes and said, "Candy, are you having an affair with Allan?"

Candy replied, "No, of course not."

"But you did, didn't you?"

"Yes," Candy replied.

It was out in the open now. Somehow, Betty had found out. The tense moment was broken when Betty abruptly left the room. She returned in an instant, carrying a three foot long axe. According to Candy's testimony, Betty did not threaten her with the axe, but vehemently ordered her never to see Allan again.

During a calm in the storm, Betty suggested that Candy pick up Alisa's bathing suit from the utility room, while she fetched a towel from the bathroom. The two women met at the entrance to the utility room. Betty passed the towel to Candy. They looked at each other. Candy blurted out, "Oh, Betty, I'm so sorry!"

As if a trigger had been pulled, Betty's repressed fury erupted. She suddenly pushed Candy into the utility room. Both women held the axe handle. Betty jerked the handle. The flat side of the blade struck Candy a glancing blow to the head. She released her grip. As she did so, she enabled Betty to raise the axe and bring it down with all her might. Candy jumped out of the way. The axe hit the utility floor linoleum and bounced, inflicting a nasty cut to Candy's toe.

Once more, the two desperate women struggled for control of the axe. Finally, Candy wrenched the axe out of Betty's hands. Without hesitation, she brought the axe down on Betty's head and then continued to rain blow after blow to Betty's body. In all, 41 wounds were inflicted.

Candy looked down at the horribly mutilated body of Betty Gore. She walked into the shower and cleaned her arms and legs. Her head hurt where the flat side of the axe had made contact. Her toe throbbed. Despite all, she acted with the cunning of a desperate animal. She gathered up her purse and Alisa's bathing suit and walked out of the Gore home. She then drove to her own home, where she changed her clothing, making sure to wear clothes similar to what she had been wearing when she killed Betty. Candy returned to the church, rejoined her children and friends, and went through the remainder of the day in a routine manner.

Back at 410 Dogwood St., Betty Gore lay butchered in her utility room. Little Bethany lay crying in her crib. Candy had left behind a bloody fingerprint on the refrigerator door and a bloody footprint on the kitchen floor.

That evening, Allan Gore phoned his wife from St. Paul, Minnesota. There was no answer. After several such calls, he contacted neighbors, who entered his home and discovered Betty's body.

Initially, homicide detectives believed a psychopath had killed the Texas housewife in broad daylight in her own home. The transient appeared to have taken a shower after the murder. The undersized bloody footprint on the kitchen floor indicated that the killer had been a very small man.

Allan Gore was routinely questioned by police about his married life. He revealed that he had had a prolonged affair with Candy Montgomery. Although there was no question that Allan was in St. Paul at the time of the crime and could not have been physically involved in the killing, there was great suspicion that he and Candy had conspired to kill Betty. However, a polygraph test and the ensuing investigation proved that Allan was telling the truth. He was guilty of adultery, but had not been involved in his wife's murder.

Candy Montgomery's fingerprints were checked against the bloody fingerprint on he refrigerator door. They were identical. Candy was arrested and charged with the murder of Betty Gore. She testified in her own defence, revealing her affair with Allan. She shocked the court by admitting that she had an affair with another man after she and Allan broke up.

Candy's attorneys argued that, despite the promiscuity of their client, despite her attempts to camouflage her crime, she was not guilty of murder. They claimed that at the time of the frenzied struggle for the axe, Candy was acting in self-defence.

The Texas jury evidently believed Candy's version of the life and death struggle which had taken place in the utility room of the Gore home. They found her not guilty.

Two months after Candy's acquittal, the Montgomerys left Texas. Three months after the conclusion of Candy's murder trial, Allan Gore married a sympathetic supporter, whom he had dated during the trial.

A WOMAN
SCORNED

In 1965, Jean and James Harris were divorced. James later died, leaving Jean to raise two young sons.

Mrs. Harris was no ordinary woman. An honors graduate of prestigious Smith College, she embarked on a teaching career which culminated in 1977, when she was appointed headmistress of exclusive Madeira School in McLean, Virginia. Cultured, witty, pleasing to the eye, Jean Harris appeared to be the consummate career woman who had carved out a happy, interesting life for herself.

Dr. Herman Tarnower, the son of Russian-Jewish immigrants, graduated from Syracuse University to become a successful suburban physician. He owned his own medical clinic in Scarsdale, N.Y. and a large home in nearby Purchase. Two servants, Suzanne and Henri van der Vrekens, lived at the doctor's Purchase estate and took care of his day to day needs.

In 1979 Dr. Tarnower received world-wide recognition when he published his best-selling book, *The Complete Scarsdale Medical Diet*. Tarnower had been a wealthy man for years. With the acclaim his book received, he achieved celebrity status.

Back in 1966, Mrs. Harris met Dr. Tarnower at a party in New York. Soon she became lover and companion to the urbane, cultured doctor. Their relationship involved more than pillow talk. Herman Tarnower and Jean Harris travelled the world for months at a time. Jean held court as the doctor's hostess at intimate dinner parties. She often stayed at the Purchase estate for weeks.

Mrs. Harris was then and is today, by her own admission, madly in love with Hy

Tarnower. The relationship over the years, while it appeared idyllic, was a fragile thing. Tarnower, a confirmed bachelor, was a completely self-centred man. Jean knew deep down that she would be his lover and companion only as long as she complied with his every whim and idiosyncrasy.

There is nothing new about the love triangle which slowly but insidiously developed. The other woman was Lynne Tryforos, a good looking nurse-secretary at Tarnower's Scarsdale Clinic.

Tarnower did little to conceal his intimacy with the younger woman. Mrs. Harris would find Lynne's nightclothes hanging in what she felt was her closet at the doctor's home. The servants would volunteer that Lynne had spent several nights with the doctor. In 1979, Dr. Tarnower vacationed with Mrs. Harris in Palm Beach. When he returned he took Lynne Tryforos on vacation to Montego Bay.

On the March night in 1980 when violence erupted to change the lives of all the members of our triangle forever, Jean Harris was 56, Lynne Tryforos was 37, and Dr. Tarnower was a healthy, vigorous 69.

There was nothing unusual about the beginning of Hy Tarnower's last evening on this good earth. Dinner was served by Suzanne van der Vrekens. Lynne and an acquaintance, Debbie Raizes, were guests. The meal broke up early and the two women left at approximately 8:30 p.m. Dr. Tarnower retired. Henri van der Vrekens, who had prepared the evening meal, also went to bed. Suzanne chose to watch television and paint a watercolor.

That afternoon Dr. Tarnower had received a rather annoying call from Mrs. Harris in Virginia. She had asked to visit with him that very night. He tried to shake her off. "It would be more convenient if you came tomorrow." Mrs. Harris pleaded, "I can't talk to you tomorrow, Hy. Please, just this once let me say when!" Tarnower replied, "Suit yourself."

Mrs. Harris left for Purchase, N.Y. in the Madeira School's blue Chrysler. It was a five hour drive. Beside her on the front seat lay a loaded .32 calibre Harrington and Richardson revolver she had purchased over a year earlier. As she drove through a storm, Mrs. Harris might have been thinking of the lengthy letter she had written Tarnower earlier that day. The letter, which belittled Lynne Tryforos in no uncertain terms, would later be used to provide motive for what was to follow.

Mrs. Harris arrived at Tarnower's Purchase estate after a tedious drive. She let herself in through a garage door which she knew was always open and made her way to the doctor's bedroom, a room she had shared with him many times over the past 14 years.

Five shots were fired. Four found their mark. Tarnower was hit in the hand, right shoulder, right arm and downward through the back, puncturing his lung and kidney.

Suzanne van der Vrekens ran to the doctor's bedroom and found him in his blood-splattered tan pyjamas. She raised the alarm, but by the time Tarnower reached a hospital he was pronounced dead.

Mrs. Harris was arrested and stood trial for her lover's murder. Initially, as the facts of the case were revealed, there was a great deal of sympathy for the defendant. It was obvious that she had felt threatened when Tarnower turned from her in favor of a younger woman. It was also apparent that the famed doctor had treated her in a cavalier fashion.

Perhaps Mrs. Harris should not have taken the witness stand in her own defence. Many believe she was responsible for her own undoing. She stated that she had not intended to shoot the doctor. It had all been a horrible mistake. She had travelled to Purchase to see him one more time before taking her own life. As she said, "I hoped it would be a quiet, pleasant last few minutes." But it was not to be.

Tarnower was asleep when Mrs. Harris entered his bedroom. When he awakened, he was in no mood to chat. Frustrated, Mrs. Harris picked up a box of curlers and threw them through a window. Tarnower, in a rage, struck her across the face. She threw a cosmetic box. He struck her a second time. Sarcastically, she invited him to strike her again. He walked away.

Calmly, Mrs. Harris opened her purse and took out her .32 calibre revolver. She raised the gun, pointed it at her head, and pulled the trigger. At that exact moment, "Hy came at me and grabbed the gun and pushed my hand away from my head and pushed it down, and I heard the gun explode."

This first shot went through the doctor's hand. The gun dropped to the floor. Tarnower went to the bathroom to tend his hand. Mrs. Harris found the revolver on the floor, just as Tarnower reappeared. He lunged at her as she picked up the revolver. Once again, it fell to the floor. Tarnower picked it up.

Mrs. Harris then begged for the gun, "Hy, please give me the gun or shoot me yourself, but for Christ's sake let me die!" He replied, "Jesus, you're crazy, get out of here!"

Mrs. Harris grabbed the revolver now resting on Tarnower's lap. Tarnower jumped on her as she fell back on the bed. Mrs. Harris felt the muzzle against her stomach. She pulled the trigger but felt no pain as the gun exploded. Tarnower fell back. Mrs. Harris claimed that she placed the gun to her head, and despite continually pulling the trigger the revolver didn't go off, although it did fire once more when she tested it away from her head.

Her wish to die was not due to Tarnower's attention to other women, Mrs. Harris claimed, but because of a deep personal and career trauma which made death more attractive than a truly exhausting life.

At her trial, prosecution attorneys stated that Mrs. Harris was the typical study of the woman scorned. Her motive was there for all the world to see in her poorly timed letter to Dr. Tarnower, in which she obviously illustrated her hatred toward her younger rival for the diet doctor's affection. She had five hours of driving with a revolver in her possession before she entered Tarnower's house, plenty of time for a calm mind to take hold of the situation.

Mrs. Harris was found guilty of second degree murder and sentenced to a minimum of 15 years imprisonment. All appeals since her conviction have failed. She is currently serving her sentence at a women's prison in Bedford Hill, N.Y.

A HOT SUMMER NIGHT

Male nurse F.W. Uterback was lying in the bed of his third floor bedroom. It was too hot to sleep on that Friday night of July 18, 1919. Suddenly, he heard strange noises emanating from the second floor of the large Colonial style mansion located in the exclusive Lakewood suburb of Cleveland. Uterback raced down the one flight of stairs to his patient's bedroom.

He found Daniel Kaber suffering from severe stab wounds about the abdomen. Uterback called an ambulance and the police.

Dan Kaber had been confined to his bed for three months by paralysis. On the night of the attack his home was occupied by Marion McArdle, his 17-year-old stepdaughter, and her girlfriend, Anna Baehr, who unfortunately had picked that one night to sleep over. Mrs. J. Brickle, the victim's 70-year-old mother-in-law, was a permanent resident.

The two girls had been awakened by the noise, but remained in their room on Uterback's instructions. Across the hall from the girls the elderly Mrs. Brickle heard nothing. Kaber's wife Eva was out of the city and was not expected back until the next afternoon.

Searching the large home, detectives found the living room in disarray. Chairs were overturned, drawers were pulled out and a buffet was scratched in the area around the lock. A quantity of silverware was missing. It appeared that robbers thought they heard Kaber moving in his bedroom. Fearing that he would come downstairs and raise the alarm, they raced upstairs and attacked him. Police found a bloodstained dagger on the living room floor. The dagger was razor sharp around its edges, but had an extremely blunt end.

Kaber, who had 24 stab wounds in his abdomen, died 14 hours after the attack. Examination of the wounds revealed that the attacker was a weak person who cut at the victim's abdomen, inflicting the large number of superficial wounds, probably with the blunt dagger. It was felt that a stronger person would have been able to kill his victim with one or two deadly strikes.

The same afternoon that her husband died, Eva Kaber returned to Cleveland. She fainted when informed of her husband's murder.

Cleveland detectives thoroughly investigated the robbery-murder. A month later they still had no suspects. It appeared that Dan Kaber's murder would remain unsolved. The victim's elderly father had other ideas. Moses Kaber called on the prestigious Pinkerton National Detective Agency and told them the details of his son's death. Money was no object. He wanted his son's death avenged.

Pinkerton agents thoroughly checked out Marion McArdle's friend Anna Baehr. She told the operatives of her own suspicions. Two days before the murder she had been in the Kaber home. A fat, creepy woman was in the house visiting Marion's mother. Anna also noticed two unsavory looking men leaving the Kaber mansion. She thought the three visitors out of character compared to the Kaber's usual acquaintances.

The thorough Pinkerton Agency found out that Eva Kaber was definitely not in the city on the day of the murder. Her one idiosyncrasy was her penchant for consulting spiritual mediums.

Male nurse F.W. Uterback appeared to be an honest, hard-working man who had never been in any difficulty with the law.

The Pinkertons were coming up dry. They surreptitiously searched the Kaber mansion, waiting until all members of the household were absent. They found an icepick which could have made the scratch marks around the lock of the buffet. The agents also recovered an unlabelled medicine bottle half filled with a golden liquid. The liquid proved to be common ginger ale, which we'll return to in a moment.

The Pinkerton organization was convinced that Dan Kaber had met his death at the hands of someone he knew rather than burglars. They contacted Eva Kaber's best friend Edith Barnes and told her of their suspicions. They enlisted her aid in searching out the truth. Edith told the operatives that Eva Kaber had a lover and had once confided to her that she had married Dan for his money. She had not slept with her husband for three years. Dan Kaber's body was exhumed and found to be laced with poison.

Agents scoured Cleveland for mediums the now suspect Eva may have visited. They came up with one old doll, a Mrs. Colaveta. Anna Baehr identified Mrs. Colaveta as the fat lady she had seen in the Kaber home two days before the murder. Things were beginning to add up. It was just possible that Eva was attempting to get rid of an unwanted husband by poisoning him. When this plan only paralyzed her husband, the impatient Eva could have arranged for someone to kill him while faking a robbery.

Meanwhile, Edith, who was still co-operating with the Pinkertons, informed them that she and Eva were taking a trip to Pittsburgh together. The two women took a room at the William Penn Hotel. That's when Edith Barnes told Eva that she too had a lover, one Jack McCoy, who would be visiting them. He would be staying at the same hotel.

A handsome Pinkerton agent showed up, posing as the fictitious Jack McCoy. He wooed Edith Barnes, often taking out both women to restaurants and theatres. After a few weeks Edith confided to Eva that she often thought of murdering her husband so she could marry Jack.

Not to worry, replied obliging Eva, she knew just how to go about it. The hook was in. Eva told Edith to call on a certain Mrs. Colaveta back in Cleveland, who would sell her a little something to hasten her husband's departure from these earthly climes.

The Pinkertons sent a lady operative to call on Mrs. Colaveta. A deal was struck. For $1,000, Mrs. Colaveta passed over a medicine bottle containing an amber liquid. It was ginger ale. Cute and effective. When the ginger ale didn't work the suckers couldn't complain to anyone without revealing that they were attempting murder.

A tap was put on Mrs. Colaveta's phone. One night she received a call from a man named Sam with a foreign accent. He was inquiring about $2,500. He also mentioned that his partner Vittorio had left for Italy.

The Pinkertons turned the case over to the Cleveland police, who closed the net. They located the missing silverware at the home of a friend of Mrs. Colaveta.

Faced with this evidence, Mrs. Colaveta talked. Eva had come to her for poison. She sold her ginger ale. When it failed to work, Eva caused a fuss. Mrs. Colaveta provided the real thing, which only paralyzed Dan Kaber. Furious, Eva demanded Dan's death or she would pull the plug on Mrs. Colaveta. The medium supplied two dim-witted killers, Sam Cala and Vittorio Pisselli. Sam, a frail, weak man had a hard time stabbing Dan Kaber with the blunt dagger, which accounted for the numerous stab wounds.

Everyone was shocked to learn that Marion McCardle and old Mrs. Brickle were in on the plot and had helped overturn furniture on the night of the killing.

Okay, let's see. Mrs. Colaveta was sentenced to life imprisonment. So was Sam Cala. Marion McArdle was found not guilty of murder. The charge against Mrs. Brickle was dropped. Vittorio Pisselli was located in Italy, tried and sentenced to life imprisonment. Ah, Eva. She received life imprisonment in the Ohio Reformatory. In 1931, after 10 years confinement, she died there of a brain tumor, still cursing her former friend, Edith Barnes.

THE MURDERING MERRY WIDOW

If you ever kill someone, don't joke about it. The practice of making light of murder most foul is in decidedly poor taste and can lead to all sorts of complications.

Mary Elizabeth Wilson, who hailed from that wellspring of infamous murderers - Merrie England - went through life with a smile on her lips and a twinkle in her eye. She also went through male companions with the same jovial air. Mary Elizabeth was a card.

Let's see now, there was a hubby, number one, John Knowles, who followed the honest but messy profession of chimney sweep. John went to that great flue in the sky unexpectedly. There were those who said that he was as healthy as a horse one day and dead as a mackerel the next. Mary Elizabeth, stout lass that she was, put on a fair to middling spread for assorted mourners.

Although Mary Elizabeth inherited a few quid upon the demise of her first husband, she soon found herself strapped for cash. Always an exceptional housekeeper, she hired out in that capacity to John George Russell. This second John lasted several years, but, alas, he too departed this mortal coil without the decency of a prolonged illness. Once more, Mary Elizabeth had the opportunity to display her culinary skill for the assorted mourners.

Years passed. Mary Elizabeth, now a matronly 65, married husband number two, Oliver Leonard, 75, a retired real estate agent. It was then that she returned to her murderous ways.

Mary Elizabeth was introduced to Leonard in the summer of 1956. He was residing at Mrs. Connolly's rooming house. Never one to mince words, Mary

Elizabeth asked Mrs. Connolly, "Has the old bastard any money?" When Mrs. Connolly replied that she thought her roomer had at least a little coin of the realm, the die was cast.

Mary Elizabeth chatted privately with Mr. Leonard for half an hour. Next day, completely smitten, Leonard gave Mrs. Connolly notice. He would soon be getting married and moving in with Mary Elizabeth. No question about it, Mary Elizabeth was a speedy worker.

On Oct. 1, 1956, Dr. John Hubert Laydon was called by Mary Elizabeth to minister to her relatively new husband. Oliver Leonard had a touch of bronchitis and arterial trouble, but otherwise seemed to be in good health. Two days later, the good doctor received a call from Mary Elizabeth. Her husband had died.

Dr. Laydon, with a certain degree of nonchalance, filled out and signed the death certificate without viewing the body. He stated the cause of death was "degeneration of the heart with some inflammation of the kidney." Before we come down hard on Dr. Laydon, it should be pointed out that at that time in England it was perfectly legal for a doctor to sign the death certificate if he had seen the patient within the past 14 days.

Mary Elizabeth collected £75 upon her husband's death, but was she satisfied? No, she was not. Leonard was hardly cold in his final resting place when she met retired engineer Ernest Wilson, who was in his seventy-sixth year. In a matter of months, Mary Elizabeth was once again a blushing bride.

It was at her wedding reception that Mary Elizabeth made her unfortunate attempt at humor. When a guest remarked that there were a lot of cakes and sandwiches left over, Mary Elizabeth, not too tactfully, responded, "Just keep them for the funeral, although I might give this one a week's extension." Knowing Mary Elizabeth's immediate past, many of her guests doubled over with laughter. The wisecrack took on a more sinister connotation a few weeks later when the new groom was buried.

On Nov. 11, 1957, Mary Elizabeth called in Dr. William Proudfoot Wallace, who thought Wilson might have some degeneration of the heart muscle. The doctor prescribed some pills and left, promising to return in three days. That same day he received an urgent call from Mary Elizabeth, informing him that Wilson was extremely ill. He was dead. Dr. Wallace attributed the death to cardio-muscular failure and myocardiac degeneration and filled in the death certificate accordingly.

Mary Elizabeth appeared to lead a charmed life regarding the unexpected deaths of those near and dear to her. If not for one anonymous acquaintance, she would no doubt have continued to bury husbands. But there is almost always someone who runs to the police with their suspicions.

The police exhumed the bodies of John Knowles, John Russell, Oliver Leonard and the recently departed Ernest Wilson. All four bodies were found to contain phosphorous, a deadly poison.

Mary Elizabeth was arrested and charged with the murder of her last two husbands. Once the press found out her address: Rectory Road, Windy Nook, County Durham she was immediately christened the Widow of Windy Nook. The name had a certain ring to it.

Mary Elizabeth stood trial at Leeds in March 1958. Crown counsel produced evidence garnered from the autopsies, indicating that Leonard and Wilson had been administered poisonous phosphorous. The autopsies also revealed that traces of bran were found in the bodies. About the only common preparation using highly inflammable phosphorous was rat and beetle poison, which are manufactured from phosphorous, wheat bran and syrup. Had the Widow of Windy Nook been killing her husband with rat poison? Other scientific evidence was produced, which showed that the odor and taste of rat poison could be neutralized when placed in beer, cider, bread and certain jams.

Mary Elizabeth had a disconcerting penchant for saying and doing the wrong things at the wrong time. She had tried to sell Wilson's gold watch on the very day he died. She had also chatted with an acquaintance that day and discussed her husband's illness. At the time this discussion took place, she knew very well Wilson was home, dead as a doornail. Then, of course, there was her tasteless joke about the sandwiches, which now came back to haunt her.

To counteract this circumstantial evidence, defence counsel pointed out that no rat poison was found at Mary Elizabeth's Windy Nook residence. They also came up with a rather fanciful theory. Evidently, certain pills, containing minute quantities of phosphorous, are often used as an aphrodisiac. The defence contended that the two deceased men had overdosed on pills in an attempt to retain their sexual prowess.

It was great stuff, but unfortunately the prosecution proved that the men would each have had to take 150 pills at one time to ingest a fatal dose. It was too much to ask the jury to believe. They retired for only one hour and 25 minutes before finding Mary Elizabeth guilty of both murders.

Mary Elizabeth Wilson was sentenced to death, but this sentence was later commuted to life imprisonment.

BLOODY TINA

It would be an understatement to say that life had not been a bowl of cherries for 16-year-old Attine Marie Cannaday. Still, that's no reason for Tina to stab her boyfriend 19 times and attempt to cart away his head for a souvenir.

Tina had it rough. She was born in Mobile, Alabama to a lady of the night, who made a few legitimate dollars in the bump and grind business. Daddy was a ne'er do well who raped Tina when she was nine years old. Tina's striptease mother divorced and remarried. She had the uncanny knack of choosing vile men. Tina's new daddy raped his 13-year-old stepdaughter.

Tina, with an I.Q. of 71, despised school and hated her horrendous home life. She ran away. At the age of 14, she married and headed for the Mississippi coast. The marriage didn't last. Eight months later, her husband obtained a divorce. Tina was on her own.

It didn't take long. By applying makeup, Tina discovered she could pass as much older. In Biloxi, she obtained a job as a stripper, the only thing she could do. Soon the management of the joint was arranging tricks for their new young stripper.

Tina, wise beyond her years, now realized that her body was a valuable asset. Men would pay for her services. Now and then, one of the johns would take more than a passing interest in her welfare. They became boyfriends for a short while, but no lasting relationship developed until she met Ronald Wojcik. Ron was different. He really seemed to care. Besides, he was a far more stable character than anyone Tina had ever met.

Ron Wojcik had joined the air force the day he turned 18. Nine years later, he was transferred to Keesler Air Force Base in Biloxi. Along the way, Ron had been married and divorced. His two children, ages four and six, spent most of their time with their mother but occasionally visited Ron at his comfortable apartment on Beach Blvd. Ron had a part-time job as bartender at the Sports Page Lounge.

For the first time in her life, Tina was totally attracted to a man. She fell hard. Her feelings were reciprocated. Ron was delighted that a sweet young thing of 16 would fall for him. Before you could say wild blue yonder, Tina moved in with Ron. It was probably the happiest few months of Tina Cannaday's entire life.

Everything was turning up roses until the day air force officials called on Ron. They informed him that while most of his personal life was his own business, the air force would not allow him to live with a juvenile. Ron, an air force career man, told Tina that she would have to move out. He insinuated that perhaps they should not see so much of each other.

Tina was devastated. The only man she ever loved was giving her the brush-off. Later when she heard that Ron was sleeping with Sandra Sowash, a barmaid at the Sports Page Lounge, Tina's feelings of affection for Ron turned to thoughts of revenge.

Throughout the early summer of 1982, Tina was in a state of depression. She thought of little else but her Ron making love to Sandra Sowash. At this low point in her existence, she met ex-con David Gray, a drifter who functioned in a haze induced by drugs and booze. Tina poured out her tale of woe to the sympathetic Dave. A strange bond developed between the two downtrodden personalities. Dave became something of Tina's protector.

On June 2, 1982, Tina and Dave were drinking in the Red Garter Lounge. A 15-year-old new girl in town, Dawn Bushart, struck up a conversation with them. Dawn was a runaway from Tuscaloosa, Alabama. As usual, Tina could talk of little else but Ron and Sandra. She asked Dave, "Will you beat him up for me? I've got a key to his apartment. Have you got a gun?"

Dave admitted that he didn't have a gun, but he did have a nice assortment of knives. That's how Dave, Tina and Dawn ended up at Ron Wojcik's apartment in the early morning of June 3, 1982.

Without a sound, they opened the front door and entered the bedroom, expecting find Ron alone. Tina was incensed to find Sandra Sowash at his side. At knifepoint, Ron and Sandra were forced into Ron's 1974 Ford van. Ron attempted to talk some reason into his former girlfriend. Tina wouldn't listen. She drove aimlessly, like a maniac. Finally, she told Dave to rape Sandra, who was still in her nightclothes. Dave did as he was told.

The van pulled into a darkened sideroad. Dave Gray forced Ron into some nearby woods. A short time passed. Dave emerged from the woods and told Tina that he had beaten up Ron. Tina wasn't satisfied. She ordered Sandra back into the van, with the ominous declaration, "I'm going to waste you."

Sandra did not take the threat lightly. She knew her life hung in the balance. Weighing the odds, she jumped from the van and ran for her life. Tina threw a knife. Sandra felt the handle of the knife hit her between the shoulders. She continued running. A few hundred yards from the van, she spotted a farmhouse. After much knocking on the door, she managed to wake up the occupants.

Meanwhile Tina had given up the chase and returned to the unconscious body of Ron Wojcik. Ron had already received a severe beating from the fists of David Gray. Tina wanted more. She took a knife from Gray's hand and told him to go back to the van.

Tina then took out her rage on the fates which had dealt her such an unfortunate hand. She plunged the knife again and again into Ron's limp body. She slit her victim's throat and continued to hack away at his neck in an attempt to remove his head. It was too difficult a job. Her rage subsided. Dripping blood, she walked back to the van.

While Tina was killing Ron, Sandra managed to tell her story to the farmer, who called police. As the sun rose that morning of June 3, police swarmed to the murder scene. The killers were long gone.

Tina headed for Slidell, Louisiana, where she had an old friend, Tim Page. As the van entered Slidell, Tina threw Ron's wallet out of the window. She had taken the money out of the wallet, but had left all Ron's personal cards and documents intact. The wallet was found and turned over to police. After scanning the identification, police knew their quarry was in or near Slidell. All the while, Tina, now totally exhausted, was asleep at Page's home.

Dawn Bushart had been let out of the van in Slidell and started hitch-hiking back to Biloxi, wondering how she had become mixed up in such a serious business. After all, she had only strolled into the bar for a drink.

The two men, David Gray and Tim Page, decided to get something to eat while Tina slept. They jumped into Ron's van. It wasn't long before the van was sighted by police. The two men were taken into custody. They led detectives to Page's home, where Tina was apprehended. Dawn was picked up, still attempting to hitch a ride to Biloxi.

Page was released, but Dave, Tina and Dawn were charged with capital murder. All three pleaded not guilty.

Dawn Bushart, fearful of receiving the death penalty, pleaded guilty to a reduced charge of manslaughter. She was sentenced to 10 years imprisonment.

David Gray was found guilty of murder and sentenced to death. At his trial, much was made of the fact that he procured and provided the murder weapon. At present, his case is proceeding through the appeal process of the State of Mississippi.

Tina Cannaday was found guilty of murder and sentenced to death. Her sentence was later commuted to life imprisonment.

LADY SUNDANCE

He called her "Lady Sundance." She called him "Nightrider." There were those who called Judith and Alvin Neeley the most sadistic, cold-blooded killers who ever roamed the highways and byways of the United States.

Judith claims she was sexually abused as a child. She ran away from home at the age of 15 to marry Alvin. If ever there was an unholy union, it was the Neeleys. Although Alvin was 26 when he met Judith, many believe she was the dominant personality.

The Neeleys lived by their wits, wandering through Tennessee, Alabama and Georgia, pulling off small thefts and passing bad cheques. In 1980, they attempted to graduate to armed robbery and were quickly apprehended. Alvin spent several months in jail, while Judith was placed in the Youth Development Centre in Rome, Georgia, where she gave birth to twins.

Two years later, Judith and Alvin were free once more. Alvin took a job at a garage and promptly absconded with the company's weekend receipts. With the proceeds of the theft, he purchased a Ford Granada for himself and a Dodge Charger for Judith. Equipped with CB radios and .38 calibre revolvers, they transformed themselves into Lady Sundance and Nightrider. It is difficult to pinpoint when the evil pair made the transition from dangerous punks to sadistic murderers, but transform they did.

In September 1982, Lisa Millican, 13, a ward of the Ethel Harpst Home for neglected children, was taken on a trip to a shopping mall in nearby Rome. Seven girls and six boys made the trip. Once at the mall, they were told to stay in groups and meet at a prearranged location for the return trip home at 8 p.m. Lisa didn't show up. Counsellors and children searched the mall, but Lisa was nowhere to be found. Police were notified.

Hours before she was reported missing, Lisa met a young woman, who struck up a conversation with her. The lady told Lisa that she was new in town and very lonely. Little Lisa, a solitary, lonely child herself, knew just how the lady felt. She accepted a drive in the country in the stranger's Dodge Charger. Once in the car, Judith Neeley's voice crackled over the airwaves, "This is Lady Sundance. Do you read me?" Nightrider read his accomplice only too well.

It is not necessary to detail the horrible fate which befell little Lisa Millican. It is enough to know that she was moved from motel to motel and sexually abused in every way imaginable. Judith was later to state that after a couple of days the little girl complied with every indignity in order to please her tormentors and avoid being killed.

For some diabolical reason known only to the perpetrators themselves, they decided to kill the child by injecting Drano and Liquid Plummr into her veins. Judith later told investigators that the caustic substances were used for no other reason than to satisfy her curiosity. Detectives theorized that the killers were trying to give the murder the appearance of an overdose.

Even as killers of a helpless child, Judith and Alvin were inept. Judith couldn't find the youngster's vein. The searing substance was injected intramuscularly. The pain must have been excruciating, but not fatal. Lisa was spirited away to remote Little River Canyon and again injected with cleaning fluid. Judith was disappointed. The child didn't die. She was then dragged to the lip of a 100-foot deep canyon. There, Judith drew her .38 revolver and shot the child in the back. She listened as Lisa Millican's body plunged to the jagged rocks below. Alvin watched from a few feet away.

Judith wanted more than sex, more than murder. She wanted the thrill of the hunt. She called police and told them where they could find the missing Lisa Millican's body. Because of the nature of the terrain, the child's mutilated body was not recovered until the next day.

Police studied the tape recording of the woman who called and told them where to find Lisa's body. They knew they were listening to the voice of a murderer, but no leads to the killer's identity were uncovered until some days after the body was found.

Not far from Rome, a man was shot in the back. The Neeleys had struck again. Twenty-six-year-old John Hancock and his fiancée, Janice Chatman, were strolling down Shorter St. in Rome. A Dodge Charger with Tennessee plates pulled up beside the young couple. The driver explained that she had just arrived in the area and was very lonely. If they wanted a ride into the countryside, they were welcome to hop in.

John and Janice had nothing better to do. They were happy to accept. Once they were inside the car, Lady Sundance told them that a friend of hers would join them with a cooler of beer. In minutes, Nightrider appeared in his Ford Granada. The two automobiles pulled into a secluded wooded lane.

Judith placed her .38 calibre pistol directly between John Hancock's eyes. She then marched him into the woods. Without warning, Hancock heard the loud report of the gun going off. At the same time, he felt a searing pain in his back. John fell to the ground, feigning death, but was conscious and well aware that the slightest movement meant a second shot and most probably death. Alvin Neeley called into the woods for his wife. Judith left the fallen Hancock where he lay. The pair sped away in their vehicles with the terrified Janice Chatman.

A few minutes later, John Hancock was able to stagger to the road and wave down a passing motorist. In hospital, police played the tape of the woman who had called in the whereabouts of Lisa Millican's body. John believed his abductor's voice and the voice on the tape were one and the same. The hunt was on for the two vehicles, but the identities of Lady Sundance and Nightrider were still unknown.

The connecting information came from the Youth Development Centre in Rome, where Judith Neeley had once been confined. Someone had called the home and threatened to kill members of the staff in retaliation for abuses received while the caller had lived there. The recipient of the call listened to the taped call from Lisa Millican's killer. It was his opinion that the same woman had made both calls.

Detectives began the dogged work of checking every girl who had been released from the institution in the previous two years. By the process of elimination, they came up with six suspects. John Hancock was shown the six photographs. He picked out Judith Neeley's photo as the woman who had shot him.

The identification was too late for Janice Chatman. She had been taken to a motel immediately after John Hancock was shot. She was handcuffed naked to a bed and sexually abused all night. Early in the morning, Judith and Alvin drove their hapless victim to a lonely area of Chattooga County and shot her in the head and back.

The wanton pair found themselves short of money. Reverting to their old method of raising money fast, they decided to pass a few worthless cheques in Murfreesboro, Tenn. They were caught within hours and quickly identified as the suspected murderers of little Lisa Millican and the abductors of Janice Chatman. Alvin couldn't wait to ingratiate himself with police. He drew maps indicating where Janice Chatman's body could be found. Alvin's maps were authentic. Janice's body was speedily recovered.

Eventually, Alvin Neeley pleaded guilty to the murder of Janice Chatman. He received one life sentence for aggravated assault and a second life sentence for murder. He is presently serving these sentences in a Georgia prison.

Judith Neeley was charged with the murder of Lisa Millican. She was found guilty and sentenced to death. While in jail, Judith gave birth to her third child.

Today, Judith Neeley is one of only two women under sentence of death in the state of Alabama. She is presently on Death Row in the Julia Tutiwiller Correctional Institute in Wetumpka, Ala. The assistant warden of the institution, Mrs. Shirlie Lobmiller, informs me, "Judith has adjusted well to the institution while her sentence is being appealed."

In compliance with a state law, her cell is checked every 30 minutes night and day. Judith has access to TV and enjoys soap operas and religious programs. Each morning, at 6:30 a.m., she is moved to a shower by a guard, but is allowed her privacy in the shower for five to seven minutes. Her mornings are spent in handicrafts. Lunch is served from 10:30 to 11:00, after which Judith takes a nap. She keeps herself clean and well-groomed, although she is compelled to wear a plain white dress.

After supper Judith watches TV. Lights are automatically turned off at 10:00 p.m. except for a solitary safety bulb, which casts a dim glow while the prisoner sleeps. Mrs. Lobmiller points out that Judith has led this enforced Spartan existence for close to six years. She adds, "You would never think Judith is the same person who committed the horrible crimes attributed to her."

Lisa Millican and Janice Chatman are not here to voice their opinions.

DOUBLE TROUBLE

Seldom have we come across a lady as cold and calculating as Marie Frazier. At the same time, you would have to walk many a crooked mile to meet anyone as pleasant and charming as our Marie.

The Frazier family lived in the factory town of Anniston, Alabama. When Marie was still in school and only 17 years of age, she married Frank Hilley. A year and a half later, the union was blessed. On Nov. 11, 1952, Michael Hilley was born. Eight years later, Marie gave birth to their only daughter, Carol.

Everyone liked Frank Hilley. He worked long and hard down at the factory, was interested in his family's welfare and loved to take in a Saturday afternoon football game. One thing everyone agrees on - Frank had never been sick a day in his life. That's why it was such a surprise when, during the late winter months of 1975, Frank complained of not feeling well. He couldn't explain it. Instead of his usual snappy gait, he had developed a shuffle. It got so Frank could hardly make it to work. Each evening he dropped into bed, exhausted.

Naturally, this change in Frank's health caused Marie some concern. She was as solicitous as she could be to her husband but nothing seemed to help. Frank was confined to his bed. On May 25, 1975, he died.

Dr. Earl Jones, who had ministered to Frank during his last weeks on earth, suggested that an autopsy be performed. Marie readily gave her consent. The autopsy revealed that lungs and kidneys were swollen. Pneumonia was evident in both lungs. The small intestine was inflamed. Dr. Jones attributed death to infectious hepatitis.

Marie was consoled somewhat with $31,140, the proceeds of a life insurance policy Frank had thoughtfully purchased at his place of employment. Life went on. Marie continued to be gainfully employed as a secretary, a position in which she was extremely capable. Her son, Mike, married and became an ordained minister to a congregation just outside Anniston.

Frank's mother was diagnosed as having cancer. Marie diligently nursed the gravely ill woman until her death on Jan. 4, 1977. Marie, ever the practical one, insured daughter Carol's life. In 1979, she began feeding her own 19-year-old daughter small quantities of arsenic. Carol became lethargic and extremely thin. Accompanied by Marie, she was taken to a series of doctors. The diagnoses ranged from a simple stomach disorder to anorexia nervosa. Occasionally, Carol was hospitalized. Marie often brought her treats to the hospital.

Carol's body eventually shrivelled up, so that she resembled a little old lady. When she lost her ability to walk, she was hospitalized on a more or less permanent basis. Finally, Carol's Aunt Freeda, her father's sister, began to suspect what no one else had even thought of. Could Marie be poisoning her own daughter? Freeda confided her suspicions to an intern, who extensively tested Carol. Sure enough, Carol had arsenic in her system. Police were notified and the bodies of Frank Hilley and his mother were exhumed. Both were laced with arsenic. While Frank's mother had been dying of cancer, she had been helped along with quantities of arsenic.

When arsenic was found in Marie's jewelry box, she was arrested. A month later, she was charged with the attempted murder of her daughter. After almost two months in jail, Marie was successful in raising bail. She promptly disappeared. Marie Hilley, suspected murderer, had become a fugitive from justice.

Marie's poisonous ways are fascinating enough, but hold on. There is more. Marie was to engage in activities which were to make headlines around the world.

After skipping bail, Marie hitched a ride, ending up in Fort Lauderdale, Florida. She had little difficulty obtaining a position with McMahon, Love, Black and Albers, an accounting firm in West Palm Beach. She falsified her application, listing previous employment which was difficult, if not impossible, to check. Marie was now using the name Lindsay Robbi Hannon. Everyone called her Robbi. She was soon a charming, efficient member of the accounting firm's staff.

Attractive Robbi Hannon met John Homan in February 1980. John, who owned a small boat building operation, was susceptible to Robbi's many charms. He had just concluded a seven year long unhappy marriage. Soon he found himself very much in love with Robbi Hannon. She told him she was 36 years old. John, 33, felt he was lucky to have such an attractive lady friend. He didn't have any idea Robbi was really 46.

Robbi told John she had a twin sister, Teri. They had been brought up in Tyler, Texas, by grandparents, but their childhood had been unhappy. Deserted by their parents, other relatives had attempted to split up the twins, but they had somehow managed to stay together until they became adults.

Robbi told John that she had been married to a Texas millionaire and had two children. Both had been killed in a car accident by a drunken driver. The millionaire's family had blamed Robbi for the death of the children. Two years after the children's death, her millionaire husband had died of a heart attack.

Our Marie could really lay it on. John was in love. Marie, alias Robbi, moved in with him that summer. By fall, when John's boat-building business failed, he and Robbi decided to move to New Hampshire. They settled in a comfortable cottage near Keene. John caught on as a tool and die maker at Findings Inc., while Robbi became a sales rep at the Central Screw Co. The following May, John married the woman he firmly believed to be a Texas heiress.

In the summer of 1982, Robbi told John the devastating news that she had a serious, life-threatening blood disease. Her performance at work deteriorated rapidly. She often had excruciating headaches and suffered from long periods of memory loss.

After much soul searching, it was decided that Robbi would consult a well-known specialist in Dallas. Her fictitious twin sister, Teri, would join her there.

While her husband thought she was in Texas, Robbi dashed over to Pompano Beach, Fla., using the name Teri Martin. Marie had switched twins. From Robbi, she now took on the persona of Teri.

Posing as Teri, she took on a job in Pompano Beach for three months. On several occasions she called John back in New Hampshire, advising him of his wife Robbi's health. She also managed to lose 30 pounds. She cut her hair and bleached it platinum blonde.

In early November, Robbi informed her husband that her condition had worsened. She was entering hospital. On Nov. 9, John received the dreadful news. His wife's twin sister Teri informed him that Robbi had died. There was little need for him to travel to Texas. Robbi had donated her body to a research institute.

Three days later, Teri arrived at the Hannon home in New Hampshire. John's wife's identical twin was somewhat thinner than Robbi. She also had blonde hair where Robbi's hair was dark. But still, the resemblance was remarkable. Indeed, everyone in Keene who saw Teri was amazed at the remarkable resemblance between her and her dead sister. Then again, identical twins are supposed to look like each other.

A touching letter in his wife's handwriting put any misgivings John might have had to rest. Together, Teri and the grieving husband, placed Robbi's obituary in the Keene *Sentinel*.

In due course, Teri found a job in nearby Brattleboro, Vermont. She was a great comfort to the grieving John. Believe it or not, folks, Teri moved in with her dead sister's husband. To this day, John swears he didn't know Teri and Robbi were one and the same woman.

This set up might have lasted for years were it not for a couple of busybodies who just couldn't swallow the story of the twin sister moving in with the grieving husband. They believed that Robbi was another fugitive who was thought to be living in New England at the time. They asked Robbi's former employer to check out the details contained in the obituary. When the details couldn't be confirmed, police were notified. Confronted with their suspicions, Teri/Robbi/Marie confessed to being Marie Hilley. She told all about her marital escapades, but swore she didn't kill or attempt to kill anyone. Three eventful years had passed since Marie Hilley had skipped bail in Anniston, Texas.

The news spread like wildfire. Everyone got a chuckle out of Marie and her ability to fool everyone, including her own husband.

Marie was returned to Alabama, where the good old southern folks didn't see that much humor in her exploits. She was found guilty of murder and attempted murder. Marie received sentences of life on the murder charge and 20 years imprisonment for the attempted murder of her daughter. Robbi/Teri won't be doing any marrying for some time. The sentences are to run consecutively.

6

ALL IN
THE FAMILY

A WEIRD GROUP

Let's face it, some families do seem to have more than their fair share of eccentrics, but you have to go some to surpass the Covells of Bandon, Oregon.

For starters, there was Arthur. An automobile accident had left Art paralyzed from the waist down. This state of affairs was devastating for the devil-may-care travelling salesman who lived for booze and broads. At a youthful 39, an age when many men believe they are at their best, Art was confined to a mattress and had to be carried whenever he wished to be mobile. Art usually started his day with a full bottle of Scotch at his side on the mattress. As the sun fell away beyond the Pacific, the bottle was always empty.

Art managed to become self-supporting. He had always dabbled in astrology as a hobby. Now, with nothing but time on his hands, he compiled horoscopes, which he sold by means of advertising in pulp magazines. Soon he was conducting a thriving business from his mattress.

Art lived with his brother Fred in the latter's old rambling house about four miles outside of Bandon. Fred was a successful chiropractor, but try as he might he couldn't help his crippled brother. Running the homestead in a nagging, annoying manner was Fred's loving, fragile wife, Ebba. Fred sort of specialized in wives. Ebba was number four. Two of the previous Mrs. Covells had passed away, while the third just went away.

Rounding out the cast of Covells was Alton, a sloven, skinny, 16-year-old, six-foot beanpole, and Lucille, a 14-year-old whose idea of an action-packed day was to get out of bed at noon. Both children were the offspring of one of Fred's previous marriages.

In 1933 the five Covells had been living under the same roof for 13 years. Art was a wizened alcoholic, who had managed to become a great success in the astrology game. The fact is his brother Fred often wondered if astrology wasn't more lucrative than manipulating tired bones. One fine summer day he nonchalantly asked his brother to cast a horoscope for his dear wife Ebba. Art was thrilled. However, he was reluctant to give the results of his effort to his brother. Evidently the horoscope indicated that Ebba was going to meet her maker on Labor Day, just a week away.

Fred didn't take the sinister prediction seriously. Labor Day dawned bright and clear. Dr. Fred surprised the rest of the family when he announced after breakfast that he would be spending the entire day at his office. Apparently he had told several patients that if he was required on Labor Day they knew where to find him. Alton and Lucille carried Uncle Art and his mattress out to his favorite spot on the lawn to work on his horoscopes. The two teenagers passed the time lolling around the yard. Ebba remained in the house alone.

At lunchtime Lucille went indoors to assist her stepmother. She didn't stay long. There was Ebba lying on the floor looking all funny. The two youngsters carried Uncle Art into the house. Just half sloshed (it was only noon), Art felt Ebba's pulse and declared that his sister-in-law was dead.

Art tried to raise Fred on his office phone, but there was no answer. He found a list of his brother's patients and called them all. None knew where Fred could be found, and no one had an office appointment with him. Finally, at three o'clock in the afternoon, Fred answered the phone and was informed that he had lost wife number four. Calmly the chiropractor said that under the circumstances he would come home immediately.

Fred took one look, confirmed the obvious, and called the local mortician. Then the strange family sat down to a hearty meal while poor Ebba rested comfortably on an upstairs bed. The undertaker eventually arrived and removed the body. Art, who was hanging around on his mattress idly swigging from his bottle of Scotch, inquired as to when the funeral would take place. He thought it strange when informed that the last rites were to occur at two o'clock the following day. Fast work, thought Uncle Art to himself.

Bright and early next morning, Fred went to work as usual, notwithstanding the fact that his wife was to be buried that afternoon. No sooner had he left the house than who should knock at the door but a big bad deputy named Malehorn. He informed Art of some distressing facts. Ebba had nasty red marks near her lips, indicating that some irritant had been pressed over her mouth. Not only that, she also had a broken neck, something not easily overlooked, especially by a chiropractor.

Malehorn just had to know. Was it possible for Fred to return home after leaving for work, kill his wife, and return to work without being seen? Arthur reluctantly had to concede that it indeed was possible.

When the doctor was questioned, his answers were far from satisfactory. He claimed that his phone hadn't rung before three, at which time he answered it. He stated that he had a terrible memory and couldn't recall the names of the patients he had told to drop in on Labor Day. He did notice that his wife had a broken neck. However, he attributed it to a fall down the stairs, which had caused death. At the end of extensive questioning Fred flared up at investigating officers, "If you think I murdered my wife, prove it!" Police knew they didn't have enough evidence to gain a conviction, but they were so sure that murder had been committed, they took all four Covells into custody.

Kept in separate cells, the four members of the family were questioned individually. All stuck to their original stories. A private detective brought into the case to assist police came up with a bright, if not sporting idea. He had the local newspaper run off a one-copy edition. The bogus headline simply stated "Covell Confesses." Correctly believing that Alton would be the weakest link in the family, detectives showed him the paper. Alton crumbled immediately.

He told of the intense dislike which his Uncle Art had for his stepmother. It had evolved because Ebba kept nagging Art about eating too much. Uncle Art had a certain power over Alton which the boy couldn't understand. His uncle had told him that he must kill his stepmother. Under his uncle's instructions he had purchased ammonia and had placed it over Ebba's mouth. In the process the strong wiry boy had broken his stepmother's neck. In this way Uncle Art made sure that his prediction concerning Ebba's death on Labor Day was certain to become a reality. Later Uncle Art, confronted with Alton's statement, confessed.

Following, in part, is his confession:

Both Alton and Lucille were at all times under control of my mind, and my will was their will. They never resisted my influence but did, without question, as I wished things done. They never argued or thought if the action was right or wrong for my influence over both was complete. They seemed incapable to resist or to think independently beyond my wishes. In regard to Ebba, I told Alton I wanted her out of the way. I told him how to do it without violence and with ammonia.

My brother Fred is entirely innocent. Lucille is innocent. Alton as an individual is innocent. I forced my will on him and made him act for me.

At the murder trial which followed, Alton received a sentence of life imprisonment. He was released, while still a young man, after serving ten years. Arthur Covell, who deteriorated rapidly while in custody, went to the gallows proclaiming to one and all that he was really John the Baptist.

TASTY SAUSAGE

If you plan to murder your wife and dispose of the body, it helps if you own your very own sausage factory. No, Adolph Louis Luetgert didn't make red-hots out of the little woman, but he did use the equipment at hand to, shall we say, liquefy his dear wife, Louise.

Adolph's parents emigrated from Germany when the subject of our study in horror was still a little boy. They settled in Chicago where Adolph soon was contributing to the family income. He tried his hand at farming, clerking, and for a while ran a saloon before he manufactured his very first sausage.

Intelligent, industrious Adolph soon had a thriving sausage factory in full production. For some years he lived high off the hog. Adolph married, but his wife died of natural causes after giving birth to a son, Arnold. Undaunted, Adolph approached the altar for a second time when he promised to love, honor, and obey one of his servants, Louise Bicknese. No one mentioned dissolve.

Louise, a woman of finely chiselled features, somewhat detracted from her appearance by wearing a perpetual scowl. She bore Adolph two sons, Louis and Elmer.

In the years directly preceding 1896 the sausage business suffered an acute recession. Business was so bad that Adolph had to lay off most of his staff, retaining only a skeleton crew to maintain the machinery and heating system. His troubled financial affairs came at a bad time, for Adolph had more than sausages on his mind. Her name was Mary Simering.

Mary, who acted as Adolph's private servant, performed all sort of private services which are not listed in the domestic's manual. She loved to frolic with Adolph in the little bedroom he had outfitted for himself right in the sausage factory.

As his heart beat faster for Mary, so his behavior towards the mother of his children suffered. Adolph treated Louise like dirt. Something had to give. What better way to resolve the problem, than to dissolve Louise?

No one saw Louise after May 1, 1897. Three days later her brother Diedrich paid a visit to her home and was surprised that no one seemed to know where she was. Adolph said that dear Louise had been missing since the first of the month. She had merely walked out of the house without saying a word. Adolph told Diedrich that in order to avoid a scandal he had paid private detectives to look for Louise, but they had not been successful so far. Diedrich informed police of Louise's disappearance.

Matters became a bit dicey when detectives questioned Frank Bialk, a night watchman at the sausage factory. Frank revealed that on the night of May 1 several strange incidents took place at the factory.

At about 9:00 p.m. Adolph gave Frank a dollar and asked him to fetch some medicine from a nearby drugstore. When Frank returned he entered the furnace room but found that the door leading to the factory proper was locked, something which had never happened before. Frank tried to gain access via an elevator, but it too was closed down. In a little while Adolph opened the factory door, retrieved his medicine and thanked Frank, who, somewhat puzzled, went back to the furnace room.

An hour later this entire procedure was repeated. Apparently Adolph had spent the best part of the night alone in the sausage factory. Furthermore Frank heard certain machinery being used. He told police that on the same night Adolph had turned on one of three steam vats used for coloring sausage. He turned off the steam at 2:00 a.m. when he finally left the factory.

When Frank reported for work the next night he noticed a vile, sticky substance in front of the middle steam vat. Fires were out in the furnace room and the ashes from the fire removed.

After hearing Frank's tale of possible horror, police made a thorough search of the sausage factory. Their terrible suspicions gained credence. The middle steam vat was filled with a brownish liquid substance which, when drained, gave up pieces of bone and two gold rings. One ring had the letters "L.L." engraved on the inside.

Now positive that they were hot on the trail of one of the most innovative murderers in the history of the United States, homicide detectives traced Adolph's past movements. They discovered that he had purchased a half drum of 350 pounds of potash from a drug wholesaler, Lord, Owen & Co., in March. Obviously Adolph had planned his wife's disappearance months in advance.

Further questioning elicited the fact that Frank had assisted his employer in dumping the potash into the middle steam vat. At one point, it became apparent to Adolph that Frank was aware of the murder which had been committed in the sausage factory. Frank swore that Adolph had told him, "Don't say a word, Frank; don't say anything about it, and I'll see that you have a good job as long as you live."

Given this loose promise, Frank helped Adolph clean up the vile substance on the floor in front of the steam vat. He also threw ashes from the furnace room onto nearby railroad tracks. Later, detectives, sifting through these ashes, recovered pieces of a steel corset and bits of human bone. There was little doubt that Adolph had boiled his wife in a solution of potash until very little remained.

Adolph was taken into custody and stood trial for Louise's murder on August 23, 1897. All the incriminating circumstantial evidence was paraded before the jury. When Emma Schiemicke testified that she and her sister had seen Adolph and his wife enter the factory on the evening of May 1, the die was cast, for Emma was the only witness who could actually place Louise in the factory on the night of the murder.

During the course of the trial disconcerting rumors persisted. Well-intentioned citizens reported that they had seen Louise alive and well throughout the United States, Mexico, and Europe. These reports no doubt were instrumental in the jury's being unable to agree on a verdict.

A second trial resulted in a conviction. Adolph Luetgert, the man who boiled his wife, was found guilty of murder and sentenced to life imprisonment.

PERFECT MURDER, ALMOST

The old man had a difficult time explaining exactly when he decided to kill his son and daughter-in-law. The idea just formed in his mind, and like a cancerous growth continued to fester and expand.

Oliver Bishop, 74, lived in a house trailer in Tampa, Florida. He and his wife had separated some years before, but Mrs. Bishop still lived in Tampa. Oliver's adult son, George, and his pretty wife, Louise, lived with Oliver.

In 1939 accepted moral standards were not what they are today, and therein lies the crunch. George and Louise were not legally married. They were third cousins, and for some reason felt that if they sought professional advice, they would be told that they shouldn't marry. Instead, they held a private ceremony and considered themselves husband and wife in every sense of the word.

This arrangement did not sit well with Oliver. The old man begged his son to leave Louise. George tried to reason with his father, explaining that he loved Louise dearly and had no intention of ever leaving her. The small house trailer left little room for privacy and the three occupants bickered incessantly.

Each spring George, who was a woodcarver by profession, would make a deal with a carnival for employment for the summer season. He and Louise would join the carnival and be gone for several months. The knowledge that they would soon be leaving made each summer tolerable. Oliver could think of little else but the fact that his son was living in sin.

As spring approached George and Louise prepared to join the carnival and leave the house trailer. At the same time Oliver was planning to kill them both.

Cunning Oliver feigned illness. The 5 ft. 6 in., 150 lb. wisp of a man complained of being tired all the time. Within a matter of weeks he gave the appearance of being a weak semi-invalid.

The night before George and Louise were to join the carnival, Oliver decided to make his move. George was in bed asleep. Oliver made his way to a woodshed where he had hidden an iron sashweight. He then returned to George's room. Louise was up, combing her hair. Oliver raised the sashweight high above his son's head and sent the iron weight crashing down on George's skull.

Louise screamed and ran from the room. Outside, the terrified woman found herself trapped by a fence which she couldn't climb over. In an instant Oliver was at her side. One blow from the iron sashweight was enough to turn slim, attractive Louise into a limp heap lying on the ground.

Oliver carried both bodies to his son's car. He then took a shovel, quick lime, and a large cardboard box with him as he drove with his unique cargo to the muddy shores of McKay Bay. Once there, he lugged the bodies onto the shore and dug a grave. The bodies were then placed inside the cardboard box, liberally sprinkled with lime, and buried.

Oliver returned to the house trailer. He noticed a few small blood stains on the rear seat of the car, and rubbed some grease into the stains. The next day, using his son's identity, he sold the car. That same day bloody clothing and bed clothing were burned.

Oliver reviewed his handiwork. As far as anyone was concerned, George and Louise had gone away with the carnival. Next winter they would simply not return. He had committed the perfect crime. Somewhere, in the back of his mind, Oliver felt that he had done it all in God's name.

Fifteen days later two men were netting crabs along the shores of McKay Bay. Their endeavors were abruptly halted when they spotted a human arm sticking out of the sand. Police were on the scene in a matter of minutes, and extracted two bodies from the remnants of an old cardboard box. Both bodies had crushed skulls. The results of an autopsy indicated that the bodies had been buried some two weeks before they were found.

In order to identify the two victims police checked all missing persons in the area. They found that a Mrs. Oliver Bishop had reported her son missing. Mrs. Bishop felt that her son, a carnival worker, would not voluntarily leave Tampa without contacting her. She told investigating officers that her son George lived with his wife and his father in a house trailer. In this way, detectives came in contact with

Oliver Bishop, who identified his son's body. However, Oliver could offer no clue as to who would want to harm his son and daughter-in-law.

Detectives decided to try to find George's missing car. By dogged police work they located the used-car lot where the vehicle had been purchased from a George Bishop. Signatures were compared. It was obvious that someone had forged George's signature on the pertinent transfer documents. The car had been sold, but the new owner was located. He gave police permission to cut away two areas of the back seat upholstery, which appeared to be stained. The stains proved to be blood mixed with grease. There seemed little doubt that George's car had been used to transport the bodies to McKay Bay. Despite this, the investigating officers were no closer to identifying the killer.

Detectives now concentrated on the personal lives of the victims. They could find no apparent enemies; certainly no one who hated the couple enough to murder them. Inquiries revealed that George and Louise were not legally married and that George's father didn't approve of the relationship.

For the first time detectives turned to Oliver Bishop as a suspect. When this line of questioning was approached, Oliver acted as though he thought the police were insane. However, when the used-car salesman identified him as the man who had sold him George's car, the old man changed his tune.

Oliver confessed that he had killed George and Louise because he couldn't stand the moral stigma attached to their relationship. He had killed in God's name.

Police were puzzled about one thing. How did a feeble, 74-year-old man, weighing 150 lbs., carry the dead weight of his son's 165-lb. body out to the car and later from the car to the shore? Oliver illustrated this feat by picking up a 180-lb. detective and carrying him away without difficulty. The elderly gentleman was far from feeble. It had all been a part of his scheme to throw police off the trail.

Oliver came very close to committing the perfect murder. Had the tides off Tampa Bay not shifted the muck covering the bodies, murder would not have been suspected. As it was, he escaped being electrocuted because of his age. Oliver Bishop received a sentence of life imprisonment for the murder of his son and daughter-in-law.

MAUDE AND CLAUDE

In the tiny town of Dowagiac, Michigan, there are few who remember the Maude Cushing case. Those who do remember are elderly, and even today are reluctant to discuss the strange series of events which enraged Dowagiac nearly seventy years ago.

It all began when Claude Cushing, a 40-year-old, respected member of the community, became ill. His wife, Maude, immediately called in a doctor, who diagnosed Claude's illness as acute stomach trouble. Despite diligent nursing by his wife and daily visits from his mother, Claude's condition worsened. He died in January 1922, on the twenty-seventh day of his illness.

The family physician, who was present when Claude breathed his last, signed the death certificate, attributing death to "stomach complaints and heart trouble."

All things considered, the untimely death of Claude Cushing should have been forgotten. By being most indiscreet, Maude Cushing gave rise to rumors which precipitated one of Michigan's most notorious murder cases.

For a few weeks following the funeral, Maude, 38, and her three young sons mourned quietly at home. Then, without fanfare, Maude quietly left town. A short while later, the Dowagiac newspaper reported that Maude had married in South Bend, Indiana, only three weeks after her husband's death. The townspeople knew the groom well. He was Emory Storick, a former bus driver from Dowagiac, who had once driven a bus from Dowagiac to the lakeside towns of St. Joseph and Benton Harbor. Before moving out of town three years previously, he had known the Cushing family well.

News of the wedding occurring so soon after Claude's untimely demise swept through the town like wildfire. Was it possible that Claude had not died from natural causes? Folks remembered that Maude had had a summer cottage at Benton Harbor. Had Emory Storick been carrying on an affair with Maude? He had plenty of opportunity when he regularly drove his bus to Benton Harbor. Maybe that was why he left town. Who knows, maybe poor Claude Cushing had caught the lovers in the act?

The rumor mill around Dowagiac performed so well that the Michigan Department of Public Safety ordered a public hearing into Claude Cushing's death. Mrs. Storick was shocked at this turn of events, pointing out that she had requested that an autopsy be performed on her husband's body, but that this step had been rejected at the insistence of her late husband's parents.

Claude's body was exhumed and the vital organs were sent to the University of Michigan. In the meantime, life for the Storicks, who had returned to Dowagiac, became unbearable in the little town. Little else was discussed in the months which followed, while the Storicks, and indeed the whole town, waited for results from the university. They were not to be disappointed. The report stated that bichloride of mercury, a poison, was found in Claude's liver, intestine, kidney, and stomach. As soon as this report was received, Maude was arrested and charged with her first husband's murder.

At the trial which followed, an array of circumstantial evidence was presented by the prosecution. This evidence was contested by the defence, but such was the hostility against Maude Cushing that much of the rebuttal evidence fell on deaf ears.

The prosecution presented Claude's mother, who stated that she had seen Maude crush two white tablets and put them in Claude's tea. It mattered little that the defence later called the family physician, who testified that he had prescribed white tablets for his patient. The impression left with the jury was that Maude had substituted poison for the doctor's prescribed tablets.

The prosecution called the lady who owned the cottage Maude had rented in Benton Harbor. She testified that she had seen Emory Storick call on Maude during the summer months. Actually, it was most natural for Emory, a close family friend of the Cushings, to pay Maude a visit. Later, one of Maude's young sons testified that he slept in the same bedroom as his mother every night during the summer.

Evidence, pertinent to the defence, which should have made an impact on the jury, failed to do so. Young Richard Cushing testified that his father always used bichloride of mercury as a throat gargle. Another son testified that he had often purchased the poison for his father at the local drugstore. An independent defence witness was found who swore that Claude had once complained to her that his throat was raw from gargling with the poison.

Despite the evidence, a Michigan jury found Maude guilty of murder in the first degree. She received the maximum sentence of life imprisonment. An appeal was launched, but the verdict was upheld.

Year after year Maude languished in prison. Her husband tenaciously worked towards vindicating her. In 1931 he found a doctor who had warned Claude to stop using bichloride of mercury because, as the doctor stated, he was slowly poisoning himself. Eight surviving members of the original jury signed a petition stating that had they been aware of the doctor's testimony at the time of the trial, they would not have found Maude guilty. A parole board considered this new evidence before turning down Maude Storick's parole.

Slowly, some people who had been sure of Maude's guilt began to have doubts. Shortly after the trial, Homer Quay, the prosecuting attorney, felt that he may have sent an innocent woman to prison. Unfortunately, after telling his niece about his doubts, he died in 1925. Years later the niece revealed her uncle's feelings about the case.

In 1949 Mrs. Alean B. Clutts, a Detroit lawyer, became interested in the case and came into possession of a note sent to Maude from Claude's mother. It stated, "I am so guilty of what I have done to you. Forgive me." Lawyer Clutts petitioned the governor of the state for a pardon, claiming that Maude was innocent. As a result of this appeal, an investigation into the conviction was instituted. Maude was given a lie-detector test which indicated that she had not poisoned her husband. The attorney general reported to the governor that there certainly was some doubt as to her guilt. Maude was offered a parole, but on the advice of her lawyer refused to accept anything but a full pardon.

On October 23, 1949, Maude walked out of prison a free woman after receiving a full pardon from the governor of Michigan. Now a grey-haired 65, she had spent 27 years in prison for a murder she didn't commit. In fact, it is doubtful that any crime took place.

Ironically, upon her release, Maude found that the little town which was so quick to convict her of nothing more than suspicious circumstances had now forgotten the famous old Cushing case. Many citizens had died during the 27 years Maude had spent in prison. Others had moved away. A few years after her release, Maude died of cancer.

DEEMING LOVED CEMENT

Fred Deeming was a boisterous, free-spending, fun-seeking fellow. He loved to dress in tweed from his head to his toes. Fred could usually be found in the local hotel regaling fellow patrons with his tales of humorous and sometimes dangerous exploits around the world. Sucking on his ornately carved meerschaum, with a mug of stout before him on the bar, Fred kept the good citizens of Rainhill, England, amused all through the summer of 1892.

Rainhill was a fitting stage for Fred and his stories. Located in Lancashire, not far from Liverpool, his audience had no way of knowing that their drinking companion, whom they knew as Albert Williams, was really an ex-con who had been convicted of robbery, extortion, arson, bigamy, fraud, and embezzlement.

Williams, as he called himself, was of average height, sported a moustache, and was of medium build. One day he just showed up, ostensibly to purchase a home for a Colonel Brooks, whom he claimed was planning to retire in Rainhill. Williams explained that both he and the colonel had recently returned to England from Australia. He neglected to point out that in reality he had a wife and four children stashed away in Birkenhead, living with one of his brothers.

Albert, fast worker that he was, noted a rather plain but well-turned-out lass clerking at a stationery store close by his hotel. Emily Mather, who lived with her widowed mother, was attracted to the tweed-bedecked Albert. Within two weeks Al had proposed to Emily. Nothing like this had ever happened to her before. Would she marry Al? You bet your life she would. Quick like a bunny, the pair became engaged.

In the meantime, Al went about securing a home for the fictional Colonel

Brooks. He rented a semi-detached, seven-room house known as Dinham Villa, with the stipulation that after the colonel occupied the house for six months the lease could be renewed. Al made one small request of the owner. It seems that Colonel Brooks had a chronic phobia about uneven floors. Al noticed that the kitchen floor was definitely uneven. Did the landlord have any objections to Al's cementing over the floor? With an eye to having a floor replaced at no expense, the owner of Dinham Villa consented to the renovations. Al immediately ordered copious quantities of cement. Later it became obvious that cement was positively Al's favorite manufactured product.

Down at the hotel Al passed the summer evenings pleasantly enough. He informed his drinking companions that his sister and her four children were planning a short visit. Fortunately, he explained, they would be able to stay at Dinham Villa as the colonel did not plan to take occupancy of the place for some time yet.

A short time later the townsfolk noted a middle-aged lady and her four offspring dashing about Dinham Villa. No doubt Al's sister and her children had arrived. Strangely enough, all five occupants of the house didn't venture far from the backyard. As Al explained it, it was all quite logical. His sister and her children would be joining her husband in California in a few days. They simply wanted to spend as much time with Al as possible before moving on. Six days after arriving, they apparently left the quiet and comfort of Dinham Villa, for they were never seen again. Once the relatives departed, Al went about laying a new cement floor. He supervised the workmen himself. In a few days the job was completed.

Al, who was chock full of schemes and ideas, informed his dear Emily and her mother that he had accepted an attractive job in Melbourne, Australia. He and Emily would sail in November, but first they would marry. On September 22 the vows were duly exchanged. Six weeks later the newlyweds bid farewell to the good folk of Rainhill and departed for Melbourne. Mrs. Mather was never to see her daughter again.

The Williamses landed in Windsor, a suburb of Melbourne. Emily was somewhat puzzled as to why her husband insisted that they use the name Mr. and Mrs. Droven. However, times were different before the turn of the century. It was not Emily's place to question her husband. If he said their name was to be Droven, then Droven it would be.

At this time Emily's letters to her mother indicated that she was having the adventure of her life. In all of them she praised her husband. Then according to neighbors, the love affair between the Drovens seemed to cool. Actually, it turned to ice water. Sometimes, late into the night, it was obvious that they were not throwing kisses at one another. Neighbors figured that it sounded more like chairs and dishes.

On December 24, a particularly loud piercing scream emanated from the Droven residence. Later, the only unusual occurrence noted by neighbors was a rather large delivery of cement to the Droven domicile. On January 5 Mr. Droven left for Sydney and informed the owners of the dwelling that he was vacating the premises. They proceeded to list the property with a rental agency, which immediately commenced to show it to prospective tenants.

As time wore on these potential tenants complained about the decidedly repugnant odor evident as soon as they entered the house. The rental-agency people were inclined to agree. They called in the police to locate the cause of the offensive smell.

In the bedroom fireplace, under freshly poured cement, the police found Emily's body. Her head had been smashed in with a blunt instrument and her throat had been slashed. On a table in the bedroom was a Bible. Inside the cover was the name of the previous owner, Mrs. E. Mather, Rainhill, England.

While the police searched for the elusive Mr. Droven they also began tracing his trail back to Rainhill. Mrs. Mather sadly confirmed that the murdered woman was no doubt her daughter. She also informed police that while Droven, whom she knew as Williams, had lived in Rainhill, he had redone the floor of Dinham Villa with cement. Not only that, but a woman and four children had stayed in the house.

Dinham Villa, which was still vacant, was searched by police, who tore up the kitchen floor. The bodies of a woman and four children were recovered. All except a baby had had their throats cut. The infant had been strangled. The victims were identified as Deeming's wife and children.

Now Deeming's murderous activities occupied the front pages of two continents. Indeed, most of the English-speaking world awaited his capture. All of this activity seems not to have bothered Deeming at all. Posing as Baron Swanston, he met a cute little number named Kate Rounsfell on the boat from Melbourne to Sydney. By the time the sweet-talking Baron disembarked, he and Kate, believe it or not, were unofficially engaged.

The pair made their way to Bathurst, where Kate introduced her fiancé to her parents. They were duly impressed. Making some excuse or other the Baron left Kate and her family and made his way to Southern Cross.

He wired Kate enough money so that she could join him. En route to her lover she was informed that the police had picked up her Baron as a suspected multiple murderer. Kate turned right around and went back to her parents. For the rest of her life she knew that she had come within a whisker of ending up under some cement floor or other.

Deeming was transported from Perth to Sydney, to Adelaide, to Melbourne. Everywhere the prisoner was taken huge crowds formed to catch a glimpse of the infamous murderer.

At his trial Deeming's attorneys attempted to prove that he was insane, but their efforts were futile. A jury brought in a verdict of guilty with a rider that, in their opinion, the prisoner was sane and knew the difference between right and wrong.

When asked if he had anything to say before sentence was passed, Deeming surprised the court by speaking for over an hour, claiming that he certainly was insane because he didn't even remember killing his wife and children back in Rainhill, England.

Deeming was hanged in Australia for the murder of Emily Mather. Had he managed to evade punishment for this crime, he would have been extradited to England to stand trial for the murder of his family.

The memorabilia of Deeming's crime have gradually been obliterated. For years his wax image was displayed in Madame Tussaud's Chamber of Horrors in London, England. In more recent years new monsters have taken his place in infamy. Dinham Villa, where five innocent people were murdered, was a sore reminder of the Deeming case. The owner of the property had it demolished, giving strict instructions that not one brick remain.

THE BANNISTER
BROOD

In 1936, the population of Pacific Junction, New Brunswick, located about 10 miles outside of Moncton, was an even dozen. Among those who called Pacific Junction home was the Lake family, which consisted of Phil, 30, his wife Bertha, 28, son Jackie, 20 months, and the baby of the family, four-month-old Betty. Big Phil Lake and his family lived in a 26 by 10 ft. home in a little clearing in the woods near the CNR railway tracks.

Eight miles away in Berry Mills lived May Bannister and her four children, Daniel, 20, Arthur, 18, Frances, 14 and Marie, 13. May Bannister had been deserted by her husband shortly after Marie's birth. The family had lived in abject poverty ever since.

They sold blueberries, cut firewood, and snared rabbits to eke out a meagre existence. Often, they wandered the streets of Moncton looking for day-old bread. None could read or write. Both boys were of below average intelligence.

Strangely enough, the members of these two families would become the main characters in a murder case which would make New Brunswick history and capture the imagination of the entire nation.

On Monday, Jan. 6, 1936, Otto Blakeney was cutting firewood near the Lakes' home. Normally, he ate his mid-day meal with the Lakes. Otto was shocked to find nothing but a smouldering burnt-out ruin where once the Lake home had stood. Upon closer examination, Otto made out the horribly burned body of Phil Lake.

He scurried down the railway track toward the CNR office. Tiny droplets of blood were clearly visible in the fresh snow. Every hundred yards or so there were larger blood smears, as if someone had fallen and risen, only to fall again. Further on, Otto came across a baby's bottle.

Exactly 471 yards from the Lake's home he sighted the frozen body of 20-month-old Jackie Lake. A few yards further on was Bertha Lake's almost nude body. The snow beside the body was thrashed, giving mute evidence that, after dropping her son and falling herself, Bertha had made vain attempts to rise before dying alone in the snow.

Otto raised the alarm and soon the RCMP was on the scene. An entire family had been wiped out in one night. Although four-month-old Betty's body was not recovered from the blackened ruins, it was assumed that it had been totally consumed by the flames. Phil's body, minus his burned off arms and legs, was readily identified by two conspicuous gold teeth. Why had someone annihilated the Lake family? The answer was soon forthcoming.

Police noted what appeared to be two sets of tracks beginning in the snow where Bertha had died in agony and leading into deep woods. Utilizing snowshoes, the police followed the tracks. They observed small holes in the deep snow beside the tracks, as if someone had used some sort of cane while trudging along.

RCMP Sgt. Bedford Peters, following closely along the trail, found a mitten. It would become the most important piece of evidence in one of the weirdest murder cases in Canadian history.

Meanwhile, CNR employee David Barron volunteered that around nightfall the day before he had seen one of the Bannister boys walking the tracks. Mounties called on the Bannister home and were greeted by Daniel. Shown the mitten found along the trail, Daniel exclaimed, "Hey, that's mine, where'd you guys get that?"

Questioned further, Daniel stated that he had loancd his mittens to his brother Arthur on the previous day. David Barron identified Arthur as the man he had seen walking along the tracks. Arthur was arrested and charged with murder.

Arthur confessed, admitting that he had visited the Lakes' home. Daniel and Frances showed up to take him home. Phil Lake made an improper advance to Frances. A brawl had ensued, in which Bertha was accidentally struck on the head by a piece of firewood thrown by her husband. Daniel then hit Phil on the head with another piece of firewood, at the same time overturning an oil lamp.

According to Arthur, the three Bannisters took off and never looked back. No doubt Bertha Lake ran from the fire and collapsed, dropping her baby, who froze to death while she died from the wound to her head. In a general way, Frances and Daniel backed up their brother's story. Daniel was taken into custody and charged with murder. Frances was held as a material witness.

The murder victims were duly buried. It was then that the Bannister-Lake case took a bizarre twist. While questioning a neighbor of the Bannisters', one Milton Trites, the police learned that there was a baby at the Bannister home. RCMP officers faced May Bannister with this information. Reluctantly, she turned the baby over to the officers. When asked who the mother of the child was, she curtly replied, "It's mine." In reality, the baby was four-month-old Betty Lake, who for a week was believed to be dead.

May had concocted a diabolic plot. In order to give the appearance of having given birth to a baby, she had sometime before purchased a doll at the Metropolitan Store in Moncton. She was seen by several people carrying a bundle, which everyone assumed was a baby. When questioned, all admitted that they had not actually seen the child. Why did May Bannister pose as the mother of a doll, and later somehow come into possession of the Lake baby?

Milton Trites had befriended the Bannisters for years. He often loaned May small amounts of money. During the previous year she had worked for him as a housekeeper. When she left his employ in November 1935, she told him she was leaving to have his baby. She did in fact go away for some time. When she returned she told Trites she had left their child in Moncton. On the day after the Lake murders she invited Trites to her home to see his baby.

It was also learned that Albert Powell, a CNR freight clerk and part-time Sunday school teacher, had conducted Sunday school classes at the Bannister home for about two years. He was often alone in the company of Marie Bannister. May had accused Powell of being responsible for Marie's fictional pregnancy.

It was obvious May Bannister was planning to blackmail two men into supporting two nonexistent babies. There was one tricky detail. At some point May had to produce a real live baby.

Evidence given by Frances Bannister further incriminated her brothers. She stated that, together with Arthur and Daniel, she arrived at the Lake house around 7 p.m. on the night of the murders. Arthur went in the house. When he came out, he passed her the baby and she started home alone. She heard a scream. Shortly after, her two brothers caught up with her.

During their investigation, the RCMP heard persistent rumors that big, tough Phil Lake could not have been overpowered by a boy with a piece of wood. Phil's body was exhumed. Doctors removed a .22 calibre bullet from his brain.

Now, the cane-like marks in the snow beside the tracks took on a new significance. Maybe they were made by a rifle. Volunteers shovelled tons of snow from the area along the trail. The tedious task paid off. The rifle was recovered and proved to be the murder weapon.

Daniel and Arthur Bannister were tried for the murder of Philip Lake. Both were found guilty and sentenced to death. On Sept. 23, 1936, the two brothers were hanged in the County Jail at Dorchester, N.B. No one claimed their bodies.

May Bannister, who no doubt hatched the plot, and ordered her dull, obedient sons to carry out her evil scheme, was found guilty of harboring a stolen child. She received the maximum sentence of three and a half years imprisonment. May served her time and returned to Berry Mills, where she lived on, a rather feared curiosity, until 1971, when she died of natural causes.

WHO CAN YOU TRUST?

What has happened to the standards by which normal folks live? Where has decency gone? Is anyone to be trusted? These are some of the questions the 332 citizens of Underwood, Minnesota, are asking themselves.

Chances are you never heard of Underwood. The tiny community is located in dairy country southwest of Duluth. Because the rich pastureland is sprinkled with lakes, the area is a popular tourist attraction. Names such as Turtle, Bass, and Otter Tail dot the map in that section of western Minnesota.

Underwood was virtually free of violent crime. In Duluth, maybe, but never in Underwood, where neighbors relied on each other through good times and bad, where doors were often left unlocked. That is, until between 6 and 7 p.m. on May 29, 1985, when 13-year-old Sara Ann Rairdon disappeared while walking the four and a half miles from school to her home just east of the town.

Sara was a popular youngster. She was an honor student attending the seventh grade. She was also a valued member of her school's track team. On the evening of her disappearance, she stayed late at school to do extra work on a home economics project.

The Rairdon family was distraught. Sara's father, mechanic John Rairdon, 38, made impassioned pleas over television, urging his daughter's abductor to return Sara safely to her family. Everyone in town knew how John felt about his family. Nine years earlier, when he and his first wife, Linda, were divorced, he obtained custody of their five children, including Sara, their only daughter. In 1975 John married his present wife, Marilyn, who brought four children from a previous marriage to the union. Together John and Marilyn had two more children.

The community of Underwood gathered around one of its own. A massive search was conducted throughout the area along County Road 122, where the child was last seen. No trace of Sara was uncovered. The community dug deep. Eight thousand dollars was raised. John Rairdon worked elbow to elbow with other members of the community late into the night, stuffing Sara's photograph into envelopes, which were sent to all 50 states and neighboring Manitoba.

Despite the search parties, despite the flyers, no trace of Sara was uncovered until July 6, over six weeks from the day of her disappearance.

About 25 miles from Underwood, a farmer noticed that his cattle were shunning a small section of his pasture. Initially, the farmer paid no attention, but when the grass grew tall in the neglected patch, he figured there was something there which discouraged the cattle from eating. He walked over and discovered the body of Sara Rairdon. Sara had died as the result of a puncture wound to the left side of her abdomen.

The community of Underwood was stunned; the Rairdons were devastated. What maniac had committed such a horrific crime? Surely the madman was an outsider. Yet there were those who pointed out that the tourist season had hardly begun when Sara went missing. Others pointed out that the back road leading from the school to her home was rarely utilized by strangers. It was beyond belief that a local resident could be the perpetrator of such a crime.

Some members of the community had difficulty coping with the tragedy which had taken place in their midst. Volunteers organized a meeting of parents and children in an attempt to better comprehend Sara's disappearance and death. John and Marilyn Rairdon attended the meeting.

Sara's funeral took place on July 9. The citizens of Underwood, along with the Rairdon family, gathered in the town's gymnasium to mourn the loss of Sara Ann. Some citizens will never forget the heart-rending scene of one of the younger Rairdon children sitting on their father's knee at the funeral service. Tears streamed down John Rairdon's face.

Shortly after the funeral, John joined a group known as Search and Find Missing Persons Inc. The aim of the group was to assist in the search of missing children. As one who had been personally touched by the death of a daughter, it was only natural that John Rairdon acted as chairman of the board of directors of the organization.

Then, in mid August, a rumor spread through the town of Underwood. It couldn't be. Had the entire community been deceived or was it all a terrible mistake? As the hours passed that Aug. 14, it became apparent that no mistake had been made. Under question by police, John Rairdon had confessed to his daughter Sara's murder.

According to court records, John revealed that he had been sexually abusing his daughter for the past five years, since she was eight. In recent months, Sara had resisted his advances. Rairdon related that on the day of her death, he had picked Sara up in his truck as she walked home from school. He drove the youngster to an abandoned farmhouse, where he attempted to have sexual relations with the child. When she resisted he became angry. He took an awl from his truck and stabbed Sara in the abdomen. John then hid Sara's body in the farmhouse, returning later that night to transfer the body to the farmer's pasture some miles away.

John Rairdon's family was understandably numb with shock. Marilyn Rairdon was completely unaware of what was taking place in her own home. Married to a man who sexually abused his own child for five years, she could only say, "He was a caring parent and husband." Later, she said, "He's going to pay for it. He'll never see his family grow up."

Social workers questioned the other Rairdon children, and satisfied themselves that none were abused by their father. Sara's school friends were also questioned. The little girl had told no one of the ordeal she was living through.

Underwood had been deceived by one of its own. The citizens felt betrayed. The hours of work, the thousands of dollars raised and spent, the strained emotions, all for naught. John Rairdon had known who had killed his daughter for the three months during which he had accepted their concern, love and assistance.

A scholarship fund was set up in Underwood in memory of Sara Ann Rairdon. Her father's confession complicated matters for the volunteers who raised $2,500 as a reward for the capture of Sara's killer. They considered donating the reward money to the scholarship fund. John Rairdon was to be on the committee to decide who should receive the scholarship.

Meanwhile, Rairdon had his day in court. He was found guilty of intrafamilial sexual abuse and guilty of murder in the first degree. John Rairdon was sentenced to 13 years imprisonment for the murder of his own daughter. The sentences are to run consecutively. The outside world has heard the last of John Rairdon for a long, long time.

A DUTIFUL
DAUGHTER

Fifteen-year-old Theresa Gresch never liked her mother. Still, that's no reason to assist in hitting her over the head with a hammer, stabbing her repeatedly and encasing her body in plaster of Paris.

Theresa's physical charms were those of a well-developed 22-year-old. She was like a frisky filly chafing at the bit to be serviced by the stallions on the other side of the fence.

Theresa's 43-year-old mother, hard-working Anna Gresch, had her own strict code of conduct. It didn't include lipstick, nylon stockings or low-cut blouses. Anna ran a tight ship. She had lost her husband some years before when Theresa was still a tyke. It wasn't easy in 1954 for a single parent to bring up a daughter in New York, particularly since Anna had to work all the time to keep the wolf from the door.

Anna put in eight hours on the assembly line at a shoe factory and worked an average of three nights a week as a charwoman in an office building. She and her daughter lived at Avenue B and 13th St. in Manhattan. It was three floors up to their cold water flat. In the half year they lived there Anna had fixed the place up and had purchased some furniture. Although it was slum living, their flat was clean and comfortable.

Although Theresa had a high I.Q. and attended high school, she had no interest in school work. Instead she craved the trappings of the mature woman. To Theresa this meant makeup, smart clothing and, above all, a boyfriend. She and her mother quarrelled over these little matters constantly.

On the night of Feb. 18, 1954, Theresa hit paydirt at a neighborhood dance. His name was Billy Snyder. Billy, an older man at 17, walked Theresa home. She poured out her tale of virginal woe. Billy understood. In fact, he could cure Theresa's particular malady for all time.

There were practical problems. Theresa's mother was between jobs in the char business and was home every night. Billy's mother was home ill, so his apartment was not available. For seven days the young couple wandered the streets of New York expressing their love for each other, but were at a complete loss as to where to consummate those sly biological urges which Theresa just had to satisfy. That sort of thing can be frustrating.

At last, Mrs. Gresch received a call to clean an office building. No sooner was she out the door than Billy scampered up those three flights of stairs into Theresa's arms and bed.

Wouldn't you know it? Mrs. Gresch finished work early. When she returned home there was Theresa, wearing nothing but a smile, in bed with Billy. Mrs. Gresch screamed, ranted and raved. Then she unceremoniously kicked Billy out of her home.

Mrs. Gresch and her wayward daughter had several heart to heart chats. It must be remembered that her daughter's welfare was the focal point of her life. When she pulled the reins too tightly Theresa threatened to run away. A compromise was reached. Billy would be allowed in the Gresch home. In return, Theresa and Billy would refrain from doing whatever they did between the sheets.

The deal worked for exactly two weeks. On the night of March 4, Mrs. Gresch wearily dragged herself up the three flights of stairs to her home. She turned the key and walked in. This was too much. Those kids had no respect. They were at it again.

A terrific argument ensued. Billy picked up a hammer and struck Mrs. Gresch about the head several times. Blood gushing from her head, she staggered into the kitchen. Billy returned to Theresa's side in bed, but it was tough to concentrate with Mrs. Gresch moaning in the kitchen.

Annoyed, Billy jumped out of bed, surveyed the situation in the kitchen and asked for Theresa's assistance. Theresa passed Billy a knife. He proceeded to stab Anna Gresch 21 times. Together the two teenagers mopped up the bloody floor and lifted the body into a laundry tub. Then they went to bed in peace and quiet.

Next morning Theresa and Billy went shopping with $13 taken from Mrs. Gresch's purse. They bought a yellow light bulb to add atmosphere to their lovemaking. They also purchased some plaster of Paris, which they mistakenly thought would act as a decomposing agent if sprinkled over the body. For four consecutive nights they had friends over to the flat for dancing and a few beers. The door to the kitchen was kept closed.

On the fourth night of partying, a friend, Richie Aylward, commented that he detected a disagreeable odor coming from the kitchen. Billy explained, "It's Theresa's mother. I killed her and she's in there rotting away."

What are good friends for? Richie helped sprinkle some more plaster of Paris on the body. He told no one what he had learned that night.

On day five, Billy felt it was time to vacate the scene. He left the flat and enlisted in the Marines, stopping long enough to phone Theresa, asking her to wait for his return.

In the days which followed, Theresa continued to throw the occasional party. When the urge struck her, she and good friend Richie made love. Theresa later pointed out that Richie was little more than a surrogate lover, keeping things warm, so to speak, for Billy's return.

The good times abruptly came to an end when neighbors complained to police of a disagreeable odor emanating from Apartment 3B. Investigating officers found the body of Anna Gresch, now encased in a solid layer of plaster of Paris.

Questioned by detectives, Theresa told the whole story. Billy was brought back to the Big Apple from Beaufort, South Carolina, where he was stationed with the marines. Faced with Theresa's confession, Billy unhesitatingly told the police, "I did it." He mentioned that Theresa had passed him the knife with which he had stabbed Anna Gresch. Theresa had neglected to include this embarrassing bit of information.

While in custody, Billy wrote often to Theresa. One line is worthy of repetition. Billy wrote, "I killed your mother." Prosecuting attorneys thrill at confiscating letters like that.

The two teenagers were brought to trial. Theresa gained some measure of fame as the youngest person to be tried for murder in New York State.

Both accused repudiated their confessions, each changing pertinent details to cast the other as the true culprit. Billy now claimed that Theresa had killed her mother and had merely enlisted his help in washing the blood off the floor and encasing the body in plaster of Paris. His lawyer had a difficult time dismissing Richie Aylward's testimony and that incriminating letter.

Theresa, for her part, swore that she never passed Billy any knife. She claimed she was in bed when the dastardly deed took place in the kitchen.

Billy was found guilty of murder in the first degree, and Theresa of murder in the second degree. She was sentenced to 20 years to life in prison. After serving 14 years Theresa was released at the relatively young age of 30. Her present whereabouts are unknown.

Billy wasn't quite as fortunate. In January 1956, after walking unassisted and chewing bubble gum, Billy Snyder was executed in Sing Sing's electric chair.

MINNIE WAS UNFAITHFUL

Everyone remembered when Ed Schroeder started acting strange. It was in the middle of June 1880, when his friends noted that the happily married, outgoing Oakland, Cal. banking executive became sullen and withdrawn. It just wasn't like Ed not to sit in on a card game with the boys or root home a nag on a Sunday afternoon. Concerned friends inquired, but Ed was noncommittal.

In an attempt to snap out of his depressed state of mind, Ed applied for two weeks' vacation from the London and San Francisco Bank where he was employed. The request for an immediate vacation was denied. Ed was fortunate not to be fired when he took the vacation anyway. Evidently, after eight years with the bank, his superiors chose to overlook this one indiscretion. When Ed returned from his unscheduled leave, nothing had changed. He still was not the old Ed acquaintances had once known and respected.

Eight years before that fateful summer of 1880, Ed had married Minnie Stebbins. Now Minnie wasn't your average run of the mill girl. Not by a long shot. No, Minnie was the daughter of bigwig Rev. Horatio Stebbins. The Reverend held the position of Regent of the University of California, trustee of Stanford University and other assorted prestigious posts.

Rev. Stebbins made it very clear that he was opposed to the match. In order to break up the romance he organized a little trip to Europe for Minnie and her aunt. They were booked to depart on June 6. On June 5 Minnie circumvented her father's scheme by becoming Mrs. Edward F. Schroeder. Defeated, the Reverend cancelled the trip.

Once the die was cast, Minnie's family accepted Ed. In the ensuing years Minnie gave birth to two children. The young couple bought a home in a middle class Oakland suburb. Sarah Gallagher, their reliable live-in maid, was like a member of the family. All was right with the world for six contented years.

What, you may ask, happened to disrupt this picture of domestic tranquillity? You won't believe this. The family came to grief all because Minnie developed a toothache. She consulted the most popular dentist in Oakland, Dr. Alfred LeFevre. This proved to be a mistake. LeFevre, the father of four children, was a handsome devil, well regarded by his patients and a pillar of the community. You get the idea, a real rock.

We have no idea how many visits it took before the dentist and his patient became intimate. We do know that Minnie had extensive work done on her teeth. She was a regular patient for two years.

On June 11, 1880, Ed returned home early from the bank. As he entered he thought he heard someone exiting by the rear door. He asked his good wife Minnie. She replied that it was the maid, Sarah Gallagher. There was something in her voice which caused Ed not to believe his wife for the very first time in their married life. That evening he could think of little else than the mysterious back door. He bugged Minnie all night until finally she blurted out, "It was Dr. LeFevre." Minnie confessed to having intercourse with the doctor in the master bedroom while the children slept peacefully in another room only a few feet away.

Ed, half-crazed with his new found knowledge, got the bright idea that he would verify how many times his wife had been intimate with the doctor by examining her dental bills. He discovered that in two years of visiting the doctor, Minnie had never received a bill. Ed consulted with Minnie's father. The very next day the two men marched into the dentist's office and demanded to see Minnie's dental bill. Dr. LeFevre couldn't produce a bill or an appointment book. It was obvious that whatever services he was performing on his dental chair came free of charge.

Ed brooded. His friends readily noticed the drastic change in his personality. Things came to a head on July 26 when Ed walked into Dr. LeFevre's office just as a Mrs. Keeney was having a tooth drilled. Ed pulled out a pistol and shot the dentist in the head. The doctor staggered, then fell. It was the most exciting dental work Mrs. Keeney ever had done.

Before he died Dr. LeFevre said, "Schroeder shot me without any provocation from me, or any cause for so doing." After he told this whopping lie, he died.

Meanwhile, Ed ran from the office and told the first policeman he could find, "I just shot a man. No man can seduce my wife and live."

Ed was taken into custody and charged with first degree murder. By the time he came to trial on Nov. 29, 1880, he had achieved the status of hero for plugging the lecherous dentist. Naturally enough, a probing Assistant District Attorney had different ideas. A man was dead. Ed had shot him while he worked on the now famous cavities of the very unfortunate Mrs. Keeney.

A gunsmith testified that Ed had purchased a pistol on July 26, the very day of the shooting. This pistol proved to be the murder weapon. The Assistant D.A. didn't need much more. Ed had the strongest possible motive for killing LeFevre. He had coolly purchased the murder weapon, indicating premeditation. A witness had observed the killing. As if this wasn't enough, Ed had confessed to killing the man who had seduced his wife.

Counteracting this veritable mountain of strong evidence, Ed's attorneys brought forth the case of provocation. An array of witnesses paraded to the stand to relate the abrupt change in Ed's behavior when he found out his wife was bedding down with her dentist. Experts testified that despite the purchase of the murder weapon on the day of the crime, Ed had been so depressed that he had killed his adversary while temporarily insane.

In directing the jury, the presiding judge pointed out that the horizontal activities of Mrs. Schroeder and her dentist could not be used as an excuse for killing a man. However if the knowledge had driven the accused man insane, the jury must acquit him.

The jury took a full three days to mull over the only question in dispute. Was Ed insane when he bought the gun and shot the dentist? After their lengthy deliberation they found Ed Schroeder not guilty.

Everyone was happy with the verdict. Minnie and Ed left the courtroom hand in hand. Because of the notoriety of the two remaining participants in the case, they left Oakland a few months after the trial and were never heard of again.

We can only assume that Minnie Schroeder never required further dental work.

SHE WASN'T A GOOD MOTHER

Can a woman murder eight of her nine children over a period of 14 years and go undetected? That's what the 70,000 citizens of the factory city of Schenectady, N.Y. are asking themselves.

Mary Beth Tinning, 44, was born in the area back in the war years when the local General Electric plants employed 45,000 workers churning out strategic war materials. That large figure has steadily declined, and today 12,000 are gainfully employed at G.E., still the largest industry by far in Schenectady. The town, adjacent to Albany, has seen better days.

Joe Tinning worked at General Electric as a systems analyst. He and Mary Beth moved frequently over the years. No one gave it much thought. The area around Albany, the state capital, is surrounded by villages and towns. It is difficult to ascertain where one stops and the next one begins. There was one thing different about the Tinnings. They suffered tragic misfortune with their children - all nine of them.

On Jan. 3, 1972, the Tinnings' new baby, Jennifer, died while still in hospital. She was eight days old. Jennifer is the only Tinning death not considered to be suspicious. Seventeen days later, on Jan. 20, two-year-old Joseph died. Understandably, the Tinnings were devastated. But there was more to come. On March 2, 1972, four-year-old Barbara died.

What a horrible experience for any family to endure. In two months less a day all three Tinning children were dead. Their deaths were attributed to natural causes.

Those who knew the Tinnings offered their sympathy. It happens. There was little anyone could do.

Nine months later, Mary Beth gave birth to a son, Timothy. On Dec. 10, 1973, 14 days after his birth, Timothy died. The cause of death noted on the death certificate is SIDS (Sudden Infant Death Syndrome). In its purest sense, SIDS is not a cause of death. It really means that the cause of death is unknown.

With Timothy's death occurring so soon after being taken home from hospital, rumors spread among the Tinnings' few acquaintances. Was it possible that there was something wrong with the Tinnings' genes, some imperfection which caused their offspring to die suddenly?

Just under two year's after this tragedy, five-month-old Nathan died. His death was attributed to acute pulmonary edema. When Nathan died on Sept. 2, 1975, various individuals in official capacities, such as doctors and social service workers, became somewhat suspicious. However, it must be pointed out that the same doctors and social workers were not necessarily involved in all the deaths. Autopsies were performed on all the Tinning children. The results were always the same. Death was attributed to natural causes.

Dr. Robert Sullivan, the Schenectady County Medical Examiner, admitted that when Nathan died, he was aware of the earlier deaths. Nathan's death was thoroughly investigated, but no evidence of foul play was found. Dr. Sullivan revealed, "The parents were doing nothing wrong. They were initiating examinations into the deaths of the children."

Joe Tinning had a responsible position at the G.E. plant. He was an avid bowler. Over the years, Mary Beth often worked as a waitress to supplement the family's income. Sometimes she served as a volunteer ambulance driver. There was absolutely nothing to distinguish the Tinnings from their neighbors. Absolutely nothing except the inexplicable deaths of their children.

After Nathan's death, three and a half years passed before Mary Beth gave birth to another child, a daughter, Mary Frances. The beat continued. Mary Frances died at age three and a half months.

Ten months later, Mary Beth had a little boy, Jonathan. He died three months later, on March 24, 1980. That same year, the Tinnings adopted a son, Michael. He died a year after Jonathan, on March 2, 1981.

Michael's death put an end to the theory that some kind of black genetic evil was at work causing the strange deaths of the Tinning children. After all, he was adopted. An autopsy was performed. The official cause of death was listed as viral pneumonia. Now, suspicions ran rampant. Although there was no proof of any wrongdoing, pediatricians and social workers advised police that should any further Tinning children die, a forensic pathologist should be called in immediately.

Eight children were dead. It seems unbelievable that, despite an extensive investigation into some of the deaths, nothing more than dark suspicions were cast in Mrs. Tinning's direction. The bodies of Timothy and Nathan were exhumed, but nothing new was found.

Over three years passed. Mary Beth became pregnant for the eighth time. She gave birth to Tami Lynne, who died four months later, on Dec. 20, 1985. This ninth death initiated a massive investigation. I have been unable to unearth just what, if anything, investigating officers uncovered. Evidently, a tip concerning Tami's death came from someone attached to the Schenectady County Social Services Department's Child Protective Unit.

On Feb. 4, 1986, Mary Beth was picked up by detectives and taken to the nearby State Police Headquarters at Loudonville. Under intensive questioning, which lasted a total of 10 hours, Mary Berth admitted killing three of her children, Timothy, Nathan and Tami.

She was duly arrested, lodged in jail and charged with two counts of second degree murder concerning Tami's death. More specifically, she was charged with one count of "having intentionally caused her daughter's death by smothering her with a pillow," and in the other count "with showing depraved indifference to human life by engaging in conduct which caused Tami Lynne's death." The maximum penalty for second degree murder in New York state is life imprisonment. The minimum penalty is from 15 to 25 years.

On March 19, after spending a month and a half in jail, Mary Beth Tinning was released on $100,000 bail. She immediately instituted court proceedings to have her confession deemed inadmissible evidence at her impending murder trial.

Mary Beth professed that her constitutional rights had been violated when the confessions were obtained. The suppression hearing into this charge was concluded in April. As a result, the details of what was said on the night Mary Beth confessed to detectives can now be made public.

The first statement, given in narrative form, describes how Mary Beth smothered Timothy, Nathan and Tami, "With a pillow, because I'm not a good mother. I'm not a good mother because of the other children." She also said, "I did not do anything to Jennifer, Joseph, Barbara, Michael, Mary Frances or Jonathan."

In a second question and answer session with detectives, Mary Beth gave more details of Tami's death. She arrived home that night, five days before Christmas in 1985, at about 8:35 p.m., after being out shopping with a friend. Her mother-in-law and father-in-law had been baby-sitting four-month-old Tami. They, as well as her friend, left at about 9:30 p.m. Mary Beth sat in a recliner chair with Tami on her lap. After a while she put the baby to bed.

Mary Beth related, "I tried to give her a bottle, but she didn't want it. She fussed and cried for about a half hour. She finally went to sleep. I then went to bed." Joe came home at 11 p.m. They chatted for a few moments.

"I was about to doze off when Tami woke up and started to cry. I got up and went to the crib and tried to do something with her to get her to stop crying. I finally used the pillow from my bed and put it over her head. I did it until she stopped crying." Mary Beth went on, "When I finally lifted the pillow off Tami, she wasn't moving. I put the pillow on the couch and then screamed for Joe and he woke up and I told Joe Tami wasn't breathing."

It was this chilling recital that Mary Beth attempted to suppress. However, a county court judge ruled that her statements would be admissible at her upcoming murder trial. He also ruled that they had been given willingly and voluntarily.

While awaiting her murder trial, Mary Beth and her faithful husband Joe moved to Ballston Spa, a tiny community about 25 miles outside Schenectady. The prosecution's case was prepared by District Attorney John Poersch. He was quick to point out, "Mrs. Tinning's rights must be protected. She is only being tried for the murder of one daughter, Tami. Joe Tinning is not a suspect in the case."

In a city where two murders a year is the average, the Tinning case was the main topic of conversation. District Attorney Poersch guards what he says, but as I left his office he assured me, "The Grand Jury made a proper indictment and I'm sure we will gain a conviction."

They did. Mary Beth Tinning was convicted of murder and sentenced to twenty years to life imprisonment, a sentence she is presently serving.

I drove to the Most Holy Redeemer Cemetery and removed the snow from the tiny markers indicating the final resting place of the Tinning children. None of them reached five years of age.

PIECES OF A PUZZLE

A small percentage of murderers insist on dissecting their victims and scattering the assorted parts hither and yon in an effort to escape detection. This distressing practice has, on occasion, puzzled me, for having completed such a tiresome task, the murderer invariably displays a marked disregard as to where he or she distributes the gruesome portions.

Take the O'Leary family of Kilkerrin, County Cork, Ireland, for example. Let's see now, there was Mrs. Hannah O'Leary, a spry little lady of 75. Unfortunately, Mr. O'Leary does not take any part in our little drama, having gone to his great reward three years previously. Before departing this mortal coil, he sired two sons, Patrick and Cornelius, and two daughters, Hannah and Mary Anne.

When Mr. O'Leary died, he left the small farm to his wife. After her death, the farm was to be passed on to the eldest son, Paddy, with certain conditions. Mary Anne was to receive £350 outright, while Cornelius and Hannah had the right of residency for life. This type of will was very common among the many small farmers of Ireland in 1927, when our macabre tale takes place.

For all intents and purposes, Paddy, who was in his mid-forties, was the head of the household. He was hard-working, stern and gruff. He was not beloved by all. Cornelius, who was called Con by everyone, was rather shiftless and preferred working for others rather than toil on the family farm. Hannah and Mary Anne were plain girls who had obviously been overlooked by the lads of the county.

On Feb. 26, 1927, a neighbor observed Paddy working on the farm. When that same neighbor called on him the next day, he was met by Con, who explained that Paddy had gone to Bandon Fair early that morning to sell a colt. That explanation was fine for day one, but as each day passed with no sign of Paddy, tongues began to wag.

A couple of things bothered those who knew the family. Neither Con, the two girls, nor even Paddy's mother, seemed to be unduly concerned about his absence, yet no one could remember Paddy ever leaving the farm for any prolonged period of time. Then there was the colt Paddy was supposed to be selling at the fair. As anyone could see, it was grazing right there on the farm.

On March 7, Paddy's disappearance was at least partially solved. Ten-year-old Frank Wash was crossing a field on the O'Leary property when he came across a potato sack. There, staring unsmiling up at him was the bashed and bruised head of Paddy O'Leary. No one clocked Frank, but he made it home in more than a canter and told his mother of his grisly find. She immediately informed police.

The Irish police took sack and head to the O'Leary farmhouse. Displaying an admirable degree of tact, they placed the head on the kitchen table for the family's inspection. No one screamed. No one fainted. Police were amazed at the calmness, even nonchalance, of the family. Con said, "That's Paddy all right." The two girls agreed. Even Mama O'Leary, looking down at the head of her eldest offspring, didn't bat an eyelash.

Does it ever rain that it doesn't pour? The very next day, a farmer nearby found one of Paddy's arms, complete with shirt-sleeve. That afternoon, Paddy's torso showed up down the road a bit. Then, horror of horrors, the O'Leary dog waddled to the front door of their farmhouse, carrying Paddy's other arm in his mouth.

The funeral was a joyous Irish affair. Paddy was "laid out" in an open coffin in the living room. It was a larger wake than usual. Many farmers from distant points of County Cork were curious about the juxtaposition of Paddy's assorted sections. As toddies were raised, there were some who felt displaying Paddy like that was not the Christian way. But never mind, everyone had a good time, except, of course, Paddy.

With the festivities out of the way, Irish detectives thought it a good idea to look into the murder. Certainly the O'Leary family's behavior was far from normal. All the members of the family were questioned. Not too bright Con was the most demonstrative. Before a question could be put to him, he declared, "Should God strike me dead, I am innocent. My hands are clean."

After he settled down, he told detectives that he last saw Paddy on Feb. 26, when his older brother said he was going to Bandon Fair. Con admitted that he and his brother didn't get along. Since the death of their father, the two brothers rarely spoke. Con said Paddy was a bully, who didn't want to pay him for working on the farm. For that reason, he usually worked elsewhere.

Con claimed that he had not been concerned about Paddy, because he expected him to show up at any moment. Hannah and Mary Ann agreed with their brother in every detail. So did Mrs. O'Leary. Because there were no discrepancies in all for statements given by members of the family, detectives felt it was possible that the entire family had taken part in the murder.

Detectives searched the O'Leary home. Paddy's bed had been made up with fresh bedding since his disappearance. The bed's wooden frame had been wiped clean, but blood was found in tiny wormholes in the wood. Blood was also found in cracks in the floorboard under the bed. No doubt Paddy had been killed as he slept. One side of his head had been crushed with a plank or pole. Because of the crowded sleeping arrangements in the house, it would have been impossible for one member of the family to have committed the murder without the others at least having knowledge of the crime.

Taking no chances, the Irish police arrested all four members of the O'Leary family and charged them with murder and conspiracy to commit murder.

Before she could be brought to trial, Mary Anne died in prison of cancer. The charges against the elderly Mrs. O'Leary were dropped. During the course of the trial, no mention was made of Mrs. O'Leary or Mary Anne. Con and Hannah stood alone.

Prosecuting attorneys put forward a great deal of damaging evidence indicating that Paddy was murdered in his bed. They even found a discarded bloody mattress on the farm. There was bad feeling between the two brothers. Although there was no way of ascertaining who had struck the fatal blows, the prosecution suggested it didn't matter which one killed and which one helped dispose of the body. Both were equally guilty. No one, other than the two on trial, was remotely suspected. No one else had been on the farm. No one else had reason.

A Mr. Travers, who often hired Con, told the court that Paddy had complained to him on several occasions about employing Con. Travers fired Con, giving as his reason Paddy's annoying calls. Con reacted like a wild man and swore revenge against his brother.

Why had Hannah consented to the murder? Several witnesses testified that Paddy was offensive and overbearing to his two sisters. Hannah told several neighbors over the years that she hated her brother.

Gradually the evidence painted a picture of a gruff, overbearing elder son alienating his entire family, until they conspired to kill him in his sleep. Only death and old age spared Mary Anne and Mrs. O'Leary from standing trial.

Defence lawyers could do little to cloud the picture of hate. They could only stress that all the evidence was circumstantial. Neither defendant testified.

It took the Irish only half an hour to find both the accused guilty of murder. When asked if he had anything to say before being sentenced, Con could only utter, "I had not hand, act or part in the murder." The presiding judge sentenced both the accused to death.

On July 28, 1928, Con O'Leary was executed. Three days before that date, Hannah O'Leary had her sentence commuted to life imprisonment. Hannah spent 14 years in prison before being released in 1942 to enter a convent.

BROTHERLY LOVE

I think I am safe in saying there was no love lost between the brothers Kirwan. Truth is, they hated each other's guts.

Laurence and Bernard lived on a 75 acre farm in Ballycloughan, about six miles from Tullamore in the midlands of Ireland. After Mother Kirwan went to her great reward in 1937, her other four sons and daughters left the farm, leaving Larry in charge. He shared the small farmhouse with hired hand John Foran.

Where was Bernie? Well, a year before Mummie's demise, Bernie had donned a mask and equipped himself with a sawed off shotgun. Thus prepared, he accosted a postman who was pedalling his bicycle down a peaceful Irish lane near Rahan. Bernie relieved the postman of £29 in cash. Arrested, the impetuous Bernie received seven years imprisonment for his trouble.

In June 1941, Bernie was paroled after serving four years of his sentence. He returned to the family farm to find things far different than when he took his enforced vacation. Larry had taken over the farm. It didn't help matters that Larry referred to older brother Bernie as "that jailbird."

Events down on the farm simmered, boiled and then exploded. Larry had had enough of his wayward brother. One rainy night he locked Bernie out of the farmhouse. Furious, Bernie knocked down the door. A violent fight took place. The two men squared off in the kitchen. One of the brothers grabbed a knife. As they wrestled on the floor, both received cuts about the hands and arms.

As a result of the fight, the two men refused to speak to each other. Larry gathered up all the food in the house and locked it in a large cupboard. Thereafter, he refused his brother food. He and Foran ate alone as Bernie sulked around the house.

Larry also hid the keys to the family automobile.

On Friday, Nov. 21, Larry and Foran attended a fair in nearby Tullamore. Larry sold a few head of cattle, receiving cash for his livestock. He bought a sack of flour and returned to the farm. After dinner, from which Bernie was excluded, Foran left on Bernie's bicycle for the nearby village of Clara to pick up a watch which was being repaired. When he returned around midnight, Larry was nowhere to be found. In Tullamore, a Miss Flannery waited in vain for Larry to show up at 8:30 that evening.

Foran questioned Bernie, who was busy ironing some clothing. His inquiries met with the rather economical reply, "Larry's gone." Foran suspected something was amiss. Bernie was wearing Larry's overalls. Besides, there was food on the table. It was not locked up as usual. Bernie even offered Foran a glass of cocoa, which was gratefully accepted. Foran then went to bed and slept like a baby until 9:30 that morning.

When he awoke, Foran again inquired about Larry.

Bernie told the hired hand that he had already been to mass that morning and met his sister, Mrs. Conroy. She told him that Larry was in Kildare taking care of a farm owned by their aunt. Foran accepted the story, but wondered why Larry hadn't taken the car for such a trip.

Later that same day, Bernie sent Foran to Clara on an insignificant errand. When Foran returned, he was sent to a far field of the farm to do rather unnecessary work. It appeared to Foran that Bernie didn't want him around the farmhouse. Soon after he was relieved of his duties and left the Kirwan farm forever.

Coincidental with Larry's absence, the good folk around Tullamore noticed that Bernie was spending money rather freely. He paid off old debts and bought a new suit, all without any visible income. Rumors spread, until word reached police that Laurence Kirwan had mysteriously vanished. A member of the force paid a visit to Bernie and was taken aback by his nonchalant attitude. Bernie didn't seem to give a damn about his missing brother. He readily admitted that he hadn't reported his brother missing to the police. He told the officer that on the night of Nov. 22, he left his brother at home and went out to visit his sister, Mrs. Conroy. He returned some time after 1 a.m. to find his brother and his own bicycle missing. He hadn't seen either since. The officer conducted a cursory search of the house and the farmyard before leaving. He was far from satisfied with Bernie's story.

In the month following Larry's disappearance, farmers of the area talked of little else. Police drained a nearby canal without results. A photograph of Larry was distributed to police agencies throughout Northern Ireland. A further search of the

Kirwan home uncovered Larry's pipe, wallet, and watch. It was well known that the missing man would never leave home without these items.

Now convinced that Larry was a murder victim, police confiscated his clothing. They were able to account for all his garments, except one overcoat. While they searched for this overcoat, who should show up in Tullamore wearing the coat but brother Bernie. He had dyed the coat a dark brown, but it was unmistakably Larry's coat. Positive that Larry could not have left the farm in the nude, police now actively searched for his body.

On May 30, Joseph Bracken and John Dunne were digging clods of turf out of Ballincur Bog, located a mile and a half from Kirwan's farm. One of the prongs of Bracken's fork caught on a half-open sack. The two men peered inside. What they saw were the decomposed remains of what had once been portions of a human body.

State pathologist Dr. McGrath could not help to identify the body. However, the sack containing the human remains was the same as those used on the Kirwan farm. It was believed that the portions of the body were those of Laurence Kirwan.

Bernie was taken into custody and charged with his brother's murder. At his trial it was proven that he had his brother's money and overcoat immediately after the disappearance. Dr. McGrath described the gruesome contents of the sack. He could only say that the sack had been in the bog for several months and that the remains were that of a person between 25 and 50 years of age. The victim had been attacked with a hatchet. Dismemberment had been performed by a person with some skill, such as a butcher. Bernie was a well-known butcher of livestock in the area.

Bernie Kirwan took the stand in his own defence. He proved to be a stubborn, arrogant witness. Bernie accounted for wearing his brother's overcoat by claiming it was really his coat, which he had loaned to his brother while he was away in prison. He stated that since his release he had been given the loan of money by a man he would not name.

Occasionally, in a tension-packed courtroom, one single question and answer crystallizes the plight of the accused. Such a moment took place in the Kirwan case when Bernie was being cross-examined. The lawyer for the prosecution led Bernie to the last time he had seen his brother alive. Laurence was standing in front of a mirror preparing himself for his date with Miss Flannery. Bernie was directly behind him. The prosecution attorney asked, "Perhaps, sir, it was your last view of your brother?"

Bernie answered, "It could have been." Suddenly the lawyer asked, "Was that the time, sir, when you struck him from behind?" There was a long pause. The color drained from Bernie's face. He struggled to gain his composure. Finally, the judge had to interject, "Well, Kirwan, what is your answer?" Bernie replied, "I didn't think I had to answer such an absurdity. I never struck the man."

Bernie never seemed to recover from the tense moment. It appeared to everyone in court that the prosecution attorney had correctly guessed the exact moment at which the first blow had been struck.

Evidently, the jury was convinced that the portions of the body found in the sack were that of Laurence Kirwan. Bernard Kirwan was found guilty and hanged for his crime on June 2, 1943.

The late Irish playwright Brendan Behan based his famous play, *The Quare Fellow*, on the Kirwan case.

A FAMILY AFFAIR

This is the tale of two families, their aspirations, their struggles and their tragedies.

Patrolman Bill McCue lived with his pretty wife Mary and their two children in an apartment in Queens, New York. The children - a boy, six years old, and an infant daughter - were the apples of their father's eye.

Bill knew that he would never own the world on a police officer's salary, but by keeping a tight rein on expenses over the years, he and Mary had managed to put away enough money to place a healthy down payment on a house in Elmont, Long Island. That year of 1962, the McCues were planning on moving into their new home. The future looked bright.

William Geiry and his wife Shirley had been married ten years. They had five children, ranging in age from two to nine. The recent history of the Geiry marriage was not a happy one, but it was improving.

William had met Shirley when he was stationed at Fort Bragg, North Carolina during the Korean War. Shirley, a native of Georgia, was then 16. She married William and returned to New York with him upon his discharge from the service.

William obtained a steady job as an accountant, but with Shirley pregnant most of the time, he just managed to keep his head above water. Shirley, an extremely beautiful woman with glistening red hair and a voluptuous figure, worked as a part-time waitress between pregnancies.

There was one fly in the ointment. After nine years of marriage Shirley disappeared for two weeks without any explanation. William loved his wife dearly. Upon her return he forced himself to forgive her.

The second time Shirley mysteriously disappeared, William decided to investigate. He called on several restaurants where his wife had worked over the years and found out she was in the habit of dropping into a bar not far from Pennsylvania Station. William's worst fears were well founded. His wife had a lover - a police officer - Patrolman Bill McCue. William was devastated.

When Shirley returned home he told her of his new-found knowledge. Exasperated, she blurted out, "Yes, it's true, but don't worry, he's married. He's got a couple of kids and he lives out in Queens."

William's common sense was overruled by his love for his beautiful Shirley. Once more he chose to overlook his wife's behavior. Nothing changed. In September, Shirley disappeared. William had the very practical problem of looking after five children while holding down a steady job. Each week he expected Shirley to return. When she didn't, he had no choice but to call the proper authorities and reluctantly have his children placed in institutions.

After six weeks Shirley returned to find the children gone. She appeared to be heartbroken, but once again confessed to seeing Patrolman McCue. Williams laid down the law. Shirley would have to prove to him that the prolonged affair was over. She would have to settle down. No more absences. Then, and only then, would the children be returned. Surprisingly, Shirley agreed to this arrangement.

From September through the holidays and into January, Shirley was the ideal wife. She rose well before William left for work. Each morning she prepared a full breakfast. Upon his return for dinner many of his favorite foods were laid out in an attractive manner. In every way imaginable Shirley was the ideal wife.

On the night of Jan. 9, William was welcomed home with a kiss and hug. A sumptuous meal was consumed in the presence of his cheerful, amusing wife. Next morning, breakfast was delicious. William was given a goodbye kiss at the door. There was little doubt in his mind, Shirley was a new woman.

After William left, Shirley met Bill McCue at a restaurant on Eighth Ave. Hand in hand that bitterly cold January morning, they walked to the Hotel Evans at 273 West 38th St. They registered as Mr. and Mrs. Bill Mason and were given the key to Room 414.

In a small apartment in Queens, Mary McCue was packing a few fragile items herself. She and Bill would run them over to their new home when he got off duty. Across the city William Geiry pored over the ledgers in an accounting office, content in the knowledge that his wife had turned over a new leaf.

Loud explosions startled occupants of the fourth floor of the Hotel Evans. They opened their doors to see Shirley Geiry run into the hall, crying hysterically, "Oh, my God, oh my God, what have I done?" Someone called police. Patrolmen Joseph Di

Giovanni and Francis Jennings were the first officers at the scene.

Shirley met them in the hall. She attempted to explain. "I was supposed to turn the gun on myself, but I lost my nerve. I couldn't do it." Patrolman Jennings entered Room 414. He was amazed. The dead man was a fellow officer he knew well. They both worked out of the same precinct. Bill McCue had been shot four times; in the heart, chest, right shoulder and left leg. When questioned, Shirley revealed that the murder weapon was in the top drawer of a bureau. The police officers retrieved a small five shot .38 calibre Smith and Wesson revolver from the drawer. It was empty.

By now homicide detectives were at the scene. Shirley again tried to explain, "We had decided to die in a love pact." Her pleas fell on deaf ears. No one believed her. At the West 30th St. station house, Shirley changed her story. "We were playing Russian roulette and he was killed." Detectives gave each other the eye. It's not an easy task to shoot yourself four times playing Russian roulette.

Shirley finally broke and gave her interrogators her third story, which is probably the truth. "I loved Bill. I loved him very much. I'd have gone anywhere with him. Anywhere he would take me. But he couldn't. He was married and had two children. I begged him to leave his wife the way I was willing to leave my husband, but he wouldn't do it." Then Shirley put the motive for her lover's murder in a nutshell. "If I couldn't have him, nobody else could either."

Mary McCue hurriedly put tissue paper around some delicate cups and saucers before dashing out to her part-time job at a factory. She and Bill needed every cent to pay for the new home they'd be moving into the next day. That's where the Rt. Rev. Monsignor Joseph A. Dunne found her to inform her that her husband had been shot to death in a hotel room by his lover.

William Geiry was summoned to the Hotel Evans by police. He was told on the phone of his wife's involvement. William calmly prepared some food before racing to the hotel. He was allowed a few words with Shirley. As they talked, Shirley sobbed that she was sorry. William took her hands and placed her fingers around a paper bag he had brought with him. It contained two sandwiches and a Thermos of coffee.

Shirley Geiry was sentenced to life imprisonment for the murder of Patrolman Bill McCue.

MARTHA REACHED HER BOILING POINT

Do we all have a breaking point? Can a series of circumstances drive us beyond the limit of our endurance? Martha Place reached her breaking point on the morning of Feb. 7, 1898 in New York City.

But let's start at the sad beginning. Willie Place, an insurance salesman who had lost his dear wife, was left with his motherless 12-year-old daughter, Ida, to guide through puberty. At the outset, Willie noticed that Ida spent most of her time brooding. Eventually, he realized that his daughter longed for the responsibility of looking after him and their home. Willie gave little Ida a free hand. It worked, after a fashion.

Soon Willie was inundated with gourmet meals. Ida turned out to be a veritable whiz at conjuring up dishes laced with Indian spices and French sauces. Sometimes Willie longed for a simple pork chop. That's not all. Ida insisted on cleaning and dusting, polishing and shining. Willie felt as if he was living in a hospital operating room.

After a while it became obvious to Willie that it wasn't natural for Ida to be performing the duties of a maid and caring for her father's every need. He decided to hire a housekeeper.

That's when our Martha enters the scenario. All her life Martha had worked hard as a mother's helper and seamstress, professions not guaranteed to produce any worthwhile degree of adventure or financial security. Besides, at 44 and developing those telltale crow's feet at the corners of both eyes, Martha felt she was riding past the Last Chance Saloon and out to pasture. She jumped at the opportunity to be housekeeper for Willie Place and his Ida.

Martha threw herself into her work and at Willie. In three months he proposed. Martha had grabbed the golden ring and caught it. She and Willie were wed.

It took a couple of years for things to curdle. For one thing, Martha and Ida just didn't get along. The teenager felt that her position had been usurped by the interloping Martha. Martha hated that kid. Then there was the realization that nothing much had changed from her housekeeping days. Now Martha was a married housekeeper. Lastly, all that business of sex, which Martha had only known by hearsay, was a disappointment. Willie was an indifferent lover.

Martha made up her mind to remedy the situation. For starters, she hired a maid, Hilda Palm, to do the heavy work around the house. She then started an all-out campaign to arouse placid Willie to greater performance on the connubial couch. Despite employing girlish charms which had lain latent for so many years, nothing seemed to interest Willie. Believe it or not, he often claimed to be suffering from headaches.

Martha grew nervous. The truth is, she probably was slowly slipping into that grey realm where it is difficult to distinguish right from wrong. Whatever, Martha's frustration was taken out on anyone with whom she came in contact, but particularly Ida. That girl could do nothing right. The two women argued incessantly.

One day Martha gathered up Ida's new bonnet, hosiery and underwear. She cut the clothing into tiny strips and left the pieces on Ida's bed. No doubt about it, Martha was operating in never never land.

Martha next attempted to make a clean break. She approached Willie, suggesting that she leave his bed and board forever. Willie thought it was a great idea, until Martha asked for $300 as sort of severance pay. Willie dickered. Would $150 be enough?

"Not by a long shot," Martha roared. It was $300 or she stayed put. Willie would have to think about it. In the meantime, Martha required $20 to run the house. Willie told her to go whistle. Martha was close to the boiling point. That temperature was reached on Feb. 7.

Willie left for his office, after refusing Martha her household money as usual. He wasn't out of the vestibule before Martha and Ida were at it again. Martha inquired of Ida, "Did he give you any money?" Ida replied in her usual good natured manner, "None of your business." Then she threw a cigarette box at her stepmother and ran to her room. Martha followed.

Where was maid Hilda Palm while all this was taking place? How did she react to living in a house where there was continual fighting? Well, Hilda was a rock. She did her work, kept her eyes open and her mouth shut. Sure, Hilda saw things on Feb. 7. Later, she would tell a jury that Mrs. Place called her upstairs to her room that morning and informed her that the house was being closed and that her services would no longer be required. Hilda was promised an extra $5 in lieu of notice and told that her mistress didn't want to be disturbed for the rest of the day. Martha also told Hilda that she was leaving her husband. Hilda took all this in her usual stolid fashion.

Martha then had Hilda deliver a message to her one friend, a Mrs. McArran, informing that startled lady that she was leaving her husband and leaving New York. Mrs. McArran was shocked. She dashed over to Martha's side. The two friends embraced. Martha told Mrs. McArran that Ida was to be sent to a boarding school. With a tear in her eye, Mrs. McArran took her leave.

Martha went upstairs. She entered Ida's room. As the angry girl lay on her bed crying, Martha tossed acid in her eyes and slowly placed a pillow over her head. Ida would cry no more.

At 6:30 p.m. Willie arrived home to a warm welcome. Martha swung an axe at his head as he entered the house. She missed but, showing a marked degree of persistence, swung the vicious weapon a second time. This time her accuracy improved somewhat. Willie suffered an ugly gash to his left arm. Finally, screaming like a banshee, Willie made it out the front door.

A neighbor called police. In moments they were on the scene and systematically searched the house. They found Ida on the bed, where she had been asphyxiated by her stepmother.

Martha was found in another room, huddled under blankets in a corner. Two gas jets in the room had been turned on, but Martha was still alive. She was carried out of the room by police and revived.

Martha was arrested and charged with Ida's murder. At her trial, she vehemently proclaimed her innocence. When asked if she was the murderer, she replied, "I did not, as God is my judge, I didn't do anything of the kind."

Martha gave her version of how the horrible accident had happened. She claimed that she and Ida had argued, after which Ida went to her room. She opened her husband's desk. Groping in the dark, she removed what she thought was a goblet of headache powders. Instead, by mistake, she had taken a goblet of acid, which Willie kept locked in his desk. He sometimes used the acid when working at his photographic hobby.

When she and Ida commenced to argue again, Martha thought she was tossing harmless headache powders in her stepdaughter's eyes, rather than acid. As Martha said from the witness stand, "Mistakes are bound to happen." Maybe so, but no one believed Martha's story. Headache powders were normally kept in the Place's bathroom and not under lock and key.

Martha Place was found guilty of murder. One cold winter's day in New York, she reached her breaking point and had to pay the price. She was the first woman to be electrocuted by the state of New York.

ALL IN THE FAMILY

There are weird families and there are weird families. The Poeschkes of Frankfurt, Germany, rank right up there with the weirdest.

Originally, Anna Poeschke fled from East Germany to the West with her two small children, Dieter and Renate. Left behind in the care of his grandmother was a second son, five-year-old Juergen. The Poeschke family settled in Frankfurt. Sixteen long years passed. Little Dieter and Renate grew up to be fine-looking, healthy adults. Dieter became an automobile mechanic and made a respectable living.

Meanwhile, back in East Germany, Juergen evolved into something of a renegade. As he grew up, he balked under the restrictions imposed by the Communist state and was forever getting into serious trouble. For one thing, he made several attempts at fleeing and was always apprehended. Once he attacked a Russian army officer. On that occasion, the family thought he might end up in jail, but Juergen was let off with a stern lecture and a suspended sentence.

A few months after this unpleasant incident, the Communists decided to rid themselves of selected troublemakers. Juergen was one of those selected. To his surprise and elation, in 1973, he was kicked out of the country. After a 16-year separation, he was reunited with his family in Frankfurt.

Of course, the tight little family unit of 16 years earlier had changed somewhat. Mother Anna lived alone. Brother Dieter, now 22, had managed to get his 15-year-old girlfriend, Sylvia, in deep trouble. As each month slipped by, Sylvia realized that whatever lunar regularity her body had become accustomed to in the past was now conspicuous by its absence. Sylvia was pregnant. When she approached Dieter with news of the impending blessed event, she was thrilled that he insisted on doing the right thing. Dieter married Sylvia. They rented a two-room apartment with the express intention of living happily ever after.

Sister Renate, now a fully-blossomed 24-year-old, had married Hans Appel, who owned a successful construction company. Hans, at 34, was a self-made man. He had started out as a stone mason and by the sweat of his brow had built up a prosperous business. Renate had been married previously, and brought a six-year-old daughter, Claudia, with her when she became as one with Hans. He, in turn, had also had an unsuccessful marriage, which contributed four-year-old Lydia to the union. It is pleasant to relate that Renate and Hans produced baby Tanja without outside help.

This, then, was the growing family in whose arms Juergen found himself upon his expulsion from East Germany. Dieter had only been married for two weeks when Juergen showed up. Because of Sylvia's delicate condition and their cramped living quarters, it was decided that Juergen would move in with Hans and Renate. Things went well for a couple of weeks. Hans, who was out of the house attending to his construction company most of the time, was later to state that he liked Juergen and made him welcome in every way.

Then the most unbelievable thing happened. I mean really, folks - the sauerkraut hit the fan.

Hans came home late one night. Before retiring, he looked in on the children. Six-year-old Claudia was wide awake. She told her daddy that she had spent a most unusual day. "How come?" inquired Hans. Claudia described how Mommie dearest and Uncle Juergen took off all their clothes and jumped into bed. They closed the bedroom door, but that didn't keep little Claudia from hearing giggles and groans coming from the bedroom. Hans stood transfixed. Brother and sister! Absurd. The child must be lying. But Claudia never told fibs.

Hans poured himself a stiff one. They couldn't be brother and sister. That had to be the answer. Next morning, after a sleepless night, Hans looked up a friend who worked for the government and had access to Juergen's personal documents. When Hans was shown a photostat of Juergen's birth certificate, he was convinced. His wife was involved in an incestuous relationship with her brother.

Hans, a man of action, decided to face Renate and Juergen with his amazing accusation. That very day, the confrontation took place. There was quite a scene but Hans noted that neither party denied the accusation. Hans ordered Juergen out of his home. Renate, never the shrinking violet, stated firmly that if Juergen left, she would leave with him. And that's how it turned out. Brother and sister walked out of the house together.

The odd couple moved in with Sylvia and Dieter. They were only in their new cramped quarters a day when pregnant Sylvia was told to mind her own business and stay in the kitchen. The noises emanating from the bedroom left little doubt in Sylvia's mind. Juergen and Renate, brother and sister, were having sex. Could anything be sicker? Yes, Sylvia's own husband, Dieter, was in that bedroom as well. The two brothers were having sex with their sister. Sylvia figured that she might have married into the wrong family.

Let's get back to poor Hans. A week passed. It was tough running the business and looking after three children. Hans decided to forgive and forget. He attempted to get in touch with Renate, but she wouldn't speak to him. He had to relay his messages to his wife through his brother-in-law, Dieter. One must remember that Hans believed Dieter was unaware of any unusual behavior on the part of Juergen and Renate. The only message Dieter related back to Hans was that Renate wanted a divorce.

On Jan. 7, 1974, Hans needed his car repaired. It was only natural that he have his brother-in-law Dieter, the auto mechanic, do the repairs. When the job was completed, Dieter drove over and picked up Hans. They planned on returning to the garage, where Hans would drop off Dieter and drive away with the vehicle.

During the rather long drive, Hans became depressed and decided to confide in Dieter. He told him of the conversation with little Claudia. While it appeared there was an incestuous relationship taking place between Renate and Juergen, he knew there just had to be some other plausible explanation. Maybe it was a one-time crazy thing that was deeply regretted by both participants. Whatever, he desperately wanted his wife back.

Dieter looked Hans in the eye and responded in the most shocking manner, "But Hans, both of us have Renate all the time." Well, folks, Hans just happened to have a neat little Beretta on him at the time. He saw red. Three shots poured into Dieter. Hans pushed him out of the car onto the street and drove home.

A pedestrian saw the body being dumped on the road. She called police and gave a rough description of the car and driver. Dieter was readily identified. It was only a matter of minutes before detectives were informing Sylvia, Renate and Juergen that someone had ventilated Dieter. You could hear the wailing for blocks. Did they know anyone who had anything against Dieter? All swore they couldn't think of a soul.

During the course of their investigation, police dug up Anna Poeschke. She listened to the description of the car and the driver being sought by police. "Why that's my daughter Renate's husband, Hans Appel. But he would have no reason to harm Dieter."

Police scurried to the Appel residence. There was Hans, having a brandy to steady his nerves. When asked if he killed Dieter, he readily confessed, and it is his story of the events that we have related here.

On July 29, a Frankfurt court listened to Hans' strange tale of incest and accepted it at face value. Justice was lenient. Although found guilty, Hans was sentenced to 21 months imprisonment.

Charges of incest were initiated against Renate and Juergen, but these charges were dropped for lack of evidence, namely the unwillingness of either party to admit to the relationship. When last heard of, Renate and Juergen were living in Wiesbaden.

Possibly the understatement of the year was delivered by Mama Poeschke when she told police, "All my children were always very affectionate toward each other."

7

FAMOUS
NAMES

D.B. COOPER

The 37 passengers responded to the announcement that Northwest Airlines Flight 305 was about to take off. Flying time for the 727 between Portland, Oregon and Seattle, Washington was 25 minutes. This flight would take much longer.

It was a trip none of the 37 passengers would ever forget. On that U.S. Thanksgiving evening of Nov. 24, 1971, one of their number would become part of American folklore, as a cross between Robin Hood and Jesse James.

Dan Cooper unobtrusively strolled aboard the aircraft. Stewardesses Florence Shaffner and Tina Mucklow welcomed him aboard. D.B. Cooper, as he came to be known due to a reporting error, took a seat by himself at the rear of the aircraft.

Moments after takeoff, D.B. pressed the button requesting a stewardess' assistance. Miss Shaffner responded. Silently D.B. handed her a folded piece of paper. Miss Shaffner, an attractive brunette, had been approached in many different ways since becoming a stewardess. This was a novel move. She was later to tell authorities, "I thought he was trying to hustle me." Then she read the note.

In simple language it was a demand for 10,000 twenty dollar bills and two sport parachutes. Otherwise the plane, its passengers and crew of six would be blown up. Miss Shaffner gulped as D.B. flipped open his suitcase and revealed two red cylinders attached to coils of wire. To this day no one knows if the contents of D.B.'s briefcase held a real bomb constructed of dynamite or merely highway flares. D.B. closed his briefcase and the contents were never seen by anyone again.

Miss Shaffner walked briskly to the cockpit and passed the note to Captain William Scott. He radioed Seattle for instructions. They, in turn, immediately contacted local police, the FBI and Northwest Airlines president Don Nyrop. Instructions were not long in coming. Tersely they were told, "Do whatever he demands."

Scott informed his passengers that there would be a slight delay in landing due to minor mechanical difficulties. Meanwhile, officials on the ground were gathering up and photographing $200,000 in twenty dollar bills.

For three hours the 727 circled Seattle before beginning its descent. Once on the ground, the passengers were informed of the real cause of the delay. They breathed a collective sigh of relief when D.B. accepted a bag from a Federal Aviation Administration official. The laundry sack contained 21 pounds of twenty dollar bills. D.B. then inspected the two parachutes brought aboard as instructed. Satisfied, he dismissed all passengers and Miss Shaffner with a wave of his hand.

Flight 305 again took to the air. D.B. dictated notes to attendant Tina Mucklow, who passed them on to Captain Scott. Cooper instructed the pilot to head for Reno at an altitude below 10,000 feet, keeping flaps down and cruising at 200 miles per hour. After being assured that his wishes would be carried out to the last detail, D.B. escorted Tina Mucklow to the cockpit and gave firm orders that no one was to leave the cockpit area.

A few minutes later a red light flashed on Scott's control panel, indicating that the plane's rear boarding ramp had been unlatched. At 8:10 p.m. a second red light indicated that the ramp was fully extended. The aircraft was behaving somewhat erratically due to the extended ramp. Scott, at a loss for words, inquired over the P.A. system, "Anything we can do for you?" There was no reply.

It is believed that D.B. parachuted over a wilderness area north of Portland, which includes the tiny village of Ariel, Washington. A snowstorm was raging outside, while the temperature was 7 below zero. The crew of the 727 continued on to Reno, landing hours later without coming out of the cockpit.

Back in Seattle, passengers and stewardess Florence Shaffner were questioned extensively. They were able to provide surprisingly little in the way of helpful information regarding D.B.'s disappearance. Most had not really seen the skyjacker and had no reason to pay particular attention to him since they were not aware a skyjacking was taking place until they had landed. Miss Shaffner did her best. D.B. had been wearing a brown business suit and sunglasses. That was pretty well it. He wasn't noteworthy in any way. The 727 was searched for clues, but D.B. left nothing behind except unanswered questions.

Did he parachute out of the aircraft at 8:10 p.m. into a driving snowstorm or did he parachute out later, extending the ramp as a subterfuge to throw police off his track? Did he survive? Above all, who in tarnation was D.B. Cooper?

For over eight years nothing was heard of D.B. Cooper. Many admired the idea of an individual planning and executing the daring skyjacking without hurting anyone. To police, he is the criminal responsible for hatching a diabolical plot which placed 42 lives in jeopardy.

Whatever your feelings, D.B. Cooper caught on. First came the t-shirts, then the movie, then the songs. You can even sip a D.B. Cooper cocktail in many western U.S. bars. No question about it, D.B. became an American folk hero.

On Feb. 12, 1980 the man without an identity again made his way into the headlines. Children on a family picnic about 32 kilometres outside of Portland found a bundle of decomposed twenty dollar bills. The FBI verified that the serial numbers of the bills, which totalled $6000, matched those of the bills handed over to D.B. eight long years before. They also verified that all the bills were from one bundle.

Did the recovered money provide any answers or did it lead to more unanswered questions? Was that rascal D.B. clever enough to toss away $6000 so that searchers would believe he died in the lonely woods upon landing, or did he really perish and was his body ravished by wild animals?

The mystery continues to intrigue Laurel and Dave Fisher, the owners of the Ariel Store and Tavern in Ariel, Washington. Each year, on the Saturday following the U.S. Thanksgiving, they celebrate D.B.'s dramatic jump on D.B. Cooper Day. Laurel tells me that there generally isn't that much excitement in Ariel, whose population is about 100, with another hundred or so "within shouting distance."

However, on D.B. Cooper Day all that changes. Over 450 patrons sign the guest book on the big day. Dave stocks up with 100 cases of beer and barrels of chili for the guests, some of whom come from as far away as England. You can purchase D.B. Cooper t-shirts and an engraved certificate attesting that you are a member of the D.B. Cooper fan club. The party starts at 10 in the morning and ends at 2 the next morning.

Did finding some of the ransom loot in 1980 put a damper on the fun in Ariel? "Not on your life," replies Laurel Fisher. "It added to the speculation. Among our customers it's about 50-50 whether old D.B. is dead or alive. We all hope he shows up for a bowl of chili and a beer on D.B. Cooper Day."

So does the FBI, Laurel, so does the FBI.

JEAN HARLOW

There are many similarities between Marilyn Monroe and Jean Harlow. Both were blonde sex symbols who achieved fame and fortune in the movies. Both had several husbands. Above all, the deaths of both ladies were surrounded by mystery and intrigue. The details of Miss Monroe's life and untimely death are well documented in some 40 books, in itself a tribute to her charismatic personality and lingering popularity. Jean Harlow's life is not as well known.

Jean was born Harlean Carpentier in Kansas City on March 3, 1911. When she was only 16, she ran away and married wealthy bond broker Charles McGrew. The young bride returned to her parents and received their blessing.

The McGrews settled down in California, where they lived off the income from a fortune inherited by McGrew. Two years later they were divorced.

Still only 18, with an outstanding figure, good looks, and almost white, flowing hair, Jean entered the entertainment world by accident. One day she drove a friend to a movie studio. A motion picture executive noticed her and sent her to the Central Casting Office. She immediately received work as an extra and was noticed by famed movie maker Hal Roach, who signed her to a five-year contract.

She worked for months in small walk on parts until 1930, when millionaire Howard Hughes chose her to play the lead in the movie *Hell's Angels*. The ensuing publicity and the movie itself made Jean Harlow a star. Overnight, young girls were copying her sultry walk. Women across the country were dying their hair platinum blonde.

Jean met Paul Bern, assistant to the head of production of M.G.M. Studios. Bern was 22 years Jean's senior. He had come up the hard way, starting off working for $3.50 per week for the Produce Exchange Co. in New York. Later he entered the Academy of Dramatic Arts and was bitten by the entertainment bug. Bern travelled to Hollywood, worked as a film cutter, became a script editor, then director, until finally at age 37 he achieved the status of supervisor at M.G.M. Soon after he was promoted to assistant of production.

Bern was well liked and respected in Hollywood. An extremely intelligent, introspective man, there were many who thought there never was a more unlikely pair than Jean Harlow and Paul Bern.

The Hollywood crowd was surprised when Harlow and Bern married. It was a sudden affair. Jean and Paul both had unbreakable schedules on July 2, 1932, the day they were wed. They didn't take a honeymoon. They waited the few months until both were free of their obligations.

In the weeks following their marriage, Paul and Jean appeared to be extremely happy. Individually they told acquaintances how thrilled they were with their married life. Paul presented Jean with a beautiful new home in Benedict Canyon in Beverly Hills.

Toward the end of August, Paul changed. He no longer appeared happy. Instead, he went into long periods of depression when he hardly spoke. Acquaintances and colleagues noticed the abrupt change in his personality.

On Sept. 5, 1932, two months after his marriage, Paul Bern put a .38 calibre pistol to his head and killed himself. The bullet entered the right temple, plowed through the brain, ending up imbedded in a wall. Paul left a note which read, "Dearest Dear: Unfortunately, this is the only way to make good the frightening wrong I have done you and wipe out my abject humility. I love you. Paul. P.S. You understand that last night was only a comedy."

Hollywood was aghast at the untimely death. What had caused such a successful man, married to one of the most glamorous women in the world, to kill himself? Rumors flew throughout the movie capitol.

An inquest into the suicide was held. The only point of contention was motive. The most widely accepted reason for Bern taking his own life proved to be an embarrassment for all concerned. Evidently, Bern had suffered from a physical deficiency which made the consummation of his marriage an impossibility. His reference to "last night being a comedy" was held to mean that a desperate Bern had attempted to consummate the marriage by artificial means. If this was true, one wonders why Bern ever married Jean Harlow.

Shortly after Bern's suicide, it was revealed that he had previously lived with movie actress Dorothy Millette. Miss Millette became mentally ill and was confined to an institution. Paul Bern paid all expenses during her illness and provided her with a living allowance after her release. Miss Millette resided in the Algonquin Hotel in New York.

The day after Bern's suicide, Dorothy was staying at the Plaza Hotel in San Francisco. She boarded the Delta King, a Sacramento River steamer sailing from San Francisco to Sacramento. A pair of shoes and a ladies' coat were found beside the steamer's railing. Two weeks later fishermen found Dorothy Millette's body. The official verdict was suicide, possibly over the loss of a great love or possibly over the loss of her only means of support.

Meanwhile, back in Hollywood, Jean Harlow was so distraught she was placed under a doctor's care. She recovered rapidly, and remained one of Hollywood's leading actresses. In 1933 she married cameraman Harold Rosson. A little over a year later she divorced Rosson, charging cruelty. Seems Harold kept the light on late at night reading. Harlow couldn't get the sleep required to enable her to go before the cameras the next day.

Jean Harlow continued to star on the screen. Beloved by all, the dynamic blonde actress had the world by the tail. Her public was shocked when, in June, 1937, her mother announced that Jean was seriously ill. Four days later Jean Harlow was dead. Apparently she had influenza which caused inflammation of the gall bladder. She died of uremic poisoning. Jean Harlow was 26.

Like Marilyn Monroe years later, the suddenness of her death gave rise to rumors of foul play, but nothing was ever uncovered to lend credence to these reports.

THE
BUGSY SIEGEL
STORY

Jennie Siegel's second child, Benjamin, was the prettiest baby that Jennie or any of her friends had ever seen. Eight days after his birth on Feb. 28, 1906, at his ritual circumcision, close friends of the Siegels had no way of knowing that little Benjamin would one day grow up and leave his home in New York's Hell's Kitchen to become a leader of organized crime in the U.S. and the leading force in the development of one of its cities, Las Vegas, Nevada. You see, little Benjamin became better known to the world as Bugsy Siegel.

One of Benjamin's close friends during his formative years was Georgie Ranft. The two youngsters were to take different paths to success but would remain friends all their lives. Georgie became Hollywood movie star George Raft, who made it big in the movie industry portraying gangsters. Young Raft didn't have to do much acting. His training ground, Hell's Kitchen, was one of the toughest slums in the world.

As a schoolboy, Benjamin pulled off many illegal criminal capers. Rolling drunks brought in a few dollars spending money. Shaking down young messengers could be lucrative in a small way.

Just short of his twenty-first birthday, while employed as a cab driver, Ben took a side trip to an isolated section of Central Park with a female passenger. He forced the girl out of the car and raped her. After the rape, Ben drove the girl to her destination. Next morning he was picked up. His fare had given police Ben's cab registration number, as well as his licence plate number. When the complainant didn't show up on the trial date, the charges were dropped. Rumor had it that several of Ben's unsavory acquaintances had convinced the girl not to testify.

With the advent of prohibition in the roaring twenties, Bugsy gravitated to the enormously profitable traffic in illegal liquor. While not a household name yet, he knew men who were. His acquaintances, later to become partners, included Charles "Lucky" Luciano, then heavily involved in narcotics, Joe Adonis, Vito Genovese, Albert Anastasia, Louis "Lepke" Buchalter and Meyer Lansky.

Bugsy, a name which was never uttered in his presence, was in and out of a series of scrapes with the law without being convicted. The young hood, who looked good, acted cool and could take care of himself, soon came to the attention of Meyer Lansky. At that time, Lansky was a young man himself, only a few rungs up the ladder.

Back in the twenties, Siegel and Lansky formed the Bugs-Meyer gang. They began modestly enough, providing a vital service to big time gangsters, guaranteeing delivery of illegal booze from the New York docks to the gangsters' warehouses. One of their customers was Arthur Flegenheimer, better known as Dutch Schultz. Another was Lucky Luciano.

The Dutchman was the dominant New York gangster of the roaring twenties. Besides his illegal trade in booze and prostitution, Schultz could arrange to have a man disappear for a price. The Bugs-Meyer gang specialized in transportation and protection, with the odd contract killing thrown in. Life was cheap. A broken leg could be arranged for $50. For $100 a body could be dispatched into the East River attached to a block of cement.

Small time gunsel Whitey Krakower introduced Bugsy to his sister Estelle. Bugsy was smitten. He and Estelle were married in 1927. In the next five years the Siegels.had two daughters, Millicent and Barbara. Bugsy moved his family into a stucco Tudor style home in the fashionable community of Scarsdale. Neighbors thought quiet Mr. Siegel was the head of a national corporation which required a good deal of travel. In a way this was true.

As the twenties gave way to the thirties, the Bugs-Meyer partnership grew in power. Lucky Luciano's organization also became prominent. Dutch Schultz remained king.

When it became known to Luciano that Tony Fabrizzo, the killer of "Mad Dog"

Coll, was planning on retiring from the mob, it was time for a meeting. When Luciano heard that Fabrizzo was planning to sell his memoirs to a publishing company, it was time for a killing. Lucky talked it over with Dutch. They decided that the Bugs-Meyer boys would do the hit.

A few days before the date of the execution, Bugsy's headquarters was bombed. Fabrizzo was strongly suspected. Bugsy was fortunate to escape with a severe gash to the forehead. While recuperating in Governeur Hospital, Bugsy hatched his great plan.

One night, with the help of henchmen, he sneaked out of his private room in the hospital and drove to Fabrizzo's home. His henchmen knocked on the door. Tony answered. His mouth opened wide and his eyes popped in horror as he looked into the muzzle of a .45 calibre submachine gun held by Bugsy Siegel. Three bullets found their mark in Fabrizzo's forehead, the exact location where Bugsy was bandaged. Bugsy made his way back to his hospital bed unseen. Next morning he was awakened to the news that Tony Fabrizzo had been shot to death on his front steps.

In 1934, the Mafia, under the executive genius of Lucky Luciano, had gained full power over organized crime in the United States. Its enforcement arm, Murder Inc., had as its president Louis "Lepke" Buchalter, sometimes called the Lord High Executioner. Lepke left the running of day to day affairs to Abe "Kid Twist" Reles.

When prohibition came to an end, the Mafia had no difficulty adjusting their closely knit organization to other profitable activities. Their biggest threat came from aggressive district attorney Thomas E. Dewey. Dutch Schultz felt that Dewey had to be killed. Wiser heads, including Luciano, believed Dewey's death would bring intolerable heat on organized crime. Luciano gave the word. To prevent Dewey's death, Dutch Schultz had to go.

The job was done efficiently at the Palace Chop House in Newark, N.J. on the night of Oct. 23, 1935. Three of the Dutchman's henchmen, Lulu Rosenkrantz, Abe Landau, and Abbadabba Berman, were killed in a fusillade of gunfire. Dutch lived long enough to make it to the hospital. When asked to identify his assassins, he gave the classic gangland reply, "I didn't see nobody." Then he died.

With Dewey continuing to aggressively prosecute gangsters in the east, the mob looked for greener untapped pastures in which to make a dishonest buck. California, in particular Hollywood, beckoned. Who else but Bugsy Siegel, with his good looks and fine family, would make a lasting impression on the glitter capital of the world? Bugsy's assignment was to ingratiate himself in the movie industry with an eye towards setting up any rackets which would prove profitable to the boys back east.

For starters, Bugsy settled his family into a mansion on McCarthy Drive, formerly owned by opera star Lawrence Tibbett. His old buddy George Raft introduced him to all the right people, passing him off as a big time businessman from the east. Respectable Mr. Siegel soon had a system set up whereby narcotics were shipped from Mexico to California to New York. He also dabbled in white slavery and the labor rackets.

Virginia Hill went from a cotton patch in Bessemer, Georgia, through three husbands to the Cotton Club in Harlem, where she met Bugsy. Bugsy fell hard. Seldom was he seen in public without his Ginny. Back at the mansion, Mrs. Siegel had enough. She filed for divorce. Ginny and Bugsy returned to Hollywood, where Ginny leased the Falcon's Lair, a mansion once owned by Rudolph Valentino.

Nosy law enforcement agencies began investigating reputable Mr. Siegel's affairs in California. Bugsy got the message. He looked for new worlds to conquer. While in Las Vegas, he got the brilliant idea of building the grandest gambling palace in the world. He would call it the Flamingo.

Bugsy travelled back east to confer with the mob. Meyer Lansky, Frank Costello and Joe Adonis agreed to the idea. Bugsy returned to Vegas with the mob's blessing. Dell Webb, who would one day own the New York Yankees, was hired on as the general contractor for the job of building the Flamingo. Construction costs went way over the proposed budget of $5.6 million.

The club was a success right from opening night. Everyone who was anyone in Hollywood attended. Despite its success, profits did not cover the vast sums Bugsy had borrowed to complete the Flamingo. To meet obligations, he held out on the share allotted to the boys back east. That was a cardinal sin in the eyes of the mob. Now it was Bugsy's turn to go.

Some say Virginia Hill had prior knowledge of the hit. She left for France after giving Bugsy the keys to her leased Moorish castle on North Linden Drive in Beverly Hills. A few days later Bugsy was in L.A. with friends Allan Smiley, Charles Hill and Jerri Mason. They decided to stay over at Ginny's home.

At 11 p.m. on June 20, 1947, Charles and Jerri retired for the night. Bugsy and Smiley sat down on opposite ends of a divan beside the fireplace. A gun roared seven times from the terrace window. Smiley, unhurt, hit the floor. Three of the seven bullets entered Bugsy's head. The man who put Las Vegas on the map was very dead.

Bugsy's old Flamingo has changed hands many times since he built it. Today it is called The Flamingo Hilton. You can still catch a flight from almost anywhere in the world to try your luck at the gambling tables just as Bugsy Siegel had predicted so many years ago. . . . How the others fared:

*Joe Adonis was deported to Italy where he died of a heart attack in 1971 at age 69.

*Albert Anastasia was shot to death in 1957 while having his hair cut in the barber shop of the Park Sheraton Hotel in New York City.

*Louis "Lepke" Buchalter was executed in Sing Sing Prison's electric chair on March 5, 1944 for the murder of Brooklyn storekeeper Joseph Rosen.

*Thomas E. Dewey served three terms as governor of New York State and twice ran unsuccessfully for the presidency of the U.S. He died in Miami of natural causes on March 16, 1971. He was 68.

*Vito Genovese died on Feb. 13, 1967 in prison at Springfield, Missouri.

*Virginia Hill married for the fourth time after Bugsy's untimely demise. She took her own life with an overdose of barbiturates near Salzburg, Austria. Ginny was 50.

*George Raft, retired from a successful acting career that included 105 movies. He died in 1980 of lung cancer at age 85.

*Abe "Kid Twist" Reles became a key witness against his former buddies. He was given police protection and placed in the Half Moon Hotel on Coney Island. Despite being heavily guarded, his body was found on the ground below his open window.

The Ladies and the Tramp

Charlie Chaplin - The Little Tramp.

The name means little to the Michael Jackson generation, but to the millions throughout the world whose memories go back more than 30 years, Charlie Chaplin is synonymous with comedic genius. Charlie's movies, both silent and talkies, which he wrote, produced and starred in, stand as classics of the cinema.

The Little Tramp was born to poverty, in London, England's Kensington district in 1889. His parents, unsuccessful vaudeville entertainers, lived from hand to mouth. When Charlie was three and his older brother, Sydney, was seven, his father died of alcoholism.

Mrs. Chaplin left the theatre in an attempt to support herself and her sons, but found that the periodic sewing jobs which came her way were not enough. Desperate and alone, Hannah Chaplin had a nervous breakdown and was institutionalized. The two boys were placed in an orphanage.

Fortunately, Hannah recovered, and her two sons were returned to her. Their life of poverty continued. Charlie sold newspapers and did odd jobs around pubs. Often, he wore nothing more than rags and roamed the streets barefoot.

In desperation, Charlie sometimes made faces, sang ditties and danced. He soon discovered that he had the ability to make people laugh or cry as he chose. Charlie developed his talent and was successful in obtaining a few small parts in English music halls.

Charlie's big break came when he joined Karno's Comedians, a well-known act which had several bookings in the U.S. While performing in New York, he was noticed by Mack Sennett of Keystone Cop fame and was lured away from the Karno troupe to make a movie. Charlie was paid $150 per week to act in a film. He was a hit and was recognized as such from the very beginning. Charlie went from $150 to $1250 a week with one raise in pay.

With stardom came the spotlight. Some resented the fact that Charlie never became a U.S. citizen. Others never cared for the Little Tramp because of his sympathy toward the Communist Party. But it was not politics that catapulted Charlie into hot water. It was, in a word, women - young women.

In 1918, when Charlie was approaching 30, he was seen regularly with cute little blonde Mildred Harris. No one would have blinked an eye were it not for one thing. Mildred was an overdeveloped 16. It became a mild scandal. But Charlie had an answer for the rumormongers. He married Mildred. The fun didn't last. The odd couple divorced in 1920.

Sixteen seems to have been Charlie's favorite number. In 1924, at the mature age of 35, he took up with Lita Gray. You guessed it. Lita was 16. After Charlie and Lita were an item, as they used to say in Hollywood, Charlie was visited by Lita's uncle who, surprise, happened to be a lawyer. Unc pointed out rather forcefully that intimacy with an underaged girl was, in legalese, statutory rape. On Nov. 24, 1924, in dreary downtown Empalme, Mexico, Lita and Charlie became husband and wife. That same afternoon, Charlie went fishing.

Charlie's indifference was a foretaste of things to come. The newlyweds simply didn't hit it off. They tolerated each other for three years until Jan. 10, 1927. That was the day Lita filed a 42-page complaint against Charlie. Let's see now, there was the little matter of intimacy before they were married, when she was underage. Then there was Charlie's abnormal sexual demands. Throw in mental cruelty and running around with other women, and you get the general idea.

Charlie caught everyone by surprise when he announced to the press that he loved his wife and was deeply hurt that she didn't care for him anymore. Eventually, the charges concerning events which had occurred before the marriage were dropped. Charlie settled out of court on the other charges and managed somehow to weather the storm.

Charlie's star shone brightly. Unlike some silent movie actors, he made the transition to talkies without any difficulty. Soon he owned a large estate and was considered one of the wealthiest men in Hollywood.

At the height of his fame, Charlie never wavered in his leanings toward the Soviet Union. Perhaps it was his impoverished youth that influenced his pro-Communist tendencies. Whatever the reason, he raised the ire of anti-Communist groups in the film industry.

In 1936, Charlie married movie star Paulette Goddard on a ship off Canton, China. They stayed together for five years before Paulette obtained a Mexican divorce.

Shortly after his divorce from Goddard, Charlie was introduced to Joan Barry, 20. Within a year, Joan contacted powerful Hollywood gossip columnist Hedda Hopper with the rather startling news that she was pregnant. Hedda, who didn't trust her own mother, took Joan to a doctor, who confirmed that Joan was indeed expecting a child. Joan claimed that Charlie Chaplin was the father, and what's more, he would not even allow her into his mansion where she had once been so very welcome.

It was all too much for Joan. She took an overdose of sleeping pills and was only saved by an alert police officer, who rushed her to hospital, where doctors pumped out her stomach. Joan was booked as a vagrant. The charges were dropped in exchange for a promise to leave town. She hopped a train for New York, but got off in Omaha and headed back to Hollywood, where she broke into Charlie's home. Police were summoned and Joan was sentenced to 90 days in jail. Charlie interceded. He had Joan transferred from the jail to a hospital in Santa Monica. In return for the favor, Joan slapped Charlie with a paternity suit.

Charlie was also charged with violation of the Mann Act (the interstate transportation of women for immoral purposes) and having denied Joan her civil rights.

Joan claimed that earlier that year Charlie had travelled to New York, where she was staying at the time. True enough, he lived at the Waldorf Towers, while she roomed elsewhere. One night she joined Charlie at the Waldorf, where sexual intercourse had taken place.

In regard to the civil rights action, Joan claimed that her rights were denied her when she was forced to leave Hollywood. She also brought the same action against the judge, lawyer and the police officers involved in the incident. The civil rights indictment was eventually dropped, but Charlie stood trial on the Mann Act violation.

Charlie hired famed Hollywood lawyer Jerry Geisler. He proved without a doubt that there was little need for Charlie to follow Joan to New York. She was constantly attempting to throw herself at him, to the point of breaking into his home in Hollywood. On the night Joan claimed they were intimate, Charlie admitted escorting her to the Waldorf, but vehemently denied that intercourse had taken place.

Joan took the witness stand. Geisler had her admit that, on one occasion when she broke into Charlie's home, she had held a pistol on the comedian for an hour and a half, after which she jumped into bed and had intercourse with Charlie.

Joan also admitted that many of her travels were financed by the richest man in the world at that time, Jean Paul Getty. She usually stayed at the fashionable Hotel Pierre while in New York - particularly convenient, since Getty owned the Pierre.

Charlie beat the rap. He was acquitted of the charge, which could have brought him a 25 year prison sentence.

Joan gave birth to her baby, Carol Ann. Blood tests performed on Joan, Charlie and Carol Ann proved conclusively that Charlie could not have been the father of the child. Despite this scientific proof, Charlie was brought to trial. Strangely, the jury could not reach a verdict. Even stranger, at a second trial, Charlie was judged to be the father of little Carol Ann. The baby was awarded $75 a week and was entitled to use the Chaplin name.

The sentimental verdict passed down by the Chaplin jury can never happen again. In 1955, California passed a law prohibiting paternity trials after blood tests have proven the impossibility of the defendant being the father.

While still on trial, Charlie, now 54, married 18-year-old Oona O'Neill, daughter of playwright Eugene O'Neill. Charlie's fourth marriage proved to be his most successful. Over the years he and Oona had seven children. But Charlie Chaplin was to have still more problems from another direction.

At the conclusion of World War II, the U.S. became enmeshed in the Cold War. Everything Communist was a lurking danger. Charlie openly supported Communist causes. In 1952, Charlie and Oona sailed for Europe on vacation. While at sea, they were informed that U.S. Attorney General James F. McGranery had announced that he was rescinding Chaplin's re-entry permit. Charlie decided not to fight. He and his family settled in Vevey, Switzerland.

Charlie was not to return to the U.S. until 20 years later. In 1972, in one of the most emotional ceremonies ever witnessed on television, Hollywood presented Charlie with an honorary Oscar "in recognition of the incalculable effect he has had in making motion pictures the art form of this century." Three years later, confined to a wheelchair, Charlie was knighted by the Queen of England.

In 1977, Sir Charles Chaplin, the Little Tramp, father of 10 children, married four times, innovative genius who had made millions laugh and cry, died peacefully at his home in Switzerland with his wife and seven of his children by his side. He was 88.

The Little Tramp from Kensington had lived a full life.

BASEBALL'S DENNY McLAIN

Ron Taylor toiled for years as a relief pitcher in the major leagues. In four appearances in two World Series, he held his opponents scoreless. Today, Ron Taylor is a medical doctor with a flourishing private practice and is team physician to the Toronto Blue Jays.

Don Getty starred as quarterback for the Edmonton Eskimos in the fifties and sixties. After football, he successfully embarked on a political career. Today, he is the premier of Alberta.

Syl Apps starred at centre ice for the Toronto Maple Leafs during their glory days of the thirties and forties. After hockey, the Leafs old captain became a member of the Ontario Legislature for 12 years, and served in the cabinet as Minister of Correctional Services before retiring to his home in Kingston.

These men were achievers in sport and in the game of life. They epitomize how we want our sports heroes to turn out after they complete their athletic careers.

Unfortunately, some athletes step off the playing field and find the game of life far different from their athletic endeavors.

Maybe the handwriting was on the wall for Denny McLain while he was still basking in the limelight as a true sports hero. One of his old Detroit Tiger teammates, Mickey Lolich, explains, "We used to say he was either going to wind up in concrete shoes or in prison. I guess he got the latter."

Denny was first noticed by the baseball world while still a youngster, pitching at Mt. Carmel High School in Chicago. No wonder. He had a 38-7 won-lost record. That same season of 1962, the Chicago White Sox gave Denny a $17,000 signing bonus and assigned him to their Harlan, Kentucky farm club.

In the minors, Denny didn't impress. His record in the minors was 5 wins and 8 losses. At the ripe old age of 18, Denny was just another gifted kid, one of thousands who played baseball with one dream in mind - to make the big leagues.

In 1963 Denny received what appeared to be a setback. At spring training, the White Sox had three rookie pitchers vying for a place on the team. One of the boys had signed for a larger bonus. The other had a better minor league record than McLain. Denny became expendable. He was exposed to the rookie draft which, in effect, meant that any other major league club could pick him up for $8000. Denny was drafted by the Detroit Tigers, who shipped him to Duluth.

In Duluth, Denny displayed the magic which was to become his trademark. He chalked up a 13 win, 2 loss record. At the end of the season, he was brought up to the Tigers.

Tiger pitching instructors taught fastballer McLain how to throw a change-up curve. Denny became a bona fide major leaguer, compiling records of 16-6 in 1965, 20-14 in 1966 and 17-18 in 1967.

His 1967 season ended on a sour note. Denny didn't win a game after Aug. 29, and the Tigers lost the pennant by one game to the Boston Red Sox. During that time, Denny was sidelined with an injured foot, which was to raise ugly questions in the not too distant future.

But all that was forgotten during the 1968 baseball season. That was Denny McLain's year. Victory after victory was savored by Denny and the delirious Detroit fans. When it was over, Denny had compiled the unbelievable record of 31 wins against 6 losses and the Tigers rolled to the American League pennant.

No pitcher had won 30 games in over three decades, since Dizzy Dean accomplished the feat in 1934. Denny's achievement was one of the great sports stories of modern times. No one has won over 30 games since. That season, baseball heaped honors on Denny. He was voted the American League's Most Valuable Player and won the Cy Young Award as Pitcher of the Year.

In 1969, he was almost as invincible. He racked up a 24-9 record with a 2.80 earned run average. Once again, he received the Cy Young Award. Denny McLain had won 108 ball games. He was 25, the toast of baseball and the world of sport.

Along the line, Denny had become an airplane pilot, a better than average organ player, and had married Sharyn Boudreau, daughter of baseball immortal, Lou Boudreau.

In 1970, Denny's salary was $90,000. His income from other sources, including television appearances, organ concerts and the banquet circuit, added up to another $100,000. Remember, this was back when the average U.S. salary was well under $9,000. The talented, all-American hero was riding high.

The rumors began in magazine articles. They were made official by Bowie Kuhn, then Commissioner of baseball. Denny McLain's off field activities dating back to 1967 were being investigated. It was alleged that Denny had invested in a bookmaking establishment in Flint, Mich. in 1967. It was further alleged that the celebrated injury to his foot had been incurred by a Mafia enforcer while collecting a $46,000 gambling debt owed by McLain. While the rumors flew, it was revealed that Denny owed $2,450 in back rent on his Lakeland, Fla. home, $779 to Consumer Power Co. in unpaid bills and several months rent on his $75,000 airplane.

After a hearing before Commissioner Kuhn, baseball's brightest star was suspended from the opening day of the 1970 season to July 1, a period of two months and 24 days.

On July 1, Denny returned to the Tigers. Over 50,000 fans, the largest crowd to fill the Detroit stadium in nine years, cheered his appearance. The bad boy of baseball was back. He wasn't his old, sharp self, but the Tigers won the game and the multitude had paid homage to their talented hero.

Denny couldn't stay out of trouble. In August, he poured a bucket of ice water over the heads of two Detroit sports writers. This time, his own organization suspended him for "conduct unbecoming a professional baseball player." A week later, after apologizing to the two writers, Denny was back in the Tigers' starting rotation. To gain relief from the hordes of creditors hounding him, he declared bankruptcy.

It was a rough season for McLain. In September, he was suspended for the balance of the 1970 season by Commissioner Kuhn for carrying a gun.

At the conclusion of the season, Denny was reinstated, but the Detroit organization had had enough of their bad boy star. The same day he was reinstated, he was traded to the Washington Senators. The end was in sight. That season in Washington, Denny suffered the most losses by a pitcher in the big leagues with 22 defeats. He was later traded to the Oakland A's, and from Oakland to the Atlanta Braves. Then began the lonely trip to the minors.

In May, 1974, 30-year-old Denny McLain was out of shape and vastly overweight. He was signed to pitch a game for the London, Ont. Majors against Kitchener. In typical McLain fashion, he showed up an hour before game time. Nine hundred and four fans attended the game. The majority were there to see with their own eyes the major league's last 30 game winner. Denny received $30 for his appearance. He had slid a long way down the ladder.

Denny spent the next few years doing sports announcing for minor league teams. He even managed to catch on as manager of an American Association team. Nothing worked. Outside businesses failed. In 1977, Denny filed a personal bankruptcy petition for the second time. He listed debts of over one million dollars and assets of $900.

Throughout Denny's glory days and bad times, his wife, Sharyn, remained at his side. They have four children. She has watched her husband deteriorate from a handsome, flamboyant sports hero to a bloated 270 pound failure. During the seventies, the sports world had had enough of Denny McLain. New heroes had taken his place, but McLain's unsuccessful battle to cope with life off the baseball diamond didn't stop.

In 1984, Denny made the headlines once more. He was indicted for racketeering, conspiracy, extortion, possession and distribution of cocaine and conspiracy to import cocaine. It was alleged that he had been involved in these activities since June 1978. In 1985, Denny was found guilty of racketeering, conspiracy, extortion, and cocaine possession. He was sentenced to 23 years in prison. As the sentence was passed, Sharyn McLain and her two daughters wept openly in court.

But Denny has bounced back. After serving almost 30 months in the Federal Correctional Institution in Talladega, Ala., his attorney was successful in having his conviction overturned. Denny was released from prison. Today he is a prosperous radio talk-show host in Detroit.

MA BARKER
AND HER BOYS

Books, plays and movies have examined her life from every conceivable angle. Probably we will never know the exact role she played in the criminal history of the U.S. Was she the simple little hillbilly woman who stuck by her boys through good times and bad, or was she the infamous mastermind behind the most successful gang of bank robbers and killers ever to roam the U.S.?

Her real name was Arizona Donnie Clark Barker, but we know her as the notorious Ma Barker, leader of the Barker-Karpis gang which terrorized the Midwest during the early thirties.

Arrie, as she was known, was born in 1872 near Springfield, Missouri and was nurtured on the daring deeds of legendary badman Jesse James. She was ten-years-old when "that dirty little coward" Bob Ford shot Jesse in the back. Jesse James would remain Arrie Barker's hero all her life.

In 1892, at the age of 20, Arrie married farm worker George Barker. The young couple moved to Aurora, Missouri, where Arrie gave birth to her four boys, Herman, Lloyd, Doc and Freddie. All the boys turned out to be sweethearts.

The Barker clan had a difficult time coaxing a living out of the soil. When the four boys were still young, they moved to Webb City, a rough, tough mining town, where they set up housekeeping in a tarpaper shack. Despite the poverty of her surroundings, Ma scrubbed her boys' faces and hustled them off to Sunday school each week. As the boys grew up, their father George had little to do with their discipline. Ma was the authority in the family.

Gradually, each one of her sons became embroiled in minor scrapes with the law. Petty theft, assault, and carrying a concealed weapon were some of the charges. In every instance Ma was able to convince a sympathetic judge that her boys were really good boys. They were released into her custody.

When Ma ran out of sympathetic judges she moved to Tulsa, Oklahoma. By this time many of her sons' friends had landed in prison for various offences. When Freddie visited one of these friends who was soon to be released, he invited him to stop over at the Barker residence in Tulsa. Eventually Ma made a business out of providing a safe hideout for criminals on the run.

In 1922, her sons slipped over the line into serious trouble with the law. Lloyd, apprehended while attempting to hold up a post office, received a sentence of 25 years imprisonment and was stashed away in Leavenworth. A few months later Doc killed a night watchman at Johns Hospital in Tulsa while attempting to heist a drug shipment. He was sentenced to life in the Oklahoma State Penitentiary.

Four years later, Freddie received a sentence of five to ten years in Kansas State Prison in Lansing for robbing a Windfield, Kansas bank. Thus Ma Barker gained the distinction of having three of her four sons incarcerated in three different prisons at the same time.

What about Herman? He was busy too. Herman was captured while robbing a bank in Missouri. He escaped and robbed a store in Newton, Kansas. Herman bungled the job, killing the police officer J.E. Marshall along the way. Surrounded by police, Herman turned his revolver on himself, sending a slug directly into his brain. Ma Barker was down to three sons.

The years took their toil on Ma. She stood only 5 ft. 1 inch. During the years her sons were in prison she became fat. Ma left her husband and took up with a lazy alcoholic, Arthur V. Dunlop. Her lover was a natural complainer who avoided work of any kind like the plague. When Freddie was paroled in 1931, he sort of inherited Dunlop, whom he despised with a passion.

Freddie had met Canadian Alvin Karpis in prison and invited him to his mother's home. Karpis and Ma took an immediate liking to each other and for the rest of her life Ma considered old Creepy Karpis "one of her boys." Like Freddie, Karpis barely tolerated Dunlop for Ma's sake.

Freddie and Karpis went to work. They robbed a store in West Plains, Missouri. Sheriff C.R. Kelly spotted the getaway car a few days later. When he saw Freddie and Karpis in the vehicle, he stopped it to investigate. The two men shot the sheriff dead. There were no witnesses, and years later Karpis was to claim that it was not he but another hood who had been with Freddie that day. Karpis stated he was blamed because the two killers had borrowed his car.

Now hunted men, Freddie and Karpis stayed on the move. They transferred Ma and Dunlop to St. Paul, Minnesota. While drunk Dunlop talked too much of his association with the Barkers. Jack Peifer murdered Dunlop as a favor to the Barker gang. Ma understood.

Doc was granted a parole. He joined Freddie, Karpis, and Ma. The gang shifted into high gear. Together with the top gunslingers of the era, they quickly became the scourge of the FBI.

They relieved the Cloud County Bank of Concordia, Kansas of $250,000. In 1933, they knocked over banks in Kansas and Nebraska for $20,000 and $151,000 respectively. The gang turned to kidnapping, successfully snatching St. Paul brewer William A. Hamm and releasing him for $100,000 cash. This caper proved to be so successful that they kidnapped Edward C. Bremer, collecting $200,000 for their trouble. It is estimated that during their spree of kidnappings and holdups, the Barker-Karpis gang took in $3,000,000. They achieved the dubious status of being the most wanted fugitives in the United States.

By 1935, the heat was on and the gang scattered. Doc was picked up in Chicago by the FBI and sent to Alcatraz. When agents searched his room they found a map of Florida, indicating where other members of the gang were holed up. The FBI surrounded a remote resort on Lake Weir. When Ma and Freddie refused to surrender they were shot to death. Ma had over $10,000 in her handbag. By sheer accident, Karpis was out fishing mackerel at the time and so saved his life.

On June 13, 1939, Doc scampered over Alcatraz's high wall. He was spotted by tower guards, who shouted a warning. Doc chose to ignore their warnings and was gunned down, dying where he fell on the shore.

The only surviving Barker son, Lloyd, sent to Leavenworth in 1922, served every minute of his 25 year sentence. Upon his release in 1947 he obtained work in a snack shop in Colorado. Two years later he was murdered by his wife.

Alvin Karpis was picked up by the FBI in New Orleans. He was sent to Alcatraz on Aug. 7, 1936 and remained there for 25 years, longer than any other prisoner in that famed institution's history. In 1962, he was transferred to McNeil Island, where he served a further seven years.

After spending a total of 33 years in prison, Karpis, like a ghost from the past, was released in December, 1968, and deported to Canada. He lived as a free man for 10 years before being found dead in his bed in Torremolinos, Spain, the last remaining member of the dreaded Barker-Karpis gang.

8
MONSTERS

THE BAD SEED

I am often asked if wanton mass murder is a recent phenomenon. Are the Mansons, Sutcliffes and Olsons the product of modern society? The truth is, the strange mental processes which motivate these modern-day monsters have always been with us.

Probably the most reprehensible mass murderer of the nineteenth century was the American teenager, Jesse Pomeroy.

Jesse's family owned a retail store in Boston and were relatively well off. The Pomeroys knew they had a troubled youngster from the very beginning. When he was only nine, Jesse displayed an aggressive attitude towards other children and took delight in making life miserable for neighborhood dogs and cats.

A brooding, introverted youngster, Jesse was cursed with grotesque features. One of his eyes was covered with a white film, the result of a cataract. There was an unsightly twist to his upper lip which gave him the appearance of wearing a perpetual snarl. Altogether, Jesse was a repulsive-looking character who, because of his innate meanness, was shunned by other youngsters.

In 1881, when Jesse was 14, several children between the ages of seven and ten were reported missing in Boston. A short time later their bodies were discovered in fields and garbage dumps. Other hapless victims were found nailed to the doorways of buildings on dark, deserted streets. Some were discovered tied to posts.

In all, the murders of 27 young boys and girls were attributed to the unknown killer. A wave of hysteria and shock, similar to that which was to envelop Atlanta, Georgia, a hundred years later, swept through Boston. Despite the concentrated efforts of the police, no clue to the identity of the murderer was immediately uncovered.

Twelve-year-old Albert Pratt's father had hired an armed bodyguard to accompany his son home from school. This precaution had received some publicity and eventually came to the attention of the killer.

Mr. Pratt received an unsigned letter in the mail telling him that his son would be the next to die. A few days after this letter was delivered, Harry Pomeroy, Jesse's younger brother, knocked on the door of Albert Pratt's classroom and told teacher William Barnes that Albert's father was outside and wanted to see his son. Mr. Barnes excused Albert from the classroom. Two days later Albert's mutilated body was found in a field outside the city.

Questioned by police, Harry Pomeroy would only say that a tall man in a blue suit had requested that he pass along the message. The next strange incident to take place in a case fraught with the unbelievable occurred when one potential victim escaped the clutches of the monster.

Nine-year-old Willie Barton was playing near a field when a big boy grabbed him and tried to take off his clothes. Willie wrenched free of the bigger boy's grasp and ran away.

Because Harry Pomeroy was already connected with the case, police thought that young Willie might be able to identify his assailant at Harry's school. Willie shrieked in horror when he spotted not Harry, but Jesse Pomeroy. The white eye, snarling lip and coarse features couldn't be missed.

Instead of denying his guilt, Jesse readily confessed to all the murders. He seemed to relish the spotlight, was defiant, and swore, "I shan't be hanged. I'll fool you all again."

At his trial, Jesse discussed his case intelligently with lawyers and the judge. At other times he swore he would kill all those who testified against him, as well as the members of the jury.

Jesse was found guilty, but insane. Unbelievably, one year later he was released from an asylum as cured. His release didn't go unnoticed by the general public. A great many petitions were forwarded to Governor Groves of Massachusetts demanding that Jesse be kept in jail. Both the governor and the presiding judge at Jesse's trial were convinced that he was cured.

A year passed. Jesse stayed close to home. There was a real fear that relatives of his victims might take matters into their own hands and kill him.

Eventually, other matters captured the public's interest. Soon Jesse Pomeroy was out of the spotlight, but not for long. One day his parents left him in charge of their store. A little girl, Alice Curran, entered the Pomeroys' store and was never seen again.

Police naturally questioned Jesse, but he vehemently denied having had anything to do with the disappearance, claiming that he was being harassed because of his past. Other children disappeared. Fields and marshes were searched, but no bodies were found.

At the rear of Pomeroys' store there was a large refuse dump. That summer neighbors claimed that an offensive odor was emanating from the refuse. The city ordered Mr. Pomeroy to remove the dump. Buried in the refuse, authorities uncovered the bodies of twelve children. As the bodies were removed Jesse watched in the yard, smiling. He was enjoying the sight.

Such a furore accompanied this second group of killings that Governor Groves, who had authorized Jesse's release, was forced to resign.

Once more Jesse confessed in detail to all the murders. He was his cocky, defiant self and swore he would seek vengeance on all who were against him.

Jesse was tried and found guilty of murder in the first degree. While a mob outside the courthouse shouted, "Lynch him!" Jesse was sentenced to death by hanging. However, there were those who thought that Jesse must certainly be insane and should not hang. They worked frantically to save him. Finally his sentence was commuted to solitary confinement for life.

Jesse Pomeroy entered prison at the age of seventeen and immediately began planning to escape. It wasn't an easy task. He was watched constantly while in solitary confinement. Cunning Jesse was a model prisoner, conforming to all the rules and spending much of his time reading. Soon he was receiving small privileges.

His mother visited him and tried to help her wicked son to escape. Once she brought him a large meat pie for Thanksgiving. At the last moment guards found some small tools baked in the pie. On another occasion Jesse complained of back trouble and asked permission to have his mother bring him an armchair. Guards found tools and hacksaws hidden in the stuffing of the chair. After this last incident Mrs. Pomeroy was not allowed to bring her son gifts.

Jesse continued to try. His next scheme took three years. He found out that the prison was heated by gas, and that a gas pipe ran directly behind his cell wall. Jesse decided to get through the wall in some way, tap the gas line, and fill his cell with gas. He would then light a match and blow the place up. He didn't seem to care if he blew himself up in the process.

Jesse talked his keepers into providing him with a few simple tools, ostensibly to work on inventing a pencil sharpener. Every night for three years Jesse scraped at the cement which held his granite block cell together. The scrapings were then kneaded into his bread, which he ate.

Finally, he broke through and made a hole in the pipe, allowing the gas to fill his cell. He had secreted away one match months before. He lit the match. The whole area exploded. Two prisoners in adjoining cells were killed. Jesse was blown through the cell door. He was found alive, but badly injured.

Jesse recovered. This time he was watched day and night in a special escape-proof cell in Charleston Prison. It was as close to living in hell as you can get on earth. Years passed. Jesse was forgotten. Many assumed he had died.

In 1924, an old man, sick, frail, but still defiant, was transferred from prison to Bridgewater State Farm. Jesse Pomeroy, the "White-Eyed Boy Murderer of Boston" had served 40 years in solitary confinement. Special security was provided at Bridgewater to prevent Jesse from escaping. He remained there until the day he died.

MEMPHIS MADMAN

For twenty-nine days during the summer of 1969 a mad killer held the city of Memphis, Tennessee, in the grip of terror. Five innocent victims, picked at random by the killer, were murdered. Total financial gain to the perpetrator of these crimes was $217.

Bernalyn and Roy Dumas lived at the Heritage Apartments on South Cooper Street in Memphis. Bernalyn, a nursing supervisor, was employed at the Baptist Memorial Hospital. Roy, a small man who had been wounded so badly in the Second World War that he was receiving a 100 per cent disability pension from the U.S. Army, worked at home. One room of the couple's first-floor apartment was Roy's accounting office.

August 14, 1969, began in a routine manner for the Dumases, but it would not be a normal day. It was destined to become Day One in Memphis's twenty-nine days of terror and the last day of life for Bernalyn and Roy Dumas.

Bernalyn caught a bus to the hospital. Roy, who had been awarded the Bronze Star, Purple Heart, and a Presidential Citation during the war, and who now weighed less than 100 pounds, rose from bed. He turned on his television set and then answered a knock on his apartment door. A young, blonde stranger pushed him aside, demanding money. Frail Roy Dumas ground his teeth in frustration. He knew he was no match for the younger man. He swore he had no money.

Roy was then shoved and pushed into his bedroom, where he was tied to the bed with his own suspenders. A pair of his wife's pantyhose served as a gag. The blonde stranger ransacked the apartment but only managed to find two items of interest. He placed Roy's hunting knife in his belt, and took a $5 bill from a dresser drawer. Later, the desperate intruder extracted a further $7 from Roy's wallet before settling down to wait for Mrs. Dumas to come home from work.

Several hours later Bernalyn let herself into the apartment. The blonde man, using the hunting knife to threaten the terrified woman, forced her into the bedroom before tying her with a scarf he found in a closet.

The now frenzied intruder raped Bernalyn before removing a $20 bill from her purse. Using a handkerchief he effectively wiped the entire apartment clean of fingerprints. Bending over his victim, the madman proceeded to strangle her with the pantyhose already placed over her mouth. It didn't take long. In a cool and calculating manner the blonde man entered Roy's room and proceeded to strangle him in the same way. All was quiet, save for the several tenants swimming in a nearby pool. No one saw the murderer leave the building. Several hours later, Mike Dumas, the dead couple's son, called on his parents and discovered their bodies.

Eleven days after the Dumas's death, on August 25, Leila Jackson, an 80-year-old widow was murdered. Mrs. Jackson had lived in the same house for a quarter of a century, supplementing her small social-security allotment by renting rooms. Her one son lived in Memphis and had a family of his own. Each week Mrs. Jackson had dinner out with her son and his wife. On the day before she was murdered, Mrs. Jackson was driven home from dinner by her son.

The following morning, after the three roomers had left for work, Mrs. Jackson put out the garbage and chatted with the mailman. An hour later the laundryman called at the Jackson house but received no answer when he rang the bell. He assumed no one was home and went on with his next delivery. Inside Leila Jackson was dead. What had transpired in that fateful hour?

After the mailman had left, Mrs. Jackson answered a knock at her front door. A blonde man inquired about a room. While showing the young man the one vacant bedroom, the elderly woman was attacked, raped, and strangled to death with one of her own dishtowels. Mrs. Jackson's billfold yielded $85. More by luck than design, the killer walked away from the murder scene without being seen by anyone. Don Jackson, a grandson of the victim, discovered the body.

The similarities between the Dumas and Jackson killings did not go unnoticed. Soon the word was out. A madman was loose in Memphis. Who would be next? The good citizens of Memphis didn't have long to wait.

Glenda Sue Harden was murdered four days after Leila Jackson. Glenda Sue was a tall, good-looking 21-year-old secretary with the Jackson Life Insurance Co. She was planning on announcing her engagement in September. The wedding that would never be was scheduled for January. These were the thoughts which crowded Glenda Sue's mind as she started up her '65 Mustang to drive home.

Suddenly a blonde man jerked open the door of her car. He held a knife to her throat as he shoved her to the passenger side of the car. He then told her to drop to the floor of the vehicle, which the terrified girl did without hesitation. Driving with one hand and keeping his knife no more than an inch from his victim's head, the blonde man drove out of the city. He turned into Riverside Park, where he spotted a heavily wooded dirt road.

The blonde man raped Glenda Sue in the car. He then marched her deeper into the woods, where he stabbed her fourteen times. Within minutes he was back in downtown Memphis with Glenda Sue's car. He managed to wipe all his fingerprints from the interior of the car and counted up his take from the vicious killing. It had been the best yet. Glenda Sue had been paid that day. The blond man was richer by $100. Elated at his newfound wealth, he abandoned Glenda Sue's car and calmly drove his car away. His movements went unobserved.

Glenda Sue's parents reported her missing when she failed to arrive home from work. Next morning her Mustang was spotted by two detectives. The authorities' worst fears were realized when Glenda Sue's body was found the following day by patrolmen searching Riverside Park.

The killer had one more card to play. He played it twelve days later as he watched Mary Christine Pickens approach her apartment building. She was carrying a purse. He followed her up the apartment building steps, staying a half-dozen paces behind. As the unsuspecting woman opened the door of her apartment, she was pushed inside. She screamed. Her attacker began stabbing her with a long hunting knife. He then ran out of the building and down the streets. Mrs. Pickens, who had just returned from grocery shopping, lay dead on the floor of her apartment.

The attack on Mrs. Pickens was quite different from the previous murders. This time many people in the building heard her screams for help. Several reacted.

Wayne Armstrong opened his apartment door, saw the killer carrying a bloody knife in his hand, and quickly slammed his door shut. He dashed to his bedroom, grabbed a pistol, and ran after the murderer, who by this time was in the street. Armstrong made quite a sight running through the streets clad only in his boxer shorts.

Henry Clay Currie took off after the fleeing man in his car but was blocked on a one-way street by a telephone company truck. Other citizens phoned police, who quickly joined the hunt. After a long, complicated chase the blonde man, who had terrorized an entire city for 29 days and had killed five innocent citizens, was taken into custody.

Once in jail the killer requested a conference with his wife, who knew nothing of her husband's murderous ways. Later it was revealed that he asked her if he should tell the truth and confess. She advised him to do so, and thus we have the details of the last minutes of the victims' lives as outlined by the killer.

Buster Putt had spent most of his early life in institutions and foster homes. In 1967 he married a girl who was pregnant with his brother's baby. His wife, Mary, was 18. He was 21. Buster never kept a job for long and never really supported his wife and child. Often his behavior was so incredible it bordered on lunacy. Two years after his marriage his wife was once again pregnant. Buster was down to selling his own blood to buy beer and purchase gasoline for his old car. For no apparent reason he decided that he needed another car. An old wreck was available for $100. Buster raised the money by murdering Glenda Sue Harden. He drove his new acquisition home but was never able to get it started again.

Buster, who confessed to all five murders, was identified by witnesses who had taken part in the wild chase from the Pickens's apartment. The knife with which he had stabbed Mrs. Pickens was found along the route of the chase. It was the hunting knife taken from the Dumas' apartment.

Buster Putt stood trial for the murder of Mrs. Pickens in October 1970 in the same courtroom where James Earl Ray pleaded guilty to the murder of Martin Luther King. Buster was found guilty and sentenced to death. Later the sentence was commuted to 99 years' imprisonment. Still later he was convicted of the Dumas slayings, receiving 199 years for each murder. It all added up to 497 years in prison, the longest sentence ever meted out in Memphis.

Buster giggled as the judge passed sentence.

HEATH WAS A CHARMER

Neville George Clevely Heath was a handsome, charming former officer and gentleman. He was also a sadist and murderer. Psychiatrists, who have a habit of indexing weird individuals, had to admit that Heath was unique.

The ten-year period of Heath's life commencing in 1936 and ending in 1946 contains a winding strain of lies, frauds, arrests, and jail sentences. In 1936 Heath joined the Royal Air Force. It took him only a year to be tossed out of the service for being absent without leave after stealing an officer's car. Soon after his discharge he was sentenced to three years in jail for passing bad cheques and stealing jewelry. Released from jail in 1939, Heath enlisted in the Royal Army Service Corps., was commissioned within a year and posted to the Middle East.

In July 1941, Heath was cashiered out of the service for again being absent without leave and passing worthless cheques. While being sent back to England, he jumped ship in Durban, South Africa. Using his overabundant gall and natural charm, Heath managed to enlist in the South African Air Force under a fictitious name. He became a pilot, was loaned to the RAF, and was shot down near the Dutch-German border.

He returned to South Africa, where he married, had a son, and promptly deserted his young family. At the conclusion of the war his wife obtained a divorce. Within a year Heath was again head over heels in hot water and was discharged from the South African Air Force. He returned to England in February 1946.

This, then, was the criminal record of Neville Heath. Although his career was spotted with lawbreaking, there is no hint of any acts of violence.

Twenty-nine-year-old Neville Heath, who called himself Lieutenant Colonel, met Yvonne Symonds. The glamorous war hero attended a dance in Chelsea. Yvonne was thrilled when after the dance Neville asked her to accompany him to the Panama Club. She was a bit surprised when our hero blurted out, "Let's find a hotel and sleep together." While the proposition was not altogether unattractive to Yvonne, she turned down the offer.

Next day Neville and Yvonne spent the entire day together. Yvonne was truly smitten with Neville's good manners and charming demeanor. To her way of thinking, good fortune had brought the perfect man into her life. That very day dashing Neville proposed marriage and Yvonne gladly accepted. When Neville suggested they prematurely consummate the union, Yvonne consented. They checked into the Pembridge Court Hotel in Notting Hill Gate as Mr. and Mrs. Lt. Col. N.G.C. Heath.

Later Yvonne was to reveal that nothing of a perverted nature went on behind the closed door of Room 4 that night. Her Neville was a kind, considerate and gentle lover. The following morning Yvonne left London for her parents' home in Worthing, her head aswirl with thoughts of love, marriage, and children. She had no way of knowing that her secret night of gentle love would in a few months be splattered over the front pages of the world's press. She also had no way of knowing that she had escaped the clutches of one of the cruelest, most vicious sadists ever to walk the stage of English crime.

Heath stayed on at the Pembridge Court Hotel. The following Thursday he accompanied Margery Gardner to an evening of dancing and drinking at the Panama Club in Kensington. Margery, at 32, was slightly older than Heath. Separated from her husband, she was attractive enough to have aspirations toward a career in the movies. She accepted Heath's invitation to spend the night with him at his hotel.

By 2:00 p.m. the following day the hotel staff had decided to enter Room 4 with a passkey. Margery's body was in plain sight of the bed. She had been horribly mutilated. Her ankles were bound together and her arms were folded behind her. Later an autopsy indicated that Margery had been lashed with a whip. Seventeen individual braided welt marks were visible all over her body. The area around her breasts had been cruelly bitten. The killer had thrust a foreign object into her vagina, but this instrument was never found or identified. All of these indignities were inflicted while the victim was still alive but most likely unconscious. Margery's face had been pressed into a pillow. Death was attributed to asphyxia due to suffocation.

Police had little trouble coming up with a prime suspect, for Heath had been registered at the hotel as Lt. Col. Heath for some time. Meanwhile, the dashing officer was off to Worthing, for a friendly visit with the unsuspecting Yvonne Symonds. Heath, still the debonair man about town, checked into the Ocean Hotel, called his girlfriend, and had lunch with her.

Next day the "engaged" couple met again. From time to time that Saturday, Heath brought up the sensational case of the body found in the hotel room back in London. He explained to Yvonne that the body had been found in his room, the very room where he and Yvonne had spent such a pleasant night a few short evenings earlier. Heath told Yvonne that he had loaned the room to a passing acquaintance and that he had spent the night elsewhere. He further explained that because it was his room the police had made him view the body, which Heath described as a "gruesome sight."

When Yvonne inquired who could do such a thing to a woman, Heath replied, quite truthfully, "A sexual maniac." That same day Heath dined with Yvonne's parents, who, like their daughter, found him to be a real charmer. Next day, as the murder case gained further notoriety in the newspapers, the Symonds became somewhat concerned about their future son-in-law. Heath assured Yvonne that he would return to London and clear up any misunderstanding which might exist. The next time Yvonne was to see her fiancé would be in the Old Bailey in London when he stood trial for murder.

Instead of returning to London, Heath travelled to Bournemouth, where he booked a room at the Tollard Royal Hotel under the improbable name of Group Captain Rupert Brooke. For eleven days the Group Captain was a fixture around the hotel. Sporting a mustard-colored jacket with grey flannels, Brooke became the hotel's most popular guest.

Doreen Marshall's family sent her to Bournemouth to recover from a bout of influenza. Doreen was staying at the Norfolk Hotel. It was her misfortune to make the acquaintance of Group Captain Rupert Brooke. On July 3 Brooke had tea, and later dinner, at his hotel with Miss Marshall. They left together. Ostensibly Brooke was walking Doreen to her hotel. She never made it.

Two mornings later the manager of the Norfolk opened Doreen's room and reported her missing to the police. He also called a colleague at the Tollard Royal, informing him that Miss Marshall had indicated that she might be dining there on the evening of July 3. The manager remembered Brooke's dinner companion and inquired as to her identity. Brooke assured the manager that his guest was not Miss Marshall. However, he did volunteer to drop in at the police station to view a photograph of the missing girl.

Group Captain Brooke identified Doreen Marshall's photo as that of the lady he had dined with on the evening of July 3. He stated that he had walked his date back to the garden area of the Norfolk Hotel. Detective Constable Souter listened to his story as he stared intently at Brooke. Suddenly it came to him. "Isn't your name Heath?" he interrupted. Brooke declared that it was not. He insisted that he was cold and wanted his jacket, which was back at the hotel. Police retrieved the jacket, and in doing so searched the pockets. They found a cloakroom ticket stub, which enabled them to claim an attache case. The case contained a leather riding whip, a blood-smeared scarf, and one pearl. The pattern of the weave of the riding whip matched the welts on Margery Gardner's body.

Heath was still denying any involvement in Doreen Marshall's disappearance when her nude body was found three days later under some rhododendron bushes not far from the centre of Bournemouth. Scattered over the general area were twenty-seven pearls from her broken necklace. The lone pearl found in Heath's attache case matched the twenty-seven found near the body. Doreen had been cut and slashed as she fought for her life. The cause of death was attributed to a deep cut in her throat. Again the killer had bitten the victim's breasts and inserted a foreign object into her vagina.

Later it was ascertained that Heath had pawned a ring and watch belonging to Doreen. Confronted with the array of damning evidence, Brooke admitted that he was in reality Neville Heath. He was immediately arrested and charged with the murders of Margery Gardner and Doreen Marshall.

On September 24, 1946, Heath stood trial for the murder of Margery Gardner. His trial lasted only three days, for there was no doubt of his guilt. The only question at issue was the matter of the accused man's sanity. Applying the hard-and-fast rules of whether Heath knew what he was doing when he committed murder and whether he knew that what he was doing was wrong, there was no question but that Heath was sane. His lawyers didn't put him on the witness stand because they feared that once a jury heard this charming, intelligent man, they would most certainly judge him to be sane. It mattered little, for the jury deliberated only fifty-nine minutes before bringing in a verdict of guilty.

On October 26, 1946, Neville Heath was asked if he had any last requests before being led to the scaffold at Pentonville Jail. He requested a shot of whisky. As it was being brought to him he said, "Under the circumstances you might make that a double." Those were his last words.

VON COSEL
BUILT A BRIDE

K**ey West** is the southernmost key in a necklace of tiny islands joined by bridges stretching into the Gulf of Mexico from Florida's mainland. It is unlike any other part of Florida.

The citizens behave far more like Caribbeans than Floridians. For years, before they were connected to the mainland by the chain of bridges, the "Conchs," as the natives are known, were practically isolated. Many of their customs are to this day celebrated in a unique manner.

Halloween is one of the biggest holidays of the year in Key West. Eight nights of merrymaking known as Fantasy Fest culminates with Halloween.

In 1931 the most beautiful girl on Key West was 21-year-old Elena Milagro Hoyos. The dark-eyed Elena's classic beauty turned more than one head when she strolled down Duval Street. Her father made his meagre living as a cigar-maker.

At this time there lived on Key West a strange man with a strange name, Karl Tanzler von Cosel. Later, weird von Cosel would be compared with another unusual chap named Frankenstein. They did have one idiosyncrasy in common. Both attempted to construct their own brides.

Von Cosel was a radiologist at the Marine Hospital. That was about the only regular thing about the 62-year-old, tall, balding man with the white goatee. While on Key West he lived alone and was an introverted, emaciated figure, never seen doing much other than walking to and from the hospital.

One balmy spring day in 1931 Elena walked into the x-ray department at Marine Hospital. Von Cosel took one look at her and was never the same again. Neither was

Key West.

The old boy fell hard. Let's have him tell it: "I was in love with her the first time I saw her. I was spellbound, transfixed." Von Cosel's knees trembled, but he managed to give Elena a chest x-ray. He was shattered to discover that his new and true love had an advanced case of tuberculosis.

Because of her illness, Elena was home a great deal of the time. Von Cosel never tired of visiting her. He perfected what he called a ray gun, which he used to give Elena treatments. Nothing helped. The beautiful girl's condition continued to worsen.

Elena's family didn't mind the eccentric old man who had obviously fallen madly in love with their daughter. That is, they didn't mind him until he proposed marriage. That was going too far. Elene's father forbade further treatments with the ray gun and insisted that von Cosel stay away from his daughter.

On October 25, 1931, Elena's parents thought their daughter might be cheered up by attending the Halloween parade, the most colorful event of the year in Key West. Unfortunately, Elena suffered a severe attack while watching the parade and was rushed home. She died before a doctor could reach her, but not before our boy von Cosel was at her side. He frantically worked over the stricken girl with his ray gun and had to be pulled away from her dead body.

Elena was buried in the city cemetery without being embalmed. After the family had recovered from their initial grief, von Cosel approached Elena's father with an unusual request. He asked if he could build a mausoleum for Elena. Permission was granted.

Soon Elena rested in her own private miniature mausoleum. He lit candles and, in the eerie light, sat beside the closed coffin, speaking to his love and writing her poems of endearment.

The thought of Elena's body deteriorating in her coffin preyed on von Cosel's mind. Finally, he could stand it no more. In the wee hours of the morning he dragged the coffin out of its resting place and lugged it to his home, located in a lonesome, almost deserted section of town.

There is little doubt that von Cosel firmly believed that Elena was not dead but in some state which allowed her to hear and appreciate what he was attempting to do.

It was now two years since Elena's death. Von Cosel used techniques he had acquired while performing surgery on wounded men during the First World War. He studied ancient Egyptian methods of preserving the dead. Then he set about the task at hand. The task was to rebuild the decomposed body of Elena Milagro Hoyos.

"I rebuilt the lost parts, bandaged the broken parts, and the destroyed parts I replaced. I put in sufficient absorbent material for packing to soak her in solutions and develop the tissues. I made these solutions very carefully."

Like Frankenstein before him, von Cosel was building a bride.

Von Cosel used plaster of Paris, beeswax, and piano wire. He installed glass eyes on the corpse and fitted the skull with human hair. He used a specially treated cheesecloth to give the skin a realistic texture. He also used cosmetics extensively. The results were remarkable. The mad radiologist had recreated a lifelike replica of the beauty that had once been a vivacious woman.

After his lifelike creature had taken form, von Cosel moved the body to a bedroom and purchased an organ. Each evening beside his replica bride he played long into the night.

For seven years von Cosel talked to and played the organ for his beautiful rebuilt and long-dead bride. Later he explained that Elena spoke to him every night.

Rumors spread throughout the community that strange things were going on at von Cosel's home. Elena's sister, Florinda Medina, heard of the horrors that had been whispered about for years. Disturbed, Florinda faced von Cosel with the unbelievable gossip.

The 71-year-old recluse did not deny the horrible accusations. Instead he invited Florinda inside and parted a curtain which concealed a bed. There lay the lifelike form of her sister in a wedding dress. Von Cosel is reported to have said, "That's Elena, I beg you to leave her to me. See how pretty she looks. Touch her little hands."

Florinda staggered back in horror, but regained her composure enough to order von Cosel to return her sister's body to the mausoleum within a week or risk arrest.

A week later police officers showed up at von Cosel's home. Nothing had changed. There lay Elena, resplendent in her wedding dress. Von Cosel explained that he slept in a second bed pushed over beside his bride, "It was good to have her beside me always."

Von Cosel was hustled off to jail. Elena's body was put on display at the Lopez Funeral Home. The fantastic story of the reconstructed bride appeared in newspapers the world over. In three days, 6,850 individuals viewed the amazing remains at the funeral home. Morticians who examined the body all agreed that von Cosel had done a remarkable job in reconstructing the corpse.

Strangely enough, the public viewed the weird case as a love story and had great sympathy for von Cosel. A check of his credentials revealed that he had never received a medical degree but had been self-taught in everything he did for a living, including the practice of radiology.

Von Cosel was charged with robbing a grave, but authorities ran into difficulty when they realized that the statute of limitations had run out on this crime.

Meanwhile, Elena's sister made arrangements to have the built-up corpse dismantled. The body was then returned to the graveyard in the middle of the night and secretly buried. Elena rests there undisturbed to this day.

Freed of criminal charges, von Cosel remained in Key West for six months. In April 1941, he left Key West forever and went to live with his sister in Zephyrhills, Florida. Five hours after his departure, at 1:45 a.m., a loud explosion shook the city cemetery. Someone had set off a timed dynamite blast, blowing the doors off Elena's mausoleum. Many believe it was von Cosel's farewell gesture to Key West.

On August 13, 1952, von Cosel died of natural causes in Zephyrhills. Police were forced to break down the door of the 83-year-old madman's home when they were informed that he had not emptied his mailbox for three days. He was found dead on the floor.

A search of the home uncovered many poems to Elena, as well as photographs of his rebuilt bride taken years before. The most startling find of all was a life-size wax replica of Elena Milagro Hoyos.

THE CLOWN
KILLED BOYS

John Wayne Gacy would grow up to be a manager of a chain of southern fried chicken stores, a successful shoe-store manager, a respected member of the Junior Chamber of Commerce, a performing clown, a precinct captain in the Democratic Party, and the owner of his own prosperous contracting business. He also was to become the most prolific mass murderer in the history of the United States.

John's formative years hold no clue to his future bizarre behavior. Gregarious, fun-loving John Gacy was an average student who took a job as a shoe salesman after graduating from Northwestern Business College in Chicago.

In 1964, when he was 22, he was so highly regarded by the shoe firm that he was transferred to Springfield, Illinois, where he was made manager of the company's retail outlet. A few months later he was dating and eventually married co-worker Marlynn Myers.

John, who always had a weight problem, tipped the scales at approximately 220 pounds and stood only 5 feet 8 inches tall. His sparkling personality more than made up for his chunky appearance. He joined the Junior Chamber of Commerce, where he was one of the hardest working and most popular members of the local chapter.

When his father-in-law offered him a job in Waterloo, Iowa, working for his chain of southern fried chicken franchise stores, John jumped at the opportunity. Soon he was effectively running the chain, often working sixteen hours a day. John joined the Jaycees and quickly became a valuable member of the organization. He was named chaplain as well as chairman of the group's prayer breakfast. Marlynn gave birth to two healthy children, a son John, and a daughter Elaine.

In the spring of 1968 the veil of respectability which shielded John Gacy's world began to crumble. A local boy claimed that while he was working for John in one of the food outlets, he had accompanied the older man to his home. Mrs. Gacy and the children were not in.

After providing his visitor with a few drinks John suggested oral sex. When the boy refused, John threatened him with a knife and fastened him to a bed with chains. Gacy proceeded to choke the young lad until he was almost unconscious, abruptly releasing him and allowing him to leave the house.

A second boy told much the same story. His experience culminated with being forced to perform unnatural sex acts. John was arrested, and after much plea bargaining, was charged with committing sodomy. Understandably, at this time his wife left him.

John was sentenced to ten years' imprisonment at the Iowa State Reformatory for men at Anamosa. Anamosa boasted one of the first Jaycee chapters formed in an American prison. John threw himself into chapter work with the same vigor he had employed at Waterloo. As a result he became president of the organization. Eighteen months after entering prison John was paroled.

Still under thirty, John returned to Chicago. For a while he lived with his mother, having gained employment as a cook in a nearby restaurant. Four months after his release, with his mother's help, John purchased his own home at 8213 West Summerdale Avenue in suburban Norwood Park.

On February 12, 1971, a short time after moving into his own home, John was charged with disorderly conduct by Chicago police. A teenaged admitted homosexual claimed that John picked him up, drove him to his home, and attempted to force him to perform unnatural sex acts. When his accuser failed to show up in court, the charges against John were dropped.

No one has ever been able to explain why the Iowa Board of Parole was not made aware that Gacy had been charged with a sex crime in another state. Still on parole on the sodomy charge, Gacy's activities certainly would have been curtailed had a routine check been carried out. Unfortunately, the board was never informed. One month later Gacy was officially discharged from parole.

On the surface it appeared that Gacy was rebuilding his life. He met Carole Hoff, the divorced mother of two little girls, who would soon become the second Mrs. Gacy. He made friends with his neighbors. Everyone liked big John Gacy.

What no one knew, and could not possibly conceive, was the horrible fact that the most prolific mass murderer in U.S. history was already killing boys and burying them under the crawlspace of his home. It is believed that the first murder took place on the night of January 3, 1972. The killings were to last for the next seven years.

After John and Carole were wed, she and her two children were to remain in the death house for the next four years. Carole was completely unaware that John could only gain sexual gratification by killing. She was well aware that her husband was forever doing carpentry jobs around the house, making additions to this, enlarging that. Many men do the same thing. She never gave it a second thought.

Around this time a strange musty odor became noticeable in the Gacy household. John claimed it was a broken sewer tile. The old tile was replaced, but the odor didn't abate until John closed off the vents leading from the crawlspace.

Meanwhile, John was a considerate husband to Carole and a good father to her two children. Around the neighborhood he gained something of a reputation as a party giver. A couple of times a year he would throw a big barbecue. It wasn't uncommon for these feasts to be attended by more than a hundred friends and neighbors. John loved to dress up as a clown and entertain the neighborhood children.

Gacy left his job as a cook and opened his own business, P.D.M. Contractors, Inc. It was successful from the beginning. John hired experienced older men for skilled tasks, but drew his manual labor from young boys who were willing to work for low wages. His construction company expanded rapidly, and soon John was bidding on and obtaining contracts worth up to $100,000. He purchased a Cadillac and became active in the Democratic Party.

All the while renovations were taking place at the Gacy home. John built a storage shed at the end of the garage. It was customary to see young boys coming and going. Everyone knew John hired them for his construction company.

Carole became disenchanted with her marriage. Her husband spent all his time either working at his business or working for the Democrats. He seemed to prefer the company of young boys to hers. She filed for divorce and left her husband on March 2, 1976.

For seven years boys and young men had been picked up by Gacy off the streets or were befriended when they applied for employment with his construction company. He gratified his strange sexual desires before killing them and burying them on his own property.

Robert Piest was a conscientious high-school student who worked in a drugstore on a part-time basis. At 8:00 p.m., when his mother called at Nissons Pharmacy in Des Plaines to pick up her son on the evening of December 11, 1978,

Robert asked her to wait in the store for a few moments. He had to talk to a man named John Gacy about a contracting job which paid quite a bit better than his present job at the drugstore. Gacy was waiting in his pickup truck in the parking lot. Robert left the store, telling his mother that he would be back in a few moments. He never returned.

Mrs. Piest searched the parking lot. She questioned Robert's friends. No one could help her. Finally she called the police. Next day detectives were extensively questioning John Gacy about the missing boy. Gacy denied having any knowledge about the disappearance. When detectives were informed of Gacy's criminal record, they obtained a warrant to search his home. It soon was being referred to as the death house.

Rows of bodies, some little more than skeletons, were found buried in the crawlspace of the house. Others were found buried under the recreation room, while still others were buried in the garage. In all, twenty-nine bodies were removed from Gacy's property. Four other victims had been thrown in nearby rivers.

Gacy's murder trial concluded on March 13, 1980, when he was convicted of murdering thirty-three young men and boys, more than any other person in U.S. history. He was sentenced to death in the electric chair, and today resides on Death Row at the Menard Correctional Centre in Illinois.

TONY PLANTED BODIES

Tony Costa was an exceptional gardener. He planted only two crops - marijuana and female bodies.

Aside from his horticultural pursuits, Tony made a precarious living as a part-time carpenter in and around Provincetown, Massachusetts. In 1969 Provincetown, located on the northern tip of Cape Cod, was a home away from home for hundreds of youths who felt that the drug scene took precedence over that dull but necessary activity known as work.

Tony married young. He was a high school student when he met 14-year-old Avis, who quickly became Mrs. Costa. In the succeeding years Avis gave birth to three children, while Tony chafed under the responsibility of providing for a family.

Tony entered the drug scene with a vengeance. He was rarely without his supply of pills. In fact, he kept such a large supply on hand that he secreted it in some woods near Truro, a few miles down the road from Provincetown.

Tony spent less and less time at home, until finally he and Avis were divorced. Free to play the field, Tony was often in the company of girls who were either visiting Provincetown or were among the hordes of youths who made the hippie resort town their home.

In January 1969, Pat Walsh and Mary Anne Wysocki were reported missing. The two girls had left Providence, Rhode Island to spend the weekend in Provincetown, but had not returned. Police traced the girls' last known movements. On Friday, Jan. 24, Pat and Mary Anne had checked into a guest house owned by Mrs. Patricia Morton, paying $24 in advance for two nights lodging.

The girls left on Saturday morning. When questioned by the police, Mrs. Morton said that she had seen a note from a permanent resident, Tony Costa, pinned to the girls' door. He had asked them for a lift to Truro. He, too, had not been seen by Mrs. Morton after Friday night. It appeared to the police that the girls had given Tony a lift in Pat's light blue 1968 Volkswagen on Saturday morning and had not been heard of since.

When Provincetown police checked with Truro's two man police force, they learned that a light blue Volks had been reported parked by woods near Truro. The Truro police informed them that when they had checked out the parked car, they had found a note on the windshield. It said, "Engine trouble, will return." They now returned to the South Truro woods and found that the Volkswagen was gone.

Upon examining the wooded area beyond the road, police found torn insurance documents and sales slips in the name of Patricia Walsh. There was the very real possibility that the two friends had wandered away from their car and become lost in the woods. Exposed to the frigid January weather, they could easily have frozen to death.

Next morning one hundred men searched the wooded area. Three hours after the search began, a slight depression in the ground was detected by the searchers. The men dug and soon uncovered a human foot. Further digging revealed a leg and two arms. Police believed they had recovered the dismembered remains of Pat Walsh. They were wrong.

Returning to Mrs. Morton's guest house, detectives found that Tony Costa had left his personal belongings in his room. Obviously he had departed in a hurry. His mother thought that he had gone to Boston. His ex-wife Avis had no idea as to his whereabouts.

Provincetown police were surprised to receive a phone call from Tony. He called from Burlington, Vermont. His mother had informed him of the body found in the Truro woods and of the two missing girls. He was calling to clear up matters. According to Tony, he had met the girls at a Provincetown bar. Pat wanted an abortion and was going to meet a man named Russell, who would accompany her and Mary Anne to Los Angeles, where she would undergo the operation. The last Tony saw of the girls, they were heading down the road towards Hyannis.

Tony returned to Provincetown driving Pat Walsh's Volkswagen. He now told police a different story. He said that he knew the two missing girls from the previous summer. They had purchased dope from him and skipped without paying. When he spotted them in Provincetown, he bought the Volkswagen from Pat for $900, paying

$300 cash and deducting $600 Pat owed him. This was the first of many stories Tony was to tell officials to account for his possession of Pat Walsh's car.

It was while interrogating Tony's acquaintances that police stumbled upon Tony's horticultural bent. Somewhere in the Truro woods he maintained a marijuana garden and had often taken girls into the woods when he watered his plants. Tony also kept his cache of drugs nearby, but none of his girlfriends had actually seen the drugs.

One girl, Marsha Mowery, was willing to lead police to Tony's garden. In freezing rain they passed by the open grave where the remnants of the still unidentified body had been uncovered. Walking along a partially obscured trail through the woods they came to a clearing. This was the site of Tony Costa's marijuana garden.

Six weeks had passed since Pat Walsh and Mary Anne Hysocki had left Mrs. Morton's guest house. On March 5 the two girls' bodies were discovered in shallow graves near Tony's garden. Both had been viciously attacked with a knife, horribly mutilated and sexually ravished. Several organs had been removed from the bodies. Clothing found in the graves identified the victims. Dental charts verified the identification. An autopsy indicated that the two girls had been shot with a .22 calibre weapon.

While removing the remains of the two girls, police uncovered another body. The dissected sections of this female body were in an advanced state of decomposition and had obviously been buried for a much longer period of time. A fingerprint check of missing girls identified the body as that of Sydney Monzon, who had been reported missing the previous May 28.

By tracing a ring found on the very first corpse, detectives were able to identify 17-year-old Susan Perry. She had at one time lived with Tony Costa and was last seen in his company.

Tony was taken into custody, but steadfastly denied any guilt in any of the four deaths. He claimed that he was being harassed and persecuted because of his involvement in the Provincetown drug scene.

Tony twisted and elaborated on his original story to cover all the circumstances concerning the murders already known by the investigating officers. He vehemently swore that his brother had loaned him the $300 he required to complete the purchase of Pat Walsh's car. At first Tony's brother verified this story, but as the case developed, he admitted that he had lied to protect his brother.

Tony had a handwritten bill of sale for the Volkswagen signed by Pat Walsh. FBI handwriting experts stated that Pat's signature was in Tony's disguised handwriting.

Gradually Tony opened up. Initially he would only admit to being on the scene while a friend killed the girls and dissected the bodies. Slowly he gravitated to helping his friend mutilate the bodies. Finally he admitted to the killings.

Tony Costa was examined by psychiatrists and adjudged to be legally sane. He was also considered to be an amoral psychopath, caring only for the fulfilment of his immediate needs with no thoughts or feelings for others. In short, a monster.

Tony was tried, found guilty of two charges of murder and sentenced to two life terms in prison with no possibility of parole. On May 12, 1974, Tony Costa fastened his leather belt over the upper bars of his cell at the Massachusetts Correction Institute at Walpole and hanged himself. He was 29.

NEW ENGLAND SERIAL KILLER

As I drove down the main street of Jewett City, Connecticut, Al Schumanski was busy at his Amoco Gas station pumping air into the rear tire of a little boy's bicycle. Hendel's Furniture Store didn't have a single customer despite the big mattress sale signs in their front window. Claire LaPointe sold gas and cigarettes at Chucky's Country Store.

"Visited Toronto years ago," Al Schumanski told me. "Is the Spaghetti Factory still there? Great place. Haven't been back for years." The little boy pedalled away toward the town square where East Main and North Main intersect. It's dry and hot in the David Hale Fanning Park where three large stones list the names of every soldier in the vicinity who served in World Wars I and II and the Korean War. There is no memorial for those who served in Vietnam.

This is small town New England, the heart and soul of the U.S. The tiny Connecticut towns are reminiscent of Norman Rockwell paintings: Danielson, Brooklyn, Canterbury, Plainfield, Jewett City, Lisbon, Griswold, Preston. They run into each other, similar, neat, sun drenched, off the beaten path. No real need to lock a door at night. Most neighbors have known each other for a lifetime. Violence and its ugly ramifications belong in Boston and New York, not in these pleasant, quaint towns.

Police Chief Thurston Fields knows pretty well every one of Jewett City's 4000 inhabitants. His five man police force keeps the peace with the aid of two patrol cars. Chief Fields assures me, "There has never been a murder in Jewett City in the 11 years I've been chief and I can't remember one before that."

On Jan. 5, 1982, the small community of Brooklyn, Conn. was shocked when Tammy Williams, 17, disappeared. Hundreds of acres of brush and swamp in the area along Route 6 were searched. Tracking dogs were used. Five hundred volunteers searched the rough terrain. No trace of Tammy was found.

On June 15, 1982, Debbie Taylor and her husband James of Jewett City ran out of gas near Danielson. Debbie walked down the highway looking for a service station, while James walked in the opposite direction. Debbie never returned. Next day she was reported missing. Four and a half months later, Debbie's body was found in a Canterbury cornfield. Her skull had been crushed.

No doubt a sex-crazed stranger had lured Debbie into his car. It was horrible. It was shocking. But after all, it was an isolated incident.

Over a year passed. Most people forgot about Debbie Taylor's fate. Most forgot about the missing Tammy Williams, but not Tammy's father. He frequented flea markets, bazaars and other public gatherings, inquiring about his missing daughter. He never turned up a clue.

On Nov. 16, 1983, Robin Stavinsky disappeared off the streets of Norwich. The attractive high school student and state discus champion had a date that day, but never kept it. A week later a jogger found her body in a wooded area on the outskirts of Norwich on Thames Hospital property. Robin had been strangled to death.

Two girls murdered and one missing in two years. Were they unrelated or were the murders the work of one deranged individual? Rumors spread throughout the Connecticut towns.

Leslie Shelley, 14, and April Brunais, 15, were last seen walking on the streets of Jewett City. When they failed to return to their respective homes on April 22, 1984, they were thought to be runaways. The two friends had run away once before for one day. This time they apparently left for good.

Seven weeks later Wendy Baribeault, 17, left her Lisbon home on Round Hill Court to make a purchase at Chucky's Country Store. She left a message for her parents telling them where she was going.

Police Chief Fields and I measured off the distance between Wendy's home and the Country Store. It is exactly 1.6 miles. Somewhere in that short distance Wendy Baribeault disappeared. Wendy was immediately reported missing. A massive search of the area uncovered her body two days later. She had been sexually attacked.

The killer's luck had run out when he murdered Wendy Baribeault. This time an alert citizen informed police that she had seen Wendy walking along the road. A man in a blue 1983 Toyota seemed to be following her. Police checked over 2000 vehicles with the State Department of Motor Vehicles. By elimination they came up with Michael Ross, 24, a man who had attacked a woman in Ohio years before.

At that time Ross pretended to run out of gas in front of a house he had picked at random. He asked to use the telephone. Once inside, he attacked the lone woman occupant. Ross had picked the wrong woman. She was an off-duty police officer who was an expert in ju jitsu. He managed to get away, but was arrested a short time later.

Michael Ross was arraigned in Ohio, but allowed to return to his Brooklyn, Conn. home when his parents posted a $1000 bond. He received psychological evaluation for two months before being brought back to Ohio, where he served four and half months in jail. He was released on Dec. 22, 1982 to spend Christmas with his parents in Connecticut.

Michael Ross was arrested and charged with the murder of Wendy Baribeault. Connecticut detectives are reluctant to discuss details, but the fact remains that almost immediately after Ross' arrest, they recovered the bodies of Tammy Williams, Leslie Shelley and April Brunais in woods beside local roads. Ross has been charged with felony murder in the deaths of all six girls. Felony murder carries the death sentence in Connecticut.

Born in Brooklyn, Michael Ross lived most of his life in eastern Connecticut. In 1977 he graduated as an honors student from nearby Killingly High School. His teachers remember him as a keen student, who was quiet and well-behaved. In 1981 he graduated from Cornell University with a major in agricultural economics.

He lived in Jewett City in a large green and white house at 158 North Main St. His girlfriend, Debbie Wallace, divorced mother of three children, lived there with him. She refuses to believe that Michael could be responsible for the brutal murders of six women. Neighbors also find it difficult to believe that the polite, well-dressed, friendly young man could be a killer.

While living in Jewett City, Ross was employed with the Prudential Insurance Co. of America as a district agent and registered representative. An official of the insurance company has stated that of the 26,000 agents employed across the U.S. by the company, nothing like Michael Ross has ever happened before.

The hamlet of Brooklyn, Conn., population 900, was incorporated in 1796. A large statue of Major General Israel Putnam, a hero of the War of Independence, adorns its main thoroughfare. A little further up the road Michael Ross' family owns and operates one of the largest businesses in town, a poultry and egg factory.

It is here that Michael grew up, an unobtrusive boy who worked hard at his father's business. His parents refuse to discuss their son since his arrest. Some of the townspeople can't believe that their town may have spawned a serial killer.

Carol Kovacs, an employee of the New England Centre for Contemporary Art, remembers well hearing the devastating news that an acquaintance had been arrested for the alleged murder of six girls. Carol knew Tammy Williams, one of the victims. She intersperses her emotions with such words as "unbelievable," "dumbfounded," "shocked" when discussing the arrest of Michael Ross.

Connecticut police are inquiring as to Michael Ross' activities in other locations. While he was attending Cornell University in Ithaca, New York, 25-year-old Vietnamese student Drung Ngoc Tu was murdered. Her body was found at the bottom of a gorge. Miss Tu was majoring in agricultural economics and lived one block from the Alpha Zeta fraternity house. Michael Ross lived at the fraternity house at the time of her murder.

Epilogue: Ross' connection with Miss Tu was dropped when he was found guilty of murdering Tammy Williams and Debbie Taylor. For these murders he was sentenced to life imprisonment.

On July 6, 1987 Michael Ross was found guilty of the murders of Robin Stavinsky, Leslie Shelley, April Brunais and Wendy Baribeault. He has been sentenced to death in Connecticut's electric chair.

THE BEAST OF JERSEY

J ersey has been described as a little bit of rustic paradise which accidentally dropped into the English Channel. The lush British island lies only 15 miles from the coast of France. It is a strange place for a man to turn into a monster.

Around 1:30 a.m. on Sunday, March 27, 1960, a woman living in a rather isolated cottage in the parish of St. Martin was awakened by the family's black Labrador. Normally, the Lab spent the night downstairs by the stove, but on this night the dog refused to leave his mistress' bedroom. Cautiously the woman went downstairs to investigate.

Once there, she was attacked by a man wearing some kind of mask. The intruder tied the helpless woman's hands behind her back. At that precise moment, her 14-year-old daughter woke up. Distracted by the young girl, the attacker relaxed his grip. The frantic woman raced out of the house across a field to a neighbor's cottage. No one was home. Unable to procure assistance and fearing for the safety of her daughter, she returned to her own cottage.

By the time she got back, her daughter had been taken to a nearby field where she was beaten about the head and brutally raped. The young girl later told police that the man had tightened a rope around her neck and seemed to derive pleasure from tightening it until she almost choked to death. At the last moment, he would loosen the rope, allowing her to breathe. She described her assailant as being between 30 and 40 years old and about 5 ft. 7 inches tall.

Police investigating the vicious attack found a partially eaten box of raw chicken on the kitchen floor, obviously placed there to distract the family dog.

A month later, another girl was attacked while asleep in her room. This time the girl screamed and frightened off her assailant. Not all victims were as fortunate. Again and again the mad rapist found his way into bedrooms in the middle of the night and led his victims out of their homes to nearby fields, where they were beaten and ravished.

In the wee hours of a Sunday morning in St. Martin, the rapist was successful in gaining entrance to the bedroom of an 11-year-old girl. He whispered in the child's ear, "Be quiet or I'll kill your mother and father." Terrified for her parents, who were asleep in the next room, the child allowed herself to be led out of the house, where she was brutally assaulted.

Nothing remotely resembling a sadistic crime wave had ever occurred on Jersey before. Realizing their limited experience in such matters, local authorities called in Scotland Yard.

The English police quickly ascertained that the attacker knew the area well. The houses he entered were in isolated areas which had good escape routes. They believed they were looking for a local man who behaved normally during the day, but turned into a monster at night. He wore a cloth mask, dressed in rough oversized clothing and entered houses he had reconnoitred some time previously.

Because of the intense police inquiries, or maybe because the madman was able to control the Mr. Hyde within him, the attacks ceased for two years.

The calm was broken at 1 a.m. on April 19, 1963. That's when a man crawled through a window and abducted a nine-year-old Chateau Clairvale boy. He led the frightened boy into some nearby fields and sexually assaulted him. The lad was then led back to his bed at knifepoint, while his younger brother slept peacefully in the same room. The boy's father heard the child's moans and soon the police were at the scene. They found size nine footprints in the soft earth outside the boy's window.

Through 1964, several more attacks took place on the island of Jersey. Little by little police learned more about the man they were seeking. He had type O blood. He wore gloves without fingers and constantly talked about smoking cigarettes. These bits of information did not aid in apprehending the attacker. After an assault on a 16-year-old mentally retarded boy, the deviate left a palm print on a bedroom windowsill.

Scotland Yard and the Jersey police came under intense pressure to bring in the mad rapist. In desperation they decided to take the palm print of every male between the ages of 19 and 60 living on the eastern end of the island where the attacks had taken place. In the months to follow a six man identification team took over 10,000 palm prints. None matched the one left on the victim's windowsill.

Thirteen men stubbornly refused to voluntarily give their palm prints. This was not to infer that one of the 13 was necessarily the mad attacker. Some of the men had airtight alibis for the times of some of the attacks. Some claimed it was against their right to privacy. However, when the killer was unveiled, he proved to be one of the men who had refused to be printed.

The mad attacker, or Beast of Jersey, as he was now called by the press, was apprehended because he went through a red light. It was July 10, 1971 when police took off after a Morris 1100 through the narrow streets along the seafront. The vehicle ended up stuck in a tomato field. The occupant fled. P.C. John Riseborough, a former rugby player, gave chase and brought down his man with a flying tackle. Riseborough knew that he had more than a traffic violator on his hands. No man drives through fences and fields to avoid being ticketed for a minor traffic violation.

Besides, there was the driver's appearance. Ted Paisnel, 46, was wearing slippers. Despite the hot July evening he had on fingerless gloves. He also wore a home-made leather sheath. Paisnel's large blue coat held a stiff black wig and a face mask. He claimed he was travelling to some kind of weird meeting but police felt sure they had captured the Beast of Jersey.

Paisnel, a building contractor, was married and was the devoted stepfather of a little boy. A search of his home, which he had built himself, uncovered a secret room. In it he had built an altar. On the altar police found glass bowls, cloves, a chalice and a china toad. He also kept a wooden dagger on the altar, along with several books on witchcraft. Ted Paisnel was a Satan worshipper.

His wife was unaware of the existence of her husband's secret room. Joan Paisnel could only volunteer that sexual relations between herself and her husband had ceased some years before.

Inside Ted's secret room, police found photographs of the homes he had terrorized. Some were taken years before the attacks, indicating that Paisnel's rapes had been planned well in advance. They also found homemade bracelets made of spikes. Several of his victims had parallel scratches on their bodies, which were identified as marks left by the bracelets. Paisnel's reference to cigarette smoking was a ruse to throw police off the trail. Ted didn't smoke.

On Nov. 24, 1971, Paisnel stood trial for his crimes. Despite defence attorneys attempts to prove him insane, he was judged by the court to be sane. Ted Paisnel was found guilty of 13 charges connected with his vicious attacks. He was sentenced to a total of 30 years in prison.

The 11-year reign of the Beast of Jersey had come to an end.

PROSTITUTE

KILLER

Richard Cottingham was employed for over a decade with the Blue Cross and Blue Shield of Greater New York. He was a valued and highly regarded member of the company's large computer staff.

Richard and his wife Janet lived in a pleasant three bedroom home in Lodi, New Jersey. They had three children, two boys, Blair and Scott, and a daughter, Jenny. Richard commuted to New York each day. Because of the nature of his employment, he had the option of reporting to work at any hour convenient to him. He normally worked from 4 p.m. to 11 p.m.

Among his colleagues, Richard Cottingham was a regular guy. Janet was the first to become aware that her husband was not what he appeared to be to the outside world.

In 1976, after Jenny's birth, 28-year-old Richard refused to have sexual intercourse with his wife. As a result, she gravitated to spending more and more time with her own friends. Richard, in turn, spent most of his time at home in his own private room. After work, he rarely drove directly home. Indeed, it was common for Richard to arrive home at dawn with the smell of alcohol on his breath. Sometimes he stayed away for several days.

One day, Richard inadvertently left his private room unlocked. Janet walked in. She was amazed to find an assortment of ladies' used underclothing and cheap jewelry scattered about the room.

No, Richard Cottingham was not normal. He was clever and cunning, but far from normal. For years he had led a double life, committing abnormal criminal acts which had not been attributed to one man.

On Dec. 16, 1977, the body of 26-year-old nurse Maryann Carr was found in the parking lot of the Quality Inn in Hackensack, N.J. Maryann, who had been married only 15 months, had been handcuffed hand and foot before being strangled to death. Despite an intensive investigation, her murder went unsolved.

Two years later, in December 1979, New York firemen were called to the Travel Inn Motor Lodge on West 42nd St. The blaze was localized in Room 417. Firemen had no trouble extinguishing the flames which originated from a double bed. When the smoke cleared, even the hard-nosed New York firemen recoiled in horror. There, on the bed, were the bodies of two nude, partially burned females. They were headless and their hands had been removed.

The investigation into the gruesome murders revealed that both girls had been prostitutes. Lighter fluid had been sprinkled over their bodies and ignited. New York detectives surmised that the strange mutilations had a purpose. With no heads, there were no teeth to check against dental records. With no hands, there were no fingerprints to compare. It would be six weeks before one of the girls would be identified. The identity of the other girl has never been established.

The man who had checked into Room 417 at the Travel Inn had given his name as Carl Wilson of Merlin, N.J. Both his name and the name of the town were fictitious. Inside, the room was clean. No fingerprints, no cigarette butts, nothing that would lead to the identity of the killer. He had checked in on Wednesday evening, Nov. 29, and for four days was rarely seen by hotel staff. The "Do not disturb" sign hung from the doorknob of 417 for almost all of those four days.

After weeks of tedious legwork, detectives identified one of the victims as Deedeh Goodarzi. Jackie, as she was known, plied her trade in Atlantic City and New York City. The beautiful five-foot six-inch Kuwait native had left Atlantic City to attend a meeting with her pimp in New York during the last week of November. She never kept the appointment. Instead, she ended up in Room 417. It has never been ascertained whether a headless corpse greeted her when she entered the room or whether she was the first of the two to die. For the time being, the Times Square Torso Murders, as they came to be known, remained unsolved.

Valorie Street found Miami too hot for comfort. She had been arrested for prostitution several times. Once more on the street, she decided to try the Big Apple. Valorie arrived in New York City on May 1, 1980. Four days later, using the name Shelly Dudley, she signed herself into the Quality Inn Motel in New Jersey. Valorie was assigned Room 132. Her nude body was found under the bed. She had been handcuffed, bitten, beaten and raped.

Twenty-five-year-old prostitute Jean Mary Ann Reyner's body was found in the Hotel Seville on May 15, 1980. She had been stabbed to death and her breasts had been removed. The police had only a composite drawing of the fictional Carl Wilson to work on, provided by employees of the Travel Inn Hotel off Times Square.

Three days later, on May 18, 1980, Leslie Ann O'Dell, 18, arrived in New York by bus from Washington, D.C. Alone in the big city, without money or friends, Leslie was approached by a friendly man who bought her breakfast. The man explained that he could put her in touch with another man who would see to it that she made plenty of money. Within 24 hours Leslie was walking the New York streets under the protection of a pimp.

Leslie, on her fourth night as a New York streetwalker, was motioned over to a blue and silver Chevy Caprice. The man, who called himself Tommy, suggested a drink at a bar in New Jersey. Leslie was happy to comply. Tommy proved to be a pleasant companion. He even seemed interested in her problems.

They left the bar and dropped into a restaurant for a bite to eat. Over coffee they negotiated, finally agreeing to the fee of $100 for a half hour of Leslie's time. Dawn was breaking when they pulled up to the Quality Inn Motel in Hasbrouck Heights, the very same motel where Valorie Street had been murdered. Tommy paid $27.77 in advance for the keys to Room 117.

Soon they were in bed. Without warning, the now wild-eyed Tommy pulled a knife from his attache case. He quickly fastened handcuffs about the helpless girl's wrists. Gruffly Tommy ordered, "You have to take it. The other girls did. You're a whore and you have to be punished."

For the next three hours, Leslie endured sexual perversions and torture rarely equalled in the annals of crime. Her attacker threatened her with a pistol if she screamed. Leslie bit her lips until blood ran down her chin as she muffled her cries of pain.

At one point, while being whipped, she fell to the floor beside Tommy's gun, which he had put down so that he could wield his whip to better advantage. Leslie picked up the gun. Tommy advanced towards her with his knife. Leslie, who had never before held a firearm, pulled the trigger again and again. Nothing happened. The gun jammed. Figuring she was about to die, she screamed at the top of her lungs.

It was 9 a.m. A maid doing her rounds heard Leslie scream and called the front desk. Todd Radner, the assistant manager, called police. Together with head housekeeper Paula De Matthews, Radner headed for Room 117. Inside, the man known as Tommy, had clamped a hand over Leslie's mouth. Radner knocked on the door.

Under instructions Leslie, leaving the chain intact, opened the door. Her eyes were black and blue, her cheeks swollen. "Everything is okay. I have no clothes on. I can't open the door." As she talked, Leslie attempted to signal that she was in trouble. Radner and De Matthews walked away.

Just then a police car arrived. Tommy saw the car pull up. He frantically dressed and gathered up his implements of torture. As he ran down the hall, Leslie hollered, "Stop him, stop him! He tried to kill me!"

Tommy, carrying a small calibre weapon, unknowingly ran directly toward Patrolman Stan Mclowic. The police officer raised his shotgun and commanded, "Hold it right there and don't move!"

The hunt for the madman who had raped, mutilated and murdered prostitutes for several years had come to an end. Tommy was identified as computer expert Richard Cottingham. Costume jewelry and bits of clothing found in his home enabled detectives to link him with the previous killings, as well as several vicious rapes that they had thought were perpetrated by several different men.

After a series of trials in New Jersey and New York, Cottingham was convicted of assault, kidnapping, rape and murder. His accumulated sentences total 250 years in Trenton State Prison, where he is currently incarcerated.

THE BODY COLLECTOR

J erry Brudos didn't smoke or drink. His I.Q. was well above average. He was a skilled electronics technician, as well as a qualified electrician. Jerry was a big man, standing an even six feet and weighing a solid 180 pounds. When he was 23, an acquaintance introduced him to his first real girlfriend, 17-year-old Ralphine Leone.

In 1962, Jerry and Ralphine wed. That same year Ralphine gave birth to a daughter, Therese. In 1967 their second child, Brian, was born. The Brudos family lived in a pleasant little house on Centre St. in Salem, Oregon.

To the outside world, Jerry appeared to be a quiet, happy family man. To Ralphine he was a considerate, sensitive husband. Unknown to Ralphine, there were two incidents in her husband's past which may have served as warning signals had she been aware of their existence.

When Jerry was 17, he became frustrated when a date repulsed his sexual advances. Enraged, he beat the girl badly with his fists. As a result, Jerry was committed to the Oregon State Mental Hospital in Salem. The terms of his commitment allowed him to attend high school during the day. Nine months later he was released to his parents.

The other incident occurred after Jerry graduated from high school and joined the U.S. Army. Stationed at Fort Gordon, Georgia, Jerry fantasized that a woman entered his barracks each night and went to bed with him. Each night he beat her unmercifully. The dreams were so real that Jerry sought out Army psychiatrists. When they heard his story, they recommended that he be discharged as not being fit for military service.

What no one knew, not his high school teachers, not the mental health people in Salem, not the army psychiatrists, and certainly not his wife, was that Jerry Brudos had been stealing ladies' underwear and high heeled shoes for years. Initially, underclothing was taken from clotheslines, but Jerry was not above entering houses while the occupants slept, in order to steal items to satisfy his fetish.

Behind his home in Salem, Jerry had a garage. He outfitted the garage with an intercom connected to the house. When Ralphine wanted him for meals, she called on the intercom. There was a hard and fast rule, Ralphine was never to enter the garage. Jerry told her he developed pictures there, and didn't want sunlight pouring in unexpectedly. Men do have hobbies. Even when her husband moved the family freezer into the garage, Ralphine put up with the inconvenience.

Jerry Brudos was a time bomb ready to explode. He paraded around in women's underclothing and high heels in the privacy of his own garage. Sometimes he took pictures of himself in the stolen clothing, but the games had become less stimulating. True, he had talked Ralphine into posing in the nude, but she did so reluctantly. No, there was no other way. He had to have his very own woman in order to act out his fantasies.

An encyclopedia saleslady knocked on Jerry Brudos' door on Jan. 26, 1968. Faking interest in purchasing books, Jerry had no trouble enticing her into the basement of his home. Once there, he hit her over the head with a plank. Then he choked her to death.

Jerry was happier than he had ever been in his life. He had his very own model. For hours he dressed and undressed the body, in his collection of women's underwear. Slowly the realization came to him. His new friend would have to leave. But surely there was something he could keep.

Jerry took a saw and cut off the left foot of his victim. It would serve him well in the weeks to follow as a form for his high heeled shoe collection. He placed the foot in the freezer for safekeeping. Jerry tied an engine block to the body. At 2 a.m., displaying unusual strength, he tossed his macabre cargo into the Willamette River. Days later he weighed down the foot and threw it into the river as well.

Jerry loved the game and could hardly wait for his next victim. Jan Susan Whitney was a 23-year-old University of Oregon student. On Nov. 26, 1968, Jan disappeared while driving her old Rambler from Eugene to McMinnville. It had been Jan's misfortune to have car trouble. It had been her fatal misfortune to encounter a monster posing as a good Samaritan. Jerry told her he could repair her car, but first he had to go into Salem to get his tools.

Jan jumped in Jerry's car and ended up in his garage in Salem. He throttled her with a leather strap. Jerry had outfitted his garage for just such an occasion. He now had the proper photographic equipment. A pulley system had been installed and a hook inserted in the ceiling. The body could be raised to a standing position. Jerry dressed and undressed his victim. To add to his many perversions, he had now become a necrophiliac.

Jerry left the body hanging there in the garage when he and his wife took a trip to Portland. While they were away, a stranger drove into the side of the garage. When Jerry came home he found a card from the police department in his mailbox. It had been a close call. Police inspected the damage. Jerry repaired the garage. The body inside had not been detected. Later, Jerry weighed it down with scrap iron and threw it in the river.

Pre-med honor student Karen Sprinker, 19, was plucked off the streets of Salem four months after Jan Whitney met her terrible fate. Her car was recovered, but gave no clue as to the owner's whereabouts.

Jerry had forced the hapless girl to his garage with a toy gun. Once there, he took pictures before strangling his victim. He then indulged in his fantasies, weighed down the body with a cylinder head and tossed it into the Long Tom River.

A month later, on April 23, 1969, Linda Dawn Salee, 22, became Jerry's fourth victim. After work, Linda had driven her Volkswagen to a shopping centre, where she purchased a birthday gift for her boyfriend. Jerry pointed his gun at Linda's head just as she was about to enter her parked car. She ended up in Jerry's garage. She too was subjected to the madness that was Jerry Brudos. That night he threw her body into the Long Tom River.

Eighteen days later a fisherman discovered Linda Salee's body. Her killer had been careless and had thrown her into a shallow section of the river. A car's transmission had been tied to the body with nylon cord and a copper wire.

While diving for other clues, police discovered another body, that of Karen Sprinker. The macabre details made the front pages of the nation's newspapers. No one was more interested than Jerry Brudos.

Despite his madness, Jerry was an intelligent, cunning adversary. He read about the bodies, but was sure he had covered his tracks and would not be apprehended. He had no intention of curtailing his bizarre activities.

In fact, Jerry had hit upon a new scheme. He discovered that by phoning the university and asking for a common female name, he could get a girl to the phone. In this way he sometimes enticed girls to meet him for coffee. So far, none had appealed to him. By interviewing Oregon State co-eds, detectives learned of the man who attempted to get blind dates.

Finally, they found one girl who had met him for coffee in her dormitory's cafeteria. When interviewed, this young girl stated that the man had kept talking about the two murder victims taken from the river. Police instructed the girl to stall her caller if he ever phoned again. Sure enough, she heard from him again. She told him it would take her some time to dry her hair. In the meantime, she called police. Detectives greeted Jerry Brudos.

A search of Jerry's garage turned up his vast array of women's underclothing and high heeled shoes. Police also discovered photos of the dead girls, as well as one shot which revealed Jerry's image in a mirror. In the same photo was a picture of one of his victims.

Once in custody, Jerry made a full confession. Seven psychiatrists conducted extensive tests. Their conclusions were unanimous. Jerry Brudos had killed in a planned and premeditated manner. He was judged to be sane.

Jerry Brudos pleaded guilty to three counts of first degree murder and was sentenced to three consecutive life sentences in Oregon State Penitentiary.

Ralphine Brudos obtained a court order forbidding her children to visit their father in prison. In 1970, she obtained a divorce.

Officials of the Oregon State Prison in Salem advise me that Brudos has made a "good institutional adjustment." Initially, as a high profile inmate whose crimes were committed against women, he was the subject of abuse by other prisoners. One inmate made an unsuccessful attempt to stab him. The Oregon State Parole Board has decreed that he will never be paroled.

ALL-AMERICAN

MONSTER

Where do the monsters lurking in our society come from? Are they the products of abusive parents? Is there insanity in the family tree? Truth is, in many cases disruptive family backgrounds have contributed to those personalities who are responsible for the most horrific of crimes.

Randall Brant Woodfield was an exception. He was a member of an extremely stable family. His father, Jack Woodfield, held a responsible position with Pacific Northwest Bell Telephone Co. Jack and his wife, Donna Jean, were thrilled when Randy was born on Dec. 26, 1950 in Salem, Oregon. They already had two daughters, Susan and Nancy. The Woodfields really wanted a boy.

And a fine boy Randy grew up to be. He was extremely handsome and it was soon obvious that he was a natural athlete. Jack Woodfield was transferred to the small town of Otter Rock, Ore., and it was here that Randy grew up, attending school in nearby Newport.

Randy excelled in track and field, baseball, basketball and football. During his teenage years, he had the reputation of being the best all-round athlete in the area. Many believed that his future lay in professional sport. Randy basked in his popularity. He dated only the prettiest and most popular girls in his high school. They considered themselves fortunate to get a date with the football team's star wide receiver. The world appeared to be the oyster of the handsome, 6 foot 2 athlete.

Other honors came Randy's way. At Newport High School, he excelled in mathematics and was accelerated into an advanced class. The Rotary Club once selected him as their Boy of the Month.

In his senior year at high school, Randy was recruited by several colleges in the northwest. He chose Treasure Valley Community College in Ontario, Ore. Randy stayed a year, did well scholastically, but it was in athletics that he excelled. He was co-captain of the football team and a star member of the Varsity basketball team. He also broke the school's record for the long jump.

At the age of 20, Randy transferred to Portland State University, feeling that at a larger school he had a better opportunity to be noticed by big league football scouts. In his new surroundings, Randy again proved to be a good student and an exceptional athlete. However, it was while attending Portland State that the image of the all-American boy began to tarnish.

On Aug. 7, 1972, Randy Woodfield was apprehended in the act of exposing himself to a young girl. Charged with indecent exposure, he was convicted but received a suspended sentence. University officials were never notified of Randy's arrest and so his reputation on campus was unaffected. During the next summer's vacation, it happened again. On June 22, 1973, he was captured by a police officer after exposing himself to a woman in Portland. Randy received a sentence of one year's probation. That winter he was arrested for public indecency and was sentenced to five years probation.

Perhaps if Randy Woodfield had received professional help with his sexual problems at this juncture, his life might have taken a far different turn. After all, this star athlete, whom most girls would consider a "catch," was receiving sexual gratification out of lurking in bushes around darkened park paths, exposing himself to unwary women. Something was definitely wrong.

But professional help was not in the offing. A far more thrilling experience was to take place in Randy's life. He was drafted by the Green Bay Packers football team.

On Feb. 20, 1974, Randy signed a professional football contract. He was to receive $16,000 for the season no matter what happened. There were bonus clauses as well. He received $3000 for signing, and would receive a further $3000 if he made the team. Of course, room, board and airline tickets to pre-season practices would all be handled by the Packer organization. The whole thing was a dream come true. Randy headed for Green Bay.

Then the bottom fell out of the dream. Randy was cut by the team. He caught on with the Packers' farm team, the Manitowac Chiefs, and played out the season in the hope of being called back up to the Packers. It never happened.

Randy returned to Portland, but never went back to university. Instead, he obtained a job tending bar. Now 25, Randy may have realized that his chance to become a professional athlete had passed. He was at a crossroads.

During that winter of 1975, Portland police were investigating a rash of strange crimes. A tall, good-looking young man was sexually assaulting and robbing young women at knifepoint in Duniway Park.

A lady police officer, acting as a decoy, was used to apprehend the attacker. He turned out to be Randy Woodfield. When searched, Randy was carrying a gun and a knife. On June 10, 1975, he was sentenced to 10 years in the Oregon State Penitentiary for armed robbery. After serving less than four years, he was released as "not being a violence risk."

Randy borrowed his mother's Volkswagen, obtained jobs tending bar in several lounges, and dated pretty girls. Randy was 30, but looked 25. Sometimes he would live with a girl for a few months, but generally he lived alone. An ex-con had told him that a good way to effect a disguise was to use band-aids on his face. Randy expanded the disguise to include a crude beard. Brandishing a tiny revolver, he held up scores of fast food operations. More often than not, he struck late at night, sexually attacking the young girls who worked at such outlets.

On Jan. 18, 1981, at around 9 o'clock, Randy was out prowling the suburbs of Salem, Oregon. It didn't matter much to him any more - women working at a fast food store, women strolling on the street, any woman would do. Four days earlier, he had attacked two children, ages eight and ten. Now the man with the physique and looks of a movie actor and the mind of a monster, was stalking the streets.

Two girls, Beth Wilmot and Shari Hull, worked for Shari's father, who owned a janitorial service. They were best friends. On this particular night they were cleaning the Trans America Title Building. Suddenly they were confronted by a man waving a revolver. He herded them into the lunch room.

For 20 minutes the intruder sexually attacked the two girls. He then forced them to lie on the floor, face down. Beth Wilmot would later relate that the next thing she remembered was a shot being fired. The attacker shot Beth in the head. The crazed gunman alternately shot the girls five times. Three bullets entered Shari's body and two were fired at Beth's head. He left, sure that his victims were dead.

Unbelievably, Beth Wilmot, with two bullet wounds in her head, got up from the floor, walked to the telephone and called an emergency hot line. An ambulance arrived in minutes. Next morning, Shari Hull died in hospital. Miraculously, Beth Wilmot survived.

Doctors found one .32 calibre flattened bullet in her hair. They surmised that the ammunition used may not have been the correct calibre for the gunman's weapon. At any rate, the bullet had not penetrated her skull. The second bullet had dug a furrow under the skin, coming to rest under her right ear. Beth had beaten the odds. As she recovered from her wounds, she gave detectives a detailed description of the killer.

Randy Woodfield was on the move. Robbing as he went, he made his way 400 miles to Mountain Gate, California, where he walked into a home and sexually attacked the occupants before shooting them to death. Donna Lee Eckard, 37, and her 14-year-old stepdaughter, Janell Jarvis, lay dead in the madman's wake. Authorities connected the California murders to the crime wave in Oregon.

Strangely enough, Randy Woodfield's name first came to the attention of investigators in a case thought unrelated to the wanton attacks on women up and down the west coast of the U.S. On Valentine's Day, 1981, Julie Reitz, 18, was found dead in her Beaverton, Ore. home. Someone had shot the girl in the back of the head as she fled nude down her front stairs in an effort to elude her killer.

Subsequent investigation indicated that Julie knew her killer. Because of this, her murder was not connected to the rash of crimes then being investigated. However, one of her slight acquaintances, Randy Woodfield, was questioned and subsequently released. He was known to drive a gold-colored Volkswagen. Several fast food holdup victims reported that their attacker had driven a gold Volkswagen.

Investigators checked out Randy's record and discovered he had been in prison on a sex-related charge. Witnesses were contacted, all of whom picked Randy Woodfield out of police lineups. Beth Wilmot had no hesitation in identifying the attacker and the killer of her best friend.

On June 3, 1981, Randy stood trial in Salem, Ore. on charges of murder, attempted murder and sodomy. Prosecuted by District Attorney Chris Van Dyke (son of comedian Dick Van Dyke), Randy Woodfield was found guilty of all charges. Randy was sentenced to life plus 90 years, with a recommendation that he not be eligible for parole until he has served 50 years.

Another trial followed on Dec. 18, 1981. Randy was found guilty of sodomy and being an ex-convict in possession of a weapon. He was sentenced to a further 35 years in prison. The judge stipulated that the 35 year sentence was to run consecutive to the sentence handed down on the murder charge. Randy Woodfield in total faces life plus 125 years in prison. The star athlete from a good family will never be a free man again.

DEATH DEALT
FINAL JUSTICE

Thirty-five miles east of Tulsa, Oklahoma, lies the peaceful little town of Locust Grove. Not much ever happens in Locust Grove; yet on a rainy evening in June 1977, one of the most horrendous crimes ever perpetrated in the U.S. took place in a Girl Scout camp located on the outskirts of the town.

It was the first day of a week-long girl scout outing at Camp Scott. One hundred and forty girls poured into the campground in buses, joining the 30 counsellors who had arrived a week earlier.

In the late afternoon it rained. By nightfall a thunderstorm had rolled in over the camp and the girls were delighted to be confined to their tents.

Next morning counsellor Carla Sue Wilhite decided to take a shower at the staff house before the rest of the camp awakened. As she walked along the trail, she noticed what looked like a bundle of sleeping bags. Walking closer, she couldn't believe her eyes. There, grotesquely positioned in one of the bags, was the body of a little girl.

Carla Sue screamed for help. Police were called and in a matter of minutes what had promised to be a bright fresh day at Camp Scott turned into the darkest day in the 50-year history of the camp.

Each of three sleeping bags contained the body of a little girl. The three victims had occupied tent number eight, the last tent in a semicircle. The bodies were examined, photographed and removed for post-mortems. Doris Milner, ten, had been strangled. Lori Lee Farmer, eight, and Michelle Guse, nine, had been beaten to death. All three youngsters had been raped.

Despite the fact that the tent was separated from seven other tents by only a few feet, no noise had been heard by other girls during the night. The bodies were found about 150 yards from their tent. Police found a nine volt red and white flashlight nearby. Someone had stuffed newspaper inside the flashlight, obviously to make the batteries fit snugly. The bit of paper was a portion of the April 17 issue of the Tulsa *World*.

Police organized civilian groups into a massive search party. Miles of thick woods around Camp Scott were scoured for any clues that might lead to the killer's identity. Nothing was uncovered by the organized search, but two squirrel hunters, Willis Ray Thompson and Johnny Russell Colvin, led police to a cave they had discovered about three miles from the camp. Inside the cave were two torn photographs and a portion of the April 17 issue of the Tulsa *World*.

Because of the newspaper found in the flashlight and a piece of the same issue of the paper found in the cave, detectives had every reason to believe the cave had been used by the killer.

Days passed, but nothing of a concrete nature turned up. Despite the lack of evidence, there was one prime suspect. His name was Gene Hart.

Hart, a full-blooded Cherokee Indian, as were many inhabitants of that part of Oklahoma, had a criminal record dating back ten years. In 1966, he kidnapped two pregnant women, drove them in his own car into secluded woods, where he tortured and raped them. One of the women managed to obtain Hart's licence number. Hart, 22, was picked up. Cord found in his car matched that used to tie up the two women. Hart was found guilty of two charges of kidnapping and one of rape. He received three ten year prison sentences. A little over two years later he was paroled.

Three months after his release Hart was caught red-handed with a knife burglarizing a Tulsa apartment. When his automobile was searched, the stolen property from several other apartments was recovered. Tried separately for each burglary, he received one sentence of from 30 to 90 years, another of from 40 to 120 years, a third of from 15 to 45 years, and another of a straight 50 years imprisonment, all sentences to run consecutively. Hart was placed in the Oklahoma State Penitentiary at McAlester, ostensibly for the balance of his natural life.

On April 25, 1973 Hart was transferred to the Mayes County Jail to appear at yet another court proceeding. He escaped, but was apprehended a month later. Four months later Hart was to stand trial for escaping and being in possession of a shotgun when apprehended. Once again, he escaped. This time he remained at large. Now, four years later, his name was brought up as a man capable of raping and killing three children.

Oklahoma is Cherokee country. It is estimated that Hart had 300 relatives living within 50 miles of Camp Scott. Before his first scrape with the law, he had been something of a local high school football hero. An expert woodsman, there is little doubt that he roamed the woods while at large, living off the land. Most natives felt that Hart was innocent of all charges and had been framed by the white man. Many had assisted him with food and shelter during his four years of freedom. Now these same people believed that Gene Hart was not capable of murdering three children.

Slowly, evidence mounted against Hart. Photos found in the cave were traced to photographer Louis Lindsey. Hart had worked for Lindsey after his parole and had ready access to the photos.

As the months passed, the U.S. Army attempted to track down the wanted man. So did penitentiary officials and bounty hunters. Even medicine men had a turn at trying to locate the fugitive. All failed.

Finally, an informant gave away Hart's hideout. He was living with an old man in an isolated shack. Heavily armed police surrounded the shack and broke down the front door. Before Hart could move he was staring into the barrel of a 12-gauge shotgun. It had been two years since the girl scouts had been murdered. Now, after six years as a fugitive, Hart was finally taken into custody.

The shack where Hart had lived with the old man was thoroughly searched. Inside, detectives found a girl's blue mirror and a corn cob pipe. These two items were traced to Karen Mitchell, a counsellor at Camp Scott. The mirror and pipe had been stolen from her tent on the night of the murders.

Strangely enough, several funds were organized to pay for Hart's defence. In the six years he had been a fugitive, he had unbelievably become somewhat of a folk hero.

His trial, the longest in Oklahoma's history, was covered by the press of several countries. Hart's defence was based solely on the premise that the white man needed an Indian as a scapegoat to pay for the tragic murders. To the disgust of law enforcement agencies throughout the country he was found not guilty. He was returned to the Oklahoma State Prison to serve out his many other sentences.

On June 4, 1979, three months after being incarcerated, Gene Hart collapsed while jogging. He had suffered a massive heart attack and died where he fell.

THE YORKSHIRE RIPPER

Kathleen and John Sutcliffe's six children grew up and one by one moved out of the family home. Their eldest son, Peter, was the last to leave 57 Cornwall Rd. in Bingley, England.

Peter was ambitious, more ambitious than the gang he ran with. They only thought of nights at the pub and birds to pick up. If a legit bird wasn't available, there were always the pros, who, for £5, would show a man a good, if hurried, time.

But Peter was different. He had met Sonia Szurma, the daughter of honest Czech immigrants. Sonia's parents were impressed with hard-working Peter, who over the years held jobs as a furnace operator, grave digger and lorry driver. On Aug. 10, 1974, on Sonia's twenty-fourth birthday, she became Mrs. Peter Sutcliffe.

Six months after his marriage, Peter, always attempting to better himself, took a driving course at the Apex School of Driving, eventually earning a Class One licence. The Sutcliffes and the Szurmas were pleased. Handsome, pleasant Peter was making his way in the world. He soon obtained a good position as a lorry driver.

What the family didn't know, what the entire country didn't know, was that something deep in the recesses of Peter Sutcliffe's mind was changing and festering and smoldering. He was developing a hatred of women, a hatred so strong that for five and a half years the mere mention of the Yorkshire Ripper sent shivers up and down the spines, not only of women, but of men as well. With the possible exception of Myra Hindley and Ian Brady, no killer was ever more hated than the Yorkshire Ripper.

On July 4, 1975, Anna Rogulskyj couldn't go to sleep until she satisfied herself that her kitten was safe and sound. The kitten was missing, but Anna felt that her boyfriend must have taken it to his apartment just a five minute walk away. Even though it was 1 a.m., she decided to set her mind at ease and travel the few blocks.

A man lurking the shadows asked, "Do you fancy it?" There was no doubt in Anna's mind what the question implied. She threw an answer over her shoulder, "Not on your life." She hurried on and soon arrived at her boyfriend's door, but no amount of knocking could get a response.

Apprehensively, Anna retraced her steps. Again, the whispered innuendo, "Do you fancy it?" Anna increased her pace. The man walked faster and caught up to her, raining three blows on her head with a ballpeen hammer. He then lifted her sweater and slashed at her midriff. A window opened, a head stuck out, "What's the matter?" The attacker ran away and the head tucked back in. The window closed.

An hour later, Anna was found on the sidewalk. Rushed to Leeds General Infirmary, she was given the last rites of the Catholic Church. A 12-hour operation saved her life. Anna spent months in hospital, and had to learn to speak and walk again. She was unable to describe her attacker. Peter Sutcliffe, the Yorkshire Ripper, the man who would terrorize a nation, had struck for the first time.

Five weeks later, Peter and a friend, Trevor Birdsall, were driving from pub to pub. Peter spotted Olive Smelt, a 46-year-old cleaning woman, who habitually spent Friday night in a pub with a female friend. Now Olive was walking home and took a shortcut down an alley. Peter stopped the car and told Trevor he was going to try and have a go. He rushed into the alley, caught up with Olive and struck her twice on the head with a hammer. He tried to cut her body with a hacksaw, but gave up when a passing car came along. He returned to Trevor in the car.

Trevor asked what had happened. Peter would only say that he had been chatting with that woman. Next day, Trevor read of the strange attack on a woman where nothing had been stolen and no sexual attack attempted. He was positive that the victim was the woman Peter had followed down the alley. He said nothing, told no one. Beating up the wife or girlfriend was the norm in his crowd. The old lady survived, didn't she? Olive Smelt was unable to describe her attacker.

In the fall of 1975, Peter was hired as a driver for the Common Road Tyre Co. in Bradford. This broadened his scope. Peter came to know Leeds' inner city Chapeltown section with its teeming watering holes and tough prostitute population like the back of his hand.

Wilma McCann sold her body whenever she could for the going rate of £5. It was her misfortune to be picked up by Peter Sutcliffe. A deal was struck. Peter drove to a secluded spot and spread his coat on the grass. Wilma lay down. That's when he struck her a vicious blow to the head and stabbed her 14 times in the chest and lower abdomen. Next morning her body was found by a milkman.

The Sutcliffe family celebrated Christmas that year of 1975. No one had any idea that obliging Peter had attempted to kill two women and had succeeded in killing a third. He gave presents to his parents, his aunts, his brothers and sisters and his wife.

On Jan. 21 of the New Year he killed again. Prostitute Emily Jackson routinely picked up a client. After a short drive, Peter asked Emily to hold a flashlight while he raised the hood of his car. As the unsuspecting girl pointed the torch, Peter struck her twice on the back of her head with a hammer. In a frenzy he stabbed his hapless victim 52 times.

Peter didn't kill for the remainder of the year, but in February 1977, he struck again. Irene Richardson's body was found near a park. She had been hit over the head with a hammer, stabbed in the neck and chest and had been horribly slashed across the lower abdomen. The newspapers of the district for the first time coined the name "Yorkshire Ripper."

Leeds detectives realized from the nature and physical characteristics of the wounds, that all three women had been murdered by the same man. One hundred detectives worked on the Richardson murder without coming up with any concrete results. Policewomen, dressed as prostitutes, roamed Chapeltown but the elusive Ripper didn't show.

Tina Atkinson was dead drunk when she picked up Peter and took him to her flat. As she sat on the edge of her bed, he struck her with his ballpeen hammer, after which he stabbed her repeatedly, slashing her across the lower abdomen. Peter drove away and tossed the incriminating hammer from his car. Two days later a man found the hammer in Cottingley Bridge. He used it for three years before finding out it was a murder weapon.

Jayne MacDonald and her boyfriend left the dance at Hofbrauhaus early so they could have some fish and chips on the way home. They lingered too long. By the time they had eaten, Jayne had missed her last bus home. The pair parted. Jayne made her way down Chapeltown Rd. with the intention of calling a taxi. Peter sneaked up behind her and struck her with his hammer. He dragged her off the street and performed his distinctive mutilations to the body.

Jayne was the Ripper's first murder victim who was not a prostitute. Whether this was a pertinent factor in the increased intensity of the Ripper investigation is not known. We do know that after Jayne's death, West Yorkshire's most famous detective, George Oldfield, was placed in charge of the investigation with one directive: Apprehend the Yorkshire Ripper.

Oldfield conducted a massive investigation. Four hundred citizens had been in the general area of the night of Jayne's murder. Three hundred and eighty were traced and cleared. One hundred and fifty two prostitutes were arrested. Over 3,500 statements were taken by police. None of these efforts produced one iota of useful information.

Late in the summer of 1977, Sonia and Peter Sutcliffe purchased a home at 6 Garden Lane, Heaton. With Sonia employed as a teacher and Peter on steady as a driver, the Sutcliffes were definitely on the way up. There was even talk of a baby.

Peter had other thoughts in mind. After being in his new home for only a week, he took off for Manchester's red light district. Jean Jordan jumped into Peter's red Corsair without hesitation. He passed over the usual £5 note and then parked behind a high hedge near municipal allotments as he was directed by Jean.

The hammer crashed against the girl's skull again and again. Peter dragged the body into the bushes, but a car arrived and he left before mutilating the body. In the days following the attack, Peter was perplexed that headlines were singularly devoid of any mention of the Ripper striking for the first time in Manchester.

He correctly figured that the body had not been discovered, but this wasn't the reason Peter decided to return to the scene of the crime. He realized that he had left a valuable clue behind. Peter had been paid in crisp, newly minted notes. The five pound note he had given Jean was one of these traceable notes. Peter had to get it back.

Eight days after the murder, he returned to find Jean's body exactly as he had left it. He stripped the body, examining every garment, but could not find the £5 note. Frantically, he searched for Jean's purse in vain. He stabbed the body again and again, as if to quell the frustration at not being able to retrieve the only clue he had ever left behind.

Next day Jean Jordan's body was found. Five days later, her purse, with the £5 intact, was turned over to police.

The Bank of England quickly confirmed that the note was one of a large supply distributed by Midland Bank of Shipley, located just outside Bradford. They had been distributed four days before the murder and had been placed in pay packets for various commercial firms in the area. The new bills had been used by 30 firms employing over 7,500 men.

One of the companies was T. and W.H. Clark Ltd., the trucking firm where Peter was at the time employed as a driver. A month after Jean Jordan was murdered, two detectives knocked at the door of Sonia and Peter Sutcliffe at 6 Garden Lane. Peter calmly told the officers that he was home on the evening of Nov. 2 when Jean Jordan had been murdered. Sonia confirmed Peter's story. Peter had also been at home eight days later when the body had been mutilated. Once again, Sonia agreed. The officers left and reported nothing unusual to incriminate Pete Sutcliffe over the thousands of others being questioned.

Peter continued killing after spending another joyous Christmas season with his family and friends. In January 1978, he murdered prostitute Yvonne Pearson in his now familiar manner. Yvonne's body was not found for two months. On the last day of January, Helen and Rita Rytka, good-looking 18-year-old twin prostitutes walked their regular beats. Helen was picked up by Peter.

The twins had an arrangement. After one completed her services, she would return to a certain location to check in with her sister. That way, through the course of the evening, they would see each other several times. On this night, Rita waited. Helen never returned. Her body was found three days later.

Someone had noticed a red Corsair in the vicinity where the body was found. Because Peter drove a red Corsair, he was once more visited by detectives. The obliging lorry driver explained that he was often in that area since he drove to work to pick up his lorry. Sonia confirmed that Peter hardly ever went out at night, which was true enough. He didn't go out often, but when he did, he killed women. Sometimes he would be gone only a half hour. The questioning detectives didn't know that Peter had already been interrogated by other officers concerning the £5 note. They left believing Peter's story. The two reports were never connected.

In May 1978, Peter cruised around with his friend Trevor. After dropping Trevor off at his home, he drove to Halifax and watched various people walking their dogs in a park. Finally, he spotted a young girl walking alone. He parked his car and accosted Josephine Whitaker, a 19-year-old clerk on her way home. Josephine was not a prostitute, but was simply in the wrong place at the wrong time.

Ten women had now been murdered at the hands of the Yorkshire Ripper. The police knew from saliva tests that the killer's blood belonged to group B, a rare type found in only six percent of the population. They knew precious little else.

George Oldfield received scores of letters from cranks, but firmly believed that one such letter was authentic. Tests on the envelope indicated that the sender was a group B secreter. Then, on June 20, 1979, the letter took a back seat to a tape recording received by Oldfield. The message on the tape was startlingly similar to letters written by the original Jack the Ripper 90 years earlier. George Oldfield was convinced that the tape was authentic.

Voice and dialect experts from the University of Leeds meticulously studied the tape and came to the conclusion that the voice had a "Geordie" accent, which is generally attributed to that area of northeast England immediately south of the Scottish border. Peter Sutcliffe did not have a Geordie accent. When a police directive was issued instructing officers to exclude anyone who didn't have a Geordie accent, Peter was off the hook.

The largest manhunt in the annals of British crime was now instituted. In all, over 150,000 individuals were questioned about the case. More than 22,000 statements were on file. The tape with the supposed Ripper's voice was played in public places, on the radio and even at soccer games. But nothing stopped Peter Sutcliffe.

In September 1979, Barbara Leach, a student at the University of Bradford, was slain in Peter's usual way. A short while later, while driving a Rover, Peter encountered 47-year-old Marguerite Walls in Farsley, a suburb of Leeds. Marguerite was strangled, a departure for the cunning Peter. He decided to throw the police off the trail by changing his tactics. He was right. Initially, the Walls murder was not attributed to the Yorkshire Ripper.

Peter's thirteenth and last victim was Jacqueline Hill of Headingly. She merely got off a bus and was followed by Peter until, in a darkened area, he struck her down with his hammer. She was his only victim in 1980.

On January 2, 1981, Peter took the precaution of taping old licence plates he had found in a junkyard over the plates on his Rover. He called Sonia and told her he'd be late. He then drove 30 miles to Sheffield, where he picked up prostitute Olivia Reivers. Peter parked in a dark area near a large stone building. Without warning, a police car pulled up. Sergeant Bob Ring and Const. Robert Hydes approached the Rover. Peter gave them a false name and told the officers he was merely parked with his girlfriend. Const. Hydes returned to his vehicle and checked out the plates with the national computer. The plates didn't belong to the Rover.

The officers returned to the car. After examining the Rover's licence plates, they found that they were taped over another set. The officers decided to take Peter and his girlfriend in for questioning. Olivia didn't realize it at the time, but the two officers had just saved her life.

Meanwhile, on the way to the police car, Peter asked if he could go around the corner of a building to relieve himself. He took the opportunity to throw his ballpeen hammer and knife behind a small storage tank.

At Hammerton Road police station Peter gave his correct name. He told police he had used the stolen plates because he was planning a robbery. He even told them he had been questioned as one of the individuals who had been paid with a new £5 note like the one found in Jean Jordan's purse. Peter was detained, but was still no more of a suspect than thousands of others who had been detained and questioned in the course of the massive investigation.

Next day, when Sgt. Bob Ring heard that the man he had brought in was being questioned by the Ripper squad, he decided to take another look at the spot where he had picked up Peter Sutcliffe. In particular, he searched the area where Peter had relieved himself. There, Bob Ring found a ballpeen hammer and a knife lying in a pile of leaves.

Word spread throughout the police hierarchy. This could be it. Inspector John Boyle conducted the questioning. He told the suspect he didn't believe his story. Early on in the questioning Boyle stated, "I think you are in serious trouble."

Peter replied rather cockily, "I think you have been leading up to it."

Boyle asked, "Leading up to what?"

"The Yorkshire Ripper," replied Peter.

"What about the Yorkshire Ripper?" the officer asked, hardly able to conceal his excitement.

The reply left little room for doubt. Peter said, "Well, it's me."

Peter Sutcliffe, 35, the man who had terrorized a country for five and a half years, confessed in detail to all his crimes. In May 1981, an English jury rejected his counsel's plea of insanity and found Peter guilty of 13 counts of murder. He was sentenced to life imprisonment and incarcerated at Parkhurst Prison on the Isle of Wight.

Since that time, due to attacks on him by fellow inmates as well as mental deterioration, he has been transferred to Broadmoor, an institution housing the criminally insane.

THE LONELY KILLER

In 1942, pretty Betty Whyte of Fraserburg, Scotland, married handsome Olav Nilsen. Their courtship had an aura of glamor. After all, it was wartime. Olav was stationed in Scotland with the Free Norwegian Forces. The couple, who would divorce in 1948, had three children; Olav, Dennis and Sylvia. No one knew then that quiet, well-behaved Dennis would become the most prolific mass murderer in the history of English crime.

Dennis joined the army in 1961, at the age of 16. He spent most of his army career in the Army Catering Corp., where he learned skills which were, in later years, to assist him in the most unusual way imaginable.

While in the service, Dennis discovered two things. He was sexually attracted to men. His comrades never learned of his secret desires, for Dennis was well aware of the ridicule heaped upon homosexuals by rough, tough army personnel. In fact, Dennis often led his colleagues in demeaning those men who appeared to be effeminate. Dennis also learned how to drink in the army. It was the one way he had of joining in, becoming one of the boys.

Eleven years later, Dennis was discharged from the army, having attained the rank of corporal. In 1972, he took a 16-week course at the Metropolitan Police Training School in North London and became a police officer. While serving with the police force, he was a practising homosexual. Unlike army life, Dennis found no camaraderie in the police force. At the end of their shifts his fellow officers went home to their families. A lonely, brooding man, Dennis left the force after one year.

For a while, Dennis was employed as a security guard, but found the work boring. Eventually, he obtained a position as clerical officer with the Department of Employment, where he would remain as a valued and conscientious employee for the next eight years.

In his spare time, Dennis picked up male companions at pubs, particularly the Wellington IV in Hampstead and the Salisbury in St. Martin's Lane. He took them to his room, but these encounters, though numerous, were of a passing nature. Dennis had no meaningful relationships, no real friends.

In 1975, Dennis received a bit of a windfall. His father whom he never knew, died in Norway, leaving him £1000. Around this time, Dennis met David Gallichan at a pub. He ended up taking the 20-year-old blonde boy home with him. Next day, they decided to live together. Within days of paying one month's rent in advance, Dennis and David moved into a pleasant flat on the ground floor at 195 Melrose Ave. French windows opened onto a long garden at the rear of the flat.

The relationship provided a period of relative contentment for Dennis. He was a faithful lover but the same could not be said of young Gallichan. It was Gallichan's promiscuity which precipitated the breakup. When both men began bringing home extracurricular lovers, the writing was on the wall. In 1977, the pair parted. Dennis Nilsen was devastated. About the only thing Dennis had left was his loyal mongrel bitch, Bleep. A year passed. He and Bleep spent the Christmas season of 1978 alone and lonely. Dennis spent Christmas Eve in a drunken stupor.

On Dec. 30, Dennis picked up a lad at the Cricklewood Arms. They spent the night together at Dennis' flat on Melrose Ave. Next morning, Dennis looked at the nude, sleeping body beside him. How pleasant it would be to have a friend over New Year's. Silently, Dennis picked up his own necktie from the floor where he had dropped it the night before. He slid it under his new friend's neck and squeezed until the struggling boy went limp. Dennis noted that the boy was still breathing. He quickly filled a bucket of water and dunked the rasping boy's head into the water. After a few minutes, he was dead.

Year's later, Dennis would relate that he bathed his victim in the bathtub, even washing his hair. The clean body was placed in the bed. Then Dennis went for a walk to clear his head. Slowly a plan formed in his tormented, twisted mind. He purchased a cooking pot, but put it away when he got home.

Dennis dressed the body in new clothing he had purchased for himself and laid it out on the floor. That day Dennis slept peacefully, getting up in the evening to watch TV. Next day he pried some floorboards from the living room and shoved his companion's body under the floor, after covering it with dirt from the garden.

A week later, Dennis retrieved the corpse, washed it once again in the bathtub and performed indignities to the body. It was then once again placed under the floorboards. Seven months later, the luckless youth's body was burned in the garden. Dennis had successfully obliterated his first victim. The body has never been identified.

After keeping a body for seven months and then disposing of it, Dennis was amazed at the ease of it all. No one seemed to miss the victim. Five months later, Dennis struck again. Ironically, his second victim was a Canadian on holidays in London.

It was Kenneth Ockendon's misfortune to meet Dennis the day he was to fly home to Toronto. Kenneth was having lunch when Dennis struck up a conversation with him. Later, the two men went sightseeing, before making their way to Dennis' flat for something to eat.

Back at the Central Hotel, Kenneth's baggage remained unclaimed. He never checked out. Dennis strangled Kenneth to death that same night. The Canadian tourist was reported missing. For a while, his mysterious disappearance was noted by the London papers, but he was never traced to civil servant Dennis Nilsen.

In the next few years, Dennis was to kill ten more young men. With the exception of his Canadian victim, none were missed. Most were wandering homosexuals. Dennis liked to wash the bodies and keep them around his flat, not only to satisfy his necrophiliac desires, but also for their mere physical presence. He often dressed the bodies and propped them up on chairs to watch TV. On occasion he spoke to them and played them his favorite records. Only four of the 12 men killed at Melrose Ave. have been identified. Other than Ockendon, they are Martyn Duffey, Billy Sutherland and Malcolm Barlow.

Dennis was now killing at a rapid rate. To make room under the floorboards, he dissected some of his victims. Other victims were dissected and placed in suitcases, which were stored in an outside shed, together with various deodorants. Still, Dennis was having difficulty disposing of the bodies as fast as he was killing. At one point in 1980, he had six bodies in various stages of dissection, both in the flat and outside in the shed.

In December 1980, Dennis built a huge bonfire beyond his garden in a vacant lot. A couple of old tires atop the fire served to disguise the odor. Dennis was housecleaning, destroying bodies.

Good thing, too. Dennis had never been a good tenant. In fact, he was a born complainer. As a result, he had often been asked to move by the agents acting for the owners of the building. In desperation, they located another apartment for their troublesome tenant and threw in £1000 as compensation for the inconvenience. It was an offer Dennis couldn't refuse. He moved into a self-contained attic flat at 23 Cranley Gardens. One can only imagine his feelings as the moving van pulled away from Melrose Ave. He had terminated 12 young lives and no one was the wiser.

Dennis Nilsen was not finished, but the business of disposing of bodies was not as easy as it had been at his previous dwelling. There was no garden, no floorboards and no shed. But Dennis was not to be denied. In the ten months between March, 1982 and January 1983, he killed three more times. Each body was dissected. Individual parts were boiled in large pots on the kitchen stove. With flesh boiled away, the remaining bones were dumped in the garbage and taken away by the garbage collector.

Larger body parts, such as the skull and leg bones, were placed in bags, which were stored in a tea chest place in the corner of the living room. A red cloth over the tea chest transformed the grave into an attractive table. Excess flesh, as well as some organs and hair, were flushed down the toilet. And that's how Dennis came to the attention of police.

The toilet clogged. Tenants complained and were told not to use the facilities until the trouble was repaired.

On Sat. Feb. 5, 1983, plumber Mike Welch showed up at 23 Cranley Gardens. Mike checked the pipes leading out of the house. There didn't seem to be any problem there. He checked outside the building, but couldn't correctly diagnose the difficulty. Mike advised one of the tenants to call an outfit named Dyno-rod. However, nothing could be done until after the weekend. Unknown to all, Dennis Nilsen was busy dissecting a body all that weekend.

On Tuesday, Michael Cattran, an engineer with Dyno-rod, arrived at 23 Cranley Gardens. He went down a 12-foot manhole outside the house and discovered the cause of the malfunction - strange looking pieces of flesh. Police were called.

When Dennis Nilsen returned home from work that night, Scotland Yard inspectors were waiting for him. He made no attempt to deny his guilt. When his flat was examined, plastic bags yielded two torsoes, two boiled heads and four arms. The tea chest contained various bones.

Dennis Nilsen admitted to 15 murders. He was tried on six counts of murder and two counts of attempted murder. Dennis was found guilty of all charges. He received eight life sentences with a recommendation that he serve not less than 25 years.

SCARY STUFF

On April 17, 1971, in the tiny village of Bisselmark, located about 40 miles east of Hamburg, Germany, a local undertaker showed up for work. It would not be your run of the mill day.

There, before his eyes, was the body of a 40-year-old woman. This alone was not an unusual sight for an undertaker. But, wait, there was a difference. The corpse was sitting up in her coffin. Her eyes were held open by two match sticks. Around the coffin, the undertaker found several burned out candles. Muddy footprints gave stark evidence that someone or something had performed a sort of ritual in the undertaker's parlor that night.

The owner of the establishment, fearing that relatives of the dead woman wouldn't appreciate the indignities to the body, hastily cleared up all evidence of the ghoulish intruder's presence. He did not inform anyone of his weird experience until much later.

Two weeks after the incident at Bisselmark, the ghoul showed up on the German island of Sylkt. He sneaked into a church and, for no apparent reason, stabbed 52-year-old Gertraud Frankle. We are sure he had no ulterior motive. Mrs. Frankle was already quite dead.

Next morning, she was found by Pastor Harold Segen, the handle of a hunting knife still protruding from her chest. The pastor called police, but nothing came of their investigation.

The ghoul, in search of fresh bodies, turned up next in the city of Flensberg, near the border of Germany and Denmark. On the morning of May 31, Marion Steiger entered the Muhlen Cemetery to visit the grave of her mother. Marion took one look at the adjacent grave and took off. Who can blame her?

Someone had dug up a recently buried male body and had extracted it from the casket. There, sitting beside the coffin with his hands on the coffin top, using it like a desk, was none other than the gentleman who had so recently been laid to rest. What's more, someone had decapitated the body and carried away the head.

Marion made it to the street before collapsing. She was taken to hospital, where she recovered from her harrowing experience.

Police had several theories. Some thought a medical student required a head to examine. Others held out for Satanists.

Three days later, Karl Konzenius, a veterinarian, whose hobby was gardening, opened the door to his small garden equipment hut. Karl saw more than fertilizer. There, lying at his feet, were two ears and a nose. The experience was distracting enough to force Karl to abruptly shut the door and call police. They searched the small hut and found other assorted small parts, such as a tongue and two eyes. It was the opinion of the police that the ghoul had wanted only a skull and had cut away as much of the head as possible.

The Flensberg police sent out a circular describing the strange incidents. They were surprised to hear from Bisselburg and Sylkt police outlining their strange experiences.

No question about it. There was a weird man travelling about the countryside.

On Nov. 7, 1971, Horst Weber was planning on a pleasant visit to the Nuremberg cemetery to pay his respects at the final resting place of a dearly beloved. Poor Horst never quite made it to his relative's grave.

Someone had dug up recently buried Steffie Weichert and removed her from her coffin. She now sat stark naked on a mound of earth staring at the terrified Horst Weber. Understandably, Horst vacated the scene. When the body was examined, it was established that the intruder had been unsuccessful in obtaining blood from the body.

The German police knew that whoever was desecrating graves and performing indignities on the bodies would resort to murder. The best they could do was to stake out as many mortuaries and graveyards as possible.

George Warmuth worked at Nuremberg's West Cemetery. He was not aware of any strange occurrences taking place in graveyards. However, in May 1972, George intuitively felt that bodies laid out in his mortuary had been disturbed. He decided to return to the mortuary in the evening in an attempt to find out who or what had gained entrance to the mortuary.

George sat in his office for a few nights without results. Then, one night, he heard a noise. Quietly, he made his way to the body room and turned on the lights. There, bending over one of the female bodies, was a black-haired, slightly built man.

He was kissing the corpse flush on the lips.

The intruder did not let the sudden light disturb him in his romantic task. George screamed at him, but the man didn't move. When George faced him directly, the man pulled out a pistol and fired. A bullet entered George's stomach, but big, strong George crawled to a telephone and managed to dial an emergency number. He lay near death for 48 hours, but gradually regained his strength and recovered.

While police were obtaining a description from George, the monster struck again. Forest Ranger Werner Beranek reported that he found two bodies inside a parked Mercedes about two miles from the town of Lindelburg. He had also seen a man drive off on a red motorcycle. Police were on the scene in a matter of minutes, examining the bodies of Marcus Adler, 24, and his fiancée, Ruth Lissy, 18.

The bullets taken from the victims' bodies matched the one removed from George Warmuth. Lip marks were found near the open wounds. The vampire, or whatever, had struck again.

Nuremberg police had their two witnesses, Warmuth and Beranek, help a police artist develop a composite picture of the wanted man. Posters were widely distributed.

Helmut Kostan, who worked at the Demerag Transport Co., thought he knew the identity of the wanted man, but he couldn't be sure. One piece of information on the posters finally convinced him. The man hadn't responded when George Warmuth screamed. Helmut felt he knew why. His suspect, co-worker Kuno Hofman, was a deaf mute.

Helmut called police and Kuno was taken into custody. The weapon which had taken the lives of Marcus Adler and Ruth Lissy was found in his room. They also recovered the skull removed from the gentleman in the graveyard at Flensberg.

Kuno had studied witchcraft and Satanism. He was of below average intelligence and readily admitted all his crimes. Because of his handicap, he had frequented houses of prostitution, but soon tired of prostitutes and longed for true love. When he started going steady with a deaf mute girl, his problems appeared to be over. However, her parents didn't approve of him. He was devastated and took up the study of witchcraft.

Kuno had drunk the blood of his victims to become tall, handsome and healthy. Doctors who examined him were quickly convinced that he was not rowing with both oars in the water.

Kuno Hofman was confined to a hospital for the criminally insane, where it is expected he will spend the rest of his life.

9

AMERICANA

CHOWCHILLA DRAMA

It started out as a great idea for a movie plot. Almost as a lark the three friends had fun planning the kidnapping. Gradually the seed of the idea took root, until three healthy, good-looking young men from reputable families were actively engaged in planning one of the most diabolical crimes ever committed.

Unbelievably, Jim Schoenfeld, 24, his brother Rick, 22, and Fred Woods, 24, were planning to kidnap a busload of children and bury them alive.

Fred's family was steeped in wealth, having interests in farming, oil, shopping centres, and amusement parks. His parents owned California Rock and Gravel Co. and lived in a huge home on a twenty-acre estate known as "The Hawthornes" near San Francisco. Fred had his own apartment in a refurbished garage on the estate.

Fred met Jim Schoenfeld while both were students at Woodside High School. The boys had one interest in common - they loved cars and were excellent mechanics.

Jim Schoenfeld's parents were not born to money, as Fred's were. His father, John Schoenfeld, had worked his way through medical school. By the time his sons were teenagers, Dr. Schoenfeld had a comfortable home, large swimming pool, and horses for the use of his boys. Jim and Rick were good students but never made a success of their several attempts at college.

In 1969 Fred Woods graduated from high school. That summer he met David Boston, 21, a student majoring in film making at San Jose State college. The two boys became friends.

Fred and David engaged in the business of purchasing and repairing old cars, which they sold at a profit. Boston, who was actively attempting to raise money to produce a feature film, appreciated the opportunity. Later Jim Schoenfeld joined Fred and Boston in the venture.

The three friends often talked about the perfect crime. Eventually their ideas crystallized into the kidnapping of a busload of children. Boston was later to swear that other than discuss the theme, thinking it had the making of a good movie, he had no further part in the plan. His place was taken by Jim's younger brother, Rick.

In late 1975 and early 1976 the three friends finalized their plans. The children had to be of grammar-school age. Older children might be too tough to handle. No more than 20 hostages would be involved to avoid crowding. They would ask for $5 million ransom.

Now the details had to be taken care of, slowly, meticulously, and intelligently. Fred bought a used 1956 International truck trailer from Palo Alto Transfer and storage Co. for $750. He returned to the same firm and purchased a 1956 Fruehauf moving van.

Using an assumed name, he then purchased three surplus shore-patrol vans from the Alameda Navy Base for $3,750. Fred rented space for his newly acquired trucks in San Jose.

Preparations were proceeding nicely. The three boys purchased a dump truck at an auction in Sacramento. Fred knew exactly what he was doing. His father owned a huge quarry which was closed down each weekend. He would have no trouble digging a large trench with a bulldozer left on the property over weekends. They would carry away the excavated earth in their own dump truck and back in the moving van with their tractor. It was a major undertaking, but they carried out the well-planned scheme without a hitch.

An entry hole was cut away in the top of the moving van. Two large batteries were positioned so that they could later be attached to fans. The kidnappers figured the batteries would last forty-eight hours. The entry hole was to be covered with a steel plate. Finally the bulldozer was used to cover the van with earth.

The boys were shocked when the weight of the earth buckled the roof. The whole thing might collapse. Fortunately, Fred had brought along lumber with which he shored up the roof from the inside. An acetylene torch was used to cut holes in the wheel wells to serve as toilets. Bread, potato chips, and water were placed inside. The floor was covered with mattresses picked up at a surplus house. All was in readiness.

The $5 million was to be dropped from an airplane. It would be picked up by one of the conspirators and taken directly to a nearby airfield, where the other two men would commandeer a plane and pilot. They would all leave the country as millionaires.

For months the boys cased schools and bus lines. Finally they chose one particular bus leaving one particular school at a certain time on a certain day. All the planning was over. The day had come.

On July 15, 1976, Ed Ray pulled up his big yellow International bus in front of Dairyland School outside Chowchilla, California. Thirty-one children, 22 girls and nine boys, clambered aboard his bus. Ed pulled away from the curb.

There was little to distinguish this day from any other of the thousands which had preceded it. Ed was about to begin his twenty-fourth year on the job. The bus continued on its route. Five children arrived home safely that afternoon, leaving 26 youngsters and Ed in the bus.

Twelve-year-old Lisa Nanette Barletta gathered up her things. Her stop would be next. Ray peered down the highway. He didn't know what to make of the white van parked in the centre of the road.

Calmly and quietly the armed man spoke to Ed through the driver's window: "Would you open the door, please?" Ed released the catch, opening the bus door. Two similarly dressed armed men jumped aboard the bus. The children squealed. Some thought it was fun. Others sensed the danger right away. One of the gunmen ordered Ed to the back of the bus as his companion took over the driver's seat. Slowly the bus started up. The third gunman jumped into the white van and drove behind the bus.

About a mile down the road the strange little caravan pulled into a thicket. The white van backed up to the door of the bus and twelve children were transferred directly from the bus into the van. Little Darla Daniels held on to her 4H achievement certificate. No one was going to touch that certificate before her mother saw it. The rest of the children were moved into the second van. Ed Ray was the last captive to leave the bus.

Both vans had partitions between the driver and cargo areas. The rear windows were painted over. Once the doors were closed the occupants were in total darkness. For eleven hours the two vans rolled through the California countryside. Some children slept. Other sobbed. Several, unable to restrain themselves, urinated in their clothing.

The two vans stopped. Ed was ordered out. He found himself in a canvas enclosure which was obviously being used to conceal the vans. Ed was told to remove his pants and boots. One of the men gave him a flashlight and pointed to a hole in the ground. The top of a ladder was sticking up out of the hole. The armed man pointed and commanded, "Go down." Slowly, Ed climbed down the ladder.

One by one the children were taken out of the vans. Each child was asked his or her name and made to part with a possession before being ordered down the ladder. Most turned over a piece of clothing. Reluctantly, Darla Daniels parted with her 4H achievement certificate.

Ed Ray flashed the beam around the enclosure. He and the children were in some kind of a furniture moving van. The floor had been outfitted with several mattresses. Ed noticed that lumber had been used to shore up the roof.

Jim, Rick, and Fred quickly connected their batteries to the fans. A large steel plate, 3/8 of an inch thick, was dropped over the hole in the moving van roof. The three kidnappers placed two hundred-pound industrial batteries on top of the steel plate. A wooden box was placed over the batteries before earth was used to cover the entire moving van.

Down below the surface, effectively buried alive, were 55-year-old Ed Ray, and 26 children ranging in age from five to 14.

Ed Ray didn't want to, but he couldn't help it. He began to sob. Then he prayed aloud to his God.

A desolate feeling enveloped Ed and the children in their eerie tomb. They found bread, potato chips, and water. All were famished.

In Chowchilla, hours earlier, the bus and its occupants were missed. Parents called the school and the police. Something crazy was going on. Whoever heard of a busload of children vanishing into thin air?

Authorities traced the bus from Dairyland School to the point where Susan Zylstra disembarked. The next stop was the home of Lisa Nanette Barletta, the first child who failed to arrive home. Somewhere between Susan's home and Lisa's home the bus had disappeared without a trace.

The word went out. Local police, as well as the California Highway Patrol, were alerted to the situation. At around 8:00 p.m. that evening a small aircraft employed in the search spotted the bus in a bamboo thicket. The bus was empty. Police realized it was possible that a mass kidnapping had taken place.

By daylight the word had spread from the tiny town in California to newspapers throughout the world. President Ford took a personal interest in the case. Officers representing federal and state agencies poured into Chowchilla to assist in the search for the missing children.

Unaware of the excitement caused by the disappearance, Ed Ray surveyed his surroundings. The van was eight feet wide, 25 feet long, and 12 feet high. His flashlight was growing dim. The fans did little to alleviate the odor and heat now that it was daylight outside.

As the day wore on the heat became unbearable. At about 4 o'clock in the afternoon, Ed and the oldest of the children, 14-year-old Mike Marshall, decided to investigate the entry hole in the roof of the van. They stacked mattresses on the floor. Ed stood on the top of the pile and tried to raise the steel plate without success. He noticed that there was a little space between the edge of the plate and the opening in the roof.

Ed pried loose one of the planks supporting the roof and managed to force it in the opening. Using the 2-by-4 as a lever, Ed, with Mike's help, was able to move the plate enough so that he could reach his arm through the opening. He felt the industrial battery on top of the plate. Painstakingly, he inched the battery to the opening while he and Mike slid the plate, creating an ever-widening space.

Finally Ed was able to force the battery through the hole into his and Mike Marshall's arms. The process was repeated with the second battery. Now they were able to remove the steel plate. They raised themselves out of the hole onto the top of the van and into a shaft-like structure which had covered the batteries. Using a piece of lumber, Mike punctured a corner of the shaft. Dirt poured in.

Ed and Mike were joined by 10-year-old Robert Gonzales and eight-year-old John Estabrook. They were literally digging their way out of a grave. Dust and grime mixed with perspiration stung their eyes but finally a tiny opening appeared. Robert Gonzales, the smallest of the group, was the first to stick his head through the opening and smell the sweet aroma of fresh air. It was early evening.

Ed Ray helped each child to the top of the stack of mattresses. There were some skinned knees and cut fingers, but all made it safely out of the tomb.

Staying close together, they approached one of the buildings of the California Rock and Gravel Co. quarry and were met by an employee, Walter Enns. Enns couldn't believe the sight before him - a swarm of filthy kids, led by an even filthier man dressed only in jockey shorts.

Ed Ray could only blurt out, "We're the ones from Chowchilla!" Someone produced a pair of overalls for Ed. The ordeal, which had lasted 30 hours, was over.

As soon as they heard of the dramatic escape, Jim Schoenfeld and Fred Woods drove to Reno International Airport, where Fred caught a plane to Vancouver. Jim planned to drive to Canada but was unable to cross the Canadian border. He headed back to California.

Meanwhile, Fred arrived in Vancouver without incident. Using the alias Ralph Lester Snider, he registered at the St. Francis Hotel on Seymour Street.

Unknown to Fred in Vancouver, investigating officers had discovered that the California Rock and Gravel Co. was owned by a man named Woods whose son was nowhere to be found. He also had no way of knowing that the buried van had been hoisted to the surface, revealing the name on the side: the Palo Alto Moving and Storage Co. When detectives contacted the company, they found out that the van had been sold to none other than Fred Woods.

The third kidnapper, Rick Schoenfeld, made a dramatic confession to his father. Dr. Schoenfeld was shattered to find out that it was his two sons and their friend who had kidnapped and very nearly killed 27 innocent people. He advised his son to turn himself in.

Dr. Schoenfeld then called a San Francisco lawyer. Rather than openly reveal his son's involvement, he asked the lawyer if he would represent one of the suspects in the case. The lawyer refused and then called the police. For the first time the name Schoenfeld was linked to the kidnapping. It was a routine matter to find out that the Schoenfeld brothers and Fred Woods were the best of friends.

The Woods family estate was searched. In Fred's apartment detectives found the entire plan for the kidnapping written out in longhand, as well as a draft of the $5 million ransom note which was never delivered.

Within days they had located the warehouse where the boys had stored the two vans used to transport the children. It was here that they had performed carpentry work and painting in preparation for the kidnapping. Among the torches, oxygen tanks and paint cans detectives found a certificate of achievement awarded to Darla Daniels for her participation in a 4H youth program in Madera County.

Rick Schoenfeld, accompanied by his family's lawyer, turned himself in to the authorities. Jim read of his brother's surrender and returned home to give himself up. He was spotted by a citizen and taken into custody before this could be arranged. A telephone call to the RCMP in Vancouver was all that was necessary to have Fred Woods picked up without incident.

A year later all three men pleaded guilty to 27 charges of kidnapping. Jim, Rick, and Fred were sentenced to life imprisonment.

THE HEX MURDER

I drove through Lebanon, Lancaster, and York, through rich prosperous farmland, deep in to Pennsylvania. This small pocket of the United States is like no other, for more than 200 years ago thousands of hard-working German farmers settled here, cleared the land, and made it bloom. Now known as Pennsylvania Dutch, they brought more than their propensity for hard work when they came from Europe. Deeply religious in the conventional sense, they are nevertheless steeped in witchcraft, superstition, and medieval demonology.

To this day many of the barns are decorated with large, colorful geometric designs - the sign of the hex. An elderly gentleman explained, "How else would you keep the evil spirits from getting at the cattle inside?"

There have been many instances in Pennsylvania Dutch country when a hex placed on an enemy resulted in sickness which defied rational explanation by bona fide medical doctors. Milk cows with well-documented milk production over a period of years have been known to dry up without explanation after having a hex placed on them. Such power has resulted in more than 20 hex murders down through the years.

On the morning of November 25, 1928, Nelson D. Rehmeyer, 60, was found dead on his kitchen floor. When police arrived on the scene they found that Rehmeyer's body had been covered by the remains of a partially burned mattress. Someone had poured water over the mattress and had extinguished the fire. A length of rope was tied around the victim's neck. Detectives figured the murder was the work of transients who had initially attempted to destroy the murder scene by burning down the house but had changed their minds at the last minute and put out the fire.

The crime might have remained unsolved had not rumors persisted throughout the rural community that there was far more to the murder than appeared on the surface. Soon police were hearing stories of witchcraft and hexes. It was rumored that 32-year-old mentally retarded John Blymyer and his friend, 14-year-old John Curry, had visited Rehmeyer on the evening before the murder.

Police heard more. It was brought to their attention that the Milton Hess family had acquired a book entitled *The Long Lost Friend*. This was no ordinary book. *The Long Lost Friend* was a coveted acquisition, at the time ranking only behind the Bible in Pennsylvania Dutch country. Not everyone owned a copy. The book revealed how to put a hex on a nasty neighbor and how to make an enemy's preserves go bad; it described in detail the incantations required to ruin an enemy's crops and hundreds of other hexes. The dead man had owned such a book. It was missing, and the Hess family was suddenly in possession of a copy.

Police questioned simple-minded John Blymyer. He was quite open with his replies to their questions. John revealed that he had been hexed years ago and that was the reason he was retarded and never felt well.

Recently he had tried to find out who had cursed him with the hex. He consulted with an old witch named Mother Noll, in nearby Marietta. It was she who told him that John Rehmeyer had placed the hex on him. Mother Noll told John that there were only two ways in which he could have the hex removed. He had to have a lock of Rehmeyer's hair buried six feet in the ground or gain possession of Rehmeyer's powerful book, *The Long Lost Friend.*

One look at big, burly Nelson Rehmeyer and the boys knew they would never have the strength to carry out their plan. They left the Rehmeyer farmhouse and next day solicited the aid of Milton Hess' son Wilburt. That same night all three men showed up at Rehmeyer's farm. Without warning they pounced on the unsuspecting Rehmeyer, overpowering him.

Incredulous at this turn of events, Rehmeyer implored his attackers to tell him what they wanted. Finally, they revealed they were after his coveted book. Rehmeyer talked the three men into letting him loose to look for the book. In an instant, he made a dash for freedom, only to be clobbered on the head by a huge piece of firewood wielded by John Curry. Blymyer fastened the rope around Rehmeyer's neck. While he was doing so, he recoiled in horror, crying out to his companions, "Oh, my God! He's dead!"

Now in a state of panic, the three men rushed upstairs, found the book they were seeking, and three one-dollar bills, which they distributed evenly. They then threw a mattress over the body, lit it, and watched the flames climb for a moment. Deciding the fire might bring aid before they got away, they extinguished it.

The three men went to the Hess home and celebrated. In their minds they had performed a commendable deed. They had slain a warlock and would live happily ever after. When taken into custody, both John Curry and Wilburt Hess told primarily the same story as Blymyer.

While the men were being held for trial, there were many who felt they were being unjustly persecuted. After all, they had killed a warlock. Some considered them folk heroes.

To add to the eerie, unbelievable circumstances of the case, Amos Hermann, district attorney of York County, promptly collapsed after hearing the three men confess. Later, his fainting was attributed to overwork, but everyone knew the real reason. The three accused had hexed their accuser.

Word of the strange murder case spread throughout the United States. By the time the trial was held, crack reporters from most of the leading newspapers in the country covered the trial.

Hess and Curry confessed during their trial that their belief in black magic was waning, but not so John Blymyer. He felt better than he had ever felt in his life, having accomplished what he had set out to do. He had relieved Rehmeyer of his prized book, and more importantly, a lock of his victim's hair was now buried under six feet of earth. It didn't matter an iota that the lock of hair was still attached to Rehmeyer.

The end result of the murder trial did not sit well with the Pennsylvania Dutch. John Blymyer and John Curry were found guilty of murder in the first degree and sentenced to life imprisonment. Wilburt Hess was found guilty of manslaughter and received a sentence of from 10 to 20 years in prison. The sentences were harsh for a feeble-minded man and a 14-year-old boy who had set out to steal a book and a lock of hair and ended up killing someone they firmly believed to be a warlock.

Later, the state of Pennsylvania had second thoughts about the sentences. Ten years after their trial, after Hess had already been released from prison, Blymyer and Curry received a full pardon and were set free.

CATHERINE GENOVESE

The neighborhood was middle class; ordinary people leading ordinary lives. The crime and violence often associated with New York City didn't apply to the Kew Gardens section of Queens. Tree-lined streets, Tudor-styled storefronts - Kew Gardens was a good place to live.

Catherine Genovese lived there. In the early hours of March 13, 1964, the 28-year-old bar manager cried out to her neighbors for help. Her plea went unheeded.

At precisely 3:20 a.m., Kitty, as she was known to everyone in the neighborhood, parked her red Fiat in the Long Island Railroad Station parking lot. She locked her car and, as usual, started walking towards the door leading to her apartment at 82-70 Austin Street. Shops along Austin Street occupy the first floor. Apartments are on the second. The entrance to Kitty's apartment was at the rear of the building, about one hundred feet from where she parked her car.

Just as she was about to proceed to her apartment she noticed a man lurking at the far end of the parking lot. Otherwise, the streets were deserted. Apprehensive about the stranger, she decided to walk along Austin Street towards a police call box. Kitty could hear the footsteps of the man following her. He was gaining rapidly. Under a streetlight, in front of a bookstore, and directly across from a ten-story apartment building, the man grabbed the terrified woman.

Kitty screamed, "Oh, my God, he stabbed me! Please help me! Please help me!"

Lights blinked on in the apartment building. Windows slid open. Someone shouted, "Let that girl alone!"

The attacker shrugged and walked down Austin Street.

No one came to Kitty's assistance. No one called the police. The windows of the apartment building slid closed. One by one the lights went out.

Down on the street, Kitty Genovese got to her feet. Staggering slightly, she slowly retraced her steps, desperately trying to get to the safety of her apartment entrance. She made it to the side of her building. To her horror her assailant had returned. Again he grabbed her and stabbed her once more.

Kitty screamed, "I'm dying, I'm dying!"

More windows opened, more lights went on. Kitty's attacker walked down Austin Street, got into his car, and drove away. Behind closed windows, apprehensive eyes peered down at the scene below. Still no one came to Kitty's assistance. One by one, like snuffed-out candles, the lights of the apartments blinked off.

Now bleeding profusely, Kitty rose once more to her feet. Staggering and falling, she made her way to the rear of her building. She managed to open the door to the building and half crawled to the foot of the stairs. Unbelievably, her assailant returned for the third time and stabbed her once more, this time fatally. Then he disappeared into the night.

At 3:50 a.m. one of Kitty's neighbors called the police. They took only two minutes to arrive at the scene. The man who had made the call explained that he had consulted with a friend by phone in another section of the city before he placed the call. Why hadn't he called earlier? He told the police he didn't want to get involved.

The investigation into Miss Genovese's death was strange and frightening in many ways. Thirty-two minutes had elapsed from the time she had parked her car in the station parking lot until the police arrived at the scene of the murder. On two occasions the killer had left and returned. Had anyone called the police, most certainly Miss Genovese would not have been killed. To summon the police by phone in that section of Queens, it is only necessary to dial zero.

Kitty's neighbors, many of whom knew her well, were interviewed by police and reporters. Incredibly, 38 individuals had witnessed the attacks and no one had called the police.

Hardened homicide detectives, who thought they had seen everything, were at a loss as to why all 38 citizens had chosen not to make a simple telephone call. They all recognized the reluctance of citizens to become involved when there was a risk of danger to themselves, but this was a different situation. An anonymous phone call from the safety of your own home cannot be considered a dangerous act.

Later the 38 reluctant witnesses gave a variety of answers:

"I put out the light, and we were able to see better."

"I don't know."

"I didn't want my husband to get involved."

"I was tired."

"Frankly, we were afraid."

"We thought it was a lovers' quarrel."

Winston Moseley, a 29-year-old business-machine operator was later charged with the Genovese murder. When questioned, he confessed to killing two other women, as well as raping and robbing scores of others. He was a married man with two children and no previous record. He had returned to kill Miss Genovese for fear that she could identify him.

At Moseley's trial, when the jury brought in a verdict of guilty with a recommendation for the death penalty, the court spectators stood up and cheered. Among those who cheered that day were several of the 38 witnesses who didn't dial zero to save Catherine Genovese's life.

THRILL KILLER

When Charlie Schmid turned 16, his well-heeled foster parents presented him with a new red convertible to go with his motorcycle. They also let him know he would be receiving a $300 a month allowance.

Charlie's parents owned the Katharine Craycroft Centre, a large nursing home in Tucson, Arizona. Charlie had his own self-contained house on the nursing-home grounds. An indifferent student, he dropped out of high school in his last year. He did achieve some acclaim in high school when he led the gymnastic team to the Arizona state championship.

After leaving high school, Charlie began to hang around a section of Tucson known as the Speedway. Here young adults could pop pills, get drunk, and have sex. No one seemed to care.

Charlie's best friend was Richie Bruns. Richie wasn't that good an influence. He had been expelled from high school on four different occasions. The two friends had money and time on their hands. They drifted in and out of minor scrapes - traffic violations, drunk and disorderly charges. Nothing serious, but enough to keep them from receiving any good citizenship citations.

Charlie, who was extremely short, would stuff his cowboy boots with paper and crushed beer cans to give himself additional height. Swaggering, confident Charlie, with his red convertible and his own home, could pretty well have any of the teenage girls who hung around the Speedway. One night he met 16-year-old Mary French at a beer party out on the desert. Mary was so drunk she could hardly talk. The pair became lovers.

In May 1962 Charlie, now 22, asked Mary French to do him a favor. He wanted to fix up his friend, John Saunders, with a date. Charlie had a particular girl in mind, 15-year-old Alleen Rowe, who happened to be Mary's neighbor.

Mary promised to try to arrange a double date but didn't hold out much hope of success. Although they knew each other, the two were not exactly close friends. Alleen was an exceptional student who planned on attending university. The girls didn't move in the same circles.

The first few times Mary asked Alleen to double date, she refused. Charlie insisted, because he had this novel idea in mind to break the monotony. He had decided to kill Alleen. Not for any particular reason, mind you, just to find out what it would be like and to see if he could get away with it. He told Mary of his plan and she did nothing to dissuade him.

On Sunday, May 31, 1964, Alleen at last agreed to the date. It was a sweltering hot day, the temperature hovering around 90 degrees. Alleen's mother, a nurse, was at work. Charlie, John Saunders, and Mary drove around to Alleen's house, picked her up, and drove to the edge of the desert. The four got out of Charlie's car and walked into the desert.

After they had travelled some distance Charlie suggested that he and Mary return to the car for a transistor radio. When they were out of sight they heard Alleen scream. She was resisting John's advances. Charlie ran back to the struggling pair. He instructed John to put his hands over Alleen's mouth. Then the boys proceeded to tie the terrified girl with wire guitar strings. Charlie then struck her repeatedly with a rock until she lay dead.

The two killers had brought along a shovel with which to dig a grave. All three friends took turns digging. It was hard work. They managed to complete a shallow grave and bury Alleen. Then they agreed between themselves that if anyone ever asked they would say that John had a date with Alleen, but when they all went to pick her up she was not at home. John was to say that he went home, while Mary and Charlie went out on a date together.

Alleen's mother called the police the following morning and reported her daughter missing. A list of Alleen's friends was given to the police, and on their very first day of checking, Charlie, John, and Mary were questioned. Their stories held up, and they were not suspected.

A month went by without any trace of Alleen. John Saunders left Tucson to join the navy. Mary French moved out of town. Months drifted into years. Once more Charlie began hanging around with Richie Bruns. Alleen Rowe was forgotten, becoming another one of scores of missing teenagers who leave Tucson each year.

In July 1964, two years after Alleen's murder, Charlie met 16-year-old Gretchen Fritz, the daughter of Dr. James Fritz, a well-known heart specialist. Although her parents were socially prominent in Tucson and her brothers and sisters attended private schools, Gretchen was a loner. She liked to drink and she liked boys.

Gretchen fell for Charlie Schmid. Soon she and Charlie were an item along the Speedway. But Gretchen wasn't like the other girls. She wanted Charlie for herself. She became possessive, a nag, and a downright pain in the neck to Charlie, who had been playing the field so long he felt it was his right. Charlie couldn't get rid of Gretchen. In a moment of weakness he had taken her out to see Alleen's grave and had told her what he had done. Now, whenever he tried to split, she warned him of the incriminating knowledge she possessed and wouldn't hesitate to use.

On August 16 Gretchen and her 13-year-old sister Wendy jumped into Gretchen's LeMans. They planned to take in a Presley movie at a local drive-in. At some point during the evening the two girls ended up at Charlie's house, where he strangled them both. Charlie placed the bodies in the trunk of Gretchen's car, drove into the desert, and hastily buried the two girls in shallow graves. He then parked the LeMans where it would be easily found.

The sister were reported missing the next day. Dr. and Mrs. Fritz knew that Gretchen might stay out all night but not 13-year-old Wendy. Two weeks later, Charlie made the mistake of confiding in Richie Bruns. He even took Richie out into the desert and showed him the graves. Bruns kept the secret for two months before telling his story to the police.

In the meantime Charlie had met and married 15-year-old Diana Lynch. A few weeks later, on November 10, 1965, Richie led the police to the bodies of the Fritz girls. Charlie was picked up and charged with murder. John Saunders was located in Northford, Connecticut, and brought back to Tucson. Mary French was located in Texas. She too was returned to Tucson for questioning regarding the still-missing Alleen Rowe.

Mary was the first to confess to the Rowe killing, describing in detail the thrill killing which she, Charlie, and Saunders had orchestrated. Saunders substantiated her story but was unable to lead police to the grave. He couldn't remember the exact location. Mary also led police out to the desert but couldn't find the gravesite.

Eventually John Saunders was found guilty of first-degree murder in the Rowe case and received a sentence of life imprisonment. Mary French was found guilty of being an accessory to murder and concealing and compounding a felony. She received a five-year prison term.

On February 15, 1966, Charlie stood trial for the murders of Gretchen and Wendy Fritz. During the course of his trial it was revealed by his foster parents that

Charlie was the offspring of a single girl who had shown up at their nursing home one day in 1942. They raised Charlie as their own child, showering him with material things, but admitted that they hadn't paid much attention to him during his teens.

After deliberating only two hours and ten minutes the jury brought in two guilty verdicts. Charlie was sentenced to death. While on death row he was charged with the murder of Alleen Rowe, despite the fact that her body had never been found. In May 1967 Charlie once more stood trial for murder. With famed lawyer F. Lee Bailey as his attorney, Charlie copped a guilty plea and received sentence of from 50 years to life in the Arizona State Penitentiary.

In the meantime two death sentences still hung over his head. With some perverted idea of helping his cause, one fine day in June Charlie told a prison official, "I want to lead the authorities to the grave of Alleen Rowe." Charlie led a group of law-enforcement officers out to the spot where he had murdered Alleen. Hampered by handcuffs, Charlie uncovered Alleen's skeletal remains under six inches of earth.

A U.S. Supreme Court ruling later abolished capital punishment, saving Charlie's life. He died of natural causes in the Arizona State Penitentiary.

THEY KILLED
THE JUDGE

J udge Joseph Peel is the very first bona fide judge we have come across who has been accused of murder. To make matters even more intriguing, Joe's victim was a judge as well.

Crime makes for strange bedfellows. In 1953, Floyd "Lucky" Holzapfel was a mechanic by profession in West Palm Beach, Florida. By inclination Lucky was an armed robber and, in later years, a moonshiner and bookmaker. It proved to be an unfortunate day when Lucky ran into Municipal Judge Joseph Peel while in court on a trivial matter.

The two men became friends. They had a lot in common. You see, the judge was selling protection, and Lucky needed all the protection he could beg, borrow, or steal. Soon the two men had an informal but profitable arrangement whereby Lucky ran a bootlegging and gambling operation unmolested by police interference. Things couldn't have been more cozy. The judge drove a Cadillac, while his wife had to be content with a Lincoln.

On July 6, 1953, Peel received something of a minor setback when he was charged with representing both sides in a divorce action. Peel's case was heard by Judge Curtis Chillingworth, a man known for his harsh treatment of anyone who tampered with the law. Peel was pleasantly surprised when he only received a public reprimand for his legal sleight of hand. Chillingworth had turned out to be not such a bad guy after all.

By 1955 Judge Joseph Peel was in hot water again. He had advised a client of his, a Mrs. Shupe, that she was legally divorced. Mrs. Shupe promptly remarried and gave birth to a baby. Then she found out that it was all a terrible mistake. Authorities routinely discovered that Mrs. Shupe was an unwitting bigamist. Mrs. Shupe screamed to high heaven and pulled the plug on Joe Peel.

Judge Joseph Peel was to appear before Judge Curtis Chillingworth to untangle the Shupe affair. This time around news drifted down to Peel that Chillingworth had stated that he was going to throw the book at his young colleague. Peel could feel the good life slipping away - disgrace, disbarment, ruin and, what's more, no more protection-racket money which was returning a cool $3,000 per week to the sticky-fingered judge. Joe decided that action as required. According to Lucky, it was on June 3, 1955, that Peel spoke to him saying, "Judge Chillingworth is going to ruin me. The fact is he personally is going to take care of me when my case comes up. We'll have to get rid of the judge."

Well, now, this was a serious matter. Even in Florida, a state known for bizarre plots and intrigues, it is not quite cricket for one judge to go around plotting the murder of another. Lucky conferred with a partner of his in the numbers racket, one Bobby Lincoln. Both men realized that without Judge Peel's protection they would be out of business. They agreed to do the job for their friend and business partner, Joe Peel.

Lucky and Bobby boarded their cabin cruiser on the night of June 15, 1955. They travelled a few miles down the coast from Riviera Beach to Judge Chillingworth's summer home at Manalapan. Joe had told the two men that the judge would be home alone that night. Lucky left the boat in a few feet of water, and while Bobby stood to one side, he approached the back door of the Chillingworth home. The pyjama-clad judge responded to his knock. Lucky pulled out his gun and said, "This is a holdup. Is there anyone else in the house?" Peel had said that the judge would be alone. Lucky was surprised when Chillingworth shouted, "Margie!" In a moment Mrs. Chillingworth entered the room. She had a robe pulled over her nightdress.

The two victims had their hands taped behind their backs. Bobby Lincoln secured tape across their mouths. Initially, the Chillingworths probably thought they were being kidnapped. Slowly the thought that a more sinister end awaited them entered their minds. They were led at gunpoint down the stairs leading to the beach. Suddenly Mrs. Chillingworth let out a loud scream. She had managed to loosen the tape across her mouth. Lucky struck the little woman a vicious blow to the head with the butt end of his gun. Bleeding from a wound in the head, Mrs. Chillingworth fell down the stairs. Bobby Lincoln lifted her into the boat, while Lucky led the judge aboard.

Lucky started the engine and headed out to sea. About two miles from shore he cut the engines. The adhesive tape was gently removed from Mrs. Chillingworth's mouth. A spear-fishing waistband was fastened around her body. Lead weights were placed in the pockets. Mrs. Chillingworth knew she was about to die. Judge Chillingworth shouted to his wife, "Remember, I love you!" Mrs. Chillingworth whispered a reply, "I love you, too." Mrs. Chillingworth made no outcry as her body disappeared in the dark depths of the Atlantic.

Judge Chillingworth struggled. Despite being bound hand and foot, the judge still managed to throw himself overboard. Lucky looked on in amazement as the judge managed to stay afloat. The problem was solved when an anchor was found at the end of a rope. The rope was tied securely around the judge's neck before the anchor was thrown overboard. As the men watched, Judge Chillingworth spun out of sight and into oblivion. Judge and Mrs. Chillingworth were never to be seen again.

To visit the scene of the crime I headed south on Route A1A. Following the Atlantic coast, it was not difficult to imagine that night 25 years earlier when Lucky Holzapfel and Bobby Lincoln made their murderous boat trip. Soon I was driving on a spit of land - to the right an inland waterway, to the left majestic estates leading down to the Atlantic. This beautiful strip of paradise is Manalapan, population 300. In 1955, 150 servants and millionaires called this tiny strip of land their summer home.

Elsewhere along the coast the past quarter century have taken their toll. Luxury hotels and condominiums dot the shoreline, but not at Manalapan. Here the palm-tree-lined driveways surrounded by well-manicured lawns remain much as they were twenty-five years earlier. At the rear of 1540 Ocean Drive, the rhythmic lapping of the Atlantic is heard against the shore as it was during the Chillingworth's night of terror.

The morning after the Chillingworth murders, two workmen found bloodstains and footprints leading from their summer home down to the sea. The Chillingworths were gone. Soon the area was swarming with police, but the bodies were never recovered.

When a list was developed of those individuals who would profit by Judge Chillingworth's death, the name of Judge Peel was mentioned. There were those around Palm Beach who felt the unsavory judge was not above murder. As no proof was available, the case was soon classified as unsolved.

Peel received a 90-day suspended sentence for his involvement in the Shupe affair. A short time later he left the bench. As the months drifted into years, his fellow conspirators, Lucky Holzapfel and Bobby Lincoln, continued their life of crime.

They murdered an informer, Lew Gene Harvey, and dumped his body in a creek. Unlike the Chillingworths, Harvey's body was found.

During the investigation into the Harvey murder, authorities began to hear rumbling about the Chillingworths from the Palm Beach underground. An undercover agent gained Lucky's confidence and actually held up a few stores and pulled some hijacking jobs with the killer. Police held the theory that if anyone knew anything connecting Joe Peel to the Chillingworth disappearance, it would be Peel's old buddy, Lucky Holzapfel.

It was now years since the Chillingworth murders. Suddenly, in December 1959, Lucky Holzapfel disappeared. Only his wife knew that he had fled to Rio de Janeiro. She let Joe Peel know that her husband needed money. Joe told her that times were tough. Secretly he had decided to kill Lucky in order to ensure his silence. Unknown to Joe Peel, Lucky's friend, the undercover agent, lured him back to the United States. In a bugged hotel room Lucky readily talked about the Chillingworth killings and the Harvey murder.

Finally, the state figured it had a case. Lucky and former Judge Joseph Peel were arrested and charged with murder. Meanwhile, Bobby Lincoln, now serving time in a federal penitentiary, read about the case. He correctly figured that it would be only a matter of time before he would be charged with murder, thereby putting him in the shadow of the electric chair. He decided to make a deal.

Bobby offered his direct evidence in return for immunity in the Chillingworth and Harvey cases. The state accepted the deal. Lucky and Joe were finished. At the murder trial which followed, Joe Peel was convicted and sentenced to life imprisonment. Lucky didn't fare as well. He was executed for his crimes in the electric chair.

THE AMITYVILLE HORROR

It is seldom that the by-product of a vicious killing receives more publicity than the actual murder. Everyone remembers Amityville, the small Long Island, N.Y. town which became a household word with the publication of Jay Anson's best-selling book, *The Amityville Horror.*

The book outlined in vivid detail the supernatural phenomena allegedly experienced by George and Kathy Lutz and their family, who purchased a large luxurious Dutch Colonial home in Amityville on Dec. 18, 1975. The Lutz family were driven from their home 28 days later by a series of strange incidents.

They reported that doors had been torn off hinges, strange smells permeated the house, pigs' eyes stared at them through windows, and other ghostly happenings occurred. All this was more than the family could take.

Although the supernatural aspects of the Amityville phenomena are now considered to be unfounded, the strange events which took place there stand out from all other haunted house stories because of one undeniable fact. The house at 112 Ocean Ave. was the site of a horrendous multiple murder in 1974.

Prior to that time, there was no talk of the supernatural at the large home on Ocean Ave. It was then occupied by the De Feo family, consisting of Ronald and Louise De Feo and their five children, Ronald, Jr., 23; Dawn, 18; Allison, 13; Mark, 11; and John, 9.

Ronald Sr. was service manager for the family business, the Brigante-Karl Buick agency on Coney Island. Their five-bedroom home was complete with swimming pool and boathouse.

Ronnie, who worked for his father at the agency, was later to tell police that he woke up on the morning of Nov. 13, 1974, dressed, and was out of the house at 4:30 a.m. He drove his 1970 Buick Electra to Coney Island, arriving at work shortly after 6 a.m. Ronald Sr. wasn't expected at work that day, as he had an appointment to take Mark to the doctor. Ronnie knew he was in for an easy day.

There was little doubt in Ronnie's mind that his parents considered him the black sheep of the family. They had good reason. Ronnie, a high school dropout, drank heavily, and while not addicted to heroin, was a periodic user. He and his father often had fist fights.

Ronnie was forever getting into trouble. His most serious difficulty had occurred the previous year when he pleaded guilty to stealing several outboard motors. Put on probation, he was often accused by his father of working at the agency only to fulfil the terms of his probation.

Despite the bad blood between father and son, the elder De Feo provided Ronnie with several hundred dollars per week in spending money. Ronnie was in the habit of picking up the tab for his drinking buddies.

Knowing that his father was taking Mark to the doctor and wouldn't be at work, Ronnie hung around the agency only until noon and then took off. He met a friend, Robert Kelske, who mentioned that when he had driven to the De Feo home that morning the two family cars were still in the driveway. This seemed to puzzle Ronnie. He was sure his father was taking Mark to the doctor. At 1:30 p.m. Ronnie visited a girlfriend, where he used the phone to call home. He was surprised to receive no answer.

Later he drove to Robert Kelske's home. He told his friend that he couldn't raise his family on the phone. The two men made a date to meet at Henry's Bar at 6 p.m. Ronnie left Kelske's and went directly to Henry's, where he passed the time by consuming vodka and 7-Up. He told several customers at the bar that he was concerned at not being able to reach his family all day.

When Kelske showed up at the bar at 6 p.m., Ronnie's first words to him were, "I'm going to have to go home and break a window to get in." He left and returned a short time later shouting, "You got to help me, you got to help me! Someone has shot my mother and father."

Ronnie Kelske, and four other men, dashed to Ronnie's car and drove the half mile to the De Feo home. Ronnie's buddies confirmed that Ronald and Louise De Feo were dead in their bed. Police were called. Officer Kenneth Greguski of the Amityville village police walked through the house. In their room, on twin beds, lay the bodies of Mark and John. Further examination of the sprawling home revealed the bodies of the two De Feo girls, Dawn and Allison. All the victims were found face down in bed. They had been shot to death.

Ronnie cried uncontrollably when he was informed that every member of his family had been slaughtered. When questioned by police, he pulled himself together and told them, "I'll help you in any way I can."

Ronnie proceeded to pinpoint his movements on the day of the tragedy much as they are related here. When police inquired why he had not returned home earlier in the day, he explained that his father had beaten him up once when he had broken a window. He didn't want to risk another beating.

Initially, there was some concern that Ronnie had escaped the murderous attack by chance. Precautions were taken in case the killer was stalking the one remaining member of the De Feo family. That night Ronnie slept on a cot at the police station.

By morning, it was established that eight bullets had been fired. Mr. and Mrs. De Feo had been shot twice, while each of the four children had been shot once. The killer had stood above his victims and fired from a distance of not more than three feet. Only Allison had turned her head to receive a bullet through the left cheek. Ballistics experts determined that all six victims had been killed with a .35 calibre Marlin rifle.

Three rifles were taken from Ronnie's room, but none were Marlins. Ronnie readily admitted owning a fourth rifle, but claimed that he had gotten rid of it. He couldn't remember the calibre. Police didn't believe that Ronnie, a gun buff, would not remember the calibre of a rifle he once owned. He became a prime suspect when detectives found two boxes in his room. One contained a .22 rifle, the other a .35 Marlin.

Under expert questioning, Ronnie's sympathetic and respectful attitude towards the dead members of his family gradually changed. He cursed his father and admitted hating his brothers and sisters. Once it was established that Ronnie had been in the house between 2 a.m. and 4 a.m. when the murders took place, he had difficulty explaining how he didn't hear eight shots being fired. Finally, he admitted to systematically killing his own family, rushing from room to room, slaughtering as he went. In Ronnie's own words, "Once I started, I couldn't stop. It went so fast."

Ronnie directed detectives to a sewer in Brooklyn, where he had disposed of the clothing he had worn while murdering his family. He also told detectives that he had thrown the murder weapon into a canal near his home. On Nov. 15, scuba divers recovered the .35 calibre Marlin.

The motive for the murder was a puzzle. It is believed that the elder De Feo kept large amounts of money in a metal box in his home. This box, which reportedly held as much as $200,000, was found empty. No money has ever shown up.

After he was arrested, Ronnie behaved in an irrational manner, attempting to gain an acquittal by proving insanity. However, psychiatrists testified that, in their opinion, he was malingering.

On Dec. 4, 1975 Ronnie De Feo was found guilty of six counts of murder and sentenced to 25 years to life imprisonment. The sentences are to run concurrently. He will be eligible for parole in 1999, when he will be 48.

THE REAL McCOY

Not many men have been welterweight and middleweight boxing champion of the world, married nine times, and still managed to spend eight years in San Quentin prison for the killing of a prospective tenth bride. Then again, there has never been anyone quite like Kid McCoy.

The Kid's real name was Norman Selby, but he was known for most of his life as Kid McCoy. He fought exactly 200 fights and lost only seven. At the turn of the century, he was one of the most famous athletes in the world. McCoy had that quality sometimes called charisma or referred to as showmanship. In any case, he definitely had magnetism in the ring and in the bedroom. Everybody loved the Kid, especially the ladies.

McCoy stood 5 ft. 11 inches, had black wavy hair, and in his prime never weighed over 157 lbs. Let's take a look at his pugilistic career first. We will get to the bedroom soon enough.

In 1896, McCoy beat Tommy Ryan in 15 brutal rounds and captured the middleweight championship of the world. A year later, he purchased a saloon in New York, which became a hangout for the sporting fraternity and actors.

McCoy was so good at his profession that it was difficult for him to find a worthy opponent in his own weight class. Occasionally a promoter would stage a fight between the Kid and a heavier man. These fights accounted for the Kid's few losses. Gentleman Jim Corbett and Jack Sharkey beat McCoy. Both men outweighed McCoy by over 40 lbs. and both held the heavyweight championship of the world.

One day a drunk sauntered into McCoy's bar and started to verbally abuse McCoy. Someone told the drunk he better watch himself - he was picking on Kid McCoy, welterweight champion of the world. The drunk didn't believe he was in the presence of the champ and continued to berate McCoy. Finally, the Kid lost his patience, and with one punch knocked out the drunk. When the poor man regained consciousness, he rubbed his chin, looked up and said, "That's the real McCoy," and so coined the phrase that is still in use today to denote a genuine article.

In affairs of the heart the Kid answered the bell nine times. All of his wives were good-looking women. Special mention goes to Julia Woodruff Crosselmire, who had three return matches with the Kid, all ending in divorce.

By 1924, the Kid had run through several fortunes and all nine marriages. The black wavy hair was now sparse, and the flat-as-a-pancake midriff had developed an ever so slight bulge. Show business friends from the old days obtained bit parts for him in the movies. In between acting assignments, he was a guard in an airplane factory and had been issued a pistol.

Now 51, the Kid still had that old charisma when it came to the ladies. Theresa W. Mors, wife of wealthy art and antique dealer Albert E. Mors, came under the Kid's spell. Theresa left Albert to live with the Kid. She filed for divorce. Her husband in turn named McCoy as correspondent.

On Aug. 12, 1924, Theresa and the Kid were both hitting the bottle pretty hard. Many believe that McCoy had learned that night that Theresa had decided not to become Mrs. McCoy number ten. That's when the Kid placed his .32 calibre pistol behind Theresa's left ear and shot her dead.

The Kid had a few more blasts of whisky, made out his will and drove to the home of his sister, Jennie Thomas. McCoy told his sister, "I just had to kill that woman."

Next morning, McCoy was still on the prowl. He made his way to the Mors' antique store on Seventh Ave. He walked inside, where customers William Ross, Sam Stern, and clerk V. C. Emden were passing the time of day. The Kid pulled out his .32 and turned on a music box. He then proceeded to wave his pistol, keeping time to the music. Suddenly he slammed the box shut and robbed the three men of their money. Ross made a sudden motion and the Kid fired, wounding Ross in the leg.

The Kid dashed for the street, where he encountered Mr. and Mrs. Sam Schapp, who owned the store next to the antique shop. Sam knew the Kid. He asked, "Norman, what the hell are you doing?" The Kid answered with two shots. One struck Sam, the other his wife. All three shot that morning by McCoy recovered from their wounds.

Police soon caught up with McCoy and took him into custody. At the time of his arrest he admitted murdering Mrs. Mors. He soon changed his story, claiming that Mrs. Mors had committed suicide.

Attorney Jerry Geisler, who would later gain fame for defending Hollywood stars during their various trials and tribulations, was in the Kid's corner. He did the best he could.

The Kid was convicted of manslaughter in the Mors affair and received from one to ten years in prison. For his early morning shooting spree he received two sentences of one to fourteen years and one sentence of six months to ten years imprisonment.

The Kid was the most popular inmate in San Quentin prison. He received gifts from all over the world. Some of his friends who stuck by him included such public figures as Damon Runyon, Lionel Barrymore, and Sophie Tucker. As a result of the intervention of Henry Ford Sr., McCoy was paroled in 1932 and given employment with the Ford organization.

The Kid lived on for eight years, but suffered bouts of depression from not being in the limelight. In April 1940, he swallowed a bottle of sleeping pills in a Detroit hotel room.

The real McCoy was down for the count.

MURDER FOR MONEY

*"T*he best laid schemes o' mice an' men gang aft a-gley."

- Robert Burns

Mr. Burns had no idea how very applicable his oft-quoted poem would be to the murder business. Down through the history of crime, murderers have planned all sorts of devious schemes to hasten the demise of friends, neighbors and relatives. More often than not, something goes wrong.

Eugene Thompson, at 35, was a successful St. Paul, Minn. lawyer in 1963. He had met his wife Carol 14 years before when both were students at St. Paul's Macalester College. Eugene and Carol married in their sophomore year. Carol dropped out of school after her marriage, while Eugene continued on to obtain his law degree from the St. Paul School of Law in 1955.

The Thompsons quickly achieved the good life. By 1963 they were the proud parents of four children, Geoffrey, 13; Patricia, 12; Margaret, nine; and Amy, six. The prosperous lawyer's family lived in a large house on Hillcrest Ave., one of St. Paul's most affluent residential neighborhoods. Eugene was active in community affairs. The family attended church regularly and spent a great deal of time in each other's company. Surely Carol Thompson, devoted wife and mother, was an unlikely murder victim.

On the cold damp morning of March 6, 1963, Eugene rose early and drove to his office. Carol saw that the children got off to school before returning to bed. At 8:25 a.m. Eugene phoned his wife. She went downstairs to answer the phone. After a brief conversation, Carol went back to bed.

Minutes after that call, Harry Nelson, the Thompson's neighbor, answered his doorbell. There before his startled eyes was the horrendous sight of Carol Thompson, covered with blood from head to toe. The nightgown-clad, desperately injured woman slumped to the floor as Nelson opened the door. Nelson called a doctor, the police and Eugene Thompson.

Dr. Fritz Pearson rushed Carol to Ancker Hospital, where she died before regaining consciousness. An autopsy indicated that Carol had been stabbed 25 times. The four inch blade of a paring knife was removed from her neck. She had also been beaten about the head with such ferocity that she suffered skull fractures and a massive brain hemorrhage.

The handle of a paring knife was found near the Thompsons' front door. The blade was later matched to the one found in Mrs. Thompson's neck. Obviously the blade had broken off during the attack. Police also found the broken pieces of a plastic pistol grip and three unfired cartridges. Detectives surmised that the pistol grip had broken and the cartridges had fallen out while Carol was being viciously pistol-whipped.

Upstairs in the bedroom, bloodstains were found on the floor and walls. The bathtub was half filled with water, indicating that Mrs. Thompson may have been surprised as she was preparing to take a bath. A door to the basement of the house was open. Presumably the assailant had entered via this route. A piece of rubber hose was found in the master bedroom but it was uncertain if the hose was in any way connected to the crime. A trail of blood led from the bedroom down the stairs and out the front door to the Nelsons' residence.

Who would do such a thing and why?

Initially, investigating officers were stymied. In scrutinizing the history of he Thompsons, detectives discovered that Mrs. Thompson's life was heavily insured. She had six policies on her life, totalling $1,061,000. Eugene was the beneficiary of all the policies. His life was insured for $460,000 with Carol named as beneficiary. When questioned about the inequality of the amounts, Eugene explained that he had planned on taking out more insurance on his own life just prior to the tragedy.

The plastic remnants found on the doorstep came from the grip of a Luger. Photos of the remnants and a similar weapon were given wide publicity. A travelling salesman, Wayne Brandt, came forward. He was sure the pistol was the same as the one that had been stolen from his apartment the previous February. He had made the grips himself.

A short time later two break and entry men were apprehended in the act of robbing a house. They confessed to a series of robberies, among them the theft of the Luger from Brandt's apartment. They claimed they had given the Luger to an acquaintance, a former boxer, Norman Mastrian. They went on to say they were present when Mastrian handed over the gun to roofing salesman Dick Anderson. Still later, they heard Anderson mention that he had killed a woman in St. Paul.

Mastrian was picked up at his suburban home in Minneapolis. Anderson was located in Phoenix, Arizona, and brought back to St. Paul.

The arrests caused a sensation in the Twin Cities. Police and the public realized that these two men never knew Mrs. Thompson and had no direct motive for the murder. There had to be more to the mysterious death of Carol Thompson. Her husband could only state, "I pray that the guilty parties be brought to justice."

Meanwhile, police kept digging. They canvassed Mastrian's friends and came up with one acquaintance who admitted that only hours after the murder he had driven Mastrian and Anderson to a farm, where Mastrian had thrown a Luger into a marsh. Police retrieved the weapon, but were still not satisfied that Mastrian and Anderson had acted alone.

Against his lawyer's advice, Anderson confessed. He related the details of one of the cruelest, most heartless crimes ever committed. Mastrian had hired him "to kill a woman in a way that would make her death appear accidental." He had never met Carol Thompson until the morning of her death. Mastrian had told him she was to be killed for insurance. That was all he knew.

Anderson gained entrance to the Thompson home at 5 a.m. and waited until Mrs. Thompson was alone in the house. He had the layout of the house and knew that the bedroom phone had been disconnected. He was to wait for the phone to ring, which would bring Carol down to the kitchen. He would then sneak up behind her and strike her with a rubber hose. Anderson had been told that an injury thus inflicted would resemble one caused by a fall in the bathtub. He was then to undress Carol, hold her under the water in the tub and fill her lungs with water by reverse artificial respiration, simulating drowning.

All was in readiness. The phone rang. Carol came downstairs and answered the phone. Anderson started up the basement stairs, but they squeaked. He feared that his victim would hear him, so he decided to wait until she returned to bed.

Anderson sneaked up to the bedroom and struck Mrs. Thompson on the head with the rubber hose. He tore the nightclothes off the stunned woman, carried her into the bathroom and placed her in the tub. Revived by the water, Carol managed to slip from her attacker's grasp and escape from the bathroom. Anderson drew the Luger and pulled the trigger, but the gun misfired. Desperately, Carol grabbed her robe around her as she dashed down the stairs to the front door. It was locked and chained.

As she fumbled with the lock, Anderson caught up. He beat the hapless woman about the head with the Luger until cartridges spilled out of the weapon and the grip broke. He then ran into the kitchen, picked up a paring knife and stabbed Mrs. Thomson until the knife fell apart. His victim slumped to the floor.

Anderson calmly walked back upstairs and washed his hands. While doing so, he idly glanced out the window and was amazed to see courageous Carol Thompson staggering across the lawn to her neighbor's house. Anderson fled and sped away in his car which was parked nearby.

After hearing this story, Mastrian revealed that Carol Thompson's husband had paid him $3000 to arrange his wife's accidental death. The motive had been the insurance money.

Thompson was arrested and, together with Mastrian and Anderson, was charged with first degree murder. All three men were found guilty and sentenced to life imprisonment.

Eugene Thompson, Norman Mastrian and Dick Anderson were paroled in 1983 after serving 20 years in prison. Thompson attempted to regain his licence to practise law. His application was refused.

A NIGHT OF HORROR

The evening started out pleasantly enough, but fate would decree that it end in a hideous web of kidnapping, rape and murder.

Mrs. Eleanor Ewell, 50, her son James, 23, a Columbia University student, together with family friends Robert and Eleanor Tyson, 50, drove to Herm's Restaurant in Plainfield, N.J. in the Ewell Cadillac. Mrs. Ewell's husband Elliot was not a member of the dinner party that balmy May evening in 1961. As executive vice president and a director of the Mack Truck Company, he had been called out of town on business. Robert Tyson, a Wall Street broker, had previously been an executive of the Mack Truck Co.

As if preordained, a series of strange unconnected events took place, which would turn the harmless dinner party into a night of horror. During dinner, Robert Tyson, who had complained of a bad head cold earlier in the day, now felt so poorly that James drove him home. James then returned to the restaurant and rejoined his mother and Mrs. Tyson.

Shortly after midnight, they left the restaurant. Mrs. Ewell complained about her son's driving. An argument broke out in the car. Enraged, James slammed on the brakes, causing the Caddy to stall. When he attempted to restart the car, the motor wouldn't turn over.

James walked the short distance to the Plainview Union Water Co. and called the Mack Truck Co. for assistance. He stayed in the company's office for some time and then left the area on foot. He assumed that an employee of his father's firm would show up to assist his mother and Mrs. Tyson.

Instead of sending someone over, the employee who had received the call at Mack Truck Co. called the Dora Cab Co. The dispatcher radioed one of his cars to drive to where the women were stalled. He was instructed to drive the stranded women home.

Cab driver Wilbur Morris was sent to pick up the two ladies. He arrived just outside the water company's property where the Caddy was parked. Morris had often driven Mrs. Ewell and recognized her sitting alone in the front seat. Mrs. Tyson, whom Morris didn't know, was sitting in the back seat. The cabbie chatted for a moment with the women and then suggested that he attempt to start the car. Try as he might, he couldn't get the engine to turn over.

Just as he was about to give up and drive the women to the Ewell residence, a black Chevy pulled up. The two male occupants offered to help. One opened the hood and fiddled around for a minute. Sure enough, when Morris turned the key the engine caught. Morris then told the women he would drive them home in their own car as soon as he parked his cab. He left the Caddy in order to park his cab, when suddenly one of the strangers jumped in the Caddy, shouting, "Come on!" to his companion, and drove away in the Caddy. The second man raced after the Caddy in the black Chevy.

Wilbur Morris hopped in his cab, radioed his dispatcher advising him of the bizarre turn of events and gave chase. He soon lost both the Chevy and the Caddy. The dispatcher at the Dora Cab Co. notified police that a kidnapping had taken place. Police were waiting for Wilbur Morris when he returned to the original kidnap site.

At 4 a.m. one of the scores of patrol cars searching for the missing Cadillac, found the vehicle about a mile from the site of the kidnapping. Under the left front wheel of the cream colored hard top convertible was the raped and broken body of Eleanor Ewell. Someone had driven back and forth over her body. In the back seat was the body of Mrs. Tyson. She too had been raped before being strangled with what appeared to be a string of her own pearls.

The prime clue to the identity of the killers was the description of their car, a black 1950 or 1951 Chevy with New Jersey licence plates. It would take months to check out the registered owners, if ever such a task could be completed. This avenue of investigation became unnecessary because of one man, Patrolman John Trembicki, an 11-year veteran of the Scotch Plains, N.J., police department.

You see, John Trembicki had, over the years, developed the habit of jotting down the licence plate numbers of vehicles he didn't feel right about. Earlier on the night of May 26, before any crime had been committed, Trembicki had spotted two black men purchasing gas for their black 1950 Chevy. He picked up his notebook and jotted down the licence number - FLC-492 - Blue Star Esso gas station.

This practice had become automatic for Trembicki over the years. Once, he was instrumental in recovering a stolen vehicle, but he had always had hopes of one day taking down the licence number of a vehicle involved in a major crime. The night of May 26, 1961 was to be Patrolman Trembicki's night.

Patrolman Trembicki's radio hummed. A black 1950 or 1951 Chevy driven by two black men was involved in a kidnapping. Trembicki was sure it was the one he had seen at the gas station. He radioed the licence number to his police station.

The vehicle was registered to 23-year-old Joey Maxey of Dunellen, N.J. Maxey was immediately picked up. He had been employed as a washer of new and used cars at a dealership for the previous two years. Maxey readily admitted that he and a friend, Lorelle Parks, had helped start the stranded Ewell Caddy, but swore he had no guilty knowledge of the murders.

Parks, 22, was taken into custody. He stated that he knew nothing of the killings, until forced to view the victims' bodies at the morgue. He then broke down shouting, "I'll talk, I'll talk! I know they're going to burn me, so it doesn't make any difference. I killed Tyson and Maxey killed the other one."

The two men had been cruising around looking for women when they came across cabbie Morris attempting to start the Cadillac. They kidnapped the two women on the spur of the moment. Mrs. Ewell and Mrs. Tyson pleaded for mercy, but were raped and killed. Maxey throttled Mrs. Ewell and drove the Cadillac over her nude body again and again. He urged Parks, "We have to kill them; make sure you kill her."

Parks tightened the string of pearls around Mrs. Tyson's neck. When he detected that she was still breathing, he looped his belt around her neck and "pulled as tight as I could. She stopped breathing, there was no doubt about it, she was dead all right. I saw Mrs. Ewell lying on the ground beneath the front wheels. She was a real mess."

After submitting to a lie detector test, Maxey grudgingly admitted involvement in the double murder.

Joseph Maxey was tried and convicted of kidnapping and murder. He received two life sentences. Today he is still incarcerated in Trenton State Penitentiary. Lorelle Parks was sentenced to life in prison for murder. He was paroled on Nov. 18, 1975, after serving 14 years behind bars.

MASSACRE AT THE HI-FI SHOP

Dale Pierre and William Andrews never adjusted to air force life. Both had been in and out of scrapes and both had applied for early discharge from the U.S. Air Force. In April 1974, they were assigned to janitorial duty at Hill Field Air Force Base near Ogden, Utah as punishment for minor infractions.

Pierre, a native of Trinidad, was a short, powerful man with delusions of grandeur. The air force wasn't for him. He would get out, make a lot of money any way he could and live in luxury. Andrews was a follower rather than a leader. Much taller than Pierre, he was the type of individual who went along with the tide. He and Pierre spent a great deal of time together performing their janitorial duties at the base.

The two men planned a robbery. Andrews owned a van. They would rob the Hi Fi Shop in Ogden and stash their loot in a storage warehouse. It should be easy. They would tie up the owner, drive the van up to the back door and be gone before anyone was the wiser.

There was some talk about what to do should there be any eyewitnesses who could later identify them. Pierre felt they should kill any such witnesses. Andrews agreed. A third airman, Keith Roberts, was brought into the scheme to help drive the van and load the equipment.

On April 23, 1974, just before 6 p.m. closing time, the three airmen drove up to the Hi Fi Shop in Ogden. They pulled into the alley behind the store. Stan Walker, 20, was in charge of the store that day. The owner was in San Francisco attending an electronics show. Stan and clerk Michelle Ansley were about to close when they looked up to see two black men armed with hand-guns.

As Stan and Michelle stood there transfixed, the door to the shop opened. In walked a mutual friend, 18-year-old Cortney Naisbitt. He was told to keep his hands high. Cortney obeyed without question. All three young people were pushed downstairs into a sound studio. Their hands were tied behind their backs and their feet secured with electric wire. Two hours passed while the robbers loaded turntables, amplifiers and speakers into Andrews' van. The three captives lay in mortal fear for their lives. It was 8 p.m.

Meanwhile, at the Naisbitt residence, Cortney's mother Carol was concerned. At around 8:30 p.m., she mentioned to her husband, Dr. Byron Naisbitt, that it wasn't like Cortney to be late for dinner. Dr. Naisbitt, an obstetrician, thought his wife was making a mountain out of a molehill. Carol didn't see it that way. She jumped in her car and did the rounds, looking for her son.

Stan Walker's father dropped by the Hi Fi Shop to see what was keeping his son. Tentatively he walked through the shop only to be confronted by the intruders. He too was tied hand and foot and placed in the downstairs sound studio.

Carol Naisbitt was the next to arrive at the Hi Fi Shop in her search for Cortney. She opened the back door and peered directly into the barrel of a revolver. Mrs. Naisbitt was tied and placed on the floor beside her son and the other captives. In all, there were now five helpless victims lying on the floor in the small basement room.

Dale Pierre produced a cup of foul smelling liquid. He propped Carol Naisbitt into a sitting position and put the cup to her lips. Carol was told the liquid would put her to sleep. She was forced to take a gulp and immediately commenced to spit, cough and vomit. Soon her mouth and lips started to burn. The liquid in the cup was Drano.

Each of the five captives were made to drink the Drano. The last, Mr. Walker, recognized the smell of the caustic. He allowed his captor to pour the liquid in his mouth but only pretended to swallow. Once his head was placed back on the floor, he silently let the liquid pour out of his mouth.

Systematically the five captives were stripped of wallets, purses and jewelry. William Andrews left the shop. Dale Pierre then stepped over the sprawled forms on the floor. He felt for Mrs. Naisbitt's head, placed his gun to the back of her head and pulled the trigger. She was killed instantly. Her son Cortney was next. Then Stan Walker was shot in the same way. His father was shot in the back of the head as well. Michelle Ansley begged for her life. Pierre untied her feet and forced her into an adjoining room. There he raped the helpless girl before returning her to the floor beside the other four victims.

One individual remained conscious throughout the nightmarish incidents in the Hi Fi Shop. Mr. Walker, despite being shot in the back of the head, never lost consciousness. Pierre sensed that he was not dead. He strung a cord around Walker's neck and tied it three times, as tight as he could. Walker tensed his neck muscles. After Pierre had finished knotting the rope, Walker found he could still breathe. Walker was playing dead. Pierre then leaned over Michelle and fired a shot into the back of her head. She died immediately.

Orren Walker believed that he was the lone survivor. Lying helpless, his mouth and lips burning from the Drano, a bullet in his head, he fought to retain consciousness and yet appear not to be breathing. His tormentor wasn't through. Pierre pushed a ball point pen into Walker's ear. He stomped on the pen once, twice, but the pen didn't enter Walker's head. He felt the pen point angle down into his throat. Then the assailant was gone.

Mrs. Walker was waiting at home, beside herself with worry. Her son Stan hadn't come home from work at the Hi Fi Shop. Her husband had gone to the shop looking for Stan and had also failed to return. Together with her strapping 16-year-old son Lynn, she decided to visit the shop. When they got there they heard Orren screaming for help. Young Lynn kicked down the door and summoned police. His father embraced him. Orren Walker had a ballpoint pen sticking out of his ear.

One other victim of the Hi Fi Shop massacre lived through the ordeal. Cortncy Naisbitt was barely breathing when rushed to hospital. Doctors were undecided whether to put him on life support systems or not. The decision was made to undertake heroic measures. After numerous operations and years in hospital and convalescent homes, Cortney recovered.

Within 24 hours the perpetrators of the heinous, senseless torture and murder were themselves apprehended. An informant at the air force base revealed that he had heard three men plan the robbery. He named Dale Pierre and William Andrews. Orren Walker identified Pierre from a photograph.

At the same time two youngsters, 12-year-old Charlie Marshall and 11-year-old Walter Grisson were hunting for empty bottles in a trash dumpster at the Hill Field Air Force Base. They found wallets, credit cards and other documents, all taken from the five victims before they were shot. The dumpster was located 30 feet from Pierre's barracks.

Pierre and Andrews were taken into custody. Pierre's room was searched. Detectives found a white envelope under a carpet. It contained a rental agreement between Dale Pierre and Wasatch Storage, located only a few blocks from the Hi Fi Shop. Pierre had rented space on April 23, the day of the murder. Inside Pierre's storage facility, detectives found the equipment carted away from the Hi Fi Shop. They also found a large bottle of Drano.

Pierre, Andrews and Roberts were charged with three counts of first degree murder and two of aggravated robbery. Pierre and Andrews were found guilty on all charges. The jury couldn't agree on the murder charges concerning Roberts. He was found guilty on the two counts of aggravated robbery.

EPILOGUE: Orren Walker - Despite his ordeal, he was not as badly injured as Cortney Naisbitt. He survived to testify against Pierre and Andrews. Mr. Walker still resides and works in the Ogden, Utah area.

Cortney Naisbitt - Near death when taken from the Hi Fi Shop basement, he miraculously survived months in a coma to graduate from high school. He is presently employed at the Hill Field Air Force Base, the same base where his assailants were stationed.

Keith Roberts received a lengthy prison sentence for aggravated assault. He was released on Nov. 10, 1987.

Dale Pierre and William Andrews - Both received three death sentences. Now 17 years after the murders, they remain in the maximum security section of the Utah State Prison. They have had five dates with Utah's firing squad, but each time have won last minute reprieves. Both men have achieved the highest privilege level obtainable in maximum security. This allows them to be out of their cells for two hours per day, as well as a further two hours a week for recreation.

AN EVE OF
DESTRUCTION

Max Keller had worked hard all his life. In 1920, at age 28, he founded the Wilmar Pickle and Relish Co. in Los Angeles, Calif. Keller's company never did throw a scare into the Heinz organization but, by rising at dawn and working until midnight, Max managed to get the company off the ground. He processed cucumbers at night and developed a sales route during the day. The company prospered.

Max, whose only diversion from the pickle business was gardening, purchased a small one bedroom home, where he could usually be seen each day manicuring his lawn and tending his flower beds.

In 1925 Max advertised for a housekeeper. A cute young thing named Eve applied for the job. Eve, 25, was everything a man could want in a housekeeper. She had flowing brown hair, saucer-like blue eyes, a voluptuous figure, and a pleasing manner. She also had a small daughter, Elsie. Never mind, Eve got the job.

Things worked out very well for everyone. A few months of living under one roof with Eve led to its logical conclusion. Max and Eve became Mr. and Mrs. Keller. Little Elsie grew to love Max. He, in turn, was so fond of the little girl that he insisted on legally adopting her.

Max's business continued to prosper. By 1940 he purchased a larger home on West Raymona Blvd. in the suburb of Wilmar. He also built a two-storey mountain lodge in the San Bernardino Mountains. To complete the picture, Max drove a Cadillac. In due course, Elsie married and moved out of the house on West Ramona.

It is most disconcerting to break up this idyllic picture of domesticity which Max

Keller had built for himself in Lotusland, but we must.

The first crack in the armor of marital bliss occurred in December, 1947. Max was 55 and Eve was 48. They had been married a good many years, when Eve accused Max of running around with blondes. Max, who had always been a good husband and an exemplary father, had never looked at another woman. Eve insisted. The idea developed into an obsession. Finally, she moved out. Max, ever the gentleman, gave her the lodge in the San Bernardino Mountains and the Cadillac.

That's where matters stood the day a neighbor, Hazel Zinnen, looked out her window and was surprised not to see Max puttering in his garden. Hazel told another neighbor, Arthur Ellsworth. Together, they went to investigate. They found the doors to the house locked and decided to force a window. There was Max, in a real pickle. He lay sprawled on the floor of his den with .38 calibre slugs in his chest and throat.

Detectives studying the murder scene noted that there was no sign of a struggle in the den or any other part of the house. A sum of money lay in full view on a table in the den, and the victim's expensive watch was on his wrist. However, Max's rather distinctive wallet was missing. A service station attendant, George Vokes, was accustomed to seeing Max take bills out of the wallet. He told police that the initials M.E.K. were embossed on the front of the wallet. Because Max's clothing was in perfect condition, police believed that he had not grappled with his killer, but had been shot without warning.

The coroner estimated that Max had been dead about two days. He put the time of death at between 8 p.m. and 11 p.m. on Thursday. Detectives went up and down West Ramona Blvd. questioning neighbors. Arthur Schmerberg said he had noticed a faint light flickering on and off at the Keller residence on Thursday night. He had paid scant attention. His mother said that Max had recently complained to her that he had noticed small items missing from his home. He had replaced the lock on both front and back doors.

Another neighbor corroborated Mrs. Schmerberg's statement, adding that she had once seen Eve sneaking out of the house when Max was not at home. In passing, Mr. Schmerberg mentioned that there had been a gas explosion fire at Max's house on New Year's Eve.

Although it was all gossip, the type which surfaces in every homicide investigation, detectives had to consider the estranged wife as a suspect. It seems that the whole neighborhood believed that Eve had acted in a ridiculous manner when she accused Max of running around. When informed of Max's murder, Eve did the decent thing. She burst into tears. She stated that she had loved her husband for many happy years, but all that had ended when he began chasing other women.

Eve accounted for her whereabouts on Thursday night. She had had a meeting with the lawyer that afternoon, did some shopping, had dinner at the Checker Inn and then took in a movie at the Fox Theatre. After the movie, at about 8:30 p.m., she returned to the Checker Inn for a hamburger. Eve, who evidently was a movie fan, took in her second movie that night, this time a twin bill at the Ritz Theatre, leaving at 11:30. She clearly remembered the names of the movies were *Decoy* and *The Time, the Place and the Girl*. In fact, Eve had forgotten her scarf and returned to the Ritz at closing time. She found the location where she had been sitting and, sure enough, retrieved the scarf from under the seat.

Detectives would take a day to check out Eve's alibi. Meanwhile, they had learned more about the explosion, which had taken place at 3 a.m. on New Year's Day. The resulting fire only scorched the underpinning of the house. Fire investigators questioned Max, who told them that his estranged wife, Eve, had gained entry to the house around 1 a.m. He had been awakened by the removal of a screen from the window. He berated her and ordered her to leave, which she did. The explosion took place two hours later. At that time Max told investigators that he thought Eve was trying to kill him.

Each step of Eve's alibi was checked out. Eve was exactly where she said she was on Thursday, with one exception. Ralph Mauldin, the assistant manager of the Ritz Theatre, informed police that the movie *Decoy* had not played on Thursday night. It had been run that Thursday as the matinee only.

Eve's small slip changed matters dramatically. She could have visited the theatre in the afternoon and planted her scarf. She had no alibi from shortly after 8:30 p.m., when she returned to the Checker Inn for a hamburger, and 11:30 p.m., when she arrived at the theatre to pick up her scarf. That Eve was a clever one and was still far from a proven murderer. All that had been proven was that she had lied and had the opportunity to commit the murder.

On May 13, 1948, 16 months after the murder, Eve married one Michael Becker. The happy couple moved into the lodge in the mountains. Eve's new obsession was the breaking of Max's will. Cunning Max had left half of his estate to his daughter Elsie and the balance to various other relatives. He left Eve zilch. Eve was in constant need of money to finance her legal battle to break Max's will.

On Oct. 24, 1948, the lodge in the mountains burned down. Eve put in a hefty insurance claim, stating that several pieces of valuable jewelry had been lost in the fire, as well as many pieces of metal furniture. Investigators couldn't find one item she claimed was in the fire. They did find an open valve on a small gas unit, which Eve said she had turned off before leaving the lodge.

There was suspicion that Eve had carted away valuable furniture, silverware and jewelry before the day of the fire. Since the mountains were dotted with deserted cabins, the authorities decided to begin their search in these cabins. After much legwork, they found a cabin in Arrowhead Highlands, which had been rented by Eve under an alias. Inside were the contents of Eve's home. She was immediately arrested and charged with arson.

Aside from Eve's involvement with events incendiary, she was above all a murder suspect. The investigation into her husband's death had never been closed. Detectives realized that Eve must have lived somewhere after her mountain lodge burned down. They found out that Eve had rented a cabin in Crestline from Hazel Zinnen. Remember her - the neighbor who found poor Max?

Detectives searched the cabin. Inside they found Max's distinctive wallet, as well as a .38 calibre Smith and Wesson revolver, which proved to be the murder weapon. Police even located a witness who swore Eve had been in possession of the murder weapon around the time of the murder.

Eve was in big trouble. She was tried and found guilty of arson. The little caper brought her a sentence of two to twenty years in Tehachapi Women's Prison. On Aug. 7, 1950, she was found guilty of murdering her husband and sentenced to life imprisonment at the same institution.

REVENGE OF THE TONGS

Her name was Bow Kum (Sweet Flower) and her murder would ignite New York's Chinatown as nothing has before or since.

At the turn of the century, New York's Chinatown was not the tourist attraction it is today. The dark narrow streets, mainly Mott, Doyers and Fell, were dotted with opium dens where, for a price, you could share a pipe guaranteed to dream your troubles away. If you tired of the pipe, you could pass the wee hours of the morning at the fan tan tables.

The Chinese of New York had long since discovered that they could best take care of their own disputes and problems by forming secret clubs or societies. These clubs, known as Tongs, sprung up throughout Chinatown. The two most powerful were the On Leong Tong or Protection Society and the Hip Sing Tong or Help Each Other Society. Initially, these Tongs served useful purposes in arbitrating domestic and legal disputes. However, it wasn't long before the Tongs themselves were selling protection, as well as being deeply involved in the illicit opium trade.

Of the two powerful Tongs in New York, the On Leong emerged as the most powerful. Under its leader, Tom Lee, it controlled most of the profitable opium dens in Chinatown. Lee saw to it that the New York police were paid off.

What did a little girl born in the Canton district of China have to do with the affairs of her countrymen in America's largest city? Bow Kum's parents were dirt poor. Another girl child to feed was considered a curse rather than a blessing. They sold their beautiful five-year-old daughter for $300, a great deal of money to the struggling family.

The little girl's owner was a slave dealer. To him, the purchase was strictly business. He would raise Bow Kum for five or six years and, if she grew to be a beauty, would sell her at a substantial profit. In China, there was a great demand for beautiful young girls who could be bought and owned without the legal encumbrances of marriage.

Bow Kum developed into a lovely young woman. Shy, but very bright, she moved with grace and poise. Her unblemished skin was like pale yellow satin. Altogether, Bow Kum was a rare beauty.

When Bow Kum was 15, her owner made a deal with a wealthy Chinese merchant from San Francisco named Low Hee Tong. Bow Kum was purchased for $3000 and sent on her way to a new life. The elderly merchant was good to her. She had more to eat and better clothing to wear than she had ever had in Canton. She spent four happy years in San Francisco's Chinatown until one day Low Hee Tong's shop was raided by the police. They found Bow Kum living above the shop. When she confessed that she was neither the wife nor daughter of the shopkeeper, they questioned her further. No matter how she tried to explain, they didn't understand that she simply belonged to Low Hee Tong. When Low Hee Tong produced a receipt for $3000, they still didn't understand.

As a result of the raid, Bow Kum was taken away from her home and placed in a mission. The good ladies of the mission attempted to explain to Bow Kum that it wasn't exactly proper to live with an elderly gentleman without benefit of marriage.

Bow Kum had an idea. If marriage was the big problem, she knew someone who might be interested. She once had met a farmer named Tchin Len in Low Hee Tong's shop. He had expressed an interest in marriage. The ladies of the mission allowed Tchin Len to visit. He was deeply moved that such a beautiful woman wanted to be his bride. In due course, the pair became engaged, and Bow Kum travelled to Tchin Len's farm to await the happy day.

Word of Bow Kum's betrothal drifted into Chinatown. Low Hee Tong was fit to be tied. He was out $3000 and wanted either Bow Kum or his money back. He approached Tchin Len, who listened to his argument and told him he would discuss it with the head lady at the mission. When that stalwart representative of all that is good and holy heard the problem, she was aghast. Women were not to be bought and sold like cattle. Tchin Len owed nothing.

Tchin Len passed the word back to Low Hee Tong. He didn't take it well. He swore he would get his money or Bow Kum. If he failed, he would kill her.

Tchin Len took the threat seriously. He sold his farm for $50,000 and moved with

Bow Kum to New York's Chinatown, secure in the belief that his adversary would not follow him. Upon arrival in New York, Tchin Len became a member of the On Leong Tong. Low Hee Tong didn't follow, but he wrote influential friends in New York's Chinatown, informing them of his situation. These friends approached the On Leong Tong, demanding that their friend back in San Francisco be paid $3000 for Bow Kum.

The On Leongs agreed to sit in judgment, hear both sides of the case and render a decision. The arguments were duly presented to the tribunal. They passed down their decision. Tchin Lee was not obliged to pay anything for his bride. The laws of the new homeland had been instrumental in removing Bow Kum from Low Hee Tong's guardianship. Tchin Len had been free to marry her without payment.

That very night, in August 1903, when the decision was reached, Tchin Len celebrated by playing fan tan. Then he made his way to his home on Mott St. He reeled back in horror when he opened the door. Beautiful Bow Kum lay sprawled on the floor. Her throat had been slit from ear to ear with a hatchet. She had also been stabbed directly in the heart with a dagger, which was stuck upright in the floor beside her body.

New York's finest investigated the ritual murder. They received little co-operation from the closed-mouthed Chinese. Finally, they dropped the case.

The On Leong Tong did not take Bow Kum's death lightly. After all, she was the wife of a Tong member. Besides, her murder was a direct result of their decision. Someone had defied the Tong's authority. They made it their business to learn the identity of the culprit. Low Hee Tong's friends, who had represented him at the tribunal, were members of an ancient fraternal society known as the Four Brothers. It was this group which had murdered Bow Kum.

The On Leongs decided that members of the Four Brothers had to be punished. On the day war was declared by the On Leongs, one of the Four Brothers was found dead in a Chinatown alleyway. His throat had been cut with a hatchet. Within two days, five more victims met the same fate, all by means of the deadly sharpened hatchet.

For retaliatory purposes, the Four Brothers recruited the Hip Sing Tong. Within weeks, the most devastating Tong war New York's Chinatown had ever known was in progress. In all, it is estimated that 100 Chinese died, the vast majority by having their throats slit by a hatchet.

Often, in darkened movie houses, when the customers left, a couple of theatregoers would be left sitting in an upright position. Their throats had been clearly slit with a hatchet. One night, five members of the On Leong Tong were found sitting like grotesque statues, all in a row, all dead.

Eventually, the Chinese themselves realized that things had gone too far. Influential Chinese scholars and wealthy merchants arranged a meeting. It wasn't easy to organize such a meeting, for the hatchet killings had bred deep hatred between the two groups. But the killings couldn't go on. In due course, the Tongs signed a treaty, bringing peace to New York's Chinatown.

The Sweet Flower, who was sold in Canton for $300 at the age of five, has long since been forgotten. But not by all. A few years ago, a man was arrested for murder in Chinatown. He had killed a man with a hatchet. When questioned he would only mumble, "Bow Kum, Bow Kum."

LADY KILLER

Harvey Glatman was a specialist. He robbed only women.

In 1945, Harvey spent a year in the Canon City, Colorado prison for a series of armed robberies perpetrated against women. Shortly after his release, he was apprehended for stealing purses from women as they walked along dimly lit streets. This time he spent five years in Sing Sing, before being paroled to his mother's loving care in Denver.

In 1957, Harvey migrated to Los Angeles where the strange desires he had bottled up in his psyche came to the surface. Nondescript, owlish Harvey, with the oversized ears, shell-rimmed glasses and large nose, did not take L.A. by storm. You see, Harvey, at age 30, was a virgin. He had tried to become acquainted with members of the opposite sex in the past, but had always been rejected. Swinging Los Angeles would be different. Besides, Harvey had a plan.

Using the alias Johnny Glynn and posing as a professional photographer, Harvey had no trouble making contact with model Judy Dull. Judy, a beautiful blonde, was only 19, but had already been married and divorced. She lived in a rather plush apartment at 1302 Sweetzer Ave. with two equally beautiful models.

Harvey met all three girls, explaining that he had an assignment for one of them. It was to pose for the cover of a detective magazine and would include some nude shots. He thought Judy Dull was exactly the type. A fee was established. The shooting would take place in the girls' apartment. Harvey explained that his studio was undergoing renovations.

On Aug. 1, 1957, Harvey pulled up in his black Dodge bearing Colorado plates. He told the girls that there was a slight change of plans. He had been able to borrow the well-equipped studio of a friend. He wouldn't have to use their apartment after all. One of the girls mentioned that Judy had appointments for later that same afternoon. Could she have a telephone number where Judy could be reached? Without hesitation, Harvey jotted down a number on a piece of paper and passed it over.

Judy and Harvey sped away. They drove to a dreary building on Melrose Ave. Judy, carrying her model's suitcase, briskly walked into a second floor apartment. She was no doubt reassured by the tripods, lights and other photographic equipment already set up. Harvey took several shots of Judy fully clothed before asking her to take off her blouse. He took more photographs. Then he suggested she slip out of her skirt.

Harvey approached Judy with a five foot piece of white sash cord. Initially, Judy objected, but Harvey calmly explained that he had to tie her up for a few shots in order to fulfil his obligations to the detective magazine. Reluctantly, Judy allowed her hands and feet to be tied and a gag to be placed over her mouth. Harvey took more pictures. He then produced a gun and informed Judy that he was going to release the gag and untie her hands and feet. If she made one sound or didn't comply with his every wish, he would shoot her in the head.

Once free of the gag, Judy pleaded for her life. She tearfully explained that she and her husband were in the midst of a divorce. She was about to receive custody of their little girl. She promised to keep Harvey's secret. She just wanted to be spared. Weird Harvey raped the terror-stricken girl and forced her to watch television with him. Every so often, Judy pleaded to be released, but Harvey was deep in thought. Finally he agreed. He would drive out to the desert, take a few more photographs and then set her free.

The pair drove for hours into the San Jacinto mountains. Harvey stated, "Just a few quick shots. Then we'll go back to the highway and you're on your own. Sorry we had to come so far but there wasn't any other way, Judy."

Harvey was lying. He realized that Judy knew his address, knew he had Colorado plates on his Dodge, and could describe him in far more detail than her roommates. Harvey once more tied Judy's hands and feet and gagged the hapless girl. He took another piece of rope and wrapped it around Judy's neck. In a minute the girl was dead. There, on the lonely desert, Harvey dug a shallow grave with his hands for Judy Dull.

Judy's roommates went to the police with the phone number given to them by photographer Johnny Glynn. It proved to be a bogus number.

Seven months later, posing as plumber George Williams, Harvey joined a lonely hearts club and managed a blind date with 24-year-old Shirley Ann Bridgeford. Shirley had recently been divorced, had two small sons and lived with her mother in Sun Valley, north of Hollywood. At the urging of her mother to "mix with new friends," she answered a lonely hearts club ad. It was Shirley's misfortune to answer an ad extolling the virtues of Harvey Glatman. As soon as Shirley entered his car, Harvey pulled out his gun. He drove into the desert and took a series of photographs before raping and killing his victim.

Shirley's mother reported her daughter missing to police. A quick check with the lonely hearts club revealed that plumber George Williams had given a fictitious name and address.

Two months later, Harvey, posing as Mr. Johnson, called a nude modelling service. He required a model for an hour or two, and was put in touch with Ruth Rita Mercado, who had her own studio. A date was set and Harvey showed up in his beat-up Dodge.

On this occasion, he didn't waste time. Ruth opened the door and stared into the barrel of Harvey's trusty black automatic. In minutes, she was tied, gagged and helpless. Harvey took his pictures. At gunpoint, he untied his quarry and led her to the Dodge. They sped into the desert. The usual outdoor pictures were taken. Ruth was raped and then murdered in the usual hideous manner with the rope draped around her neck. Acquaintances reported Ruth Mercado's disappearance to police.

Harvey was confident. After all, hadn't he had his way with three lovely women? No one had the slightest idea why they had disappeared. In fact, no one even knew they were dead.

Harvey was referred to model Lorraine Vigil by another model. Lorraine was newly arrived in Hollywood from San Francisco and was eager for work. Harvey called at Lorraine's apartment. During the drive to his non-existent studio, Lorraine sized up her companion. He didn't seem right. She couldn't quite categorize her anxiety, but this strange man just didn't act like a professional photographer. When she realized her silent companion was leaving the city far behind, she knew her instincts were correct.

Lorraine didn't have long to wait. Harvey braked the car, pulled out his gun and told her he would kill her unless she complied with his every desire. Lorraine replied, "All right, just please don't hurt me." When Harvey took out his rope, Lorraine pleaded not to be tied up. She promised over and over that she would obey his every wish. Lorraine knew that she was in a life and death situation. The previous three victims possibly felt they would be spared. Lorraine knew better. This man was going to kill her.

Without warning, she pushed Harvey's gun aside. The two desperately struggled for possession of the weapon. The gun went off, but only slightly seared

Lorraine's thigh. She moaned and slumped against him, feigning death. Harvey stared at the gun in a stupor. Slowly, Lorraine inched her hand toward the door handle on Harvey's side of the car. She moved the handle mechanism until she knew the door was ajar. Then, with all her strength, she shoved Harvey out the door.

The force of her thrust landed her on top of the gunman. Desperately, she fought to get control of the gun. Her teeth clamped down on Harvey's gun hand. With a yelp, he let go. Lorraine pounced on the gun, picked it up, pointed it and fired it at Harvey. The gun jammed. As Harvey crouched like an animal, about to attack Lorraine, the courageous girl had one stroke of incredible good luck that day.

Tom Mulligan of the State Highway Patrol drove up on his motorcycle at that moment. Instantly realizing what was taking place, he barked at Harvey, "You stay right where you are!"

Harvey confessed in detail to his crimes and led police to the three lonely graves in the desert. On Aug. 18, 1953, Harvey Glatman was quietly strapped into the gas chamber in San Diego and put to death.

CATCH ME
IF YOU CAN

When Robert Erler moved from Phoenix, Arizona to Dania, Florida, it was only natural that a police officer acquaintance in Dania talked Bob into carving out a career for himself as a law enforcement officer. After all, Bob had served as a Green Beret in Vietnam from 1963 to 1966.

True enough, he and his wife Pat were having marital difficulties. That's why the Erlers decided to start life anew in southern Florida in the first place. A month after they settled in Dania, Pat gave birth to a baby boy. Little Bobby was his father's pride and joy.

Bob joined the Dania police force and proved to be an efficient, capable officer. However, his marital difficulties went from bad to worse. Pat simply wasn't the type to stay home day after day with her young son. Besides, she spent far more money than the young police officer earned. Gradually, the Erlers fell deeper and deeper into debt, which led to constant bickering. Despite this, the young couple continued to live beyond their means. Bob rented a new three bedroom mobile home, purchased a new Dodge Dart and an extensive wardrobe for his wife. Nothing satisfied Pat. One day, after a particularly nasty argument, she simply walked out.

In the course of his police work, Bob had become friends with Jim Walsh, a colleague on the nearby Hollywood, Fla., police force. Jim convinced Bob to join the larger, more modern Hollywood force.

While serving with the Hollywood police, Bob gained a degree of notoriety for his uncanny ability to smell out trouble. On more than one occasion, while on patrol, he merely looked at a speeding vehicle and declared that it was stolen. When licence numbers were checked, he proved to be correct far more often than he was wrong. Soon his fellow officers were calling him "Super Cop." No question about it, Robert Erler had a bright future as a law enforcement officer.

During the early morning hours of Aug. 12, 1968, Bob was on patrol. Later, in his police report, he described how he pulled up at a Shell service station at the corner of I-95 and Sheridan St. As he was leaving his patrol car, a blue 1968 Ford Falcon drove up. The occupants, a man and woman, told Bob that they had seen someone lying on the road a short distance away.

Bob radioed headquarters. As he was doing so, the blue Falcon drove away. Unable to see the licence number as the car sped away, Bob decided to proceed up the road, where he sighted the body of a young white female lying in the ditch. Bob radioed the exact location of the body to headquarters. In a matter of minutes, investigating officers were on the scene and had cordoned off the area. Bob typed out his report of discovery of the body and the investigation was turned over to the detective bureau.

During that early Monday morning, further developments took place. At precisely 8:18 a.m., the Hollywood police department received a phone call. The call was taped.

"I'd like to report a murder."

"A what?"

"Murder."

"A murder?"

"I just killed three people."

"Are you serious?" asked the officer.

"I'm serious. Please catch me. Please."

"Where are you, son?"

"I'm going to kill 'em tonight, too. Please."

"Where are you?" the officer persisted.

The caller hung up. Twelve minutes later, at precisely 8:30 a.m., the phone rang again.

"If you want to find those bodies, go down to the airport."

"Lauderdale Airport?" the officer asked.

"There's one in the water and one on a sidestreet."

"Route 1?" the officer asked.

"The Shell gas station. Hurry up, please."

"Okay."

414

The caller hung up. The strange phone calls were taken seriously. Before they could be acted upon, Bob Erler had found one victim, a young girl, who was obviously the one referred to as the victim beside the ditch.

The Fort Lauderdale police soon located a 1960 green Falcon near the Fort Lauderdale airport. Slumped over the steering wheel was a woman, who had been shot several times in the head. Miraculously, she was still alive.

From documents found in the vehicle, it was ascertained that the victim was 42-year-old Dorothy Clark, who had arrived in Florida from Clarkston, Georgia. Further investigation indicated that the dead girl found beside the road was Merylin Eileen Clark, her 12-year-old daughter.

Three weeks earlier, Dorothy and her daughter had left Georgia and were touring Florida while Dorothy sought employment.

The emotional calls received from the killer had mentioned three victims. He had also stated that he would kill that night. Investigating officers decided to inform the public of the danger through the media. Because of the phone calls, the press dubbed the murderer the "Catch Me Killer." Despite the madman's threats, there would be no third victim.

On the afternoon of the murder, an autopsy was performed on Merylin Clark. She had been shot five times directly in the head with a .22 calibre weapon. Meanwhile, her mother, Dorothy, lay in hospital near death. With each passing day, it became evident that this remarkable woman would survive.

A month after the attack, Mrs. Clark was strong enough to be interviewed by Hollywood detectives. She told them that she and her daughter had attempted to sleep on the beach at Dania. A police officer had approached and told her that sleeping on the beach was prohibited. On that particular night, swarms of mosquitoes were in the area. When the officer suggested that she and her daughter were welcome to spend the night in his air conditioned trailer, they jumped at the opportunity.

Mrs. Clark followed her benefactor in her car. They drove into a trailer park. The police officer's trailer was large and well appointed. She and her daughter flopped down on two separate couches. Suddenly, the officer stripped naked, made lewd suggestions, waved a .22 calibre pistol at the startled pair and demanded their money.

Dorothy and her daughter ran from the trailer and jumped into their car. Before they could start up, the police officer jumped in beside them. As they drove, Merylin Clark was shot five times in the head and thrown from the car. Near the airport,

Dorothy was ordered to stop. She, too, was shot five times in the head. The killer never for a moment believed that Mrs. Clark could possibly survive the shooting.

Investigating officers were stunned. Had one of their own been involved in one of the most senseless, cruel crimes they had ever investigated?

With Mrs. Clark's eyewitness report, the investigation swung into full gear. Hollywood detectives consulted with Dania Police Chief Parton. These discussions revealed that a Dania police officer had left that force and joined the Hollywood Police some months before the assault on the Clarks. What's more, the same police officer had been the one to find Merylin Clark's body - Super Cop Bob Erler.

Hollywood detectives learned that Erler had resigned from the Hollywood force three weeks after the murders. Strangely enough, the trailer he had rented at the Bell Trailer Court had been taken over by the Dania Police Chief for the use of his son.

The trailer had been refurnished by the Chief's son, but he told authorities that when he took possession of the trailer, he had thrown away several .22 calibre shells. Police, standing in front of Erler's trailer, had a clear view of the highway leading to the International Airport. They could also see a revolving Shell gasoline sign. Nearby was a public telephone booth. The evidence against Erler mounted. Personal friends now listened to the Catch Me tapes. Without being told of the status of the investigation, they identified the voice as that of Bob Erler. When Mrs. Clark identified Erler from a photograph as her attacker, police felt they had more than enough to act.

Erler was located in Phoenix and returned to Florida, where he was charged with the murder of Merylin Clark. Despite maintaining his innocence, Bob Erler was tried, found guilty of second degree murder and sentenced to 99 years and six months at hard labor at the Florida State Prison.

The existence of an ex-police officer in prison can be a living hell. Erler was no exception. He was beaten unmercifully on several occasions. However, his life still had many strange turns to take. After serving three years in the maximum security prison, Erler was transferred to the medium security institution at Belle Glade. A few months later, he escaped by climbing a wall and, in the dark, swimming an alligator-infested moat to gain his freedom.

Seven months later Erler was apprehended by the Mississippi Highway Patrol. After a six mile chase, Erler's car careened off the road. As he fled by foot, he was shot in the left hip. At the time of his apprehension, he was armed with a .357 Magnum revolver.

Back in prison, Bob Erler became deeply involved in religion. In 1977, under terms of an interstate agreement, Erler was transferred to an Arizona prison, where he could be close to his immediate family. While confined, he openly confessed to the murder of 12-year-old Merylin Clark and the attempted murder of Dorothy Clark. He has since been paroled, remarried and is presently an ordained minister in Arizona.

VITO AND
THE MAFIA

Mafia - the very word conjures up images of gambling, murder, and gangsterism. It wasn't always that way.

Legend has it that the secret society had its origin in 1282 in Palermo, Italy, when a drunken French sergeant, Pierre Druet, raped and killed a Sicilian girl in the shadows of a church where she was about to be married. All of Sicily was outraged at the atrocity. Sicilians banded together to hunt down Frenchmen under the battle cry "Morte alla Francia Italia anela" - Death to all of France is Italy's cry! The first letter of each Italian word was used to form the word Mafia.

Initially the Mafia was a patriotic society formed to assist the oppressed. By the 19th century it was an evil organization, extorting money from those it pretended to protect, spreading its influence to many parts of the world, notably the United States.

The organization had many leaders over the years. This is the story of one of them, Vito Genovese.

Vito was 15 and living in his home village of Nola near Naples when his father, Phillipo, sent for him to come to America. Once in the U.S., it didn't take long for Vito to realize that construction work along New York's lower east side was not for him.

Soon he was running errands for the mob. In 1915 his pal, Mike Miranda, sponsored him into the Mafia. Two years later, when he was 19, he was arrested for carrying a gun and sentenced to 60 days in jail. Forty-two years were to pass before Vito Genovese would again see the inside of a jail cell.

With fellow hoodlums Miranda and Anthony Strollo (known as Tony Bender), Vito established a profitable protection racket in Queens. If you didn't want your store robbed or damaged, you paid protection to Vito and his boys. They called it insurance.

Charles (Lucky) Luciano, then riding high in the honored society, gave Vito a house of prostitution to run. It didn't take long for him to build the lone establishment into a chain. Vito, extortionist and pimp, was now netting thousands of dollars a week.

In 1926 Vito married Anna Ragone. Their marriage was to last until Anna died of tuberculosis in 1931. During these years Vito owned the numbers racket in New York. The supply of cash flowing into his coffers each week increased dramatically.

A year after his first wife's death, Vito married for the second time. His bride was attractive brunette, Anna Petillo.

By 1933 Vito, 35, was a well-established underworld figure in New York. For four years the money rolled in, but in 1937 he recognized the danger signals. Special Prosecutor Thomas E. Dewey began looking into Vito's affairs. Vito left Anna in charge of his various business interests, and took off for Italy. She ran the numbers racket from a luxurious apartment at 29 Washington Square W. in Manhattan. Above her dwelled Eleanor Roosevelt, wife of the President of the U.S.

Anna often visited Vito in Italy, sometimes carrying upwards of $100,000 cash on her person. Vito was a big man in Fascist Italy. He contributed a quarter of a million dollars toward the construction of a municipal building in Nola. Benito Mussolini invested him with the title of Commendatore, Italy's highest civilian award.

Back home, Genovese's unpatriotic gestures did not go unnoticed. Journalist Carlo Tresca wrote several newspaper articles criticizing Vito's fraternization with an enemy of the U.S. On Jan. 11, 1943, Tresca was shot to death on the streets of New York. No one has ever been brought to trial for the killing.

When Allied forces overran Italy, Vito was arrested and returned to the U.S. The State of New York now felt that it had enough on Vito to charge him with a murder which had taken place in 1934.

Ernest (the Hawk) Rupolo, a one-eyed killer, told authorities how Genovese had ordered Ferdinand Boccia and Willie Gallo killed. Rupolo was given the contract on Gallo, but bungled the job. Two other killers were successful in murdering Boccia.

Now, years later, Rupolo found himself in jail for the attempted murder of another man. He decided to sing after the State agreed to drop his 40 to 80 year prison sentence.

Vito was brought to trial, but was acquitted. According to New York State law, Rupolo's testimony that Vito ordered Gallo and Boccia executed was not enough. It is necessary to have a second witness who had nothing to do with the actual commission of the crime. Later it was revealed that there had been a second witness. Hoodlum Peter La Tempa, who had been present when Vito passed the death sentences, had been held in jail for his own protection before Vito's trial. Vito's henchmen killed him, although his death was officially listed as "an overdose of sedative."

Perhaps Vito Genovese's finest hour occurred after his acquittal. A top echelon Mafia meeting was held on June 24, 1946 at the Hotel Diplomat in New York to honor Vito and set Mafia policy for the years ahead. Around the table sat the infamous names of American crime - Albert Anastasia, Frank Costello, Joe Profaci and John Dioguardi. It was agreed to let Rupolo live rather than execute him and bring more attention to the Mafia.

In 1947 Vito moved to Atlantic Highlands, New Jersey, where he purchased a mansion and spent several hundred thousand dollars redecorating it. The king now had his castle.

Five years later, when Vito's wife sued for divorce, she described the interior of her home. "The furniture was imported Chinese teakwood. All of our furniture was made to order. We had 24 karat gold and platinum dishes." Anna's wardrobe included a full-length mink coat, a Persian lamb coat, an ermine coat, and assorted mink stoles.

A year after the divorce Vito sold his mansion and moved to a modest clapboard house. He urged his colleagues in the Mafia to maintain a low profile as well.

From time to time internal strife rocked the organization. Albert Anastasia was assassinated by two gunmen as he sat in a barber's chair in the Park Sheraton Hotel in mid-town Manhattan. Frank Costello was grazed in the head by an assassin's bullet as he left his apartment building.

Vito called a crime convention, possibly the largest collection of top U.S. gangsters ever assembled. On Nov. 14, 1957 they came from all over the U.S. and Cuba to the village of Apalachin, N.Y., where mobster Joseph Barbara had a hilltop estate. State police received a tip that the convention was to take place and raided the estate. Fifty-seven mobsters, who collectively controlled the narcotics trade, prostitution and extortion rackets in the U.S., were picked up.

Not one carried a gun. As a cover story they claimed they were only paying a social call on their sick friend, Joe Barbara.

By this time the U.S. government felt it had gathered up enough evidence against Vito to gain a conviction. He was indicted on charges of masterminding an international narcotics syndicate that smuggled heroin and cocaine into the U.S. from Cuba, Puerto Rico and Mexico.

After a 19-week trial, Vito was sentenced to 15 years imprisonment. On Feb. 13, 1969, Vito Genovese died of natural causes at the Medical Centre for Federal Prisoners in Springfield, Missouri.

MIKE AND DORA

Long before the Capones and the O'Banions ran the rackets in Chicago, another man, virtually unknown today, held the Windy City in the palms of his ham-like paws.

Big Mike McDonald specialized in gambling, politics and prostitution. Regardless of who actually practised these worthy pursuits, Mike skimmed off 60% of the take. Twenty percent was placed in a fund to pay off police and politicians, while the remaining 40% went into the private coffers of Big Mike McDonald.

In 1893, Mike backed Harvey Calvin for mayor of Chicago. When Calvin won, Mike became unofficial king of the city. His chain of gambling emporiums ran day and night. Mike also owned legitimate enterprises such as the extremely profitable newspaper, the Chicago Globe, as well as large portions of real estate in downtown Chicago.

Alas, while fortunate in the world of legitimate and illegitimate finance, Mike was unlucky in love. His first wife is a relatively unknown quantity since she was married to Mike before he rose to prominence in the rackets. We do know that she was not a faithful soul. To a man of Mike's strict Catholic background, a sin of this magnitude could not be tolerated. Before the fat fell squarely into the fire, Mrs. McDonald number one died of natural causes.

Mike married for the second time. The object of his affection was Mary Noonan, a winsome Irish colleen who immediately found herself in a pack of trouble.

The McDonalds lived in luxurious digs above one of Mike's gambling dens. One night the police, who should have known better, raided the gambling joint. A lone cop wandered upstairs into Mary's kitchen. That was a mistake. Mary shot him between the eyes without saying a word. Big Mike arranged to have Mary appear in front of a benevolent judge who stated, "The defendant was justified in killing the invader of her home."

Mary presented Mike with two fine offspring and he presented her with a huge mansion on Ashland Ave. complete with an army of servants. There would be no more nosy cops interrupting Mary while she puttered around in the kitchen.

Now, folks, you would think Mary would be content with her lot. She had everything a woman could desire, but she lacked one fulfilment which certain ladies desire. She wanted variety. Unknown to the most powerful man in Chicago, Mary was seeing minstrel singer Billy Arlington on the side.

In a moment of emotional impetuousness, Mary and Billy ran away. Initially Big Mike was devastated; then he was furious. He hired private detectives to track down the lovebirds. It didn't take long. They were found living in the Palace Hotel in San Francisco.

Mike raced to San Francisco, broke into his wife's suite, and pulled out a pistol, fully intending to kill Billy Arlington right then and there. Mary, good sport that she was, slipped between the two men and implored her husband not to do anything rash. Actually, she did more than implore. She begged and prayed. Mike saw the light, put away the pistol, gathered up the wayward Mary and returned to Chicago. All was forgiven.

Mike, a deeply religious man despite his nefarious enterprises, thought that a little religion would be good for what ailed Mary. He built her a beautiful chapel in their home and enlisted the aid of young Father Joseph Moysant to hear Mary's rather lengthy confessions and minister to her spiritual needs each week.

Father Moysant ministered to more than Mary's spiritual needs. The pair took off and didn't stop until they reached Paris, France.

Mary and Joe lived in Paris for six years before the defrocked priest had second thoughts about the whole thing. He left Mary and entered a monastery. Mary returned home, but Mike, who had divorced her in the intervening years, refused to see her or let her see the two children. After all, enough is enough.

Mike was a glutton for punishment. He met buxom Dora Feldman and was truly smitten. There was a small problem. Dora was married to a professional baseball player named Sam Barcley. Not to worry. Mike would fix everything. He had a little chat with Sam, gave him $30,000 and told him to get a divorce. Sam said, "Right away, sir."

There is little doubt that Mike was deeply in love with Dora. In order to marry her he converted to the Jewish faith. For some time things went along just fine. Mike built a larger mansion for Dora than the one he had built for the now forgotten Mary. Furniture was imported from all over the world. Servants were hired. Dressmakers outfitted Dora with expensive gowns. A large bank account was placed at her disposal.

Would you believe that Dora wasn't the type to enjoy such luxuries? No, Dora proved to be a homebody. She shunned Chicago's night life and showed little inclination to spend money.

However, Dora was inclined in another direction. Webster Guerin was a tall blonde boy who lived down the street. He was 16. Initially, Dora inveigled the unsuspecting Webster into doing odd jobs around the McDonald mansion. It didn't take long before Webster was performing more personal tasks for Dora.

Folks, they were at it all the time. Big Mike would leave his stately home in the morning. Sneaky Webster would be in the sack with Dora before Mike was at his office. This state of affairs didn't go on for a few weeks or months. No, siree, it went on for years.

Webster graduated from high school and college, all the while seeing Dora at every opportunity. When he graduated as a commercial artist, Dora put up the money for well-equipped offices for her lover.

It was a terrible blow to Dora's pride when rumors reached her ears that Webster had a girlfriend his own age whom he intended to marry. Private detectives verified her worst fears.

Dora confronted Webster. He confessed to his indiscretions but swore he would drop his girlfriend and return to Dora's side on an exclusive basis. That satisfied Dora for awhile. When once more she found out that Webster had taken up with another woman, she marched into his office on Feb. 21, 1907 and shot him twice, once in the stomach and once in the neck. Webster sunk to the floor, very dead.

Dora readily confessed to the police, not only relating details of the killing but of her lengthy affair with the victim. When news of the murder reached Big Mike, who was now 66 years old, he was hurt beyond belief. He went to bed and stayed there for weeks. A born softie, he put up $50,000 bail for Dora, who showed up at his sickbed begging for forgiveness. Big Mike wouldn't speak to her. His condition worsened until he was taken to hospital, where he died on Aug. 9, 1907. Mike left Dora one third of his multi-million dollar estate. The balance was left to his two children.

In 1908 Dora stood trial for Webster's murder. After deliberating for over six hours the jury found her not guilty. Many believed that Big Mike's influence with judge and jury reached from the grave to bribe them into acquitting the one true love of his life, Dora Feldman McDonald.

MADELINE'S MURDEROUS WAYS

We are forever reading about beautiful young girls who make their way to Hollywood and New York to get their start in movies and plays. Their talents are discovered. Success, fame and riches follow. Rarely do we hear about the vast majority who meet with frustration, failure, and sometimes tragedy. This is the story of one such girl.

Madeline Webb graduated in the top third of her class from the Oklahoma Agricultural and Mechanics College in her hometown of Stillwater, Okla. But it wasn't only in the brains department that Madeline excelled. She was a looker with a capital L. Madeline had flaming red hair and a figure that would make the old town clock spin backwards.

Upon graduation, Madeline married her hometown sweetheart, but things simply didn't work out. Mostly it was Madeline's fault. She had a deep-seated desire to become an actress and wouldn't be satisfied until she gave it her best shot. Hubby disagreed. Divorce followed.

Free to strike it rich on her own, Madeline left for Hollywood. Once there, she found out that her stunning good looks and limited singing and dancing abilities were not enough. There were thousands of beautiful girls in movieland.

Madeline decided to try New York. Again she had difficulty breaking into the entertainment industry, but was able to obtain sporadic jobs as a model. Sometimes she caught on with the chorus of an off-Broadway play for a few months, but in general things went from bad to worse. For two years Madeline lived in sleazy hotels. When she had a half decent job she moved to a better place. When times got tough she moved on.

While employed for several months, Madeline lived at the Woodrow Hotel. It was there she met Mrs. Susan Reich, who had immigrated to the U.S. from Vienna. Mrs. Reich, a woman in her mid-fifties, had once been a beauty herself and took an immediate liking to the struggling young actress. Mrs. Reich, who lived in a suite of rooms with her mother and her husband, was continually performing some kindness for Madeline. The two women became very close friends, until once again Madeline couldn't afford the comfortable hotel and moved to cheaper, less attractive accommodations.

That's where matters stood for some months until one day in March 1942, when Mrs. Reich received a phone call from her old friend Madeline. Madeline invited the older woman to have tea with her at the elegant Hotel Sutton. She informed Mrs. Reich that she and her husband were living there. Mrs. Reich was glad to receive the call and remarked to her mother that Madeline must have married well as the Sutton was an expensive hotel.

On March 3, Mrs. Reich left her mother at the Woodrow to visit with Madeline. When she failed to return, her mother called the Sutton several times, until finally she convinced the manager that someone should look in on Room 207, where her daughter was to meet with Madeline Webb Leopold.

The manager sent a bell boy to 207 to investigate. He opened the door and gazed upon the body of Mrs. Susan Reich lying on the floor. Her arms were tied behind her back with wire and her ankles were bound with the same wire. Wide strips of adhesive tape had been placed over her mouth and a lady's scarf was wound around her neck. The body was stripped of the expensive jewelry Mrs. Reich was known to wear. Four coffee cups, several cinnamon buns, and an unopened one pound box of chocolates were on a table near the body.

The death room had been rented to Mr. and Mrs. Ted Leopold of Euclid Ave., Miami Beach. A check with Florida police revealed that the address was a vacant lot.

Mrs. Reich's mother told the police of her daughter's friendship with Madeline Webb, and was able to supply them with a picture of the aspiring actress.

The Leopolds had been living at the Sutton since Feb. 20. Detectives learned that a smalltime thief named Eli Shonbrun had stolen a valuable ring just a day before Mr. and Mrs. Leopold checked into the Sutton. A police shot of Shonbrun was shown to the employees of the hotel. They identified Shonbrun as the man they knew as Ted Leopold, husband of the beautiful Madeline.

Meanwhile, police found the store which had sold the wire used to tie Mrs.

Reich' wrists and ankles. The clerk swore that Eli Shonbrun was the man who had purchased the wire.

Delving into Shonbrun's past, detectives learned that he, like Madeline, had longed for a career as a singer but had never been able to make a living at his specialty. When he met Madeline he fell deeply in love. He abandoned his wife and seven-year-old son to move in with his true love. Together they worked when they could, but more often lived by their wits and the proceeds of petty crime. For the first time in years, Madeline had someone who really cared. She loved Eli with a passion.

In the course of the investigation into Shonbrun's background, detectives came across his uncle, Harry Hirschl, who bought and sold second hand jewelry. Police tailed Hirschl. He led them to a hock shop, where he sold a ring with the diamond missing. This ring proved to be one which had been torn from Mrs. Reich's finger.

Hirschl was picked up. To save his own skin, he sang like a canary. He told detectives that his nephew, Shonbrun, had brought him the ring, but it was too expensive an item for him to sell without raising suspicion. The two men decided to extract the diamond. They then agreed to meet soon after Hirschl sold the unmounted ring, but Shonbrun never showed up.

Hirschl admitted knowledge of the plan to lure Mrs. Reich to the Hotel Sutton, but swore it was only to rob her, not to murder her. Shonbrun and Madeline were flat broke and badly in need of money. Madeline remembered her old friend and her penchant for wearing expensive jewelry. The plan was hatched. The fourth person involved, accounting for the fourth coffee cup in the room, was an ex-con, John Cullen, a friend of Shonbrun's. Hirschl swore he wasn't in the room when the murder took place, but had been told the details when Shonbrun gave him the ring to sell.

He told police that Mrs. Reich had walked into the room. She chatted with Madeline, Shonbrun and Cullen for a few moments. Madeline excused herself and went into the bathroom. Shonbrun demanded that Mrs. Reich hand over her jewelry. The conspirators firmly believed she would do so without question. Instead, Mrs. Reich screamed. Madeline ran out of the hotel into the street. The two men slapped adhesive tape over their victim's mouth and then throttled her with Madeline's scarf.

Five days after the murder, Cullen was picked up on the streets of New York. He gave police the address of Madeline and Shonbrun. They were taken into custody without incident.

Shonbrun co-operated with the police in every way. He readily admitted his part in the murder and turned over the diamond he had removed from Mrs. Reich's ring.

He insisted that Madeline knew nothing of the plot to steal Mrs. Reich's jewelry and swore she was out of the room when the attack occurred.

All three participants in the killing were brought to trial and all were found guilty of murder. Shonbrun and Cullen were executed in Sing Sing's electric chair. Madeline was sentenced to life imprisonment, eventually being paroled at the age of 54.

Oh, yes, the unopened box of chocolates found on the table beside the body. It was a gift from Mrs. Reich to her dear friend, Madeline Webb.

YVONNE WAS
A NAG

John Westly made one large mistake when he married Yvonne Casey on Oct. 28, 1947. It had seemed like such a great idea at the time. You see, John was about to go into the chicken raising and butchering business in a big way in St. Petersburg, Florida. He had the farm already picked out, but there was one fly in the ointment. He needed additional cash to purchase his initial flock of 2000 New Hampshire Reds.

Enter Yvonne with the cash. *Voila*, John obtained a wife and his chicken farm in one fell swoop. At the outset John took great pride in his well-equipped farm. One wall of his butchering shed was outfitted with a cutting board, drainage equipment, sink, and an array of sharp knives and cleavers.

Everything would have been jim dandy if only Yvonne hadn't badgered him about paying back the money she had loaned him to go into business. All that winter Yvonne talked of little else but the loan. Actually, she shouted a lot. On one occasion John called the police, who drove out to the farm to quiet down the bickering couple. It was enough to get on a man's nerves.

Yvonne really should have known better. During the war she had been married to a man named Casey. At that time she was employed at the army's Drew Airfield near Tampa. We can only assume that she and Casey shouted at each other, which may have led to their divorce. The Caseys had a married daughter living in Lowell, Mass.

Let's get back to John and the immediate problem of the nagging Yvonne. There was one absolutely final way to keep the loquacious one silent. I mean forever. John looked down the wall of his butchering shed. He had the instruments of death at hand. It would be simple. A blow to the head, dismemberment, disposal of the body in some old burlap sacks and no one would ever be the wiser.

On Oct. 2, 1947 two fishermen off the St. Petersburg shore of Tampa Bay found a sack. They peeked inside and were greeted with the disconcerting sight of a severed arm and leg. Police were called and immediately addressed the problem of identifying the body.

St. Petersburg coroner John T. Fisher established that the human limbs were the right arm and leg of a female approximately 40 years old. The fingers of the dead woman were so wrinkled and decomposed that identification officers could only obtain an unclear fingerprint. Police also found several pieces of water-soaked newspapers in the sack. They proved to be various issues of the St. Petersburg *Times* and the St. Petersburg *Independence.*

At this point the investigation bogged down. In desperation police turned to the public for assistance in identifying the dead woman. Literally hundreds of citizens responded, reporting strange and unusual events, all of which contributed nothing of a material nature to the investigation.

Meanwhile, trace evidence was providing some results. The sack in which the dismembered limbs were found was carefully brushed. The area near the seams yielded 22 small seeds which proved to be oats. Under floodlights and with the use of a magnifying glass, four minute feathers were extracted from the weave of the sack with a pair of tweezers. The reddish brown feathers were chicken feathers.

Placed under ultraviolet lights, the following message which could not be seen by the naked eye now became visible: "To remove ink, soak and scrub thoroughly in warm water, then boil in soapy water until white." The bleaching instructions enabled detectives to trace the bag to the Western Grain Co. Officials of the company informed police that the sack had contained one of their products, Baby Chick Scratch Feed. However, the product was so widely distributed that it was impossible to trace the bag to its original dealer.

When officials of the grain company identified the feathers as those of New Hampshire Reds, investigating officers knew they were faced with the tedious task of locating all chicken farms in Florida which raised New Hampshire Reds and used Baby Chick Scratch Feed.

On Oct. 20, eighteen days after the original grisly discovery, two fishermen, Clyde Gibbs and Cliff Castillo, spotted a sack caught on a mangrove island in Tampa Bay. Police opened the sack and found the left arm and left leg of a female. Doctors established that the contents of both sacks had been severed from the same body.

Despite the thorough investigation conducted by police, the break in the case came from a casual remark made by a citizen to Patrolman Ralph Meiners. When he was told that a man named John Westly of 417 20th St. South raised New Hampshire Reds and that his wife hadn't been seen lately, Meiners passed the information along to his superiors.

Detectives drove out to the Westly farm and inquired about Mrs. Westly. John explained, "She sure ain't here now. She went up to Massachusetts to visit her married daughter. She left on Sept. 28. Her daughter by her first husband just had a baby."

Later that day police phoned Lowell, Mass. and spoke to Yvonne's daughter. She had not given birth and her mother was certainly not visiting with her.

Once again, police questioned John Westly. He readily admitted that he had lied. John explained that his wife had left him, possibly for another man. He had told his friends, as well as the police, that she was away visiting her daughter in order to save face.

John also admitted that he had had monumental battles with his wife concerning her loan to him. He had finally paid her before she ran off. As proof of this transaction he produced a receipt signed by Yvonne. When officers pointed out that the receipt was in a masculine hand, John calmly stated that he had written out the receipt for Yvonne's signature. Our John had an answer for everything.

While John Westly was being questioned, authorities found out that Yvonne had once worked at Drew Airfield during the war. Her fingerprints were on file. The severed right hand of the victim was flown to Washington, where identification experts were able to obtain a set of clear prints by taking layers of skin from the dead woman's fingers. They matched those of Yvonne. Finally, the body was identified.

A meticulous search of the chicken operation revealed plenty. In Westly's butchering shed a stack of old newspapers were found. Missing from the stack were those exact issues which had been stuffed into the sack with the victim's limbs. John used Baby Chick Scratch Feed for his New Hampshire Reds. There were several empty sacks around the shed. A hammer and a pair of John's trousers were found under the front seat of his car. Both were bloodstained. Handwriting experts claimed that Yvonne Westly's signature was a crude attempt by John to simulate his wife's writing.

On Dec. 16, 1947 John was brought to trial for murder in Clearwater, Fla. It took the jury only one hour and 35 minutes to return a verdict of murder in the first degree. John Westly was sentenced to life imprisonment.

DEATH AT SEA

Murderers have contrived to stash their victims in some weird and wonderful locales. Would you believe submerged in oil on a freighter in the middle of the Atlantic Ocean?

In 1914 Germany was still purchasing oil from the U.S. The German freighter, *Gertrude Schultz*, pulled into Galveston, Texas, where it was hurriedly converted into a tanker. Aside from loading the hold with drums of oil, 20 full tanks from railway tankers were lashed to the decks.

Six days out to sea a storm of hurricane proportions developed. One of the oil tanks sprung a leak. Captain Karl Mueller sent a young seaman to report how much oil had leaked out of the tank. The seaman looked inside and shouted, "There's a woman in there - floating face upward on the oil! A naked woman!"

The Captain had the tank drained and received another surprise. The tank contained not one naked woman, but two. They were attractive blondes in their early twenties. A woman's diamond-studded wristwatch was also found. Both girls had been shot to death, one through the head and the other through the left breast.

Once in Hamburg, Mueller reported his gruesome discovery to the police. The owners of the *Gertrude Schultz* were anxious to clear up the mystery. Realizing how slow the governments of Germany and the U.S. could be in such matters, they authorized Capt. Mueller to employ a private detective.

The *Gertrude Schultz* set out for the U.S. She docked in Houston, where Capt. Mueller hired a private detective with the appropriate name of Joe Hunter.

Hunter received word from Germany that the wristwatch found in the tank had been sold by a Danzig jeweller. He was also informed that there were no girls missing from that German city around the time of the murder. In Galveston, Hunter learned that 20 tank cars of oil had been taken from a train which had originated in Chicago and placed on the *Gertrude Schultz*.

The train had been loaded with oil in Texas before continuing on to Galveston. Hunter believed that the girls could have been murdered anywhere along the line. He travelled to Chicago and checked with the police. No missing girls matched the description of the murdered girls.

Hunter decided to check at each railway yard where the train had stopped on its way from Chicago to Galveston. After questioning 20 yardmasters, he hit paydirt in East St. Louis, Illinois.

The yardmaster remembered the train, which was made up of 20 empty tankcars. One had a broken axle and had to be replaced. He replaced it with another tankcar, which had a minor defect in the riveting. The yardmaster had it repaired before making the substitution.

Hunter checked with the repair shop. The repaired plate was in the same location as the one which had given way, during the storm at sea. He contacted the St. Louis police and found that a girl had been reported missing two weeks before the Gertrude Schultz put out to sea.

The report read: "Adele Drucker, 23, 5 feet 6 inches, 125 pounds, blonde. Reported by Mrs. Ella Abington, East St. Louis." A note attached to the report stated that a male member of the family had informed police that Adele was no longer missing. She had returned to Germany.

Hunter looked up Ella Abington, a pleasant, middle-aged woman who told the following story. The missing girl was the daughter of her divorced husband's recently deceased brother, Hans Drucker, who had died a year before in Germany. Mrs. Abington went on to relate that her former husband Oscar and his brother Hans had been the sons of a wealthy steel manufacturer in Danzig. Oscar had immigrated to the United States years before, while Hans remained in Germany to help run the family business. Hans had married and had two beautiful daughters, Adele and Ida, who had often visited their aunt and uncle in America. When elderly Herr Drucker died, he left the business to Hans.

When Hans died, it was decided his two daughters would be better off in the U.S. They planned on staying with Mrs. Abington, even though she had obtained a divorce from Oscar, who had remarried and was living in Chicago.

Eight months previously, Adele arrived from Germany and took up residence with Mrs. Abington. One day she told Mrs. Abington that she was going to Chicago to visit her Uncle Oscar. She planned on doing some shopping in St. Louis and continuing on by train. Mrs. Abington never heard from Adele again.

Alarmed, she travelled to Chicago and confronted her former husband, who told her that he had expected Adele, but that the girl never arrived. Ida never did come over from Germany. Mrs. Abington assumed that the trip was cancelled because of the war. Mrs. Abington reported Adele missing to the police and had no idea who had called them about Adele's return to Germany.

When Mrs. Abington returned from Chicago, she learned that her son had turned over Adele's unpacked trunks to an expressman, who had a note signed by Adele instructing him to pick up the trunks. Mrs. Abington was unable to trace the moving company. Hunter travelled to Chicago for a little chat with Oscar Drucker. Oscar told Hunter that Adele never arrived in Chicago.

Hamburg police wired Hunter. He was on the right track. They confirmed that the two murdered girls were Adele and Ida Drucker. Ida had left her home on July 12, 1914, arriving in New York City two weeks later. Adele had left a month earlier.

The tenacious Hunter returned to St. Louis to check moving companies. Sure enough, he found the man who had picked up Adele's trunks. His name was Jack Alf. He had been instructed by Adele Drucker to move the trunks to a dimly lit street, just off the railway tracks. Alf even had a receipt signed by Adele, indicating that she received the trunks.

Hunter scampered over to the address on the receipt. There he met landlord George Lundy. Lundy had taken a vacation the previous summer and had sublet his cottage to a Mr. Berger. When he returned, Berger had already vacated the premises, but had left the place in a terrible mess. He obviously had female company during Lundy's absence. Lundy found half-burned letters and a bloody mattress in the yard. They were still outside in a garbage dump.

Crawling through the garbage, Hunter found portions of letters which revealed that Adele had agreed to keep house for Mr. Berger and that her sister Ida would soon join her. Hunter also found partly burned female underclothing, which Mrs. Abington identified as belonging to Adele Drucker.

Lundy described Mr. Berger. The description fit Oscar Drucker down to the last detail. Hunter faced Drucker with portions of letters he had written inviting his two nieces to visit.

Oscar broke down. He told Hunter how his father had left his complete fortune to his brother Hans. When Hans died he left everything to his two daughters. In Oscar's mind he had twice been cheated out of financial security. Oscar decided to have his two nieces come under his influence and in some way fleece them of their fortune.

Adele suspected that her uncle was up to something when she found out he was living under an assumed name. Oscar shot her in the head. The very next day Ida arrived. Oscar killed her an hour after her arrival. That night he carried the two bodies to the railway siding and dropped them into the empty tanker.

Hunter travelled by train to St. Louis with his prisoner. Oscar escaped from the moving train by jumping out of the bathroom window. Despite a massive search, he got away. A year later, his second wife informed police that he was living in Tijuana, Mexico. Joe Hunter, accompanied by a U.S. marshal, approached Oscar in a bar. Oscar, who was downing a drink, had his back turned to Hunter. Hunter identified himself. Oscar spun around, firing wildly. His shots went astray. At the same time, Joe Hunter fired his .32 calibre revolver.

Oscar Drucker, the man who killed his two nieces, was dead on the barroom floor.

◆

HORROR AT STARVED ROCK LODGE

The boy scout troop walked carefully over the rugged terrain of an isolated portion of Starved Rock State Park. The huge Illinois recreation area was not only ideal for enthusiastic scouts, it was also the location of Starved Rock Lodge, a plush resort frequented by wealthy guests from Chicago.

Three scouts ventured into a small cave. The sight which greeted them on that April day in 1960 would remain forever etched in their memories. The battered bodies of three middle-aged women lay grotesquely sprawled on the floor of the cave. State police were notified and were soon on the scene.

The three women had been savagely beaten about the head. Two of the victims were tied together at the ankles and wrists with white cord. Their clothing had been pulled above their waists and their underclothes had been torn off. The third woman's clothing had not been touched.

Initially the hideous crime was considered to be sexually motivated. The women's jewelry was intact. Small amounts of money had not been removed from their purses. A heavy, bloodstained tree branch found beside the bodies was obviously the murder weapon.

Police recovered a camera with a broken strap nearby. Film inside the camera was developed in the hope that it might contain a picture of the murderer or at least a clue to his identity. However, the photos depicted only scenic views of the area.

The three women had been guests at Starved Rock Lodge. They were readily identified as Mrs. Mildred Lindquist, 50, Mrs. Lillian Oetting, 50, and Mrs. Frances Murphy, 47. All three were the wives of prominent Chicago businessmen and had travelled the 90 miles to the park in Mrs. Murphy's station wagon. They had checked into the lodge, had lunch, and were last seen walking together through the park.

The murder scene was thoroughly studied for clues. There was little of value. The murder weapon had obviously been picked up at the spur of the moment and used as a club. The only material item the killer might have left behind were the strips of cord used to tie two of the victims.

Guests and employees of the lodge were questioned, but no one could offer any information about the murders. All employees consented to take a lie detector test. All passed without difficulty. Sexual deviates recently released from prison were interviewed. None were near the park at the time of the murders. For some time it was believed that Chicago gangsters may have fulfilled a murder contract in order to gain revenge on the husbands of the dead women. This tangent of the investigation proved fruitless.

Four months after the murders, Illinois detectives returned to square one. Using a microscope, they examined the pieces of cord used to tie the women. Most pieces of the cord were made up of 20 strands. Only one piece had 12 strands. A search of the lodge uncovered pieces of cord in almost every room. All were manufactured with 20 strands, except for pieces found in the kitchen. Some of these were composed of 12 strands.

A check of records indicated that Starved Rock Lodge purchased their cord from a Chicago store, which in turn bought it from January and Wood, a factory in Maysville, Kentucky. Factory employees identified the cord as having been manufactured at their facility. They used a distinctive white dye which they easily recognized.

Detectives felt that it was possible that an employee of the lodge had committed the crimes. They decided to conduct another series of lie detector tests. This time expert John Reid of Chicago was solicited to bring equipment to the lodge and conduct the tests under controlled conditions. All the tests indicated that the employees tested had no guilty knowledge of the murders.

It was now six months since the tragedy. Several members of the lodge staff were no longer employed there. Police located them for retesting. This tedious task brought into the sphere of the investigation a former dishwasher at the lodge,

Chester Weger. Weger had taken a lie detector test previously and had passed. This time his test proved to be far from normal. The results indicated very definitely that Weger had guilty knowledge of the triple slayings.

Authorities were stumped as to how Weger had passed the previous test. They decided to set him free and keep him under constant surveillance. Meanwhile, detectives delved into Weger's past. He had once been in the U.S. Marines, where he had learned seafaring knots identical to those used to tie two of the victims.

Although he professed to have been off duty, miles from the park on the day the crime was committed, detectives now learned that he had been a substitute dishwasher for an acquaintance who wanted time off that day. Faced with this last bit of incriminating evidence, Weger stated that he had initially been in error. It was true; he was working at the lodge on the day of the crime. In fact, he was washing dishes at the time of the killings, and could not possibly have been the murderer.

Detectives had a difficult time proving or disproving Weger's claim. They tracked down every guest who had stayed at the lodge on the day of the triple murder. Weger's photograph, among others, was shown to each guest in the hope that someone had seen him outside the lodge. This was a time consuming task. Many of the guests lived hundreds of miles from the resort. One by one they were located and interviewed. Sure enough, one woman recognized Weger as the man she had passed on one of the paths near the murder scene around the time of the murders.

Weger was taken into custody, and interrogated. Detectives played it straight. They told the pale nervous suspect every bit of evidence they had pointing to him as the guilty man. At the conclusion of the interrogation Weger blurted out, "There's no use my trying to deny anything after that - you got me cold!"

Weger stated that he was a married man with two children. Heavily in debt, he realized his dishwashing job would never allow him to get out of his financial difficulties. He slipped out of the lodge unseen with the intention of snatching purses from unwary ladies along the resort's many isolated paths. He grabbed at Mrs. Murphy's camera, mistaking it for a handbag. The strap broke.

Weger claimed he then picked up the heavy branch and threatened the women. He ordered them to turn around and lie down while he tied them. The women complied. Weger stated that suddenly "the one with the camera broke loose from the string and hit me hard over the back of the head with a pair of binoculars. As she struck me, I raised my club and gave it to her. Then I hit the other two. I didn't want them telling on me."

Weger went on to say that he dragged the three women into the nearby cave. He pulled and tugged at their clothing to make it appear to be a sexually motivated crime.

How did Weger manage to beat the first lie detector test? "That was a cinch," he explained. "I stuffed myself with aspirin and Coke. I should have done that on my next test." Why did he bother to drag his victims into a cave? Weger had an answer for that one as well. At the time of the murders he observed a low flying red and white Piper Cub circling overhead. He thought the bodies would be seen from the air and decided to conceal them.

An investigation into this aspect of his confession checked out. A red and white Piper piloted by Homer Charbonneau had taken off on the day in question. Airport records verified the date and time. Charbonneau distinctly remembered circling the area several times.

Taken to Starved Rock Park, Chester Weger reenacted his senseless crime. Weger was charged with the murder of Mrs. Oetting. At his trial he repudiated his detailed confession, claiming he was innocent and had been coerced into saying what the police wanted to hear.

On the afternoon of March 4, 1961, the jury retired to reach a verdict. It was Weger's birthday. He was 22. Nine hours later the jury returned with a verdict of guilty. Weger was sentenced to life imprisonment, which was considered a victory for the defence at the time. The state had strongly urged that Weger be executed.

Chester Weger, Prisoner Number 01114, is still incarcerated at the Statesville Correctional Centre at Joliet, Ill., which has been his home for the past 30 years. Prison officials inform me that he is a quiet man who keeps to himself. He is now the longest serving inmate in the institution. Each year he is eligible for parole. Each year parole is refused.

THE ZEBRA KILLERS

Richard Hague and his attractive wife, Quita, left their apartment on Chestnut St. in San Francisco to go for a walk. All was right with the world. Christmas was only a couple of months away. Richard, 30, was a mining engineer; Quita a reporter with a local paper.

As the Hagues walked hand in hand, two black men blocked their way. One had a gun. He pointed the weapon at Richard's chest and forced the young couple into the cargo door of a parked van containing two confederates. Quickly, the two captives were tied and driven to an isolated area near railroad tracks.

Quita Hague was marched towards the tracks and was struck with one vicious blow with a machete, which ended her life. Richard was beaten about the head with a wrench and stabbed in the face with a knife. He was left for dead. Somehow, Richard Hague survived. He regained consciousness and, with hands still tied behind his back, staggered to a highway where a passing motorist stopped and gave assistance.

No one knew it at the time, but Quita and Richard Hague had just become the first victims of a San Francisco group of Black Muslims who advocated the death of all whites, including women and children. In the months to follow, the crimes of this small group of men would become infamous throughout the world as the Zebra killings. Zebra was the code name given to a special wave length on the police radio, when a task force was formed some months later solely for the purpose of apprehending the wanton killers of white San Francisco citizens.

Frances Rose, 28, a student at the University of California Extension campus, drove up to the university gates in her gold and black Mustang. As she slowed down, a young man waved at her to stop. He obviously wanted a lift. He approached the car, pulled open the passenger door and fired four times. Frances Rose's death was instantaneous. The killer walked away, but this time luck was against the murderer.

Officers Thomas O'Connell and William Kelly were patrolling near the university. Speeding toward the scene of the shooting, they spotted Jesse Lee Cooks walking on the sidewalk. They found an automatic weapon in Jesse's belt. It proved to be the gun which had taken the life of Frances Rose. Jesse was convicted and sent away for life. There was now one less member of the killing squad in San Francisco, but Jesse's arrest did nothing to stop the carnage.

Thirty-five days after Quita Hague had been hacked to death, Saleem Erakat, a shopkeeper, was forced into a corner at the back of his store. A member of the assassination squad then placed a gun behind Saleem's right ear and pulled the trigger. The shopkeeper died instantly.

Paul Dancik, a small-time hoodlum, was gunned down as he used a public telephone. With Dancik's death came the first concrete indication that the wanton killings were connected. A .32 calibre slug removed from Saleem Erakat's head had been fired from the same weapon used to kill Paul Dancik. There was one other connecting factor. Witnesses who had seen men leaving the various crime sites, as well as Richard Hague, who had survived, agreed on one thing - the killers were black. All the victims were white.

Arthur Agnos was employed as a consultant with the California State Legislature's Joint Commission on Aging. On Dec. 13, 1973 he attended a meeting. He chatted with two lady friends as he made his way to his parked Volkswagen. Two slugs tore into Arthur's back. He staggered. The women ran. So did the attacker. Rushed to Mission Emergency Hospital, Arthur survived the attack after undergoing operations on his lungs, spleen and kidneys.

That same night the madmen struck again. Marietta Di Girolamo, 31, grew tired of waiting for her date. She decided to go to a neighborhood bar for a drink. As she walked, she failed to notice the men in the black Cadillac stalking her. One of the men got out of the car and approached Marietta. As he did so, he extracted a .32 calibre automatic pistol from his waistband. Without a word, he shoved the terrified girl into a doorway and began shooting. Marietta Di Girolamo was dead on arrival at Mission Emergency Hospital.

Eighty-one-year-old Ilario Bertuccio was shot to death as he strolled home from his janitorial job at a 7-Up plant. Soon after Neal Maynihan and Mildren Hasler were shot dead in the streets. Cartridge casings recovered from the scenes of the latest crimes matched those found near the four previous murders.

On Jan. 28, 1974, four innocent victims, Tana Smith, Vincent Wollin, John Bambic and Jane Holly were shot to death. Strangers in life, they would be forever linked in death as innocent victims in the most infamous night in San Francisco's criminal history. A fifth victim, Roxanne McMillan, survived a shot directly in her chest and another in her back. The killers were now using a different .32 calibre weapon.

Rewards were offered. A police task force was formed, but still the killings continued. Thomas Rainwater and Linda Story attended the Salvation Army Officers Training School in San Francisco. On April 1, 1974, they left the school together and walked down the street. A young man rushed past them. He stopped suddenly, wheeled and drew a gun. The roar of gunfire pierced the silence. Thomas took two slugs in the back. So did Linda. Thomas ran 50 feet before falling to the ground. Linda screamed. The assailant fired a shot in her direction, but missed. Then he ran away. Thomas Rainwater lay dead on the sidewalk. Linda Story survived.

San Francisco's black community was as incensed as the white community. What maniacs were loose, spreading their particular brand of horror? Many blacks accompanied whites as bodyguards on the streets at night.

Nick Shields was loading the cargo space of his Vega. He never knew what hit him. Three slugs slammed into his body. He died beside his car. Nick Shields was the last victim of the wanton murderers.

The Zebra killers were not tracked down, nor was clever deduction on the part of detectives instrumental in bringing them to justice. The arrests of the four men dedicated to killing was as devoid of drama as was their own method of dispensing death. One of their own number, Anthony Harris, made a deal for reward money and the promise of immunity from prosecution. In this way detectives garnered enough evidence to arrest Larry Green, 23, Jesse Cook, 30 (already serving time for the murder of Frances Rose), J.C. Simon, 28, and Manuel Moore, 30. Their trial was the longest ever held in California, lasting one year and three days.

The jury took only 18 hours to find all the defendants guilty of murder as well as a series of other charges arising out of the Zebra killings. All four received life sentences. They are presently serving their time in prison.

I WANT TO LIVE

Barbara Graham didn't have an easy childhood. She was born in the slums of Oakland, California, on June 26, 1923. Her mother, Hortense, was confined to an institution for wayward girls when Barbara was two.

While Mama Hortense was enjoying her involuntary vacation, Barbara's father died, leaving the child without mother or father. She was temporarily placed in the care of distant relatives. Upon being released, Hortense remarried and took Barbara once more under her wing.

Evidently, Hortense's maternal contributions were not received that well. Barbara was nine when she ran away for the first time. She was found, whipped and returned to live with her mother and stepfather. By the age of 13, Barbara had run away from home several times. In the process, she had discovered boys.

In her early teens, it was evident that Barbara was developing into a beautiful woman. Unable to cope with her curvaceous offspring, Hortense enrolled Barbara in a convent. She did rather well in school, but was a holy terror when her mother brought her home for any length of time. Hortense had Barbara confined to her old alma mater, that school for wayward girls. Barbara served two years. By the time she was release, she had developed into a rare beauty.

Barbara attempted to travel the straight and narrow. She attended high school, then business college and, on completion of her course, obtained employment as a file clerk.

However, her wild streak wasn't to be denied. By the time she was 16 she was picked up in Long Beach for disorderly conduct. A short time later she became pregnant, married and soon divorced. Barbara's former mother-in-law raised her child.

At this point in her life, Barbara Graham had become one of thousands of girls with better than average looks who drifts from city to city, working in bars, dipping into prostitution and getting into trouble. In San Francisco, Barbara became a full-time prostitute. After several arrests, she drifted to Chicago.

It was here, at the age of 23, that she became acquainted with fringe underworld characters. Barbara worked the dice tables for several hoods and was the trusted friend of several others. When she provided two small-time hoodlums who had beaten up a madame with a bogus alibi, her status with the gangs was secure. Unfortunately for Barbara, her perjury was exposed. She was tried, convicted and sentenced to one year in jail.

Upon her release, Barbara headed for Tonopah, Nevada, where she had some decent friends. Once again, in her turbulent existence, Barbara was attempting to change the direction of her life, but it was not to be. When she lost her job as a waitress, she took off for Chicago and the life she knew best. From Chicago she drifted to Los Angeles. In the process, Barbara married, divorced and married again for the third time.

Her third husband, Henry Graham, was a spineless, alcoholic bartender. Barbara gave birth to their child in 1951. Two years later, she left her baby with Henry's mother and obtained a divorce.

In 1953, Barbara gained employment in a gambling den operated by Emmett Perkins, who was known to be a buddy of Jack Santo. The two men had a long string of arrests for everything from hijacking to murder. Barbara Graham graduated from the school of hard knocks to post-graduate work in serious crime.

The two men had heard that an old lady, Mrs. Mabel Monahan, 63, kept a fortune in cash and jewelry in her Burbank home. Mrs. Monahan was a fragile lady who lived alone. She was lame and walked with a cane. The rumor, which spread throughout the underworld, was unfounded. She had no great fortune in her home.

Perkins and Santo approached Barbara with their plan to rob the old lady. They explained that there would be nothing to it. Barbara's job would be to ring the door bell. When the old lady answered the door, Santo and Perkins, together with gang members John True and Baxter Shorter, would force her back into the house. Once they tied, blindfolded and gagged Mrs. Monahan, it would be an easy matter for them to find out the location of the money and jewels.

Everything went wrong. There are two versions of what transpired when Mrs. Monahan answered her door that night. The result, however, was that Mrs. Monahan was tortured and beaten to death with her own cane. She couldn't reveal the hiding place of any valuables, because they didn't exist.

Using underworld contacts, it didn't take police long to locate the four suspects still alive in the Monahan murder. Before he could be taken into custody, Baxter Shorter had been taken for a ride by unknown hoods and was never seen or heard of again. Perkins and Santo were tried, found guilty and sentenced to death.

John True turned state's evidence and saved his skin. He testified that Barbara had performed the actual killing. He swore that Barbara had wrestled the elderly woman to the ground, held her hair in one hand, while beating her to death with the butt of a pistol and the old woman's own cane. All the while, Mrs. Monahan pleaded for her life.

The jury was asked to believe that Barbara, who stood five feet three inches and weighed 118 pounds had taken it upon herself to mercilessly beat Mrs. Monahan to death, while four husky hoods nonchalantly stood by. Unlike her confederates, Barbara had no history of violent crime.

Barbara did, however, have a propensity for making matters worse than they already were. She came up with a phoney alibi. Barbara swore she was with her former husband, Henry Graham, on March 9, the night of the murder. She positively remembered the date because the argument she had that night with Henry led to their divorce. Henry proved to be no help. He declared that the argument took place on March 7. So much for Barbara's alibi.

A fellow inmate, serving time for manslaughter, was enlisted to get the truth out of Barbara. She and Barbara became good friends. When she told Barbara she could arrange an alibi for a price, Barbara fell for it. The inmate, who had been guaranteed her freedom, arranged a meeting between Barbara and an undercover policeman. His conversation with Barbara was taped. Barbara promised to pay him $25,000 if he would testify that he had spent the night of March 9 with her in a hotel in Encino. The plot was exposed in open court. The jury was left with the idea that only a guilty woman would resort to purchasing an alibi.

John True and the female inmate were set free. Barbara was sentenced to death.

To this day, many believe that while Barbara was definitely in the Monahan home on the night of the murder, she did not commit it. It matters little now.

On the morning of June 3, 1955, Perkins and Santo, seated side by side, were put to death in California's gas chamber. That afternoon, protesting her innocence to the end, Barbara Graham met the same fate.

In 1958, the Barbara Graham story was made into a motion picture entitled *I Want to Live*, starring the late screen actress, Susan Hayward. Miss Hayward's performance won her an Academy Award for her outstanding portrayal of Barbara Graham's turbulent life.

HAND OF DEATH

Ruth Wheeler's two older sisters, Pearl, 24, and Adelaide, 18, had attended Merchants' and Bankers' Business College in New York. As a result of their education, both girls had secured well-paying jobs. Fifteen-year-old Ruth planned on following in their footsteps.

The three Wheeler girls lived with their widowed mother at 313 West 134th St. Each week, they turned over a portion of their pay to their mother. In 1910, all things considered, there were many New Yorkers far worse off than the close-knit Wheeler family.

Ruth was thrilled when Sherman Estey, the principal of the college, called her to report for a job interview. He had received a postcard requesting a stenographer at a real estate office. The card was signed A.W. Wolter, 224 East 75th St. Estey had received other cards from Wolter, but each time he sent a girl to the address, there had been no one in.

Maybe this morning of March 24 would be different. Ruth dressed up in her very best clothing, kissed her mother goodbye and left the apartment.

That evening, Adelaide returned home at 5:30. Pearl came in at 7:30. But where was auburn-haired Ruth? Mother and daughters were frantic. Pearl told Adelaide to stay with their mother. She would go out to find their younger sister. Pearl knew that there were night classes at the college and that Mr. Estey would be there.

From Estey, she received the address of Ruth's job interview. When she appeared at the shabby address, she could find no Wolter listed among the rusty mailboxes in the vestibule. She rang the janitor, John Mohl, who told her there was an A. Wolter living on the top floor back. In fact, that very morning, a young girl with auburn hair had inquired about Wolter. Mohl had directed her to his apartment.

Pearl raced up the stairs and knocked on Wolter's door. A woman, clad only in her nightclothes, answered. As the door opened, Pearl detected the unmistakable odor of fresh paint. The woman didn't answer, but directed her to a bedroom. There on the bed, practically naked, was Albert Wolter.

Albert, 18, was a good-looking young man with a full head of bright blonde hair. He looked up from his bed quizzically at this intrusion of his privacy.

"I am here to get my sister, Ruth Wheeler," Pearl blurted out.

"I don't know what you're talking about. Never heard of her."

Later, Pearl Wheeler was to state that a strange feeling came over her, a feeling that her sister was in that apartment. Pearl kept her head. She beat a hasty retreat to the closest drug store and called police.

In moments, police were at the scene. Together with Pearl and Mohl, they knocked on Wolter's door. Albert invited them all inside. He denied ever knowing Ruth Wheeler. He also denied sending the postcard to her college. Wolter claimed that he was an unemployed bookkeeper and had been out looking for a job until 3:00 that afternoon. At that time, he returned home and busied himself painting the fireplace.

Wolter showed the officers around the apartment. He pointed out that his kitchen window opened onto a fire escape shared by the next apartment. He appeared to have nothing to hide. None of the other tenants in the building could shed any light on the whereabouts of the missing girl. In fact, there was only janitor Mohl's word that a girl matching Ruth's description had been to the building that day. Pearl steadfastly insisted that she felt her sister's presence in the Wolter apartment. That wasn't enough. Later that might, Ruth was officially listed as missing.

Bright and early next morning, Pearl and Adelaide were pestering police to once more search Wolter's apartment. This time, Wolter wasn't present. Mohl used his passkey to gain entrance. Under old clothing in a bureau drawer, police found a rubber stamp, which read, "A.W. Wolter," as well as an ink pad. The signature matched that on the card sent to Mr. Estey at the college.

Police waited for Wolter and his live-in lady friend to return. They were taken into custody and questioned. On Wolter's person police found a notebook. In it was the name, nationality, occupation, education and salary requested by Ruth Wheeler. It was obvious to the investigators that Wolter had gone through the ruse of interviewing the unsuspecting Ruth.

Within an hour of finding this direct link to the missing girl, John Mohl, in a state of hysteria, rushed into the 67th St. police station. Wolter's immediate neighbor, who shared his fire escape, had noticed two burlap bags on the fire escape beside the window. Irritated, he kicked both bags over the side to the alleyway below and informed janitor Mohl. Mohl went down to remove the unsightly bags. Before lugging them away, he opened the smaller of the two. The bag contained ashes, a partially burned undershirt and some hairpins. The larger bag yielded a partially burned human skull.

An army of detectives swarmed over the Wolter apartment. Naturally enough, the fireplace came under close scrutiny. The fireplace opening had been covered with a metal sheet, which had a round hole in the centre to fit a small stovepipe. The pipe had long since been removed and the remaining opening was now covered with a common lithograph.

Coroner Herman W. Holtzhauser removed the metal front of the fireplace. There lay what was left of Ruth Wheeler; a portion of two legs and the charred remains of an arm. A signet ring bearing the initials R.A.W. confirmed the identity of the victim. The ring was one of Ruth's prized possessions.

From the physical evidence, forensic experts were able to ascertain that Ruth had been raped, strangled and gagged before death. Professor John H. Larkin of Columbia University examined the victim's lungs and found them to be full of smoke. He concluded that Ruth had been burned while still alive.

Who was the man who had committed such a horrible crime? Albert Wolter, faced with the overwhelming evidence pointing to his guilt, did not flinch. He professed to know nothing of Ruth Wheeler and her terrible fate. Wolter had arrived in America from Germany three years earlier. He had secured employment with a piano manufacturer, but lost his job when he was caught stealing. At the time of his arrest, he was little more than a bum. He had picked up his lady friend, Katchen Mueller, in a dance hall. Katchen worked in a restaurant and was her lover's sole support.

It was theorized that Wolter raped and strangled Ruth Wheeler and then attempted to burn the body in the fireplace. When this effort proved too difficult, he placed what he could in the two burlap bags, leaving everything behind the fireplace's metal front. This was the reason nothing was discovered during the preliminary search of the apartment. No one dismantled the metal fireplace screen.

In order to disguise the smell of burnt flesh, Wolter had painted the fireplace several times. When he realized the sooner or later, someone would surely look behind the metal screen, he decided to dispose of the body in the burlap bags. All of this was done in the middle of the night in order not to arouse the suspicion of Katchen Mueller. Wolter went to trial admitting nothing. Despite the abundance of evidence, the defence contended that it was possible that Ruth had been killed by someone who had lured her to Wolter's apartment without his knowledge.

All reasonable doubt disappeared when Dr. George S. Huntington, professor of anatomy, took the witness stand. In one of the most dramatic scenarios ever to take place in a courtroom, Dr. Huntington produced the preserved left hand of Ruth Wheeler. Hanging down from the clenched fist were ten human hairs. They were not the distinctive auburn hair of the victim. As everyone in the courtroom stared from the light blonde hair grotesquely hanging from the hand to the light blonde hair of Albert Wolter, it was obvious who had killed Ruth Wheeler.

At 5 a.m. on Jan. 29, 1912, Albert Wolter, still proclaiming his innocence, was strapped into Sing Sing's electric chair, where he paid for his crime with his life.

THE

MOUNTAIN MAN

C laude Dallas had a reputation for being honest, personable, loyal and hard-working. He was also a cold-blooded killer.

In 1970, Claude showed up in Paradise Hill, Nevada. That's the portion of Nevada you never see when you visit Reno or Las Vegas. If ever a place was misnamed, it is Paradise Hill. It's dry. It's dusty. It's desert country. Coyotes yowl and rabbits scurry from sagebrush to sagebrush. A little higher up on the mountains ringing Paradise Valley, cattle graze and are the area's main industry.

When Claude appeared on the scene, he was already a seasoned cowhand. At 5 ft. 10 in. and 165 pounds, he was wiry tough. A man had to be tough around Paradise Hill. Every house in the area contained a couple of guns within easy reach.

Claude had no trouble obtaining employment as a cowhand with one of the big ranches in the area. Soon he gained a reputation as a hard worker and an expert in the use of firearms. Claude was popular among the locals, but never did mix that much. He liked to go out into the Owyhee Desert for long periods of time by himself.

About the only really close friendship Claude developed in Paradise Hill was the bar owner George Nielsen. For years, the 60-year-old boisterous George was something of a father to Claude. They drank most nights, although George was the drinker of the two. Claude like to nurse his beer at the Paradise Hill Bar.

After five years of being a cowboy, Claude turned his enthusiasm for hard work to trapping. He strung his lines in Nevada and across state boundaries into Oregon and Idaho. He trapped coyotes, foxes and bobcats. Bobcats were fetching $200 a pelt in 1975.

No one knows how it started, but Claude was different when it came to trapping. He had no regard for the conservation laws governing his livelihood. He shot wild mustangs to bait his traps illegally. He wasn't above shooting an animal and ringing the carcass with traps.

During his years as a trapper, Claude became an expert at living in the wild. He learned how to subsist off the land. The abundance of pheasants, quail and deer helped. But even here, Claude flouted the law. He always killed more than he could eat.

Over the years, Claude's reputation for disregarding the game laws and for being a true wild west mountain man kept pace. Down at the Paradise Hill Bar, he and George would often laugh at what Claude would do to one of those game wardens if they ever became too uppity.

A friend of Claude's, Jim Stevens, had no way of knowing that someone had lodged a complaint against Claude's illegal trapping practices. Jim enjoyed the mountain man's company. Besides, he was an avid collector of Indian relics and jumped at the chance to spend some time with Claude in the desert country whenever possible. On these occasions, he would bring Claude his mail and groceries.

Jim drove over bumpy terrain and then walked for several hours before arriving at Bull Camp, where he met Claude. A few moments later, they were joined by two Idaho game wardens.

Game warden Bill Pogue, 50, had received a complaint about Claude Dallas poaching in the Owyhee Desert. He had picked up colleague Conley Elms, a giant of a man who tipped the scales at 265 pounds. Elms, 34, had many friends and no known enemies.

Before Jim Stevens could say a word, Pogue asked for his Smith and Wesson. Jim readily handed over his weapon to the game warden, who unloaded it and returned shells and gun to the owner. Pogue noted bobcat skins around the camp and told Claude what they both knew very well - the trapping season wasn't open yet. The tension between the officers and the trapper rose. Jim Stevens looked away. Suddenly a shot rang out. Jim whirled to see Claude bent over in combat style and Bill Pogue on the ground. Claude aimed at Conley Elms and the big man fell. The mountain man then went to his tent, picked up his rifle and proceeded to shoot both dead men in the head.

Jim Stevens thought he might be next, but he was wrong. According to his later testimony, all he could say was, "Why, Claude, why?" His friend answered, "I didn't want to be arrested. They were gonna put the cuffs on me."

With Jim's help, Claude disposed of Elms' body in a nearby river and carried Pogue's body to Jim's vehicle. The two men drove to the Paradise Hill Bar and woke up proprietor George Nielsen. Claude told George that he had just killed two game wardens and wanted to borrow his pickup truck to dispose of one of the bodies. George readily agreed. In minutes, the body was transferred to George's truck. Claude drove into the desert. Some hours later, he dropped off the truck at the bar. Then the mountain man disappeared.

Next day, Jim Stevens and George Nielsen, fearful because of their involvement in the crime, decided to inform attorney Richard Lagarza, who called police immediately.

Utilizing helicopters, police located and recovered Conley Elms' body from the river. The hunt was on for mountain man Claude Dallas. It was to be one of the most extensive manhunts in U.S. history. Claude was spotted all over North America, but the mountain man stayed at large for a year and a half before he was taken into custody near his regular stomping grounds of Paradise Hill. Eventually, Claude revealed the location of Bill Pogue's body.

After Claude's arrest, a strange phenomenon took place among the citizens of Paradise Hill and its environs. Many thought Bill Pogue had been too aggressive in carrying out the letter of the law. Claude claimed it was a "them or me situation." He professed to having killed in self-defence. Others felt that likable Claude Dallas wouldn't kill two men unless he was provoked.

Claude Dallas' trial began on Sept. 15, 1982. The result was not a foregone conclusion. Warden Pogue's reputation for being a stern officer was meticulously reviewed. The jury, after being out for 45 hours, the longest deliberation in Idaho history, reached their verdict. Unbelievably, Claude Dallas was found guilty only of voluntary manslaughter. There were those who felt the verdict was a travesty of justice.

In passing sentence, the presiding judge dismissed the self-defence theory as so much rubbish. He sentenced Claude to 30 years imprisonment in the Idaho State Prison.

On the quiet Sunday night of March 30, 1986, Claude Dallas proceeded to a certain area in the prison yard. Administrative Assistant Steven Crossman figures that Claude had noticed a small area of the prison fence that was not visible to the guards in the tower. Although he had been searched minutes before, he obviously had wire cutters hidden in the prison yard. Claude cut his way through two wire fences. It is believed a confederate drove him away from the prison area in a matter of minutes.

When asked if he had any theories as to Claude Dallas' whereabouts, prison official Crossman said, "We figure he made for the desert country around a little place called Paradise Hill. They call him a survivalist down there. We call him a killer."

Dallas managed to elude capture for a full year before being apprehended outside a convenience store in Riverside, California. He is presently back in prison serving his 30-year-term.

BEHIND HER BACK

Ingenious husbands are always attempting to find new ways to murder unwanted wives. Just when I am certain that I have related every possible wife disposal method, another bizarre modus operandi is brought to my attention.

Today's quaint but deadly yarn has its beginnings at noon on March 9, 1963. That's when 27-year-old Della Rose dashed out of her car parked in the Fordham section of little old New York, claiming that his wife was dead or at least near death. Someone in the fast growing crowd called police, who managed to get to the scene within three minutes. Della was right. His wife Gloria was indeed very dead.

Detectives found Gloria Rose slumped over the steering wheel. There was a hole as big as a baseball in the dead woman's back. The front seat of the car had a large section out, indicating that the fatal shot had torn through the seat and into Gloria's back.

When the rear door of the Ford was opened, investigating officers observed that the floor mat was bunched up and resting against the back of the front seat. Gingerly, they picked up the crumpled mat. Underneath lay a double-barrelled shotgun.

Someone had set a booby trap for Gloria Rose. The stock of the shotgun had been partially sawed away. So had the barrels of the weapon. The relatively large weapon had been cut down to fit the exact space needed to prop the shotgun at an angle which would cause it to discharge directly into the driver's back. The end of the muzzle had been placed in a hole carved out in the back of the front seat.

A length of wire had been used to hold the shotgun in place against the seat. Venetian blind cord was attached to each trigger. The cord led to a metal cleat under the rear seat. A forward adjustment to the front seat would put the muzzle of the gun forward and cause the cord to tighten, thereby discharging the gun. Someone had devised a diabolical death machine for Gloria Rose. Even in the Big Apple, this was a bit different.

Della Rose was beside himself with grief. The weeping, near-faint Della was taken to a station house for questioning. He repeated over and over, "It's all my fault," which was enough to raise the eyebrows of the streetwise New York detectives. Della went on. Evidently, his wife was backing into a parking space. Della looked out the back to make sure she didn't hit the car already parked at the curb.

As he turned around, he spotted a large lump on the floor in the back. He asked Gloria, "What's this?" Gloria replied, "What's what?" Then, according to Della, he reached over the back seat and, feeling something under the floor mat, attempted to lift it up. As he did so, there was a terrible explosion and his wife slumped dead over the wheel.

Well, now, this threw a completely different light on the entire matter. The infernal machine had not worked as the assassin had planned. Detectives sympathized with Della and inquired if he knew who would want his wife dead. Wiping away his tears, Della had a few ideas about that one.

He told detectives that he had been married for about a year and a half. A month before his marriage, several men had beaten him up with the warning that this was only a sample of what would happen if he married Gloria. They also told him that they had been hired by Santo Mordante, Gloria's old boyfriend. Della had reported the assault. Police had questioned Mordante at the time, but had insufficient evidence to lay a charge. Another event Della was quick to relate was the recent break in at his apartment. Six months earlier, thieves had looted his place of clothing, a radio and his car keys. As a matter of routine, police checked Della's story. It was verified in every detail.

The investigation was progressing nicely. If Della's keys had been stolen, the assassin could have entered the car at any time to set up his killing device. Della confirmed that his wife always adjusted the driver's seat forward, as she was accustomed to driving with the steering wheel almost touching her chest. Obviously, something had gone wrong.

Della confirmed that his wife had left their apartment alone at 9 a.m. to meet a friend, Sally Nunzio. After shopping with Sally, she returned home around 11 a.m. Together they drove to his doctor's office to pick up his medical records. This was a necessity, as he was undergoing treatment for an injured back. His back had been troubling him ever since he had taken a bad fall sometime previously. Della's doctor had died and his new physician required his records. Once again, police routinely checked out his story. Sally Nunzio and Della's new physician corroborated his story in every detail.

Meanwhile, police located Gloria's former boyfriend, Santo Mordante. He swore that he had never hired anyone to beat up Della and had been annoyed when he was questioned about it well over a year earlier. He also stated that he had not spoken to nor seen Gloria since her marriage. In fact, he was now a happily married man himself and was indignant at being interrogated concerning a casual girlfriend he had not seen in close to two years.

Experiments with the booby trap indicated that it would not fire when the front seat was adjusted forward. Whoever set the device had used a bit too much Venetian blind cord. The adjusted seat drew the cord taut but did not exert enough pressure to pull the triggers. Detectives asked Della to demonstrate exactly how he had pulled at the device, setting it off. Della was more than anxious to oblige.

A detective sat in the driver's seat. Della sat beside him. A broom had been set up underneath the rear floor mat to simulate the shotgun. Della turned his head slowly and placed his arm over the back seat. He told detectives that it was at this point he noticed the lump on the back floor. At this precise moment, his interrogators asked him to freeze. His exact position was noted by all present.

Della was then taken from the car and a detective of identical height was place in the passenger seat. Once in position, the detective was asked if he could see the bulge on the back floor. Dramatically, he replied that he could see only the top of the back seat. In order to get a view of the rear floor, the detective had to almost stand and crane his head forward. It simply couldn't have happened the way Della had related.

Accused of killing his wife, Della lost his composure. He blurted out, "Oh, God forgive me . . . I loved her so much!"

Della went on to say that he had been acting strangely and that Gloria wanted to put him in a hospital for treatment. He explained that she had threatened to leave him if he didn't enter hospital. Della decided to kill his wife rather than lose her. He purchased the shotgun at a Sears Roebuck store and proceeded to cut down the stock and the barrels. He was well aware that his wife always adjusted the seat forward when she entered the car.

After Gloria went to sleep on Friday night, he went out to his car and set up the killing machine. He then went back to his wife's side in bed. Next morning, when Gloria jumped in her car, Della listened for the report of the double barrel shotgun. Nothing happened. Still, Della figured any jar or bump would set off the triggers. When his wife returned home safe and sound, he knew something was drastically wrong with the mechanism.

When they went out together, Della decided to do the job himself. He reached over, pulled at the shotgun, applying the needed pressure on the cord. The weapon exploded and Gloria Rose was no more.

Ironically, police discovered that Della had been wrong about his wife attempting to have him institutionalized because of his strange behavior. Gloria's family revealed that she had been merely coercing Della into going into hospital to have his injured back properly treated.

In one way, she succeeded. Della was tried and convicted of murder. He was sentenced to life imprisonment, where we can only assume he had sufficient time to clear up his back trouble.

MADMAN
AT THE DOOR

This is the story of one family whose home was invaded by a madman. The Romaines lived on a pleasant street in the peaceful town of Leonia, N.J. What happened to them could happen to anyone.

On Jan. 8, 1975, 28-year-old Didi Wiseman's washing machine was being repaired. She dressed her four-year-old son Bobby, bundled up her laundry and headed for her parents' home at 124 Glenwood Ave. Didi's trip was planned. Her mother, Edwina, her sister, Retta and Retta's boyfriend, Frank Welby, would be busy that morning, and would not be home.

As a result, Didi had volunteered to stay with her 90-year-old bedridden grandmother, Blanche Smith. Another sister, Retta's twin, Randi, planned to leave the house later that morning to visit their father in the hospital. DeWitt Romaine had suffered a massive heart attack but was now recovering in the hospital. The Romaines had experienced sickness, but they also knew great joy. There were a close and loving family.

Shortly after Didi arrived, Randi left for the hospital. Didi prepared lunch for herself and her grandmother. Around 1:30 p.m. there was a knock on the front door. Didi answered. A swarthy man with a receding forehead stated, "I am a John Hancock salesman. Is anyone else at home?" Didi immediately thought something was wrong, but was reassured by the appearance of a small boy with the stranger. Didi correctly thought that the youngster, whom she estimated to be around 12 years old, must be the man's son.

Abruptly, Didi Wiseman was pushed back into the house. The stranger pulled a revolver out of his pocket and, pointing it at little Bobby's head, announced, "This is a robbery. Do as I say and you won't get hurt." Holding Didi firmly by the hair, and now threatening her with a knife held to her throat, he marched her upstairs to make certain Mrs. Smith was an invalid.

The man thrust Didi onto a bed and wrapped adhesive tape around and around her head after putting a kneesock in her mouth. Her nostrils were left exposed, allowing the terrified woman to breathe. Then the intruder hogtied his victim and undressed her. As he stripped her, he ripped her engagement and wedding rings from her fingers. Little Bobby Wiseman was undressed and made to lie beside his mother. Later, Didi would relate that she could feel her son's body beside her and tried in every way she could to comfort the child.

Didi was convinced that she was about to be raped when the doorbell rang. Randi Romaine was home from visiting her father in the hospital. The man grabbed her by the hair and put a pistol to her head as she walked into the house. She passed over $5, all the money she possessed. Accompanied by the stranger and his son, Randi was led upstairs and into the room where her sister and nephew lay bound and naked. She was then ordered to undress. Randi did as she was told. She was tied. Using his adhesive tape, the intruder taped her eyes and put a gag in her mouth. Randi managed to ask, "Are you going to kill us?" The man's son replied, "No."

A few minutes passed. Edwin Romaine, her daughter Retta, and Frank Welby returned home. They were greeted by a swarthy man who pointed a gun at them and commanded, "Do as I say and you won't get hurt."

The three captives were pushed and shoved into the living room. All three were forced to lie on the floor. While the man tied and stripped the two women of their rings, the boy held a gun to Frank's temple. He removed Frank's belt and used it to tie his hands. The doorbell rang.

It was 21-year-old nurse Maria Fasching, who had the misfortune to ring the bell that day. She often dropped around to look in on the elderly Mrs. Smith. She, too, was tied, but not gagged.

Frank Welby was told to get to his feet. He found that he could see his feet and so was able to half hop at the gunman's command. Frank, who stood 6 feet 3 inches tall, thought of somehow attacking the gunman, but felt he had little chance of success. He was forced down into the basement. Once there, he was tied more securely and told to lie on the floor beside the furnace.

Maria Fasching was then forced at gunpoint into the basement. Here the intruder raped her and slit her throat. Maria's screams for help sent chills through the other bound and gagged occupants of the house. In the living room, Retta Romaine, now sure they would all be killed, inched her way under a sofa. Her mother, Edwina, drawing on resources brought to bear by hysteria, pulled her hands free from the cords which bound them. Screaming like a madwoman, she hopped out of her home.

A neighbor spotted her and called police. Sgt. Robert MacDougall responded to the call. Edwina was still screaming in front of the house. As MacDougall cut her legs free, she told him of her ordeal and the madman inside. Walking into the living room, he spotted a trembling hand slowly emerging from underneath the sofa. MacDougall shouted, "Come out with your hands up!" Retta's day of terror had come to an end. MacDougall found Bobby, his mother Didi and Randi, all bound and totally naked. Reinforcements arrived, and it was these officers who found Frank Welby and the body of Maria Fasching in the basement.

The man and boy, who had terrorized a family and killed a nurse, had managed to get away as Mrs. Romaine stood screaming in front of her home.

Some distance from the Romaines', the killer threw away his bloodied shirt. The shirt was recovered. It had been manufactured by the Enro Shirt Co., who, as luck would have it, sold their entire production to one retail outlet, Berg Brothers of Philadelphia. It was reasonable to assume that the owner of the shirt most probably resided in that city. From the laundry mark, the shirt was traced to Bright Sun Cleaners. Proprietor Joseph Fisher knew the owner of the shirt.

"That's Joe Kallinger's shirt," he said, without hesitation. Evidently, Kallinger, a shoemaker by profession, always spilled a certain chemical he worked with on his shirts, which gave them a distinctive odor. Several of his victims in the Romaine home had commented on the unmistakable odor.

Police wanted Joe Kallinger badly. He and his son had pulled off four sex robberies in the previous six weeks. Now the owner of the smelly shirt had murdered and had to be stopped.

Police checked on Kallinger. They found out that Joe had been born in an orphanage and had been adopted at the age of 18 months. His adoptive father had died years earlier, but not before he taught Joe the shoemaking trade. Joe owned his own shop and made a comfortable living. He had married for the first time when only 16 and had two children, a daughter, Anna, now 20, and a son Stephen, 18. After four years of marriage, the Kallingers divorced. Mrs. Kallinger obtained custody of Anna, while Stephen was brought up by his father.

Joe married Betty Bomgard in 1958. They had five children; Joe Jr., who had died at age 14; Mary Jo, 16; Michael, 13; James, 11; and Bonnie Sue, two. Two years before his death, Joe Jr., Mary Jo and Michael walked into a police station and accused their father of abusing them. They displayed scars where their father had whipped and burned them. Kallinger was tried, found guilty and sentenced to 11 months imprisonment.

When Joe Jr. was later found dead under suspicious circumstances, his father was closely questioned by police. However, no direct evidence involving Joe with his son's death was uncovered and the investigation wound down.

Now, for the second time, Joe Kallinger was a prime murder suspect. His photograph was viewed by victims of his four sex attacks, as well as the Romaine family. All picked him as the vicious intruder. It was his 13-year-old son Michael who had accompanied him on his assaults.

Joe Kallinger was picked up at his home by police. A search of the Kallinger residence uncovered several items stolen from the five homes he had looted. Kallinger was charged with armed robbery, wounding, kidnapping, rape, theft and murder.

Kallinger proved to be an interesting study. Other than the child abuse charges brought against him by his children, he had not been in any previous serious trouble. Even these charges are a bit tarnished. After the fact, the three children recanted their accusations, claiming they were attempting to gain revenge on their father for being such a strict disciplinarian.

Joe attempted to prove himself insane in order to escape punishment. He underwent psychiatric examination by a number of doctors, many of whom gave conflicting opinions regarding their patient's sanity. Joe's favorite yarn was that God had sent him to earth to help people whose brains were lopsided because of poorly designed shoes. He claimed the devil was constantly chasing him, but could never catch him because, as everyone knew, he was a butterfly.

Butterfly or no, Joe Kallinger was found fit to stand trial for his crimes. On Sept. 18, 1975, a jury took less than an hour to find him guilty of robbery, burglary and kidnapping. He was sentenced to 30 to 80 years imprisonment. A year later, he stood trial for armed robbery, breaking and entering, possession of a dangerous weapon, assault with a dangerous weapon, open lewdness, contributing to the delinquency of a minor and murder. He was found guilty and sentenced to life imprisonment.

Michael Kallinger, a minor, never stood trial nor gave evidence. He was sent to an institution for boys for an indefinite period.

In 1984, Joseph Kallinger confessed to murdering his son, Joe Jr., years earlier and another boy, Jose Collazo, age 11. He was tried for these two crimes and received two further life sentences. He is presently serving these sentences at Fairview State Prison in Pennsylvania.

MURDER
AT THE OPERA

The curtain at the Metropolitan Opera House in New York came down at the conclusion of the ballet Don Quixote. As the applause subsided for Russian dancers Valery and Galina Panov, violinist Helen Hagnes Mintiks placed her violin under her chair and walked away to her death.

Helen was raised in Aldergrove, B.C., about 30 miles east of Vancouver. As a child, her musical gifts were obvious. At three, she was winning prizes at music festivals. As she grew up, she continued to strive for a musical career. Helen attended Western Washington University and later received her bachelors and masters degrees from the Juilliard School of Music in New York City.

Europe beckoned. Helen studied at the Cigiana Academy in Siena, Italy and at the Institute for Advanced Musical Training in Montreux, Switzerland. On her return from Europe, she met and wed American sculptor, Janis Mintiks.

On July 23, 1980, Helen was performing at the Met. At intermission, she placed her violin under her chair. It was precisely 9:29 p.m. At 1 a.m., her husband grew apprehensive. He called police when colleagues showed up at his apartment inquiring about his wife's whereabouts.

By 3 a.m. police were taking the disappearance seriously. When they heard that Helen had left her violin behind, they knew something was amiss. No musician would leave the orchestra pit for any length of time without his or her instrument.

What had happened to Helen from the moment she left her chair? No one seemed to know. Throughout the wee hours of that morning, detectives learned that

Helen had her early roots in Canada. Maybe she unexpectedly returned to British Columbia. Her husband, Janis, was distraught and mystified. A fellow musician had seen Helen leave her violin behind. None of this information proved fruitful, although detectives heard that Helen planned to spend intermission looking for Valery Panov.

Around 8 a.m., a maintenance man told detectives that he had found a pair of women's shoes on the sixth floor roof. He had been there to routinely turn on an air conditioning fan. Once on the sixth floor, a detective peered down one of the shafts leading three storeys below. There, at the base of the shaft, lay Helen's nude body. Her hands were tied behind her back. A rag was stuffed in her mouth.

This was the stuff of sensational headlines. A beautiful blonde violinist thrown to her death down an air conditioning shaft at the famous Metropolitan Opera House. Within hours, police were no longer looking for a killer. They were hunting the 'Phantom of the Opera'.

In reality, police knew they had a high profile crime on their hands. They also realized it wouldn't be easy to solve. The interior of the Met is a jungle of catwalks, hallways, dressing rooms, storage space, closets and literally scores of other dark, little used areas. Over 300 stage hands and other behind the scenes employees were on the premises at the time of the killing, not to mention an audience of over 3000 patrons out front enjoying the performance.

Police felt someone within the building had murdered Helen. The largest number of officers ever deployed to investigate a single murder case in New York was assembled to work on the Met murder case.

After interviewing scores of opera employees, detectives found a woman who had seen Helen after she left the orchestra pit. The woman had been with Helen on elevator number 12. She told detectives a man had also been on the elevator. He and Helen had spoken to each other. Helen had asked him for directions to Panov's dressing room. Helen and the man got off at C level. That was all the woman knew. She gave police a vague description of a white man, whom she supposed worked at the Met.

Meanwhile, an autopsy indicated that Helen had been alive when she was thrown down the air conditioning shaft. She had not been raped. The time of death was established at no more than one and a half hours after Helen left the orchestra.

And so Helen Hagnes Mintiks, gifted violinists, was murdered. Her death came at the same time as the ballet *Miss Julie* was being performed on the stage. As closely as they could estimate, police believed Miss Julie died on stage at the same time that

Helen plunged three storeys to her death.

The first real break in the case came when police found a fingerprint at the crime scene. The entire staff of the Metropolitan Opera House was asked to submit to fingerprinting. At the same time, they were photographed and asked to fill out a questionnaire, stating where they were during the crucial hours around the time of Helen's death.

Two employees refused to have their prints taken. They had moral objections and were quickly eliminated as suspects. A third man, stagehand Craig Crimmons, 21, submitted to being fingerprinted, but acted extremely nervous. His print matched the one found on a pipe at the scene of the crime.

Crimmons was questioned on several occasions. Police were sure they had their man and they were right. Crimmons confessed. He told of meeting Helen by chance on the elevator. He pretended to help her find Panov's dressing room. After they got off the elevator, he made a crude suggestion to Helen. She hauled off and slapped him.

The man took out a hammer and threatened the terrified woman. He forced her to walk down five flights of stairs. On a small landing, Helen attempted to fight her way to freedom. Crimmons held the hammer in a threatening manner and Helen subsided. He commanded her to strip and she complied. Crimmons attempted intercourse, but was unsuccessful. Helen was told to dress. One more, she complied.

We will never know what thoughts raced through Helen's mind at that moment. Maybe she felt that her luck had changed. She had avoided being raped. Now to escape with her life.

Helen was forced to walk up stairs to level A, the first floor, then up more stairs to the third floor. Here the pair scuffled briefly. Helen's bobby pins and her pen were found on the floor. Up to the sixth floor they walked. The roar of air conditioning made conversation difficult.

Helen's hands were tied behind her back and her ankles were bound together. Crimmons left her, but not for long. He turned. Helen had managed to loosen the ropes around her ankles. Quickly, Crimmons rushed to her side. This time he tied her more securely and stuffed a rag in her mouth. He then took a knife and cut away his victim's clothing. The clothing was thrown down an air shaft.

Now the killer was in a dilemma. Helen squirmed. Surely to let her live would lead to his identification. Helen was picked up and thrown to her death.

Crimmons was tried for the murder of Helen Hagnes Mintiks. In June 1981, he faced two separate murder charges. After 11 hours of deliberation, a New York jury acquitted Crimmons on a charge of intentional murder. However, he was convicted of murder committed during the commission of a felony - in this case, rape.

Craig Crimmons was sentenced to 20 years to life imprisonment. He is currently incarcerated at the Ossining Correctional Facility, better known as Sing Sing.

BEATING A BULLY

When he was just a kid, no one liked Kenrex McElroy. His name was Kenneth Rex McElroy, but everyone down Skidmore, Missouri way called him Kenrex.

Kenrex was a handful right from the beginning. Just for fun, he would douse a cat with kerosene and set the poor creature on fire. A big, burly youth, he had no trouble beating up any kid who chose not to have similar opinions on any subject. By the time he was in sixth grade, he had had enough of school and never did learn to read.

Kenrex grew up to be a farmer, and a rather prosperous one at that. There is a longstanding rumor around town that ol' Kenrex did more hog rustling than farming. At any rate, he always carried a large wad with him whenever he drove into town. On those occasions, the 450 citizens of Skidmore stood aside, and with good reason, too. Kenrex, all 230 pounds of him, usually sported a rifle or shotgun. And he didn't mind using it one little bit.

He frightened half the population of the town the day he shot up the side of the garage on Main St. Then there was the time he sprayed the grocery store ceiling with shotgun pellets. There didn't seem to be much anyone could do. Sure, the local law could take their lives in their hands and slap Kenrex in jail for a few days. But who would testify against him knowing what awaited them upon the town bully's release?

If Kenrex's social life left a lot to be desired, so did his marital escapades. He went through several wives and sired a total of 12 children. Sooner or later, all his wives, with one exception, left him.

Things got worse. Kenrex shot Romaine Henry in the leg for no better reason than that he had heard a rumor that Henry had bad-mouthed him. If Kenrex knew the truth, according to his logic, he would have to shoot all 450 residents of Skidmore.

One day in July 1981, Kenrex got into an argument with 72-year-old grocer Ernest Bowencamps. The argument came to an abrupt halt when Kenrex gave the grocer a shotgun blast in the face. Miraculously, Ernest survived. This time the blatancy of the attack and the seriousness of the injury predicated legal action.

Kenrex was arrested and convicted of the assault, the only time he was convicted of anything. However, he was soon free after posting a large bond. A few days later, the town bully strolled into town and swaggered down Main St. carrying a rifle, just as bold as brass.

It was too much. The town had suffered too long. About 75 good citizens held a little meeting in the American Legion Town Hall. We do not know exactly what went on at that meeting, but we do know that certain things were decided.

Right after the meeting, the menfolk of Skidmore retired to D and G's on Main St., the local watering hole and poolroom. Bellys up to the bar, they ordered beers from bartender Red Smith and were surprised when they were told that there would be no charge for beer that day.

Kenrex McElroy and his wife Trena sat quietly at the bar. Big Kenrex sucked on a beer. He had never seen that many people in the bar that early in the morning. A couple of locals picked up cues and began shooting eight ball. The place took on an eerie silence. The locals stopped drinking. About the only noise was the sharp crack of the balls on the pool table.

Kenrex and Trena felt uneasy. They left the bar and strolled outside to their pickup truck. En masse, the Skidmore men followed. The truck was surrounded. No one argued. No one explained. Trena McElroy is the only one who will talk about what happened next.

"A man walked across the street, pulled a rifle out of his pickup and started firing. He fired four times and I pleaded with him to stop." But the man didn't stop. Many in the crowd took refuge in doorways. Some dashed around corners. Others simply watched as slugs tore into Kenneth Rex McElroy. Big, 46-year-old Kenrex slumped over the steering wheel. He wouldn't bother anyone anymore. He was very dead.

Surely, members of the group surrounding the truck would be arrested. Surely, the gunman, who made no attempt to leave the scene, would be charged with murder. No such thing happened. A grand jury refused to indict anyone for the killing. Not one person in a crowd estimated to consist of between 60 and 80 individuals, could be found who would corroborate Mrs. McElroy's eyewitness account of the execution.

Nodaway County prosecutor David Baird had the unusual experience of prosecuting Kenrex only a few weeks earlier. It was he who gained the only conviction on Kenrex's record. Now he would be in charge of prosecuting Kenrex's killer.

The wheels of justice turn slowly. First, a circuit judge called a grand jury (equivalent to our preliminary hearing). A jury of 12, requiring a majority of nine, has to decide if there is probable cause that someone committed a felony. The suspected party is then indicted and stands trial. Sixty witnesses were called over a period of ten days. The grand jury failed to indict anyone.

The second judicial body to be assembled was a Missouri coroner's jury. Six citizens make up the jury. They listened to several witnesses, including the deceased's wife, Trena. She actually named the man who pulled the trigger. The jury ruled that the deceased was killed by person or persons unknown.

Finally, the federal system got into the act. A grand jury was impaneled in Kansas City. They too failed to indict.

Things haven't changed that much down Skidmore way since the McElroy killing. Red Smith doesn't tend bar any more at the D and G. In fact, the D and G is under new ownership. Robin Montgomery bought the bar, which she naturally enough calls the Robin's Nest.

People are a bit reluctant to talk about the McElroy case. Q. Goslee is typical. When I asked him what kind of a man Kenrex McElroy was, Goslee answered without hesitation, "Kind of a bully, but he ain't no more."

10

AROUND THE WORLD

A DEADLY FRIEND
(SOUTH AFRICA)

Marthinius Rossouw was born in Cape Town, South Africa, in 1938. Being the son of a railway worker it was quite natural that by the time he was 16 he was employed as a laborer on the railway. Trying to upgrade himself, he moved from job to menial job, until finally he gravitated to the diamond mines. In January 1961 he met Dietrich Von Schauroth; the meeting was destined to change both their lives.

Von Schauroth had a far different background from Rossouw's. He had legitimately inherited the title of baron from his father. He lived with his wife in a luxurious, palatial home, deriving a large income from investments in sheep farming and diamonds.

These two men from such different walks of life became dear friends. In the months following their first meeting they were seldom apart. Von Schauroth was a generous friend. He always treated his less educated and less cultured buddy with courtesy and respect. Maybe more important, he always picked up all the tabs for food and liquor.

On the morning of March 25, 1961, Dietrich Von Schauroth's body was found in an open field near Milnerton, five miles north of Cape Town. He had been shot twice in the head with a Beretta pistol. Within the next 48 hours the investigation into Dietrich's death led to his dear friend Rossouw. Because he gave conflicting stories about his activities on the night of the murder, Rossouw was held for questioning and finally arrested for murder. His trial, which started on September 12, 1961, may be one of the strangest ever held anywhere.

Rossouw pleaded not guilty to murder but confessed that he had shot his friend. He claimed that he had pulled the trigger because Von Schauroth had pleaded with him to do it. Looking at it from his point of view, he had aided his friend in committing suicide.

Let's start at the beginning.

While it appeared that Von Schauroth was a wealthy man, it was uncovered that he had made several disastrous business deals and was, in effect, broke. In the several months previous to his death, he had insured his life for over £200,000, making his wife the beneficiary. He realized that none of the policies would pay off if he committed suicide, so he decided to ask his friend to kill him.

At first Rossouw thought the whole idea was some sadistic joke. Then on the night of March 24, Von Schauroth informed Rossouw that he was serious and that the time was now. The two friends drove out to a deserted area near Milnerton, where Von Schauroth parked his car. Both men got out of the vehicle. Von Schauroth produced the Beretta and gave it to Rossouw.

Rossouw claimed he objected. Von Schauroth pleaded with him, explaining that he was broke and didn't want to live any longer. If his friend would only pull the trigger, he would leave his wife a wealthy woman. Von Schauroth told Rossouw that there was £5,000 in it for him. All he had to do was show up at Von Schauroth's bank on the day after the shooting and collect. The arrangements had already been made; no questions would be asked.

Von Schauroth turned his back on his friend and said, "Shoot me." Rossouw said, "Goodbye friend, we shall meet again." With this brief exchange he pumped two slugs into Von Schauroth's head. You could hear a pin drop in court at this incredible conversation was being recalled.

To add further credence to the story, a letter had been confiscated from Rossouw's wife, Johanna. A guard had noticed it tucked between the pages of a book as she was leaving her husband's jail cell. The letter was most enlightening. It was read aloud in court by the attorney general while Johanna sobbed.

Dearest darling,

I do not know what will happen to me. If I am lucky I shall get a few years' imprisonment but dearest, if it so happens that I am condemned to death, remember that in spite of all our troubles I always loved you. Your own husband has shot Dietrich Von Schauroth. It was also a bitter experience for me, but I released him from his troubles. He had no happiness. I relieved him of his troubles.

The letter amounted to a remarkable written confession, which tended to verify Rossouw's claim that Von Schauroth had asked to be shot. It was also a confession of murder.

The prosecution was quick to point out that even if Rossouw's story was true, it was still a matter of cold-blooded murder without extenuating circumstances in the eyes of the law. The jury evidently agreed. They took only one hour to find Rossouw guilty of murder. He was sentenced to death.

An interesting sidelight to this strange case was the disposal of the insurance money. The insurance companies felt that Rossouw's story was true and, despite the murder conviction, that Von Schauroth was instrumental in hastening his own death. Von Schauroth's estate ended up accepting a settlement of only £10,000.

On June 19, 1962, Rossouw walked to the gallows singing "Nearer My God to Thee."

STRANGER THAN FICTION (AUSTRALIA)

How to commit the perfect murder? Since Cain slew Abel, perpetrators of the most horrendous of all crimes have been trying to come up with novel approaches. Detective-fiction writers rack their brains to discover original ways for murderers to kill their victims. Seldom has any real-life killer followed the example of a fictional murderer - but it has happened.

In the late 1920s a mystery writer in Western Australia, Arthur Upfield, was searching for a way in which his fictional detective, Napoleon Bonaparte, could solve a murder. In the story Upfield's killer shot his victim, then took the body into dense, burned-over woodland. A huge white-hot wood fire effectively burned the corpse. Upfield's killer then pounded the victim's ashes into a powder in a large vat. The fictional killer then sifted the remains through a sieve, thereby retrieving the victim's false teeth, a bullet, and some small bones.

The burned carcass of a kangaroo was dragged over the scene and left on top of the scattered powder. The bullet, bones, and teeth were disposed of at a distant location.

The plot for the perfect crime was so airtight that Napoleon Bonaparte couldn't find a clue. There didn't seem to be a loophole whereby the case could be solved. Upfield described the plot to his friends, asking them to help Bonaparte out of his dilemma. Despite the offer of a pound reward, no one was able to come up with a solution.

Louis Carron, a ranch hand who worked at a large camel-breeding spread at Narndee Station, thought he had the answer. Why not have a small hole develop in the sieve, unknown to the killer, and let a piece of bone and some identifying object, such as a belt buckle, fall through? Bonaparte would establish that a body had existed and trace the buckle back to the victim.

Carron received his pound and an autographed copy of the book which followed - *The Sands of Windee*. Our story should end here, but it doesn't. A short time later Louis Carron disappeared. Upfield reported the coincidental disappearance to the police in Perth, the closest city to Narndee Station.

Ranch hands have been known to pull up stakes without notifying their friends or their employers, but Carron was different. He had a girlfriend in Perth whom he planned to marry. She swore to the police that she and Louis had not had a lover's squabble, and she could think of no reason why her boyfriend had dropped out of sight. She mentioned another revealing fact. She told the police that Louis had a distrust of banks and always carried a large amount of money in gold coins on his person. He had a little bag in which he carried his gold. It opened by means of a drawstring which ran through a metal ring.

The investigating officers now had a possible reason for the disappearance. Could Carron have been killed for his money? They traced his last paycheque and discovered it had been cashed three days after his reported disappearance. The signature on the back of the cheque was a forgery. In fact, the forgery wasn't very good. Someone had put a little circle over the 'i' in Louis instead of the dot which Carron always used.

The police checked the handwriting of all Carron's fellow ranch hands, and sure enough, they found one who circled the 'i' rather than dotting it.

Joe Williams had two 'i's in his name, and he always put a little circle over them. When questioned he admitted having quarrelled with Carron. He even admitted to disliking the man intensely but claimed he had nothing to do with his disappearance. Joe could account for all his time at the ranch and, therefore, could not have had anything to do with the murder of Louis Carron, if a murder had in fact taken place.

Was it possible that whoever forged Carron's paycheque was cunning enough to put little circles over the 'i's, so that Joe Williams, who had openly quarrelled with Carron, would be suspected? The police thought that this might have been the case. If so, one of Carron's 50 fellow ranch hands would have had knowledge of William's writing habits and Carron's large bag of gold coins.

The police searched the burned bush area around Narndee Station. After a month of hard work they found an almost completely burned copy of *The Sands of Windee*. It occurred to the police that the killer might have been following the plot of the book to dispose of the body of the very man who was instrumental in providing the author with the solution to the fictional murder.

Around the time that the book was found, police received word that ranch hand Snowy Rowles was spending far too much money in Perth. A secret search of his quarters revealed 50 gold coins, not proof of murder, but strong circumstantial evidence. The temptation to spend the gold coins had proved too much for Rowles. He continued to live it up in Perth.

A year had passed since Louis Carron had disappeared. The search in the burned bush area around Narndee Station was carried on sporadically until finally police found the carcass of a burned kangaroo, lying on a caked bed of ashes. At the police laboratory in Perth the ashes were minutely examined. A small human bone was discovered among the ashes, as well as a metal ring. Louis Carron's girlfriend identified the ring as a part of the bag in which he kept his gold coins.

Rowles was picked up and confronted with the burned book, the metal ring, and the bone fragment. After some sparring, he confessed to killing Carron. He had borrowed *The Sands of Windee* from Carron and thought the plot was foolproof. Just as in the fictional solution, he had somehow missed the small hole in the sieve which had allowed the bone fragment and the metal ring to be found a year later.

Yes, he got the bright idea to put a circle over the 'i' in Louis's signature so that Joe Williams would be suspected.

Snowy Rowles stood trial for murder, was convicted, and executed.

By providing Upfield with the solution to a fictional plot, Carron unwittingly gave his killer the idea that led to his murder. Ironically, the murderer followed the book in every detail, even to inadvertently providing police with the same clues as the fictional killer had.

BULLET FOR
A BIKER
(FRANCE)

Every twenty minutes of every day a Frenchman or Frenchwoman dies from alcoholism. In some parts of France alcohol is guzzled by the man of the house, sipped by the lady of the house, and added to the children's milk to warm the cockles of their hearts on their way to school.

In the tiny village of Saint-Macaire-en-Mauges near Cholet, in western France, the Bauvier family existed in less than ideal conditions. Each day Papa Bauvier blessed the dawn with a full tumbler of locally distilled pure alcohol. Papa gradually went downhill as the day wore on. By nightfall, Mama Bauvier strapped him to his bed. This had the effect of curtailing Papa's annoying little habit of strolling through the Bauvier's two sparse rooms striking out wildly at anything that moved.

In order to endure Papa's ungentlemanly conduct Mama Bauvier was not averse to testing the local grog herself. She never became a confirmed alcoholic but sort of went around in a stupor all day long.

Into this rather unstable marriage were born two daughters, Leone and Georgette. Both attended the village school, but it was soon apparent that the two children did not have similar abilities. Leone was a pleasant little girl, although she was far from attractive. Her nose was decidedly oversize, and her eyes were placed just a touch too far apart. She got along well enough with her fellow pupils and her teacher, but she was a slow learner.

Georgette was another kettle of fish. She seemed to absorb her schoolwork without effort. She was two years older than Leone. By the time both girls were teenagers, their future paths were well defined. Georgette, at 18, left home and entered a nearby convent to become a nun. It is difficult from this distance to ascertain if Georgette's motives were entirely religious or if she would have joined a high-wire act to get away from her drooling, wild, alcoholic father. Her motives matter little. Georgette became a nun.

Leone left school at the age of 14. She worked in a shoe factory and it was her salary which kept the booze on the table and a roof, such as it was, over the Bauvier's collective heads. Now, at the age of 16, she not only lacked her older sister's companionship, she also was continually unfavorably compared to the success of the family - Georgette, the nun. With Papa swinging at her and Mama screaming at her, is it any wonder Leone sought out the companionship of boys her own age?

In 1950, at the age of 18, Leone found an escape in the arms of the local rural lads, who were only too willing to oblige in any way they could. Leone worked hard all day and was abused at home, but at night she was loved.

Saint-Macaire-en-Mauges was not the largest hamlet in the world. Leone soon became known as a loose woman. She didn't care, for she always hoped that one of her lovers would turn out to be serious. Once she even came close. A boy in the French Air Force fell in love with her. She was crazy about him. They planned to marry. A month later he was killed in an accident. Leone became so despondent she contemplated suicide. Then, one night while attending a dance at Cholet, she met Emile Clenet.

Emile was a good-looking, muscular lad of 22, who made his living working as a mechanic in a garage in Nantes. The young people were immediately attracted to each other. As they danced together, all night, Leone thought of love, marriage, and children. Emile thought of a roll in the hay. Leone wouldn't hear of it. She insisted on a hotel room.

That very first night Emile and Leone gratified their strong physical attraction for each other. Thereafter, each Sunday afternoon, Emile would leave Nantes on his motorcycle and drive halfway towards Cholet. Leone would pedal her little ankles off driving her bicycle to meet her lover at the appointed spot. All week Emile worked in the garage, but each Sunday he made love to Leone far into the night.

Leone was deeply in love with Emile. Emile, while at first infatuated with his new romance, little by little began to tire of a regular diet of Leone. Soon he was looking at other girls. Then he took to directing cutting remarks towards Leone, which hurt her to the quick.

Leone became pregnant and was thrilled at the thought of having Emile's baby. She convinced herself that the impending blessed event would bring Emile back to her. She thought she heard the faint peal of wedding bells. Emile, rascal that he was, did not take kindly to the news that he was soon to become a papa. He instructed Leone to have an abortion. Heartbroken, the simple peasant girl did as she was told.

We will never know Leone's intention when she purchased a .22 automatic pistol from the gun shop. Possibly she contemplated suicide. Maybe she had other motives. Later, she was not able to express her true feelings, but after the abortion she carried the pistol in her purse at all times.

The affair, which was not surviving by the slimmest of threads, came thundering down around Leone's head. During one of those chill French autumns, Emile casually mentioned that he was leaving France for good. He had accepted a position in North Africa. Leone asked her lover point blank, "Then you have no intention of ever marrying me?"

"No, never," came the crushing reply.

At long last, the truth was evident to Leone. As the lovers prepared to part, Leone got on her bicycle. Emile mounted his motorcycle. Leone dismounted and went to her lover's side. "Kiss me for the last time, Emile." As she said the words, she draped one arm around her lover's neck and drew his cheek to hers. With her other hand, she extracted the pistol from her purse and placed it gently against Emile's neck. As she kissed him, she squeezed the trigger.

The police picked Leone up at the convent where her sister Georgette was a nun.

Leone's murder trial was not dramatic. All the pertinent facts of the case were openly attested to by the parties involved. The defence attempted to illustrate Leone's upbringing by dragging her incoherent father to the witness stand.

Ironically, Leone was still being compared to her sister, just as her mother used to do when they were children. The prosecution emphasized that her poor upbringing did not excuse her actions. Didn't Georgette come from the same home, and as everyone could see, Georgette had become a nun.

Leone was sentenced to life in Haguenau Prison.

WHERE'S SAM?
(NEW ZEALAND)

Every country in the world has its infamous rural crimes. While murder down on the farm is rare, the ones which do occur are often classics.

New Zealand's entrée into the cowardly art of annihilation took place in 1933 in a district known as Ruawaro, about 60 miles south of Auckland. Here dairy farms spread for miles; cattle contentedly roam the fields. The hardworking farmers are oblivious to the tensions and stresses of their urban counterparts in Auckland.

Sam Lakey and his wife, Christobel, were middle-aged, industrious farmers. They toiled from sun-up to sundown, providing for their dairy herd. Like most farmers, their chores on the farm were repetitious, being carried out at the same time each day.

On Sunday, October 15, 1933 at 4 o'clock, the Lakeys' immediate neighbor, Mrs. Stevens, saw the couple drive their 35 cows to the cowshed for milking. This procedure was followed at 4 o'clock each day, but on this particular day Mrs. Stevens' nonchalant glance towards the Lakey farm was to take on an unexpected importance. Other than their killer, Mrs. Stevens was the last person to see the Lakeys alive.

Later Mrs. Stevens saw the cows outside in their paddock. She assumed the animals had been turned out after being milked. Next morning Mrs. Stevens and her husband rose bright and early to milk their own cows, as was their custom. They were taken aback when they noticed that the Lakey cows were still in their paddock. For the first time something unusual had been observed at the Lakey farm.

Mr. Stevens, together with another neighbor, walked over to the Lakey farm. Receiving no response to their shouts, they entered the house.

The morning fire had not been lit. The previous evening's meal was still on the stove, and the Lakeys' bed had not been slept in. Above all, the Lakeys' cows were moving about uncomfortably in the paddock. They had not been milked, a chore no dairy farmer would neglect. The Lakeys were nowhere to be found.

Mr. Stevens contacted the police. News of the disappearance spread throughout the district. In the close-knit farm community it seemed inconceivable that a normal, well-established couple could simply vanish. Surely they had met with foul play.

This theory soon proved to be tragically accurate when Mrs. Lakey's body was found under some old sacks beside the farm's duck pond. Although Mrs. Lakey's body was on dry land, her head was submerged in the pond. The upper portion of her body was badly bruised and cut. An autopsy indicated that death was due to drowning. It was obvious to the authorities that she had been beaten unconscious before being placed face down in the pond.

No sign of Sam Lakey could be found. No one could believe that the steady, hard-working farmer had killed his wife and fled. All the farmers in the district were questioned, but Sam had not been seen.

A neighboring farmer, Bill Bayly, came up with a plausible theory. He suggested that Mrs. Lakey may have fallen, striking her head on some rocks, tumbling face first into the pond. Sam may have panicked, thinking that he might be accused of his wife's murder. He could have decided to cover the body and disappear.

Police considered this theory, but dismissed it, believing that despite the panic Sam would not leave without taking some of his worldly goods with him. Other than a double-barreled shotgun and a rifle, nothing was missing from the farmhouse.

Investigating officers formed the opinion that Sam had definitely met with foul play. With this in mind they scanned the area for known enemies of the Lakeys. They were surprised to discover that there was bad blood between none other than Bill Bayly and the missing Sam.

When questioned, Bayly passed off the disagreements as minor, but to detectives the differences appeared far more serious. Some months before the murder Bayly had made a deal with Sam. He would graze some sheep on Lakey's land with the understanding that some of the meat would be turned over to Sam when the animals were butchered. The two men argued bitterly when Sam accused Bayly of holding out on his portion of the lamb.

Another item of contention occurred when Sam asked Bayly for permission to cut a road through his property. Bayly vehemently refused. There was no doubt about it. There was no love lost between the two men. Bill Bayly became a suspect.

Detectives searched Bayly's farm, where they discovered several old wooden farm implements which had been recently whittled. The stained shavings from the implements were found on the ground. When sent to a lab in Auckland the stains on the shavings or chips proved to be human blood. Someone had gone over the farm, paring away bloodstains. Bayly's bloodstained knife was also found.

All of these incriminating bits of evidence convinced the New Zealand police that Bayly was the killer. Still, they were faced with a perplexing problem - where was the body of Sam Lakey?

Police began the meticulous search for clues for which the old murder case is remembered to this day. Scattered about the district were small swamps, called water holes by the local farmers. One of these water holes was located no more than 140 yards from Bayly's farmhouse. It was decided to probe for foreign objects under the soft, mudlike soil of the water hole. In this way detectives found the shotgun and rifle missing from the Lakey home.

Meanwhile, criminologists at the Criminal Registration Department in Wellington had produced blown-up photographs of Bayly's knife illustrating every nick and groove in the steel. They did the same thing with the bloodstained shavings found on the floor of Bayly's barn. The indentations in the knife matched exactly those in the shavings. There was no doubt whatever that Bayly's knife had been used to cut away the bloodstained wood.

Detectives proceeded to take apart Bayly's farm piece by piece in a search for clues. Stuck to a shovel they found bits of ashes containing traces of bone and charcoal. For the first time police had an indication that Bayly might have burned Sam's body.

In conjunction with this find, a neighbor now remembered seeing great billows of smoke emanating from Bayly's cowshed on the night of the Lakeys' disappearance. In some nearby bushes police found one half of a charred benzine drum. Fragments of burned bone adhered to the drum.

The discovery which put the lid on the case occurred when police found a makeshift grave containing artificial teeth, pieces of clothing, and bone fragments. In all, fifty-five pieces of ribs, vertebrae, bits of skull, and a thighbone were recovered.

Bill Bayly was arrested and charged with the murder of Sam Lakey. His trial began in Auckland on May 21, 1934, and lasted 29 days. More than three hundred gruesome exhibits were displayed at the sensational trial, while a total of 77 witnesses were called.

The prosecution maintained that Bayly literally obliterated Sam's body by burning it in the intense heat of the benzine drum. The effectiveness of this procedure was illustrated by the burning of a lamb in the same manner. After the inferno died down only the ashes remained. The prosecution also maintained that Bayly intended the same fate for Mrs. Lakey, but didn't have time to finish the job and had to leave her submerged in the duck pond.

After deliberating only one hour, the New Zealand jury found Bayly guilty. He was executed at Mount Eden Gaol, Auckland, on July 30, 1934.

DID MRS. KIRWAN DROWN?
(IRELAND)

There may not be greater strain placed upon our mental faculties than to study those rare murder cases where, despite the jury's verdict, we are still left with the perplexing dilemma - was the defendant really guilty? Today's nostalgic trip down the murderous highways and byways of the past has baffled students of the macabre for over a hundred years.

An island, aptly called Ireland's Eye, lies about a mile off the harbor of Howth in County Dublin, Ireland. Years ago its fine stretch of sandy beach and lush vegetation made it a picturesque setting for family outings.

A Howth fisherman, Patrick Nangle, picked up extra income by ferrying families and young couple across to the island for picnics. It was his custom to get a pickup time from his fares when he dropped them off.

On Monday, September 6, 1852, Patrick delivered 35-year-old William Kirwan and his attractive 30-year-old wife, Marie Louisa, to Ireland's Eye. It was not the first time Patrick had delivered the Kirwans to the island. Kirwan was an artist from Dublin who was spending six weeks in Howth. He obviously found the scenery of Ireland's Eye a perfect subject for his brush and palette.

To pass the time, his wife often swam while he painted. The Kirwans had been married for twelve years but had not been blessed with a family. This was to be the last day of their holiday. They were scheduled to return to Dublin the following day. Marie Louisa would never leave Ireland's Eye alive.

At approximately 7:00 p.m. a fishing boat glided past the island. The only man above deck was the steersman, Thomas Larkin. The sea was calm, all was quiet, when suddenly the pastoral quiet was shattered by a blood-curdling scream, which seemed to emanate from Ireland's Eye.

Larkin could see the shoreline plainly in the fading light but could see no living thing. About five minutes later he heard another piercing scream. The boat was now farther from the island, and so the scream was not as loud. A few minutes later he heard a third, faint scream and then all was quiet. Larkin was so unnerved that he later mentioned the screams to his mates belowdeck, who had quite naturally heard nothing.

While walking through her garden in Howth, Alicia Abernethy heard the screams a mile across the water. Catherine Flood, a domestic working in Howth, opened the back door to take a break from her work. She too heard the horrible screams. Hugh Campbell happened to be staring out over the water when he heard the screams. All three natives of Howth mentioned the incident to acquaintances.

Patrick Nagle left Howth to pick up the Kirwans. He arrived at the island at about 8:00 p.m., accompanied by his cousin Michael and two local men who had gone along for the ride.

Kirwan was waiting for the boat, but Marie Louise was nowhere to be seen. Quite naturally, Nangle asked where she was. Kirwan replied, "I have not seen her for the last hour and a half." The fisherman displayed some displeasure. He did not relish the idea of hunting for an irresponsible woman with darkness falling over the island.

Kirwan pointed towards a narrow creek called the Long Hole and explained, "She went that way. I was sketching at the time. She did not like to bathe where I told her to."

All the men spread out, searching and shouting for Mrs. Kirwan. Marie Louisa's body was found by Patrick Nangle on a large protruding rock in the Long Hole. She was lying on her back on a sheet with her feet in a small pool of water, while her head hung grotesquely over the edge of the rock. Her wet bulky bathing suit was crumpled up under her armpits, leaving almost her entire body exposed. Patrick covered the lower portion of the body with the sheet.

Soon Kirwan was at his wife's side. "Oh, Marie, Marie!" was all he could say. He refused to leave the body while the men brought the boat around to the Long Hole to take Marie Louisa back to Howth.

The body of Marie Louisa received some very unprofessional handling, even for 1852. She was taken to her lodgings, for we must remember the Kirwans were on vacation in Howth for six weeks. Kirwan arranged to have two local ladies wash his wife's body. They objected, correctly pointing out that it was customary for the police to be called first in cases of accidental death. Kirwan would hear none of it and demanded that they wash the body. This was done.

Marie Louisa was prepared for burial. Later these women were to state that her face was covered with blood. There were cuts above the right eye, on the cheek and forehead, as well as a cut on the right breast.

The morning after the tragedy the coroner ordered a medical examination. Here again, a certain laxity occurred. A medical student named Hamilton examined the body. He admittedly conducted only a superficial examination and concluded that Mrs. Kirwan had died through accidental drowning.

That afternoon an inquest into the death was held at Howth. Kirwan told of his sketching trip to Ireland's Eye, of his wife's habit of swimming while he painted, and of finding the body. Hamilton, the medical student, testified that death was due to accidental drowning. The jury agreed, and Marie Louisa was duly buried.

As so often happens in small communities, the citizens of Howth felt that justice had taken a holiday. What about the blood-curdling screams heard by no less than four independent individuals? What about the cuts about Mrs. Kirwan's head? No mention of these facts was made at the inquest.

The notoriety of the accident uncovered a choice bit of evidence which, though not directly related to Mrs. Kirwan's death, did much to place Kirwan on trial for murder. It was revealed that he was leading a double life. In Dublin, during the 12 years of his marriage to Marie Louisa, he had kept a mistress, one Teresa Kenny, who bore him a total of seven little Kirwans. It must be added that Kirwan maintained a fine home in a suburb of Dublin, complete with maid, for his second wife, who was also called Mrs. Kirwan.

Unsuspecting wives have been killed for less reason. The Kirwans' landlady in Howth now knew why Kirwan spent three nights out of each week in Dublin.

William Kirwan was arrested and charged with the murder of his wife. His trial opened on Wednesday, December 8, 1852, in Dublin. In contrast to the inquest, Kirwan's trial was a meticulous procedure, every detail being thrashed about by defence and prosecution.

The prosecution made much of the cuts about the victim's head, Mr. Kirwan's morals, and the terrible screams heard shortly before the body was found. Kirwan claimed he had heard nothing. There was also some evidence that Kirwan mistreated his wife, both in Dublin and in Howth.

The defence stated that Marie Louisa was an epileptic and could have accidentally met her death having a seizure while swimming.

It was one of those trials where everyone figured that the defendant had killed his wife in order to be able to live full time with his mistress. Yet, where was that clincher, that fact which puts the case to rest? It wasn't forthcoming.

Marie Louisa's body was exhumed 31 days after her death. An autopsy was performed, but no signs of violence were found on the body. A doctor testifying for the prosecution confirmed that a water-soaked sheet held over the mouth and nose could result in drowning without leaving telltale marks on the body.

To counteract this argument, the defence insisted that an epileptic seizure could also result in drowning without external signs of violence.

Medical evidence swung back and forth, but in the end there was one fact the jury could not dismiss from their minds. The horrible screams heard minutes apart, echoing across the water from the tiny island, were compatible with murder. The jury knew that whatever else was true, Kirwan was lying when he stated he hadn't heard the screams when four reputable citizens heard them from up to a mile away.

Kirwan was found guilty and sentenced to death. His sentence was later commuted to life imprisonment. Twenty-five years after his conviction, Kirwan, now an old, stooped, bearded man, was released. He travelled to Liverpool, where he purchased passage to the United States. And so William Kirwan sailed into oblivion.

WAYWARD PRIEST
(FRANCE)

As a general rule, gentlemen of the cloth have enough to do saving souls without going around killing people. But, as we all know, it is the exception to the rule that makes life so very interesting.

The 400 citizens of the tiny French village of Uruffe, France, were delighted when Cure Guy Desnoyers was assigned to their village to assist their aged abbé in his divine tasks. At 31, Father Desnoyers was somewhat older than the average novice priest, having spent the first two years of his education pursuing a medical degree. Father Desnoyers' parents could not afford to financially assist their son. As a result, he had to leave the field of medicine, eventually to arrive at ecclesiastical pursuits. He brought to the village a smattering of medical knowledge and a flair for the theatre.

Father Desnoyers was soon dispensing quasi-medical advice for minor ailments. He also organized a teenage theatre group. When the abbé went to that great parish in the sky, Father Desnoyers became the village's chief spiritual leader, a position he was to retain for six years.

In August 1956, an incident took place in Uruffe which would have far-reaching effects on Father Desnoyers' religious career. Nineteen-year-old Regine Fays checked her lunar calculations one more time. There was no doubt about it. She was pregnant. Before too long her condition would be evident to anyone with average eyesight. Regine had to tell someone. After much soul searching, she chose her mother. Her mother cried. Uruffe girls didn't do such things. In Paris, yes, but not in their own little village. There would be a scandal. Worse, a disgrace on the Fays' good family name.

When Madame Fays had spent her wrath, she faced her fallen daughter and gingerly inquired, "Who's the father?" Regine refused to tell. She would never give away the identity of the father of her child. When Papa Fays heard that he would soon be a grandpere, he too begged for the name of the impregnator. Regine declared that she would go to the grave with her secret.

That night as they were lying side by side in bed, Mama and Papa Fays discussed the mystery and came up with a solution. Their daughter had made love to a stranger. Maybe someone who was merely passing through the village. Who knows, she might not even be aware of her lover's name. Mon Dieu, what is the world coming to!

Months passed. Regine could no longer conceal her delicate condition. Tongues wagged. The word spread. It was a juicy scandal. Truth to tell, Mama and Papa Fays wouldn't have made it through that fall if it hadn't been for Father Desnoyers. The kindly priest spent many an evening comforting the parents of the disgraced girl.

On Saturday, Dec. 1, Father Desnoyers had dinner at the Fays' home. He told Monsieur Fays that he would be travelling to Applemont to visit his parents on Monday. M. Fays remarked that he too would be away from the village that day. He was travelling to Commercy to purchase a carriage for his expected grandchild.

On Sunday, Father Desnoyers conducted services and showed a movie at the village hall. At the movie's conclusion he announced that on the next day he would be visiting his parents for a few days.

Bright and early the next morning, Father Desnoyers raced away in his Citroen. M. Fays left for Commercy by bus. That evening at 6 p.m., Regine told her mother that she was going for a walk. Some villagers saw her strolling through town. While she was out, her father came home with the new baby carriage.

A few hours passed. Regine failed to return home. Monsieur and Madame Fays became worried. They took to the streets, inquiring about their daughter. Some people had seen her walking, but that was all. In desperation, they called Father Desnoyers in Applemont. He told them not to worry, but was himself disturbed enough to return to Uruffe immediately. By 10 p.m. that night he was in the Fays home.

A search party was organized. Over a hundred volunteers trampled across roads and frozen fields throughout the wee hours of that cold December morning. Searchers didn't find Regine. Father Desnoyers, accompanied by three men in his Citroen, came across a crumpled heap about three kilometres from the village. Regine lay partially nude under her overcoat. She had been shot in the back of the neck. Her abdomen had been slashed open. Beside her on the road was a 6 mm.

cartridge case. Not far from her body lay the body of her newborn child. The baby had been stabbed several times. Both mother and child were dead.

Father Desnoyers took charge. He advised the villagers to guard the bodies while he returned to Uruffe for the police. Police from Nancy had been assisting in the search, and it was these officers who returned with Father Desnoyers to the scene of the macabre murders. Before they could begin their investigation, the good father dropped to his knees and prayed at the top of his voice for the fallen girl.

The bodies were removed and examined by medical experts. Unbelievably, Regine had been subjected to a Caesarean operation performed by someone with some medical knowledge but no skill. Her unborn child had been taken from her body after she was dead. Doctors stated that the child was alive when delivered and subsequently stabbed to death. Rarely had such a repulsive, heartless act taken place in the annals of crime.

Commissaire Jean Chapuis from Nancy headed the investigation. He found out immediately that there was only one registered automatic pistol in Uruffe. It was owned by none other than Father Guy Desnoyers.

Chapuis received a strange visitor at his makeshift office. She was a young girl of the village who would only divulge her information with the understanding that Chapuis would never reveal her identity. He agreed, and the young girl told how she had been a virgin until Father Desnoyers had his way with her in the presbytery. She believed that other girls of the village had been shorn of their virginity by the priest. She also believed that Father Desnoyers was the father of Regine Fays' baby.

Chapuis called on Father Desnoyers and asked him to produce his pistol. Ballistic evidence proved that the automatic was the murder weapon. Father Desnoyers maintained his innocence for some time before suddenly exclaiming, "It was I!" He then went on to dictate a formal statement revealing that he had been intimate with Regine on 31 occasions. He admitted killing the helpless girl and using his pocket knife to perform the Caesarean operation.

At the movies held on Sunday night at Uruffe, he had arranged a clandestine rendezvous with Regine for Monday night at 7 p.m. Regine kept the appointment. She got into his car and they drove away, stopping three kilometres from the village. Regine was puzzled as to why he wanted to meet with her. Father Desnoyers told his astonished interrogators that he informed the girl he wished to give her absolution.

Regine ridiculed him and ran from the car. Father Desnoyers ran after the fleeing girl, firing two shots into the back of her neck. He conveniently claimed that he had no memory of what transpired after the shooting, stating that he came to his senses wiping blood from his pocket knife. He then raced to his parents' home in Applemont in plenty of time to receive M. Fays' phone call. Later, Father Desnoyers revealed that on that cold winter night he had baptized his baby daughter before killing her.

When his confession became public knowledge, Guy Desnoyers was defrocked as a priest of the Roman Catholic Church and excommunicated. His murder trial was nothing more than a formal stage for one of the most horrendous crimes ever committed. Father Desnoyers was found guilty of murder and sentenced to life imprisonment at hard labor.

After being confined for 22 years, Guy Desnoyers was freed in August 1978, due to an amnesty granted by the French government.

CANNIBALISM
(THE ATLANTIC)

When wealthy Australian Harry J. Want purchased the yacht *Mignonette*, he had no idea he was about to precipitate a sensational murder trial and at the same time alter the culinary habits of three true blue English sailors.

Harry bought the 52-foot yacht in England. He was desirous of having his new possession brought back to his home in Sydney, Australia. He let it be known in that spring of 1884 that he was looking for a capable sailor to take charge of the journey. Thirty-one-year-old Thomas Dudley applied for, and was successful in obtaining, the position of captain. From other applicants Dudley picked his crew, experienced sailors Edwin Stephens, 36, and Edmund Brooks, 33. The cabin boy was Richard Parker, 17.

The *Mignonette* was overhauled and supplies taken aboard at Southampton. On May 17, she sailed for Madeira and from there, on June 2, she set sail on the long journey to Australia. The first weeks of the small yacht's voyage were uneventful, but on July 5 the weather worsened. Gales and heavy seas battered the *Mignonette* until her starboard side caved in.

The four men scampered aboard a 13-foot long lifeboat. They were able to grab a few navigational instruments and two tins of turnips before abandoning the yacht. Within five minutes the Mignonette disappeared in the heavy seas.

Thomas Dudley took stock of the desperate situation. They were in the middle of the South Atlantic, well off travelled shipping routes. Two tins of turnips stood between the men in the lifeboat and starvation. They had no water. South America lay some 2000 miles away. Their situation appeared hopeless.

The four men made a crude sail from their shirts and attempted to head toward South America. Four days later, half-starved from their ration of tinned turnips, which can be trying at the best of times, they captured a turtle. The turtle, with the exception of the skin and shell, was devoured in the next few days. By July 18, the few drops of water they had managed to catch in their oilskins were gone. So were those dreadful turnips and the turtle.

For the next five days, the men had absolutely nothing to eat or drink. Dudley approached Stephens and Brooks. He suggested that they draw lots to see which man would be killed so that the remaining men could survive by drinking human blood and eating human flesh. The captain's suggestion was not received favorably. Young Parker, being a lowly cabin boy, was not consulted.

On the same day that this rather horrid idea met with rejection, Dudley wrote to his wife. He told her how very sorry he was to have undertaken such a perilous journey. He had signed on strictly for the remuneration. He went on to tell her that their plight was desperate and that all four would soon be dead. He closed by expressing his love.

Soon after Dudley wrote what he thought would be his last act of consequence, Richard Parker took ill. Parker couldn't stand his thirst. He commenced to drink sea water and as a result rapidly grew weaker. He lay outstretched on the bottom of the boat with his arms over his eyes.

Three torturous days passed. Once more Dudley approached the two older men about drawing lots. Brooks expressed the opinion that they should all die together. Stephens didn't agree with Dudley but didn't object strenuously to the idea. Dudley went a bit further. Maybe lots wasn't the only solution. After all, the boy Parker was obviously about to die anyway. By killing him the rest might survive. Dudley felt that if they weren't rescued by the next morning, the only thing to do would be to kill Parker.

Next morning, Dudley gave the high sign to his two companions. Brooks would have none of it. He went forward and placed an oilskin over his head. Stephens positioned himself so that Parker couldn't move his legs. He had agreed to hold the boy's legs should there be a struggle. Dudley said a short prayer. Then he opened his penknife and bent over the cabin boy. "Now, Dick, my boy, your time has come." Barely conscious, Parker inquired, "What me, sir?" Dudley responded "Yes, my boy." Then he plunged the two-inch blade into the side of Parker's neck, killing him painlessly and instantly.

Any type of utensil within reach was used to capture the blood from Parker's neck. Brooks, while not taking part in the killing, wasn't above quenching his thirst with Parker's blood. Parker's liver and heart were then extracted and ravenously consumed. For four more days the survivors subsisted on the flesh of Richard Parker.

On July 29, the small lifeboat was sighted by the German barque Montezuma. The three men were so weak that they had to be raised aboard the barque by means of ropes. Only Brooks could walk. No effort had been made to dispose of what was left of Richard Parker. Two German sailors threw the remains overboard. With the little lifeboat in tow, the Montezuma made her way to Falmouth, England.

During the voyage home, the three men, while still in terrible condition, regained some strength. They readily told their German rescuers of their adventures, including the killing and eating of Richard Parker.

Once in port, Captain Dudley and his crew of two went directly to the authorities reporting their lost yacht, as well as their ordeal at sea, including the consumption of the cabin boy. It was obvious that the men didn't feel they had committed any crime.

That very night they were arrested and taken into custody. Within days their adventures on the high seas were being retold throughout England and wherever men go down to the sea in ships. Dudley had the unexpected thrill of personally presenting his wife with the hastily written letter he firmly believed would be his last meaningful act on earth. The three men told similar stories, all verifying the details as outlined here. The court unanimously ruled that Brooks had not taken part in the killing. Charges against him were dropped.

Dudley and Stephens were charged with the murder of Richard Parker. Throughout the land there was much sympathy for the accused pair. During their trial both men testified, as did Brooks. Defence attorneys pointed out that, while in the lifeboat, the two accused discussed the fact that they had wives and children back home in England, while Parker had no dependents. Parker was surely at death's door when he was killed. So weak was he that although he knew he was about to die, he did not have the strength to struggle. It was stressed that had the two accused not killed Parker, they would surely have perished during the four days that elapsed before they were rescued. Parker, by far the weakest, would have died first.

In essence, the defence pleaded that under these particular unique circumstances, the accused had the right to kill. The Crown argued that the accused had no right under any circumstances to measure the value of life. They chose to eliminate the youngest and most unresisting and had in fact committed murder.

Thomas Dudley and Edwin Stephens were found guilty and sentenced to death. That same afternoon the Home Secretary advised Queen Victoria to "respite the prisoners until further significance of her pleasure." Within four weeks their sentences were commuted to six months imprisonment. So ended the strange adventure of the sailors of the good yacht *Mignonette*.

During the trial of Dudley and Stephens in 1884, Edgar Allen Poe's novelette, *The Narrative of Arthur Gordon Pym*, published in 1838, was passed around in court. Poe's story vividly described castaways in a similar position to the accused men standing trial. In Poe's story the men drew lots. The unlucky man who lost the draw consented to being stabbed in the back. By an astounding coincidence, his name was Richard Parker.

THE KILLING MACHINE (SCOTLAND)

Scotland has nurtured its share of evil men. Maybe Peter Manuel was the nastiest of all. During his criminal career he was responsible for snuffing out the lives of nine innocent individuals. Manuel, a muscular, dark-complexioned youth, lived in Glasgow. His family, decent, hard-working people, stuck by their wayward son to the bitter end.

By the time he was 12, Manuel was breaking into houses and stealing anything of value. For some strange reason, he never rushed his work, but took his time, usually opening canned fruit and other food he found in the house and eating heartily before departing. By the age of 19, he had spent time in ten different correctional facilities.

On the nights of March 3, 4, and 8, 1946, three women were attacked on the outskirts of Glasgow. In two cases, Manuel viciously beat the women, but was interrupted before he could ravish them. On the third occasion, the unfortunate victim was raped. As a known criminal in the area, Manuel was placed in an identification lineup. The two women who were not raped positively identified him. The third woman had not seen her attacker. However, while Manuel was in custody, police were able to gather enough scientific evidence from the scene of the rape to bring their suspect to trial. Manuel was found guilty and sentenced to eight years imprisonment. With time off for good behavior, he was released after serving six years.

Upon his release from prison, Manuel met Anna O'Hara, a bus conductress, to whom he soon became engaged. He obtained employment and, to all outward appearances, seemed to be going straight. Manuel and Anna were scheduled to wed on July 30, 1955, but the wedding never took place. Anna and her family discovered Manuel's unsavory past. The wedding was cancelled. Anna refused to marry a jailbird.

On the night he was to be married, Manuel attacked a woman in the suburb of Birkenshaw. This time he carried a knife. The woman talked Manuel into releasing her and went to the police. She was able to identify her attacker. Manuel was taken into custody and charged with assault.

Acting as his own defence counsel, Manuel made an extremely good impression on the jury. Taking the witness stand in his own defence, he put forward the view that the lady in question was really his girlfriend. She was taking this vindictive action to gain revenge for his trying to break off their relationship. The jury brought in the unique Scottish verdict of "Not Proven." Manuel walked out of court a free man.

At this point in his criminal career, Peter Manuel had stolen, lied, assaulted, injured and raped. His status was soon to change. It was time to kill.

On Jan. 2, 1956, Anne Knielands, 18, of East Kilbride had a date to meet Andrew Murnin, a young Scottish soldier, in nearby Capelrig. It was Scotland's rather rowdy New Year's holidays, Hogmanay. The young soldier was partying with some friends and simply forgot his date with Anne. Somewhat disappointed, Anne decided to visit old family friends in Capelrig, the Simpsons.

The Simpsons were no ordinary family and deserve mention. Pat Simpson, 47, had lost his arm when he fell under a train at the age of eight. The Simpsons had 17 children, but there was an explanation. Both had been married before. Between them, they had brought ten children to their union. A further seven were the product of their own marriage.

At 8:40 p.m., after passing the time of day, Anne Knielands left the Simpson household. Two days later, George Gribton was taking his daily walk along the East Kilbride golf course when he discovered Anne's body near the fifth fairway. From the physical evidence at the scene, police were able to ascertain that she had been attacked, but had managed to break free of her attacker and run in the darkness down an embankment, over a barbed wire fence and across a field before being overtaken by her pursuer. Her underclothing had been ripped from her body, but she had not been sexually attacked. Several articles of her clothing had been spread over a wide area.

As a previously convicted rapist, Manuel was questioned about the Anne Knielands murder. He told a simple story. On Jan. 2, he had been home all night. There was nothing to connect him with the killing. Months passed.

To keep his hand in, Manuel pulled a few robberies. On one occasion, he was interrupted during the commission of a robbery. While running away from the scene, he ripped his pants on a barbed wire fence. When the police caught up with him, the piece of cloth found on the fence perfectly matched the tear in his pants. Manuel was arrested but was released on bail.

Mr. and Mrs. William Watt and their 16-year-old daughter Vivienne lived at 5 Fennsbank Ave., Burnside. On Sept. 9, Bill, who owned his own bakery, went on vacation with his black Labrador, Queenie. He loved to go fishing at Lochgilphead, near Argyll, where he often stayed at the Cairnbaan Hotel. It was some 90 miles of twists and curves around Loch Lomand.

While Bill was away, Mrs. Watt's sister, Mrs. George Brown, came to spend a night or two at the Watts' home. Eight days after Bill left on his vacation, his wife, sister-in-law and daughter were shot to death with a .38 calibre pistol as they lay sleeping in bed. There was some evidence that Vivienne had awakened when her aunt and mother had been shot. She had put up a struggle before being killed.

Unfortunately for Bill Watt, two eyewitnesses swore that on the night of the killing, they had seen him and Queenie driving the 30 miles between his hotel and his home. Poor Mr. Watt. Devastated at losing everyone near and dear to him, he was arrested and taken into custody.

Most researchers of the Manuel case believe that there was someone in a vehicle similar to Mr. Watt's maroon Vauxhall driving toward Burnside that night. No doubt there was a dog in the car. However, it definitely was not Bill Watt and his dog Queenie. The man has never come forward, nor has he been found, but the strange coincidence was to haunt Bill Watt for weeks before he was exonerated and released. Peter Manuel must have enjoyed the lark.

Once again, Manuel was questioned. In fact, his father Samuel claimed police were harassing his son. He threatened to take the matter to his member of parliament. While Peter enjoyed Mr. Watt's predicament, he did not appreciate all the attention which had been directed to that unfortunate man. Manuel attempted to remedy the situation. He contacted Bill Watt's lawyer, Lawrence Dowdall, and told him that he had been approached by a man who wanted him to get rid of a .38 calibre pistol. Manuel claimed that this man had described the interior of the Watts' home to him. He, in turn, described it to the lawyer. This information was turned over to the police, but of course the suspect named by Manuel had nothing whatever to do with the crime.

Meanwhile, Manuel, who had been out on bail on the breaking and entering charge, was found guilty and sentenced to a year in jail. On Nov. 30, 1957, he was released from prison.

Three days later, Manuel travelled to Newcastle looking for employment. On Dec. 7, he hailed a cab. Cab driver Sydney Dunn, 36, didn't know his fare was a mass murderer. He would never know. Peter Manuel shot him in the head, slashed his throat, and for some reason known only to himself, smashed in every window in the cab. Dunn's body and cab were found next day on the lonely moors near Edmundbyers.

Peter Manuel was now a killing machine. Isabelle Cooke of Glasgow became his sixth victim only 20 days after Sydney Dunn's murder. When Isabelle failed to return home, Mr. Cooke notified police. Pieces of her clothing were found near a footpath, but police were unable to ascertain the fate of the missing girl. Peter Manuel had buried her body in a nearby plowed field.

Nothing could stop the killing machine. It was New Year's Eve. Mr. and Mrs. Peter Smart and their ten-year-old son were anticipating the 70-mile drive to Ancrum to visit Mr. Smart's parents. The family never showed up. They were all dead. Peter Manuel had claimed his seventh, eighth and ninth victims.

On Jan. 6, Mr. Smart's employers called police, who broke into the Smarts' home and found the bodies. Neighbors stated that they hadn't become suspicious because the house had appeared to be occupied. Blinds were up one day, down the next. Newspapers were taken in each day. Inside the house, police found evidence that the Smarts' killer had remained for days after the murders. He had eaten heartily.

Once again, Manuel was suspected and questioned, but this time it was different. Mr. Smart's employers had paid his expense account in new pound notes. They had a record of the serial numbers of these bills. The money was traced to pound notes which Peter Manual had spent in a pub the day after the triple murder.

Manuel was arrested. The jig was up. He gave a detailed account of all of his crimes and led police to the plowed field, where Isabelle Cooke's body was recovered.

Peter Manuel was hanged at Glasgow's Barlinnie Prison on July 11, 1958.

DUTCH TREAT
(HOLLAND)

This is the story of four Dutch boys and how three of them deliberately planned the murder of the fourth. The three perpetrators of the crime, ranging in age from 15 to 17, were so cool and calculating that they even staged a murder rehearsal before the actual killing took place.

Theo Mastwijk, 14, was no angel. He did so poorly at the school he attended in his hometown of Soest, Holland, that there was some talk of having him transferred to our equivalent of a reform school. When a government official met with Theo's father and discussed the transfer, the boy promised to straighten out.

Theo was scared silly, but that didn't stop him from getting into more trouble. Using a borrowed motorcycle, he raced through the streets of Soest. In Holland it is against the law for anyone under the age of 16 to ride a motorcycle. Theo was picked up by police. In order to save his own skin, he told them that a buddy of his named Hendrick had stolen some paint. Theo was photographed in his loud shirt with its distinctive pattern and sent home. In the ensuing weeks, he took part in several small robberies in the area. He was suspected by police, but, as they had no proof, he was never taken into custody.

Theo had met Hendrick at a teenage snack bar in Soest. Although Theo was two years younger than Hendrick, he was accepted as an equal by the older boy because of his reputation.

Hendrick was a bright, intelligent lad, if somewhat aloof and cold. He disliked animals and was often reprimanded for breaking the beaks of ducks. On one occasion, he strangled a cat. In the summer of 1959, his family moved two miles north of Soest to Baarn.

A hundred years earlier, when Holland was one of the chief commercial powers of the world, many wealthy Dutch industrialists built mansions in Baarn. By 1959, several of these mansions had been converted into institutions or divided into offices. Some were still partially in use as homes.

Hendrick became friends with two schoolmates, Boudewijn, 17, and his brother Evout, 15. Boudewijn and Evout lived in one of the old mansions set on five acres of well-kept grounds. The rather unattractive structure contained 30 rooms, not counting closets, bathrooms and cellars. Ten rooms had been partitioned and were in use as offices. The boys' family lived in the rest of the house, although some of the rooms were not entered for months at a time. Topping off the mansion was a small dome.

Hendrick, Boudewijn and Evout were inseparable. They attended school together. One was rarely seen without the other two. No one remembers how it started or who was the first to suggest it, but somehow the boys decided to steal for the sheer adventure of the exercise. Of course, this was old hat for Hendrick, who had often broken into warehouses.

One pleasant summer night in June 1960, Hendrick forced open the window of a warehouse in Soest. He and Evout climbed in. Boudewijn acted as lookout. Soon the three boys were scampering away with tins of peaches, apricots and strawberries. Nothing had ever tasted as good.

Three weeks later, the police called on Hendrick. Their inquiries had nothing to do with the recent warehouse robbery. It had come to their attention that sometime earlier, a quantity of paint had been stolen. Hendrick was offended at being accused. After questioning him for an hour, the police left.

Meanwhile that summer, Theo was being harassed by police. They were sure he was responsible for a series of minor robberies. Theo knew that it was only a matter of time before he would be picked up. He discussed the matter with friends. Everyone agreed that he should eventually try to get out of Holland. In the meantime, he should at least leave his home. Several of Theo's acquaintances were very interested in his predicament, since he made no bones about the fact that if he was picked up, his only way of staying out of jail would be to inform on friends in exchange for his freedom.

Rumors of Theo's dilemma reached Hendrick. He discussed the matter with Boudewijn and Evout. While Theo posed no threat to the brothers, they knew that he and Hendrick had taken part in burglarizing warehouses. To protect their friend, they offered to hide Theo in their parents' mansion.

On the night of June 23, the three boys escorted Theo up through the mansion to a room under the dome. The boys had equipped the room with an old mattress and a night pan. Theo, who had never before met the two brothers, was grateful. Each day the brothers would share their food with Theo or would steal food from their parents' pantry. The plan was to hide Theo until the search for him died down. He would then be smuggled across the border into Belgium. Theo was to stay in his hiding place for 40 days.

Life went on outside the mansion. The school term drew to a close. The boys took summer jobs. Sometimes, for the fun of it, they would rob a warehouse. June gave way to July.

The three boys often discussed Theo. What if their plan worked and they were successful in smuggling him into Belgium? What was to stop Theo from returning? Now Boudewijn and Evout were implicated as well. It seemed to them that more drastic measures had to be taken. They decided, plain and simple, to kill Theo Mastwijk.

An overdose of sleeping pills would be the best method. No blood, no fuss. It had to be done before Aug. 2, when the two brothers were scheduled to leave on vacation to Nauchatel with their parents. A deep grave was dug in the backyard. Quicklime was easily stolen from a construction site. All was in readiness. An entire box of sleeping pills was dissolved in a bottle of beer. Theo was grateful as usual. The three boys left the dome. When they returned two hours later to pick up the body, they were shocked to find Theo alive and well. The pills had made him nauseous and caused him to vomit.

Why was there not a more extensive search conducted for Theo Mastwijk? It was a matter of luck. Hendrick and a friend had asked a lorry driver if they could accompany him to Antwerp for a visit. The lorry driver agreed. Before the two boys arrived in Antwerp, they quarrelled and separated. Hendrick returned to Soest alone. Police showed the lorry driver a photograph of the missing Theo Mastwijk. The lorry driver swore he was the boy he had dropped off in Antwerp. The search for Theo was called off. He had obviously left the country.

The three boys were more intent than ever on killing Theo. Hendrick obtained a piece of pink clothesline rope. He practised on each brother, looping the rope over their heads from behind. They, in turn, used Hendrick as a model. It seemed easy enough.

On Aug. 1, 1960, Theo was told the time had come for him to be smuggled out of the country. He dressed rapidly, putting on the distinctive shirt he loved so well. It was midnight. The brothers' parents were out of the mansion. Down a series of winding steps, Theo followed his friends.

Once out in the garden, Boudewijn held Theo's hands while Hendrick quickly slung the rope around Theo's neck and pulled with all his might. The rope tightened and then slipped out of his hands. Hendrick picked up a shovel and struck Theo on the head over and over until he lay still. Then he and Boudewijn lowered Theo into his grave, poured quicklime over the body and covered it with earth. Evout, who had stood watch, was delighted with the night's work. Next day, the brothers went on vacation with their parents.

Months passed. Hendrick left Baarn and obtained employment in Limberg. Boudewijn and Evout did well at school that year. Boudewijn graduated and enrolled at the University of Amsterdam.

On Oct. 27, 1961, 15 months after the murder, a plumber, repairing an underground pipe discovered the skeletal remains of Theo Mastwijk. The discovery caused a sensation throughout Holland. A small scrap of the victim's shirt found with the skeleton was the only clue police had to aid in the identification of the victim. They went back into their old files and found that Theo Mastwijk had been reported missing a year and a half earlier. He had once driven a motorcycle while underage and had been photographed by police. There, in the picture, was the boy wearing a distinctively patterned sport shirt. The shirt was identical to the scrap of shirt found with the body. According to the missing person's report, a boy named Hendrick had been the last person to see Theo alive.

Hendrick was located, questioned, and immediately confessed. Boudewijn and Evout were picked up and confessed as well. Their trial, which revealed in chilling detail the cold-blooded actions of the participants, held Holland spellbound for months. The three boys agreed to all the particulars of their deadly scheme, with one exception. Hendrick claimed that it was Boudewijn who delivered the deadly blows to Theo's head with the shovel, while Boudewijn claimed it was Hendrick who actually struck the blows. It matters little. Both boys were found equally responsible.

On April 11, 1963, sentences were passed on the three defendants. Hendrick was sentenced to nine years imprisonment, Boudewijn to nine years as well. Evout, who had been 15 at the time of the murder, was sentenced to six years imprisonment.

THE REVEREND

JIM JONES
(GUYANA)

Who can forget the horrific photographs of the more than 900 corpses decomposing in the intense heat of the Guyana jungle? Almost nine years have passed since that Nov. 18, 1978 when vague news dispatches hinted at the mass suicide of some obscure religious cult in a jungle commune. The dispatches also alluded to the possible murder of a United States congressman.

The individual behind the horror story, which was soon to make headlines around the world, was the Reverend Jim Jones.

Jones was born in Lynn, Indiana in 1931. He was the son of an army veteran who was gassed in the First World War. Jones' father was an enthusiastic member of the Ku Klux Klan.

In 1951, the 20-year-old Jones attended Butler University, a school operated by the Disciples of Christ. He took courses at Butler off and on for the next 10 years, receiving his B.S. degree in education in 1961. However, in 1958, Jones founded his own interdenominational Christian Assembly of God Church. By 1960, his Peoples' Temple, located in Los Angeles, was a bona fide congregation of the Disciples of Christ, which had a membership of almost a million and a half, mostly living in the Midwest states.

From 1961 to 1963, Jones performed missionary work in Brazil, organizing orphanages. There is evidence that he visited Guyana while in South America and, quite possibly, it was during this period that the seeds of his own colony in the jungle took root in his mind.

Upon his return from Brazil, Jones displayed a degree of entrepreneurial acumen by forming two non-profit organizations with headquarters in Indianapolis. The Wings of Deliverance was organized to spread the word of God, while the Jim-Lu-Mar Corp. was formed to purchase every money-making venture that was available. The latter company's elongated name was made up of his own first name as well as that of his mother, Lynette, and wife, Marceline.

During the sixties, Jones operated out of Ukiah, a small town located about 100 miles north of San Francisco. His headquarters, known simply as the Peoples' Church, became a money-making machine. The strategically located church afforded Jones and his followers the opportunity to swoop down on weekends to San Francisco and Los Angeles to spread the word, win followers, and raise hard cash.

Sometimes the group would return to headquarters richer by as much as $40,000. Members of the congregation turned over their social security cheques to Jones. As the flock grew, so did the routine amount of cash flowing into the church's coffers. Many members, completely enraptured with the charismatic Jones, turned over their entire life savings. Some cashed in their life insurance policies. Others moved into the church's dormitories to live.

Jones wasn't above slick hucksterism. Photographs of "The Father," as he was now called by his followers, were considered to have healing powers. These bogus medical aids fetched a pretty penny, as did other religious artifacts.

In 1971, Jones purchased a former synagogue and moved the centre of his operations to San Francisco. The Peoples' Temple held their opening service with much fanfare. Scores of gospel singers raised their voices in praise of the Lord. Angela Davis spoke. The Peoples' Temple appeared to be a model of what God fearing folks could achieve. It boasted a day-care centre, an infirmary, a printing press, a carpentry shop and facilities to feed hundreds of the poor each day.

Soon, the devoted congregation and its dynamic leader were being lauded by the media as a fine example of an efficiently operated pure charity. Jones' photograph, depicting him handing over sizable cheques to worthwhile causes, often appeared in the press. His now 8000-member church also became politically powerful. At the snap of a finger, Jones could muster hundreds of followers to work on a political campaign. Many dignitaries wooed the religious leader, sometimes for manpower, sometimes for substantial donations.

In 1973, Jones dispatched 20 members of the Peoples' Church to Guyana, with the express purpose of finding a site for an agricultural mission. A year later, Father Jones leased 27,000 acres in the jungle near the town of Port Kaituma from the government of Guyana. The commune was called Jonestown after its founder.

As the colony was populated, glowing reports were received by relatives back in the States. Crops were flourishing, housing was more than adequate, and above all, the individual freedom that the disciples enjoyed was lauded by all. The Minister of Foreign Affairs for Guyana reported on Jonestown, "Peace and love in action."

In 1975, Rev. Jim Jones was named one of the most outstanding clergymen in the U.S. by an interfaith organization, Religion in American Life. The following year he was named "Humanitarian of the Year" by the Los Angeles *Herald*. That same year he was appointed to the San Francisco Housing Authority by his good friend, Mayor George Moscone. In January 1977, Jones received the annual Martin Luther King Jr. Humanitarian Award.

In the midst of this praise, there were some ominous rumblings. A few members dropped out of the congregation. Others sued, claiming they were brainwashed, beaten and stripped of their wealth. A handful of journalists made their way to Jonestown. Their stories were far from complimentary. They told of poor living conditions and disillusioned members. After their reports appeared in California papers, many of these journalists were threatened. The adverse publicity initiated an investigation of the commune by the government of Guyana. They reported "Not one confirmation of an allegation of mistreatment."

California Congressman Leo Ryan, 53, was serving his fourth term when he became interested in the Jonestown commune and reports that its members were being abused and being denied their civil rights. He decided to look into the matter.

This was not Ryan's first excursion into a high profile, well-publicized investigation. It was he who strongly and successfully petitioned for the release from prison of his constituent Patty Hearst. In 1965, he made a trip to Newfoundland and came away denouncing the hunting of seal pups. The International Wild Life Foundation named him Man of the Year for that effort.

Ryan's entourage, including aides, lawyers, a Guyanese government official, newspaper reporters and a T.V. crew from NBC landed at the closest airstrip, Port Kaituma. Only Ryan and four members of his party were allowed to proceed immediately to Jonestown. The remainder of the entourage were made to wait four hours before they too were transported over the muddy single lane road to Jonestown.

Initial impressions of the commune were favorable. Food appeared to be plentiful. The Ryan group clapped to gospel music as they finished a pleasant meal. Members of the congregation conversed with Congressman Ryan. They told him they were experiencing the happiest years of their lives. Throughout the informal introduction to Jonestown, benevolent Father Jim Jones presided, volunteering his views when asked.

Later, only Ryan and his four original party members were allowed to spend the night at the commune. The balance were transported back to Port Kaituma in a dump truck. Next morning, they returned to Jonestown and were escorted around the compound by Marceline Jones. Impressive nurseries and classrooms were shown to the newsmen. Curiously, some buildings were shut tight. Newsmen were were told the inhabitants were sleeping and were not to be disturbed.

Questioned by the reporters, Jones denied the veracity of the bad press he had lately received back in the U.S. He vehemently denied the allegations by former members of his flock of poor treatment. During the questioning, word drifted down to Jones and his interrogators that several members of the commune wanted to leave with Congressman Ryan and his group. Jones flew into a rage. Tension mounted. But no one prevented the dissident members from leaving.

As Ryan talked to the disturbed Jones, a member of the commune pulled a knife and attempted to stab the congressman. While he was being disarmed, the attacker was wounded. Much blood was spilled on Ryan, who was noticeably shaken by the experience.

Finally, Ryan, his entourage of officials, newsmen and defectors, boarded the dump truck for the return trip to the airstrip at Fort Kaituma. Later, newsmen were to state that at this point they believed that Jones was an unstable character, but they were under the impression that he was sincere in his desire to do good for his fellow man. True, there were some flaws to Jonestown, but that was to be expected. Sixteen homesick dissidents out of 900 members was not out of the ordinary. No one seemed to be there against their will, no one appeared to be mistreated.

We can only surmise at the state of mind of Jim Jones. Unstable, paranoid Jones believed the adverse publicity generated by the stories the newsmen would file would spell the ruination of his colony in the jungle. He also believed that the dissidents who joined Ryan and his group were only the beginning of a wave of dissension that would sweep Jonestown. He determined to force the world to sit up and take notice.

The small planes landed at the Fort Kaituma airstrip to take the visitors home.

The dump truck which had originally carried the Ryan group to the landing strip pulled up with a tractor and flatbed. The truck parked, but the tractor towing the flatbed drove up between the two aircraft. Suddenly, the men on the tractor and flatbed opened fire. Airplane tires were punctured. Jonestown defector Patricia Parks lay dead. Also killed in the rain of gunfire were San Francisco *Examiner* photographer Greg Robinson, NBC cameraman Bob Brown, NBC correspondent Don Harris, and Congressman Leo Ryan. Others were wounded, some severely.

While the Guyanese police looked on from a distance, one of the defectors pointed out that Larry Layton, posing as a defector, had opened fire on his fellow commune brothers. When uninjured Dick Dwyer, head of the U.S. Embassy in Georgetown, Guyana, and himself a member of the ill-fated mission, was told this, he insisted that the police arrest Layton on the spot.

The slow-to-react Guyanese police, together with soldiers, assisted the wounded. After a night of horror, the Ryan party was flown to safety in Georgetown.

Back in Jonestown, an unbelievable scenario was taking place. Cyanide was mixed with Kool-Aid and quickly distributed to members of the commune. Mothers forced the liquid down their children's mouths. No one refused to take the poison. Black and white, young and old, people who had fled the ghettos and streets of America for the jungles of Guyana, were committing mass suicide. They had followed their charismatic leader, who had promised them a better life. Instead, he led them to death. All 913 died.

On Dec. 2, 1986, 41-year-old Larry Layton was convicted of conspiring to murder a U.S. congressman. He faces life imprisonment. He was the only person ever tried for the incident which took a total of 918 lives.

UNHOLY DUO
(GERMANY)

Frau Mathilda Ladestock and her lover, a Russian who lived under the alias of Hans Just, planned and committed the almost perfect murder. The unholy duo made only one mistake. They didn't figure on Minna Stablein, who simply loved to play amateur detective.

All of the characters in today's rather gruesome little drama lived and loved in the slums of Berlin in 1923. Mattie and Hans had one child, a boy, Horst. Mattie's first hubby died defending the Fatherland during World War I, leaving her with a small pension.

Hans made a fair living as an engraver, but had the habit of dropping into bars on payday and partaking of enough schnapps to refloat the *Titanic*. He would then stagger home and punch Mattie about their grimy two-room apartment just for kicks. When sober, Hans was dull, but thank goodness, gentle.

Down the hall lived the 60-year-old widowed superintendent of the tenement, Frau Rochling, who took a liking to Mattie and spent a great deal of time in the latter's apartment. Hans didn't care for Frau Rochling and, on those occasions when he came home higher than a kite, he would order the older woman from his home, be it ever so humble.

During that winter of 1923, Frau Rochling had a dispute with the owners of the tenement. As a result they presented her with an eviction notice effective the following April 1. Frau Rochling thought her landlord might attempt to seize some of her belongings, so she asked Mattie to store several pieces in her apartment. In return, Mattie would have the use of the furniture. As Mattie's apartment was practically barren, she jumped at the chance.

Everyone was happy with the arrangement. Now when Frau Rochling visited, she could sit on her own sofa. As a result, her visits became more frequent. She seemed always to be underfoot. Soon Mattie was extremely annoyed with her presence, as was Hans.

One day when Frau Rochling walked in unannounced and found that Mattie had opened a linen chest belonging to her and was using her prized linens, she went into a rage. Hans pacified the distraught woman, assuring her that he would pay for anything missing or soiled that very night.

While gulping down a hot plate of borscht at supper that evening, Mattie blurted out what had been on her mind for some time, "Oh, if only that Rochling woman would die!" Mattie went on to suggest a drowning. Hans wouldn't heart of it. "How about poison?" ventured Mattie. Hans thought it would be fine. That evening Hans paid Frau Rochling for damages to her linens. While she drank some tea, Mattie slipped 20 aspirins into the brew. Next day Frau Rochling remarked that she hadn't felt so well in years.

No, there had to be another way. On the evening of Feb. 19 Mattie poured several courage-producing litres of beer into Hans and then presented him with a practical cutting instrument, a hatchet. When Frau Rochling called, the sozzled Hans attacked her with the hatchet, killing the poor woman instantly with a few well-aimed blows to the head.

Busy as beavers, the conspirators warmed to the task at hand. Conscientious Mattie had a new saw and kitchen knife at the ready. The work took all night. Off came the head, arms and legs. All assorted parts, including two sections of torso, were boiled in large pots. The hot, disagreeable labor completed, the pair wrapped their gruesome cargo in old pillowslips and bits of old clothing they found around the apartment. Little Horst slept peacefully in the bedroom.

Hans washed down the apartment. Then he and Mattie made two trips each carrying what remained of poor Frau Rochling in shopping bags. These were thrown over bridges far from the apartment. The next night they entered the dead woman's apartment and moved the remainder of her belongings into their own apartment, hanging her key on the hook outside her door.

Frau Rochling's absence didn't cause any undue alarm. Her sudden disappearance seemed obvious. Realizing that she was being forced out of the apartment in about 40 days, she had cleaned out the place and skipped away, probably owing some rent. A few days after Frau Rochling's departure, Mattie and Hans also moved to a new apartment.

On Feb. 26 a rag-wrapped parcel was found beside Berlin's Muhlendamm Lock. It contained half a human torso. Police were stymied, particularly after their forensic lab revealed that the torso had been boiled.

In desperation, investigating officers displayed the materials which had been used to wrap the torso. A pillowslip, brown shawl, chenille cover, a piece of faded blue material, some string and two safety pins were exhibited in the window of a leading department store. Thousands stared at the morbid items. Several persons with good intentions came forward, but all were mistaken. Two months passed. Someone had committed the perfect murder.

Hold it. Enter our amateur detective, Minna Stablein. Minna called on the Missing Persons Department of the Berlin Police. She wanted to know what had become of Frau Rochling, who had been superintendent of the building where she lived. She reported that the missing Frau Rochling had generally kept to herself, but had one good friend in the apartment, Mathilda Ladestock. Minna revealed that she had asked Mattie about Frau Rochling's absence and was told that Mattie had no idea of her whereabouts.

Minna couldn't believe that the two friends would not have kept in touch. She took it upon herself to ask neighbors if they had seen anyone move Frau Rochling's belongings. No one had. She even interviewed the landlord. He knew nothing. When Mattie and Hans moved in the middle of the night, Minna watched in hiding and noted that several pieces of Frau Rochling's furniture moved with them.

It didn't add up, so Minna went to the police. Detectives showed her the materials which had been wrapped around the torso. The faded blue material had been a piece of a frock worn by little Horst. Berlin police visited Mattie and Hans' former apartment. Bits of soiled wallpaper were taken away for laboratory examination.

Mattie and Hans were taken into custody. Furniture and other belongings found in their new apartment were identified as the property of Frau Rochling. The wallpaper taken from their former apartment was stained with human blood. Tenants who lived directly above Mattie and Hans told police that on the night of the alleged murder they heard noises best described as sawing and hacking, which continued all night.

Faced with this type of incriminating evidence, Mattie and Hans confessed. They told of Frau Rochling's ingratiating herself in their lives so that, despite frequent quarrels, there seemed to be no other way to jettison their unwanted friend than to kill her.

Hans underwent psychiatric testing and was adjudged to be a moron, completely dominated by his aggressive lover Mattie. He stood trial for Frau Rochling's murder and was found guilty. In deference to his mental deficiencies, he received the relatively light sentence of six years imprisonment. Upon his release he was deported to Russia as an undesirable alien.

Mattie was convicted of attempted murder. Remember the 20 aspirins? She was sentenced to nine years imprisonment, and was released in 1933 after serving her complete sentence.

The odd couple had come within an ace of committing the perfect murder. If only it hadn't been for that meddling Minna Stablein...

MURDER IN CAPE TOWN
(SOUTH AFRICA)

As we all know, triangles are three-cornered geometric forms. Substitute individuals for corners and you have a love triangle.

Come along with me now to Cape Town, South Africa and meet the characters who combined to produce a love triangle so hot that it erupted into bloody murder.

Marlene Lehnberg was brought up by strict religious parents. She was an excellent pupil, whose teachers were disappointed when she chose not to pursue a university education. Instead, attractive Marlene moved out of her parents' Cape Town home and moved into Stowell Lodge in nearby Rondebosch. She obtained clerical employment at the Orthopedic Workshop, an organization which outfitted, assisted, and otherwise dealt with individuals who had lost limbs.

Her boss was tall, well-preserved, 47-year-old Christiaan van der Linde. In 1973, Chris had been married for 25 years to his 46-year-old wife, Susanna. They had three adult children. Theirs was considered to be an ideal marriage. That is, it was right up until 17-year-old Marlene began working with Chris.

Despite the 30-year age difference, Marlene fell hard for her suave employer. Chris, in turn, not only failed to put up adequate defences to ward off Marlene's advances, he actually encouraged her attention. Within weeks Marlene and Chris were whipping over to Stowell Lodge at every opportunity to satisfy those oh so natural biological urges which are wont to plague us mortals.

Marlene swore undying obedience, servitude, loyalty and whatever to Chris. She urged him to tell all to his wife, obtain a divorce, marry her and live happily ever after. Chris simply didn't see it that way. Yes, he loved Marlene dearly, particularly on those occasions when they were between the sheets over at the Lodge, but he just couldn't leave his wife. Not after 25 years of marital bliss.

There matters simmered and boiled until September 1974, when Marlene phoned Susanna for an appointment and then drove out to the van der Linde home for a meeting. She told Susanna that she was on intimate terms with Chris, that they loved each other, and asked what she intended to do about it. Susanna was understandably taken aback by the knowledge of her husband's infidelity but, in the true tradition of the wronged wife, she clearly and quite loudly told Marlene that she had no intention of giving Chris a divorce.

When Chris heard of the meeting between mistress and wife, he was furious at Marlene, but not furious enough to terminate those pleasant trysts in Marlene's room. Heavens, no.

Marlene became depressed at the hopelessness of her situation. Chris wouldn't leave his wife, Susanna wouldn't divorce him, and all the while Marlene couldn't live without her man. She thought and thought. There had to be a solution. Well, now, there was one way. Why hadn't she thought of it sooner? It was so very simple. She could kill Susanna.

With this rather positive attitude, she approached Marthinus Choegor, a 33-year-old destitute black cripple, who had lost his leg in a car accident and was an out patient at the Orthopedic Workshop where Marlene was employed. In the past Marlene had displayed some semblance of kindness toward Marthinus, who had been born to poverty and subservience to the white man in a country where blacks were treated as inferiors. Initially, Marthinus was appalled at the suggestion put forth by Marlene, namely that he kill Susanna van der Linde.

To fully comprehend Marthinus' predicament, we must touch on his circumstances. Later, psychiatrists were to make much of his state of mind at the time he was approached by Marlene. He had a wife and two children who were living in squalor. Because of his crude artificial leg and use of a crutch, he could obtain only the most menial of jobs.

Marthinus' intelligence was well below average. This young white girl who had been so kind to him now offered him money, a radio and a car, riches far beyond his wildest dreams. In addition, Marlene had offered to fulfil another dream. She promised Marthinus that once the killing had taken place, she would have sex with him.

Twice Marthinus mustered up enough courage to approach the van der Linde home and twice his courage failed him. The first time he went as far as knocking on the front door, but when he saw Susanna part the drapes and look at him, he ran away. On his second attempt, police picked him up and questioned him as a vagrant before releasing him. On that occasion poor Marthinus had just enough time to get rid of the hammer he was carrying.

Marlene was furious at Marthinus' failure. In desperation, on Nov. 4, 1974, she drove her accomplice out to Susanna's house. This time the odd couple came equipped with a pistol. Marlene had no trouble gaining entrance to the home on 66 Gladstone St. Susanna let her in. Marthinus followed.

When Susanna saw Marthinus, she became frightened and ran to the telephone. Marlene crashed the pistol against Susanna's left jaw. She screamed for Marthinus to choke Susanna. Later Marthinus would say he obeyed as if hypnotized. Susanna lay on the floor being throttled when Marlene passed Marthinus a pair of scissors, at the same time commanding him to stab the now helpless Susanna. Seven times the scissors plunged into Susanna's chest. Her life's blood spilled out on her living room floor.

Marlene drove Marthinus to his corrugated tin hovel. She then drove to Johannesburg, where she had taken up residence a few days earlier in order to establish an alibi for the time of the murder.

Later that morning Chris van der Linde couldn't reach his wife by phone. He called his daughter Zelda, who drove to her mother's home and walked into the house of carnage.

It didn't take long. Police remembered detaining the distinctive derelict with the artificial leg close to Gladstone St. On the morning of the murder a neighbor had seen such a man using a crutch walk up the steps to the van der Linde residence accompanied by a white girl.

A few questions thrown at employees of the Orthopedic Workshop revealed the close relationship between the 19-year-old Marlene and her 49-year-old lover, Chris van der Linde. Marthinus and Marlene were picked up by police.

Within 24 hours both suspects confessed to the murder. Both agreed to all details except one. Marlene insisted that she had never entered the murder house but had remained outside in her car.

On March 4, 1975 the accused pair stood trial for murder. The jury chose to believe that Marlene was in the van der Linde home and took an active part in the actual murder.

Marthinus Choegor didn't get his money, radio, car or sex. He was sentenced to 15 years imprisonment.

Marlene Lehnberg didn't get the man she loved. Instead she received a sentence of 20 years in prison.

Christiaan van der Linde, who was the catalyst which caused the death of one person and ruined the life of two others, had no guilty knowledge of the murder and was never accused of any crime.

DINGO MURDER
(AUSTRALIA)

Did a preacher's wife kill her two-month-old daughter? Or did a wild dog carry off the baby, as the mother has steadfastly claimed?

The disappearance of Azaria Chamberlain is Australia's most sensational murder case. It has been dubbed "The Dingo Baby Case" by the press of the world.

To properly comprehend the locale of the alleged crime, one must realize that Ayers Rock is located in central Australia. Much as Niagara Falls is Canada's foremost tourist site, Ayers Rock may be considered one of Australia's prime natural attractions. The monolith is roughly 340 metres high and nine kilometres in circumference. The huge rock changes color dramatically as the sun rises and sets. Thousands of visitors clamber over the sleeping giant each year.

In August 1980, the Chamberlains drove for three days to reach isolated Ayers Rock. The family consisted of Michael, 36, a Seventh Day Adventist preacher, his wife of 10 years, Lindy, 32, and their three children, Aiden, six, Reagan, four, and baby Azaria, two months.

The two boys helped their father pitch their four-man pup tent about 20 metres from a public barbecue area. The tent was accessible through a zippered front flap.

It was an exciting day. The family took pictures of the huge rock from various angles. Despite the cramped quarters, everyone had a good night's sleep. Next morning, the mercury rose to 120 degrees F. Michael and his two sons climbed to the top of the rock and visited the various tourist attractions at the base. They then returned to their campsite.

Reagan fell asleep. Little Azaria was wrapped in several blankets and placed in a bassinet at the rear of the tent. The zippered flap was left open because Aiden was hungry and Lindy knew she would be putting him to bed as soon as he had something to eat. Lindy was about 20 metres from the tent, attempting to open a tin of beans, when Michael thought he heard the baby cry. Lindy said she would check.

As she approached the tent, according to her later statements, she saw a dingo (wild dog) emerge through the unzipped flap of the tent. The animal shook its head as if it was carrying something in its mouth. Lindy screamed. "The dingo has got my baby!"

Within minutes, a search party was organized, but the only trace of Azaria were scattered blankets found in and round the front of the tent. Lindy and Michael Chamberlain did everything they could to assist authorities in finding their child. Lindy described her little daughter's clothing. The child weighed 10 pounds, which was considered a heavy load for a dingo to carry. The tawny beast is roughly the size of a small German shepherd.

A few days after the tragedy, the Chamberlains left for their home in Mount Isa in Queensland. Eight days after the disappearance, tourist Wallace Goodwin was walking along the west side of Ayers Rock when he came across a pile of infant's clothing. Goodwin realized the importance of his find and immediately notified police.

The clothing was quickly identified as belonging to the missing child. The area around the collar of the child's jumpsuit was bloodstained, as was her tiny singlet. He other garments were free of blood. Strangely enough, Lindy insisted that Azaria was wearing a jacket. This jacket was not found in the relatively neat pile of clothing discovered by Goodwin. No sign of a body or portions of a body were in evidence.

The discovery of the clothing gave rise to all sorts of sinister theories. Suddenly, the tragedy of a child being dragged away by a dingo was suspect. It is impossible for a dog to undress a two-month-old baby.

A coroner's inquest into the disappearance revealed stunning facts. The child's clothing was devoid of dingo hairs. There was no saliva present on the clothing, nor did the tiny garments appear to be torn or shredded. It was clear to all that a human being had undressed the child. It was also strongly insinuated that because the clothing was found several kilometres from the Chamberlains' tent, a human had placed the clothing where it was eventually found.

Summing up, the coroner concluded that after the dingo had killed and absconded with the child, the body had been found and undressed by an unknown person. It was then buried and the clothing placed at the base of the rock. The coroner offered his sympathy to the Chamberlains.

Many did not agree with the conclusions of the coroner's inquest. It just didn't seem possible that a dingo could kill an infant without getting hair and saliva on the baby's clothing.

Utilizing dolls, various experiments were conducted by experts. They concluded that the bloodstains on the jumpsuit and singlet were compatible with the child's neck being cut, rather than from head injuries inflicted by a dog. The clothing was sent to London, England, where experts, using ultraviolet fluorescent photography, uncovered bloody handprint impressions. From the position of these prints, they concluded that the child was held after she was cut and the blood flowed. The sum total of all these experiments indicated that Azaria had met her death by having her throat slashed by a cutting instrument.

A year after the disappearance, the case was officially reopened. The Chamberlain's car was confiscated and minutely examined. At a second coroner's inquest, it was revealed that blood traces were found in the car. The blood was identified as being fetal blood, meaning that of a baby under six months old. A pair of scissors was found in the car. The cutting edge had traces of fetal blood. Once again, experts, this time imported from England, confirmed that there was no way a dingo could have come in contact with Azaria Chamberlain without leaving hair or saliva traces on her clothing.

As a result of this second coroner's inquest, Lindy Chamberlain was charged with the murder of her baby and her husband Michael was charged with being an accessory after the fact of murder.

On Sept. 13, 1982, the Chamberlains stood trial. Lindy was seven months pregnant. Once more, the evidence already described was put before a jury. Prof. Malcolm Chaikin, head of the School of Textile Technology at the University of New South Wales, stated from the witness stand that the child's jumpsuit had been damaged by scissors and not by the teeth of a dog. He had come to his dramatic conclusion by using a dead rabbit, dressed in a jumpsuit and utilizing a machine with dogs' teeth attached. He had failed to produce the same type of damage as found on the dead girl's garment.

The trial lasted seven weeks. The jury deliberated for under seven hours. Both defendants were found guilty; Lindy of murder, Michael of being an accessory after the fact. Lindy was sentenced to life imprisonment at hard labor, while Michael received a suspended sentence at hard labor.

In the years which had elapsed since the tragedy, Lindy never deviated from her original bizarre story of the dingo dog. She insisted that every detail was true, right down to the missing jacket she claimed her daughter was wearing at the time of the disappearance. Lindy gave birth to her fourth child, Kahlia, while in prison. On April 29, 1983, her appeal against conviction was dismissed. Meanwhile, her husband fought with every resource at his disposal to help secure her freedom.

In February 1986 a tourist was reported to have fallen off Ayers Rock. Unbelievably, during the search for the tourist, police found a tattered white jacket. It proved to be Azaria Chamberlain's jacket, the jacket which Lindy swore she had been wearing when she disappeared six years earlier. Most of the scientific evidence, including the blood evidence which convicted Lindy Chamberlain, was based on the premise that the jacket didn't exist. Authorities agree that had the jacket been found at the time of the trial, a conviction would not have been possible.

Three days after the discovery of the jacket, Lindy Chamberlain was released from prison and a further inquest into the case has been ordered. Northern Territories Attorney General Marshal Perron has stated that regardless of the outcome of the new inquiry, Mrs. Chamberlain would not be returned to jail. He further stated that her release did not recognize her innocence, but was done in order that she might have access to legal advice in preparing for the upcoming inquiry.

In May 1986, a royal commission inquiry found "numerous and formidable obstacles" for "acceptance of the prosecution's evidence" and concluded that a dingo "may have taken" the baby.

Lindy Chamberlain and her husband received an official pardon. A year later her conviction was officially overturned. At the same time, her husband's conviction was dismissed as well.

On July 16, 1991, the Chamberlains were awarded $369,000 (Cdn) by the government of Australia. Much of this damage award will go to legal fees - in all, the Chamberlains have retained 17 lawyers. The case has been the subject of three documentaries, eight books, and the movie *A Cry in the Dark*.

KILLER IN MANILA
(PHILIPPINES)

Tall, handsome George Murray kept his eyes open. As a criminal investigator for the U.S. Army in the European theatre during the Second World War, he learned plenty. Near the conclusion of hostilities, the Kansas City native was transferred to the Philippines.

When the war came to an end, Murray decided to put his store of knowledge to practical use. He obtained financial backing and soon became a big time arms smuggler. He never returned to the U.S. Instead, he entered a world of secret ships with hidden cargoes and clandestine meetings with agents of other countries. Within a few short years George Murray was a wealthy man.

George acquired a beautiful Filipino wife, the former Esther del Rosario. Quite possibly Esther thought Murray a convenient way out of her predicament. Her husband had died of natural causes some time earlier, leaving her with four small children. Whatever her original motives, Esther soon found herself very much in love with her swashbuckling husband.

As the wife of a man who made his living in the shadows, Esther learned not to ask questions concerning his business dealings. She resented the fact that George was away from home for long periods of time, but relished those intervals he spent at her side.

As for George, he dealt with dangerous and often violent men on a daily basis, but the rewards were substantial. He had a luxurious home, a chauffeur-equipped Cadillac and a long, sleek yacht. In fact, you might say George had the world by the tail. However, there was one fly in the ointment.

Her name was Carol Varga.

George met Carol in 1947, when he rented out his yacht, appropriately named

Mistress, to a movie company filming sea scenes for the movie *Sagur*. Carol had a starring role in the film.

Gorgeous Carol had heard of George's reputation before meeting him. Our boy's physical appearance did nothing to lessen her interest. Here was a man actually leading the kind of life often depicted on the screen. To say Carol and George were attracted to each other would be an understatement. For two years the lovers met at every opportunity. That is, right up until the night of Aug. 13, 1949.

George spent the early evening in his wife's arms, dancing at their palatial home. These were the moments Esther cherished. At 11 p.m. George told his wife that he had to drive into Manila on business. As usual, Esther didn't ask questions.

As he had on so many nights, George backed his Caddy out of the garage and sped to the Riviera night club, where Carol was waiting. The clandestine meetings, the subterfuge, and the lies he told his wife were getting on his nerves. This night he asked Carol to marry him. She quite logically responded that she would be most happy to marry him were he not already encumbered by a wife. That was good enough for George. While we cannot read his mind, we know that when he wanted something, he would let nothing stand in his way. After all, he was a man of action.

At 4 a.m. George returned to his home in suburban Rizal. He undressed and went directly to bed. Soon he was fast asleep.

A short time later, a revolver was placed between George's eyes. The noise of the report ricocheted through the large house. Outside, George's three boxers started to bark. A second shot was aimed directly into the mouth of the now dead man. The third shot plowed through the neck, most likely because the head jerked back from the force of the second bullet. A fourth bullet made its way though George's heart. Someone definitely did not like George Murray.

Mrs. Murray called police. When they arrived, she greeted them with her four frightened children at her side. She explained that at the time the shots were fired, she was downstairs making coffee. Her husband had awakened her when he returned from Manila. He had fallen asleep, but she had difficulty sleeping, so she went downstairs for coffee.

When she heard the shots, she ran upstairs, passing her maid Maria Naral, understandably running downstairs. Esther looked in the children's rooms. Thank heaven, they were unharmed. She raced to her own room, threw open the door and screamed, "George, what has happened?" George didn't answer.

Attempting to gather her wits about her, she sent her eldest daughter to wake up chauffeur Jose Tagle and tell him to fetch a doctor. Tagle, who slept in a separate wing of the house, dressed and followed her instructions.

When asked if her husband had any enemies, Mrs. Murray readily volunteered that George must have had scores of enemies. Police didn't take long to trace the dead man's nefarious business dealings from the time he was discharged from the U.S. Army to the day of his death. In fact, word drifted down to the working detectives to be discreet. George had greased the palms of many a politician in his dealings to procure U.S. Army surplus materials.

Initially, the investigation concentrated on business enemies, but there was disconcerting physical evidence about the Murray home. The window to the master bedroom was open. The dog's kennel was directly below the window. Surely, had the killer gained entrance to the home via the window, the dogs would have caused a racket. Yet they had not barked until after the shots were fired.

It had been drizzling rain all that night. The earth around the Murray home was extremely soft, but there were no footprints outside, nor was the carpeted bedroom floor soiled in any way.

Most startling of all, maid Maria Naral could not be found. Mrs. Murray stated that the last time she had seen Maria had been when she passed her on the stairs. The poor girl had been scared out of her wits and apparently planned on never returning.

Within days, police found Maria in a nearby house owned by the Murrays. She had quite a story to tell. On the morning of the murder, Mrs. Murray had knocked on her door. One of the younger children wouldn't sleep and wanted to stay with Maria. Mrs. Murray left the child and closed the door. About 30 seconds later, Maria heard loud explosions which she thought was a car backfiring. She got out of bed and met Mrs. Murray at the threshold of the master bedroom. Maria peered in and saw the bleeding body of George Murray.

Mrs. Murray told Maria, "If anybody asks you any questions, tell them the shots you heard were the backfiring of a car and that you also heard the dogs bark. Tell them I was in the kitchen." Maria added significantly that on the night of the murder, she had closed and locked the window to the master bedroom before retiring for the night.

After the meeting in the hall, Mrs. Murray had accompanied Maria to the nearby vacant house with the instructions, "You stay there and don't let yourself be seen."

Chauffeur Tagle was questioned more closely. He now stated that he had been awakened by the shots. He had peered out of his bedroom window, located over the garage, and had seen a woman step onto the master bedroom balcony and toss something into the kennels. A search of the kennels uncovered a revolver, which proved to be the murder weapon.

George Murray had underestimated his wife's knowledge of his affair with Carol Varga. Both husband and wife had planned on killing each other at approximately the same time. Esther struck first.

Throughout her murder trial, Mrs. Murray stuck to her story that an intruder must have entered her home and killed her husband. No one believed her. Esther Murray was found guilty of the murder of her husband and was sentenced to life imprisonment.

PICTURE PERFECT
(MEXICO)

Police officer Manuel Cardano, one of Mexico City's finest, earned a few extra pesos for keeping an eye on Casa Numero 17 on the Avenida Insurgentes. In fact, the lady of the house, Senorita Jacinta Abnaz, had given Dardano a key to the back door so that he could drop in daily to check her valuable furnishings, paintings and jewelry.

While thus moonlighting one day in 1931, Cardano was shocked to find the interior of the pink stucco home in shambles. A human wrecking machine had gone through the house, ripping chesterfields, breaking china, slashing paintings and in general demolishing the inside of the once attractive, well-appointed home. Amid the debris lay the body of beautiful Jacinta Abnaz. She had been beaten to death about the head.

Cardano called his superiors. In minutes, the house was swarming with detectives, a doctor and a police photographer. Cardano explained his rather unique relationship with the deceased. His story was accepted at face value. Cardano was completely exonerated of any guilty knowledge of the crime.

Detectives delved into the strange life of the dead woman. They learned that Jacinta was born in one of the poorer sections of the Yucatan Peninsula. However, her father was a wealthy plantation owner, who died when she was 23 years old. Left with a sizable fortune and no longer encumbered by the restraints of an overprotective father, Jacinta moved to Mexico City.

The beautiful but shy young girl had some difficulty breaking into Mexican society. She enrolled at the University of Mexico, where she took courses in medicine and psychology. As a hobby, she also studied astrology and hypnotism. Yet even at university, Jacinta had difficulty cultivating friends. She was remembered as a loner.

One room of Jacinta's home was covered with photographs of prominent Mexican men. Doctors, politicians, industrialists and high-ranking army personnel smiled down from the walls. An examination of the backs of the photographs revealed inscriptions of endearment, such as, "To the one and only woman who made me forget the outside world," and "To the greatest astrologer in Mexico."

Police investigated the dead woman's connection with astrology and hypnotism. They found out that she was a part-time professional astrologer and often received clients at her home. Detectives systematically and tactfully checked out each prominent Mexican whose picture appeared on Jacinta's wall. Each man was amazed to be involved in a murder investigation. All admitted that the photographs were of them, but stated vehemently that the inscriptions were forgeries. Many of the men had never known the dead woman. A few had attended hypnotic sessions at Jacinta's home. Certainly, none of the men had been romantically involved with Jacinta, nor had any of them given her a photograph.

Experts agreed that the inscriptions on the back of the photographs had been written by Jacinta herself. When the men were asked who had taken the pictures, police discovered that the photographer in all cases was the same man, Miguel Alvarez. Maybe the strangest twist in a case fraught with strange twists was that, besides being a well-known photographer in Mexico City, Miguel was also the official police photographer. It was he who had taken the photographs of Jacinta Abnaz's body. Why hadn't he told police of his connection with the dead woman?

The veteran police photographer was detained for questioning. He told a remarkable story. Over a year earlier, he had received a phone call from Jacinta requesting that he do some photographic work for her. Miguel went to Jacinta's home with the finished work.

Upon entering the house, Miguel found the lights low, soft music playing and Jacinta, now clad in a seductive, low-cut dress, pouring drinks. Before the night was over, Miguel and Jacinta were frolicking under Mexico's twinkling stars. Miguel became Jacinta's lover. However, he was quick to point out that he loved his wife and children. It was just that, darn it all, she was so beautiful and had such a nice home and bought him such expensive presents and purchased his photographs at such exorbitant prices - gee whiz, what was a fellow to do?

All was not a rose garden. Jacinta had a few little quirks. She had her lover make copies of his photographs of prominent men and adorned her walls with these portraits. She inscribed them herself. She even wrote letters to herself declaring undying love and forged the names of prominent Mexicans to these letters. Sometimes she insisted that Miguel call her princess. Let's face it, Jacinta was a little kinky.

The beginning of the end of Miguel and Jacinta's strange relationship occurred when Jacinta set up a hidden microphone and recorded Miguel's lovemaking. According to Miguel, during this particular session, Jacinta implored her lover to kiss her feet and talk to her as if to a goddess.

On the morning of the murder, Jacinta played the tape to Miguel. She also presented him with divorce papers and a marriage certificate. Her scheme was simple enough. Miguel was to divorce his wife and marry her. Jacinta, dressed in silk gown and jade necklace, demanded that Miguel get down on his knees and wash her feet.

Instead, Miguel saw red. He killed his lover then and there. Miguel swore that he had an overwhelming urge to destroy everything Jacinta owned. Like a madman, he roared through the house, wreaking destruction.

Police searched Miguel's apartment. They recovered a blood-stained shirt and trousers. There was little doubt that his strange story was true.

As a matter of routine, Miguel's fingerprints were checked. Surprise of surprises, the 10-year veteran police photographer was not Miguel Alvarez at all. He was Pedro Gallegos, who had years before served a prison term for robbery. Faced with this evidence, Miguel readily admitted his true identity. He had completely reformed over 10 years earlier and had built up a prosperous photography business over and above his police work. His marriage had been a successful one. That is, until he received that fateful phone call from Jacinta.

Miguel, or Pedro if you like, goes down in history as the only man who not only returned to the scene of his crime, but was the official photographer of the crime scene as well.

Miguel was tried and found guilty of murder. He was sentenced to 30 years imprisonment, but did not serve out his sentence. He was shot to death sometime later, while attempting to escape.

If you are ever vacationing in Chichen-itza, Mexico, you may visit a restored astronomical observatory among the ancient Mayan ruins. We have Jacinta to thank for the restored observatory. She willed her fortune to the Mexican government for that purpose. And why not? For a large portion of her adult life, she wanted only to be treated as a Mayan princess.

THE FIVE-FOOT SPEAR
(Germany)

Kurt Rheiners was disgusted. Here he was, 36 years old and everywhere he went he was inundated with one topic of conversation - sex. It seemed to Kurt that he had missed the boat. Sure, his wife Petra was a good woman. After all, they had been happily married for 11 years and had a fine 10-year-old son, but that wasn't the point. His sex life was a definite bore. Besides, it appeared to Kurt that all the younger people in Hanover, West Germany, were doing what comes naturally all the time.

Take his best friend, pastry cook Norbert Splett, for example. In 1972, Norbert was a virile 20. His girlfriend, plump, luscious Anna Drucker performed in every which way for Norbert. And how did Kurt know these intimate details? Because Norbert wasn't averse to telling him, that's how. Sometimes, just to keep up with his friend, Kurt would make up fictional orgies in which he took part.

In 1972, there were scores of encounter magazines in West Germany advertising sexual adventures. All one had to do was contact the code number under the photo and delights would be delivered to your door like pizza. Kurt told his friend that he often obtained his kicks through these advertisements. In reality, he was far too chicken to attempt such liaisons.

In June, Kurt, a plumber by profession, convinced Petra to take a vacation with their son. After 11 years of marriage, it would do them both good. Well, folks, Petra wasn't over the horizon before Kurt was fantasizing orgies with beautiful, willing frauleins.

He slugged back schnapps after schnapps down at the Ant Tavern, his usual hangout. Sometimes, just for fun, he threw back 40 glasses of beer at one sitting. Trouble was, most of the young stuff congregated at the many discos in town. Kurt felt out of place in such establishments. Things simply were not working out the way things were supposed to when the Queen Bee leaves the hive.

During the late afternoon of June 20, Anna and Norbert joined Kurt down at the tavern. All three went at that delightful German beer as if it was going out of style. The afternoon gave way to evening. Our trio switched to schnapps. By midnight, when the three friends left the Ant, Anna was a giggling mass of jolly fun.

Next morning, Otto Hoffman, another of Kurt's acquaintances, dropped by to see how his pal was making out without Petra around the house. When no one answered his knock, he simply opened the door and walked in.

Otto would never forget the horrible scene. There was Kurt, naked as the day he was born, lying on his stomach with a five-foot spear sticking out of his back. Otto couldn't see the blade of the spear for the simple reason that it had been driven completely through poor Kurt.

Otto was understandably stunned. His eyes swept the living room. There were empty glasses, plates of food and piles of clothing everywhere, certain signs that a wild party had taken place.

Gathering his senses, Otto ran to his friend's side. There was no sign of life. Then, attempting to make things look as good as possible for his friend, he grabbed Kurt's bloody pants and attempted to pull them over the dead man's legs, but found the task too difficult and gave up. It dawned on Otto. Kurt had been murdered, probably by one of those people who advertise in those encounter magazines. Kurt was always bragging about the wild parties he had with them. No doubt this was one party that got out of hand.

Otto called police. When they arrived, poor Otto was still trying to pull Kurt's bloody pants over his legs. The policemen took one look at the scene and figured they had the murderer. Otto was handcuffed to a radiator. They then called their superiors at headquarters, informing them that a man had been killed with a spear. It was some time before anyone took the officers seriously. It wasn't that often that people were speared to death in 1972.

An hour later, homicide detectives, accompanied by a doctor, showed up at Kurt's home. The doctor confirmed what everyone knew. No question about it, Kurt had been killed with a spear. The blade had entered Kurt's back, had gone through the heart and left lung and emerged through the skin of the chest. The angle of the blade indicated that the spear had not been thrown, but had been hand-held.

The doctor, who proved to be a wealth of information, had still more details to reveal, some of a rather delicate nature. You see, folks, from the physical evidence, the doctor was able to ascertain that Kurt had been having intercourse at the time of death. The spear had been plunged into his back while he was thus engaged on the sofa. We can only assume that he died happy. Because the blade had gone all the way through his body, there was a possibility at Kurt's lady friend might have a superficial wound, or at least a scratch on her chest. One wonders how she escaped dying of shock.

As an afterthought, Otto was released from the nasty radiator. A few questions, and he was exonerated from taking any part in the crime.

Before anyone knew that Norbert Splett had been in Kurt's company the night before, Norbert strolled into police headquarters. He didn't mince words. "I killed him, I killed my best friend. He was raping my fiancée."

Norbert went on to tell about the drinking bout at the Ant Tavern. When they left the tavern, Kurt suggested they continue drinking at his home. Everyone agreed. They proceeded to Kurt's place, where they dug up the unappetizing combination of sausages and cognac. Kurt suggested a novel game of cards. Anyone who got the jack or ace of hearts had to take off an article of clothing.

Soon, Kurt, Norbert and the giggling Anna were stark naked. That's when Norbert fell ill. He excused himself and proceeded to the bathroom. When he returned, there were Kurt and Anna on the sofa in that oh, so embarrassing position. It appeared to Kurt that Anna was fighting to protect her honor or whatever. Norbert picked up the decorative spear and plunged it into Kurt's back. Kurt stopped doing whatever he was doing and fell off the sofa onto the floor. Anna stopped giggling.

Norbert was detained. Police picked Anna up at Norbert's apartment. She told exactly the same story as her boyfriend. In fact, it was so similar that police believed the two lovers had discussed the details before Norbert showed up at the police station.

There were questionable areas. No money was found on Kurt, although a waiter at the Ant Tavern stated he had been carrying a wad of bills in his pocket the night before. Both Norbert and Anna's fingerprints were found throughout the house, but the spear had been wiped clean of prints. Anna had long, sharp fingernails. Kurt's body was free of any sign of scratches, indicating that she had not tried to fight him off.

While the investigation was at its height, who should show up but Mrs. Kurt Rheiners. The vacation was definitely over. To her credit, Petra stood up for her dead husband, regardless of his embarrassing exit. She blamed the sexual revolution for his death. She felt their marriage was a good one, but that Kurt and men like him felt they were missing something in life and did foolish things. She stated that there usually was a fairly large sum of money kept in the house. This money may have been the real motive behind Kurt's death.

On May 22, 1973, Norbert Splett was found guilty of unpremeditated murder with extenuating circumstances. He was sentenced to ten years imprisonment. The charges against Anna Drucker were dropped. She never stood trial.

And, no, I was unable to find out if Anna had a scratch on her chest.

11

QUESTIONABLE CASES

DELAYED JUSTICE

The murders which shocked the tiny New England town of Fort Fairfield, Maine, 20 years ago may never be solved to anyone's satisfaction. The scenario reads like a tangled plot of an Agatha Christie whodunit.

There were two murders within two months. A wayward citizen of the town was a suspect. So was an Air Force lieutenant. A prominent citizen of the county also came under suspicion. Throw in the attractive teenage daughter of a convict, mix well with a poem sent to a newspaper and you begin to get some idea of the intrigue which enveloped this otherwise peaceful rural community.

Fort Fairfield is in potato country. The rich soil which gives sustenance to New Brunswick's potato processing industry stretches across the international boundary into Aroostook County, Maine. The Interstate Food Processing Corp. is the largest employer in Fort Fairfield. The town's population hovers around 4000.

On the day after Christmas, 1964, 14-year-old Cyrus Everett, a newspaper delivery boy for the Bangor *Daily News*, started out from his home on Presque Isle St. at 5:15 p.m. to make collections. Within hours, Cyrus Everett would be dead.

As the evening wore on, Cyrus' mother began to worry. Cyrus had never been late before. By 9 o'clock Mrs. Everett was frantic. She had called all her son's friends. Finally, she called her pastor, Rev. John Goodhart. Together they drove along Cyrus' paper route. An hour later they called police.

Investigating officers ascertained that Cyrus was carrying a Northern National Bank purse containing between $12 and $20 in coins and bills when he was last seen along his route. Naturally they were interested in the last homes where Cyrus had been seen alive and well. One of the occupants of these homes was Philip Adams, who had a lengthy police record. Adams was questioned but not detained.

On the day following the disappearance, Adams reported that he had been attacked by a man in Jerry's Gym, a ramshackle building located close to Adams' home. Red marks on Adams' throat gave credence to his story. A truck, which had been seen near the gym, was later located. There were bloodstains on the front seat. These seemingly unrelated events were to take on more sinister connotations much later. At the time police were looking for a missing teenager.

Local authorities were baffled. No youngster had ever run away from Fort Fairfield. Cyrus Everett was a conscientious, well-behaved teenager, who had acted normally in every way right up to the time of his disappearance. Weeks passed. Cyrus was listed as a missing person with Maine authorities.

During the time that Cyrus was missing, Shirley Harrison, a Portland housewife with a wide reputation for extra-sensory perception, gave a lecture to a group of funeral directors at the Holiday Inn in Portland. She brought up the missing Cyrus Everett case, stating emphatically that the boy was dead and had been murdered. She said that he would be found under a log in a swampy area near the Chaney Place. Her prediction would prove to be eerily correct.

Two months after Cyrus Everett went missing, the town of Fort Fairfield experienced its second shock. Donna Mauch, 24, a pretty brunette cocktail waitress employed at the Plymouth Hotel in Fort Fairfield, rented the very same apartment which Philip Adams had lived in at the time of Cyrus Everett's disappearance.

Donna moved in on Feb. 15, 1965. Nine days later, when she failed to show up for work at the hotel, her brother called at the apartment. He found his sister's body in the living room behind the sofa. Donna was fully clothed. Her head, wrapped in a towel, was lying in a pool of blood.

An autopsy indicated that Donna died of a "fractured skull and brain lacerations." She had been beaten to death with an instrument which has never been recovered.

The town buzzed with rumors. Cyrus Everett was last seen calling on a certain apartment. Donna Mauch moved into that very apartment and was murdered nine days later. Was it a mere coincidence or was there a more sinister connection?

Events were soon to unfold which would pose more questions than answers. On May 3, 1965, three youngsters playing in a swampy area known as Chaney's Grove found Cyrus Everett's body. It was partially held down under an 800 pound tree trunk. The body was found lying on its back, arms extended above the head. Cyrus' jacket and shirt were bunched up over the upper portion of his torso, indicating that he might have been dragged by the legs to the huge stump.

Then began a series of blunders which contributed to a classic case of a bungled investigation. An autopsy, performed the day after the body was found, incorrectly indicated that the body was too decomposed to determine "anatomical evidence of the cause of death." This statement converted what had obviously been a murder into an accidental death. It was pointed out that the boy might have been playing on the tree trunk, tipping it over and may accidentally have been pinned underneath.

Few believed the accidental death theory. All that summer, rumors spread throughout Aroostook County. One vicious rumor making the rounds was that a prominent politician, known to have a drinking problem, had been out driving with Donna Mauch on the night of Cyrus Everett's disappearance. Driving while drunk, the politician hit Cyrus. He then dragged the boy's body into the nearby swamp. Two months later he killed Donna to insure her silence. The theory held no matter. At the time of Cyrus' death, the politician was in an institution "drying out."

To quell the rumors once and for all, Attorney General Richard Dubord issued an official statement: "A complete autopsy and State laboratory examination disclosed there were no fractures, or any other indications of violence or foul play on the body." This statement effectively brought the investigation into the boy's death to a close.

Incensed at the lackadaisical attitude of certain officials, Fort Fairfield Town Manager Leonard Kyle elicited the aid of an experienced investigator, Otis LaBree. In a matter of days LaBree established that Everett had been a murder victim. He concluded that the position of the body was not consistent with accidental death. The clothing of the dead boy indicated that he had been dragged to the location where he was found.

As a result of LaBree's findings, Cyrus Everett's body was exhumed. Dr. Michael Luongo, one of the top pathologists in the U.S., performed the autopsy. Dr. Luongo detected a skull fracture. He believed the victim had been beaten to death.

Meanwhile, the investigation into the murder of Donna Mauch was being actively pursued. Twice divorced Donna had had many boyfriends. At the time of her death her beau was First Lieutenant Kenneth Fore, a member of the U.S.A.F. attached to nearby Loring Air Force Base. Fore was a young bachelor. He had loaned Donna his sportscar while he was on temporary duty in Texas. When he returned, he learned that Donna had dated other air force men, using his car.

He and Donna had argued. On the morning before her death, he had removed his T.V. and other personal belongings from her apartment. Fore had also made assorted threats to other personnel on the base who had dated Donna. When questioned, he could provide no airtight alibi for the night of Donna's murder. True enough, he was officially on duty at the air force base that night, but he was unobserved for long periods of time, and could have made his way to Fort Fairfield, killed Donna and returned without being seen.

Fore was taken into custody and tried for Donna's murder. The evidence pointing to his guilt was woefully thin. On the night of the murder it was 25 degrees below zero. Fore's car was inoperable. He was acquitted after going through the ordeal of a murder trial, knowing full well that he was innocent.

Why did a private investigator have to be brought into Fort Fairfield to prove that murder had taken place in the case of Cyrus Everett? The answer lies with a newspaperman named Kingdon Harvey, who until 1979 was owner and editor of the Fort Fairfield *Review*. Kingdon Harvey has been described as stubborn, obstinate, totally fair and, above all, a great old time newspaperman. His beloved Fort Fairfield *Review*, published weekly, has never had a circulation of more than 2000.

In 1965, when the official report stated that Cyrus Everett's death was an accident, Harvey was furious. He ran a picture of the boy and his tombstone on the front page of the Review. Many believe it was this pressure that was instrumental in bringing Otis LaBree into the case. After LaBree proved that murder had been done, Harvey ran the names of Donna Mauch and Cyrus Everett on the front page of his little newspaper for two years.

When Lt. Fore was arrested, Miss Mauch's name was deleted. When the lieutenant was acquitted, crusty King Harvey placed Donna Mauch's name back on the front page. In 1968, even King Harvey ceased in his efforts to urge officialdom to take action to solve the murder cases. In 1980 Harvey suffered a series of strokes and today lives in a convalescent home. His son, Tom Harvey, a former schoolteacher, has taken over the family newspaper.

Years passed. In fact, 20 years. Fort Fairfield's population has not increased. Potatoes remain the chief crop. In recent years there has been talk of bringing in broccoli to give the area some economic flexibility. The old Everett-Mauch murders were forgotten.

One day in 1984 Tom Harvey, editor of the Fort Fairfield *Review*, received a poem in the mail alluding to the old murders. It had been sent anonymously from the Somers Correctional Institution in Somers, Conn. Philip Adams, one of the men who had been questioned regarding the disappearance of Cyrus Everett, was an inmate of the institution. Subsequent investigation by Harvey indicated that Adams had written the poem.

Adams, 42, had a long criminal record, dating back to 1957 when he was only 15. His current incarceration was the result of attacking a ten-year-old boy in Wallingford, Conn. To prevent the youngster from revealing the details of a sexual attack, he had punched the boy in the face and choked him, leaving him unconscious. The boy spent nine days in the hospital. On another occasion Adams had been convicted of sodomizing a nine-year-old boy in Fort Fairfield. Adams, a native of Fort Fairfield, had been in and out of reform schools and training centres throughout his formative years.

In 1965, exactly 46 days after Cyrus Everett was murdered, Adams voluntarily committed himself to the Bangor Mental Hospital. He was released on Feb. 18, six days before Donna Mauch was found murdered in her apartment.

Twenty years later he was writing poems about the old murder cases. Tom Harvey informed police of the poem, which was immediately brought to the attention of District Attorney John McAlwee. McAlwee asked Harvey to sit on his potentially explosive story for six weeks. Harvey agreed. Meanwhile, McAlwee was pursuing the old case from another angle.

Karen Sprague, Philip Adams' former wife, had remarried. Her daughter, Jodie, now an attractive 18-year-old student at Fort Fairfield High School, expressed an interest in contacting her biological father, from whom she had been separated since she was a child. Initially they corresponded. Eventually a meeting was set up.

Jodie visited the correctional institution accompanied by her stepfather. Phil Adams let his daughter know that he would soon be coming up for parole. He suggested that when he was released they could live together, maybe start life anew in Alaska. Other visits took place. Jodie wanted to know more about her father, specifically if he was responsible for the murders in Fort Fairfield. Adams reply was ambiguous but startling, "I'm not saying I did do it and I'm not saying I didn't." Subsequent visits brought forth intimate knowledge of the old crimes. Jodie and her stepfather consulted a lawyer, who advised them to pass along the information to D.A. John McAlwee.

McAlwee felt sure his man was ready to talk. He faced the mammoth task of piecing together two separate investigations which had taken place twenty years apart into a cohesive case for the state of Maine.

Phil Adams waived extradition and was brought back to Maine in January 1985 to stand trial for the murder of Donna Mauch. The Cyrus Everett case was not mentioned during the trial.

The state slowly but surely presented its circumstantial case. The most startling evidence was that of Wayne Adams, brother of the accused. He revealed that Phil phoned him on April 16, 1984, stating, "There's something you've been waiting to hear for 20 years." Phil went on to reveal that on the night of the Mauch murder he had attempted to borrow money from his parents. When they refused he went to Donna's apartment looking for money. She was asleep on the sofa. As he searched the apartment she woke and he killed her. Phil said he covered her face with the towel because she looked at him.

Adams' 18-year-old daughter Jodie told of getting to know her father while he served time. He never actually confessed the killing to her, but he told her he had spent the night in Mauch's apartment and had found her body when he awoke.

Jodie's mother testified that she was a high school student at the time of the Mauch murder. Phil Adams gave her a watch as a gift the day after Donna Mauch was killed. He told her he had purchased the watch at a pawnshop weeks earlier. Later he asked her to return the watch. When she gave it to him, he threw it away, telling her he would get her another one.

Donna Mauch's watch was missing when her body was found. Her mother now testified that Donna was wearing a watch the last time she saw her daughter alive. The inference was not lost on the jury. Did Adams rip the watch off Donna's wrist and present it to his girlfriend as a gift? Did he later think better of it and dispose of the damning evidence?

Jodie's sister Kelly testified that her father confessed to her that he had killed Donna, but afterwards claimed he was only kidding.

Evidently the jury believed he wasn't kidding. Phil Adams was found guilty of the murder of Donna Mauch. He has been sentenced to life imprisonment.

In an anteroom in the courtroom during the Adams murder trial sat a man who was not called to give evidence. Col. Kenneth Fore of the U.S. Air Force, now in charge of security at a U.S. missile installation at Cosimo, Sicily, had been flown over from Italy by District Attorney McAlwee in case his evidence was required. Col. Fore never expressed his feelings when he watched a man convicted of the murder he had stood accused of committing twenty years before.

CIRCUMSTANTIAL EVIDENCE

I has been said that the best example of circumstantial evidence was expounded by an English judge, who pointed out that when Robinson Crusoe spotted Friday's fresh footprints in the sand on his desolate island, it was logical to assume that the island was occupied by a fellow human being. Despite the strength of circumstantial evidence, juries demand an abundance of such evidence before being convinced of a defendant's guilt.

A murder case which rested entirely on circumstantial evidence occurred in 1952 in the tiny English village of Barlaston, Staffordshire, a hamlet more famous for Wedgewood china than acts of violence.

At precisely 6:18 p.m. on Wednesday, July 16, 1952, Fred Wiltshaw, 59, returned home to find his wife Alice, 62, dead on the hall floor. The sight which greeted him was not a pleasant one. Alice was lying in a pool of her own blood. Her head had been bludgeoned beyond recognition. A bloody poker lay beside the body. A large earthen vase had been smashed to pieces. Quite possibly the vase had been brought down on the victim's head.

The Wiltshaw's hall led to the kitchen, which was in a shambles. The entire room was bloodstained. Two wooden logs lay on the floor. Both were bloodied, with tufts of grey hair adhering to them. Vegetables and a broken saucepan littered the floor. A shoe print, made up of distinctive parallel lines, was visible on the kitchen floor.

Observing the scene of violence, Fred had difficulty controlling his emotions. He managed to call his immediate neighbor, Dr. Harold Browne, who was at his side in two minutes. Dr. Browne took one look, comforted Wiltshaw and called the police.

Initially there was no evidence that anything was missing from the home and thus no apparent motive for the vicious attack. Fred Wiltshaw, the respected owner of a pottery firm in Stoke, was an unlikely suspect. His activities on the day of the murder were scrupulously traced. Fred had left for his business in Stoke at 9:30 a.m. in his automobile. His gardener-chauffeur, Roy Shenton, had reported for work as usual at 8 a.m. Two daily maids, Ada Barlow and Florence Dorrell, arrived for work at 8:15 a.m.

On the day Mrs. Wiltshaw was murdered, the two maids left at 3:30 p.m., after washing the kitchen floor and placing vegetables in a saucepan for the evening meal. These were later found scattered on the kitchen floor.

Roy Shenton, who had only been employed with the Wiltshaws for ten weeks, took up his gardening duties at 8 a.m. He was around the house all day. He observed John Matthews delivering the evening paper shortly after 5 o'clock. At roughly the same time he nodded to the village constable, John Bigham, as he strolled past the Wiltshaw home. At 5:22 Shenton observed Mrs. Wiltshaw talking on the telephone. A few minutes later Shenton hopped on his bicycle and peddled home, passing the time of day with neighbors as he went.

Fred Wiltshaw left his business in Stoke at 4:15 and drove to the Trentham Golf Club near his home, where he played bridge with friends until 6:16. At 6:18 he pulled into his driveway and walked in upon the violent scene of death.

The statements of the two maids, Roy Shenton, Fred Wiltshaw, and Dr. Browne were corroborated by other individuals. In particular, the neighbor who had talked to the victim on the telephone confirmed the time of the conversation as being 5:22. Thus it was certain that Mrs. Wiltshaw had been killed between 5:22 and 6:18, a period of 56 minutes.

Who had killed Alice Wiltshaw and why? Scotland Yard was requested to enter the case and provide the answers. In their own meticulous way, they attempted to reconstruct the crime from the physical evidence in the Wiltshaw home.

They deduced that the killer had approached the house by a little-used back path. He walked through the door which was always unlocked and proceeded upstairs, where he knew some jewels were kept in a drawer. He helped himself to a few pieces which he felt would not be missed.

Downstairs, Mrs. Wiltshaw picked up her saucepan to cook the vegetables for the evening meal. Suddenly, she heard the intruder just as he was leaving the house. There was a confrontation. The thief picked up a log and struck Mrs. Wiltshaw. The saucepan and vegetables flew in the air. So did the log. He picked up a second log and struck the staggering woman again. She slumped to the floor while he made for the back door.

The realization dawned on him. Mrs. Wiltshaw had recognized him. He must be certain of her death. Desperately, he lurched into the living room and grabbed a poker from its stand. Meanwhile, Mrs. Wiltshaw had staggered out into the hall. Once again, this time with the poker, she received vicious blows to the head until she was dead. The killer dropped the poker beside the body and ran out the back door and down the secluded path without being seen.

This theory accounted for all the physical evidence, but did little to identify the killer. None of the people associated with Mrs. Wiltshaw could be the murderer. It had to be someone else.

Detectives believed that only one other person would have the intimate knowledge of the Wiltshaws' habits and would know when the servants were on the premises. This man was Leslie Green, who had been the Wiltshaws' gardener-chauffeur prior to their hiring Roy Shenton.

While attempting to trace Green, detectives found that he had left his wife and had run away with an Irish nurse. When his name and photo appeared in the press, he walked into the Longton police station and offered to clear up any misunderstanding.

Subsequent investigation into Green's activities uncovered an array of circumstantial evidence pointing to his guilt. Green knew the Wiltshaws and their habits. He and his girlfriend had spent one night in a rooming house. A few pieces of Mrs. Wiltshaw's jewelry were found hidden in their room. The shoeprint on the Wiltshaws' kitchen floor matched Green's shoe. An old raincoat belonging to Mr. Wiltshaw was found in Green's possession. It was believed that this coat was used to cover his bloodstained clothing. When Green walked into the police station he had scratches on his arms and wrists which could have been inflicted by a woman struggling for her life.

In his defence, Green claimed that his shoes were not the only ones which could have made the print on the Wiltshaws' kitchen floor. He admitted stealing Mr. Wiltshaw's raincoat before being dismissed from his job as gardener-chauffeur. Green also claimed that he had received the incriminating scratches on his arms while gardening. He could not, however, account for the stolen jewelry being in a room occupied by him and his girlfriend, except to offer the lame explanation that others had occupied the same room since the murder.

Green swore that he was drinking in the Station Hotel in Stafford, some ten miles from Barlaston, at the time the crime was committed. However, after police questioned patrons and hotel staff, Green's alibi did not stand up.

Leslie Green was tried and convicted of Mrs. Wiltshaw's murder. Green never confessed, but left notes to his wife and detectives implying that they had the right man. He was hanged on Dec. 23, 1952 without appealing either verdict or sentence.

SLAIN PRIEST

It is rare that a man of the cloth is a murder victim. After all, why pick a victim who might very well have important connections in high places? This is the story of a man accused of murdering a priest.

On Feb. 4, 1924, Hubert Dahme, the rather slight, grey haired pastor of St. Joseph's Church, left his home in Bridgeport, Conn., for his evening walk. It was a rather disagreeable evening, but the weather never deterred Father Dahme. Each evening he would leave his home at 7:45, walk briskly through the downtown area and arrive back home at 8:45. This evening was no different.

Father Dahme, head down against the stormy wind, waved greetings to passersby. About 10 minutes into his walk, a man quickly strode up behind the priest. Several witnesses observed the incident. The man raised his arm, pointed a gun and fired directly into the back of Father Dahme's head. The assailant quickly ran up a side street. Father Dahme lay dead on the sidewalk.

Naturally enough, the murder of Father Dahme threw the citizens of Bridgeport into a frenzy. After all, a priest had been shot to death on a busy thoroughfare. The public demanded that the culprit be brought to justice without delay.

Police immediately interviewed several people who had witnessed the shooting. All agreed that the killer was a young man of medium height, who had been wearing an overcoat and a peaked cap. Three days after the murder, police had the extremely common description and nothing else. They were stymied. Father Dahme had no apparent enemies. Robbery had not been attempted, nor was it ever considered as a possible motive. Everyone knew Father Dahme never carried any appreciable amount of money on his person.

Two weeks later, police apprehended a suspect. Harold Israel was a 28-year-old alcoholic tramp. He had recently been kicked out of the army for excessive drinking. Israel and two other discharged soldiers were living in the sleazy Norfolk Hotel when he was picked up.

Initially, Israel claimed that he was at a movie at the time of the murder. He even remembered the name of the epic - *The Leather Pushers*. When asked to tell the plot of the movie, Israel could only remember that it was a boxing story.

Against this rather flimsy alibi, the police had a mountain of evidence. An empty. .32 calibre revolver cartridge was found in the bathroom of Israel's apartment. Israel stood 5 ft. 8 inches tall. When arrested, he was wearing an overcoat and peaked cap. In the pocket of the overcoat police found a .32 calibre revolver. While the damaged slug fragments could not be matched to the weapon found in Israel's coat, it was the same calibre weapon used to kill Father Dahme.

Four eyewitnesses positively identified Harold Israel as the man they saw approach the priest, raise the gun and fire. Three other witnesses identified Israel as the man they saw fleeing the scene of the crime. A lone witness swore he saw Israel leaning exhausted against a wall some distance from the murder site.

A waitress serving customers in a hamburger joint recalled waving to Israel through her front window at 10 minutes to eight. She knew him well as he often ate in her establishment. Her statement added fuel to the overwhelming evidence that Israel could not have been at a movie at the time of the murder.

During his first night in custody, Israel cracked under extensive questioning. "Yes, yes, I shot the guy! Now for Chrissake, leave me alone." He went on to elaborate that he was depressed on the night of the murder. His companions had left for New York. He would soon be evicted from his rooms. He hadn't eaten for two days. Strolling around Bridgeport, he felt that life had let him down and decided to kill the first person he met. That unfortunate persons happened to be Father Dahme. Israel claimed he pulled the gun out of his pocket, shot the priest in the head and ran away.

After confessing, Israel led police along his escape route. He pointed to the spot where he had leaned against the building to rest. It was the exact location indicated by one of the witnesses.

On the surface, there was little doubt that Harold Israel was the guilty party and deserved to be executed. State Attorney Homer Cummings was slated to prosecute the obviously guilty Israel. Cummings reviewed the case. The more he thought about it, the more he felt something was wrong. Does a hungry man go without food for two days when he has a perfectly saleable revolver in his pocket? Surely he would have at least pawned the gun.

According to Israel's confession, he shot Father Dahme as they met on the street. If this was so, the priest would have been shot in the face, not in the back of the head by someone who had sneaked up on him.

Delving further, Cummings found out that once Israel had had a good night's sleep, he had repudiated his signed confession. The conscientious attorney interviewed Israel. The accused man told the lawyer that he had been questioned or hours. He had had no food, no sleep, and even more important to an alcoholic, nothing to drink. Everything was promised to him once he confessed. Israel told Cummings he would have turned in his mother to escape the questions and the lights.

Why had Israel led police over his supposed escape route? Israel explained that he merely responded to questions. At the time he was practically asleep. To questions such as, "Did you turn right here?" he would nod. Cummings was convinced that he was dealing with an innocent man who had been caught up in a murder case he knew nothing about.

Cummings questioned the detectives who had recovered the .32 calibre shell in Israel's bathroom. They revealed that there had been scores of shells on the bathroom floor. Israel and his two soldier friends had each owned .32 calibre revolvers. They had set up targets in the yard outside their bathroom window and shot at them from the window. Israel's landlady confirmed that she had often complained of the noise.

Cummings went to the trouble of finding acquaintances who had seen the movie *The Leather Pushers*. When asked about the plot, most replied that it was about boxing, the same answer as Israel had given. Evidently, *The Leather Pushers* had been one boring movie, particularly for a hungry drunk bum who only wanted to get in out of the cold.

Cummings and members of his staff re-enacted the crime. They placed themselves where the witnesses had been standing on Feb. 4. Cummings played the murderer. Another man took the part of Father Dahme. All agreed they could not make out the identifying features of the killer.

Why had the witnesses erred? Cummings interviewed them. All had initially stated that they had only seen a male form leave the scene. Later, when police asked if the suspect had an overcoat and peaked cap, they had agreed.

Cummings looked in at the hamburger stand where the waitress said she waved through the window at Israel. She was the only witness who knew him personally. Once again Cummings re-enacted the scene. A man walked by the window, but he was impossible to identify. A layer of steam on the window made a vague image of anyone walking by outside.

Why had the witness lied? Further probing revealed that a lawyer had discussed a $3,000 reward with her. The waitress felt Israel was guilty anyway and saw a chance of obtaining easy money.

On May 27, 1924, State Attorney Homer Cummings went into court and, before an astonished courtroom, demolished his own case. He concluded by asking the court to "let this man go free."

The court agreed. Israel was set free. Homer Cummings went on to become the youngest attorney general in United States' history. Harold Israel sobered up. He later married, went into the lumber business and became a prosperous, law-abiding citizen.

The murder of Father Dahme remains unsolved.

RARE DEFENCE

Seldom does a sane person murder with no discernible motive. Such a murder took place in Mineola, N.Y. on April 19, 1947. The Papa Affair, as it came to be known, would be long forgotten were it not for the unusual theory put forward by defence counsel in order to account for his client's lack of motive.

Tony Papa was a 27-year-old laborer employed at a button factory in Mineola. He lived with his wife Frances and their 8-month old daughter in a pleasant, if modest, apartment on Willis Ave. Just around the corner lived the Fusco family, the Papas' best friends. The Fuscos had three children, Lena, 11, Billy, 10, and Rose Marie, five. In fact, it was Filomena Fusco who had introduced Frances and Tony years before. The two families remained dear friends. Little Rose Marie had been the flower girl at the Papas' wedding in 1945.

Tony didn't work on Saturdays. He loved to garden and, on the day in question, spent most of the day gardening at his allotment some distance from his home. At a little after 6 p.m., Tony returned home complaining of a headache. He had half a glass of wine with his supper, most of which remained uneaten. He took a couple of aspirins.

Little Rose Marie Fusco was visiting. Tony was very fond of the little girl and she in turn loved to spend time in his company. Mrs. Fusco and Lena dropped by. After some discussion, Mrs. Fusco mentioned that she had to deliver some shirts to an acquaintance and asked Frances to accompany her. While they talked, Tony read a comic book to Rose Marie.

Finally, Mrs. Fusco left with Rose Marie. It was agreed that she would put Rose Marie and Billy to bed. Lena and Frances would join them in a few minutes and together they would take a walk and deliver the shirts. Mr. Fusco was at a movie and was never a factor in the events which were to follow. Tony was moderately upset that his wife was dashing out, leaving him at home when he was not feeling well. He made them promise to be back in a half hour.

Tony read the paper. It was now 10:15 p.m. They had been gone an hour. He went downstairs to a candy store and had a chocolate sundae, a two dipper with chocolate syrup, walnuts and whipped cream.

Tony proceeded to the Fusco home, which was really two flats. The lower flat was occupied by the Fuscos and the upper was rented to a family named Jaffee. Tony tried the front door. It was locked. He went around to the back door. It too was locked. He noticed that a side window was broken, reached in and unfastened the latch. As he did so, he released the window, which fell down. A jagged piece of glass inflicted a nasty cut to his left hand. The cut bled profusely. Tony walked to his home, dripping blood all the way.

Once there, he washed the cut, bandaged the hand and headed back to the Fuscos. He crawled through the window into a vacant bedroom normally occupied by Lena Fusco. Tony walked out of the bedroom through the kitchen, noting that there was a butcher knife on the kitchen table. He proceeded into the bedroom where Billy and Rose Marie lay asleep in the same double bed. The light was on. Tony turned it out, plunging the room into darkness. He picked up Rose Marie and carried her into Mr. and Mrs. Fusco's empty bedroom without disturbing Billy.

Rose Marie's pyjama bottoms and panties were removed. They were later found intertwined lying on a trunk in the bedroom. It appeared that they had been pulled off together. Rose Marie woke up. She began to cry. Tony rushed to the kitchen, grabbed the 12-inch butcher knife and slashed the helpless child's neck four times. Splattered with blood, Tony opened the back door and went home. He removed his bloody clothing, bathed and went down to the street. He tossed the murder weapon beside some nearby trees.

Tony then met his wife, Mrs. Fusco and Lena returning from their stroll. He acted normal in every way. His wife mildly admonished him for leaving their baby daughter alone.

Frances and Tony went home. When Mrs. Fusco approached her house she was alarmed to find her door open. She dashed into the bedrooms, took one look at Rose Marie dead on the bed and fainted. Some minutes later, when she regained consciousness, she hysterically sought assistance.

In minutes, swarms of investigating officers were at the scene. Tony was immediately suspected. There was a trail of blood from the Fuscos' windows to his home. Tony was taken into custody and charged with the murder of Rose Marie Fusco.

His trial began on Sept. 8, 1947. The prosecution presented their case much as it is outlined here. They could only theorize as to motive. As Rose Marie was not sexually interfered with in any way, it was their contention that Tony had intended to sexually molest the child, but her crying frightened him and he killed her to avoid detection.

Tony had confessed in detail to police, outlining step by step the tragic events of the evening from the time he came home for supper until the body was discovered by Mrs. Fusco. He could not remember taking off the child's pyjama bottoms. Defence attorneys theorized that they came off as the child struggled. Above all, Tony could give no reason why he had killed Rose Marie.

Tony took the witness stand in his own defence. He told of crawling through the broken window, taking Rose Marie out of her bed, but now his story changed. He claimed that the child crawled over his shoulder and fell downward, striking her head on the floor. As he clutched her it was possible that her pyjamas and panties could have come off. When he noticed that her eyes weren't open, he went to the kitchen to get some water. Then his memory went blank. He had no recollection of killing the child. The next thing he remembered was feeling the bloodied knife which he had tucked inside his sweater. He threw it away before meeting his wife.

That in substance was Tony's story. His attorneys put forward a startling and unique reason for Tony's behavior. They reviewed his entire life. Tony was a difficult child who had been shuttled from one reform school to another. He entered the work force, but could only hold on to a job for a few months at a time. He had been in the army and navy, and had been discharged from both services because of misbehavior.

Still, the fact remained. Tony had no record as a sex offender and was extremely fond of his victim. Why did he kill five-year-old Rose Marie Fusco? Defence attorneys presented an array of distinguished doctors in an attempt to demonstrate a reason beyond Tony's conscious control which would account for the killing. Dr. E.M. Abrahamson, a chemical engineer, a doctor of philosophy, as well as a medical doctor, was an impressive expert witness. He had performed a sugar tolerance test on Tony. The results of this test indicated to Dr. Abrahamson that Tony had a condition known as hyperinsulinism.

The doctor explained that Tony had an overactive pancreas, producing too much insulin, with the result that some time after he took a large amount of sugar into his blood, his blood sugar readings were abnormally low. During the actual testing, Tony became extremely pale and was very sensitive in the area of the pancreas. Dr. Abrahamson went on to state that low blood sugar in certain individuals might produce coma. It also might produce convulsions. Patients with hyperinsulinism generally have peculiar personalities. When the blood sugar is terribly depressed the brain cannot function properly.

In essence, Dr. Abrahamson felt that a person suffering from an attack of hyperinsulinism could not deliberately plan or premeditate a murder. Yet, in a short while that same person could return to normal.

Other doctors concurred with Dr. Abrahamson. Dr. Richard Hoffman, noted neuropsychiatrist, also came to the conclusion that Tony had the condition known as hyperinsulinism. He stated from the witness stand, "It's a condition in which there are periodic attacks of an overproduction of that substance in the pancreas which burns the blood sugar and leaves the brain incapable of normal functions."

It was all too much for the Papa jury. They found Tony guilty of murder in the first degree. All appeals failed. On July 1, 1948, Anthony Papa was executed in Sing Sing's electric chair at Ossining, N.Y.

INNOCENT OR GUILTY?

It is unusual for a man to stand trial for murder when it is uncertain where and when the crime took place, or if a murder was committed at all. Strange as it first appears, these circumstances did occur back in 1905 in Nashville, Tennessee.

Oscar Mangrum, 35, was the not too bright owner of a barber shop down Nashville way. His wife of nine years, the former Rosa Mason, was an attractive woman of 33 when our little tale of intrigue and possible mayhem took place. The couple had no children.

They had a room and board arrangement at Mrs. Cullom's comfortable establishment on Sixth Ave.

Rosa was quite unlike her husband in many ways. Oscar was an introvert; Rosa was a bubbly, outgoing personality. Where he was content, she was ambitious. To fulfil her energetic nature, Rosa threw herself into working for philanthropic organizations, often heading up charitable fund-raising drives in cities other than Nashville. It was not unusual for Rosa to travel alone to New Orleans, St. Louis and Chicago. She was extremely successful and grew financially independent of her husband. In fact, Rosa sported several diamond rings which were way beyond what the average barber could afford in 1905.

The Mangrums had a friend, their family physician, J. Herman Feist. It was an open secret among their acquaintances that handsome Dr. Feist had more than a professional interest in pretty Rosa. She, in turn, appeared to encourage the attention. Oscar wasn't exactly unaware of what was taking place behind his back. He spoke to Rosa. She seemed to take the matter lightly, but promised to cool it if her friendship with the doctor was a source of embarrassment to her husband.

There matters stood until Dec. 14, 1905. For several days Rosa had been planning a business trip to Chicago. She would leave on the 8 p.m. train and arrive in Chicago the next morning. Rosa mentioned to her brother, J.H. Mason, a cashier at the First National Bank, that she had obtained an upper berth for the trip. Her sister, Mrs. Logan Trousdale, thought she was working too hard and should slow down.

It was a Saturday night, a busy one down at the barber shop. Rosa told Oscar it wasn't necessary for him to accompany her to the station. She caught a hack and promised to call him the next day when she arrived at her destination. Oscar was never to see his wife alive again.

When Rosa failed to call him, Oscar phoned the Hotel Newberry in Chicago. His wife had not been there for several months. Distraught and somewhat suspicious, Oscar called his brother-in-law at the bank. He was informed that Rosa had withdrawn her entire savings, the substantial sum of $1,433.62, the day before she left for Chicago. Oscar searched her rooms at Mrs. Cullom's and discovered that Rosa had taken all her jewelry and a trunkful of clothing. The thought occurred to him that his wife might have left him for good. Oscar, naturally enough, thought of Dr. Feist, but that worthy gentleman was still in Nashville, attending to his practice as usual.

Weeks passed. Oscar approached Dr. Feist, imploring the doctor to tell him anything he knew about his missing wife. Feist swore he knew nothing. When Rosa's sister spoke to the doctor, she received the same answer.

On Jan. 26, 43 days after Rosa left for Chicago, steamboat pilot George Spence found her body floating in the Ohio River, near Cairo, Ill. Oscar read about the unidentified body in the newspaper and rushed to Cairo. He positively identified his Rosa.

An autopsy served only to add to the mystery. Doctors agreed that the dead woman had been in the water for a lengthy period of time. They could not, however, ascertain when death had occurred, nor could they find the cause of death. The dead woman had not drowned. There were no marks on her body. Her internal organs were healthy.

Had she met with an accident? Had she committed suicide or had she been murdered? If murder had taken place, where was the foul deed committed? The location of the Ohio River, where the body was recovered, was 265 miles from Nashville. Rosa's money and jewels were not found on her body.

The dead woman's movements were traced. The hack driver, who picked her up in Nashville, was located. He swore he dropped her off at the railway station. Rosa's trunk was recovered from the train depot in Chicago, where it had rested since Dec. 15, the day after she disappeared. It seemed that Rosa had checked her trunk and boarded the train for Chicago.

In Nashville, nasty rumors circulated about Dr. Feist's relationship with Rosa. He was seen in Nashville each day in December, but there were those who believed the doctor could have robbed and murdered Rosa at night. Maybe poison was used. The doctor could have thrown Rosa into the river without ever leaving Nashville during daylight hours. Many came forward with information that they had seen Dr. Feist and Rosa in compromising circumstances. It was all only gossip before, but now the relationship took on far more serious connotations.

Based on these innuendoes and rumors, Dr. Feist was arrested and charged with Rosa's murder. His trial was the most sensational to take place in the Southern U.S. in years.

During his trial, evidence was produced indicating that Dr. Feist had never had more than $159 on deposit in his bank at any one time. He had often borrowed money from Rosa. While it was never established what the doctor did with his substantial income, many believed he bet heavily on the horses.

Other doctors occupying the Wilcox Building, where Dr. Feist had his practice, swore that they had seen Rosa and the doctor embrace on several occasions. One had even warned Feist to be more discreet. As the trial progressed, there was little doubt that hanky panky had taken place between the doctor and Rosa, but hanky panky does not a murder case make. There was more.

E.H. Mitchell, a livery stable owner, stated that he received a call from a Dr. S.A. Bean at approximately 8:30 p.m. on Dec. 14. The doctor asked that a rig be delivered to him at the Wilcox Building. Mitchell complied and met Dr. Bean. Next day, he again met Dr. Bean when he picked up his rig, which was mud-splattered inside and out. There was no Dr. Bean listed in Nashville. Mitchell swore that the man he met was Dr. Feist. The defence produced a myriad of witnesses who swore that Mitchell was a habitual liar.

Five passengers had boarded the sleeper car on the night of Dec. 14. Rosa supposedly had Upper 7. Understandably, neither the Pullman conductor nor the porter could remember anything about the passengers. The prosecution insisted that Rosa had checked her trunk through to Chicago, but had not boarded the train. On some ruse or other, Dr. Feist had enticed her into his rented rig and later that night robbed, killed and tossed her into the river. They claimed the body had floated the

265 miles to where it was found.

Defence counsel believed Rosa had boarded the train and, for some reason known only to herself, disembarked at Evansville, Ill. Here she was murdered for her possessions and thrown into the Ohio River, where she was later found.

The presiding judge reminded the jury that there was really no proof that Rosa Mangrum had been murdered. If she had been murdered, there was no proof that the crime had taken place in the jurisdiction in which the trial was being held. Despite these warnings, Dr. Feist was found guilty of murder.

Dr. Feist appealed. It took a full year for the appeal to reach the state supreme court. That august body declared that murder had not been proven and reversed the jury's decision. Dr. Feist was not tried again. He immediately left Nashville and never returned.

Was Dr. Feist innocent or guilty? Would a man of his intelligence hire a rig from a man who could later identify him? Very unlikely.

Then again, there are those suspicious souls who relish the convoluted. They claim the wily doctor, deeply in debt, talked Rosa into withdrawing all her money. He had her pack her clothing on the pretence that they were running away together. She purchased a single ticket. To allay suspicion, he told her he would buy his own ticket. At the last minute, after the trunk was checked, he talked her out of taking the train. He then killed her and submerged her body on one of the rivers around Nashville. The doctor had over a month and a half to lug the body the 265 miles to where it was found.

Of course, we will never know whether Dr. Feist was guilty or not. He died without telling a soul.

UNIDENTIFIED BONES

Skeletons have a most distressing habit of popping up in the strangest places. Over the years we have related tales of inconsiderate skeletons which were discovered in the basements of homes, in trucks, in the foundations of restaurants, in abandoned caves and in assorted watery graves.

Come along with me now to the tiny town of Heavener, Oklahoma. Heavener is no great shakes now. In 1907, it resembled Horse Fly, B.C. on a Monday night. About three miles from Heavener, as the crow flies, some children playing in the woods came across a human skeleton, an old hat, some burnt rocks, cooking utensils and empty tin cans.

U.S. marshals, who were the main law enforcement officers at the time, attempted to identify the gruesome find. Their inquiries revealed that one Bud Terry, 23, had disappeared several months earlier. Bud hailed from Caulksville, some 70 miles away in neighboring Arkansas. He was an orphan who had been brought up by his aunt, Mrs. Julia Knotts.

Bud had left his aunt's home to seek employment at Bates Sawmill, located near Heavener. He was hired by Bates as a lumber checker. His co-workers were two local lads, Will Stiles and Millard Vaught. The mill also employed Louis McKibben, 27, who was the sawer and Sam Swider, 42, who ran the board shop.

One day, Bud Terry simply didn't show up for work and was officially listed as missing. The usual inquiries were made, but no trace of Bud was found. Months passed. Bud's disappearance was treated as something of a local mystery.

When the skeleton was discovered, there were those who said it might very well be that of the missing Bud Terry. Still, there was no evidence that a crime had been committed and no real investigation followed the morbid discovery.

Two years later, in 1909, Sam Swider was convicted of larceny and sentenced to five years in the Oklahoma State Penitentiary. Sam served two years in prison before having a little tete-a-tete with the warden. He told the warden that back in 1907, he had witnessed Vaught, Bates and Stiles kill Bud Terry. His friend, Louis McKibben, verified that every word Swider uttered was the absolute truth. He too, had witnessed the murder.

The warden passed on the information to the proper authorities. The three men, Vaught, Bates and Stiles, were transported to Poteau, Oklahoma, to stand trial for the murder of Bud Terry.

On May 7, 1912, the trial began. It proved to be sensational. There was direct evidence that the three men on trial were guilty, yet there was strong proof that at least one had an ironclad alibi.

Ready? Here we go.

Mrs. Julia Knotts positively identified the skeleton as that of her nephew, Bud. She identified a gold filling in one of his front teeth. She also stated that Bud had broken his left leg above the ankle when he was 12. She pointed out that the skeleton, which was centre stage in the courtroom, had an identical break at that exact location.

Sam related how Bud's murder had occurred. The six men, Vaught, Bates, Stiles, McKibben, Bud Terry and he had attended a fair about 40 miles away in Mena, Arkansas. They returned to Heavener by train. All were a little tipsy as they made their way to the sawmill by wagon. Periodically, they stopped to wet their whistles.

While taking a swig of the best homebrew money could buy, Bates said to Vaught, "I understand you have been telling people that you have been playing around with my wife." Vaught replied that he had never said such a thing and that he had no reason for spreading such malicious gossip. What's more, he wanted to know who had told Bates these lies. Bates replied, "Bud Terry told me."

When faced with the accusations, Bud didn't deny it. An argument ensued. Furious, Vaught grabbed a plank out of the wagon and swung it down on Bud's skull. Bates and Stiles encouraged him and cheered as the plank crushed Bud's skull.

As Sam related the details of the vicious attack, members of the jury could see for themselves the gaping, jagged hole in the skull before their eyes.

The narrative continued. Vaught, Bates and Stiles then lifted Bud's body onto the wagon. At the same time, they threatened Sam and McKibben with death if they related what they had seen. The men drove the body a few miles into the woods, propped it up in a sitting position, built a fire encircled with rocks and spread a few pots and empty tin cans around the simulated camping site. They wanted to make it look as if a derelict had met a violent death in a hobo camp. Once again, the three men warned Sam and McKibben that they wouldn't hesitate to kill them if they uttered one word of the murder.

Why was Sam telling all at this late date? Sam explained that while in prison his conscience had bothered him to the extent that he just didn't care anymore. He had to tell, even if it meant death. McKibben took the witness stand and corroborated Sam's accusations in every detail.

All three accused men testified on their own behalf. Vaught stated that the story of a drinking party while returning from the fair was basically true, with one exception. Bud had not returned from the fair. He had often complained that he suffered from consumption. As a result, he headed south for his health. Vaught and his fellow accused never believed that Bud was missing, nor that it was his skeleton that was found at the old campsite.

In fact, when the men were returning to the sawmill at the conclusion of the Mena fair, Vaught had taken a side trip. He had travelled to his parents' home, obtaining a lift there on a wagon with six or seven other individuals. Among the group was an elderly lady who had won a rocking chair at the fair for having given birth to more babies than anyone in attendance that year.

Sure enough, the defence was able to trace the old lady. She took the stand in Vaught's defence and swore that his story was accurate. So did several other occupants of the wagon. The elderly lady had served Vaught his supper when they arrived at her home. All this had taken place during the exact time span when Sam Swider claimed Vaught and his two friends were killing Bud Terry.

Vaught's alibi was a strong one. However, so was the fact that the skeleton was identified as Bud Terry and that two men with apparently nothing to gain claimed to have seen the defendants commit the crime.

After deliberating 48 hours, the jury failed to agree. They did volunteer that they had no doubt the three men had killed Bud Terry. However, in order to gain a conviction of murder, the prosecution had to prove premeditation. The jury didn't believe the crime was premeditated, but was precipitated by a spontaneous argument fuelled by alcohol. They also couldn't convict the defendants on a manslaughter charge as the judge had instructed them that the statute of limitations prevented a conviction on this charge. A second trial was held. The same evidence was presented with the same results. Even the judge agreed that the men were guilty, but by a quirk of the law were being set free.

The three men walked out of court legally free, but things did not go well with them. Bates, once the owner of a prosperous business, was ostracized by his customers. His business failed. The other two defendants, once respectable, hard-working members of the community, were now shunned by former friends. Bates, in particular, was incensed at being treated as a murderer, and devoted his every moment attempting to vindicate himself and his co-defendants.

Then fate interceded. One R.E. McClelland of Los Angeles had been made aware of the missing Bud Terry by a brother who lived in Oklahoma. McClelland was admitted to the Los Angeles County Hospital. Here he met a fellow patient, none other than Bud Terry. Terry immediately wrote back home.

In August 1917, ten years after his supposed murder and five years after three men stood trial for that murder, Bud Terry returned alive and well to his home town. There was really no mystery to his disappearance. He had suffered from tuberculosis and had received medical advice to change climate. He had innocently moved from Oklahoma to Louisiana to Texas to California. Bud admitted his only sin had been in not keeping in touch with his dear Aunt Julia.

Sam Swider and Louis McKibben were confronted by Bud Terry. They immediately confessed that they had fabricated their entire story. But why? Sam thought he might have his sentence reduced if he were responsible for bringing the culprits of an unsolved crime to justice. McKibben had gone along for no more reason than to help out an old friend.

They made a terrible mistake. Both men pleaded guilty to perjury. Each received a sentence of 25 years in the Oklahoma State Prison. McKibben died there in 1925. Sam served his sentence and was released, only to be convicted of counterfeiting. He ended his days behind bars in Leavenworth, Kansas.

Bates, Vaught and Stiles left Oklahoma after their names were cleared. They went separate ways and were never heard of again. Bud Terry lived on for some years, eventually dying of tuberculosis.

Which leaves us with the perplexing question - whose skeleton was that, anyway? The puzzle has never been solved.

JUSTICE WAS BLIND

Γhis tale of murder most foul is an oldie but a goodie. It all happened in Merrie England back in the summer of 1835.

Jonathan May, a Devonshire farmer, attended the Moretonhampstead Fair, about seven miles from his home. Like most farmers of the area, Jonathan combined a little business with the good times the fair afforded. He sold a few cowhides to the local tannery and paid a bill he owed to a cobbler. He then attempted to purchase sheep, but found the price too high and decided not to buy them.

After taking in the fair, Jonathan dined at the White Hart Hotel, leaving just before 10 p.m. The proprietor of the hotel, Sam Cann, wished him a safe trip home. Jonathan mounted his trusted steed and was last seen peacefully cantering along the Exeter turnpike on the way home to his farm.

Two hours later, a man named Taverner came across Jonathan's saddled but riderless horse. He brought the horse to Moretonhampstead, where it was readily identified as belonging to Jonathan May. A group of men organized a search party. It wasn't long before they found Jonathan lying unconscious on the edge of the Exeter road. He had taken a severe beating and died from his injuries the next day.

The area where the attack had taken place was thoroughly examined. May, a big, robust man, had obviously put up a gallant struggle. Scuff marks and bloodstains were found for 60 paces from where Jonathan had been pulled off his horse. He had been beaten to death with a club or stick. Since it was known that Jonathan had been carrying a relatively large sum of money with him to purchase sheep, and since no money was found on his body, robbery was the apparent motive. A double set of footprints led from the scene of the attack across neighboring plowed fields.

The same fair which attracted hard-working, God-fearing farm folk of the region, had also attracted scores of low life characters out to make a fast buck. There was no scarcity of suspects in the May killing. In all, eight persons were taken into custody. One fine gentleman, George Avery, had the rather distressing experience of being placed under arrest while in bed with one Elizabeth Harris. Although George turned out to be innocent of Jonathan's murder, he was found guilty of another unrelated charge. The interruption of his sex life was therefore not without some redeeming feature. George's paramour Liz was released, but was to play a major role in the drama yet to unfold.

Andrew Carpenter, one of the eight suspects, wasn't nearly as fortunate as George. A 36-year-old linen pedlar, Andrew had attended the fair and had been seen talking to Jonathan May. When searched, he was found to be carrying an unusually large amount of money for a pedlar.

The lower portion of Carpenter's trousers were blood spattered. Investigation revealed that the trousers had been cleaned on the day before the attack on Jonathan and were seen to be bloody on the day after. Andrew Carpenter was arrested, charged with Jonathan's murder and lodged in jail to await trial.

While Carpenter languished in jail, his version of the circumstantial evidence against him was checked and proved to be completely true. The Irish linen company verified that they had indeed sent their representative a large amount of money for services rendered. A butcher, who had returned to his home village, was located. He told authorities that on the morning of the fair, he and Carpenter had engaged in horseplay. He had good-naturedly squirted cow's blood on Carpenter's pants. Andrew Carpenter was set free, but the process had taken nine long months.

Another suspect, Thomas Oliver, a young, good-looking petty criminal, had been seen with Jonathan before he left the fair. In the days after the murder, he had bragged about the successful robbery. Oliver was arrested with Jonathan's murder.

The other man to eventually stand trial for murder was Edmund Galley, a short, stout, ugly man, who made a strange companion in crime to the rather natty Thomas Oliver. The main evidence against Galley was that he had been seen drinking with Jonathan May on the day of the murder.

More damaging was the evidence of Elizabeth Harris. Remember her - the bed mate of George Avery? Well, folks, Elizabeth now stated that after fun and games in bed with George, she had gone out on the Exeter road to catch a stage coach. She missed the stage, but witnessed the murder of Jonathan May. Having nothing better to do that night, Elizabeth returned to the everloving arms of George Avery. She might still be there if those annoying officials had not taken him away the next morning. Elizabeth now positively identified Thomas Oliver and Edmund Galley as the culprits.

In July 1836, a year after the murder, Oliver and Galley stood trial for Jonathan May's murder. It was a foregone conclusion that both men were guilty, although Galley claimed innocence throughout. The jury took only ten minutes to return a guilty verdict against both accused.

Before sentence could be passed, Oliver jumped to his feet, turned to his fellow prisoner Galley and shouted, "You are innocent, but you will be hung innocently!"

Galley, now pale and haggard after months in a jail cell, could only say, "My Lord, I have never been at the Moretonhampstead Fair in my life." Before he could continue, Oliver interrupted, "My Lord, do you think, if I was going out to do a deed like that, I should take a weak little fellow like this for my companion? This man had nothing to do with it. He is innocent."

The presiding judge was not to be deterred. He continued, "The sentence is . . ."

Once more, Oliver sprang to his feet, "My Lord, do not send an innocent man to the trap! The man at my side is as innocent of this murder as you are. I declare that the other prisoner is innocent. I know who it was who did the deed. His name is John Longley. He is a good-looking young man and no more like this man than a candle."

The judge attempted to go on, but Oliver would not be denied. "The evidence is false. He is not the man. I have never seen this man until I entered prison." Despite the dramatic outburst, the judge went on to sentence both men to be hanged. The double execution was to take place within 48 hours.

Next day, Oliver's lawyer, pleading for a respite for both prisoners, was successful in gaining a reprieve of 14 days for Galley. Oliver was hanged. On the scaffold, he confessed his part in the murder, but again swore that Galley was innocent.

Further reprieves were granted Galley. His lawyer even came up with five witnesses who swore he was working at a fair in Kent on the night Jonathan was murdered. Unfortunately, these witnesses were of the vagrant variety, and held little persuasive clout with the court. Finally, the Home Secretary ruled that it would be cruel to hang Galley after such a lengthy delay. His sentence was commuted to transportation for life, which in those days meant a fate worse than death - Australia.

Galley was shipped off down under, and there the Jonathan May case should have ended forever. John Longley, the man accused by Oliver, had also been sent to Australia for an unrelated crime. Years passed. Galley became a trustee. In 1846, 11 years after the murder, he was given a ticket of leave, which enabled him to change employment. For a while, he was a horse driver, then a bricklayer. In 1860, he obtained employment on a huge sheep farm in New South Wales.

Edmund Galley was getting old, but a new element had entered his life. Now, 30 years after being exiled to a strange land and a new life, he fell in love. The lady of his choice had seven children. Rumors had come to his attention that one John Longley, somewhere in Australia, was bragging about getting away with murder years before in England.

Galley wrote to the senior magistrate in Exeter to review his case in order for him to obtain permission to marry. It was now 42 years since the murder, but Magistrate Thomas Latimer remembered it well. He wrote to Galley, advising him that although many of the participants in his trial were now dead, he would take up his cause. Soon, a campaign was under way to prove Galley's innocence.

Just as everyone had been certain of his guilt so many years before, now many believed Galley innocent. By 1879, the old murder case had become a cause celebre throughout England. The case was debated in the House of Commons. Unfortunately, at the height of the fervor, John Longley died. The opportunity to hear a confession from the murderer's own lips was no longer possible.

In 1881, Edmund Galley was finally declared innocent and granted a free pardon. After much debate in the House of Commons, he was awarded £1000 compensation for his wrongful conviction.

FRENCHY'S FALL

The man carved a cross in the woman's thigh. Then he left squalid room 31 of the equally squalid East River Hotel, pausing only long enough to use his key to lock the door from the outside.

Behind the locked door of room 31 that April 24, 1891, lay the slashed and dead body of Carrie Brown. Carrie, a former actress, who had stubbed her toe while climbing the ladder of success, was about 60. It was hard to tell. Years of drink and dissipation had aged Carrie far beyond her years.

When tipsy, which was pretty well all the time, Carrie would recite Shakespeare until the booze ran out. As a result, the elderly prostitute was known to her friends and clients as Ol' Shakespeare.

When Carrie failed to show up next morning, night clerk Eddie Harrington used his master key to open room 31. Eddie called police. A bloody kitchen knife was found beside the bed where the mutilated body lay. Carrie had been strangled and viciously slashed. As a parting gesture, the killer had carved the hideous cross on her thigh.

Detectives traced the victim's last known movements. She had arrived at the hotel around 11 p.m. with a young male companion, who registered as "C. Knick." He and Carrie were assigned room 31. A few hours later, the mysterious C. Knick was seen leaving the hotel. Despite an extensive manhunt for the mystery man, he was never identified or located.

It wasn't a difficult task to round up Carrie's customers. Many could account for their activities on the night of the murder. Others had been too drunk to remember one way or another.

Into the police dragnet fell one character known only as Frenchy, who professed not to speak or understand English. Eventually, Frenchy's identity was established. He hailed from Algeria, spoke Arabic, and his real name was Ameer Ben Ali.

Gradually, like the foundations of a building under construction, the pieces fit into place until police had a veritable fortress of evidence pointing to Frenchy as the killer of Carrie Brown. Admittedly, he was not the mystery man who had spent part of the night with Carrie. However, it was proven that Frenchy had occupied room 33, directly across the hall from the murder room.

Evidence supporting the official theory was strong. Minuscule blood traces were found on both sides of the door of room 33. Tiny drops were found on the floor of Frenchy's room and on a blanket of his bed. Scrapings from under his fingernails indicated the presence of blood. Frenchy could not satisfactorily explain the bloodstains. When questioned, Carrie's fellow prostitutes told police that Frenchy was one of their fallen comrade's regular customers.

Frenchy was charged with Carrie Brown's murder. As such cases rank, the murder of a down-and-out prostitute in the Big Apple normally doesn't rate more news space than a pothole on 42nd St. For some reason, the trial of the Algerian captured the imagination of the public. A failure in life, Carrie Brown was to occupy centre stage in death.

The trial opened with the prosecution attorneys parading a galaxy of recently washed and sobered witnesses, who swore that Frenchy regularly roamed the halls of the run-down hotel looking for female companionship. However, the most damaging evidence came from an expert witness. Dr. W. Formand had conducted tests of blood found in the murder room, in the hall and on the door of room 33. He found that all the samples contained intestinal contests of food elements at the identical degree of digestion. The inference was that all the blood had originated from the same source - the abdominal wounds of the deceased. The doctor left no room for doubt. He stated from the witness stand that he would stake his life on the accuracy of his blood tests.

To counteract this testimony, the defence placed their own experts on the witness stand. They stated that their testing left much room for doubt. The blood samples did not necessarily all emanate from the dead woman's intestine. When pressed, they all admitted that Dr. Formand was the most respected man in his field.

The defence took that ever dangerous step of putting the defendant on the witness stand. To the question, "Did you kill Carrie Brown?" Frenchy lifted his arms above his head and screamed in Arabic. "I am innocent! I am innocent! Allah is Allah, Allah is great! Oh, Allah, help me! Allah, save me! I implore Allah to help me!"

Despite the impassioned plea, Allah deserted Ameer Ben Ali. He was found guilty and sentenced to spend the rest of his natural life behind Sing Sing Prison's cold walls.

That should have been that, but it wasn't. Newspapermen, as well as conscientious detectives, felt that the mystery man who was never located was a better suspect than Ameer Ben Ali. As the years drifted by, they uncovered new evidence and sifted through prosecution evidence as it was presented at the trial. To add credence to their suspicions, every so often the police would receive word from sailors that the real murderer of Carrie Brown had quietly caught a ship sometime after the murder and ended up in the Far East. These reports were never verified, but they were disconcerting.

It is rare for hard-nosed New York detectives to spend their time attempting to free destitute convicted murderers. However, in this case, they worked diligently gathering evidence in Ameer's favor. They submitted an application to the governor of the state requesting that Ameer Ben Ali be pardoned.

Police discovered that a man who fit the description of the mystery man had lived and worked in Cranford, New Jersey. This man had been absent from his room on the night of the murder. Several days later he disappeared from the area and had not been seen since. When his abandoned room was searched, police found a brass key bearing a tag marked 31. The key fit the murder room.

Various witnesses, including reporters and police officers, who had been at the scene of the crime minutes after the door was opened, submitted affidavits stating that they had examined the hall and the doors leading into both rooms. They swore there were no bloodstains in the hall or on the doors. They suggested that the stains which were tested had materialized as a result of the coroner moving the body. It was noted that there was no blood on the doorknob of room 33. Had Ali been the killer, surely he would have bloodied the door handle when he went back to his room. It was further felt that the minute amount of blood found under Ali's nails could have originated from a number of sources other than the abdomen of Carrie Brown.

Gov. Odell studied the application and reported, "To refuse relief under such circumstances would be plainly a denial of justice, and after careful consideration of all the facts, I have reached the conclusion that it is clearly my duty to order the prisoner's release."

On April 16, 1902, a week short of 11 years after someone carved a cross in Ol' Shakespeare's thigh, Ameer Ben Ali's sentence was commuted. The Algerian paid for his transportation back to his native land.

12

MERRIE ENGLAND

STICKY-FINGERED BUTLER

The suspects are gathered in a Victorian parlor. With belt drawn tight around his English Burberry, the Scotland Yard Inspector points an accusing finger at the butler and exclaims, "The butler did it!" All eyes focus on the culprit who drops his tray of tea and crumpets and he blurts out his reasons for killing the master.

This familiar scenario of the English butler has been repeated hundreds of times in detective fiction and grade B movies. There is probably no more maligned profession than that of the hard-working English butler.

Men such as Roy Fontaine have done much to perpetuate this myth. You see, Fontaine was a butler, and he actually did do it.

Born Archibald Hall on July 17, 1924, to a middle-class Glasgow couple, Hall proved to be nothing but trouble to his parents from the age of 13 when he was admonished by a Glasgow judge for breaking and entering. There were two younger children in the family, a daughter, Violet, and a son, Donald.

While still in his teens, Archibald fancied the well-known actress Joan Fontaine and began calling himself Roy Fontaine. The name stuck.

Roy Fontaine was one of those men who early in life make up their minds to travel through life first class without the encumbrance of honest labor. Roy became one of the most successful criminals in Scotland and England. He was an accomplished con man and professional thief. Between capers he spent money lavishly. Friends and relatives were the recipients of expensive gifts.

Roy gained fame among London's criminal element for obtaining responsible jobs as a butler with forged letters of reference. Once employed, he would case his employer's mansion for valuables and advise confederates when and how to gain entrance. Often they would clean out the entire estate of anything of value. On other occasions Roy would leave the employ of some wealthy landowner and return months later to ransack the house. He was an avid reader and became expert on many topics, specializing in antiques and objects of art. A fastidious dresser, Roy was a charming dinner companion. Indeed, over the years many of his employers thought themselves fortunate to acquire such a cultivated and well-informed butler.

From 1943 on, Roy was to be in and out of prison for the rest of his life. Each time he was apprehended and incarcerated he plunged into reading and studying. Upon gaining his freedom, he would take a vacation to shake the latest institution out of his system. Then he would continue his criminal pursuits. For more than thirty years, Roy's pattern of living didn't change. He saw the inside of scores of prisons, but upon his release he would rob the rich and live off the proceeds of his criminal life.

In 1977, suave, debonair Roy Fontaine presented his forged credentials to 74-year-old Lady Peggy Hudson, the widow of a former member of parliament. Lady Hudson, who lived on a huge estate near Waterbeck, Dumfriesshire, considered herself lucky to acquire such a distinguished, well-informed butler as Roy Fontaine. As a condition of his employment, Roy had the use of an automobile, lived in a furnished flat on the estate, and received £20 a week for doing a minimum of work.

Around this time, David Wright, an ex-con who had known Roy in prison, contacted him. With the blessing of Lady Hudson, Roy was able to secure a job for Wright on the estate as a gardener and handyman. Lady Hudson, who seems to have had an uncanny knack for gathering unsavory characters around her, took a liking to Wright from his first day on the job.

The few pounds Wright earned were squandered on the ponies. He pleaded with Roy to rob the estate. Roy felt he had a good setup and wasn't prepared to jeopardize his position, at least not for the time being. When Roy caught Wright stealing a statuette from the house, the pair had a fierce argument which culminated in Wright's stalking off the estate.

That night, while Lady Hudson was away from the estate, Wright took a potshot at Roy while he slept in bed. The shot missed, but just barely. The slug plowed into the headboard of the bed only inches from Roy's scalp. The pair grappled, and Roy was successful in gaining possession of Wright's .22-calibre rifle and calming down the younger man.

Next day Wright told Roy that if he didn't agree to strip Lady Hudson's estate of all its valuables, he would inform her that her butler was a professional thief. Roy was later to confess that his stay as Lady Hudson's butler was the happiest period of his life. He enjoyed walking the dogs, fishing, purchasing fine wines, and driving his mistress over the countryside. This may have been true, but most probably he was waiting for the proper moment to strike. One thing he knew for sure: David Wright wasn't going to ruin the best setup he ever had.

Pretending to let bygones by bygones, Roy went hunting with Wright on the following day. As Wright was engrossed in aiming at a rabbit, Roy sneaked up behind him and fired three slugs into Wright's body at close range. As Wright lay in the grass groaning, Roy shot the dying man once more. He lay still. Roy dragged the body to a nearby stream and covered it with rocks. Roy Fontaine had graduated to murder.

In September 1977, a jealous former girlfriend of Roy's found out about his cushy job and informed the police, who felt it was their duty to let Lady Hudson know that she had an ex-con as a butler. Lady Hudson, who almost certainly would have become a victim sooner or later, fired Fontaine on the spot. No one, not the police or Lady Hudson, had any idea that a murderer was being thrown off the estate.

Roy rented a cottage at Newton Arlosh, near Carlisle, paying £120 in advance for three months' rent. He then looked around for new fish to fry. Roy applied for the job of butler to Mr. and Mrs. Walter Travers Scott-Elliot of 22 Richmond Court, London. The Scott-Elliots were loaded. They maintained homes in France, Italy, and Switzerland, besides their London residence. Roy's forged references again passed muster. He was deemed to be the most accomplished applicant by far.

When Roy walked into the Scott-Elliot's residence he couldn't believe his eyes. He was gazing upon more riches than he had ever seen in one place in his life. Antiques, jewelry and paintings, which would make any international collector envious, were stuffed into the dwelling.

Walter Travers Scott-Elliot was a doddering 82-year-old. Soon the ever-efficient butler, Roy Fontaine, became an indispensable member of the family. As soon as he was sure the trusting Scott-Elliots felt he was above reproach, he contacted two old underworld friends, Mary Coggle and Michael Kitto.

Initially it was Roy's idea to swindle the Scott-Elliots out of at least £100,000. The rich old gentleman had bank accounts all over the world. A man of Roy's intelligence would have no trouble organizing such a swindle.

One day, when he was certain that Mrs. Scott-Elliot was spending the night away from her home, Roy invited Kitto to stay overnight. Roy showed Kitto around the house. He was particularly interested in showing his friend the vast treasures which were to be theirs if only they were patient and clever enough.

The two men entered Mrs. Scott-Elliot's bedroom. Then something happened which could not have been anticipated. Standing in front of the two crooks was a wide-awake, staring Mrs. Scott-Elliot.

The terrified woman demanded an explanation. Roy panicked and struck Mrs. Scott-Elliot a stinging blow to the head. She fell to the floor, where Kitto held her fast. Roy then pressed a pillow into her face until she made no further sounds. Mrs. Scott-Elliot was dead. The pair of desperate men then placed the body in a sleeping position in her own bed. Suddenly they heard the shuffling footsteps of old Scott-Elliot. As Kitto hid, Roy met the old gentleman at the door and explained that he too thought he heard noises and had entered Mrs. Scott-Elliot's bedroom to investigate. Obviously he was wrong. Mrs. Scott-Elliot was sleeping soundly. The old gent looked over Roy's shoulder to his wife's dead body and agreed. Wishing Roy a good night, he returned to bed.

Next day, Roy and Kitto contacted Mary Coggle. They told her what had happened and welcomed her as a fellow conspirator. The trio rented a car. Each had a part to play. To anyone who didn't know the Scott-Elliots, Roy would be their godson. Kitto was to be their chauffeur, and Mary would be Mrs. Scott-Elliot. Mrs. Scott-Elliot's body was placed in the trunk of the car. The scenario was as weird and strange as any fictional plot.

Senile Scott-Elliot, who was accustomed to taking massive doses of medication, wasn't too sharp at the best of times. That evening, stuffed with sleeping pills, the old gent was half-dragged to the car and placed in the back seat beside Mary Coggle, who was dressed in his late wife's clothing. The doped-up old man slumbered. That night the three desperados and Scott-Elliot stayed at Newton Arlosh, where Roy had rented a cottage.

Next day they buried Mrs. Scott-Elliot near Braco, Perthshire. Mary wore Mrs. Scott-Elliot's £4,000 mink coat as she helped dig the grave. Mr. Scott-Elliot dozed in the car, unaware of what was going on around him. The four then returned the 150 miles to the cottage at Newton Arlosh.

That same night, Roy, Kitto, and Mary decided that Mr. Scott-Elliot must die. After awakening in the morning, they drove to Blair Atholl, where they took rooms at the Tilt Hotel. Next morning all four had breakfast, after which Scott-Elliot paid the bill with a personal cheque. The pathetic old gentleman never for a moment realized that he was in any danger, and at all times, in his befuddled mind, thought he was travelling with his wife.

The strange entourage travelled beyond Inverness to a lonely stretch of road where Scott-Elliot was enticed into the bushes and strangled with a scarf. The two men buried the body. They then drove back to Inverness, eventually making their way to Perth and on to Edinburgh.

Mary Coggle caused Roy some concern. She drank heavily each evening, but, much worse, she had grabbed a handful of rings and jewelry from the Scott-Elliot's residence and insisted on wearing these items. She rarely took Mrs. Scott-Elliot's mink coat off her back.

The trio returned to Roy's rented cottage at Newton Arlosh. Once there, Roy and Kitto faced Mary. She had to let them dispose of the jewelry and mink coat she was wearing. Otherwise she would bring suspicion to all three of them. They even proposed selling Mrs. Scott-Elliot's belongings and giving Mary the proceeds to purchase a new coat. She wouldn't hear of it.

Roy pretended to agree to let Mary keep the coat and jewelry. Secretly he decided that Mary had to be silenced. Kitto agreed. Kitto held the struggling Mary, while Roy rained blows upon her head with a fireplace poker. That night they drove into Scotland and threw Mary's body off a bridge near Lockerbie, Dumfriesshire. The two friends had a couple of drinks before heading back to Newton Arlosh. For Roy Fontaine it was murder number four.

The pair now proceeded to systematically strip the Scott-Elliots' home. Cutlery, antiques of every description, silver, clocks, china, all were carried way and sold to dealers. During December and early January of 1978 the two men lived like kings, taking in the best night life London and Edinburgh had to offer. It was round after round of wine, women, and song.

Christmas was spent with Roy's family. As usual he distributed the most expensive presents. All his family were happy to see him in such good spirits.

On January 13, Roy's younger brother Donald was released from prison, having completed a three-year sentence for housebreaking. Donald was eager to join his brother; Roy, on the other hand, had a hard time tolerating the sloppy, unsophisticated Donald. Donald stuck with his brother and Kitto for a few days. It didn't take him long to figure out that his hosts must be in on something big in order to be spending money like drunken sailors. Donald's prying questions didn't sit well with the two murderers. Donald had become a threat. He had to go. Without warning, both men strangled Donald until he was dead. They placed his body in the trunk of their car, which had previously been occupied by the bodies of Mrs. Scott-Elliot and Mary Coggle.

The two killers then drove as far as North Berwick, where they procured rooms at the Blenheim House Hotel. Later they came down to the lobby and chatted with the owner of the establishment, Mr. Norman White. Mr. White didn't mind chatting; it was a quiet night. The two men seemed to be volunteering too much information. Something in their manner made White suspicious. Quietly he called the police, who discovered that the guests' automobile plates had been removed from another vehicle.

The two officers drove to the Blenheim House and asked the two strangers to accompany them to the North Berwick Police Station. One of the officers drove Roy's rented car back to the police station. All the while Donald's body rested in the trunk.

Once back at the police station, Roy asked to use the washroom. He was surprised that no officer accompanied him. Slowly he opened the washroom window and let himself out. He hailed a cab and made good his escape, only to be picked up at a roadblock. Upon being returned to the police station Roy was informed that a body had been discovered in the trunk of his car. When searched by police Roy was found to be carrying several pieces of jewelry from the Scott-Elliot estate.

Little by little Roy and Kitto revealed the details of their private horror story. Roy eventually led police to the bodies of David Wright and Mr. and Mrs. Scott-Elliot. Mary Coggle's body had been found by the time the two men were arrested. They informed police of their involvement in the Coggle murder as well.

On May 2, 1978, Roy Fontaine and Michael Kitto were sentenced to life imprisonment for their crimes. They are serving their time as you read this account of their exploits.

WAGE BATTEL

English law didn't just happen. It evolved over hundreds of years and is constantly in a state of change. Those cases which were instrumental in precipitating major changes in the law are some of the most celebrated of all time.

We have to go back a long way to the very last case when a man twice stood trial for the same murder after having been found not guilty in his first trial.

The year was 1817, the locale a small village near Birmingham, England. Life was hard, and for most a meagre living was wrested from the soil.

Mary Ashford was an attractive, healthy, 20-year-old housekeeper and servant to her uncle, James Coleman. Her father, a laborer, also lived with the Colemans at Langley Heath.

On the evening of May 26, Mary was excited in anticipation of a dance at Tyburn. She made elaborate plans. First, she had to walk to Birmingham to make some purchases for her uncle. Instead of coming all the way back to Langley Heath, she would stop at the house of her friend, Hannah Cox, who lived in Erdington, located halfway between Birmingham and Langley Heath.

Mary left for Birmingham in her usual working clothes, a multicolored frock, black woollen stockings, and black shoes. Jauntily bouncing down the country road, she carried a sack which contained a white muslin dress and white stockings. Hannah was to lend her friend a pair of white shoes to go with her outfit. These were Mary's dancing clothes. She dropped off the sack, proceeded to Birmingham where she conducted her uncle's business and returned to Hannah's house. By 6:00 p.m. she was changing her clothes to attend the dance.

The two friends walked the two miles to Byburn, arriving at approximately 7:30 p.m. The Three Tuns, a large roadhouse, was crowded with local farmlads and their girlfriends from the surrounding countryside. Mary was far more popular than Hannah. She was on the dance floor almost all night.

Abraham Thornton, the son of a prosperous builder from Castle Bromich, paid particular attention to Mary and monopolized most of her time. Thornton stood about 5 feet, 6 inches, had broad shoulders, a bull neck, and an oversized head; altogether not a very attractive fellow.

Shortly after 11:00 p.m. Mary and Hannah started for home. They were accompanied by two boys. Ben Carter, a neighbor of Hannah's, was with her; Abraham Thornton walked with Mary. After a few minutes Carter decided to return to the dance. Hannah, Mary, and Abraham continued until they came to a crossroads leading to Hannah's house. Mary decided to continue on, telling Hannah that she would stay at her grandfather's, who lived a bit farther up the road. The friends parted.

At 4:00 a.m. Hannah was awakened by a knock at her door. Mary wanted her work clothes, explaining to the startled Hannah that she had to be at her uncle's in an hour or so. She changed in the kitchen, forgetting to return the white dancing shoes. She mentioned that she had slept most of the night at her grandfather's, insinuating that a good portion of the elapsed time was spent in the company of young Abraham Thornton.

Mary took off in a rush for home. Three different farmers, early risers heading for their fields, saw her. She left the main road to take a well-known footpath home.

At about 6:00 a.m., George Jackson, a road worker walking along the footpath, found a bundle containing Mary's dancing clothes. A little farther on he found her blood-splattered white shoes. Close by the clothing was a water-filled pit. At the edge of this pit Jackson observed a small puddle of blood.

After Jackson raised the alarm, the pit was dragged and Mary's body was uncovered. Authorities investigating at the scene observed two sets of footprints in the soft cultivated soil beside the footpath. The footprints had been made by a man and woman. From the distance between the individual prints it was obvious that whoever made the male prints had been running after Mary. At the edge of the pit a man's footprint was gouged into the earth much deeper than the others. Some thought it indicated that the man now held a weight, presumably Mary's body, which he threw into the pit. Preliminary examination of the body indicated that Mary had been raped.

By 10:00 a.m. that same day Abraham Thornton was arrested and charged with Mary Ashford's murder. His boots were immediately checked against the footprints in the field. They matched perfectly.

Thornton stated that after Hannah left them at about midnight, he and Mary walked for some time. They left the road and walked through some fields, stopping at intervals to talk. As it was getting close to 4:00 a.m., Mary went back to Hannah's to get her working clothes. Thornton said he waited for her on the village green. When she failed to return, he leisurely walked to his father's home at Castle Bromwich, arriving there about 5:00 a.m.

When arrested, Thornton's shirt was blood-stained. Later he admitted that his stops to talk with Mary were not exactly for the purpose of conversation. They had been intimate on several occasions during the early morning hours. He steadfastly denied having raped the girl.

On August 8 Thornton stood trial for murder. The prosecution contended that Thornton tried for hours to talk and coerce Mary into having intercourse with him. He didn't succeed. When she left to retrieve her working clothes from Hannah, he waited for her. He surprised the girl, raped her, and then, seeing his victim running hysterically, he grew alarmed and took after her. He caught up with her at the edge of the pit and struck her, causing her to faint. Thornton picked her up and threw her into the pit. At least, that's what the prosecution contended.

Thornton's defence painfully elicited from the coroner that nothing was found during his examination of the body which was inconsistent with consenting intercourse. All the blood at the scene and on Thornton's shirt proved to be menstrual blood. Mary had not been beaten in any way.

The defence called a series of witnesses, all with nothing to gain and all respected farmers who had lived in the area most of their lives. If anything, they only felt contempt for the prisoner, yet they testified on his behalf.

It was a mile and a quarter from Hannah's house to the pit where Mary's body was found. Witnesses saw Thornton casually walking towards his home at Castle Bromwich miles beyond the pit at the exact time that Mary must have been murdered. One was a man up to milk his cows. Another was a farm lady who casually stood in her doorway and observed Thornton walking up the road. Another man, John Haydon, a gameskeeper, testified that he knew Thornton well. He met him that fateful morning and inquired what he was doing up so early. "To take a wench home," came the straightforward reply. All of this was taking place at the exact time Mary was traversing that mile and a quarter and getting herself murdered.

The jury took only six minutes to find Thornton not guilty.

The Thornton-Ashford case normally should have ended here, but it was far from over. Thornton had been assumed guilty from the morning Mary's body had been dragged from the pit. The horrible aspects of the case, coupled with Thornton's rather unattractive appearance, almost dictated that he should be guilty. The public felt that justice had not been done and that a murderer had been set free.

In 1817 it was still possible for a victim's next of kin to lodge an appeal within a year and a day of the murder. The action was called "suing out an appeal." It was not often used, but it was law. In the infamous Thornton case, William Ashford, Mary's eldest brother, brought such an action against the man who was just acquitted of killing his sister.

On October 9, 1817, Abraham Thornton was again arrested and placed in jail. More than a month later he again stood trial for Mary's murder. This time the defendant's lawyers pulled one out of the hat. They invoked a privilege which had not been used since the reign of Charles I - the right to "wage battel." In effect, this ancient law allowed the accused to toss a gauntlet on the floor of the court, indicating that he was invoking his right to "wage battel." Which meant that the appellee, in this case Thornton, and the appellant, William Ashford, would engage in a supervised battle until one party was either killed or indicated that he had lost. If Thornton won he would be acquitted.

While all of England discussed little else, Thornton threw down his gauntlet. After many legal hassles and delays, on April 20, 1818, Ashford, faced with a fight which would probably result in his death, withdrew his suit against Thornton. Thornton, in turn, withdrew his right to "engage battel."

Abraham Thornton walked out of court a free man, but he found no peace. The public never forgave him for ruining the reputation of a murdered girl. Many still thought he was the true murderer. He became so notorious and hated that when he booked passage on the Independence, bound for New York, all the other passengers turned in their tickets and the voyage was cancelled.

Thornton did eventually make his way to the United States. He prospered and married settling in Baltimore, where he died in 1860. Mary Ashford's murder has never been solved.

On the day Thornton was set free, the attorney general gave notice in the House of Commons that he would bring in a bill to abolish trials by "battel" and appeals of murder. The following year the bill received royal assent was was passed into law.

GUY FAWKES NIGHT

From time to time many of us wish that we could start life over. If only by some magic the clock could be turned back, we would explore different avenues and take different turns. But alas, this is not possible. The more adventuresome among us attempt drastic change in order to carve out a new life. There are several recorded cases of men and women, caught up in a life they could no longer tolerate, who managed to effectively disappear. They literally began life anew in another location.

These very thoughts kept dancing through Alfred Arthur Rouse's mind. The wives, the debts, and the intrigue were too much. Arthur decided to do something about it, and what he did became a classic in the annals of crime.

Arthur was born in London on April 6, 1894. His parents were divorced when he was only six. They shipped their son off to live with an aunt. Arthur was a bright, cheerful lad, who did well at school and was liked by his chums. After finishing school, he obtained a position as an office boy with a west-end dry goods store. He advanced rapidly in the store and was soon one of their best salesmen. Along the way he became acquainted with a girl in the office, Lily May Watkins. It wasn't long before Lily was Arthur's girlfriend.

In 1914, within a week after the First World War was declared, Arthur joined the army. He became a private in the 24th Queen's Territorial Regiment. Impetuous, 20-year-old Arthur married Lily on November 29, 1914. Three and a half months later he was shipped to France. For two months Arthur was engaged in some of the fiercest battles which took place during the entire war.

Then, on May 25, 1915, Arthur was seriously wounded by shell fragments. He was hit in the left temple and above the left knee. Sent back home as a cripple, he managed to keep his sense of humor and cheerfulness, which had always been his trademark. In 1916, he was considered to be 100 per cent disabled and received a small pension.

Despite his wounds, he never became discouraged and worked hard until, in 1920, he was making a fine living. Other than some scar tissue in the area of his left temple, his war wounds were not evident. Miraculously, Arthur had recovered so that he was completely mobile.

Now employed as a successful commercial traveller, Arthur prospered from 1920 through 1927. The Rouses owned their own comfortable home on Buxted Road. Arthur appeared to be the perfect family man, puttering about his home and garden. Art also was a regular at the local tennis club. Lily was the perfect wife, constantly cleaning their quaint little home.

This picture of matrimonial bliss may have been accurate as far as Mrs. Rouse was concerned, but in Arthur's case it was as false as a two-headed penny. You see, Arthur had been playing the field all along. In 1920 he met, wooed, and won pretty 15-year-old Helen Campbell. As fate or luck or whatever controls such thing would have it, Helen became, as they used to say in those days, heavy laden with child.

Helen gave birth in a private home. The baby lived only five weeks. Arthur continued his relationship with Helen, cautiously avoiding parenthood until shortly after November 1924. That was the month Art bigamously tied the knot with Helen at St. Mary's Church, Islington. After the ceremony Helen again became pregnant.

One fine day, while driving about, Arthur stopped to give a lift to 17-year-old Nellie Tucker. That rascal Arthur ended up giving Nellie more than a lift. The pair became lovers. Meanwhile, Helen gave birth to a bouncing baby boy who was aptly christened Arthur, Jr. Thereafter, when Arthur and Nellie went for little motor trips into the country, they often took along Arthur, Jr.

For years Art somehow kept his three lives running smoothly. Helen Campbell, who had been employed throughout her married life, had managed to save a bit of money. When she informed Art that she was about to purchase part ownership in a restaurant, he vehemently disapproved of the idea. The pair argued so bitterly that they decided to separate. Wouldn't you know it, Nellie Tucker picked this inopportune time to give birth to a baby girl. In order to get Art to financially assist her in bringing up the child she obtained a maintenance order against him in 1928. They say it never rains but it pours. Helen Campbell obtained a maintenance order against Arthur for the support of Arthur, Jr.

Goodness, everything was becoming complicated. In fact, with court appearances and the like, it was impossible for Art to keep his three families separate. This state of affairs came to a head in the Rouse's living room, when Helen Campbell and Lily faced each other, eyeball to eyeball. Helen clutched a marriage certificate dated 1920 in one hot little hand and Arthur, Jr., in the other. Lily fetched her marriage certificate dated 1914, thereby proving to Helen that she was the only legitimate claimant to Arthur's matrimonial obligations.

It is a tribute to the common sense of the two women that once they knew the truth, they calmly discussed their mutual problem. The ladies decided that Arthur, Jr., needed to live in his father's home. Helen turned over her son to Lily Rouse. Lily became extremely attached to the boy, and we have every reason to believe that young Arthur liked his Aunt Lily.

With babies, wives, and finances swimming through his head, one would think that Arthur would make an honest effort to curtail his amorous ways. Not so. Arthur picked this rather inappropriate time in his life to fall in love. The object of his affection was Ivy Muriel Jenkins, called "Paddy" by everyone, including Art. Before you could say Numero Quatro, Paddy was going on long drives with Art in his shiny black Morris. She fell in love with Art, and most probably for the first time in his life he felt genuine love for a woman. Paddy, who never doubted for a moment that Arthur was single, took her boyfriend home to Gellygaer, Wales, to meet her parents.

Mr. Jenkins was not a country bumpkin. He owned a small profitable colliery and was a man who appreciated his family. It was his custom to offer a small share of his colliery to each new member of the family. One can only imagine Arthur Rouse's thoughts as he listened attentively to Mr. Jenkins accepting him at face value. The matter of a few hundred pounds to acquire his shares would pose no problem. Arthur assured Mr. Jenkins that it would be a mere formality.

At the time, Arthur was dead broke and was being pressed by everyone for payment of overdue bills. Paddy assured Art that her family had been favorably impressed. The lovers returned to London.

During subsequent visits to Wales, Art informed Mr. Jenkins that after they were married he and Paddy would be moving into a comfortable home at Kingston-on-Thames. Later, when Paddy told her father that she and Arthur had become man and wife during a quiet ceremony held on June 12, he was pleased with the news. Four months later Paddy returned to Gellygaer quite ill and very pregnant.

To add to his problems, Arthur received the rather distressing news that Nellie

Tucker was pregnant again. Nellie gave birth to her second daughter in October, just as Paddy arrived back home to be with her parents during her difficult pregnancy.

Pregnancies, babies, girlfriends, wives, it was enough to drive a man crazy. Arthur became edgy. He and his one legitimate wife, Lily, started to bicker. Young Arthur, Jr., now six years old, seemed to be always under foot.

Then tragedy struck. On November 5, 1930 two cousins, Alfred Brown and William Bailey, were walking the roads near Hardingstone. The two men were returning home from a Bonfire Night dance at Northampton. It was Guy Fawkes Night. Effigies of Fawkes were being burned on bonfires all over England.

Brown and Bailey turned the corner of the main London Road and proceeded along Hardingstone Lane. As soon as they did so a man walked by them, coming from the opposite direction. Both men later recalled that the stranger was bareheaded. So popular were hats in England in 1930 that anyone not wearing one in the evening would be conspicuous. As the stranger walked by, the cousins' attention was drawn to a bonfire about 600 yards ahead of them. The stranger, who was now 20 yards behind them, shouted, "It looks as if somebody has got a bonfire up there." The two men ran towards the fire.

They came upon a car completely engulfed in flames. The two men fetched the police. As the flames died down and were doused with water, it was obvious that a badly burned body was in the passenger seat of the vehicle. The right arm was burned off at the elbow and the right leg was burned off at the ankle. The left leg had somehow become doubled up under the torso.

Early the next morning the licence number of the Morris Minor was checked. The vehicle belonged to Mr. Alfred Arthur Rouse of 14 Buxted Road, London. Had some terrible accident taken place, horribly burning Arthur Rouse to death? It was not that uncommon for motor vehicles to catch fire and burn in 1930. Then again, if the burned body wasn't that of Arthur Rouse, who was he and how did he end up in Arthur's car on a quiet country road on Guy Fawkes Night?

Arthur was at Gellygaer, Wales, visiting his pregnant 'wife' Paddy and her respectable family. Next day when the newspapers were delivered to the Jenkins' residence, there was quite a commotion. There, for all the Jenkins family to see, was a picture of Arthur's burned-out car. You just don't walk away and leave a burning car. If there is a body in the car it is considered only proper to notify the police. The Jenkins family's stares and questions were too much for Arthur. He took off by bus for London. Other people had read the newspapers that day. One of them spotted Arthur boarding the bus, carrying a briefcase with the initials "A.A.R." on its side. He called the police.

Detectives intercepted the bus at Hammersmith Bridge Road. One of the detective asked, "Are you Mr. Rouse?"

"Yes, that is right," came the reply.

"We are police officers, and I want you to accompany me to the police station."

Arthur replied, "Very well. I am glad it is over. I was going to Scotland Yard about it. I am responsible. I am very glad it is over. I have had no sleep."

Right from the beginning Arthur insisted on telling his story to anyone who would listen. It never varied. He claimed that the man in the car was a hitch-hiker. Arthur had picked him up near St. Albans. At first their journey was uneventful. Later a policeman had pulled them over and spoke to Arthur about a defective rear light. As they drove through the night Arthur said he became somewhat sleepy. He also thought the engine of his Morris might be acting up. He pulled over, informing his passenger that he was going into the nearby woods to relieve himself. He asked the stranger if he would pour some gasoline into the tank of the car. Arthur customarily carried a large can of gasoline in the vehicle. As Arthur was taking his leave the stranger asked for a cigarette. Arthur tossed him a cigar. Next thing he knew the whole vehicle was a blazing inferno. The man must have started the whole thing when he lit the cigar.

Arthur tried to approach the car, but the heat was too intense. He admitted that he was the hatless man seen by the two cousins. He hadn't stopped because his first impulse had been to hail a truck which might be able to help. Why had he gone to Wales rather than go to the police? Arthur said he was in a state of panic and admitted that he had acted badly. He had been on his way to Wales originally, and it seemed most natural for him to follow through with his plans. He had hitched a ride part way and then went the rest of the way by bus.

That was Arthur's story. There were many who believed it word for word. Others thought it was a complete fabrication.

Arthur was arrested and charged with murder. His trial began on January 26, 1931, at the old County Hall at Northampton. The bizarre nature of the case attracted world-wide attention. More than 2000 applications for seats were received by the court. The old County Hall seated 60.

Arthur took the witness stand and told substantially the same story as has already been related here. The prosecution bore down heavily on the theory that Arthur had clumsily tried to disappear by substituting his victim's body for his own. Yet would anyone do all this and then continue to his wife's home, carrying his initialled briefcase? These were hardly the actions of a man trying to disappear.

The briefcase proved to be an embarrassment. Does one usually take a briefcase out of the car when one is going to relieve himself? Arthur claimed he didn't trust the stranger and took the briefcase as a precaution against theft.

The prosecution brought out the fact that Arthur was something of an amateur mechanic and knew how to get up a car so that it would burn furiously from the moment it was lit.

Several yards from the car police found a mallet. Arthur admitted that the mallet belonged to him but could offer no explanation as to how it got outside the car. The Crown felt that the victim had been rendered unconscious by repeated blows to the head with the mallet which had then simply been thrown away.

The jury took only one hour and fifteen minutes to reach their verdict, and during that time they had lunch. Their verdict was guilty.

The decision of the jury satisfied many but still left some questions unanswered. What was the motive for the crime, and who was the victim? Many felt Arthur's story could very well be true.

All appeals and reprieves were refused. Arthur Rouse was hanged on March 10, 1931.

The following day his confession was released to the press and was published. It is reproduced here word for word:

"It was the Agnes Kesson case at Epson in June which first set me thinking. It showed that it was possible to beat the police if you were careful enough.

"Since I read about that case I kept thinking of various plans. I tried to hit on something new. I did not want to do murder just for the sake of it.

"I was in a tangle in various ways. Nellie Tucker was expecting another child of which I would be the father and I was expecting to hear from 'Paddy' Jenkins similar news. There were other difficulties and I was fed up. I wanted to start afresh.

"I let the matter drop from my mind for a while, but in the autumn of last year something happened which made me think again.

"A man spoke to me near the Swan and Pyramid public house in Whetstone High Road. He was down-and-out and told the usual hard luck story. I took him into the public house and he had some beer. I had lemonade. Of course, I paid for the drinks.

"He told me he usually hung about there. I met him once again and stood him a couple of drinks. He did not tell me his name, but he did say he had no relations and was looking for work. He said he had been to Peterborough, Norwich, Hull, and other places trying to get work, and that he was in the habit of getting lifts on lorries.

"He was the sort of man no one would miss, and I thought he would suit the plan I had in mind. I worked out the whole thing in my mind, and as it was then early in November, I suddenly realized that I should do it on November 5, which was Bonfire Night, when a fire would not be noticed so much.

"I think it was on November 2 or 3 that I searched out the man. He was having a drink of beer and we talked. When I said I intended to go to Leicester on the Wednesday night, he said he would be glad of a lift up there. This is what I thought he would say.

"I made an appointment with him for the Wednesday night for about eight o'clock. I met him outside the Swan and Pyramid, and we went into the bar. He had more beer, and I again had lemonade.

"I asked him if he would like something to drink on the journey, and he said he would. I bought a bottle of whiskey. Then we both got into the car, which was outside the public house.

"We drove first of all to my house in Buxted Road. I got out, leaving the man in the car.

"My wife was in. She had seen me draw up near the house and asked me who it was I had in the car. I said it was a man I knew, but she suspected it was a woman.

"I said, 'All right. I'll drive close up in front of the house, as I am turning round, to let you see it is a man.'

"I did so, as I drove out of Buxted Road, so that my wife could see for herself and have no grounds for jealousy.

"So far as I remember, it was about 8:30 p.m. when I started off for the north with a man in the car, though I might be mistaken about the time. I drove slowly because I wanted it to be late when I did what I had in mind. I don't think I travelled more than fifteen miles an hour.

"I stopped at St. Albans partly for a rest and partly to fill the time. The man switched out the lights by mistake and a policeman spoke to me, as is already well known.

"During the journey the man drank the whisky neat from the bottle and was getting quite fuzzled. We talked a lot, but he did not tell me who he actually was. I did not care.

"I turned into Hardingstone Lane because it was quiet and near a main road, where I could get a lift from a lorry afterwards. I pulled the car up.

"The man was half-dozing - the effect of the whisky. I looked at him and then gripped him by the throat with my hand. I pressed his head against the back of the seat. He slid down, his hat falling off. I saw he had a bald patch on the crown of his head.

"He just gurgled. I pressed his throat hard. My grip is very strong.

"I used my right hand only because it is very powerful. People have always said I have a terrific grip. He did not resist. It was all very sudden. The man did not realize what was happening. I pushed his face back. After making a peculiar noise, the man was silent, and I thought he was dead or unconscious.

"Then I got out of the car, taking my attache case, the can of petrol, and the mallet with me. I walked about ten yards in front of the car and opened the can, using the mallet to do so. I threw the mallet away and made a trail of petrol to the car. I took the mallet away with one purpose in view.

"Also I poured petrol over the man and loosened the petrol union joint and took off the top of the carburetor. I put the petrol can in the back of the car.

"I ran to the beginning of the petrol trail and put a match to it. The flame rushed to the car, which caught fire at once.

"Petrol was leaking from the bottom of the car. That was the petrol I had poured over the man and the petrol that was dripping from the union joint and carburetor.

"The fire was very quick, and the whole thing was a mass of flames in a few seconds. I ran away. I was running when I came near the two men, but I started to walk then. It is not true that I came out of the ditch when the men saw me. I was on the grass verge. I did shout to them there must be a 'bonfire over there.'

"I did not expect to see anyone in the lane at that time of night. It surprised me and I decided to change my plans.

"I had intended to walk through to Northampton and to get a train to Scotland. But when the men saw me I hesitated and went the other way. The men were right when they said they saw me hesitate.

"I left my hat in the car. When I was driving, I nearly always did so with my hat off. I forgot, in the excitement, to take it out of the car.

"I went to Wales because I had to go somewhere, and I did not know what to do. I did not think there would be much fuss in the papers about the thing, but pictures of the car with long accounts were published, and I left Wales.

"I was not going to Scotland, as I said. I just went back to London because I thought it was the best thing to do. London is big.

"In my attache case was my (army) identity disc, which the police still have. I intended to put it on the man in the car so that people would think it was me. I forgot to do so.

"I knew that no one would find out that the man had been strangled, because the fire would be so fierce that no traces of that would be left.

"I am not able to give any more help regarding the man who was burned in the car. I never asked his name. There was no reason why I should do so."

And so ended the life of Arthur Rouse. His victim has not been identified to this day.

THE BLACK PANTHER

He was called the Black Panther - a mysterious British criminal who specialized in robbing sub-post offices while wearing an ominous shoulder-length black hood. He was a small man, standing no more than five and a half feet, but he was strong, wiry, and quick as a panther. He operated in England in the early seventies, gaining access to sub-post offices by drilling holes in windowframes with a half-inch brace-and-bit drill.

Not very daring stuff, you might say, but before he was through the Black Panther was to take four lives and be responsible for the most extensive and expensive manhunt ever to take place in England until another reprehensible character known as the Yorkshire Ripper came upon the scene.

On the night of February 15, 1974, the Black Panther gained entrance to a sub-post office operated by Donald Skepper in New Park, Harrowgate. Skepper, fifty, a former pilot, occupied the corner shop with his wife, Johanna, and their 18-year-old son, Richard. The Panther, dressed entirely in black, forced Richard to accompany him to his parents' room. Donald Skepper woke up to face the terrifying sight of the black-clad intruder waving his shotgun.

Taking in the situation at a glance, Skepper decided to take a chance. He swung his body as if to get out of bed. It was a mistake. The shotgun roared, and Donald Skepper was thrown back on his bed, dead. Quick as a cat, the Panther was gone. He had killed for the first time. Donald Skepper would not be his last victim.

Seven months later, on September 6, 1974, in the village of Higher Baxenden, near Accington, sub-post master Derk Astin was awakened in the middle of the night.

He resisted the Panther's demands and was shot dead.

Only two months were to pass before this strange criminal struck again. This time one of the Panther's victims survived. It was 7:00 p.m. Sidney and Margaret Grayland were closing up for the day when Sidney had occasion to open the back door of the shop. There he stood, face to face with the black-clad hooded Panther. Without warning the loud report of a shot broke the still of the evening. Sidney Grayland slumped dead on the storeroom floor. Margaret rushed to her husband's side, only to be dealt a stunning blow to the head. The Panther rained blow after blow upon the woman's head until she fell unconscious in a bloody heap. Four hours later, two policemen making their rounds discovered the Graylands. Margaret was rushed to hospital and survived the attack but could offer little assistance in identifying her husband's murderer.

There are close to 25,000 sub-post offices in England. Most are run by middle-aged couples, many of whom live over their shops. Were none safe? Circulars went out to all sub-post offices, alerting proprietors to be on the watch for the man now known as the Black Panther. Horrific as the three post office murders were, it would be another type of criminal activity which would catapult the Black Panther into national notoriety. He would try his hand at that most dreaded of all crimes - kidnapping.

The tiny village of Highley in Shropshire was home to the wealthy Whittle family. Ronald Whittle had been left a thriving transportation business by his late father. The family home was occupied by his sister Lesley Whittle, seventeen, and his mother Dorothy. Ronald, with a family of his own, lived at the other end of the village.

On the night of January 13, 1975, Dorothy Whittle was out visiting friends. Lesley was alone at home. When Dorothy returned at 1:30 a.m., Lesley was nowhere to be found. So began the strangest kidnapping ever to take place in England. Whoever had spirited Lesley away had left a coil of Dymo tape behind. The message on the tape demanded £50,000 in small used bills. Police were immediately called in by Ronald Whittle.

A news leak took place, and the kidnapping received wide publicity. To this point no connection was made between the three murders of sub-post office proprietors and the kidnapping of Lesley Whittle.

In the 48 hours immediately following his sister's disappearance, Ronald Whittle received several communications from the kidnapper, instructing him on the method to be used to deliver the ransom money. The drop would be made on the night of January 15 just outside the Dudley Zoo.

Just before the transfer of monies was to take place, something went wrong, as it so often does at this most crucial of all moments in the course of a kidnapping. The Panther parked his Morris 1300 a little distance from the zoo. He made his way through a carpark but ran into Gerald Smith, a security guard, who asked the Panther for identification. Without warning, six shots were fired. All six found their mark, but Smith, who amazingly never lost consciousness, managed to raise the alarm. It was too late. The kidnapper had escaped on foot. Ironically, his Morris was to remain locked and undisturbed for some time. In it were Lesley Whittle's slippers, Dymo tape, and a tape-recording of Lesley's last words.

Two days later Scotland Yard released the information that the murders of sub-postoffice proprietors Skepper, Askin, and Grayland, as well as the attempted murders of Mrs. Grayland and Gerald Smith were all committed by the same man, the man who had kidnapped Lesley Whittle. A massive manhunt, the most extensive undertaken in England up to that time, was conducted through the combined efforts of several law-enforcement agencies. Where was Lesley Whittle? Above all, was she alive or dead?

On the night Lesley was kidnapped, she was forced to leave her home at gunpoint, wearing only slippers and a housecoat. She was taken to Kidsgrove and coerced into going down a manhole in Bathpool Park. She descended a rusty ladder down into the bowels of the Bathpool drainage system. Urged on by the Panther, she entered a damp, dark tunnel. They proceeded until they reached the main shaft of the drainage complex. Down the shaft the terrified, shivering girl walked, until she and the Panther came to a small platform. The platform was equipped with a sleeping bag, food, and a torch. This would be Lesley's resting place until, as her kidnapper assured her, she would be released after her family paid the ransom for her freedom. Before leaving the girl the Panther tied a noose around her neck and attached it to a metal ladder. The diabolical device could not be removed without proper tools.

We have two versions of the horrible fate which befell Lesley. The Panther was later to state that Lesley fell off her platform and hanged herself. The Crown was to prove that the Panther, thwarted in his attempt to collect the ransom money, pushed the girl off the platform and callously watched as she hanged.

Months passed before a piece of Dymo tape was found by children in Blackpool Park. The tape, which contained the words, "Drop suitcase into hole," led police to search the park area. An adventuresome constable slowly descended into the dark drainage tunnel. His torch illuminated the body of Lesley Whittle grotesquely hanging by the neck.

The Panther was to remain at large for a further nine months. Then, on the night of December 11, 1975, at approximately 11:00 p.m., Constables Tony White and Stuart McKenzie were patrolling the streets of Mansfield Woodhouse. The two young constables decided to question a suspicious-looking man carrying a valise. Before they could get through the preliminaries, the stranger barked, "Don't move." In his hands he held a sawed-off shotgun.

The Panther forced the two policemen into their own vehicle and instructed them to drive. Constable White waited for his opportunity. The moment the shotgun wasn't pointed directly at his head he lunged for his adversary. In an instant the two constables had the Black Panther in custody. Aside from his shotgun, the Panther was carrying two knives, two razors, a strangle cord, and a bottle of ammonia. Within hours he was identified as Donald Neilson, a former soldier who had learned to kill while serving in Africa with the King's Own Yorkshire Light Infantry.

On June 14, 1976, Neilson was tried at Oxford. He confessed to all his crimes, with the exception of the murder of Lesley Whittle. He always claimed her death was an accident. Despite this, he was found guilty of all four murders and received one sentence of 21 years and three life sentences.

In passing sentence the English judge attached a rider - "In your case, life must mean life. If you are ever released from prison, it should only be on account of great age or infirmity."

WIGWAM MURDER

In the normal course of events Joan Wolfe should have married a shopkeeper from her hometown of Tunbridge Wells in England. She should have had a home alive with the voices of children and grandchildren. But what should have been was never to be.

Joan was a teenager in 1941 when soldiers from every corner of the British Empire converged on England for final training before being sent into battle. She was a religious, well-behaved youngster who was completely captivated by the glamorous uniforms of the Canadians and Australians who swarmed over the countryside.

Perhaps her morals were not of the highest standards, but times were different then, and who are we to judge? Many of these soldiers would never see their homes again but would lie forever in Holland, France, and Italy. Besides, they had delightful accents and were so worldly compared to the local boys.

By the time Joan met August Sangret she had had casual affairs with several soldiers. In fact, at the age of nineteen she was what is commonly called "a camp follower."

Joan Wolfe was a notch above the other girls, who hung around the military camps. She didn't drink, smoke, or use profane language. Rarely did a day pass that Joan didn't pray to her God. When she sinned she asked for forgiveness. Sometimes she asked for understanding, too.

August Sangret, 28, from Battleford, Saskatchewan, was half Cree Indian and half French. He had jet-black hair, was dark skinned and, in his Canadian army uniform, was an altogether attractive young man. August could neither read nor write.

Joan was nearly destitute when she strolled into a pub in Godalming, Surrey. The pub, located only a few miles from Jasper Military Camp, was crawling with soldiers. August struck up a conversation with Joan. She talked a great deal. He was a great listener. Joan never hinted to him that she hadn't eaten since morning, nor did she tell him that she had no place to stay that night.

The young couple went for a walk. They wandered to the edge of the town, where August gently kissed Joan's cheek. The kiss led to several more. In a deserted field the Canadian soldier and the 19-year-old English girl were intimate.

Joan was too embarrassed to tell her new boyfriend that she had no place to sleep. She told him she was going to catch the train for Guildford. August walked Joan to the station. That night she slept on a bench.

All that July of 1942 Joan saw August at every opportunity. She told him she loved him. He, in turn, promised to marry her as soon as he received permission from the army.

Towards the end of July Joan fainted on the street. Police placed her in the Warren Road Hospital in Guildford. Joan felt she was pregnant, but doctors told her it was too early to make a positive diagnosis.

She signed herself out of the hospital and continued her romance with August. August was sympathetic when she told him she had no place to stay. He came up with a novel solution to the problem.

August would build a wigwam in the woods behind the army camp. He proceeded to cut down three large branches from nearby trees, forming the frame of a wigwam. This he covered with blankets. Joan and August made love in their new home.

Joan was now positive she was pregnant. August didn't seem to mind. He repeated his promise of marriage, but as the weeks drifted by Joan realized that her inquiries brought a rather lame response: August claimed that he had not yet received permission to marry from the Canadian army.

As the summer waned Joan suffered a minor inconvenience. Military police stumbled upon the wigwam. The lovers were made to move on. August simply built another wigwam in another area. When this location was discovered Joan moved into a deserted cricket pavilion on a green in Thursley. After a few days, a groundskeeper chanced upon her and evicted her. She resorted to sleeping in the woods.

August brought her cakes and pies from the camp, but their relationship was undergoing a change. August sometimes grew sullen. Sometimes he shouted at her. He seemed rougher in his love-making. Joan worried that her lover was tiring of her.

On October 7, 1942, soldiers were carrying out manoeuvres on Hankley Common, Godalming. One of them spotted a hand sticking out of a sand dune on the top of a hill. Police were called. Soon Scotland Yard pathologists were gingerly excavating the body of a young girl who had been murdered approximately three weeks earlier. Joan Wolfe was at rest at last.

The shallow grave had offered little protection from the elements. Pathologists ascertained that the body had been dragged to the hilltop about two or three days after death. Joan Wolfe's shoes, her purse, and bits of jewelry were scattered all over the hill.

A large stake was found with small strands of blonde hair imbedded in the bark. These strands were compared with Joan's hair and were found to be identical. Police felt that the stake was the murder weapon. Joan had been struck from behind; the blow crushed her skull. She had also been stabbed three times in the head and several times on the arms and hands.

It is believed that Joan had been attacked with a knife and had raised her arms to ward off the blows. Finally, though badly injured, she had run from the assailant until he caught up with her and delivered the lethal blow to her skull. The stab wounds to the arms were distinctive. They had been made by a knife with a slight hook or break at the end of the blade.

Detectives immediately learned that August Sangret had been the dead girl's boyfriend. Questioned extensively, he told of his relationship with Joan. For five consecutive days August talked as secretaries took down every word of his 17,000-word statement. His uniforms were confiscated and checked for bloodstains, but the clothing had been thoroughly washed and the tests proved to be inconclusive. No knives were found among his possessions.

Although August had not been told of Joan's death when he signed his lengthy statement, he said, "I suppose you have found her. Everything points to me. I guess I shall get the blame."

Although his statement detailed his relationship with the dead girl, it was in no way a confession of murder. August was released. Even though Scotland yard felt certain he was the murderer, they also knew they didn't have a case that would stand up in court.

Detectives discovered that a soldier, Private Crowle, had sometime earlier been in the woods picking blackberries when he found a knife sticking in a birch tree. Close by he noticed a wigwam. Crowle pulled the knife out of the tree, noting that it had a distinctive beak tip. He turned the knife over to his corporal. Later the knife was identified as belonging to Sangret and was returned to him. Suspicious and incriminating, but in the opinion of Scotland Yard still not enough to enable them to proceed.

Then one of those unrelated events occurred which so often are instrumental in providing police with the one element they need to tie up a murder case. A drain was blocked at the army camp. The soldier assigned to repair the drain reached down and dislodged papers and cigarette butts. The drain remained clogged. He reached down again and extracted a black-handled knife. The blade had a distinctive beak or curve at the end. It was identified as the one which had been found near the wigwam and returned to Sangret.

Sangret was arrested and charged with Joan Wolfe's murder. He was tried in February 1943. During his trial pathologists demonstrated how Sangret's distinctive knife fit exactly the stab wounds to Joan's skull.

August Sangret was found guilty of murder. Although the jury added a strong recommendation to mercy, he was hanged at Wandsworth Gaol in April 1943.

THE TEACUP PUZZLE

On July 9, 1940, police were called to a pleasant upper middle class home in Matfield, Kent, England. The sight that greeted them was not a pleasant one. Three bodies were scattered about the garden.

Let's see, there were the occupants of the cottage, Mrs. Dorothy Fisher and her adult daughter Freda, as well as their maid, Mrs. Saunders. Mrs. Fisher and Freda had been shot while facing their attacker, while Mrs. Saunders had been mowed down from the rear. There was plenty of blood about the garden, but no sign of a weapon.

Scotland Yard detectives were called to the murder scene, where they observed a great deal of broken china and a tea tray near Mrs. Saunders' body. Each piece was gathered up and put together by the Yard's lab technicians. They ended up with four complete tea cups and saucers. A search of the garden area turned up one other clue, a woman's glove. The glove was tried on each body and did not fit.

Now, if you have been paying attention, you should by now have deduced, as Scotland Yard did, that a fourth woman had been present for tea and had shot the three victims just as tea was about to be served. Unknowingly, this fourth woman had left her glove behind.

Mrs. Fisher was separated from her husband, who lived on a farm in Oxfordshire. He was immediately notified of his wife's death, but could offer no clue to her killer's identity. Detectives are sometimes known not to take a suspect's word at face value. They checked out Fisher's whereabouts on the day of the massacre and found that he was in his London office all that day. He could not possibly have been the killer.

They also discovered that Fisher was living with a 35-year-old widow, Mrs. Florence Ransome, but were disappointed to learn that Florence and Mrs. Fisher got along, as the British say, famously. Mrs. Ransome, who seemed to have the best of all worlds, often visited Mrs. Fisher. No one could ever remember a harsh word passing between the two women. Mrs. Ransome appeared to be in the clear.

Famed pathologist Sir Bernard Spilsbury added to the mystery by revealing that all three women had been shot with a single barrel shotgun, hardly a lady's weapon. The cunning killer, using the single action weapon, had to load and reload three times as she, or perhaps he, slew the hapless victims one by one. The killer also must have retrieved the shotgun casings, as none were found at the scene of the crime.

There you have it - broken teacups, retrieved shell casings, a lady's glove, and all those bodies. In true Agatha Christie fashion, can we solve the mystery of who killed the three ladies in the garden? Let's get to it, shall we?

Detectives interviewed Mrs. Ransome. She stated quite simply that the Yard boys were barking up the wrong tree. She had been on the farm in Oxfordshire on July 9, the day of the multiple murder. She pointed out that it was impossible to travel from Oxfordshire to Matfield in one day. She tried on the glove found at the murder scene. While Mrs. Ransome thought it was decidedly small, everyone else thought it fit nicely.

Inquiries were made at the railway station. Detectives found that it was indeed quite possible to travel from Oxfordshire to Matfield and back in one day.

Things began to heat up for Mrs. Ransome. A hired hand on her farm told detectives that Mr. Fisher owned a .410 single barrel shotgun. On July 8 Mrs. Ransome had practised shooting on the farm. The next day, the all-important ninth, she was nowhere to be seen.

Mr. Fisher's shotgun was confiscated and taken back to the Yard's lab in London. Without the shotgun casings, it was impossible to ascertain if it was the murder weapon.

Detectives kept scratching and came up with a tradesman who identified Mrs. Ransome as the well-dressed lady he had seen lugging the unwieldy shotgun to the Matfield station on the day of the murder.

Motive, motive, we must have a motive. After all, what would Agatha think?

Delving deeper into Mrs. Ransome's past, those nosy Yard detectives discovered that although she appeared to be contented with her lot in life, she had confided to intimate friends that she dearly wanted to become Mrs. Fisher. As the original Mrs. Fisher was in extremely good health, she might very well have decided to kill the obstacle to her happiness.

Detectives figured Mrs. Ransome lugged the unwieldy shotgun to Mrs. Fisher's home. As all the tea party guests were well acquainted, she could have offered some excuse for having the shotgun with her, possibly taking it to a shop later for repairs.

When Mrs. Saunders brought in her tea tray, the carnage started. Mrs. Ransome had to shoot reload, shoot, reload, and shoot again. Mrs. Fisher was the prime target, but Mrs. Ransome planned to leave no witnesses. Freda and Mrs. Saunders had to die because they were there.

Mrs. Ransome then gathered up the three shotgun casings and left for her farm a Oxfordshire. She either never thought of the fourth cup on Mrs. Saunders' tray or simply didn't care. In the confusion and turmoil which must have taken place in that garden, Mrs. Ransome dropped one glove. She had to have a certain amount of guile to leave with the shotgun casings, which she probably threw off the train along with her one remaining glove on the way home.

On Nov. 8, 1940 Mrs. Ransome stood accused of multiple murder in England's famous Old Bailey. She pleaded not guilty. We have already mentioned the pertinent facts pointing to her guilt. The defence had other ideas.

Mrs. Ransome professed her innocence throughout. She claimed that she had not been in Matfield on July 9, and that the tradesman who had identified her was undoubtedly mistaken as so many eyewitnesses have been in the past. She claimed that malicious gossip of friends and neighbors was not proof of motive. Mrs. Ransome swore that she got along extremely well with Mrs. Fisher. It was true she had access to a .410 single action shotgun, but there were thousands of these guns in farmhouses throughout England.

The jury retired to reach their verdict. Surprisingly, they took only 47 minutes to find Mrs. Ransome guilty.

A panel of psychiatrists examined Mrs. Ransome and found her to be mentally ill. One might wonder why she didn't plead insanity, but it was thought by her lawyers that the act of retrieving the shell casings clearly demonstrated that she had her wits about her and knew very well at the time that what she was doing was wrong. The striker-pin marks on the casings would have definitely pointed to the murder weapon. Mrs. Ransome knew this and was intent on carrying away the casings from the scene of the crime.

Who knows, if it hadn't been for that fourth shattered teacup and the misplaced lady's glove, Scotland Yard might have concentrated their hunt on a man. Today, Mrs. Ransome might have been the second Mrs. Fisher, and at the age of 78, be a kindly little grey haired lady conducting tea parties of her own. Instead, she was detained in Broadmoor, an asylum for the criminally insane, where she died several years later.

TWENTY YEARS LATER

Some men have the capacity to commit the most reprehensible acts without a second thought. Then there are those whose guilty consciences gnaw at the very essence of their being until they must tell all or go mad.

Let's turn back the pages of time to 1838 and peek in on Willie Sheward. Willie was a tailor by trade and a confirmed imbiber by inclination. Hardly a day went by when Willie wasn't well into his cups by mid-day.

Waistcoats were repaired with trembling hands. Patches were applied in a haphazard manner. No wonder Willie's tailoring enterprise didn't flourish. The good folks of Norwich, England had better things to do with their clothing than to put them in the hands of a drunken tailor.

If you discount Johnny Barleycorn, Willie did have one friend in this world, his housekeeper, Martha Francis. Martha, dear Martha, at 43 was a member of the over the hill gang, who for years had kept her eyes wide open in the search for an eligible bachelor. Prospects were not that numerous in Norwich town.

Gradually, Martha lowered her standards. Willie wasn't that bad. True enough, every couple of years he declared himself bankrupt. True enough, he was intoxicated more often than he was sober. But a girl can't have everything. Maybe a stern hand and a sharp tongue would divert Willie from the rocky path he had chosen.

The not-so-young couple duly wed. Martha soon found out that a sharp tongue brought only a quick retort. A stern hand brought Willie's crashing onto her jaw. Year after dreary year, life went on. In an attempt to increase their tailoring business, Willie and Martha moved to a new location, St. Martins-at-Palace. Nothing changed.

Business was mediocre. Bickering was constant.

Summer of 1851 came to Norwich. The Shewards had been unhappily married for 13 years when neighbors and acquaintances noticed that Martha wasn't around any more. Inquiries as to her whereabouts brought forth the information that she had run away with another man. As Martha had often threatened to do that very thing, Willie's explanation was readily accepted.

But of course Martha, dear Martha, had not run away. She had yelled, cajoled and otherwise made life miserable for Willie once too often. Fortified with the false courage of alcohol, Willie plunged his tailor's shears into his wife's chest. He was immediately racked with remorse and pleaded for those shears to evict themselves from Martha's bosom and return to their rightful place on his tailor's bench. He begged his dead wife to return to life. He cried like a child. All requests went unanswered.

Willie looked down at the crumpled form at his feet. He made up his mind. No one would ever know the terrible thing he had done. When darkness fell over Norwich that June night so many years ago, Willie went about dismembering his wife's body. All night he worked. He sobered up, rested, then returned to his grim task.

Next morning, Willie took a few small portions of Martha out of the house and threw them away. He bent over his tailor's bench all that day, but when night fell he returned to the task at hand. Martha's head was put in a large saucepan and set to boil on the stove. Later Willie wrote, "I then broke it up and distributed it about Thorpe. I put the hands and feet in the same saucepan, in the hope that they might boil to pieces."

Every day at sundown Willie continued his macabre task. "On Friday I disposed of all the remains of the body. On Sunday morning I burnt all the sheets, nightgown and pillowcases and all that had blood about them. Her long hair I cut with a pair of scissors into small pieces and they blew away as I walked along."

Finally Martha was no more. Willie appeared to be in the clear, but annoying events took place which caused him some anxiety. Since plunging the shears into Martha's chest, Willie had not taken a drop of liquor. He didn't dare for fear of talking about what he had done. Life without booze was a strain.

Then there was the day a dog was seen running down the street with a human foot. A search of the area turned up a human hand. Police gave these portions to doctors who, after examining them, declared that the possible murder victim was a female between the ages of 16 and 26. They were simply wrong. Martha was 56 when she was killed. The foot and hand were preserved and nothing further was done about the gruesome find. Willie drew a sigh of relief, but not for long.

About six months after Martha's demise, stone sober Willie answered a knock at his door. He was greeted by a constable. Willie froze. The constable explained that Martha's aunt had gone to her great reward, leaving her niece what amounted to a fortune of £300. Willie explained that he had no idea where Martha could be located which, if you dismiss the hand and foot, was true enough.

Ten years passed without any further inquiries about Martha. Willie became frustrated with the tailoring trade and turned to pawnbroking. His bad luck held. Business under the three balls was no better than the tailoring game. Displaying a flair for the romantic, Willie decided to marry, trying the knot with the second Mrs. Sheward on St. Valentine's Day in 1862.

The marriage was a mistake. In Willie's mind his second wife could do nothing right. Compared to the late Martha, she ran a distant second. Dear Martha, who had bickered and argued with Willie for 13 years, had, with the passage of time, become a saintly figure in Willie's memory. Now truly in love with the woman he had murdered, Willie took to the bottle with a vengeance. Some hard drinkers fall off the wagon. Willie dove. In no time at all he was hitting the sauce with the same singleness of purpose he had displayed at the time of Martha's passing 17 years before.

As the Christmas season of 1868 approached, the second Mrs. Sheward suggested that Willie visit his sister in London. Willie was only too pleased to get away and spend Christmas sloshed to the gills with his sister's family.

On Dec. 28 he left his sister's home and pub crawled throughout London. On New Year's Day Willie could think of nothing but his dead, dismembered wife Martha. Almost 20 years after Martha's death, Willie was torn by a guilty conscience. He tried a few more pubs, but it was no use.

Willie walked into a divisional office of the London Metropolitan Police and asked to speak to the man in charge. Insp. Davis first detected the pungent aroma of alcohol before raising his head to peer at the slightly drunk man before him.

"I want to give myself up," Willie said.

"What for?" asked Davis.

"For the murder of my first wife, Martha," Willie replied.

Initially, the inspector thought he was dealing with a crank, but that all changed when Willie explained how he had killed and dismembered Martha, topping it all with, "Some of it is still preserved in spirits of wine at the Guildhall in Norwich."

Within hours the foot and hand, which had been pickled almost as long as Willie, were being examined by eminent physicians. They proclaimed that the parts were those of a woman in her fifties.

The strange murder and Willie's subsequent trial caused a sensation in London. Sober once again, Willie attempted to retract his confession, but he had gone too far. It took the jury only one hour and fifteen minutes to find him guilty.

On April 23, 1869, Willie Sheward was hanged in Norwich Castle.

JUST FOR THE
DOUGH

Elizabeth Fenning was not a good-looking girl, but that is not to say she was without redeeming features. She had an abundance of faith. She also had a striking figure.

Elizabeth, 22, was gainfully employed by Orlibar and Margaret Turner as cook-housekeeper at their home at 38 Chancery Lane, London, England. The household consisted of the Turners, their married son Robert and his wife, Charlotte. Orlibar was a bookbinder. A young apprentice, Roger Gadsden, lived on the premises. The Turners also employed Sarah Peer as a general maid. A nephew, Thomas King, was a frequent visitor to the Turner home.

These, then, are the characters who appeared so briefly on our criminal stage way back in 1812, but, alas, will be remembered forever because . . . ah, but that would be telling. Let's get on with it, shall we?

Elizabeth became engaged to be married. She thought of little else but the happiness which the future promised. However, the path to marital bliss had a few rough spots. You might even say potholes. For one thing, Roger Gadsden had a thing on for Elizabeth. He always seemed to be within arm's reach of the curvaceous cook. In fact, lecherous Roger sometimes made unwelcome overtures to Elizabeth. On occasion he went further. Let's face it, Liz found herself wrestling with randy Roger every time they were alone.

Come closer - this gets a bit risqué.

Liz was undressing one night when who do you think marched right into her bedroom? If you guessed randy Roger, you would be 100% correct. Well, folks, Liz was in the process of protecting her honor, when Charlotte Turner strolled in to the bedroom. Gadsden, the cad, said that Liz had invited him in for fun and games. Despite Liz's vehement denial of this dastardly lie, Charlotte chose to believe Gadsden. She chastised Liz and hinted that her services might not be required by the Turner family in the future.

Liz was understandably upset. She spoke to Margaret Turner, whom she considered to be her real mistress. Margaret sympathized with her cook's plight and assured our Liz that she would not be relieved of her duties. Still, a girl shouldn't be treated that way, especially since she was scheduled to marry in a few months.

Nothing untoward happened for a few weeks. Then, one fine day, Liz decided to make some dumplings. Don't ask my why, she just decided to make dumplings to accompany the beefsteak pie she planned on serving at the evening meal.

Liz proceeded to gather together the necessary ingredients. Margaret Turner left the kitchen to do some work upstairs. Sarah Peer was already upstairs, sewing. By the time Margaret returned to the kitchen, Liz had the dumpling dough in a pan. In due course the dumplings were put in a pot to boil, while Margaret busied herself making a sauce for the dumplings.

If you are reading this rather distasteful culinary exercise before breakfast, it is permissible to take a short recess, eat breakfast, and continue later. If, however, it is your good fortune to be absorbing this tale after partaking of breakfast, please continue.

All of this action in the kitchen took some time, as you well know if you've ever made dumplings. Anyway, the crux of the scenario was this - Margaret Turner was later to state that Liz was the only one in the kitchen and had not left the room for a minute.

Liz denied this. She swore that she had gone out of the kitchen for several minutes to accept a load of coal, which was delivered to the house. The other members of the household thought that the coal had been delivered the next day. The coal merchant, who kept no detailed records of deliveries, could not say with certainty which day he had delivered the coal.

Those disagreeable dumplings were finally served. Wouldn't you know it? Everyone took violently ill, the one exception being Sarah Peer, who had not eaten the dumplings, but made do with the equally unappetizing beefsteak pie.

Orlibar Turner called in Dr. John Marshall, who did the medical profession proud by unhesitatingly declaring, "Arsenic poisoning." Orlibar revealed that he kept arsenic under lock and key in his desk. He took a look. The arsenic was gone. No one had taken the packets by mistake. Both were marked, "Arsenic, Deadly Poison." Dr. Marshall rendered assistance to his patients and left with the promise that he would return the next day.

Orlibar found the dish in which the dumplings were made. When Dr. Marshall returned the next day, he examined the dish and once again exclaimed, "Arsenic poisoning."

This was no laughing matter. All of the victims of the poisoning survived, but in those days in England, attempted murder was a capital offence. The culprit, if proven guilty, stood a good chance of being hanged.

The police were called. Liz was interviewed. She swore she had not laced the dumplings with arsenic. She also swore that she was out of the kitchen, giving the perpetrator of the crime an opportunity to slip the arsenic into the dumpling dough. Besides, Sarah Peer had purchased milk for the dumplings. Maybe that was the source of the arsenic.

The Turners were interviewed. They stuck to their story that Liz was the only one in the kitchen all day and the only one who could have placed arsenic into the dough. Milk that was left unused was tested. It was free of arsenic. No, the poison was in the dough. Apparently the only one who had the opportunity to place it there was our Liz.

Liz was taken into custody and charged with the attempted murder of the Turner family. That's where the faith comes in. Liz displayed no fear of her upcoming trial. As she said, "Have no fear, I am not guilty and the good God will never suffer a poor girl to go to the gallows for another's fault."

On April 11, 1812, Elizabeth Fenning stood trial for attempted murder. Much of the evidence already reviewed was presented to the court. In summing up, the judge stated that it had been proven that the dumpling dough was the substance which contained the arsenic and that Liz and Liz alone had mixed the dough. Liz was summarily found guilty and sentenced to hang.

For two months, Liz awaited her June date with the hangman. Most of the time she was comforted by a chaplain, who implored her to cleanse her soul by confessing.

The day arrived - June 26, 1812, Liz's last day on earth. She had finished making her wedding dress and chose to wear it for her execution. She wore a solitary white rose near her right breast. A huge crowd roared at the sight of the pathetic young girl, for there was much talk that the Crown might very well be hanging an innocent girl.

It would be pleasant to report that a sheriff on a white steed broke through the crowd and presented a last minute reprieve to the hangman. That didn't happen. The trap door swung open. Wedding dress and all, Liz plunged to her death.

Fifty years later, in Chelmsford, Essex, a man lay on his deathbed. Remember Thomas King, the Turners' nephew? He confessed to attempting to murder the Turner family. King had asked the Turners for a loan of money. When they refused, he sought revenge. He saw a servant girl leave her kitchen to take delivery of some coal. In the few minutes she was absent from the kitchen, he took arsenic out of this uncle's desk and tossed it into a pan containing dough. He remembered well the servant girl's name - Elizabeth Fenning.

SECRET IN THE SAUNA

Michael Telling was born to wealth. His family, the Vesteys, rank as one of the half-dozen wealthiest families in England.

Michael was never a stable lad. Oh, I don't know, he did little things like breaking a milk bottle over the parson's daughter's head. Then there was the time he lay down stark naked in the middle of the road and simply refused to move. From the time his parents divorced in 1953, when he was only three years old, he was a troubled child.

When his mother married an Australian, Michael accompanied the newlyweds down under. In the spring of 1976, he met a waitress, Alison Webber. Michael and Alison married and returned to England to live. There was much talk of married life making a man of him. Someone even mentioned wild oats having been sown.

Once in England, Michael was advised by Vestey lawyers that he was entitled to funds from a family trust. He was given an allowance of £1200 a month as well as the use of several credit cards. The dear boy was also given the use of an expense-free home in the seaside resort of Maidencombe.

But I ask you, did money and all the comforts of life help the Telling marriage? No, it did not. To be blunt, Michael remained a spoiled brat. In 1979, Alison gave birth to a son, Matthew, in an attempt to save the marriage. The birth of the child did nothing to make a man of his father. A year later, Alison and Michael were divorced. It was great fun, but it was just one of those things.

Michael busied himself with hobbies, such as photography. When he tired of that, he became a motorcycle enthusiast. That's how he met Monika Zumsteg. He was in San Francisco, picking up a Harley-Davidson and ran into a friendly couple who asked him to join them and their daughter for dinner. Monika was the daughter.

Michael was smitten, and with good reason. Monika had large brown eyes, full lips, a flawless complexion, and an hourglass figure. She was short, slightly over 5 ft. tall, which suited Michael, who was not much taller.

Monika kept her ears wide open. During the course of the dinner, it became obvious that her parents' guest was an extremely wealthy young man. Two nights later, Monika and Michael were doing what comes naturally in bed at the St. Francis Hotel. Michael cancelled his return flight to England and stayed as long as he could between the sheets with Monika. Finally, he returned home, but kept in daily touch with his true love by telephone.

Would she marry him when his divorce became final, Michael wanted to know. You bet your boots she would. Better still, she would leave for England right away. They could shack up while waiting for the divorce to be finalized. What could be more convenient?

And that's exactly what happened. Monika and Michael lived together, happy as larks until 1981, when they married.

As soon as they became husband and wife, a distinct change came over Monika. Sex became a thing of the past. Drinking bouts were the order of the day. Monika favored vodka, except for breakfast, when orange juice liberally laced with Benedictine put each fresh sunrise in its proper perspective. Although she received a liberal allowance from Michael and lacked nothing of a material nature, she was always in need of cash. The reason was Monika's cocaine habit, which she fed with a vengeance.

It didn't take too many months of married life for Michael to realize that he was married to a hellion who had obviously concealed her darker side from him before the marital knot had been secured. Still, Michael loved Monika in his own way, and chose to overlook her faults in the interest of keeping their marriage intact. This was not an easy task, especially after Michael found out that Monika was bisexual. How did he discover this oh so personal trait?

Three doors down the street from the Tellings, there lived a solicitor, his wife Rosemary and their three children. Rosemary and Monika were carrying on a sexual relationship. In fact, the two ladies belonged to a secret club called Us Girls, which met exclusively for female fun and games.

One night Michael returned home earlier than expected and caught his wife and Rosemary together on the couch. You can say what you want about Michael, but he was a real gentleman. He suggested that the ladies continue their activities in the privacy of an upstairs bedroom.

In fact, there is some evidence later gathered from Rosemary's diary, that she and Monika had Michael's blessing in their lesbian activities. She claims he encouraged the relationship in order to keep Monika. As for Monika, she planned on remaining married to Michael for two years, no matter what. She was well aware that the Vesteys paid off divorced wives after two years of marital bliss.

Michael thought a change of scenery away from Rosemary would do his wife a world of good. The Tellings moved to the Buckinghamshire village of Bledlow Ridge, about 15 miles west of London. Within days, Monika made the acquaintance of a lesbian pizza parlor waitress named Karen in nearby High Wycombe.

Monika and Karen became an item. At one rather boisterous party, Michael was so angered by Monika's behavior that he drove his custom-built Mini right into another vehicle. This infuriated Monika. She called police to search their home for firearms. Police found an illegal weapon, which Michael had brought over from Australia. The weapon was confiscated and Michael was fined £6000.

By February 1983, Michael had given up. He and Monika simply couldn't get along. Michael took a quick trip to Australia to consult with his stepfather about his marital woes. Each day he called Monika. More often than not, she answered the phone from her bedroom. Sometimes she let Michael speak to her female companion. Now folks, that was just too much.

Michael returned to England carrying a Marlin 303 rifle and a diamond necklace for Monika. Pleased as punch, Monica actually made love with her husband on the night of his arrival. Next morning, when she asked him to leave so that she could continue with her regular sex life, he didn't say a word. Instead, Michael retreated to the bedroom and returned with the marlin. He levelled it at Monika and fired. As she lay on the floor, he cocked the rifle twice more and fired. Two bullets entered her chest and one entered her throat.

Like many men who kill their wives, Michael was immediately sorry. What's more, he didn't know what in the world to do next. As a result, he did absolutely nothing for the next few days, if you discount the many kisses he allegedly showered on his very dead wife.

Michael moved Monika's body to an outbuilding. That very day, he installed an electric air freshener in the tiny building which he had partially converted into a sauna bath. Carpet cleaners were called in to shampoo the living room rug where Monika had so recently reposed. Michael then hired a neighbor, Mrs. Richardson, to cook and tidy up the house for him.

To while away the time, Michael played around with his expensive CB radio. In this way he met a lonely woman who lived in the same area. Ten days after Monika's death, Michael and his new friend met for dinner. They became constant companions. Michael showered expensive presents on his new friend. Spring turned into summer.

Michael developed another friend through his CB radio. This lady had no objection to sexual intercourse. She was completely unaware that a few yards away, the body of Monika Telling sat propped up in an outbuilding.

In August, Michael was informed by the Vestey trustees that his home was due to be refurbished. They suggested that he go on vacation. In a moment of anguish Michael blurted out to his housekeeper, Mrs. Richardson, that he had killed his wife. "What's more," Michael said, "the body is stinking in the sauna!" Mrs. Richardson didn't believe him and admonished him for his foolish talk.

Two days later, Michael placed Monika's body in a van and drove towards Maidencombe. When darkness fell, he dragged the body into some woods and chopped off Monika's head. He then propped the headless body in a sitting position against a tree. After placing Monika's head in a polyethylene bag, he lugged it back to the van. Later, at home, he put the bag in the trunk of his Mini.

On Sept. 3, five months after his murder, a motorist intent of relieving himself came across the headless body of Monika Telling. That night, Mrs. Richardson and Michael watched the news of the gruesome find on the telly. Now Mrs. Richardson couldn't get Michael's admission of murder out of her mind. She spoke to her husband and together they went to the police.

The body was quickly identified as being that of Monika Telling. When Michael was confronted, he quickly confessed, stating, "I had 101 reasons for killing Monika." It all poured out, the drinking, the other men, the other women. It had been a nightmare. Michael had snapped.

In June 1984, Michael Telling stood trial. He pleaded guilty to the charge of manslaughter. After a sensational nine day trial, he was found guilty and sentenced to life imprisonment.

13

THE
WILD WEST

BILLY THE KID

The movies have made the men who pushed back the frontiers of North American civilization so appealing and glamorous that it is really a shame to shatter images nurtured and developed since childhood.

It is distressing to report that the gunslingers who roamed the West didn't spend their time seeking out bad men to shoot down in fair gunfights. In the main they were psychopathic killers. Their stories are so distorted by legend that it is difficult to distinguish fact from fiction, but we will try.

Henry McCarty was born in New York City on November 23, 1859. He had one brother, Joe, who never handled a firearm in his life. Joe lived until 1930 and spent many a happy afternoon in his waning years spinning yarns about his famous brother, Billy the Kid.

The boys' father died while they were still small children. Mrs. McCarty headed west and became Mrs. William H. Antrim in 1873. She ran a boarding house in Silver City, New Mexico. A little over a year later she died of tuberculosis.

At the age of fifteen Henry McCarty was on his own. His first brush with the law involved the theft of some clothing from two elderly Chinese merchants. While in jail for this offence he escaped by climbing through the chimney of the jailhouse. Henry headed for Arizona, where he worked as a ranch hand for three years. Then he killed his first man.

Using the surname of his stepfather, Henry Antrim got into a fistfight in a saloon in Camp Grant, Arizona, with a big man named F.P. Cahill. Henry was taking a beating. With the bigger man on top of him, he managed to pull his gun from its holster and fire. Cahill fell over dead. A coroner's jury found Antrim criminally responsible, but by then Henry was long gone.

It was at this time in his life that Henry Antrim changed his name. He took the first name and initial of his stepfather, William H., and added the last name Bonney. His nickname, "The Kid", was a common one in those days. And so Billy the Kid was created.

A happy-go-lucky reckless boy with an infectious smile, Billy was also totally amoral, lacking even the semblance of a conscience. He worked as a cowpoke and ranch hand whenever the mood struck him.

Powerful men hired cowhands like Billy to enforce their own rules. The stakes were high. General stores in frontier communities made their owners wealthy men. So did banks. The U.S. government dispensed lucrative beef contracts in order to fulfil their trade obligations to the Apache Indians. Beef on the hoof was a valuable commodity and relatively easy to steal. Ranch owners needed protection, and men like Billy were their insurance policies.

One such man, John H. Tunstall, owned a bank and general store in Lincoln, New Mexico. He also raised cattle with the financial backing of John Chisum, who was literally the king of cattlemen in New Mexico. Another faction owned a bank and general store in Lincoln. They too raised cattle. The ensuing struggle for power became known as the Lincoln County War.

One fine day in 1878 Tunstall and a group of his men, including Billy the Kid, were ambushed. As the men rode into the trap a flock of wild turkeys scrambled across their path. Billy let out a yell, and together with John Middleton, took off after the wild game. They were both out of sight when the sound of gunfire made them pull up. Still in hiding, they observed what took place. All the riders had put spurs to their horses and managed to escape. All except their boss, Tunstall. He was forced to dismount. Jesse Evans, no older than the Kid himself, calmly shot the older man through the chest. A foreman named Morton then shot the already dead man in the head before bashing in his skull with the butt of a rifle.

When news of the ambush and cold-blooded killing spread, Tunstall's friends and financial backers formed a posse to mete out their own brand of revenge. Billy the Kid rode with the posse.

It took the posse several days of hard riding to catch up with the killers. A wild gunfight took place. Morton and one of his men, Frank Baker, managed to escape but were later surrounded in an old shack. The siege lasted two days. Finally, with the promise that their lives would be spared, they surrendered to the posse. Their bullet-riddled bodies were found later by some sheepherders.

The posse continued to hunt and kill Tunstall's enemies until their own leader, Dick Brewer, was killed. The organized posse disbanded, but many of its number stayed together. At the gang's head was the boy with the infectious smile, Billy the Kid.

Despite warrants having been issued for the arrest of the gang members, they lived openly in Lincoln. On April Fool's Day, 1878, Billy and his boys ambushed the town sheriff. Unsuspectingly walking towards the courthouse, Sheriff Brady fell under a barrage of bullets. His deputy, George Hindman, died later of his wounds. During the melee Billy received a superficial wound in his side.

Now that sheriffs were being gunned down on Main Street, the situation required stern measures to bring it under control. Law-abiding citizens were appalled at the lack of safety in the small towns of the West.

Official word was brought to the attention of none other than the president of the United States, Rutherford B. Hayes. The president had the governor of New Mexico removed from office. In his place he installed a former Civil War general, Lew Wallace. At the time of his appointment he was in the midst of writing a book. He will forever be remembered as the author of the biblical classic *Ben Hur*.

Soon after Wallace became governor, Billy found himself being pursued by a posse. The posse caught up to him and surrounded his gang of eighteen men in a house owned by a friend. Forty men pumped bullets into the house and finally set it on fire. During the battle Billy lost five of his men and managed to kill two members of the posse.

The new governor was furious. He decided to contact Billy directly. A meeting was set up and the two far different men met eyeball to eyeball.

Wallace told Billy that if he remained a bandit he would surely be shot to death. He offered Billy a deal: "If you will stand trial like a man, you'll either go free or you'll be convicted. If you're convicted, I'll get you pardoned."

Billy replied, "No court in New Mexico would give me a fair deal. No, I'll go ahead and die with my boots on."

So much for deals.

In 1880 a new sheriff was elected in Lincoln County. Pat Garrett was a former friend of Billy's who swore that as sheriff his prime objective was to bring Billy to justice. He set up a network of spies to keep informed of Billy's activities. When he found out that Billy was heading for Fort Sumner, he got there first.

The Kid and his gang rode in. Garrett and his men opened fire, killing Tom O'Folliard but the rest of the gang got away. Two days later, Garrett had Billy cornered in an old cabin. Cold, tired and hungry, Billy the Kid surrendered to Garrett.

In March 1881, the Kid stood trial for the murder of one Buckshot Roberts but was acquitted. He was then tried for the murder of Sheriff Brady. This time he was found guilty and sentenced to hang on May 13. Billy awaited death on the second floor of a former store, where he was segregated from the other prisoners. He was guarded day and night by Deputy Sheriff J. W. Bell and Deputy Marshall Robert Olinger.

On April 28, just two weeks before the death sentence was to be carried out, Pat Garrett was out of town collecting taxes. That evening the other prisoners, escorted by Olinger, were herded across the street to a restaurant for supper. Billy, now being guarded only by Bell, asked to be taken to the outhouse. Bell led his handcuffed and leg-shackled prisoner outside. It is believed a friend smuggled a gun into the privy. The pair were retracing their steps to the second floor when Billy turned and shot Bell dead. He then dashed to a gun rack and grabbed a shotgun. Meanwhile Olinger had heard the shot and was running back across the street. Billy ran to a window and killed Olinger with a blast from the shotgun. Citizens who heard the shots ran for their lives.

Billy commandeered an old man, Godfrey Gauss, to help him out of his leg irons. Once free of the irons, he mounted a horse and galloped out of town, laughing and shooting like a madman.

Billy was now the most wanted man in a land of wanted men. Newspapers clamored for his capture. Garrett took the escape as a personal insult. Again, his informers provided him with clues as to Billy's whereabouts. Word drifted back that Billy had been seen around Pete Maxwell's house at Fort Sumner. Together with two deputies, Garrett rode up to Maxwell's late one night. The two deputies covered the house from the outside while Garrett was admitted by Maxwell. He was making initial inquiries when a man's form appeared in the doorway. Clad only in underwear, the man carried a revolver and a butcher knife.

"Who is here?" the intruder inquired.

Garrett recognized the voice of Billy the Kid. When he didn't receive an immediate answer Billy raised his revolver. As he did so Garrett fired twice and Billy fell dead at his feet. It was July 14, 1881.

Pat Garrett lived another twenty-seven years before being shot in the back. An acquaintance, Wayne Brazil, stood trial for his murder, but was acquitted.

Lew Wallace's book *Ben Hur* was published in 1880 while he was still governor of New Mexico. The following year he was appointed Minister to Turkey. For years after its publication *Ben Hur* ranked second only to the Bible in popularity in the

English language. Two movies have been made based on Wallace's bestseller.

In this area he is far outranked by Billy the Kid. More than twenty movies have been produced about the baby-faced killer with the infectious smile, including the recent *Young Guns* and its sequel *Young Guns II*.

SAM'S GOLD COINS

Saloons, shootouts, and loose women - the phenomenon known as the American Wild West may never be duplicated. Adventuresome, reckless men pushed westward, expanding the bounds of civilization. The lawless conditions spawned famous outlaws, as well as lesser known criminals.

Let's take a look at Sam Yeager. Sam was a handsome devil, whose early entry into the criminal world was nurtured by his dear father. The elder Yeager made his living posing as a medical doctor who had developed a cure-all known as Dr. Yeager's Wonderful Liniment for Man and Beast. Everyone felt good after a dose of the wonderful liniment. It didn't have any healing power, but its alcoholic content was higher than most of the hootch being peddled at the local saloon.

While Daddy gathered a crowd around him with his Wonderful Liniment pitch, Sam would relieve the suckers of their wallets. Unfortunately, one day Sam attempted to pick the pocket of a hayseed who had taken the precaution of sewing an open safety pin into his pocket. Sam pricked his finger, gave out a yell, and the jig was up. Our hero had four years to contemplate the error of his ways while detained in a federal prison near Wellsboro, Pennsylvania.

Somewhere along the line Sam learned the art of engraving. In 1872, when he was twenty-nine and freshly released from prison, he decided that picking pockets was not for him. There had to be an easier way to make money. It was all so very simple when one thought about it. That's exactly what Sam would do - make money.

Sam proceeded to manufacture ten-dollar gold coins, known as Eagles, which were in wide circulation at the time. His ten-mould die could turn out five hundred coins before lunch each day. The coins were perfect specimens, identical to the real thing in every detail, with one exception - they weren't gold. Sam produced his spurious loot by using poor copper thinly plated with an alloy of nine parts gold and one part silver-copper.

Sam packed up his equipment and headed west, where he correctly figured it would be an easy matter to place his phony coins into circulation. He planned to distribute the coins through the most popular saloon in each town. What bartender could resist purchasing one hundred gold Eagles at half price?

Wouldn't you know it? With such a foolproof scheme in mind, Sam rode into South Pass City, Wyoming, and met a lady, Molly Morris. Now Molly wasn't your average pink-cheeked, calico-swishing innocent of the West. No, Molly was something else. Built along the lines of an hourglass, there was more naked flesh cascading out of the top of Molly's gown than there is water roaring over Niagara Falls. Pretty as a picture, the more than adequately endowed Molly made a fine living as a greeter at Happy Halligan's Saloon. She also plied her talents from a horizontal position in one of the rooms above the bar. Molly wouldn't turn a trick for less than a hundred dollars and was considered the best and most expensive lady of the evening in South Pass City.

Three evenings and three hundred phony dollars later, Sam proposed to Molly. Now you must understand that while Sam appeared to be a well-heeled fine fellow, Molly, in her particular profession, was not unaccustomed to receiving proposals. Many an outlaw and miner, pockets bulging with nuggets, had professed undying love to Molly, which wasn't difficult to do whilst frolicking between the sheets. No, no, a thousand times, no. Molly wanted more tangible proof of Sam's love. A nice home near Denver, Colorado, and a hundred thousand dollars in genuine cash is so much more comforting to a girl than mere promises. Sam agreed. He revealed the details of his counterfeiting business to Molly and swore he would raise the hundred thousand dollars in a few months. They would both live happily ever after.

Sam hit such Wyoming towns as Split Rock, Hanna, Horse Creek, and Encampment, selling from 100 to 500 phony ten-dollar gold pieces for five dollars each. He always returned to Molly, to whom he entrusted his genuine cash. Sam expanded into Colorado, where his operation proved to be as successful as in Wyoming. That is, until July 16, 1872.

On the day Sam ran into an honest bartender, Clements Murray, in the small town of Virginia Dale. As soon as Sam left the saloon, Clements called Marshal Elijah Gates. Sam, who figured that everyone had his price, tried to bribe Gates, but it was no use. Three days later, he stood trial before the only lawyer in town, Gilbert McCain, who acted as judge.

Gilbert took one look at the perfect Eagles, and with nothing but larceny in his heart, decided that he had stumbled onto a good thing. Gilbert gave Sam the high sign - just leave everything to him and things would work out. That same day Sam was convicted and sentenced to ten years in Colorado State Prison at Canon City.

The very next morning Marshal Gates was transporting his prisoner from Virginia Dale to prison, when suddenly a ten-gauge shotgun blast felled the marshal. He was dead before he hit the ground.

Gilbert McCain was the culprit. While he cut Sam's wrists loose he explained that scores of outlaws had threatened to get even with the marshal over the years. They would be suspected of his murder. In the meantime Gilbert suggested that he and Sam become partners. Gilbert figured that if Sam agreed to work beyond lunch he could turn out a thousand coins a day. With Gilbert placing the coins in circulation, the partnership could clear a cool $5,000 a day.

For the next few months Sam slaved over his portable forge, manufacturing perfect ten-dollar gold pieces. Gilbert dashed about Wyoming and Colorado selling the coins at half price. The partners returned to South Pass City, where Sam turned over $70,000 to Molly before bedding down for a night of lust and sin. It wouldn't be long before Sam reached his objective of $100,000 and Molly would be his forever.

The next day the partners hit the trail once more. Just to keep his hand in, Sam decided to approach a bartender in Sterling, Colorado. As luck would have it, Sam hit another honest bartender. He pulled a gun and held Sam captive until someone fetched Marshal Henry Larney. Henry unceremoniously threw Sam in the local lockup, where he was to remain until a circuit judge arrived in town. Gilbert heard about his partner's plight and did the honorable thing. He headed out of town as fast as his horse could carry him.

One fine night, while the good citizens of Sterling slept soundly, Sam approached his lone guard, one Ron Shively. Sam let Roy know that he was wearing a secret money belt containing $1,000. It would all be his if Roy would just take care of two minor details. Sam wanted a fresh horse parked outside the jail. He also wouldn't mind if Roy carelessly walked by his cell close enough so that Sam could extract Roy's gun from his holster. Within fifteen minutes Sam was galloping out of town, heading for South Pass City and the comforting embrace of Molly Morris.

A few days later Sam roared up to Happy Halligan's Saloon. Taking the steps three at a time, he dashed up to Molly's room. What was this?! A male voice coming from Molly's room? Could it be his partner Gilbert's voice? Was Gilbert saying, "Sam will be put away for ten years"? Was Molly replying, "I never intended to marry the runt anyway"?

It was all too much. Sam threw open the door. His betrothed and his partner were, shame to say, in bed. Sam shot twice. Molly and Gilbert were dead.

In an instant, Sam was apprehended by the patrons of the saloon. Soon half the town was at the scene. A lynch mob dragged Sam across the road to a stable. A rope was tossed over a cross-beam, and one of the slickest coin counterfeiters the United States ever produced was unceremoniously hanged.

Later one of the town stalwarts was heard to state, "We would have forgiven Sam for shooting Gilbert McCain, but no one was going to get away with shooting the finest whore in South Pass City."

DOC HOLLIDAY

Doc Holliday holds a unique position in the folklore of the Wild West. Unlike most western badmen, he never robbed a bank or held up a stagecoach. Doc was a dentist by profession and a gambler by inclination.

John Henry Holliday first saw the light of day in Georgia in 1852. As a teenager he was intrigued by guns. By practising every day he became a crack shot. His family sent him to Baltimore, where Holliday took a course in dentistry. At the age of twenty, John Henry returned as a full-fledged dentist and opened a practice in Atlanta.

The slim, blonde, good-looking young man with the twinkling blue eyes appeared to have everything in the world to live for. One day a persistent nagging cough necessitated a visit to a doctor. The routine visit turned out to be a nightmare. Holliday was told that he was dying of tuberculosis. The doctor informed him that if he stayed in Georgia he could expect to live only a few months. A move to a drier climate might give him a few years.

Holliday took the advice and moved to Dallas, Texas. As the cough grew worse, Doc's practice suffered. Dentistry, crude as it was in those days, wasn't enhanced by the dentist coughing in the patient's face.

Doc looked around for some other way to make a living and decided to become a gambler.

Doc studied the various card games for months, until he felt he knew how to detect the cheats and sleight-of-hand artists who risked their lives every time they sat down at a table. Many a confrontation was settled right then and there with revolvers roaring at close range. Doc didn't have to brush up on shooting; he was already a lightning-fast draw.

In 1875 Doc killed his first man over a card game. While charges were never brought against him for the shooting, he thought it would be in his best interest to leave Dallas. Doc moved to Jacksboro, where he promptly killed two men in gunfights. Now constantly on the move, he touched down in Denver, Colorado, where he managed to put three additional notches on his gun.

As a doomed man, Doc Holliday always shot first and asked questions later. His disregard for his own life was nurtured by the fact that he felt he didn't have long to live anyway.

Doc drifted into Fort Griffin, Texas, where he met a dance-hall lady who answered to the descriptive moniker "Big Nosed Kate." Kate fell hard for Doc Holliday, and while Doc didn't exactly reciprocate, he didn't discourage her either.

At this time Doc met lawman Wyatt Earp, who was passing through Fort Griffin tracking down a train robber. The two men were to form a close relationship which was to last throughout Doc's life.

Doc was at his regular table playing poker one night, when a local man, Ed Bailey, accused him of cheating. Bailey drew his gun. Doc leaped across the table, brandishing a razor-sharp knife. Within a minute, Bailey lay dead on the saloon floor. Doc was taken into custody. To protect him from a possible lynch mob, he was temporarily stashed away in a hotel with a deputy guarding him around the clock.

Big Nosed Kate sensed that Bailey's friends would attempt to lynch her man. She decided to take matters into her own hands. Kate set fire to the back of the hotel. During the confusion caused by the fire, she marched into Doc's room with six-shooters already drawn and disarmed the guard. The pair took off on waiting horses.

They didn't stop running until they hit Dodge City, Kansas, where Doc again practised dentistry for a short while. Big Nosed Kate posed as his respectable wife. The only fly in the ointment was the fact that Kate and Doc didn't get along. They fought like cat and dog, but Doc always was ready for a reconciliation. He never forgot that Kate had probably saved his life.

Dodge City was a rough, tough shipping point for the Longhorn cattle which had been driven up from Texas. It was the end of the trail for thirsty, sex-starved cowboys who had just been paid off. As a gambler, Doc flourished in Dodge City. It was here that he again ran into Wyatt Earp, who was now Deputy Marshal of Dodge.

On one occasion, a group of drunken Texas cowboys shot up the main street of Dodge and cornered Earp in a saloon. Wyatt figured he was a goner. Just as the cowboys were about to kill him, the saloon doors swung open and there, behind them, stood Doc Holliday, with guns already drawn. As the cowboys turned, Wyatt drew his guns. The two friends marched the cowboys down to the jail. Next day, with everyone sober, Earp issued the cowboys their guns as they were ushered out of town.

From that time on, Wyatt Earp and Doc Holliday were bosom buddies. When the discovery of silver brought prosperity to Tombstone, Arizona, Wyatt Earp and his brothers accepted various law-enforcement positions there. Doc and Big Nosed Kate followed them to gun-totin' Tombstone.

As a local gambler with a bad reputation, from time to time Holliday was accused of crimes he knew nothing about. Once, just outside Tombstone, some masked men held up a stagecoach carrying gold bullion. The bandits didn't get the gold, but managed to kill the stage driver and a passenger. Doc's enemies spread the rumor that he was the trigger-happy gunsel.

When Big Nosed Kate got dead drunk after one of her frequent spats with Doc, some of his adversaries got her to sign an affidavit stating that Doc had taken part in the robbery and had, in fact, killed the two men. Next day Holliday was arrested and charged with murder. His buddy, Wyatt Earp, put up $5,000 in cash, a fortune in those days, to secure Doc's release on bail.

At the inquest which followed, Kate admitted she had signed the affidavit, but swore she was so drunk she had no idea what she was signing. Wyatt Earp testified that Holliday couldn't have taken part in the robbery because they were together at the time of the robbery. Doc was released and the $5,000 was returned to Wyatt.

Doc Holliday never forgave Kate for signing that affidavit. She had saved his life once, but was now responsible for almost having him hanged. Doc figured the slate was clean. He gave her $1,000 and sent her packing.

At this time Wyatt Earp and his four brothers were deeply involved in politics. All of them made their living as law-enforcement officers and, as a result, were active in local elections. Like most politicians, they had some enemies. Two sets of brothers, the Clantons and the McLowerys, their friend Billy Claiborne, and Sheriff John Behan, all despised the four Earp brothers and Doc Holliday.

In October 1881, the whole kit and caboodle found themselves in Tombstone at the same time. All day the Clanton-McLowery faction hurled insults at the Earps and Holliday. Next day, Virgil Earp, who was city marshal, asked the sheriff for assistance in settling down the unruly men. The sheriff refused to interfere.

On October 25, probably the most famous Wild West gun battle in history took place. The Battle of the O.K. Corral has been immortalized in stories, songs, plays, and movies.

The entire gunfight, involving nine men, took about thirty seconds. After it was over, Frank and Tom McLowery were dead. Billy Clanton lay dying on the ground. Ike Clanton and Billy Claiborne turned tail and took off. Virgil Earp had a leg wound, while his brother Morgan had been hit in the left shoulder. Doc Holliday had a superficial bullet crease across his back. Wyatt had emerged uninjured.

After the battle Doc and Wyatt had to get out of Arizona. They went to Colorado, where they decided to go their separate ways. Eventually, Doc was arrested for the murder of Frank Stilwell. Ironically, he was innocent of any guilty knowledge of this crime. Again Wyatt Earp came to the rescue. He arranged to have Doc arrested for a confidence swindle, which effectively held up his extradition to Arizona. It was felt that Doc's enemies would have him killed before he ever got to trial. Later the governor of Colorado flatly refused to extradite Holliday, and he went free.

Doc drifted to Deadwood in the Dakota Territory. By this time his reputation as a killer followed him wherever he went. Shortly after arriving in Deadwood, he added fuel to the fire by killing a bartender. He moved on and tried his luck in Leadville, Colorado, where he dealt faro for a time. In his later years he was to stand trial twice more for killings. Each time he pleaded self-defence, and each time he was acquitted.

As his tubercular condition worsened, he was constantly coughing. Finally, in September 1887 he was confined to bed. Doc knew he was dying. The idea of dying in bed with his boots off appealed to his sense of humor. Just before he closed his eyes for the last time on November 8, 1887, he said, "This is funny."

Texas

BEN THOMPSON

Texas Ben Thompson was one of those rare individuals who squeezed twenty-four hours of living into every day of his life. He was in succession a printer, soldier, gambler, and law-enforcement officer. He also was a cold-blooded killer.

Born in Knottingley, England, on November 11, 1842, Ben emigrated to Austin, Texas, with his family when he was nine years old. His father eked out a precarious living as a fisherman on the Colorado River. Ben and his brother Billy peddled fish door to door, but Ben continued his schooling until he was 15, which was something of an accomplishment for that time.

When he was 13, Ben argued with a friend, 15-year-old Joe Brown. Ben ran home and returned with his single-barreled shotgun to settle the dispute. Without hesitation he fired at the fleeing, terrified Brown who, while not seriously wounded, had the painful experience of receiving several pellets in his backside.

Ben was tried for shooting Brown. He was found guilty of aggravated assault and sentenced to sixty days' imprisonment and was fined $100. Ben served the sentence and was working off the fine when Governor Hardin R. Runnels heard of the case and cancelled the balance of the fine.

Ben became a printer and worked for the Southern Intelligencer for two years, during which time he gained a local reputation for never backing off a fight. He craved excitement and had no difficulty in finding it.

In 1858 a band of Comanches raided Austin and carried off five children. Ben

Thompson was one of the first men to mount his horse and give pursuit. He and his companions caught up to the Indians, killed several and rescued all the children, although one youngster died the next day. Ben Thompson had killed his first man.

Ben accepted a position with a bookbinding firm in New Orleans in 1860. While he was on a horse-drawn streetcar, an inebriated Frenchman, Emile De Tour, began annoying a female passenger. Ben suggested that he desist. De Tour paid no heed. He should have known better. Infuriated, Ben announced, "Leave that girl alone! I will assume to protect her." De Tour swung. Ben ducked and, at the same time, plunged a knife into the Frenchman's side.

De Tour recovered from his wounds and set about looking for Ben to settle the score. He suggested a duel. After much haggling, the two men agreed to face each other in a darkened room using only knives. In three minutes De Tour was dead. Ben was now a fugitive, but with the help of friends made his way to Houston and eventually to his home in Austin. Once in Austin, Ben turned to gambling, a profession he was to pursue for the rest of his life.

With the outbreak of war, Ben immediately joined the Confederate Army as a private in the Second Regiment Texas Cavalry. Within months he was in trouble. Sergeant William Vance accused him of stealing rations. Ben denied the accusation and Vance drew his pistol. Ben drew his six-shooter and both men fired. Vance missed. Ben's shot went through Vance and through another soldier's leg.

When Lieutenant George Hagler charged at Ben with his sword, Ben fired once more and Hagler fell. Finally, a Captain Hamner arrived on the scene and asked Ben to surrender. Ben turned over his pistol, remarking, "Captain, I surrender to you and would have yielded to them had they sought to arrest me instead of killing me." A few weeks later Lieutenant Hagler died. The other wounded men recovered.

Despite being chained to the guardhouse floor, Ben managed to set fire to the place and escape. He was never tried for his involvement in Hagler's death. In fact, he later re-enlisted and, on one of his leaves, married respectable, well-to-do Catherine Moore of Austin.

While in Austin, Ben (now a lieutenant) together with Captain John Rapp, was given the responsibility of recruiting a company of young soldiers. Rapp became embroiled in an argument with one John Coombs. Ben came to his colleague's assistance and shot Coombs dead. Both men were taken into custody, but later were allowed to rejoin their regiment in Waco, where they remained until the end of the war.

At the conclusion of the war Ben was placed in the Austin jail, waiting for someone in authority to decide just what charges to bring against him. With the help of two guards, he escaped and joined Emperor Maximilian, who was attempting to regain his throne in Mexico. Ben fought gallantly for the unfortunate Emperor. He had risen to the rank of Major when the Emperor's cause was lost and Maximilian was executed.

Ben returned to his Texas home. Awaiting him there was the old charge of killing John Coombs. Ben gave himself up and was tried and acquitted.

He next received the gambling concession at Coe and Bowles Saloon, one of the finest in Austin. By 1868 he had opened several other gambling concessions and was, by the standards of the day, considered well-to-do.

Still, it seemed Ben couldn't stay out of trouble. In succeeding years he was charged with threatening a magistrate's life and the attempted murder of another man, for which he spent two years in Huntsville Prison.

Upon his release Ben didn't take long to get into serious trouble again. While attending a play in Austin he argued with theatre owner Mark Wilson. Witnesses said Wilson fired first, but when the smoke cleared it was Wilson who lay dead on the floor with three slugs in his body. Ben turned himself in, was charged with Wilson's murder, but was found not guilty.

To everyone's surprise Ben decided to run for the office of city marshal of Austin. He lost, but two years later ran again and this time was victorious. Ben took his duties seriously, devoting all his time and energy to his office. Crime dropped to an all-time low in Austin.

While marshal, Ben crossed paths with an old gambling adversary, Jack Harris of San Antonio, a well-known theatre owner. The outcome was predictable. Ben shot Harris dead. Next morning, Ben turned himself in. He resigned his position as city marshal, stood trial, and once again was found not guilty. Ben returned home.

As I stood in Austin looking up the broad modern expanse of Congress Street leading to the state capitol buildings, it was not difficult to imagine the exuberance with which the citizens of Austin greeted their returning native son. Ben and his wife were treated as celebrities. Brass bands, state officials, and waving flags ushered the flamboyant former marshal along his way. It was Texas Ben Thompson's finest hour.

Tragedy was soon to follow. While visiting San Antonio with an old friend, King Fisher, Ben entered the Vaudeville Theatre. Once inside, he and Fisher met Joe Foster and Billy Simms, friends and partners of Jack Harris, the man Ben had killed.

An argument ensued. For the first and only time in his life Ben lost a gunfight. He and Fisher were killed in a hail of bullets. Great controversy followed Ben's death.

Was he the instigator of the gunfight or was he assassinated? It matters little, for Texas Ben Thompson, aged 41, died as he had lived - by the gun.

THE BROTHERS D'AUTREMONT

J esse, Frank, Butch, and Sundance had all gone to that great shootout in the sky by the time the D'Autremont brothers of Oregon decided to revive the fading art of robbing mail trains in 1923. Ray and Roy D'Autremont were twins in their early twenties. Brother Hugh was a few years younger. They should have known better. Everything went wrong.

The old mail train reduced speed as it approached the Siskiyou Tunnel located near the Oregon-California border. As the engine slowly emerged from the tunnel, two of the brothers smartly raised themselves up into the engine. Brandishing revolvers, one of them barked, "Hands up!"

Sidney Bates, the engineer, looked at the revolver pointed directly at his mouth. Up went his hands. Marving Seng, the fireman, had the same experience. The train was stopped and both men were ordered out of the cab.

Suddenly the mail-car door opened. The mail clerk, Edwin Daugherty, peeked out. "What's going on?" he inquired, only to be greeted by a hail of bullets passing perilously close to his face. Daugherty slammed the mail-car door shut.

The third D'Autremont brother lugged a blasting machine to the mail-car door. He set the explosive and ran for cover. At that precise moment brakeman Charles Johnson came running towards the action from the far end of the stalled express. He received the full force of the blast and was killed instantly, as was Daugherty inside the mail car.

The bandits panicked. Shots were fired. Bates and Seng were shot dead when they stood with their hands raised above their heads. The contents of the mail car were now forgotten. The three brothers thought only of escape. Behind them four dead men lay sprawled across the Southern Pacific tracks.

Officials examining the area surrounding the murders uncovered a Colt .45 automatic, obviously thrown away by one of the killers. An old pair of blue denim overalls were found in some bushes. Days passed with no trace of the fugitives.

Meanwhile detectives had given the denim overalls to California University for analysis. Curled up in the bib of the overalls lab technicians found a tiny ball of paper. Under microscopic examination the paper proved to be a receipt, Number 236-L, for a registered parcel posted in Eugene, Oregon. Detectives examined back records at Eugene and discovered that the person sending the registered parcel was Roy D'Autremont.

The father of the three boys was questioned, but he didn't know where his sons could be located. Detectives found a cabin in the Oregon woods where the boys had lived for several weeks. They even located the gunsmith who had sold the murder weapon to Roy D'Autremont.

Despite the widespread publicity given to the manhunt and the fact that the killers' identities were known, no new developments took place for more than three years.

In 1926, Sgt. Thomas Reynolds, a soldier home on leave from the Philippines, was standing in line buying a stamp in a San Francisco post office when he noticed some wanted posters on a bulletin board. He recognized the the face of Hugh D'Autremont. He had known him as Private Brice in the Philippines. The soldier contacted police, who flew to Manila and confirmed that Brice was in reality D'Autremont. He was brought back to the United States.

A few weeks later Albert Cullingworth was reading his Sunday newspaper. He turned to the magazine section which featured the D'Autremont manhunt. He recognized Ray and Roy as the men he had worked with two years previously at a mill in Steubenville, Ohio. He informed police, who learned that the two brothers, now called Goodwin, were still in Steubenville. They were arrested and charged with murder.

In order to escape the death penalty, the brothers confessed to the multiple murder, were found guilty and sentenced to life imprisonment in the Oregon State Penitentiary at Salem.

They didn't fare well. Hugh was paroled in 1958 after serving 31 years in prison.

He died a year later. Roy was declared insane and was transferred to an Oregon mental institution, where he resides to this day. Ray was paroled in 1961. His whereabouts are unknown.

14

POTPOURRI

SMUTTY NOSE

The Isle of Shoals lies approximately ten miles southeast of Portsmouth, New Hampshire. The remote group of tiny islands is a tourist attraction which draws thousands of visitors each summer to its shores. They come to gaze at the rustic beauty of the rock-encrusted islands.

The second largest of these islands (less than half a mile long) has the quaint name of Smutty Nose and juts out into the Atlantic in the shape of a giant nose. Over a hundred years ago murder so vile took place on Smutty Nose. Because of a lingering doubt, it remains to this day as one of New England's most sensational murder cases.

In March 1873 the Shoals were inhabited by only a few fishermen. They were Scandinavians who couldn't resist the rich fishing grounds surrounding the islands. They built homes on the bleak rocks and lived a hard-working, lonely, and isolated existence. The largest island, Appledore, was inhabited by two Norwegian families, the Thaxters and the Ingerbredsens.

John and Maren Hontvet lived on Smutty Nose, having emigrated from Norway five years previously. Later John's brother, Matthew, joined them. Maren's brother, Ivan Christensen, and his wife, Anethe, were added to the small fishing community a few months later. The family circle was completed when Maren's sister, Karen, a spinster of 38, also settled on Smutty Nose. The close-knit group were all related by blood or marriage, had the same country of origin and the same occupation. The fact that they lived side by side in such isolation made them a homogenous group.

At the break of dawn on March 5, John Hontvet, his brother Matthew, and Ivan Christensen headed out in John's schooner, the Clara Bella. They were finished fishing for the day when a storm came up. Rather than risk bucking a headwind and going back to Smutty Nose, they decided to put in at Portsmouth. The men were going to take the opportunity to purchase bait which was coming in by train that night from Boston. The heavy seas prevented them from making it back to the island. On a wharf in Portsmouth they met an old acquaintance, Louis Wagner, a Prussian who had at one time worked for John. The men chatted awhile, and John inquired if Louis would be interested in helping them load the bait later on. Louis said that he would give them a hand and asked if they would be returning to Smutty Nose that night. The men assured him they would not chance the rough seas.

No one thought anything further about the conversation, except that when the bait did arrive after midnight the men couldn't find Louis anywhere and they did the job without his help.

Meanwhile, back at Smutty Nose, darkness came to the dreary island. The three women, Maren, Anethe, and Karen, knew that the men might not return because of the storm. They decided to make supper in case the storm abated. When the storm didn't let up they figured that the three men had pulled into Portsmouth and wouldn't be back that night. They agreed to sleep in one house to keep each other company. All slept in downstairs rooms, Karen on a couch in the kitchen and Maren and Anethe together in a bedroom. They had not bothered to lock the door of the house as there seemed little reason to do so.

Almost simultaneously the girls heard the noise of someone entering the house. Karen called out, "John, is that you?" Then the sounds of a vicious fight came from the kitchen. Maren went to open the kitchen door but it was locked from the inside. She screamed and pounded on the door, but it did no good. From behind the locked door, Karen screamed again, "John kills me!" In her horror Karen thought the intruder was her brother-in-law John. Finally the kitchen door burst open and Karen staggered into Maren's arms. Maren could only make out the figure of a man in the dim light. The intruder picked up a chair and lashed out at the two women, who took the blows to their shoulders and heads, but managed to retreat to the bedroom and close the door behind them. In the bedroom Anethe was paralyzed with fear.

Maren told Anethe to climb out the window and scream for help. The terrified woman managed to get out, and then Maren heard her holler "Louis, Louis!" She had run right into the assailant. He swung an axe and Anethe sank dead to the ground. Maren then begged Karen to dash out the back door and run from the house, but the other woman had already taken a fearful beating and couldn't move. Maren fled in the cold March air, wearing only her nightdress. She hid at the edge of the island under a huge rock.

The next morning she was spotted by Jorge Ingerbredsen from Appledore Island. An examination of the murder scene revealed the movements of the killer.

After Maren escaped he got at Karen, and as she tried to flee through the window he struck her a vicious blow to the head with the axe. The intruder then searched the entire house, opening every trunk and drawer, looking for money. He managed to find $20, which was the only thing missing from the house. Then noticing the food already prepared, he fixed himself a meal, sat down and ate it. Blood smears were on knives, forks, dishes, and he even brewed himself a pot of tea, leaving bloodstains on the handle of the teapot. Only then did he go outside to the well, and wash the blood from his hands. It was evident that the killer took his time, knowing that he wouldn't be interrupted by the return of the men.

When Maren told her story suspicion immediately fell on Louis Wagner. He was arrested the night following the attack and was charged with murder. The facts as they unfolded pointed to Wagner being the killer. The most damaging was Maren's identification of him, but there was other evidence. Louis knew there would be no men on the island that night. At 7:30 on the night of the killings, James Burke left his dory at a dock in Portsmouth. By 8:30 it was gone, the inference being that Wagner stole the dory, rowed the ten miles to Smutty Nose, and then rowed back to the mainland. Wagner owed his landlady $15 for a month's back rent. When drinking in the waterfront saloons he had often mentioned to friends that he was getting so hard up for money that he would kill for it. He also mentioned that he heard that Hontvet was saving to buy a boat and had $600 stashed away in his house. When arrested he was desperately trying to get a berth on a ship out of Boston.

Wagner was returned to Alfred, Maine, to stand trial. A crowd estimated at 10,000 met the train in Portsmouth. Feeling against Wagner ran so high that there was some fear that he would be lynched. At his trial a further piece of evidence was produced. A button belonging to one of the murder victims was found on his person when he was arrested. The best Louis could do with that one was to claim that he must have picked up the button when he once worked for the Hontvets. The jury took only 55 minutes to find Louis guilty. A series of reprieves followed. Louis steadfastly proclaimed his innocence, saying that John and Maren Hontvet were the murderers.

No positive evidence has ever been uncovered to support Wagner's claim. Between the time of his trial and June 25, 1875, when Louis Wagner walked calmly to the gallows, a small minority of people started to wonder. If three experienced fishermen couldn't make it back to Smutty Nose in a schooner that fateful night, how could Louis Wagner go out and return in a rowboat?

DID JOHNSON
DO IT?

On the morning of September 6, 1911 in Madison, Wisconsin, Mr. and Mrs. Martin Lemberger stared down at the vacant cot of their seven-year-old daughter, Annie. The Lembergers had two other children, Alois, nine, and Martin, Jr., six. Their home was small and Lemberger was not a wealthy man, so the initial dread of kidnapping for ransom was not considered.

The police studied the scene of the crime. Mrs. Lemberger stated that all doors and windows had been locked from the inside the night before, and all except the window by Annie's cot were still locked the next morning. The window beside the cot had a small triangular piece of the pane broken out. Police believed the abductor had broken the pane, stuck his hand in, and opened the lock from the inside. They felt he carried the child out, through the window. Below Annie's window police found evidence of scuffled footprints.

An immediate search for the missing child was instituted by the police. Vacant lots, culverts, and abandoned buildings were searched, but no trace of little Annie could be found. A further mass search was planned for the following Saturday. In response to an appeal by the chief of police, a huge crowd gathered to scour the entire area foot by foot. Feelings in Madison were running high - official rewards were offered and private contributions were made to obtain expert detectives to work on the case. The day the extensive search took place Annie's body was found in nearby Lake Manona.

An autopsy of the child's body revealed a wound behind her left ear. No water was in her lungs, indicating that the child was either unconscious or dead before being thrown into the lake. She had not been sexually interfered with in any way.

At this point the authorities were puzzled as to the motive for the killing. It was a senseless murder, for it appeared no one could gain anything from the death of the little girl.

A week after the crime had been committed the police still had no concrete clues to pursue. They routinely checked out all the known characters in Madison. One name kept coming up - John A. Johnson. Johnson lived close by the Lemberger home and from the very day the little girl was reported missing he became conspicuous by being one of the very first to volunteer for the search party. Johnson's character and mental capacity were suspect - he was a lazy, feeble-minded bum who hung around bar-rooms and let his wife support him. After Annie's body was taken from the lake Johnson began loitering around the undertaker's parlor. Finally the police brought him in for questioning. His notorious past was uncovered. He had been committed to insane asylums twice for sexual offences against young girls, and had been sentenced to jail for non-support of his wife and children.

At first Johnson stuck to his alibi for the night of the kidnapping. He claimed that he had gone to bed at 9 o'clock that night and had not left his house until the next morning. His wife corroborated his statement, saying that she had stayed up with one of her daughters who happened to be sick that night and it would have been impossible for her husband to leave the house without her having seen him. Johnson's two daughters, Bertha and Selma, verified their mother's story.

Despite the alibi, Johnson was arrested and charged with murder. Detectives grilled him constantly in relays until he finally broke down and confessed. Here is his confession:

"I had been drinking hard the last two months and on this night I went to bed drunk. Sometime after one o'clock I awoke and wanted another drink of whisky. I got out of bed and dressed quietly and crept downstairs and got my shoes from behind the stove. When I got outside I put them on with the intention of going to some saloon close by and begging for a drink.

"I walked up Francis Street as far as the Lemberger house which is four doors away from my home. When I reached there I remembered I had often looked into the window of the little cottage and seen the Lemberger children going to bed. Some devilish impulse caused me to step over to the window and reach my hand through the broken pane and raise it. I lifted Annie out without making any noise and the cold air awakened her and she saw me and yelled, "Johnson!" I hit her with my fist and began to run. She kept making a noise and I kept hitting her until she was limp in my arms. By that time I had reached the middle of the vacant lot and I laid her down in the weeds to catch my breath and get my bearings.

"In a few seconds I began to realize what I had done and I thought I had better throw the body into the lake. I walked to the bay, five blocks away, and by keeping in the shadows of the barns and fences I got there without anyone seeing me. I threw the body as far as possible out into the water and then ran home. I took off my shoes and put them back and got upstairs without waking any of the family. I want to plead guilty and make this confession so I will be taken to prison today."

Johnson insisted that the trial be held without delay, and that he be taken from the jail to the Waupun Penitentiary that same day.

The authorities explained the seriousness of the course Johnson wanted them to follow, but he insisted and they complied. Without delay, Judge Donovan of the Municipal Court for Dade County sentenced Johnson to life in prison at hard labor, and he was rushed away to serve his sentence.

Months turned into years, and Johnson languished in prison, a broken and forgotten man. Every so often he would write a letter to someone connected with his case, pleading that he was innocent, but no one paid any attention. Ten years went by, and one day Johnson sent one of his pathetic letters to a former judge with the unlikely name of A.O. Stolen. Stolen went to visit Johnson, studied the record, and was convinced of Johnson's innocence.

Stolen put together a pardon application for Johnson. Pressure was put on the state to conduct a hearing into the application. When the hearing was granted on September 27, 1921, A.O. Stolen appeared on behalf of Johnson. He brought out the fact that the hole in the window was too small to allow Johnson's hand to get in to undo the lock. Again, Johnson's wife and daughters stated that he was home at the time the crime was committed.

Why had Johnson confessed? He told his story.

Years before he had witnessed a lynching where the victim was riddled with bullets, his body cut down and stabbed. When questioning him the detectives found out about this fear and told him there was a mob outside just waiting to get at him. This preyed on his mind, and when they told him the one way to save his skin was to confess, he jumped at the chance. All this evidence was convincing enough, but it is doubtful if it alone would gain a pardon for an already convicted man.

Then a strange thing happened. While the hearing was in progress Mr. Stolen received a phone call. It was from a Mrs. Mae Sorenson. She told Stolen she could tell him who killed Annie Lemberger if he could guarantee her protection from the murderer. Stolen actually got the judge who was conducting the hearings out of bed and had him open his court in the middle of the night to take Mrs. Sorenson's testimony. The following day she formally gave her evidence from a witness stand before a crowded courtroom.

She was a good friend of Mrs. Lemberger, and on the morning of September 6, 1911, more than ten years earlier, she had gone to the Lemberger home to console her friend over the disappearance of Annie. She found Mrs. Lemberger in the kitchen burning a bloodsoaked nightgown belonging to Annie. On the day that Annie was buried, Alois Lemberger went to Mrs. Sorenson and told her what had really happened to Annie. Alois said that her father had been drinking with other men that night in the kitchen of their home. Annie got out of bed to get a drink of water. While in the kitchen her father asked her to give him a poker. Annie couldn't find it, and in a drunken rage her father struck her behind the ear with a beer bottle. As the child fell she hit her head against the kitchen stove and lay on the floor, unconscious. Lemberger then carried her to her cot and later Annie's mother found her dead. The body was hidden in the basement, and the next night Lemberger disposed of it in the lake.

The Lembergers were called to the witness stand and hotly denied these damaging accusations. Martin Lemberger was arrested as he left the witness stand. He was charged with second-degree murder, and on January 5, 1922, Lemberger's preliminary hearing was held. His lawyer was quick to point out that Wisconsin law provides that a charge of second-degree murder is outlawed after ten years. The charge against Lemberger was dropped and he was released that very day.

Johnson's sentence was commuted to expire immediately. On February 17, 1922, after serving more than ten years in prison for a crime he didn't commit, he was released.

The state of Wisconsin allows compensation to people wrongly sent to jail. A.O. Stolen tried on several occasions to gain compensation for Johnson, but each time he was refused based on the grounds that Johnson had contributed to his own conviction. Johnson was given a job by the city of Madison. Now a broken man and in ill-health, he aged rapidly and passed away in the 1930s.

TEACHER, DOCTOR, KILLER

It is refreshing to report that Edward Rulloff was a Canadian. You see, everyone who met Edward came away convinced that he was a genius. They had good reason. Edward had a more than passing command of Greek, Latin, German, French, Hebrew, and only God knows what other languages. Bring up geology and Edward could talk for an hour on the distinctive qualities of fossils found in Archeozoic strata as opposed to Paleozoic. Mention works of art and Ed could give a learned dissertation on anything from the time of the Etruscans to Rembrandt. Ed was just that kind of guy.

Born Edward Howard Rulloffson in the tiny hamlet of Hammond River, close to Saint John, New Brunswick, in 1819, there is little about Ed's early years to give any indication of his checkered future. Formal education was not readily available in Hammond River, but Ed's folks knew they had a rare one when, at the age of four, their little pride and joy was reading anything he could lay his chubby hands on. When he was twelve he received some formal education, but left the routine of the classroom for the relatively exciting life of a clerk in a law firm in Saint John.

It was a matter of some concern when the home of the senior partner of the law firm was robbed. Several fine suits were among the stolen items. Concern turned to downright embarrassment when the senior partner spotted Ed wearing one of his stolen suits. The little indiscretion was instrumental in sending Ed to the local jail for two years.

Upon his release Rulloff left the Picture Province, never to return. He next pops to the surface in 1842 in Dryden, New York. Now a strapping young man of 23, Ed had a noteworthy appearance; his outstanding features were to haunt him to his dying day. Ed stood 5 feet 8 inches, weighed 180 pounds, had dark hair and a broad, full face. Two things distinguished him from other men. He had an oversized head and the distance between his eyes was greater than average.

Obviously a well-educated man of superior intelligence, Edward Rulloff stood out in Dryden like a virgin at a hustler's convention. Soon he was offered the teacher's job at a small private school in the village. Ed accepted the position. In a short time the village experienced the unheard of: Their young folk arrived early and stayed late at school. The teacher was so interesting that the little ones would rather learn than go home. Ed was an instant success.

Professor Rulloff took a shine to one of his pupils, 16-year-old Harriet Schutt. Harriet behaved like a 13-year-old but looked like 23. The only thing Harriet possessed which wasn't in full bloom was her brain. She fell hard for the professor.

The lovers planned to marry. This idea did not sit well with Harriet's older and larger brothers. William, Edward, and Ephraim didn't approve. They just didn't cotton to the high and mighty professor. In the end, true love overcame all. Ed and Harriet tied the knot on December 31, 1843.

Two things happened after the holy union - Ed left his teaching position, and due to the loose licensing of the times became a self-proclaimed doctor. While he had a gentle hand with patients he had nothing but abuse for Harriet. Ed was moody and quick-tempered. In fact, sometimes he just plain punched Harriet in the face for the fun of it.

The not-so-idyllic couple moved to Lansing where the former professor was a huge success as a doctor. One day Dr. Rulloff was summoned to Ithaca to minister to the wife and child of his brother-in-law, William Schutt. Ed later explained to Harriet, "They called me in too late." Both mother and child died.

Despite the doctor's harsh treatment of his wife, their marriage did have its moments. Harriet had a baby in April 1845. Two months later, on June 23, a series of events took place which were later to come under close scrutiny. Neighbors noted that the Rulloff's blinds were closed.

Around noon Dr. Rulloff emerged from the house and called on his immediate neighbors, the Robertsons, and asked for the loan of their horse and wagon. Ed explained that his wife's uncle had called on them the night before and taken Mrs. Rulloff and the baby on a visit to Motts Corners, a tiny village between Lake Cayuga and Lake Seneca. The uncle had limited accommodations at Motts Corners. To make room for his guests he had given the doctor a large crate of household effects. Now the doctor wanted to return the crate and pick up his family.

Sounds like a complicated plan to facilitate an overnight visit. The Robertsons loaned Rulloff the horse and wagon. Mr. Robertson even gave Ed a hand placing the heavy crate on the wagon. Rulloff tapped old Bessie on the rump and drove away.

Later it was learned that he never did go to Motts Corners but travelled through Ithaca to the shores of Lake Cayuga and then returned home to Lansing. Mr. Robertson was mildly surprised when he saw the doctor pull up in front of his house with the big crate still in tow. He was even more surprised when the doctor had no trouble taking the crate single-handed from the wagon into the house. The doctor then returned the horse and wagon. While doing so, he advised the Robertsons that he and his family were taking a vacation for a week or two.

Dr. Rulloff fled. Soon Harriet's brothers were making inquiries about their sister's absence. They were sure she had met with foul play at the hands of her husband. They contacted police, who picked up the good doctor in Cleveland. Ed's oversized head and distinctive eyes had made him easy to find. Dr. Rulloff was brought back to Ithaca, but since there was no body and no direct evidence that murder had taken place, the murder charges were not pressed. Ed was charged with abduction, found guilty, and convicted. In January 1846 he was sentenced to ten years in prison in Auburn. Back in the mid-nineteenth century, ten years meant ten years. Dr. Rulloff spent every minute behind bars.

When the doctor stepped out of prison authorities tapped him on the shoulder and informed him that they had decided to try him for the murder of his wife after all. While Ed was serving his time, Lake Cayuga had been dragged several times in the search for the bodies of his wife and child. They were never found. However, it was revealed that at about the time of the Rulloffs' disappearance, the bodies of a woman and child had been sold to the Geneva Medical College on a no-questions-asked basis.

Dr. Rulloff was again placed behind bars to await trial. Within days he escaped. Sleeping in barns and culverts, Rulloff managed to remain at large, but all was not peaches and cream. One night it was so cold that his big toe froze. In that flamboyant way of his, Rulloff brazenly called at a drug store in Jamestown. Displaying an amazing knowledge of pharmacology to the owner he talked the pharmacist into letting him concoct his own prescription for frost-bite. The remedy obviously didn't work. Later Rulloff amputated his own big toe.

The doctor made his way to Ohio where he obtained a position as a teacher, but as luck would have it, a former convict recognized that oversized head and informed the police. Again Dr. Rulloff was returned to Ithaca. Feelings ran so high against him that there was some fear of lynching. Authorities transferred their prisoner to Auburn Penitentiary for safekeeping.

Despite the strong suspicion of guilt against him and his escape from jail, there was some reluctance to prosecute Rulloff. The evidence against him would have a hard time standing up in court under cross-examination. Remember the deaths of William Schutt's wife and baby? It was felt that these two unfortunates had been murder victims as well. After fourteen years the bodies were exhumed and found to contain poison. Here again there was little proof that the doctor had administered it to the Schutts. Dr. Rulloff was not charged. He walked out of jail a free man.

You would think Rulloff would call it a day. After all, he had probably killed four people, spent ten years in prison, and had successful careers both as a teacher and doctor behind him. But our boy was not content to let sleeping dogs lie.

In 1864 Dr. Rulloff made his way to Brooklyn. He brought Bill Dexter and Albert Jarvis, two ex-cons, with him. As the leader of the three, the doctor planned robberies and sent his two colleagues out to pull them off. They were successful, making enough from their break-ins to keep the doctor in coffee and cakes. Of course, this wasn't nearly enough to keep Ed sufficiently stimulated.

Using the alias "Professor E.C. Howard," Ed opened an office in Hoboken, New Jersey, and taught English to immigrants. Hold on, that's not all. As Professor Edward Leurio, an eminent philologist (one who scientifically studies languages), he was busily engaged in developing a universal written language. Professor Leurio maintained offices at 170 Third Avenue in Manhattan.

There is little doubt that in this latter effort Rulloff was dead serious. In learned circles he was accepted at face value, and his work was received with a certain degree of respect.

Of course, no one realized that this intelligent, hard-working scholar was being financed through the commission of robberies. To his professor friends he talked of saving mankind by perfecting a universal language. With his ex-cons he discussed how they would break into the next warehouse.

The whole unreal set-up erupted in violence on the night of August 21, 1870. Dexter and Jarvis had entered the premises of Halbert Bros., a silk shop in Binghamton, New York. Unknown to them, two clerks, Fred Mirrick and Gilbert Burrows, were sleeping in the store. They woke up and rushed the burglars. The scuffle which followed was abruptly terminated when a fifth man approached, brandishing a revolver. Rulloff had been outside the building and at the first sign of trouble came to his colleagues' rescue. Rulloff raised his revolver and pressed the trigger. A bullet went crashing into Mirrick's forehead, killing him instantly. Rulloff then calmly shot Burrows.

The three desperate men ran out of the store. Badly wounded, Burrows staggered out of the store to the home of the chief of police, only three blocks away.

The cold-blooded murder shocked the entire country. Police were baffled by the one clue found at the scene of the killing. One of the robbers had lost his shoe. The shoe was stuffed with paper in the space normally occupied by the big toe.

Two days after Mirrick's murder two bodies were found floating in the Shenango River. Clerk Burrows identified them as the two burglars. They were later identified as William Dexter and Albert Jarvis. Rulloff made no attempt to flee. Through his association with the dead men he was readily traced and apprehended.

The strange shoe found at the scene of the Mirrick murder, coupled with Rulloff's missing big toe, placed him squarely at the scene of the crime. On January 5, 1871, Rulloff stood trial for Mirrick's murder at Binghamton, New York. The facts surrounding Rulloff's career were widely publicized. He was called the Educated Murderer. He had killed seven people in his wild and unusual career. Rulloff was convicted and sentenced to hang.

During his last days he confessed to killing his wife and child. He had taken them to Lake Cayuga with Robertson's horse and wagon, stolen a rowboat and, after attaching stones to their bodies, had dumped them overboard. The bodies have never been recovered. He also confessed to killing Mrs. Schutt and her baby. He did it because of William Schutt's opposition to his marriage.

Swearing and refusing all spiritual assistance, Edward Howard Rulloffson was hanged in front of the Binghamton Jail on May 17, 1871.

COUNT DE LACY

Patrick O'Brien de Lacy had everything a bright young Irish lad should have. He had a twinkle in his eye, a spring in his step, and a tongue that could charm the birds out of the trees. Besides, he was handsome. One thing Pat didn't have was money. As an ambitious teenager in southern Ireland at the turn of the century, he decided to cure this deficiency by travel and adventure. He knew the money would come.

By 1905 Pat had travelled to Warsaw, where assorted confidence schemes set him up with enough cash to move on to Vilna, Poland, posing as wealthy Count de Lacy. In Vilna Pat hit the jackpot. One of the most eligible females in all of Poland fell for the good-looking Irishman with the winning ways. The young damsel's father was the fabulously wealthy General Buturlin, who owned several estates throughout Europe. The General's family consisted of himself, his wife, his independently wealthy son, Captain Buturlin, and of course, the object of our Pat's affection.

Now it behooves me to be cruel. The general's daughter was not a looker. She peered at the world through beady eyes, which gave the appearance of being three-quarters closed. When she wasn't squinting she was constantly dabbing at her pointed nose, which seemed to be forever dripping. She bore a distinct resemblance to a mouse suffering perpetually from the Hong Kong flu.

Pat knew a fortune when he saw it, even though it resembled a mouse. He pursued the general's daughter until she caught him. The couple were married in Vilna, and as custom would have it, a substantial dowry went along with the bride.

Pat was in the chips. Accompanied by Countess de Lacy, he moved to St. Petersburg, Russia, where they lived high off the hog. Firmly ensconced in a luxury hotel, he and the Countess entertained lavishly. On occasion members of Russian royalty would be his guests. He and the Countess were in turn invited to many of Russia's social functions of the season. With little coming in to replenish his wife's dowry, it became obvious to Pat that a day of reckoning was soon at hand. What to do? Well, Pat thought and thought before he came up with his rather unique solution.

First he would kill the general's son, who would of course leave his not inconsiderable wealth to the general, as he had no family of his own. Then Pat would kill the general, who would leave everything to his wife, who would be the next to die. She would have only one surviving offspring to leave three individual fortunes to, and that would be Pat's wife, the Countess de Lacy. What a coup! Pat would have huge estates all over Europe. Life would be one big round of parties. It beat southern Ireland.

Pat looked around for a method by which to annihilate his in-laws. It didn't take him long to notice the obvious. Hundreds were dying each day of cholera in St. Petersburg. If he could make it appear that his in-laws had caught the dreaded disease, he would be home free.

Pat looked up Dr. Panchenko, a respected but poor member of the important sounding Laboratory of Plague Cultures, which was busy searching for a cure for the plague. The doctor was one of those men who was eager and willing to devote his life to research but unfortunately was never able to raise the funds to pursue his true vocation. Knowing this, Pat was quite open with the medic.

Pat explained that he required cholera germs, which would somehow be used to infect Captain Buturlin. For this service Pat promised £1,000. The general's death would be worth £5,000. The doc became absolutely glassy-eyed upon learning that when the general's wife was safely tucked under the good soil of Russia, he would be the recipient of a cool £50,000. As they say in sporting circles, the package came to 56,000 big ones. It was all too much for the impoverished doctor to pass up. He accepted Pat's proposition without reservation.

Dr. Panchenko had no difficulty obtaining the deadly bacteria from the Laboratory of Plague Cultures. He turned over two tubes of cholera endotoxin to Pat, who quickly urged his wife to invite her brother to St. Petersburg. Captain Buturlin was delighted to visit with his sister.

When he arrived his food was liberally spiked with the deadly bacteria. Nothing happened. Pat was furious. He then learned that the captain had taken the precaution of obtaining an inoculation against cholera before leaving Poland. Nothing would do but Dr. Panchenko would have to come up with a new goody to send the Captain along his way.

The resourceful medic produced diphtheria toxin, which he insisted on personally injecting into the unsuspecting captain. Pat had no difficulty arranging for himself, his wife and the captain to receive inoculations from the doctor. The plans were for the doctor to call at Pat's hotel suite and perform the triple header. To allay any suspicion, the initial inoculations were harmless. The second visit also was a dry run. On the doctor's third visit he injected Captain Buturlin with the deadly diphtheria toxin. In no time at all the captain was seriously ill. Despite all efforts to save his life, he passed away, an obvious victim of the disease rife in St. Petersburg. Captain Buturlin was duly buried without his death causing any suspicion.

Preparations were underway to murder the general when Dr. Panchenko made a fatal mistake. Apparently the good doctor had a mistress, one Madame Muravieva, who helped the man of medicine while away the evenings when he wasn't busy fooling around with deadly bacteria. It was the doctor's misfortune to have a mistress who shared her favors with others.

One fine Russian evening, the Madame, while pursuing decidedly earthly pleasures with the doctor, couldn't help but wonder at her lover's new-found generosity. Every time the doctor met with de Lacy, she would receive a lavish gift. It was a puzzle. All her lover and de Lacy ever talked about was a Captain Buturlin. Madame Muravieva mentioned the interesting coincidence to her other lover. He figured it out. He correctly surmised that de Lacy and Dr. Panchenko had killed Captain Buturlin. Being a rival of the doctor's, he had no misgivings about taking his suspicious information to the police.

That same evening police picked up Panchenko. Before the sun had risen over St. Petersburg the doctor had made a complete confession. Madame Muravieva, who had really let the cat out of the bag, as well as de Lacy and the doctor, were charged with the murder of Captain Buturlin.

All three stood trial for murder in January 1911. Madame Muravieva was acquitted, as it was a certainty that she had not taken part in the plot to annihilate the entire Buturlin family. De Lacy and Panchenko were found guilty. Panchenko received a sentence of fifteen years' imprisonment, while de Lacy received life.

Strangely enough, General Buturlin financed his son-in-law's defence, despite the fact the accused had killed his son and was planning to kill everyone he held near and dear. General Buturlin and his daughter attended every day of the trial. The day after de Lacy was pronounced guilty, his wife was found wandering the streets of St. Petersburg screaming hysterically. Her mind had snapped. She returned to Vilna, where she died a few months later without regaining her reason.

TRY, TRY AGAIN

December of 1932 wasn't the happiest of times for Tony Marino. Despite the impending Yuletide season with its message of joy to the world, Tony just couldn't see the silver lining in the dark clouds.

Tony was the sole proprietor of Marino's Bar on Third Avenue in New York. The bar was not the classiest place in the world. Let's be truthful. During the Depression it was a step below sleazy. A faded sign proclaimed that Grade A1 Whisky was 15 cents a shot. You could get two slugs for a quarter.

Business was lousy in the gut-rot selling game. Tony cried the blues to his two best friends, his bartender Red Murphy, and his best paying customer, Frank Pasqua, an undertaker.

Both these upstanding gentlemen were hurting too. The Depression had made Red's tips as scarce as hen's teeth. Frank was feeling the pinch in his own way. Families of the dear departed had the annoying but frugal habit of spending only $12 for bottom-of-the-line caskets. Gone were the good old days when he moved expensive mahogany jobs at least a couple of times a week.

The three friends were belly up to the bar one day when they decided there just had to be a way to turn over a fast buck. That's when Michael Malloy staggered into the bar. Mike rarely walked, having developed a staggering gait many years before when he gave up drinking water. This son of Eire made a dubious living sweeping out bars and performing odd jobs in saloons along Third Avenue.

Tony took a look at Mike and idly mentioned to Red that it was a shame the little old drunk didn't have a friend or relative in the world. Frank volunteered that if Mike met with an accident there would be no one to mourn the poor man. The three friends agreed that it would be a good idea to insure Mike's life and then murder him.

Frank knew an insurance salesman who had a reputation for cutting through red tape with a sharp but crooked knife. Before you could say double indemnity, the boys had Mike's life insured for $1,200 without the little Irishman's knowledge. Tony was named beneficiary. All the conspirators had to do was kill Mike and make his death appear to be an unfortunate accident.

What better time to start than right now?

The first thing the boys set up was a few free drinks of genuine A1 15-cent whisky for Mike. Once he was pleasantly pickled, Red slipped him a healthy double blast of radiator antifreeze. Mike licked his lips.

Four shots of pure antifreeze later Mike was singing Irish ballads at the top of his voice. On the fifth slug he hit the floor with a dull thud. When Tony closed the bar he checked out old Mike. Mike's heart was beating, but just.

The boys decided to split a bottle and wait for Mike to go to the great green which lies beyond. They waited and they waited.

As the sun peeked through the canyons of New York, little Mike Malloy blinked. Then he cursed. Then he got up. Mike was fine.

Foiled in their first attempt, the boys believed that if at first you don't succeed, try, try again. Credit for attempt number two goes to Frank Pasqua. Frank purchased a tin of sardines, opened the can, and let those little fishes sit for several days.

There would be no mistake this time. Frank shredded the can into little needle-sharp filings, which bartender Red mixed gently with the bad sardines. Mike was then served a ptomaine-and-tin sandwich which would have knocked over a horse. Mike merely grinned and asked for a shot of whisky to wash down the delicacy.

The three partners in crime were amazed. It was obvious that Mike had a lead-lined stomach capable of digesting anything from antifreeze to tin. A more direct, deadly scheme had to be devised.

After observing Christmas and New Year's, the three men went back to work. Tony brought his good friend, cabdriver Hershey Green, into the conspiracy. Hershey would do practically anything for a hundred dishonest dollars. The plan was simple enough. They would get Mike drunk, a ritual which took place every night anyway. They would then drop him off at some deserted spot where he would freeze to death.

The perfect night presented itself during the first week in January. A cold, miserable sleet storm was raging outside, while inside Mike had slumped over Tony's bar. Tony and Frank hustled the unconscious form into Hershey's cab. Hershey drove to a deserted section of Claremont Park.

They took off Mike's coat and shirt and dumped him in some bushes a few feet from the road. For good measure they poured a few gallons of water over Mike's inert form. Shivering, the men scrambled back into the cab. They took one last look at Mike. Little mounds of sleet were piling up around his body.

Next morning Tony searched through the papers for news of a body found in the park. There was nothing. Later, he had Hershey drive up to the park. There was no trace of the little drunk.

That evening Mike Malloy walked into Tony's bar. He had a funny story to tell. He had awakened in Claremont Park and had no idea how he got there. Everyone had a good laugh, except Tony, who had somehow contracted a nasty cold.

A council of war was held. All conspirators attended. It was decided that Mike would be taken to an isolated strip of roadway, where he would be propped up while Hershey ran him down with his cab.

Again, the drunken Mike was hustled into Hershey's cab. This time the plotters made their way to deserted Baychester Avenue. Mike was held upright by Tony and Frank. At the last minute they jumped out of the way of Hershey's cab. Mike flew through the air like a rag doll. The three men sped away in the cab.

Next morning the boys were absolutely distraught when no news of the hit and run could be found in the papers. They called all the hospitals, but no Mike.

About three weeks later Mike walked into Tony's bar. He had a story to tell. He had been hit by a car and had spent three weeks in hospital. His name had not appeared on the accident list due to a clerical error. But all that was behind him now. Mike assured everyone that he was fit as a fiddle and would appreciate a shot of whisky.

They say Tony Marino put his head on the bar and cried.

The plotters would try one last time. Tony elicited the aid of another friend, Dan Kreisberg, a former fruit dealer. Dan became a buddy of Mike's, which wasn't that difficult as long as he provided the dogged little Irishman with 15-cent whisky. Dan invited Mike to his room, where, with the help of Red Murphy, he hooked up a rubber hose to a gas jet. This time Mike didn't have a chance.

There was great joy in the back room of Tony's that night. Frank explained to the gathering of the clan that a down-and-out doctor had signed the death certificate attributing Mike's demise to pneumonia. Mike was buried the following day in one of Frank Pasqua's $12 specials.

The insurance company turned over $1,200 to Frank, and that's when the trouble started. The money didn't go that far, considering the number of partners. Everyone was dissatisfied with his cut.

Dan Kreisberg asked friends how much he should get. After all, Dan was proud of the fact that he had accomplished in a few minutes what everyone else had failed to do in three months. Then there was Hershey. He complained to everyone who would listen that he had dented a fender when he had hit Mike and should be entitled to damages over and above the paltry $100 he had received for his failed attempts.

With everyone going around complaining, it wasn't long before the law got wind of the murder scheme. They found out that the deceased Mike Malloy had indeed been insured, and that the beneficiary was Tony Marino. Mike's body was exhumed. It was discovered that he had not died of pneumonia but had been gassed. The gang was rounded up and sang like so many canaries in an aviary.

Tony Marino, Frank Pasqua, Red Murphy, and Dan Kreisberg were put to death in Sing Sing's electric chair. Only Hershey Green was spared. He received a twenty-year prison sentence.